PARKER AND MEL[L]

THE MODERN LAW OF TRUSTS

AUSTRALIA
The Law Book Company
Brisbane · Sydney · Melbourne · Perth

CANADA
Carswell
Ottawa · Toronto · Calgary · Montreal · Vancouver

AGENTS
Steimatzky's Agency Ltd., Tel Aviv;
N.M. Tripathi (Private) Ltd., Bombay;
Eastern Law House (Private) Ltd., Calcutta;
M.P.P. House, Bangalore;
Universal Book Traders, Delhi;
Aditya Books, Delhi;
MacMillan Shuppan KK, Tokyo;
Pakistan Law House, Karachi, Lahore

PARKER AND MELLOWS:

THE MODERN LAW OF TRUSTS

Sixth Edition

by

A. J. OAKLEY, M.A., LL.B.,
of Lincoln's Inn, Barrister,
Fellow of Trinity Hall, Cambridge,
Lecturer in Law at The University of Cambridge

LONDON
SWEET & MAXWELL
1994

First Edition	1966
Second Edition	1970
Third Edition	1975
Fourth Edition	1979
Fifth Edition	1983
Sixth Edition	1994

Published in 1994 by
Sweet & Maxwell Ltd. of
South Quay Plaza, 183 Marsh Wall,
London E14 9FT.
Typeset by Interactive Sciences, Gloucester.
Printed in England by
Clays Ltd., St Ives plc.

ACIP catalogue record for this book is
available from the British Library
ISBN—042148750X

No natural forests were destroyed
to make this product;
only farmed timber was used.

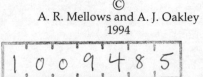

PREFACE

In the preface to the first edition of this work in 1966, its authors stated that the law of trusts "is a branch of the law which is developing at a rapid pace and which is highly relevant to modern conditions, not merely to a bygone age". The accuracy of this statement was demonstrated by the fact that four further editions rapidly followed, culminating in the fifth edition in 1983. The absence of any new edition since then has certainly not been due to any slowing down in the development of the law of trusts but rather to the unexpected and untimely death of Professor Parker in 1987. This sixth edition is the first which has not been prepared by Professor Parker and Professor Mellows. However, the immense debt which this edition owes to their scholarship and erudition will be apparent to anyone familiar with its predecessors and will continue to be apparent for many editions to come.

This work has always been noted for its clarity of expression and for this reason as much as possible of the original text has been retained. This edition follows the same order as its predecessor, save for the fact that the Chapters on Trusts of Imperfect Obligation and on Avoiding a Conflict of Interest have been incorporated into, respectively, the Chapters on Express Private Trusts and on Constructive Trusts; further, some of the material formerly covered in the Chapter on Implied or Resulting Trusts has been transferred to the Chapter on Constructive Trusts because of my different views as to its correct classification. The Chapter on Express Private Trusts has been considerably expanded, in particular by the inclusion of a section on The Beneficiary Principle, and the Chapter on Constructive Trusts has been completely rewritten in order to incorporate material from my own book *Constructive Trusts* and in order to reflect the much greater importance of this topic in the last two decades. It is because of the incorporation of this additional material that this edition is somewhat longer than its predecessor. Substantial rewriting of the Chapters on The Taxation of a Trust and on Breach of Trust has been necessitated by, respectively, legislative reform and recent case law, some of which has had to be incorporated at the proof stage. I have resisted the temptation to incorporate separate Chapters on Pension Funds and on The Trust in the Conflict of Laws, preferring to incorporate the relevant material elsewhere in the most appropriate place; however, there is little doubt that separate Chapters dealing with these topics will be necessary in future editions.

In the preface to the fifth edition, its authors drew attention to the then recent Twenty-Third Report of the Law Reform Committee on the powers and duties of trustees and expressed the hope that "by the time that the next edition of this work is published most of its recommendations will be reflected in legislation, which we can discuss in the main body of the text". This hope has proved to be unjustified since, to the great disappointment of all trust lawyers, no steps have yet been taken to enact these important recommendations. This edition has, like its predecessor, therefore referred to these recommendations only in the footnotes so that no one will be confused into thinking that there is a present legislative base for them. The absence of any reforming legislation explains why the Chapters dealing with the powers and duties of trustees are those which have changed the least.

I would like to thank Professor Mellows for allowing me to prepare this edition. I hope that he will not be unduly disappointed with the result, for which I alone am responsible. I would also like to thank those of my colleagues and former colleagues with whom I have discussed the subject-matter of this work over the years and in particular Mr. J. D. R. Adams, Registrar of Civil Appeals, Professor David Hayton, Professor of Law in the University of London at King's College, and Mr. Charles Harpum, Fellow of Downing College Cambridge and a Law Commissioner for England and Wales. I would also like to thank the publishers for producing the Index and the Tables of Cases and Statutes and for their general efficiency and rapidity.

The law has been stated from the sources which were available to me on January 31, 1994 although it has been possible to incorporate a certain amount of subsequent material at the proof stage.

August 1, 1994
Trinity Hall,
Cambridge.

A. J. Oakley

CONTENTS

9. CHARITABLE TRUSTS 296

10. THE APPOINTMENT, RETIREMENT AND REMOVAL OF TRUSTEES 360

11. ACTION ON APPOINTMENT AS TRUSTEE 383

12. THE ADMINISTRATION OF A TRUST 386

TABLE OF CASES

TABLE OF STATUTES

xlvi　　　　　　　　TABLE OF STATUTES

Statutory Instruments

CHAPTER 1

INTRODUCTION

THE TRUST TODAY

EVER since the trust was invented, no lawyer has been able to give a comprehensive service to his client without a thorough grasp of the subject. This is more true today than it has ever been. Throughout its history the trust has been used by lawyers as a device to circumvent inconvenient rules of law.

In medieval times a "use", which was the forerunner of the trust, was brought into existence as a result of a transfer of property by its owner to third parties to the use either of himself or some other beneficiary. The third parties then became the owners of the property in the eyes of the law but they held their legal title to the property for the benefit of the transferor and/or any other nominated beneficiary. There were several circumstances in which this device was used.

Before 1540,[1] it was not possible to leave freehold land by will. However, if a landowner wished to achieve the same result, he could convey the land during his lifetime to third parties[2] to the use of himself during the remainder of his life and thereafter to the use of the intended beneficiary. The landowner would continue to derive the benefit from his land for as long as he lived and on his death the intended beneficiary would automatically become entitled.

Similarly, from the Thirteenth Century onwards the Statutes of Mortmain[3] imposed prohibitions on gifts of land to corporations (the usual donees were ecclesiastical foundations) in an attempt to prevent land being taken out of circulation more or less permanently, thus depriving feudal lords of their revenue therefrom.[4] These statutes could often be avoided by taking advantage of a use. Thus a conveyance of land to third parties to the use of the corporation in question was effective to circumvent the prohibition until 1391.[5]

However, the use was probably employed most frequently as a device to avoid feudal taxes. It was the medieval equivalent of a "tax avoidance

---

[1] Prior to the enactment of the Statute of Wills 1540.

[2] There was always a plurality of trustees so that on the death of any one of them the others would take the property by survivorship and so avoid the difficulties which would otherwise have arisen if a sole trustee died.

[3] Culminating in the Statute De Viris Religiosis 1279.

[4] By this time most of the feudal taxes worth collecting were levied on inheritances; ecclesiastical foundations never died (hence the name Mortmain ("dead hand")).

[5] When the device was prohibited by 15 Ric. II (1391), c. 5.

scheme". On the death of a person who held land as a tenant in knight service,[6] an adult heir would have to pay the feudal lord a fixed sum before he could claim his inheritance and a year's profits of the land in question, although after 1267 this latter sum only had to be paid if the feudal lord in question was the King.[7] An infant heir was in an even worse position since the feudal lord would be entitled to use the land for his own benefit[8] until the infant reached the age of majority[9] and the infant had either to submit to the feudal lord's choice of a spouse or, if he could not endure the thought of spending a lifetime locked in the arms of the lord's choice,[10] to compensate the lord for the value to him of the marriage[11]; further, at the end of the wardship, the infant had to pay the feudal lord a half year's profits of the land, although after 1215 this sum only had to be paid if the feudal lord in question was the King.[12] All these disadvantages could be avoided if, before his death, the tenant in knight service conveyed his land to third parties to the use of himself during the remainder of his life and thereafter to the use of his heir. Following his death, the third parties would transfer the land to the heir but, because he had not actually received the land by way of inheritance, the feudal lord would not be able to claim any of the rights mentioned above.

Because the effect of uses was to deprive feudal lords in general and the King in particular of a substantial proportion of their feudal revenues, uses were understandably unpopular with the Crown which consequently attempted to abolish the advantages of the use by the enactment of the Statute of Uses 1536.[13] However, the effect of this Statute was short-lived[14] and by the Eighteenth Century the use had returned under the name of the trust.[15] By then all the feudal taxes mentioned above had been abolished[16] and so no longer had to be avoided. However, in subsequent centuries the trust was used to tie up land or wealth for succeeding generations of a family and to make

---

[6] The basic tenure by means of which land was held by persons other than subsistence farmers and agricultural labourers.

[7] Statute of Marlborough 1267, c. 16.

[8] This right was formally recognised in the Assize of Northampton 1176 c. 4; Magna Carta 1215, cc. 4,5 prohibited feudal lords from destroying the capital value of the inheritance but they were entitled to its entire income.

[9] 21 for males, usually 14 for females (unless the death occurred when the female was already over 14 and unmarried, in which case she came of age at 16 or upon earlier marriage).

[10] The lord could not put forward the most unattractive girl he could find in the hope that the infant would refuse and so give the lord a right to compensation. Magna Carta 1215 c. 3 contained a list of defects in a potential spouse which prevented the lord from putting her forward.

[11] Magna Carta 1215, c. 3.

[12] Magna Carta 1215, c. 3.

[13] This "executed" the use by transferring the legal title from the third parties to the beneficiary. As a result none of the devices described in the text continued to work.

[14] It remained in force until 1925 but the effect of its provisions was rapidly circumvented.

[15] The Statute of Uses was held only to "execute" the first of two or more successive uses. Consequently, if land was transferred "unto and to the use of" third parties (to the third parties to their own use) to the use of (or on trust for) the intended beneficiary, the third parties retained the legal title which they held on trust for the intended beneficiaries.

[16] These were abolished by Military Tenures Abolition Act 1660.

provision for dependants. It also had other purposes. For example, the common law rule, which was of general application, that a married woman could not hold property in her own right during the marriage[17] could be overcome by vesting that property in trustees to hold upon trust for her. Likewise, unincorporated associations such as clubs, friendly societies and trade unions, which are not themselves legal entities and so cannot hold property, would not have developed as they have if it had not been possible for property to be held by trustees on their behalf. Finally, in this century, the trust has once again come to be used as a means of creating "tax avoidance schemes".

The principal uses of the trust today are these:

1. To enable property, particularly land, to be held for persons who cannot themselves hold it. Thus the legal title to land cannot be vested in an infant[18] but there is no objection to land being held upon trust for an infant. Statute has now adopted this principle, to the extent that a purported conveyance of a legal estate to an infant operates as an agreement for valuable consideration to create a settlement of that land on the infant and in the meantime to hold the land on trust for the infant.[19]

2. To enable a person to make provision for dependants privately. The most obvious examples are provision made by a man for his mistress or his illegitimate child. During his lifetime there is no problem, but if a man provides for a mistress or an illegitimate child by will, the circumstances may well leak out, for when probate has been obtained a will becomes a public document, and is open to public inspection. But a trust deed escapes publicity of this sort.

3. To tie up property so that it can benefit persons in succession. An outright gift may be made to a parent, in the *hope* that on the parent's death that property will go to his child, but there is no guarantee that it will do so. A gift to trustees to hold on trust for the parent for life with remainder to the child will ensure[20] that the child derives a benefit. It is not normally possible to ensure that the person ultimately entitled will receive the very property that is settled, for the trustees will almost always have the power to sell that property and to re-invest the proceeds. But it is possible virtually to ensure that the person ultimately entitled does receive the benefit which is derived from that property.

4. To protect family property from wastrels. A person may feel that an outright gift of money to a surviving spouse or child will lead to its being dissipated. A gift of that money to trustees to hold upon trust to pay either the income or only a limited proportion of the capital to the surviving spouse or child will probably

---

[17] This restriction, which seems to date from the beginning of the Thirteenth Century, did not prevent the property descending to the married woman's heirs on her death.

[18] Law of Property Act 1925, s.19.

[19] Settled Land Act 1925, s.27.

[20] Unless the child agrees, after reaching the age of majority, to bring the trust to an end prematurely.

prevent this. The trustees may be given a discretion as to the amount (if any) which they may pay over at any one time; another possibility is for property to be given to trustees to hold upon trust for a beneficiary in such a way that it will be preserved if the beneficiary goes bankrupt.[21]

5. To make a gift to take effect in the future in the light of circumstances which have not yet arisen and so are not yet known. If, for example, a person has three young daughters, he may by will set up a trust whereby a sum of money is given to trustees for them to distribute among the daughters, either as they think fit, or having regard to stated factors. They might, for example, in due course decide to give one-quarter each to two of the daughters who had married well and one-half to the poorer unmarried daughter.

6. To make provision, particularly by will, for causes or for non-human objects. By means of a trust money can be donated for the furtherance of education or for the purpose of maintaining a beloved animal such as a favourite dog or cat.

7. To enable two or more persons to own land. One of the more curious features of English land law is that not more than one person may be the absolute and beneficial owner of land, but that if two or more persons wish to own land jointly, they may only do so by means of a trust.[22] Since the Second World War it has become increasingly common for married couples (and for that matter unmarried couples living in a de facto relationship) to have the family home vested in their joint names—indeed, building societies and banks normally make a mortgage advance conditional on this being done. Substantially more than half of the residential property in the country must now be owned jointly in this way so that, technically, well over half the houses in the country are held on trust—though this fact would surprise most of their occupants.[23]

8. To provide pensions for retired employees and their dependants. Since the Second World War pension schemes have become increasingly common and are now regarded as an essential part of virtually every contract of employment and an important factor for the self-employed.[24] Pension schemes for employees are either non-contributory, in which case the whole of the money is provided by the employer, or contributory, in which case both the employer and the employee pay into the fund. Self-employed persons take out personal pension schemes, facilitated by generous tax concessions, which are also available to employees

---

[21] This device is known as a protective trust.

[22] Either under a "trust for sale" or under a "settlement within the Settled Land Act 1925".

[23] This has come to be so much a matter of course that some solicitors are now thought to have given up explaining the provisions of conveyances of land which declare the trusts upon which the property is to be held so that the fact that the property is to be held on trust may never even have been mentioned to the purchasers.

[24] British pension funds are now worth in excess of £275 billion.

who wish to "top-up" the pension arising out of their employment. In the vast majority of cases, pension funds are held by trustees with the objective, usually but sadly not always[25] achieved, of assuring the employee that his pension will in fact be forthcoming and that in the meantime his employer cannot in any way dispose of the money. The funds contributed towards personal pension schemes are similarly invariably held by trust corporations.

9. To facilitate investment through unit trusts and investment trusts. The objective of such trusts is to enable the small investor to acquire a small stake in a large portfolio of investments and thus to spread his risk across a substantial range of stocks and shares. Further, such portfolios are sufficiently large for their investments to be supervised on a full-time basis. In the case of a unit trust, the promoter, usually the future manager, of the unit trust invites the public to subscribe for units of a fixed initial value. The funds so obtained are invested in the stock market, either entirely generally or with at least the majority of the holdings in a particular nominated sphere, such as in companies engaged in shipping. The investments so purchased are vested in trustees, usually in a trust corporation. The trustees receive the dividends on the investments which, after payment of their administration expenses and the remuneration of the manager (usually a percentage of the value of the fund), are distributed among the investors in proportion to the number of units held or reinvested to increase the total value of the fund and so of the individual units in the fund. The manager, who is responsible for selecting the original investments and changing them when he feels this to be appropriate, is obliged to buy back the units at any time at a price fixed by reference to the total value of the fund at any one time. He will offer for sale any units so bought back at a slightly higher price. There are consequently at any one time two different prices at which units are respectively bought back and sold. An investment trust works in a broadly similar way with two important distinctions. First, the fund is not divided into units so that the capital subscribed can be of any amount which the manager is prepared to accept. Secondly, the individual investors can only deal with their investments on the stock exchange (the manager is not under any obligation to buy them back); this consequently means that the price paid will depend on market forces rather than being directly related to the total value of the fund at any one time. The importance of investment

---

[25] The systematic looting by the late Robert Maxwell of the pension fund established to provide pensions for ex-employees of "The Daily Mirror" caused great concern among employees in general; pension fund administration then became the subject of a Committee of Inquiry, the Pensions Law Reform Committee, which reported in the autumn of 1993 and came down on the side of continuing the utilisation of the trust vehicle.

vehicles of this kind for the small investor cannot be overesti-mated.[26]

10. To minimise the incidence of income tax, capital gains tax and inheritance tax. There are numerous possible "tax avoidance schemes" and a high proportion of them involve a trust in one way or another.[27] One example will suffice for the moment. A person with a high income[28] will pay income tax of 40 per cent on any investment income. If, however, the investment is transferred to trustees on trust for five members of his family, each of whom is only of modest means and so pays either no income tax at all or income tax at a lower rate, a substantial saving of tax will be made. The minimum saving, without taking into account the administration expenses of the trust, will be 15 per cent of the income (the difference between the 40 per cent tax otherwise payable and the 25 per cent basic rate of tax[29]) and even greater savings will be made if any of the five has not enough other income to use up his personal allowance[30] and 20 per cent tax band.[31]

11. To protect the environment. In other jurisdictions, the trust has developed a role in environmental protection law. In the United States of America, under the so-called "public trust doctrine", each State has a fiduciary obligation to ensure that public lands which constitute the coastline, the bays of the sea, and the tidal rivers and their beds are made continuously available for the members of the public at large. In Canada, "the "trusteed" environmental fund" has been developed so as to provide an assurance for the State that, following the termination of some environmentally harmful activity such as mining or logging, the post closure land reclamation will be adequately financed. The party carrying out the activity makes periodic payments to trustees who, like the trustees of a pension fund, invest these payments for return and the accumulated fund is the primary or immediate source for meeting the costs of reclamation.[32] This interesting use of the trust concept in a field which is today of such enormous international importance and interest could undoubtedly be adopted in this jurisdiction in appropriate circumstances.

One of the great advantages of a trust is the flexibility of purpose for

[26] Unit trusts and investment trusts are often incorporated in which case they are governed by the Companies Acts 1985 and 1989. All such investment vehicles are in any event subject, in addition to the normal provisions of trust law and company law, to special legislation designed to protect the public against fraud.
[27] Such schemes "involve" trusts because in the majority of cases they will necessitate either the setting up of a trust or the breaking of an existing trust or a combination of the two.
[28] In 1994–95 income tax is payable at 40 per cent on any taxable income over £23,700.
[29] Payable in 1994–95 on taxable income between £3,001 and £23,700.
[30] £3,445 for a single person in 1994–95.
[31] Payable in 1994–95 on the first £3,000 of taxable income.
[32] See D. W. M. Waters in *Equity, Fiduciaries and Trusts 1993* (ed. Waters (1993)) 383.

which it can be used. Another is that the rules which govern a trust are by and large the same whatever the purpose for which it is employed. The remainder of this book attempts to explain those rules.

I. DEFINITION OF A TRUST

Difficulty has been found in providing a comprehensive definition of a trust, but various attempts have been made. The following may be considered:

(1) Coke's definition

Lord Coke defined a trust as "a confidence reposed in some other, not issuing out of the land but as a thing collateral thereto, annexed in privity to the estate of the land, and to the person touching the land, for which *cestui que trust* has no remedy but by subpoena in the Chancery."[33] The language may require elucidation. When Coke says it is collateral to land not issuing out of it he means that it differs from a legal interest: a legal interest continues to subsist even on the purchase for value without notice of that interest, whereas an equitable interest such as a trust does not, and it is, for that reason, collateral. When he says it is annexed in privity to the estate he means that the trust will only continue while the estate continues. By annexation in privity to the person it is shown that a purchaser for value of the legal estate without notice of the trust takes free of it.

It has to be said, however, that there are some objections to Coke's formulation. First, what is a "confidence"? This expression does not explain precisely the meaning of "trust". Secondly, the definition imports the idea of a reliance placed by one person in another person. But this may not be universally correct. The *cestui que trust* (or "beneficiary") may be a baby in arms or unborn or ignorant of the trust. The trust in such cases may still be effective but the *cestui que trust* will place no "reliance" in the trustee. Thirdly, it applies only to real property, whereas the subject-matter of a trust may be personal property also. And, finally, it is procedurally out of date: the Court of Chancery no longer exists and all branches of the High Court have jurisdiction in equity.[34] Nevertheless this early definition still deserves a mention: subject to the criticisms that can be made it is as useful as most modern definitions.

(2) Underhill's definition

Sir Arthur Underhill described a trust as "an equitable obligation binding a person (who is called a trustee) to deal with property over which he has control (which is called trust property), for the benefit of persons (who are called beneficiaries or *cestuis que trust*[35]), of whom he

---

[33] Co. Litt. 272b.

[34] Supreme Court of Judicature (Consolidation) Act 1925, s.4(4).

[35] This is the plural: "*Cestuis que trustent*" is "hopelessly wrong": Sweet (1910) 26 L.Q.R. 196.

may himself be one and any one of whom may enforce the obligation."[36]

As a comprehensive definition of all kinds of trusts it may be objected that it does not in terms cover charitable trusts, and, moreover, does not provide for the so-called "trust of imperfect obligation,"[37] such as a trust "for the maintenance and support of my dog Fido"; this may well amount to a valid trust but it is of imperfect obligation because Fido cannot enforce it. The editors of Underhill have pointed out that charitable trusts are outside the scope of the book but, in any case, are covered by the definition, because such a trust is for the benefit of persons, namely the public, on whose behalf the Attorney-General may enforce it.[38] And trusts of imperfect obligation are not referred to because they are acknowledged to be "anomalous and exceptional."[39]

(3) Lewin's definition

A rather more comprehensive definition is that adopted in the present edition of Lewin's *Trusts*.[40] It is based on a definition given by Mayo J. in *Re Scott*.[41] According to this formulation, "the word 'trust' refers to the duty or aggregate accumulation of obligations that rest upon a person described as trustee. The responsibilities are in relation to property held by him, or under his control. That property he will be compelled by a court in its equitable jurisdiction to administer in the manner lawfully prescribed by the trust instrument, or where there be no specific provision written or oral, or to the extent that such provision is invalid or lacking, in accordance with equitable principles. As a consequence the administration will be in such a manner that the consequential benefits and advantages accrue, not to the trustee, but to the persons called *cestuis que trust*, or beneficiaries, if there be any; if not, for some purpose which the law will recognise and enforce. A trustee may be a beneficiary, in which case advantages will accrue in his favour to the extent of his beneficial interest."[42]

(4) A recent statutory definition

The Hague Convention on the Law Applicable to Trusts and on their Recognition, incorporated into English law by the Recognition of Trusts Act 1987, contains in Article 2 the following definition of a trust:

---

[36] Underhill & Hayton, *Law of Trusts and Trustees* (14th ed.) p. 1. The definition was approved by Cohen J. in *Re Marshall's Will Trusts* [1945] Ch. 217 at p. 219 and by Romer L.J. in *Green* v. *Russell* [1959] 2 Q.B. 226 at p. 241.

[37] See *post*. p. 112.

[38] See *post*. p. 296.

[39] See *post*. p. 112.

[40] (16th ed.), p. 1.

[41] [1948] S.A.S.R. 193 at p. 196.

[42] For a similar and well-known definition see Keeton *Law of Trusts* (11th ed.), p. 2. For other definitions by text writers, see Halsbury's *Laws of England* (4th ed.), Vol. 48 p. 272, American Law Institute, *Restatement of the Law of Trusts* p. 6, para. 2. For judicial definitions, see *Sturt* v. *Mellish* (1743) 2 Atk. 610 at p. 612, *per* Lord Hardwicke L.C.; *Burgess* v. *Wheate* (1759) 1 Eden 177 at p. 223, *per* Lord Mansfield C.J.: *Re Williams* [1897] 2 Ch. 12. at p. 19 (C.A.) *per* Lindley L.J. As to the meaning of "trust" and "trustee" in T.A. 1925, see *ibid*, s.68(17).

"For the purposes of this Convention, the term 'trust' refers to the legal relationships created—*inter vivos* or on death—by a person, the settlor, when assets have been placed under the control of a trustee for the benefit of a beneficiary or for a specified purpose. A trust has the following characteristics—*a* the assets constitute a separate fund and are not part of the trustee's own estate; *b* title to the trust assets stands in the name of the trustee or in the name of another person on behalf of the trustee; *c* the trustee has the power and the duty, in respect of which he is accountable, to manage, employ or dispose of the assets in accordance with the terms of the trust and the special duties imposed upon him by law. The reservation by the settlor of certain rights and powers, and the fact that the trustee may himself have rights as a beneficiary, are not necessarily inconsistent with the existence of a trust."

Because the source of this definition is an international convention which necessarily has to be capable of being applied to a number of different systems of law, its format inevitably has to include references to a number of features of a trust not mentioned in the definitions already considered and cannot include specific references to features which apply only in respect of English law, such as the fact that the trustee is compellable by a court acting under its equitable jurisdiction. Nevertheless, although like Lewin's definition it does not roll off the tongue as easily as the definition propounded by Underhill, its comprehensive nature cannot be disputed; no trust recognised by English law falls outside the four corners of this most recent of the many attempts to define a trust.

Trusts "in the higher sense" and trusts "in the lower sense"

It should be clear from the definitions offered that the type of trust with which we are concerned is an equitable obligation which is enforceable in the courts.[43] There is, however, no magic in the word "trust," as Lord O'Hagan once said,[44] and it can mean different things in different contexts. For example, a person may be in a position of trust without being a trustee in the equitable sense, and terms such as "anti-trust" or "trust territories" are not intended as relating to a trust enforceable in a court of equity. By the same token, a trust in the conventional legal sense may be created without using the word "trust."[45] In each case it is necessary to consider whether such a trust was intended.[46]

This basic question of definition arose for decision in *Tito* v. *Waddell*

---

[43] This is the general rule, but one exception is provided by the so-called "trust of imperfect obligation," *e.g.* a trust to maintain a monument or tomb or a particular animal. Such a trust is not enforceable, but nevertheless, anomalously, is valid: see *post*, p. 112.

[44] *Kinloch* v *Secretary of State for India in Council* (1882) 7 App. Cas. 619 at p. 630.

[45] *Tito* v.*Waddell* (*No. 2*) [1977] Ch. 106 at p. 211, *per* Megarry V.-C.

[46] See *post*, p. 90.

(*No.* 2),[47] a case which Megarry V.C. aptly described as "litigation on the grand scale."[48] The case involved Ocean Island, a small island in the Pacific. It was called Banaba by its inhabitants and they themselves were known as Banabans. The island was formerly part of the Gilbert and Ellice Islands protectorate which subsequently became a colony. At the beginning of this century phosphate was discovered on the island, and royalties for mining the phosphate were paid to the islanders. As time passed the Banabans sought increases in the royalties. Some increases were paid but they were considerably less than what the Banabans claimed. The Banabans continued to make various claims politically and internationally but when they failed, brought these proceedings. They claimed that the rates of royalty payable under certain transactions had been less than the proper rates and accordingly that the Crown as the responsible authority was subject to a trust or fiduciary duty for the benefit of the plaintiffs or their predecessors, and was liable for breach thereof.

The question whether there was a trust or fiduciary duty involved the construction of various agreements and ordinances as well as other documentation. In the result, it was held that there was not. The essential elements of the decision for purpose of definition[49] appear to be as follows:

1. Although the word "trust" was occasionally used with reference to the Crown or its agents it did not create a trust enforceable in the courts (what Megarry V.C. described as a "trust in the lower sense" or "true trust") but rather a trust "in the higher sense" by which was meant a governmental obligation which was not enforceable in the courts.[50]
2. Such a trust "in the higher sense" involved the discharge under the direction of the Crown.[51] There might be many means available of persuading the Crown, for example by international pressure, to honour its governmental obligations, and it might be more than a mere obligation, but it was not enforceable by the court.[52]
3. Although various ordinances imposed statutory duties they did not impose fiduciary obligations. It will be seen later that in some cases a person may be in a fiduciary position even though he is not a trustee in the proper sense of the word (for example, an agent or a partner or a company director) and he will be liable if he is in breach of his fiduciary obligations.[53] The relationship

---

[47] [1977] Ch. 106.

[48] *Ibid.* at p. 123. The report of Megarry V.C.s. judgment runs to 241 pages. The Vice-Chancellor also held a view of the *locus in quo.*

[49] For other aspects of the decision, see *post*, pp. 222, 593.

[50] Adopting the language of Lord Selborne L.C. in *Kinloch* v. *Secretary of State for India in Council, supra* at p. 625.

[51] *Tito* v. *Waddell (No.* 2) *ibid.* at p. 216.

[52] *Ibid.* at p. 217.

[53] See *post.* pp. 221 *et seq.*

from which the fiduciary obligations arise may be equitable or legal or statutory, but it is required that it be a relationship with enforceable legal consequences.[54] However, as Megarry V.C. held, "a trust in the higher sense or governmental obligation lacks this characteristic and where the primary obligation itself is one which the courts will not enforce, then . . . it [cannot] of itself give rise to a secondary obligation which is enforceable by the courts."[55]

4. If a duty is imposed by statute (such as the ordinances in this case) to perform certain functions it does not, as a general rule, impose fiduciary obligations, nor is it to be presumed to impose any. It has to be shown that the statute imposes such obligations.[56]

It may suffice to say that this book is concerned with "trusts in the lower sense" or "true trusts" and with those situations which give rise to enforceable fiduciary obligations.

II. Subject Matter of a Trust

Any property can form the subject matter of a trust, whether that property be tangible, that is to say a chose in possession such as a freehold or leasehold estate, or intangible, that is to say a chose in action such as a share or the benefit of a covenant or simple contract. It is evident from these illustrations that it makes no difference whether the property in question is realty or personalty. Furthermore, it makes no difference whether the interest subject to the trust is a legal estate or an equitable interest. If the legal estate in property is held by trustees on trust, the interests of the beneficiaries are necessarily equitable. If any beneficiary assigns his equitable interest to a third party to hold on quite different trusts, that equitable interest will constitute the subject matter of the second trust (technically a sub-trust and therefore subject to certain special rules which will be considered later[57]); the legal estate will remain vested in the original trustees.[58] However, property subject to a trust must be capable of being identified. Consequently, a liability cannot, without more, be the subject matter of a trust. If a creditor suggests to his debtor and the debtor agrees that, instead of repaying the loan, the debtor should hold the sum in question on trust for a third party, a valid trust will only arise if the debtor segregates the appropriate sum from his other assets by, for example, opening a new bank

---

[54] *Ibid.* at p. 224.
[55] *Ibid.* at p. 225.
[56] *Ibid.* at p. 235; see also *Swain* v.*The Law Society* [1982] 3 W.L.R. 261, H.L. (in exercising a statutory power the Law Society was performing not a private duty but a public duty for breach of which there was no remedy in breach of trust or equitable account); see further *post*, p. 223.
[57] See *post*, p. 35.
[58] See *Gilbert* v. *Overton* (1804) 2 H. & M. 110.

account for the purpose. If he fails to do this, something which in practice is highly likely since if the debtor had the assets to segregate he could equally easily have repaid the loan on the spot, the third party will be unable to point to any property subject to any trust and so will have no remedy.[59]

The precise nature of the interest of the beneficiary in the trust property has always been difficult to define.[60] On the one hand, the beneficiary has a proprietary interest in the subject matter of the trust because he can recover it from anyone into whose hands it passes other than a bona fide purchaser for value of a legal estate therein without notice of the interest of the beneficiary; on the other hand, given that if the property does reach the hands of such a person it cannot be recovered by the beneficiary, whose only option will then be to bring a personal action against his trustees for breach of trust, his interest is certainly not a right *in rem*. The best view is that his interest is a true hybrid—substantially more than a right *in personam* but substantially less than a right *in rem*. This is reflected by the decided cases, which regard the beneficiary as owner of the trust property for some purposes but not for others. Thus in *Baker* v. *Archer-Shee*,[61] the beneficiary was held to be the real owner of the trust assets for income tax purposes. On the other hand, in *Schalit* v. *Joseph Nadler*,[62] a beneficiary was held unable to distrain for rent due under a lease of the trust property granted by the trustee. The Divisional Court stated that "(t)he right of the *cestui que trust* whose trustee has demised property subject to the trust is not to the rent, but to an account from the trustees of the profits received from the trust".[63] Both these decisions appear to accord with principle.

III. Distinction from Other Legal Concepts

1. *Contract*

The general rule is that a contract is not enforceable by a person who is not a party to the contract, whereas a trust can be enforced by a bene-

---

[59] Exactly this situation arose in *M'Fadden* v. *Jenkyns* (1842) 1 Ph. 153; however, despite the fact that all three parties had clearly intended the debtor to be the trustee, Lord Lyndhurst L.C. generously found that the effect of the agreement was that the creditor held his right to sue the debtor on trust for the third party, thus providing her with a remedy against his personal representatives. The creditor can of course create such a situation intentionally; in *Barclays Bank* v. *Willowbrook International* (1987) 1 F.T.L.R. 386, a creditor charged to the bank a debt which was due to be repaid and the Court of Appeal held that any repayments made by the debtor were held by the creditor on constructive trust for the bank.

[60] See Latham (1954) 32 Can B.R. 520 on the question generally.

[61] [1927] A.C. 844.

[62] [1933] 2 K.B. 79.

[63] *Ibid.* at p. 83.

ficiary who is not (indeed he rarely is) a party to the instrument creating the trust. The rule of contract is one of general application and seems to have been firmly established by *Midland Silicones* v. *Scruttons*[64] and *Beswick* v. *Beswick*[65] but there are some recognised exceptions to it which are founded in statute.[66] They have no particular relevance to the law of trusts.

In addition, however, to the intervention of statute into the general law of privity of contract, the rigidity of the rule itself has also been mitigated in some (though rather small and uncertain) degree by recourse to the concept of the trust and this requires some discussion. For although the rule remains intact that only a person who is a party to a contract can sue upon it, yet if one of the parties expressly or impliedly contracts as *trustee* for a third party the latter is entitled to the benefit of that contract. Therefore if a contracting party enters into a contract as trustee for a third party, the third party, as beneficiary of the trust, will be entitled to the benefit of the contract. In the event that the other party breaches the contract, the machinery for its enforcement may take a number of forms. The trustee can recover on behalf of the third party beneficiary the damages suffered by the latter as well as the nominal damages suffered by himself.[67] Alternatively, the third party beneficiary can sue as *cestui que trust* joining the trustee as co-plaintiff and, if the trustee declines to be joined in that capacity, he can be joined with the other party to the contract as a co-defendant.[68]

No difficulty will arise if there is an express declaration of trust, or an assignment of the benefit of the contract to trustees. The real difficulty is to know when a trust is to be *implied* and this is shown by the way in which the case-law has developed. One of the earlier cases is *Re Flavell*[69] where articles of partnership provided that an annuity should be paid by the surviving partner to the widow of his co-partner. It was held that this created a trust of the annuity in favour of the widow which was free from the claims of the co-partner's creditors. Again, *Les Affréteurs Réunis S.A.* v. *Leopold Walford (London)*[70] the decision was to a

---

[64] [1962] A.C. 446. Cf. *New Zealand Shipping Co.* v. *A.M. Satterthwaite & Co.; The Eurymedon* [1975] A.C. 154, P.C., where a stevedore was allowed to claim the benefit of limitation clauses in a bill of lading: cf. also *Jackson* v. *Horizon Holidays* [1975] 1 W.L.R. 1468, C.A., where it was held that the plaintiff had made a contract for a family holiday, and though only he could sue for damages for breaches of that contract, he could sue for damages not only for his own discomfort and distress but for that suffered by his wife and children by reason of the defendant's breach of contract to provide them with the holiday contracted for; but see *Woodar Investment Development* v. *Wimpey Construction U.K.* [1980] 1 W.L.R. 277, H.L. rejecting the opinion of Lord Denning M.R. in *Jackson's* case so far as he suggested that a third party could sue on a contract.

[65] [1968] A.C. 58.

[66] See, *e.g.* Married Women's Property Act 1882, s.11; Marine Insurance Act 1906, s.14(2); Law of Property Act 1925, ss.47(1),56; Occupiers' Liability Act 1957, s.3; Road Traffic Act 1972, s.148(4).

[67] See *Gregory and Parker* v. *Williams* (1871) 3 Mer. 582; *Lloyd's* v. *Harper* (1880) 16 Ch.D. 290.

[68] See *Vandepitte* v. *Preferred Accident Insurance Corpn. of New York* [1933] A.C. 70 at p. 79.

[69] (1883) 25 Ch.D. 89.

[70] [1919] A.C. 801.

like effect although in this case the position was simplified by an agreement enabling the third party to sue.

The principles at stake were later discussed in *Harmer* v. *Armstrong*,[71] where there was a contract for the sale of the copyright in certain periodicals and the plaintiff for whose benefit the contract had been made claimed specific performance of the contract. The Court of Appeal held that the plaintiff as *cestui que trust* of the agreement could himself specifically enforce it. Lawrence L.J. said that there were two distinct rules as to neither of which there could be any reasonable doubt: (i) that the law does not recognise any *jus quaesitum tertio* arising by way of *contract*; (ii) that such a right may be conferred by way of a proprietary interest under a *trust*.[72] These dicta appear to suggest that it is easy to discover whether or not a trust in favour of a third party has been created. But in fact it is by no means easy, for there are other cases where the court has declined to imply the existence of a trust although it might be thought that if the court had been so disposed the implication could easily have been made. Thus, in *Vandepitte* v. *Preferred Accident Insurance Corpn. of New York*,[73] a car owner had insured his car in British Columbia against third party risks with the defendant and it was agreed that the policy should cover all persons driving with his consent. His daughter, while driving the car with his consent, injured the plaintiff and the plaintiff obtained judgment against her in an action of negligence. The judgment was not satisfied. Under the relevant Act in British Columbia a plaintiff, if he failed to recover his damages against a guilty motorist, could avail himself of any rights which the motorist enjoyed against the insurance company. The question was whether the daughter was a beneficiary under the policy. She was not a party to the contract of insurance: the result, therefore, depended on the presence or absence of a trust. The Privy Council held that no trust had been proved: the intention to prove a trust had to be affirmatively shown and this had not been done.

A similar result occurred in *Re Schebsman*.[74] A company agreed with its employee, in consideration of his retirement, to pay certain sums to him and after his death to his wife and child. He went bankrupt and soon afterwards died. The question was whether the trustee in bankruptcy could "intercept" the money which the employers were willing to pay to the wife and child. The Court of Appeal held that the employee had not entered into the contract as a trustee for his wife and child. However, although the wife and child could not have enforced the contract against the company, the company were nevertheless free to perform the terms of the contract and make the required payments. Since the employee would not have been able to intercept the payments, the trustee in bankruptcy could be in no better position. Du Parcq L.J. said that unless an intention to create a trust is clearly to be collected from the language used and the circumstances of the case the

---

[71] [1934] Ch. 65.
[72] *Ibid.* at pp. 87–88; *cf.* Romer L.J. at pp. 93-94.
[73] [1933] A.C. 70.
[74] [1944] Ch. 83.

court ought not to be "astute" to discover implications of such an intention.[75]

A like reluctance to imply a trust was manifested in *Swain* v. *The Law Society*.[76] This case concerned the master policy which The Law Society had arranged under statutory powers for indemnity insurance and which was compulsory for all practising solicitors. It had been agreed that a proportion of the commission earned by the insurance brokers in arranging the insurance should be paid to The Law Society which would apply it for the benefit of the profession as a whole. Two solicitors were dissatisfied with the scheme and claimed (*inter alia*) that The Law Society was a trustee of the benefit of the master policy contract for the benefit of all individual solicitors and was, therefore, accountable for the proportion of the commission which it received. Reliance was placed on the fact that the policy contract stated that the policy was entered into "on behalf of" solicitors and former solicitors, and these words, it was claimed, imputed an intention to create a trust. The House of Lords (reversing the Court of Appeal) rejected this argument. It was held that these words clearly did not *express* a trust and they did not necessarily *imply* a trust. As Lord Brightman said,[77] "it would indeed, be surprising if a society of lawyers, who above all might be expected to make their intention clear in a document they compose, should have failed to express the existence of a trust if that was what they intended to create." Moreover, it was unnecessary, as had been argued, to imply a trust to secure the commercial viability of the scheme; this was a statutory indemnity scheme, the policy had statutory authority, and accordingly all persons insured had a direct remedy against the insurers if they declined to perform their obligations.

These cases indicate that it may, in practice, be extremely difficult to provide a test by which it can be determined whether a contracting party is entering into a contract as trustee for a third party.[78] Indeed the view has been expressed that the way in which the court will decide a novel case is almost entirely unpredictable.[79]

The suggestion has also been made, as a reason for this difficulty, that trusteeship is too highly charged with magic to admit of an accurate test. "There is a vast deal of magic in words and among the words most highly charged with magic to be found is the word 'trustee'. "[80] However, whether or not this is the true reason, it would appear from

---

[75] *Ibid.* at p. 104.

[76] [1982] 3 W.L.R. 261.

[77] *Ibid.* at p. 276.

[78] In addition to the cases mentioned in the text see *Tomlinson* v. *Gill* (1756) Amb. 330; *Gregory and Parker* v. *Williams* (1817) 3 Mer. 582; *Lloyd's* v. *Harper* (1880) 16 Ch.D. 290; *Royal Exchange Assurance* v. *Hope* [1928] Ch. 179; *Re Gordon* [1940] Ch. 851; *Re Webb* [1941] Ch. 225. In these cases a trust was established. This was also held to be the position in *Fletcher* v. *Fletcher* (1844) 4 Hare 67: see *post*, p. 85. See also *Colyear* v. *Lady Mulgrave* (1836) 2 Keen 81; *Re Engelbach's Estate* [1924] 2 Ch. 348; *Re Sinclair's Life Policy* [1938] Ch. 799; *Re Foster (No. 1)* [1938] 3 All E.R. 357. In these cases a trust was *not* established.

[79] Williams (1944) 7 M.L.R. 123.

[80] Corbin (1930) 46 L.Q.R. 20.

decisions like *Re Schebsman* and *Swain* v. *The Law Society* that the courts are now reluctant to interpret a contract as creating a trust in the absence of the clearest possible evidence that a trust is intended. It is certainly unwise to place any reliance on the trust concept as providing a loophole in the principle of privity of contract.[81] It is also noteworthy that no reliance was placed on the trust concept in the decision of the House of Lords in *Beswick* v. *Beswick*[82] where relief was only obtained as a result of the particular facts of that case. A nephew was employed by his uncle in his business as a coal merchant. An agreement was made between them whereby the uncle assigned the business to the nephew in return for the latter's promise to pay the uncle £6 10s. 0d. a week for the rest of his life and when he died to pay the uncle's widow an annuity of £5 a week. The uncle died, and after making one payment to the widow, the nephew stopped all payments. The widow sued the nephew both in her personal capacity and as administratrix of her husband's estate. It was held that she had no claim in the former capacity because she was not a party to the contract. But because she was administratrix she could enforce the provisions of the agreement for the benefit of herself in her personal capacity by specific performance. If she had not been the administratrix of the promisee she would have been without a remedy. The case shows up the unsatisfactory state of the law regarding third party beneficiaries.[83]

A further allied problem arises out of the principle that equity will not assist a volunteer who is not a party to the contract even though it is made by means of a deed. Despite the arguments of academic writers that in such a case an enforceable trust of the benefit of the contract may have been constituted, thereby obviating the application of the equitable principle, the court continues to uphold this principle—not perhaps surprisingly in view of the fact that it was enunciated long ago by Lord Eldon and is supported by a body of case-law in the intervening years.[84]

2. Debt

It has already been seen that a liability cannot, without more, be the subject matter of a trust and that a debtor will only be able to create a valid trust of the sum which he owes in favour of his creditor or of a

---

[81] See also, generally, in addition to the articles mentioned in notes 79 and 80, Williston (1902) 15 H.L.R. 767; Dowrick (1956) 19 M.L.R. 374; Scamell (1955) 8 Cur. Leg. Pro. 131; Elliott (1956) 20 Conv. (N.S.) 43, 114; Andrews (1959) Conv. (N.S.) 179; Elliott (1960) 76 L.Q.R. 100; Hornby (1962) 79 L.Q.R. 228; Matheson (1966) 29 M.L.R. 397; Lee (1969) 85 L.Q.R. 213; Barton (1975) 91 L.Q.R. 236; Meagher and Lehane (1976) 92 L.Q.R. 427; Friend (1982) Conv. 280.

[82] [1968] A.C. 58. See also *Jackson* v. *Horizon Holidays* [1975] 1 W.L.R. 1468, (C.A.) where it was held that the plaintiff was entitled to damages for himself and family by reason of breach of contract. The notion of a trust arising was, however, rejected: see *ante*; p. 13, n. 64, *cf. Woodar Investment Development Ltd* v. *Wimpey Construction U.K. Ltd.* [1980] 1 W.L.R. 277, H.L.

[83] See (1967) 83 L.Q.R. 465.

[84] This matter is discussed further, *post*, p. 77, in relation to "Completely and Incompletely Constituted Trusts."

third party if he segregates the appropriate sum from his other assets.[85] Such a trust will clearly come into existence where the debtor makes an express declaration of trust in respect of duly segregated assets. The effect of the creation of such a trust will be to give its beneficiary an advantage over the other creditors of the debtor in the event of his bankruptcy—this is because the proprietary right of the beneficiary will enjoy priority over the purely personal rights of any unsecured creditors. For this reason, in the event that the debtor does subsequently become insolvent, such a trust will be vulnerable to challenge under the Insolvency Act 1986[86] on the grounds that it amounts to preferential treatment (technically known as a "preference") of the beneficiary vis-à-vis the other creditors. However, if consideration is given to the possibility of the debtor's insolvency at the time when the debt is first created, it is sometimes possible for the creditor to obtain a priority which cannot be successfully challenged.

There is in principle no reason why the same transaction should not give rise both to a trust and to a debt; a loan for a specific purpose can be made on terms that the sum advanced will be held on trust for the lender unless and until that purpose is carried out. What is crucial in such circumstances is the intention of the parties. In *Barclays Bank* v. *Quistclose Investments*[87] a company which was substantially indebted to the bank needed funds in order to pay a dividend on its shares. Quistclose Investments advanced the necessary funds on the basis that they were only to be used for this purpose and they were paid into a separate account at the bank, which was made aware of the arrangement. The company went into liquidation before the dividend had been paid. If Quistclose Investments was no more than a creditor of the company, then the funds in the bank belonged to the company and the bank would be entitled to set off the credit balance of the account against the substantially greater indebtedness of the company.[88] If, on the other hand, the funds were held on trust for Quistclose Investments, its proprietary interest therein would enjoy priority over the rights of the bank. The House of Lords held that arrangements for the payment of a person's creditors by a third person give rise to "a relationship of a fiduciary character or trust, in favour, as a primary trust, of the creditors, and secondarily, if the primary trust fails, of the third person"[89] Once the primary purpose was fulfilled, the third person would be no more than an unsecured creditor. However, there was "no difficulty in recognising the co-existence in one transaction of legal and equitable rights and remedies".[90] Since the purpose for which the funds had been advanced had failed, the funds were still held on trust for Quistclose Investments, whose beneficial interest was binding on the bank because it had been aware of the basis on which the funds had

---

[85] See *ante*, p. 11.
[86] s.239 in the case of companies, s.340 in the case of individuals.
[87] [1970] A.C. 567.
[88] Banks have a statutory right to amalgamate the balances of the different accounts held with them.
[89] (1970) A.C. 567 at p. 580.
[90] *Ibid.* at p. 581.

been transferred. Although there is some controversy as to the precise nature of the secondary trust,[91] *Barclays Bank* v. *Quistclose Investments* has been applied both where part of the funds advanced had indeed been used for the specific purpose in question, the court holding that the creditor was entitled to recover what was left,[92] and where the funds, although advanced for a specific purpose, were paid not by way of loan but rather in satisfaction of a contractual debt.[93] In this latter case Peter Gibson J. stated that:

> "the principle in all these cases is that equity fastens on the conscience of the person who receives from another property transferred for a specific purpose only and not therefore for the recipient's own purposes, so that such person will not be permitted to treat the property as his own or to use it for other than the stated purpose".[94]

While it seems tolerably clear that the common intention of the parties is an essential prerequisite of what has become known as a "*Quistclose* Trust," it is equally possible for proprietary rights to be conferred on someone who would normally be no more than an unsecured creditor as a result of the unilateral act of one of the parties. It is clearly possible for a purchaser who is paying for goods in advance to specify that the funds remitted are to remain his property in equity unless and until the goods are actually supplied. Such a reservation will clearly bind the vendor and his trustee in bankruptcy but will not, however, bind any bank in which the funds have been deposited unless they are clearly segregated in what the bank knows to be a trust account. It is also possible for proprietary rights to be created as a result of a unilateral act of the potential debtor. In *Re Kayford*[95] a mail-order company in financial difficulties became concerned as to its ability to provide the goods for which its customers were paying in advance. It consequently opened a "Customers' Trust Deposit Account" into which all purchase moneys received from customers were paid and were withdrawn only as and when their orders could be fulfilled. Shortly afterwards the company went into liquidation. Megarry J. held that the funds in this bank account were held on trust for the customers; by paying the purchase moneys into the trust account, the company had prevented the customers from ever becoming creditors so no question of a preference arose. *Re Kayford* has been followed.[96] However, its principle will clearly not apply where the recipient of the funds has contemplated the possibility of making further drawings therefrom.[97] More generally, given that the customers had no intention of becoming

---

[91] It has variously been classified as an express trust, a resulting trust, and a constructive trust. See P. Millett Q.C.: 101 L.Q.R. (1985) 269 and C.E.F. Rickett: 107 L.Q.R. (1991) 608 & in *Equity, Fiduciaries and Trusts 1993* (ed. Waters) 325.

[92] *Re EVTR* (1987) B.C.L.C. 647.

[93] *Carreras Rothmans* v. *Freeman Matthews Treasure* [1985] Ch. 207.

[94] *Ibid.* at p. 222

[95] [1975] 1 W.L.R. 279.

[96] In *Re Chelsea Cloisters* (1981) 41 P. & C.R. 98.

[97] *Re Multi Guarantee Co.* [1987] B.C.L.C. 257.

anything more than general creditors, it is not easy to see why the
unilateral creation of proprietary rights in their favour does not amount
to a preference; if the only reason why they did not become creditors
was the same unilateral act of the company, that cannot be a sufficient
reason for the absence of a preference.[98]

Finally, it must be emphasised that, in the absence of any of the
special circumstances considered in the preceding two paragraphs, the
liability of a debtor, whether the debt in question is contractual or non-
contractual, is a personal liability and does not confer any proprietary
rights on the creditor. In *Re Sharpe (a bankrupt)*[99] the bankrupt
purchased a property with the help of a sum lent to him by his aunt as
part of an arrangement whereby the aunt was to live in the property for
the rest of her life. Browne-Wilkinson J., while finding in her favour on
another ground, rejected her claim to a beneficial interest in the
property by virtue of her loan advance, holding that where "moneys are
advanced by loan there can be no question of the lender being entitled
to an interest in the property".[1] He distinguished on the grounds of its
"very special" facts the earlier decision in *Hussey* v. *Palmer*[2] where, in a
similar situation, the Court of Appeal had been unable to agree as to
whether the payment in question had been made by way of loan or by
way of direct contribution to the building of an extension and had, by a
majority, imposed a constructive trust on the basis of a principle[3] which
is no longer regarded as good law.[4] While it is sometimes difficult to
decide, in the context of family arrangements, whether a particular
payment has been made by way of loan or by way of contribution to the
acquisition of the property in question, once the intention of the parties
has actually been established the two possibilities are mutually
exclusive.

3. *Estates of Deceased Persons*

In a sense the legal personal representative—an executor in the case of a
person nominated as such in a will, otherwise an administrator—of a
deceased person is a trustee for the creditors and beneficiaries claiming
under the deceased; he holds the real and personal estate for their
benefit and not his own. Moreover, by virtue of section 69 of the Trustee
Act 1925, the provisions of the Act also apply to personal representatives.[5] But it would be an error to equate their legal position, because
certain differences still persist, primarily as the result of other statutory
enactments. For example, an action by a beneficiary to recover *trust*
property or in respect of any breach of trust cannot, in the absence of

---

[98] See W. Goodhart and G. Jones: 43 M.L.R. (1980) 489.
[99] [1980] 1 W.L.R. 219.
  [1] *Ibid.* at p. 223.
  [2] [1972] 1 W.L.R. 1286.
  [3] That a constructive trust is a general equitable remedy which can be invoked in order to
     do justice in the individual case. See *post*, pp. 218 & 281.
  [4] See *post*, p. 281.
  [5] See also Administration of Estates Act 1925, ss.33, 39.

fraud or retention of the property by the trustee,[6] be brought after the expiration of six years.[7] Personal representatives are subject to a different period of limitation, namely, twelve years for a claim to personal estate,[8] and six years for actions to recover arrears of interest in respect of legacies.[9] On the other hand, the exception relating to fraud and to property retained by the trustee applies to personal representatives just as it does to trustees.[10] The authority of personal representatives in handling pure personalty is *several*, whereas that of trustees is *joint*.[11] However, over realty (which includes since 1925, for this purpose, leaseholds)[12] the authority of personal representatives, like that of trustees, is joint.[13] The difference lies in the fact that one of a number of personal representatives can give a valid title to a purchaser or pledgee of pure personalty; one of a number of co-trustees cannot: all must act.

The *functions* of personal representatives are also different from those of trustees. The duty of trustees is to administer a trust on behalf of beneficiaries, some of whom may be minors or unborn, and this may be a long continuing process, since many years may elapse before a trust is brought to an end. On the other hand, the primary duty of personal representatives is to wind up the estate by paying debts and inheritance tax, and applying the net residue to the persons beneficially entitled to it under the will or intestacy[14] or to trustees, who may be themselves, to hold on trust. Furthermore, whereas a beneficiary has an equitable interest in the trust property as soon as the trust takes effect,[15] a legatee or devisee or person entitled on intestacy has no proprietary interest (legal or equitable) whilst the assets of the state remain in course of administration. All he has is a right to require the deceased's estate to be duly administered by the personal representatives.[16]

It follows that although a personal representative has, like a trustee, fiduciary duties to perform, those duties are owed to the estate as a whole; it does not, therefore, necessarily follow that the duty of an executor in the course of administering an estate is subject to the trustee's duty of holding the balance evenly between the benefici-

---

[6] Limitation Act 1980, s.21(1).

[7] *Ibid.* s.21(3) and see *post*, p. 593.

[8] *Ibid.* s.22.

[9] *Ibid.*

[10] *Ibid.* See also *post*, p. 592.

[11] *Jacomb* v. *Harwood* (1751) 2 Ves. Sen. 265; *Attenborough* v. *Solomon* [1913] A.C. 76. It has been recommended that the power should also be joint in the case of personal representatives (Law Reform Committee on the Powers and Duties of Trustees (23rd Report, Cmnd. 8733 (1982)). For historical reasons, see 1 Spence's *Equitable Jurisdiction* (1846), p. 578. *Collier* v. *Hollinshead* (1984) 272 E.G. 941.

[12] Administration of Estates Act 1925, s.3(1), 54.

[13] *Ibid.* s.2(2).

[14] Considered in more detail *post*, p. 367.

[15] At any rate, in the case of a "fixed trust," but not in the case of a "discretionary trust": see *post*, p. 156.

[16] *Commissioner of Stamp Duties (Queensland)* v. *Livingston* [1965] A.C. 694: *Eastbourne Mutual B.S.* v. *Hastings Corporation* [1965] 1 W.L.R. 861; *Lall* v. *Lall* [1965] 1 W.L.R. 1249; *Re Leigh's Will Trusts* [1970] Ch. 277. See further, Mellows, *Law of Succession* (5th ed.), p. 411.

aries.[17] In *Re Hayes's Will Trusts*[18] it was accordingly held that where executors exercised a testamentary power of sale in favour of one of the children of the testator at an estate duty valuation, his other children could not attack the valuation on the ground that the executors did not consider the question of holding the balance evenly between the beneficiaries.

Personal representative becoming trustee. It is a question of some complexity to determine the time when, and the circumstances in which, a personal representative may become a trustee in cases where he has been appointed to both offices. It must be emphasised at the outset, however, that a personal representative holds his office as such for all time unless the grant to him is limited or the court revokes it.[19] The question is whether he has exhausted all his duties and functions as such and taken on himself the character of a trustee.

No problem will arise if the technically correct practice is followed in cases where trusts of *land* are designed to continue after completion of the administration of the estate, namely that the personal representatives vest the property, by means of a document known as an assent,[20] in themselves as trustees[21] (the situation is exactly the same where the personal representatives are also beneficially entitled to the property under the will or intestacy in question). Where such a written assent is made, it is clear that there is a change in their character from personal representatives to trustees (or beneficial owners), even though liability *qua* personal representative may still persist. However, until 1964, it was generally accepted that such a written assent was not actually necessary in such circumstances and that, when the estate had been fully administered in the sense that all funeral and testamentary expenses and all debts and liabilities had been discharged and the residue ascertained, the personal representatives became trustees[22] or, alternatively, could exercise their statutory powers to appoint new trustees in their place[23] (or became beneficial owners). However, this generally accepted practice was first doubted[24] and subsequently in 1964 rejected in *Re King's Will Trusts*,[25] where it was held that an express written assent is necessary in every case. Although this decision is a little difficult to reconcile with the wording of the appropriate statutory

---

[17] *Re Hayes's Will Trusts* [1971] 1 W.L.R. 758 at p. 764; and see *post*, p. 461, for discussion of *trustees'* duty in this respect.
[18] *Supra.*
[19] See *Attenborough* v. *Solomon* [1913] A.C. 76 and see generally *post, infra.*
[20] See *Attenborough* v. *Solomon* [1913] A.C. 76 at p. 83.
[21] As in *Re Bowden* (1890) 45 Ch.D. 444; *Re Swain* [1891] 3 Ch. 233; *Re Timmis* [1902] 1 Ch. 176; *Re Oliver* [1927] 2 Ch. 323 (where property was to be held for persons in succession); and as in *Re Claremont* [1923] 2 K.B. 718 (where the property was to be held on trust for sale).
[22] *Re Ponder* [1921] 2 Ch. 59, *Re Pitt* (1928) 44 T.L.R. 371.
[23] *Re Cockburn's Will Trusts* [1957] Ch. 438.
[24] *Harvell* v. *Foster* [1954] 2 Q.B. 367.
[25] [1964] Ch. 542.

provision,[26] such an express assent is clearly in practice more desirable because it admits of no doubt as to the precise capacity in which the land in question is being held. At the time, however, the decision in *Re King's Will Trusts* had the effect of rendering technically defective the title to any land which had been administered in accordance with what had previously been regarded as the accepted practice and many of these titles had to be put in order by the time-consuming and expensive process of obtaining the necessary written assent, sometimes many years after the estate in question had been administered. Now that more than thirty years have passed, virtually all the defective titles which have not already been rectified must now be hidden behind the present root of title to the land in question[27] and so are in practice completely irrelevant. Whether or not the decision in *Re King's Will Trusts* is actually correct,[28] any assent relating to a legal estate in land is now invariably made in writing. However, the Court of Appeal has since established that an assent to the vesting of an *equitable* interest need not be in writing but can be inferred by conduct[29] and it has always been clear that assents in writing are not necessary in the case of pure personalty[30]; assents to the vesting of such property by the personal representatives in themselves, whether as trustees or as beneficial owners, can be implied and can be taken to have occurred as soon as the administration has been completed.

4. *Agency*

The relationship between principal and agent has some resemblances to the relationship between trustee and beneficiary. For example, agents are liable to their principals, as are trustees to their beneficiaries, for any secret profits made out of the property or business entrusted to them and in such circumstances their respective positions may coincide.[31] The main difference, from which other consequences follow, is that the relationship between principal and agent is primarily that of creditor and debtor. So a trustee has full title to the property vested in him[32]: an agent has not. Agents act on behalf of the principal and subject to his control: trustees do not.[33] Agency is based on agreement: it is not necessary that there should be—indeed there rarely is—an agreement between trustee and beneficiary.

---

[26] Administration of Estates Act 1925 s.36(4).

[27] Only where the title to the land in question is still unregistered and where there has been no disposition for value since 1964 is it likely that any technical defect in title created by the decision in *Re King's Will Trusts* will still cause any problems.

[28] The Court of Appeal assumed that *Re King's Will Trusts* had been correctly decided (but in fact distinguished it) in *Re Edwards's Will Trusts* (1982) Ch. 30, C.A.

[29] *Re Edwards's Will Trusts* [1982] Ch. 30, C.A..

[30] Because Administration of Estates Act 1925 s.36 applies only to realty (which includes, for this purpose, leaseholds).

[31] See *post.* pp. 221, 225.

[32] See *ante*, p. 7.

[33] See *post*, p. 520.

5. *Equitable Charges*

This distinction is that a charge merely imposes a liability on the property which is subject to it; a trust imposes a fiduciary character on the owner of the property.[34] This has a number of consequences. Thus, if property is held subject to a charge and the chargee satisfies the charge he will hold the property beneficially,[35] whereas a trustee will, on the termination of the trust, hold the property on a resulting trust.[36] Again, a chargee is not accountable for rents and profits during the subsistence of the charge,[37] whereas a trustee is.[38] On the other hand, a basic similarity consists in the fact that both are equitable interests and may, therefore, be overridden on a purchase for value of the legal estate.[39]

6. *Conditions*

A condition may, in certain carefully defined circumstances, operate as a trust. Property may be given to a person on condition that he does something or confers a benefit on somebody. But it is only if that condition can, or must necessarily, be fulfilled or satisfied out of the property that it will take effect as a trust.[40] This will not be its effect if the duty is merely collateral.[41]

7. *Powers*

The basic distinction, subject however to much elaboration, between a trust and a power is that a trust is imperative whereas a power is discretionary. Almost all trusts involve the exercise of a power or discretion by the trustees. In many cases this does not affect beneficial entitlement. So, depending on the circumstances of the particular trust, trustees will often have powers which include those to vary the investments of the trust[42]; to grant a lease of property which is subject to the trust[43]; to settle claims[44]; to apply income for the support of an infant beneficiary or to accumulate it[45]; to apply to the court for

---

[34] *Cunningham* v. *Foot* (1878) 3 App. Cas. 974 at pp. 992–993, *per* Lord O'Hagan.

[35] *Re Oliver* (1890) 62 L.T. 533.

[36] See *post*, p. 201.

[37] *Re Oliver, supra.*

[38] See *post*, p. 430.

[39] *Parker* v. *Judkin* [1931] 1 Ch. 475.

[40] *Att.-Gen* v. *Wax Chandlers Co.* (1873) L.R. 6 H.L. 1; *Cunningham* v. *Foot* (1878) 3 App. Cas. 974 at p. 995, *per* Lord O'Hagan.

[41] See *Re Brace* [1954] 1 W.L.R. 955 (house devised to a daughter on condition that "she provides a home" for another daughter: no trust arose). *Cf. Re Frame* [1939] Ch. 700 (a condition in a will that a legatee should adopt the testator's daughter did constitute a trust); *Re Niyazi's Will Trusts* [1978] 1 W.L.R. 910 (the words "on condition that" were held apt to create a trust). *Cf. Swain* v. *The Law Society* [1982] 3 W.L.R. 261, H.L.: (the words "on behalf of" did not express or imply a trust); see *ante*, p. 15 and *post*, p. 223.

[42] See *post*, p. 431.

[43] Law of Property Act 1925, s.28; Settled Land Act 1925, s.41.

[44] Trustee Act 1925, s.15.

[45] See *post*, p. 483.

guidance as to the execution of the trust[46]; and to insure trust property.[47] Trustees or any other persons designated in the trust instrument for this purpose may have other powers, such as those to remove trustees and to appoint new ones.[48] Indeed it is of the fundamental nature of a trust that a trustee is not a puppet at the end of a wire pulled by the settlor or the beneficiaries,[49] but is a person who is to exercise an independent judgment over a wide field. These administrative powers of trustees will each be fully discussed in due course in the appropriate Chapter.

However, the trustees' discretion need not be limited to the administrative and other matters just indicated but can extend to beneficial entitlement. Trustees can be given a power to select which person or persons shall receive the benefit of the property subject to the trust. Such a power can be either wholly unrestricted or restricted to an already defined class of persons.[50] Alternatively, in a situation where the trust instrument provides that each member of a class of beneficiaries is to receive some benefit, the trustees may be given the power to determine how much each beneficiary will actually receive and, in relation to income, whether it is distributed or accumulated.[51] These powers relating to the existence and extent of beneficial enjoyment can also be conferred on persons who are not themselves trustees; such persons are known as donees of a power. In such circumstances, the trustees hold the property for whatever beneficiaries and to whatever extent the donee of the power in question indicates. The precise nature and interrelation of powers and discretions of this type are discussed fully in Chapter 4.[52] For present purposes, all that is necessary is an outline of the different categories of trusts and powers relating to beneficial entitlement.

Where a person has a right, but is not under any obligation, to make a selection relating to the beneficial enjoyment of property, he is said to hold a mere power. The traditional view is that, in the event that the person entitled to make the selection fails to do so, the court cannot step in and decide the beneficial enjoyment of the property in question; in other words, when a mere power is not exercised, that power cannot be executed by the court. However, a distinction has recently been drawn between mere powers held by trustees (a "fiduciary power"), and mere

---

[46] See post, p. 393.

[47] Trustee Act 1925, s.19. The position is surprising. Trustees are under no duty to insure (Re McEacharn (1911) 103 L.T. 900) and the statutory power is only to insure for a sum up to three quarters of the value of the property. Express powers of insuring usually allow the cover to be effected in the full reinstatement value.

[48] See post, p. 366.

[49] It is in this respect that the position of a trustee differs from that of a nominee, who is often under an express or implied contractual obligation to comply in all respects with the beneficiary's directions.

[50] Such powers are known respectively as general powers and special powers. A third category, the hybrid or intermediate power, has evolved much more recently; such powers are exerciseable in favour of anyone except already defined persons or classes of persons (see Re Manisty's Settlement [1974] Ch. 17).

[51] See post, p. 130.

[52] See post, p. 130.

powers held by anyone else (a "non-fiduciary power" or a "personal power"). It has now been held[53] that in the event that a fiduciary power is not exercised, the court will in appropriate circumstances step in and execute that power. However, the court is still unable to step in and execute a non-fiduciary or personal power.

Where, on the other hand, a person not only has a right but is also under an obligation to make a selection relating to the beneficial enjoyment of property, he is said to hold a "trust power", an apparently contradictory term which indicates that, contrary to the basic distinction between a trust and power, the power in question is imperative rather than discretionary. A trust power can only arise where the selection is to be made from an already defined class of persons. In this situation, it has always been held that, in the event that the person entitled to make the selection fails to do so, the court can and will step in and decide the beneficial enjoyment of the property in question; in other words, if a trust power is not exercised, the court can and will execute that power.[54] Rather confusingly, two quite distinct situations are described as giving rise to the creation of a trust power. First, where a trustee is under a duty to make a selection relating to the beneficial enjoyment of property vested in him; this situation is more usually described as a discretionary trust. Secondly, where a person who is not a trustee is under a duty to make a selection relating to the beneficial enjoyment of property which is not vested in him; this situation is also described as a "power in the nature of a trust". Given the very considerable differences between trusts and powers, it is most unfortunate that both discretionary trusts and powers in the nature of a trust have been described by the same name; the confusion thus caused has at times even extended to the members of the House of Lords.[55]

Precisely which of the various different kinds of trusts and powers outlined above has been created in any given case is a question of construction of the language of the deed or will in question. Such instruments should ideally be drafted in such a way as to leave no room for doubt. However, in the majority of the cases which have come before the courts, the wording of the instrument in question has given rise to considerable doubt which has had to be resolved by the application of a number of rules of construction developed for the purpose. These rules and the other important distinctions between trusts and powers, particularly the different rights of the beneficiaries of a trust and the persons in whose favour a power is able to be exercised, will be discussed fully in Chapter 4.[56]

---

[53] In *Mettoy Pension Trustees* v. *Evans* [1990] 1 W.L.R. 1587.

[54] Traditionally, by dividing the property equally among the members of the class; however, other methods of executing a trust power have become established as a result of the decision of the House of Lords in *McPhail* v. *Doulton* [1991] A.C. 424.

[55] Particularly in *McPhail* v. *Doulton* [1991] A.C. 424.

[56] See *post*, p. 130.

CHAPTER 2

CLASSIFICATION OF TRUSTS

I. STATUTORY, EXPRESS, IMPLIED, RESULTING AND CONSTRUCTIVE TRUSTS

TRUSTS may be created (i) by statute—these are *statutory* trusts; (ii) intentionally by an act of the settlor—*express* trusts; (iii) impliedly, *i.e.* arising from the presumed intention of the settlor—*implied or resulting* trusts, or (iv) by operation of law—*constructive* trusts.[1]

1. *Statutory Trusts*

A number of trusts have been expressly created or implied by statute. The following examples[2] may be taken:

(a) Under section 34 of the Law of Property Act 1925, whenever land is conveyed to persons in undivided shares it vests in the first four persons named on a statutory trust for sale for all the grantees beneficially as tenants in common.

(b) Under section 36 of the Law of Property Act 1925, where land is conveyed to joint tenants, it vests in the first four named on a statutory trust for sale for all the grantees beneficially as joint tenants.

(c) Under section 33 of the Administration of Estates Act 1925, on the death of a person intestate, his property vests in his personal representatives upon trust for sale and division between the spouse and issue of the intestate or other relatives specified in the Act.[3]

2. *Express Trusts*

An express trust is created by express declaration of the settlor. It may be by will, deed, writing or by parol.[4] Whichever form is used, it is a trust which has been intentionally created by the settlor. A trust will

---

[1] For a well-known classification, see *Cook* v. *Fountain* (1676) 3 Swanst. 585, *per* Lord Nottingham L.C. *Cf. Soar* v. *Ashwell* [1893] 2 Q.B. 390; *Re Llanover Settled Estates* [1926] Ch. 626.

[2] For further examples see S.L.A. 1925, s. 36; L.P.A. 1925, s. 19.

[3] See *post*, p. 366.

[4] See *post*, p. 35 for cases where writing is necessary.

indeed still be regarded as express even where the settlor has, for example, expressed himself ambiguously if the court concludes, upon a true construction of the instrument, that a trust was *intended* by the settlor. Thus words of prayer, entreaty or expectation, known as precatory words, may be held to create an express trust.[5] Furthermore, a power to distribute property among a class of persons may possibly be construed as indicating an intention to create an express trust in favour of that class if there is no gift over in default of appointment; the question in each case is one entirely of construction of the relevant instrument.[6]

3. *Implied or Resulting Trusts*

These are trusts arising from the unexpressed but presumed intention of the settlor. Such trusts are often known as implied or resulting trusts because the beneficial interest may "result" to the settlor or his estate. Thus, to take two examples only at this stage: first, where the settlor of an express trust fails to deal effectually with the whole of the beneficial interest the court will imply that so much of the beneficial interest as is undisposed of will be held on trust for the settlor himself; and, secondly, where a purchase is made in another person's name, a similar resulting trust may arise in favour of the person who provided the purchase-money.[7]

4. *Constructive Trusts*

Constructive trusts arise by operation of law. Unlike all other trusts, a constructive trust is imposed by the court as a result of the conduct of the trustee and therefore arises quite independently of the intention of any of the parties. To give an example, in one case the trustee of leasehold property used his position, on the determination of the lease, to induce the landlord to renew the lease to him. This was held to be an attempt to obtain a personal advantage for himself and was accordingly antagonistic to the beneficiaries' interest; it was an act of bad faith and the trustee was directed to hold the new lease upon the same trusts as he held the old lease.[8]

II. SIMPLE AND SPECIAL TRUSTS

1. *Simple Trusts*

A simple trust arises where a trustee is simply a repository of the trust property with no active duties to perform.[9] If a settlor transfers property to trustees to hold on trust for a nominated beneficiary absolutely, the trust is a simple trust. The only duty which the trustee has to perform is

---

[5] See *post*, p. 90.
[6] See *post*, p. 137.
[7] See further *post*, p. 189.
[8] *Keech* v. *Sandford* (1726) Sel. Cas. t. King 61 and see also generally *post*, p. 242.
[9] *Underhill* v. *Hayton*, *Law of Trusts and Trustees* (14th ed., (1987)) pp. 29–30.

to transfer the whole or some part of the property to the beneficiary if the latter so directs.[10] In such a case, he is known as a bare trustee.

2. *Special Trusts*

A special trust arises where the trustee is appointed to carry out a purpose designated by the settlor and must exert himself actively in the performance of the trust.[11] He is called an active trustee. Thus if the trust created is that the trustee is to collect the rents and profits of the trust property, to pay the cost of repairs and insurance, and pay the residue of the rents and profits to a nominated beneficiary for his lifetime and, on his death, hold the property on trust for someone else absolutely, the trust is a special one until the life tenant dies because the trustee has active duties to perform during that period. On the death of the life tenant, however, the trust becomes a simple trust and the trustee a bare trustee because the only duty remaining to him is to transfer the trust property to the other beneficiary in the manner and to the extent that the latter directs.

Special trusts are subdivided into ministerial and discretionary trusts. The former require for their performance no more than ordinary business intelligence on the part of the trustees, such as the collection of the rents and profits of the trust property. The latter require the exercise of a discretion on the part of the trustees. For example, where money is simply left to trustees to divide up at their absolute discretion between a number of local charities such as the Dogs' Home, the Cats' Home, and the Home for Distressed Gentlewomen, the trust in question is discretionary. A trust is similarly discretionary where the trustees have a discretion to determine the amount of income, if any, to be paid to each member of a class of beneficiaries.[12] Discretionary trusts are considered in detail in Chapter 4.

III. EXECUTED AND EXECUTORY TRUSTS

A trust is *executed* in the technical sense of the expression when all the terms of the trust are specified in the trust instrument or declaration that constitutes it. On the other hand, a trust is *executory* where, although the trust property is vested in the trustees or is the subject of an enforceable agreement to so vest it, the instrument or declaration requires the execution of a further instrument setting out the detailed terms of the trust. The distinction between the two is that in the case of an executed trust the settlor has, in the language of the Nineteenth Century, been his own conveyancer,[13] whereas in the case of an executory trust he has not. A conventional, if old-fashioned, example of an executory trust is marriage articles from which a formal marriage settlement is later to be prepared.[14] A modern example is a pension

---

[10] See *Christie* v. *Ovington* (1875) 1Ch. D. 279; *Re Cunningham and Frayling* [1891] 2 Ch. 567.
[11] See n. 9.
[12] See *post*, p. 130.
[13] *Egerton* v. *Brownlow* (1853) 4 H.L.C. 1 at p. 210, *per* Lord St. Leonards.
[14] For further discussion, see *post*, p. 55.

scheme established by an interim deed of trust which provides for the subsequent execution of a definitive deed of trust. In one such case,[15] the definitive deed of trust was duly executed but its validity was challenged when questions arose as to the entitlement to surplus funds. Scott J. in fact found the definitive deed valid but stated that, had he not done so, the interim deed would have been upheld as a valid executory trust capable of being executed by a court order; this would have had the effect of providing rules corresponding to those in the definitive deed by means of which the questions as to the surplus funds would have been able to be resolved.

IV. COMPLETELY AND INCOMPLETELY CONSTITUTED TRUSTS

A trust which is described as completely constituted is one which has been perfectly created by the settlor either declaring himself to be a trustee of the property in question or vesting that property in the intended trustees by means of the appropriate formalities so that nothing more remains to be done by him. Both executed and executory trusts are inevitably completely constituted trusts. But if, on the other hand, something still remains to be done by the settlor, the trust in question is imperfect and is said to be incompletely constituted, which is another way of saying that, because there is as yet no valid trust, no interest of a proprietary nature has yet vested in the beneficiary. This will be the case where the settlor has undertaken to vest title to the trust property in the intended trustees but has not yet complied with all the formalities required for a transfer of the property in question. In such circumstances, the only conceivable remedies of the beneficiaries will be contractual rather than proprietary.[16]

V. FIXED AND DISCRETIONARY TRUSTS

Discretionary trusts have already been mentioned as one of the two forms of "special trusts". They must also be contrasted with fixed trusts, trusts in favour of pre-determined beneficiaries or classes of beneficiaries. In the case of a fixed trust, each of the beneficiaries is entitled in equity to a fixed pre-determined share of the trust property and his rights thereto may be enforced against the trustees. In the case of a discretionary trust, on the other hand, the trustees have to exercise one or more discretions vested in them by the settlor before any individual beneficiary has a right to any part of the trust property; the discretion vested in the trustees may merely be that of deciding in what proportions, if any, the trust property is to be divided among the members of a pre-determined class; at the other extreme, the discretion vested in the trustees may be that of deciding the membership of the class itself. Whatever the discretion, unless and until it is exercised, no

---

[15] *Davis* v. *Richards & Wallington Industries* [1990] 1 W.L.R. 1511.
[16] For further discussion, see *post*, p. 58.

individual beneficiary or potential beneficiary has any proprietary rights.[17]

VI. PRIVATE AND PUBLIC TRUSTS

A private trust aims to benefit either one person or a defined number of persons. A public or charitable trust aims, in general, to achieve a purpose which will benefit society or some considerable section of it. Because of their public nature, charitable trusts enjoy a number of privileges not shared by private trusts, for example, in relation to perpetuity and certainty and—most important today—with regard to liability to tax and rates.[18]

VII. NEW CLASSIFICATIONS?

The traditional classification of implied, resulting and constructive trusts, which has generally been thought to be workable, has been the subject of considerable judicial comment in recent years.

In the first place, a subdivision of resulting trusts has been suggested. The suggestion was made by Megarry J. in *Re Vandervell's Trusts (No. 2)*[19] where he made a distinction between a "presumed resulting trust" and an "automatic resulting trust". The first class of case would arise when a purchase is made in another person's name but not on trust; there is then a rebuttable presumption that the other holds the property on a resulting trust for the real purchaser. In such a case there is an implied or presumed intention to that effect which can be rebutted by evidence to the contrary.[20] The second class of case is where a transfer has been made on trusts which leave the whole or part of the beneficial interest undisposed of (for example, because the trusts are ineffective or incomplete). Here the transferee automatically holds on a resulting trust for the transferor to the extent that the beneficial interest is not disposed of. In such a case, according to Megarry J., the resulting trust "does not depend on any intentions or presumptions, but is the automatic consequence of [the transferor's] failure to dispose of what is vested in him".[21] Such is an example of an "automatic resulting trust".

On the face of it, the distinction between "presumed" and "automatic" resulting trusts appears to accord with common sense but it is fair to say that, in the same way as a presumed resulting trust is said to be created by implication as the result of a purchase in the name of another, so also an intention could be implied on the part of a settlor that the settled property should result to him in so far as he has failed to dispose of it. The implication of an intention does not appear to be markedly more artificial in the one case than in the other. This point is

---

[17] They do, however, have a right to compel the due administration of the trust and can share in the fund on a premature determination. See *post*, p. 156.
[18] The distinctions are discussed *post*, p. 296.
[19] [1974] Ch. 269, at pp. 294, 295. Megarry J.'s decision was reversed by the Court of Appeal ([1974] Ch. 269), but no comment was made on the judge's formulation.
[20] See *post*, p. 195 for the ways in which it may be rebutted.
[21] [1974] Ch. 269, at 294.

open to debate but it is doubtful whether it has any particular practical, as opposed to theoretical, significance.

Secondly, there have been a number of attempts to bring the concepts of resulting and constructive trusts closer together. These attempts, which will be considered in Chapter 8, were largely initiated by Lord Denning M.R. in a series of cases decided in the years immediately before and after 1970. In *Cooke* v. *Head*[22] he stated that

> "whenever two parties by their joint efforts acquire property to be used for their joint benefit, the courts may impose or impute a constructive or resulting trust",[23]

while in *Hussey* v. *Palmer*[24] he said that, although

> "the plaintiff alleged that there was a resulting trust. I should have thought that the trust in this case, if there was one, was more in the nature of a constructive trust: but this is more a matter of words than anything else. The two run together."[25]

The expressed intention of Lord Denning M.R. was to convert the constructive trust into a remedy for unjust enrichment and thus incorporate into English law what had long been the attitude of the courts of the United States of America towards the constructive trust. Indeed in *Hussey* v. *Palmer*, following the passage which has just been cited, Lord Denning M.R. continued:

> "By whatever name it is described, it is a trust imposed by law whenever justice and good conscience require it. It is a liberal process, founded upon large principles of equity . . . It is an equitable remedy by which the court can enable an aggrieved party to obtain restitution."[26]

Subsequent decisions rejected the approach manifested in this series of cases and English law seems for the moment to have reverted to its traditional approach towards the constructive trust. However, there are now some signs that English law may be about to make some further move, of a more limited nature than that made in the years immediately before and after 1970, towards a more remedial approach. The Court of Appeal has recently stated[27] that "there is a good arguable case" that circumstances may arise in which "the court will be prepared to impose a constructive trust de novo as a foundation for the grant of equitable remedy by way of account or otherwise", classifying such a trust as a "remedial constructive trust".

Whatever the fate of this possible new development, however, the

---

[22] [1972] 1 W.L.R. 518.
[23] *Ibid.* at p. 520.
[24] [1972] 1 W.L.R. 1286.
[25] *Ibid.* at p. 1289.
[26] *Ibid.* at pp. 1289–1290.
[27] In *Metall und Rohstoff A.G.* v. *Donaldson Lufkin & Jenrette* [1989] 3 W.L.R. 563 at p. 621.

series of decisions handed down immediately before and after 1970 has had a lasting influence on the law governing joint enterprises entered into by the members of a family unit. It is in this area of the law that the concepts of resulting and constructive trusts have been brought closer together as a result of the development of what has become known as "the common intention constructive trust" which contains elements both of resulting trusts and of constructive trusts. If two parties make direct contributions to the acquisition of a property in which they intend to live, the principles of "presumed" resulting trusts will give each of them a beneficial interest in proportion to his respective contribution, provided that the contrary is not stated in the conveyance by means of which the property is conveyed to one or both of them. However, if one of the parties is subsequently encouraged by the other to believe that he or she will acquire an enhanced beneficial interest in the property by making contributions of a less direct nature towards the repayment of the mortgage or the subsequent improvement of the property (a straightforward illustration is the payment by one of the parties of all the day to day household expenses so that the other can more easily make the repayments of the mortgage), any attempt subsequently to deprive that party of the enhanced beneficial interest which he or she has been encouraged to expect will be regarded as unconscionable and will lead either to the imposition of a constructive trust or to the invocation of the principle of equitable proprietary estoppel.[28] This development has in no sense undermined the traditional categories of resulting and constructive trusts which have already been mentioned. What it has done is to produce a new type of trust which contains features of both types of trust. As will be seen in Chapter 8, it is thought that this may in the end lead to the development of a general principle of unconscionability to replace both the "common intention constructive trust" and the principle of proprietary estoppel. For the moment, however, the "common intention constructive trust" has undoubtedly brought closer together certain aspects of resulting and constructive trusts which are co-existing in a clearly defined but rather unexpected manner.

---

[28] See particularly *Lloyds Bank* v. *Rosset* [1990] 2 W.L.R. 867, H.L., discussed *post*, p. 282.

CHAPTER 3

EXPRESS PRIVATE TRUSTS

I. CAPACITY TO CREATE A TRUST

IN general, if a person has a power of disposition over a particular type of property, he can create a trust of it. Accordingly, any person over the age of 18[1] may create an express trust of any property which is capable of disposition, unless he is suffering from mental incapacity, and he may also create a trust of certain types of property of which he cannot dispose. If a company grants a pension to a retired director, and includes in the pension agreement a provision that the pension is non-assignable, the retired director may nevertheless be able to create a valid trust of the benefit of that agreement. So far as concerns mental incapacity, the position depends on whether the settlor is incapable of managing his affairs, and a receiver has been appointed under sections 94 and 99 of the Mental Health Act 1983. Where a receiver has been appointed it is thought that any purported trust would be void.[2] The court may, however, either on the application of another person or on its own initiative direct the creation of a trust of a mental patient's property.[3] Further, since January 1, 1970, the court has been able to make a will on behalf of the patient,[4] and it can vary any trust which is made at any time until the patient's death.[5] In exercising these powers, the court must principally consider what the patient would have been likely to have done if he had not been incapable.[6]

Even where there is no receiver, a trust will be set aside if it can be shown that the settlor did not understand the nature of the act in which he was engaged.[7] It seems that the burden of proof will always lie at the outset upon the person seeking to set the trust aside, but where there is a long history of mental illness, this burden will be easily discharged, and the court will then require evidence that the trust was created during a lucid interval.[8] Where the trust was created for valuable con-

---

[1] Family Law Reform Act 1969, s.1(1).
[2] There is no authority under the 1983 Act, but see *Re Marshall* [1920] 1 Ch. 284, a decision on the Lunacy Act 1890.
[3] Mental Health Act 1983, s.96(1)(*d*).
[4] *Ibid.* ss.96(1)(*e*), 97.
[5] *Ibid.*
[6] *Re T.B.* [1967] Ch. 247, *Re D.(J.)* [1982] Ch. 237.
[7] *Re Beaney* [1978] 1 W.L.R 770, *Simpson* v. *Simpson* [1992] 1 F.L.R 601 (cases of *inter vivas* gifts which upset the balance of the estate being held void).
[8] See *Cleare* v. *Cleare* (1869) 1 P. & D. 655; *Chambers and Yatman* v. *Queen's Proctor* (1840) 2 Curt. 415.

sideration, it will not be set aside if the person providing the consideration was unaware of the mental incapacity at the time when the trust was made.[9]

A person under the age of 18 cannot hold land,[10] although he can own an equitable interest in land. A minor cannot, therefore, create a settlement of a legal estate in land, for this has never been vested in him, but he can create a trust of property which he does hold, including equitable interests. The trust is voidable until shortly after the minor attains the age of 18, and if he does not repudiate it the trust will become fully binding.[11]

It was previously possible for a female minor aged 17 or over to make a binding settlement, but this power no longer exists.[12]

In order to create even a voidable trust, a minor must be old enough to appreciate the nature of his act. If he is too young to appreciate this the act is void, and where property has been transferred, the recipient will hold upon a resulting trust[13] for the infant. Little does the unsuspecting adult who has a sticky bag of sweets pushed into his hand by a toddler appreciate that thereafter he holds them on a resulting trust.[14] The same principle would apply where a person suffering from mental incapacity seeks to create a trust which is void, and transfers property to a trustee. Therefore, although full capacity is required before a fully binding express trust can be created, a resulting trust may arise as a result of a person's involuntary actions.

II. STATUTORY REQUIREMENTS FOR THE CREATION OF AN EXPRESS TRUST

Certain statutory provisions governing the creation of a trust demand consideration because these require writing. When these provisions are inapplicable the trust may be created orally. It may indeed be thought surprising that, as will be seen, a declaration of trust must be evidenced by writing if it relates to a square foot of land, but need not be if it relates to millions of pounds worth of cash or investments.

1. *Law of Property Act* 1925, *s.*53(1)(b)[15]

This provides that a declaration of trust respecting any land or any interest therein[16] must be manifested and proved by some writing

---

[9] *Price* v. *Berrington* (1851) 3 Mac. & G. 486.

[10] Law of Property Act 1925, s.1(6); Family Law Reform Act 1969, s.1.

[11] *Edwards* v. *Carter* [1893] A.C. 360.

[12] The power was conferred by the Infant Settlements Act 1855, but this has been repealed by the Family Law Reform Act 1969, s.11(a).

[13] See *post*, p. 201.

[14] Presumably he should sell them and convert them into authorised investments: see *post*, p. 430.

[15] This replaces Statute of Frauds 1677, s.4 (in part), s.7.

[16] This includes freehold and leasehold property: Law of Property Act 1925, s.205(1)(ix); and also apparently a share in the proceeds of sale of land: Law of Property (Miscellaneous Provisions) Act 1989, s.2(6).

signed by some person who is able to declare such trust, or by his will.[17] It will be observed that a declaration of trust should in effect be merely *evidenced* by writing; it has not necessarily to be made in writing. And the evidence may take the most diverse forms,[18] provided that it contains all the terms of the trust (*i.e.* parties, property and the way in which the property is to be dealt with[19]). Writing will still be required even if the land is abroad and is unnecessary according to the *lex situs*, because this is a rule of evidence which must be complied with in an English court.[20] It will also be noticed that this provision does not sanction signature by an agent.

Resulting, implied and constructive trusts are exempt from these requirements.[21]

2. *Law of Property Act* 1925, s.53(1)(c)[22]

It is enacted that a disposition of an equitable interest or trust subsisting at the time of the disposition must be in writing and signed by the person disposing of the same or by his agent lawfully authorised in writing, or by his will. It is therefore required that an assignment of an equitable interest or trust must be *in writing*, not merely evidenced by writing; but the writing need not in all cases be completely detailed and, for example, if the assignee is to hold in a fiduciary capacity, the writing need not comprise particulars of the trust.[23] At the same time, it appears to be unnecessary that the writing be contained in one document; a number of documents may be joined together for the purpose of satisfying the statute, provided that they are sufficiently interconnected.[24] Section 53(1)(*c*), however, does not cover the area of law covered by subsection (1)(*b*) because that deals only with the creation of trusts, not with their disposition. The creation and operation of resulting, implied and constructive trusts are exempt from this requirement but any disposition of interests arising thereunder must comply with the section.[25]

Section 53(1)(*c*) therefore has to be complied with where an existing equitable interest or trust is being disposed of but not where a wholly new equitable interest or trust is being created. What is the position where the beneficiary of an existing trust declares that he is holding his beneficial interest on sub-trust for a third party? This looks like the

---

[17] If made by will and intended only to operate after death, it must comply with the Wills Act 1837, s.9; *post*, p. 44.

[18] e.g. the memorandum may be in correspondence (*Foster* v. *Hale* (1798) 3 Ves. Jun. 696); a recital in an instrument (*Re Hoyle* [1893] 1 Ch. 84); an answer to interrogatories (*Hampton* v. *Spencer* (1693) 2 Vern. 288); or a telegram (*McBlain* v. *Cross* (1871) 25 L.T. 804).

[19] *Forster* v. *Hale, ante.*

[20] *Rochefoucauld* v. *Boustead* [1897] 1 Ch. 196, at p. 207.

[21] L.P.A. 1925, s.53(2), and see *post*, p. 42.

[22] This replaces the Statute of Frauds 1677, s.9. See, generally, G. Battersby (1979) Conv. 17.

[23] *Re Tyler* [1967] 1 W.L.R. 1269.

[24] *Re Danish Bacon Co. Staff Pension Fund Trusts* [1971] 1 W.L.R. 248. This was, *per* Megarry J., a novel question on which there appeared to be no previous direct authority.

[25] *Post*, p. 42.

creation of a wholly new equitable interest or trust and so it might be anticipated that section 53(1)(c) does not have to be complied with. However, it has been held[26] that, unless the person declaring the sub-trust has reserved some active duties,[27] he "disappears from the picture"[28] and the original trustee thereafter holds directly on trust for the sub-beneficiary. In such a case, the declaration of the sub-trust has in effect amounted to an outright disposition of the interest of the original beneficiary; it is consequently thought[29] that the creation of such a sub-trust has to comply with the requirements of section 53(1)(c).

While it is therefore still to be established whether or not the creation of a sub-trust amounts to a "disposition" for the purposes of section 53(1)(c), other aspects of the meaning of this term have had to be considered by the House of Lords. In *Grey* v. *I.R.C.*[30] the settlor, having made six settlements, *orally* directed the trustees to hold 18,000 £1 shares which had already been transferred to them on the trusts of these settlements. The trustees then executed six declarations of trust: they were all in similar form and each recited that the trustees were holders of shares, the settlor's oral direction and their acceptance of the trust reposed in them by that direction. These transactions amounted to an ingenious exercise to avoid payment of stamp duty normally chargeable on transfer of shares[31]; but, as it happened, the six declarations of trust were assessed to *ad valorem* stamp duty, and the exercise failed. It was held that the directions given by the settlor were in fact *dispositions* by him of his equitable interest in the shares within the meaning of the section and, because they were not made in writing as required by the

---

[26] This was stated in *Grainge* v. *Wilberforce* (1889) 5 T.L.R. 436 at p. 437 and held by the Court of Appeal in *Re Lashmar* [1891] 1 Ch. 258.

[27] In which case, as was held in *Onslow* v. *Wallis* (1849) 1 Mac. & G. 506, a wholly new trust will have been created; the classic example of such active duties is the duty to pay the rents and profits of the trust property to the sub-beneficiary, thus restricting his rights to call for the capital; whether the fact that an apparently passive sub-trust is for persons by way of succession makes it active is unclear but in *Re Lashmar supra* Fry L. J. stated that it did not do so.

[28] *Grey* v. *I.R.C.* [1958] Ch. 375 at p. 382 (Upjohn J.).

[29] There has been no relevant authority since 1925. G. Battersby *op. cit.* adopts the view stated in the text. B. Green in (1984) 37 M.L.R. 385 suggests that all sub-trusts, whether active or passive, have to comply with s.53(1)(c).

[30] [1960] A.C. 1.

[31] Stamp duty is a tax which is payable on documents, so that where a transaction is properly effected orally, no duty is payable. A method of avoiding duty was evolved some time ago, whereby the settlor orally makes a declaration of trust, and some time later signs a document merely recording what he has done. As long as these two events are separate—see *Cohen and Moore* v. *I.R.C.* [1933] 2 K.B. 126—as the trust is effected by the oral declaration, no duty is payable. *Grey* v. *I.R.C.* was an attempt to extend this principle. It really consisted of three stages:
(a) a transfer by the settlor of the shares to the trustees to hold as nominees on his behalf (because there was no change in the beneficial interest, duty of only 50p was payable);
(b) the oral direction to the trustees (no duty);
(c) subsequent declarations of trust.
Without s.53(1)(c), the oral declaration would have been sufficient to pass the equitable interest, and so no duty would have been payable. But by virtue of the requirement of s.53(1)(c), the disposition had to be in writing, and the disposition was not effective until the declarations of trust were signed. Duty was therefore payable.

provision, were ineffective; but they became effective on the execution of the later declarations of trust. The word "disposition" had to be given the wide meaning which it bears in normal usage and the declarations of trust were, accordingly, rightly assessed.

It had been persuasively argued that section 53 was merely a consolidation of three sections of the Statute of Frauds 1677, *viz.* sections 3, 7 and 9, and, so treated, the term "disposition" was merely the equivalent of the former words of section 9—"grants and assignments"—which would not cover the transaction concerned. It was, as Lord Radcliffe said, a "nice question" whether a parol declaration of trust was or was not within the mischief of that section. The point had never been decided and perhaps never would be. But the question was only relevant if section 53 was to be treated as a true consolidation of these three sections of the Statute of Frauds and as governed, therefore, by the general principle that a consolidating Act is not to be read as effecting change in the existing law unless the words are too clear to admit of any other construction. The House of Lords held, however, that it was impossible to regard section 53 as a consolidating enactment in this sense. The Law of Property Act was no doubt strictly a consolidating statute but what it consolidated was not merely the Law of Property Act 1922, but also the Law of Property (Amendment) Act 1924. The sections of the Statute of Frauds were untouched by the 1922 Act but were repealed and re-enacted in altered form by the 1924 Act. So it was held, there was no direct link between section 53(1)(c) and section 9 of the Statute of Frauds: the link was broken by the changes introduced by the 1924 Act and it was those changes, not the original statute, that section 53 must be taken as consolidating. If so, it was inadmissible to allow the construction of the word "disposition" to be limited or controlled by any meaning attached to "grants and assignments" in section 9 of the old statute.[32]

The word "disposition" was thus given a wide meaning in *Grey* v. *I.R.C.* It has, however, subsequently been made clear that a disclaimer of an equitable interest is not caught by the section and so does not have to be in writing. This was held in *Re Paradise Motor Company*[33] where a verbal disclaimer by a person to whom shares had been given in such a way as to give him an equitable interest therein was held to be effective and to disentitle him from claiming in the liquidation of the company in question. It has also been stated that the right of an employee to nominate a person to receive moneys payable under a pension fund in the event of his death prior to becoming entitled to receive his pension is not caught by the section. In *Re Danish Bacon Company Staff Pension Fund*,[34] Megarry J. held that such a right did not amount to a testamentary disposition and so did not have to comply with the formal requirements for wills[35] and stated that he "very much

---

[32] [1960] A.C. 1 at 17–18.

[33] [1968] 1 W.L.R. 1125.

[34] [1971] 1 W.L.R. 248 at p. 256.

[35] See *post*, pp. 44. On this point, the decision of Megarry J. was confirmed and applied by the Privy Council in *Baird* v. *Baird* [1990] 2 A.C. 548.

doubted" whether the right was caught by section 53(1)(c). He doubted
not only whether such a nomination could properly be described as a
disposition, given that it had no more than a mere possibility of
disposing of anything, but also whether the interest of the person at the
time of making the nomination could properly be described as
"subsisting". His view seems entirely justified. However, given that he
was able to hold that there was sufficient writing in any event,[36] he did
not actually have to decide the point. Section 53(1)(c) was also given a
narrow construction by the House of Lords in *Vandervell* v. *I.R.C.*[37] and
by the Court of Appeal in *Re Vandervell's Trusts (No. 2).*[38] Both these
cases (and a third case which also went to the House of Lords) arose out
of an ill-advised endowment in favour of the Royal College of Surgeons.

The facts of this unfortunate litigation require fairly detailed examination.[39] Vandervell had during his lifetime been a very successful
businessman. He ran a private products company in which he was
beneficially entitled to virtually all the shares, and he could declare
dividends as and when he pleased. In 1949 he declared trusts in favour
of his children, which he did by forming a trustee company and
transferring money and shares to the trustee company to be held in
trust for his children (the so-called "children's settlement"). In 1958 he
decided to found a chair of pharmacology at the Royal College of
Surgeons and to endow it by providing £150,000. He then directed his
bank, who held shares in his products company as his nominee, to
transfer the shares to the College, not however by direct gift, but by
requiring the College at the date of transfer to grant to his trustee
company an option to re-purchase the shares for £5,000 (a figure much
less than market value) at any time within five years. The purpose of
this transaction was that when £150,000 had been raised, he or his
trustee company would be able to regain the shares which could be
used for other purposes. From 1958 to 1961 the products company
declared dividends on the shares which were more than sufficient to
found the chair at the College. Unfortunately, Vandervell failed to
specify the trusts on which the trustee company was to hold the option.
(It appeared that he had not made up his mind whether the option
should be held in trust for his children or the employees of his products
company.) The Revenue thereupon argued that Vandervell was liable to
surtax on the dividends,[40] the reason being that he had failed to define
the trusts on which the option was to be held. Subsequently, in
Vandervell v. *I.R.C.*[41] the House of Lords, by a majority of three to two,
held that as no trusts of the option had been declared, there was a

---

[36] *Supra.*
[37] [1967] 2 A.C. 291.
[38] [1974] Ch. 269.
[39] The judgment of Lord Denning M.R. in *Re Vandervell's Trusts (No. 2), supra,* contains an
incisive statement of the facts.
[40] Amounting to £250,000; under the Income Tax Act 1952, s.415. What are now known as
higher rates of income tax were then known as surtax.
[41] [1967] 2 A.C. 291; applied, as between different parties, in *Re Vandervell's Trusts (No. 2)*
[1974] Ch. 269, with regard to the period 1958–61; see *infra.*

resulting trust in favour of Vandervell and, therefore, he had been rightly assessed.

This was sufficient to dispose of the case, but the Revenue also argued that in any event section 53(1)(c) had not been complied with. At the outset Vandervell had held the equitable beneficial interest in the shares which were in the name of his bank; he had never transferred that equitable interest to the College in the manner required by section 53(1)(c); consequently, the beneficial interest was still vested in him and he was for that reason liable to surtax on the dividends declared thereon. However, the House of Lords rejected this contention, holding that section 53(1)(c) has no application where the holder of the equitable interest also controls the legal interest and intends that both should be transferred to a third party beneficially. In other words, section 53(1)(c) only applies to the disposition of an existing equitable interest when that interest is both before and after the disposition vested in someone other than the holder of the legal interest. The House of Lords had little alternative but to reach this conclusion since otherwise nominees would no longer have been able to pass a beneficial interest to a third party in the absence of a written disposition by or on behalf of the beneficiary.[42] However, the reasons enunciated by the House are less than wholly convincing[43] and it may be that the decision is best regarded as having been taken on policy grounds.

The decision thus taken does at least place a necessary limitation on the scope of section 53(1)(c).

However, the actual decision in *Vandervell* v. *I.R.C.* that there was a resulting trust with the consequential serious tax liability for Vandervell led directly to *Re Vandervell's Trusts (No. 2)*[44] which involved section 53(1)(c) in another way. To resume the recital of the sequence of events. Thus far, the trusts of the option to repurchase had not been specified and the option itself had not been exercised. In October 1961, however, the trustee company exercised the option. They paid £5,000 from money of the children's settlement to the College. Accordingly, they became legal owners of the shares themselves, no longer merely of the option to re-purchase the shares. But at this stage Vandervell did not expressly declare the trusts on which the shares of dividends should be held. Only in January 1965 did he execute a deed transferring to the trustee company such interest as he might have in the shares or dividends, expressly declaring that the trustee company was to hold them on the trusts of the children's settlement. He died in 1967.

---

[42] In particular, the practice whereby brokers who are holding shares on behalf of their clients resell them on the strength of oral instructions would have required some reconsideration in the event that the House of Lords had reached the opposite conclusion.

[43] Lord Upjohn (with whom Lord Pearce agreed) had recourse to the mischief rule of statutory interpretation in order to hold that the section was enacted to prevent fraud on those truly entitled and so could not apply to an absolutely entitled beneficiary, an argument which casts some doubt on the conclusion reached in *Grey* v. *I.R.C.*, while Lord Wilberforce begged the question by holding that Mr. Vandervell had done all in his power to transfer his beneficial interest and so could rely on the Rule in *Re Rose* (see *post*, p. 60) *et seq.* (see G.H. Jones (1966) 24 C.L.J. 19.)

[44] [1974] Ch. 269.

Re Vandervell's Trusts (No. 2) concerned the period between October 1961 and January 1965. The Revenue, on the basis that Vandervell had not divested himself of his interest in the shares or the option until January 1965, assessed his estate to surtax in respect of the dividends received during this period.[45] The Revenue was not, however, a party to *Re Vandervell's Trusts (No. 2)*.[46] What had happened was that Vandervell had made no provision in his will for his children because, as he thought, he had sufficiently provided for them in the children's settlement. The executors of the will on behalf of the beneficiaries of the will claimed that they were entitled to all moneys received by the trustee company as dividends between October 1961 and January 1965 thereby ousting the claims of the children. The executors' appeal against the revenue assessment was stood over pending the action against the trustee company.

It has been mentioned that the moneys for the exercise of the option were provided from the children's settlement. It was also a fact that thereafter all dividends received by the trustee company were paid by them to the children's settlement and treated as part of the funds of that settlement. Furthermore, the solicitors for the trustee company had written a letter to the Revenue stating that the shares would be held on the trusts of the children's settlement. The Revenue admitted that all these dealings, which were done with Vandervell's approval, showed that Vandervell and the trustee company *intended* that the shares should be held on trust for the children's settlement, but it was argued that this intention was unavailing, the reasons being as follows: (1) that until October 1961 Vandervell had an equitable interest under a resulting trust[47]; (2) that he himself never disposed of that interest until January 1965; and (3) that in any case any disposition prior to January 1965 would have been a disposition of an equitable interest which, by virtue of section 53(1)(c) of the Law of Property Act 1925, had to be in writing. The Court of Appeal rejected this argument as fallacious and held (*inter alia*)[48] that the dealings with the moneys during this period not only showed an intention to create but actually created a trust of the shares in favour of the children's settlement which, because it involved pure personalty, could be created without writing.[49] Section 53(1)(c) was, therefore, irrelevant.

Such was the decision, but some doubts must remain. In the first place, it appears dubious whether a valid trust of the shares was completely constituted by the events referred to.[50] In the second place, with regard to section 53(1)(c), while there is no doubt that both Vandervell and the trustee company *intended* that the shares should be

---

[45] Amounting to £628,229.

[46] The Revenue had failed in their application to be joined in the proceedings: *Re Vandervell's Trusts* [1971] A.C. 912. In the result, paradoxically, the executors had the duty of fighting the Revenue's battle for them, because if the Revenue succeeded the executors would have to meet the surtax assessments.

[47] See *Vandervell v. I.R.C.* [1967] 2 A.C. 291, *supra*.

[48] See further, *post*, pp. 63, 75.

[49] The Law of Property Act 1925, s.53(1)(b), applies only to trusts of land. See *ante*, p. 34.

[50] See *post*, p. 63.

held on trust for the children's settlement, it is difficult to infer that Vandervell could have intended to dispose or did dispose of his equitable interest under the resulting trust of the option since he was unaware that he had such an interest until January 1965 when the first instance decision was handed down in *Vandervell* v. *I.R.C.*. Further, even if the necessary intention can be inferred to have existed prior to January 1965, why did the decision in *Grey* v. *I.R.C.*, where the settlor was also trying to dispose of an interest under a resulting trust, not oblige him to dispose of his equitable interest in writing in accordance with section 53(1)(c)?[51] The Court of Appeal held that Vandervell's interest under the resulting trust had been extinguished when the gap in the beneficial ownership which had given rise to it was filled by the creation or declaration of a valid trust. The gap in the beneficial ownership had only existed until the option was exercised; as soon as this had occured, a valid trust of the shares was created in favour of the children's settlement. It is possible to confine this proposition to the situation where an option is held on trust; in this case *Re Vandervell's Trusts (No. 2)* merely decides that, where an option is held on resulting trust, a direction by the beneficiary to the trustees to declare new trusts of the property which they receive by exercising the option does not require writing. However, the formulations of this principle in the judgments are not actually restricted to options and so at least suggest that, where any property is held on resulting trust, a direction by the beneficiary to the trustees to declare new trusts of that property does not require writing; if this is indeed the case, then it is not easy to see any satisfactory distinction between *Re Vandervell's Trusts (No. 2)* and *Grey* v. *I.R.C.*, where a similar direction by the beneficiary of a resulting trust to the trustees to hold the property on new trusts was held to require writing.

Leave to appeal to the House of Lords was granted in *Re Vandervell's Trusts (No. 2)* but no appeal was in fact made, perhaps unfortunately for legal theory but presumably not for the Vandervell trustees.

The present state of the law may be summarised as follows.

1. Section 53(1)(c) has to be complied with where an existing equitable interest or trust is being disposed of but not where a wholly new equitable interest or trust is being created. A declaration of an active sub-trust amounts to the creation of a new trust, while a declaration of a passive sub-trust seems in effect to amount to an outright disposition and so is thought to have to comply with the requirements of the section.
2. The term "disposition" in section 53(1)(c) has the wide meaning which it bears in normal usage and consequently includes a direction to trustees to hold on new trusts but not a disclaimer.
3. Section 53(1)(c) has no application where the holder of the equitable interest also controls the legal interest and intends that

---

[51] See the summary of the argument by Stephenson L. J. in *Re Vandervell's Trusts (No. 2)* [1974] Ch. 269 at pp. 322–323. The point had not been argued before Megarry J. at first instance.

both should be transferred to a third party beneficially; thus the section only applies to the disposition of an existing equitable interest when that interest is both before and after the disposition vested in someone other than the holder of the legal interest.

4. Where an option is held on resulting trust, a direction by the beneficiary to the trustees to declare new trusts of the property which they receive by exercising the option does not require writing.

5. It may be that the above proposition is not confined to options in which case, where any property is held on resulting trust, a direction by the beneficiary to the trustees to declare new trusts of that property does not require writing.

3. *Law of Property Act* 1925, *s*.53(2)

This subsection provides that section 53 as a whole does not apply to the creation or operation of resulting, implied or constructive trusts.[52] This provision clearly exempts such trusts from section 53(1)(*b*). This is illustrated by *Hodgson* v. *Marks*.[53] An elderly widow was persuaded by her lodger to convey her house into his name on the spurious grounds that this would prevent him from being turned out of the house after her death. He subsequently sold and conveyed the property to third parties without revealing that he had no beneficial interest therein. The Court of Appeal held that he had held the property on resulting trust for the widow; such a trust arose without any need to comply with the statutory formalities required by section 53(1)(*b*) and so was capable of binding the third parties.[54] Section 53(2) is, however, interpreted extremely literally in relation to section 53(1)(*c*); although resulting, implied and constructive trusts can come into existence and operate without any need for writing, any disposition of an interest arising under such a trust must comply with the section—this is demonstrated by *Grey* v *I.R.C.*, where what was being disposed of by the settlor was an interest arising under a resulting trust. It has, however, been suggested that section 53(2) may enable equitable interests to be disposed of without any need for writing where the disposition in question is by way of constructive sub-trust arising as the result of the formation of a specifically enforceable contract of sale.

This possibility was canvassed in another decision of the House of Lords, *Oughtred* v. *I.R.C.*[55] Shares in a private company were settled on trust for a mother for life and subject thereto for her son. They agreed to exchange other shares in the same company to which the mother was absolutely entitled for the son's equitable remainder, thus enlarging her life interest into absolute ownership. The existence of this specifically

---

[52] See *ante*, p. 35.

[53] [1971] Ch. 892.

[54] It was in fact held to bind the third parties on the grounds that the widow had an overriding interest under the Land Registration Act 1925 s.70(1)(*g*).

[55] [1960] A.C. 206.

enforceable contract automatically gave rise to a constructive trust[56] (or more strictly sub-trust) under which the son held his equitable remainder on constructive trust for his mother. It was argued that as a result of the creation of this passive sub-trust the son had "disappeared from the picture" and his equitable remainder had passed to his mother; since by virtue of section 53(2) no writing was necessary for the creation of this constructive sub-trust, the mother had therefore acquired an absolute beneficial interest in the shares without the use of any instrument on which stamp duty could be levied (although the trustees had subsequently transferred the legal title to the shares to her, this had transferred only the bare legal title, in respect of which only a nominal duty of 50p was payable). The majority of the House of Lords, however, accepted the Revenue's contention that this transfer had to be stamped *ad valorem*. The reasoning behind this decision was stated by Lord Jenkins, who held that, if the subject matter of a sale is such that the full title to it can only be transferred by an instrument, then any instrument executed by way of transfer ranks for the purposes of stamp duty as a conveyance upon sale. He stated that, in the case of a contract for the sale of land, "a constructive trust in favour of the purchaser arises on the conclusion of the contract for sale, but (so far as I know) it has never been held on this account that a conveyance subsequently executed in performance of the contract is not stampable *ad valorem* on a transfer on sale".[57]

On this basis, the scope of section 53(2) was not directly in issue. However, Lord Radcliffe, who dissented, accepted the contention that the mother had acquired the equitable remainder without any writing having been used.[58] On the other hand, Lord Cohen (also dissenting) and Lord Denning both stated by way of dicta[59] that, although the constructive sub-trust had come into existence without any need for writing, the interest arising thereunder could not be transferred without complying with section 53(1)(c). This view, which at first sight appears consistent with *Grey* v. *I.R.C.*, in fact overlooks the point that the son's "disappearance from the picture" must have caused his interest to pass to his mother automatically by operation of law. Consequently, the view of Lord Radcliffe seems preferable and has been adopted in a number of subsequent decisions. In *Re Holt's Settlement*[60] Megarry J. held that, when beneficiaries of a trust agree, for valuable consideration, to a variation of the beneficial interests, their existing interests (which are necessarily equitable) are varied without any need for any writing. In *D.H.N. Food Distributors* v. *Tower Hamlets L.B.C.*[61] two members of the Court of Appeal accepted that, where the transaction in question was not a gift, an equitable interest in land could

---

[56] Under a specifically enforceable contract of sale, the purchaser acquires an immediate equitable interest in the subject matter which takes effect behind a constructive trust. See *post*, p. 292. *et seq.*
[57] [1960] A.C. 206 at p. 240.
[58] *Ibid.* at p. 228.
[59] *Ibid.* at pp. 230, 233.
[60] [1976] 1 Ch. 100 at p. 116.
[61] [1976] 1 W.L.R. 852, *per* Goff L. J. at p. 865, *per* Shaw L. J. at p. 867.

pass without writing. Lord Wilberforce went even further in *Chinn* v. *Collins*,[62] where he stated that, as soon as there was an agreement for the sale of the equitable interest in shares in a public company (which were held by nominees) followed by payment of the price, "the equitable title passed at once to the purchaser". This contract was not even specifically enforceable so that this enunciation of principle is even wider than that of Lord Radcliffe.

Consequently, while the matter certainly cannot be regarded as settled, it appears increasingly probable that where an equitable interest becomes subject to a constructive sub-trust as a result of the creation of a specifically enforceable contract of sale, that equitable interest will, by virtue of section 53(2), immediately vest in the purchaser without any need for writing. However, if this principle indeed exists, it is now limited to pure personalty, because all contracts for the sale of land are now required to be in writing.[63]

4. *Law of Property* Act 1925 s.55

This section provides (*inter alia*) that nothing in section 53 is to invalidate dispositions by will or affect any interest validly created before the commencement of the Act, or the acquisition of title by adverse possession, or affect the law relating to part performance (now abolished by the Law of Property (Miscellaneous Provisions) Act 1989).

5. *Wills* Act 1837, s.9

This section (as substituted by section 17 of the Administration of Justice Act 1982) provides that no will shall be valid unless (a) it is in writing and signed by the testator or by some other person in his presence and by his direction; and (b) it appears that the testator intended by his signature to give effect to the will; and (c) the signature is made or acknowledged by the testator in the presence of two or more witnesses present at the same time; and (d) each witness either, (i) attests and signs the will or (ii) acknowledges his signature in the presence of the testator (but not necessarily in the presence of any other witness), but no form of attestation shall be necessary. A will executed without these formalities is void; this applies both to an equitable interest and to a legal estate disposed of by the will.

6. *Equity will not Allow a Statute to be Used as an Instrument of Fraud*

The courts will not allow the statutory provisions mentioned above, any more than they would allow the relevant sections of the Statute of Frauds 1677, to be applied in such a way as to achieve a fraudulent purpose. A basic equitable maxim is that equity will not allow a statute to be used as a "cloak" or "engine" for fraud. No doubt an important

---

[62] [1981] A.C. 533, at p. 548.
[63] Under the Law of Property (Miscellaneous Provisions) Act 1989 s.2.

principle behind the statutory provisions already mentioned—indeed this was particularly true of the Statute of Frauds itself—is the prevention of fraud. But it is easy to visualise a situation where an automatic application of the statutes would have the unintended effect of allowing fraud by one party to succeed and in such circumstances the court will intervene for a party's protection under the umbrella of the equitable maxim. Thus in *Bannister* v. *Bannister*,[64] the defendant sold and conveyed two adjoining cottages to the plaintiff on the basis that she could continue to occupy one of them rent free for as long as she wished. When he subsequently sought to evict her on the basis that the conveyance did not mention her right of occupation, she successfully counterclaimed for a declaration that the plaintiff held the cottage on trust for her for her lifetime. The Court of Appeal classified as fraudulent the conduct of the plaintiff in attempting to rely on the absence of the writing which section 53(1)(*b*) of the Law of Property Act 1925 requires for the creation of the interest claimed by the defendant and imposed a constructive trust under which he held the property on trust for her for her lifetime. The relevant authorities will be considered more fully in the Chapter on Constructive Trusts.[65] Similarly, if a testator makes a gift of property in his will on the strength of a promise by the recipient that he will hold that property on trust for a third party, equity will prevent any attempt by the recipient to rely on the absence of any mention of this trust in the will and, despite the testator's failure to comply with section 9 of the Wills Act 1837, will hold the recipient to his promise by obliging him to carry out the trust. Trusts of this type are known as secret trusts and will be discussed in detail in the next section.[66]

7. Secret Trusts

Of some importance in connection with this maxim of equity is the law relating to secret trusts. When a person dies his will becomes open to public inspection and secret trusts usually arise when a testator wishes to make provision for somebody but does not want the whole world to know about it, sometimes because the provision is for the testator's mistress or illegitimate children. In the usual way the secret trust will arise under the will itself, but this does not exhaust the possibilities, and the same principles will apply to a case where a testator has decided not to make a will,[67] or, alternatively, revoke a will he has already made[68] on the strength of a promise by someone to dispose of property in a specified manner. Usually the disposition is to be made *inter vivos* but a secret trust may also arise where a testator has made a will in favour of a person on the basis that that person will himself later dispose of the property by will elsewhere.[69] The method by which the

---

[64] [1948] W.N. 261.
[65] See *post*, p. 277. *et seq.*
[66] See *post*.
[67] *Re Gardner* [1920] 2 Ch. 523.
[68] *Tharp* v. *Tharp* [1916] 1 Ch. 142.
[69] *Ottaway* v. *Norman* [1972] Ch. 698.

trustee is to carry out the obligation, whether by making a will in favour of the secret beneficiary or by some form of *inter vivos* disposition, is immaterial.[70]

The original basis of the jurisdiction was that equity would not allow the Wills Act 1837 to be used as an instrument of fraud.[71] But this is clearly not now the sole ground on which such trusts are enforced, because in many cases—as will be seen from some of the decisions discussed in the text—there is no question of fraud. Nevertheless, the prevention of fraud was, and may still be in some cases, a decisive factor and this makes it appropriate to discuss the subject at this stage.[72]

Basis of secret trusts. A secret trust is essentially an equitable obligation communicated to an intended trustee in the testator's lifetime. In enforcing such a trust it might be thought that equity directly contradicts the terms of section 9 of the Wills Act 1837,[73] but this is not so, because the basis of the doctrine of secret trusts is that the trust operates outside the will: indeed, the Act is not concerned with the trust at all. As Viscount Sumner said in the leading case of *Blackwell* v. *Blackwell*[74]:

> "For the prevention of fraud equity fastens on the conscience of the legatee a trust which otherwise would be inoperative: in other words, it makes him do what the will has nothing to do with, it lets him take what the will gives him, and then makes him apply it as the Court of Conscience directs, and it does so in order to give effect to the wishes of the testator, which would not otherwise be effectual."

The basis of the doctrine is the existence of a validly executed will which passes the title of property to the intended trustee and the acceptance by the latter of an equitable obligation in the testator's lifetime; he is thereupon bound by that obligation. This basis principle is illustrated by *Re Young*.[75] Here one of the intended beneficiaries under a secret trust had witnessed the will and the question was whether he forfeited his legacy under section 15 of the Wills Act 1837.[76] Danckwerts J. held there was no forfeiture because the whole theory of the formation of a secret trust was that the Act had nothing to do with the matter. The forms required by the Wills Act were to be entirely disregarded because the beneficiary did not take by virtue of the gift in the will but by virtue of a secret trust imposed on an apparent beneficiary who did take under the will and who was bound by the trust.[77] It

---

[70] *Ibid.* at p. 711.

[71] *Drakeford* v. *Wilks* [1747] 3 Atk. 539; *McCormick* v. *Grogan* (1869) L.R. 4 H.L. at pp. 88–89, 97; *Blackwell* v. *Blackwell* [1929] A.C. 318, at pp. 334–335.

[72] See generally Fleming (1947) 12 Conv. (N.S.) 28; Sheridan (1951) 67 L.Q.R. 314; Oakley, *Constructive Trusts* (2nd ed. (1987)) 112–140.

[73] As substituted by Administration of Justice Act, 1982, s.17.

[74] [1929] A.C. 318, 335.

[75] [1951] Ch. 344.

[76] This provides that a witness to a will cannot take a benefit under it.

[77] *Ibid.* at p. 350.

was also held in *Re Gardner (No. 2)*,[78] for the same reason, that the interest of a secret beneficiary who predeceases the testator will not lapse (although the case seems to have been wrongly decided for another reason, namely that the trust could not take effect until the testator's death and the secret beneficiary would have no interest until that date). However, it does appear that if it is the devisee or legatee *who accepts the secret trust* who precedeases the testator the trust will not take effect where the trust in question is fully secret. In such circumstances it seems that the beneficiary will not be able to establish his title because the devise or bequest on which the trust is based has itself failed.[79] On the other hand, where the trust in question is half-secret, the trust will take effect because a gift to a person who takes as trustee on the face of a will never lapses by reason of his predecease.[80]

The subject of secret trusts has to be divided into two parts; (i) fully secret trusts and (ii) half-secret trusts.

(1) Fully secret trusts

These are trusts which are fully concealed by the testator. They will arise where on the face of the will the alleged trustee takes absolutely and beneficially. If property is given by will to X absolutely and a communication is made to X by the testator during his lifetime that he is to hold the property on specified trusts, and provided also that X accepts the trust, a fully secret trust which is enforceable will come into being.[81]

Evidence, oral[82] or written, is admissible to show the terms of a trust—even in the form of a memorandum made by the trustee after the testator's death[83]—and if it is satisfactorily established by such evidence, the trust will be enforced.

In *McCormick* v. *Grogan*[84] Lord Westbury said[85] that the "clearest and most indisputable evidence" was required to set up a secret trust contrary to the absolute terms of a disposition, words which indicate a

---

[78] [1923] 2 Ch. 230.

[79] *Re Maddock* [1902] 2 Ch. 220 at p. 231; *cf. Blackwell* v. *Blackwell* [1929] A.C. 318 at p. 328, *per* Lord Buckmaster.

[80] *Re Smirthwaite's Trusts* (1871) L.R. 11 Eq. 251.

[81] In *Ottaway* v. *Norman* [1972] Ch. 698, 711, Brightman J. stated the essential requirements of a secret trust as follows: (i) the intention of the testator to subject the primary donee to an obligation in favour of the secondary donee; (ii) communication of that intention to the primary donee, and (iii) the acceptance of that obligation by the primary donee either expressly or by acquiescence. By "primary donee" the judge referred to the person on whom such a trust was imposed, and by "secondary donee" he referred to the beneficiary under that trust.

[82] At any rate, if the trust relates to personal property, *sed quaere* if the trust concerns land; see *post*, p. 54.

[83] *Re Gardner's Will Trusts* [1936] 3 All E.R. 938 (admissible because not against trustees' personal or proprietary interests). See Civil Evidence Act 1968, s.2, which admits such evidence in any case. See also *Shenton* v. *Tyler* [1939] Ch. 620 (interrogatories to widow admissible); *cf.* (1939) 2 M.L.R. 319; (1939) 55 L.Q.R. 330; (1940) 56 L.Q.R. 137. However, although evidence is admissible, even in the trustee's favour, it may have little weight if it is uncorroborated or if the donee is not only a trustee but also stands in a professional or quasi-professional relationship to the testator: see *Re Tyler* [1967] 1 W.L.R. 1269. See *post*, p. 54 for cases where writing may be necessary.

[84] (1869) L.R. 4 H.L. 82.

[85] *Ibid.* at pp. 97, 98.

very high standard of proof. They were, however, interpreted by Brightman J. in *Ottaway* v. *Norman*[86] to mean merely that "clear evidence" is needed before the court will assume that the testator did not mean what he said but intended that the gift should be held by the beneficiary subject to a secret trust. In this case it was held that the evidence was sufficiently cogent to establish that the alleged trustee was under an obligation to dispose of a bungalow by will in favour of the secret beneficiary. Brightman J. was also of the opinion that the standard of proof to establish a secret trust was "perhaps" analogous to that which the court requires for the rectification of a written instrument. On the other hand, in *Re Snowden*,[87] Megarry V.-C considered that the standard of proof for rectification was not the appropriate analogy.[88] He thought that, in the absence of fraud[89] or other special circumstances, the standard of proof of a secret trust was merely the ordinary civil standard of proof (namely, balance of probability) to establish an ordinary trust. The testarix had left her residuary estate to her brother who subsequently died leaving his estate to his only son. There was some evidence that the testatrix had said that the brother would "know what to do" and "would deal with everything" for her, but it was held that although there was some arrangement between the parties it amounted only to a moral obligation which was not intended to be binding and accordingly the brother took the residue free from any secret trust and on his death it passed to his son absolutely.

The doctrine of fully secret trusts has a fairly lengthy history: its basis was established as long ago as the eighteenth century. Thus, in *Drakeford* v. *Wilks*,[90] the testatrix bequeathed a bond to the plaintiff. She was then induced to make a new will by which she bequeathed the bond to a third party on the strength of a promise by him that on his death the bond would go to the plaintiff. It was held that the plaintiff could compel the performance of the trust.

The general principles now governing fully secret trusts are clearly established,[91] subject only to the possible doubt as to the standard of proof required to establish such trusts which has just been considered.

1. It is essential to show that the testator did in fact communicate the trust during his lifetime to the legatee or devisee and that the latter expressly or impliedly accepted it. If the devisee or legatee only hears of the trust after the testator's death the secret trust will fail and he will take absolutely (assuming that the gift is to him in absolute terms). There is no fraud on his part in this event. There is what appears to be an absolute gift to him; he can, therefore, set

---

[86] [1972] Ch. 698 at p. 712.
[87] [1979] Ch. 528.
[88] "Strong" evidence is required in a rectification action to contradict the evidence of the instrument: *ibid.*, at p. 535.
[89] See Hodge (1980) Conv. 341.
[90] (1747) 3 Atk. 539.
[91] See also the formulation by Brightman J. in *Ottaway* v. *Norman* [1972] Ch. 698 at p. 711 cited at p. 47, n. 81, *ante*.

up section 9 of the Wills Act 1837,[92] and say that any later communication (for example, in an unattested document) does not
comply with the Act. So in *Wallgrave* v. *Tebbs*[93] the legatees only
knew of the trusts after the testator's death, and since they took
absolutely on the face of the will, the absolute bequest to them
could not be impeached.

2. The communication of the trust and its acceptance may be made
   either before or after the date of the will provided it is made
   during the life of the testator. In the well-known case of *Moss* v.
   Cooper,[94] for example, the communication was made after the
   execution of the will and, moreover, by an agent for the testator,
   and Wood V.C. held it to be effectual.

3. If the fully secret trust is *accepted* by the trustee as trustee, but the
   actual objects are not communicated during the testator's life, the
   trust will not take effect and the trustee will hold the property for
   the residuary devisee or legatee or, if there is no gift of residue in
   the will, in favour of the persons entitled on intestacy. Thus in *Re
   Boyes*[95] the testator made an absolute gift of property to his
   executor. The testator had previously told him that he wished him
   to hold the property according to directions which he would
   communicate by letter. He agreed. These directions were not,
   however, given to the testator, but after his death two unattested
   documents were found in which the testator stated that he
   wished a particular person to have the property. Kay J. decided
   that the executor held the property for the testator's next-of-kin,
   there being no gift of residue in this case.

4. Communication and acceptance of the trust may be effected
   constructively. In *Re Boyes*[96] Kay J. expressed the view that a trust
   put in writing and placed in the trustees' hands in a sealed
   envelope would constitute communication and acceptance at the
   date of delivery for this purpose. And in *Re Keen*,[97] the Court of
   Appeal accepted this view: this was a case of a half-secret trust
   but it would seem that if the rule applies to half-secret trusts it
   should also apply to fully secret trusts.

5. It is, of course, required that the property which forms the subject
   of the intended secret trust should be certain: this is a rule which
   applies generally in the law of trusts.[98] For example, in *Ottaway* v.
   Norman[99] it was contended that the alleged trustee was under an
   obligation to dispose of whatever part of the testator's money was
   left at her own death in favour of the secret beneficiary.[1] It was

---

[92] As substituted by the Administration of Justice Act 1982, s.17.
[93] (1855) 2 K. & J. 313.
[94] (1861) 1 J. & H. 352.
[95] (1884) 26 Ch.D. 531 and see *Re Hawksley's Settlement* [1934] Ch. 384.
[96] *Supra.*
[97] [1937] Ch. 236.
[98] See p. 94, *post.*
[99] [1972] Ch. 698.
[1] For another aspect of the decision where it was held that a secret trust did arise in
respect of other property, see p. 48 *ante.*

held that there was insufficient evidence to establish this obligation and the claim failed. It was, however, also said that if the alleged trustee had the right to mingle his own money with that derived from the testator, there would be no ascertainable property on which the trust could bite at death. It is highly questionable whether a secret trust whose subject matter is insufficiently certain should be upheld and, to the extent that *Ottaway* v. *Norman* suggests that such a trust is possible, it is hoped that it is not followed.

(2) Half-secret trusts

These arise where the trustee takes as trustee on the face of the will, but the terms of the trust are not in fact specified. If property is, for example, given to a person upon trust "for purposes which I have communicated to him" or "for purposes with which he is fully acquainted," a half-secret trust will arise. Here, as in the case of a fully secret trust, certain governing principles can be stated, but one of them raises considerable doubt.

1. It is clearly established that evidence cannot be adduced to contradict the terms of the will. Accordingly, if the will points to a future communication, *e.g.* "to my trustees for purposes which I will communicate to them," evidence cannot be admitted of communications made before the will was executed. Similarly, if the will points to a contemporaneous or past communication, evidence cannot be admitted of a communication after the will was executed. The first and governing rule is that one has to consider the terms of the will to see what communications are admissible, and the other principles applicable to half-secret trusts take effect subject to this.[2] It should, however, be noticed at this stage that it appears, in the present state of the law, that future communications, whether or not the will points to them, are not, in any event, admissible.[3]

2. Where the communication of the trust is made before or at the same time as the execution of the will, evidence is admissible to show the terms of the trust and the trustee is bound by it. A leading case is *Blackwell* v. *Blackwell*.[4] A testator by codicil bequeathed a legacy to five persons upon trust to invest at their discretion and "to apply the income . . . for the purposes indicated by me to them" and to apply capital "to such person or persons indicated by me to them." Before the codicil was executed the objects of the trust were communicated to the five persons. The House of Lords held that evidence of the communication was admissible to show the terms of the trust and the trustees were bound.

3. The principle governing communication made subsequently to

---

[2] See *e.g. Re Keen* [1937] Ch. 236; *Re Tyler* [1967] 1 W.L.R. 1269.
[3] *Infra.*
[4] [1929] A. C. 318. See also to a like effect *Re Fleetwood* (1880) 15 Ch.D. 594; *Re Huxtable* [1902] 2 Ch. 793, C.A.

the will, yet before the testator's death, is extremely difficult to state. The leading case on this question if *Re Keen*,[5] a decision of the Court of Appeal, but from which unfortunately it is a matter of some difficulty to extract the precise *ratio decidendi*. The facts were that the testator gave a sum of money to his executors "to be held upon trust and disposed of by them among such person, persons or charities as may be notified by me to them or either of them during my lifetime." Shortly before the will the testator had given one of the executors a sealed envelope containing the name of the intended beneficiary and directed that it was not to be opened before his death. The view expressed in *Re Boyes*[6] was accepted that the handing over of this sealed envelope was a sufficient communication at the date of delivery. Therefore the communication was made *before* the will. This necessarily meant considering the words used in the will in the light of the first governing rule mentioned above that evidence is not admissible to contradict the terms of the will, so that if a will points to a future communication evidence is inadmissible of a communication before the will is executed and vice versa. The court held that the terms of the will quoted above could only be considered as pointing to a future definition of trusts which had not at the date of the will been established; in other words, the will pointed to a future communication. In fact, as already held, the trusts had been communicated before the will, the handing over of a sealed envelope being a sufficient communication for this purpose. Accordingly, by reason of the terms of the will, evidence of a communication made before the will was executed was not admissible. If this is the only ground of the decision there can be no dispute with it. But Lord Wright M.R. went on to discuss the question on a broader basis and held that, even if the words of the will could be construed as pointing to a past as well as a future communication, they would be equally ineffective on the grounds that no testator can validly reserve to himself a power to make future unattested dispositions. If this statement is to be treated as part of the *ratio decidendi* (and from the general tenor of the judgment it may well be so) it means that communications made after the will but during the testator's lifetime are not in any event admissible to show the terms of the trust, or, stated in other words, that a half-secret trust will not be effectual if the terms of the trust are communicated subsequently to the execution of the will.

There are also dicta, although these are clearly *obiter*, in *Blackwell* v. *Blackwell* which are apparently to the same effect. Thus Viscount Sumner said in this case[7]: "The limits, beyond which the rules as to unspecified trusts must not be carried, have often been discussed. A testator cannot reserve to himself a power

---

[5] [1937] Ch. 236.
[6] (1884) 26 Ch.D. 531.
[7] [1929] A.C. 318, 339.

of making future unwitnessed dispositions by merely naming a trustee and leaving the purposes of the trust to be supplied afterwards. . . . To hold otherwise would indeed be to enable the testator to 'give the go-by' to the requirements of the Wills Act because he did not choose to comply with them."

But there are not only the decision in *Re Keen*[8] and the dicta in *Blackwell* v. *Blackwell*; there is also the earlier case of *Johnson* v. *Ball*.[9] Here a testator gave the proceeds of a policy of assurance to two trustees to "hold the same upon the uses appointed by letter signed by them and myself." No such letter complying with the precise terms of the will at any time existed though there had been other communications before and after the making of the will. It would have been sufficient to hold that the latter communications did not accord with the formalities prescribed by the will and were inadmissible for that reason. But Parker V.C. was not content to do this. He chose to hold on a more general basis that the communication of the trust was not admissible in evidence because a testator could not by will prospectively create for himself a power to dispose of his property by an instrument not duly executed as a will or codicil. The same principle was adopted in *Re Bateman's Will Trusts*[10] by Pennycuick V.C., who thought the position to be "really clear."

In view of the foregoing it is no easy task to state the true principles on subsequent communications. There is no doubt that judicial opinion is against their admissibility. However, it is submitted that this opinion is fallacious.[11] The basis of secret trusts—half-secret as well as fully secret—is that the trusts operate outside the will. The only necessity is that the will be validly made in accordance with the Wills Act; the Act is not concerned with the enforceability of the trust. The essence of the matter is or should be simply (i) a validly executed will which passes to the intended trustee the title to the property and (ii) the acceptance by the latter of an obligation in the lifetime of the testator, before or after the execution of the will, but before the testator's death, by which he is equitably bound. A further reason for saying that a subsequent communication should be possible is that such a communication is, as has been seen, effectual in a fully secret trust and it might be thought somewhat inconsistent if this is not possible in a half-secret trust.

It appears that there has been some confusion in *Re Keen* and the other cases between the equitable doctrine of secret trusts and the probate doctrine of incorporation by reference. This doctrine of probate means that it is possible to incorporate in a will, which

---

[8] [1937] Ch. 236.
[9] (1851) 5 De G. & Sm. 85.
[10] [1970] 1 W.L.R. 1463.
[11] See also Holdsworth (1937) 53 L.Q.R. 501; Snell (28th ed.), p. 113, Hanbury and Maudsley (11th ed.), p. 261; Keeton and Sheridan (10th ed.), p. 78; *Cf.* the Irish and American law which admits such communications: see Sheridan (1951) 67 L.Q.R. 314 (Irish); *Restatement of Law of Trusts*, p. 43 (American).

has been validly made, a document which is not executed in accordance with the Wills Act. For the doctrine to apply, however, the document must be in existence at the date of the will and must be specifically referred to in the will. These conditions must be satisfied because, if not, that other rule comes into play, that a testator cannot prospectively reserve to himself a power to dispose of his property by an instrument not duly executed as a will or codicil.[12] But this rule is concerned purely with the validity of the will itself and the documents to be incorporated within it; it does not or should not relate to secret trusts which, according to true principle, operate outside the will.[13]

4. Those named as trustees[14]—and they will, of course, be named as such in a half-secret trust—cannot generally take beneficially. If a half-secret trust fails for any reason the trustees will hold the property on trust for the residuary legatee or devisee if there is a gift of residue in the will; if there is no such residuary gift they will hold for those entitled on intestacy. In principle if the trustees are themselves so entitled, they should be able to take beneficially. However, it has been stated that they are prohibited from doing so. In *Re Rees*[15]; the trustee was named as such on the face of the will and directed to dispose of the estate in accordance with the testator's directions. The Court of Appeal held that he could not adduce evidence to show that he was, in fact, intended to be one of the beneficiaries and went on to state that a half-secret trustee can never take beneficially. This seems unnecessarily harsh but is recognised as the law at present.[16]

5. If a testator wishes to carry out his purpose by making a number of secret trusts piecemeal he must take the trustees into his confidence as to every addition to the secret object. Thus, in *Re Colin Cooper*[17] a testator by will bequeathed £5,000 to two trustees "upon trusts already communicated to them." He had in fact communicated the nature of such trusts to them. By a further will he purported to increase the sum to be devoted to the secret trust to £10,000 without informing the trustees. The result was that although the first instalment of £5,000 could be devoted to the secret trusts, the second instalment could not. This case involved a half-secret trust, but it seems clear that the principle of the decision should also apply to a fully secret trust.

---

[12] See, *e.g. Re Jones* [1942] Ch. 328; *Re Edwards' Will Trusts* [1948] Ch. 440; *Re Schintz's Will Trusts* [1951] Ch. 870.

[13] *Cf.* Matthews (1979) Conv. 360.

[14] If the testator's directions are expressed *not* to create a trust they will of course take beneficially: *Re Falkiner* [1924] 1 Ch. 88; *Re Stirling* [1954] 1 W.L.R. 763. See also *Irvine v. Sullivan* (1869) L.R. 8 Eq. 673. On the other hand if the terms of the will do not create a trust but they agree with the testator to hold on trust, the trust will be enforceable as a fully secret trust: *Re Spencer's Will* (1887) 57 L.T. 519.

[15] [1950] Ch. 204; followed in *Re Pugh's Will Trusts* [1967] 1 W.L.R. 1262, but distinguished in *Re Tyler* [1967] 1 W. L. R. 1269.

[16] *Re Tyler* [1967] 1 W.L.R. 1269.

[17] [1939] Ch. 811.

(3) Gifts to concurrent owners on fully secret trusts

According to the law as it stands at the present time, it is necessary to make a distinction, which appears to be totally unjustified,[18] between joint tenancies and tenancies in common. It must be stressed that the rules apply only to fully secret trusts.

(a) Joint tenants. An antecedent promise merely by one of the joint tenants on the strength of which the will is made, binds both or all joint tenants. The reason is stated to be that no person can claim an interest under a fraud committed by another. But a subsequent promise by one of the joint tenants alone, on the strength of which the will is left unrevoked, binds only the one who promised if the other joint tenant or tenants know nothing of the matter until the testator's death. The reason is stated to be that the gift is not tainted with any fraud in procuring the execution of the will,[19] but this explanation is inadequate: although there may be no fraud in the execution of the will, there may be fraud which induces the testator not to *revoke* his will once made.

(b) Tenants in common. An antecedent promise by one of the tenants in common, where the other knows nothing of the matter until after the testator's death, binds only the one who promised. A gift to tenants in common is therefore distinguishable in this respect from a similar gift to joint tenants. Furthermore, a subsequent promise by one of the tenants in common will bind only him. The reason stated for these rules is that to hold otherwise would enable one beneficiary to deprive the rest of their benefits by setting up a secret trust.[20]

The difference can be seen to lie in an antecedent promise: whether this binds both will depend on whether they are joint tenants or tenants in common. Although reasons have been judicially expressed, they appear to be completely lacking in merit.

(4) Express trust or constructive trust?

Secret trusts have been dealt with here under the heading of express trusts, but the view has been expressed that they—or at least fully secret trusts—are really constructive.[21] The point is of importance because it will determine whether a secret trust of land requires to be evidenced in writing under section 53(1)(*b*) of the Law of Property Act 1925 and whether a secret trust of a subsisting equitable interest requires to be made in writing under section 53(1)(*c*) of the same Act.[22] Apparently, it will if it is express, but it will not if it is constructive.[23] It seems self-evident that a half-secret trust must be express because the trustees are actually named by the will even though the objects of the trust are not

---

[18] See Perrins (1972) 88 L.Q.R. 225.

[19] See the discussion by Farwell J. in *Re Stead* [1900] 1 Ch. 237 at 241 where the cases in support of these propositions are reviewed.

[20] See n. 19 *ante.*

[21] Nathan and Marshall (7th ed.), p. 431. Subsequent editions have taken a different view (see Hayton & Marshall (9th ed. (1991)), p. 105).

[22] See *ante*, p. 34.

[23] L.P.A. 1925, s.53(2), see *ante*, p. 42.

specified, and evidence in writing for such trusts if they relate to land will be required.[24] There is, however, perhaps more to be said for including a fully secret trust among constructive trusts because the existence of the trust is fully concealed. But even here it seems that a trust has *been declared*, albeit in secrecy, and because of that must be express. If so it will also need to be evidenced in writing if it relates to land and made in writing if it relates to a subsisting equitable interest. But there remains a possibility: it may be open to the court to say, with regard to both fully secret and half-secret trusts, that it will not allow section 53(1) to be used as an instrument of fraud.[25] The argument would be that if a fraudulent purpose[26] would otherwise be effected, the court could impose a constructive trust upon the alleged trustee, and that that trust would be enforceable notwithstanding the absence of writing. This would have the result that what is *ex hypothesi* an (unenforceable) express trust would be transmuted into a constructive trust which could be enforced. There seems to be no objection in principle to such a result.[27] Thus if the trustee seeks to raise the absence of writing in order to claim the property himself, a constructive trust should be imposed. But there will be no such fraud where the trustee is faced by conflicting claims from those beneficially entitled under the secret trust and those otherwise entitled to the property. In such a case, in the absence of the statutory formalities, he should hold the property for those otherwise entitled thereto.

III. EXECUTED AND EXECUTORY TRUSTS

The basic distinction between such trusts has already been mentioned[28]: we are now concerned with amplifying this distinction and also with distinguishing both such trusts from trusts which are completely or incompletely constituted. An executed trust arises when the settlor has defined in the trust instrument precisely what interests are to be taken by the beneficiaries.[29] An executory trust, on the other hand, arises where the instrument or declaration requires the subsequent execution of a further instrument and does not itself define precisely the terms of that instrument.[30]

The practical importance of the distinction between executed and executory trusts lies in the field of construction although since 1925 the position is no longer of as much importance as it used to be.[31] The construction of an executed trust is governed by rules of law, whereas

---

[24] This was the decision in *Re Baillie* (1886) 2 T.L.R. 660; see also Sheridan (1951) 67 L.Q.R. 314.

[25] See *ante*, p. 44.

[26] In the meaning discussed *ante*, p. 45.

[27] It is perhaps fair to point out that in some modern cases such as *Ottaway* v. *Norman* [1972] Ch. 698 (discussed *ante*, p. 48) which involved real property, and where documentary evidence was lacking, the question was not considered.

[28] See *ante*, p. 28.

[29] See *Egerton* v. *Brownlow* (1853) 4 H.L.C. 1, at p. 210, *per* Lord St. Leonards.

[30] Nevertheless the directions as to the trusts to be defined must not be too ambiguous; if they are there will be no executory trust: *Re Flavel's Will Trusts* [1969] 1 W.L.R. 444.

[31] See *post*, p. 57.

executory trusts are construed more liberally and always with a view to carrying out the settlor's true intention. This may be illustrated by comparing two cases. On the one hand, in *Re Bostock's Settlement*,[32] the settlor had omitted certain words of limitation which, if they had been inserted, would have given the fee simple to the beneficiaries. It was held that, in the absence of such words, the beneficiaries took only a life estate even though it was probably intended that the beneficiaries should take the fee simple. This was a case of an executed trust and in the absence of the necessary technical expressions the limitation was construed according to rules of law. On the other hand, in *Glenorchy* v. *Bosville*[33] the testator devised real property to trustees upon trust to convey the estate, after the marriage of his grand-daughter, to the use of her for life, remainder to the use of her husband for life, remainder to the use of the issue of her body. Under the rule of construction known as the rule in *Shelley's Case*[34] the grand-daughter would have taken an estate tail if this had been an executed trust. But as this was a case of an executory trust the court could look into the true intention of the testator. His intention was clearly to provide for the children of the marriage, and it was held that the trustees should, regardless of the rule in *Shelley's Case*, convey the property to the grand-daughter for life, remainder to her first and other sons in tail, remainder to her daughter.

These cases illustrate the practical importance of the distinction between executed and executory trusts in matters of construction. But there is one case where it might be argued that the distinction is not as clear-cut as is often thought. This case is *Re Arden*[35] where it was held, in effect, that the use of an untechnical expression by the creator of an executed trust gave the court a loophole for applying a construction in accordance with the real intentions of the settlor. Here the settlor had used the word "absolutely," and Clauson J. held that the use of this word entitled him to decide that the beneficiary in whose favour it was used took an equitable fee simple, though if it had been omitted, it was acknowledged that he would only have taken a life estate. If this decision is correct, and doubts may be entertained as to that, an untechnical expression may be given a technical meaning even in an executed trust, but the lack of such an expression—as in *Re Bostock's Settlement*[36]—has the effect prescribed by law.

1. *Marriage Articles*

One class of executory trusts has been given special treatment. These are executory trusts arising under marriage articles. In such a case the presumption is that the intention of the settlor was to provide for the issue of the marriage, so that despite any technical rule of construction

---

[32] [1921] 2 Ch. 469.
[33] (1733) Cas. *t*. Talb. 3, see also *Papillon* v. *Voice* (1728) P.Wms. 471.
[34] (1581) 1 Co.Rep. 88b. This case will not apply to instruments taking effect after 1925: see *post*, p. 57.
[35] [1935] Ch. 326.
[36] [1921] Ch. 469.

the husband and wife will normally take life interests.[37] And the presumption will apply unless the parties clearly intended to create some other interest. This presumption is a strong one and will only be rebutted by the clearest evidence to the contrary. It was particularly significant in the application of the rule in *Shelley's Case*. In a limitation of land before 1926 for a person for life, remainder to the heirs of his body, he would have taken an estate tail by reason of the rule of construction established by this case. But if an executory trust on these lines was contained in marriage articles the court would strive to avoid this construction and give only a life estate. For otherwise he could bar the entail, that is, bar his successors' interest, and thereby convert his interest into a fee simple, thus defeating his issue. But in the case of other executory trusts, which will normally arise under wills, the court, although it will, of course, construe the instrument with a view to ascertaining the settlor's true intention, will consider the whole question of construction on its merits. So, in the ancient case of *Sweetapple* v. *Bindon*[38] a testator gave £300 to trustees upon trust to lay it out in the purchase of land and settle the land to "the only use of a person and her children," and if she died without issue "the land to be divided between her brothers and sisters then living." The question of construction, since this was an executory trust under a will, was approached on these lines: there was no overriding necessity to give her a life interest and it was held that she took an estate tail.

2. *Effect of 1925 Legislation*

The whole of the foregoing still applies in principle but it—and the cases given in illustration—must now be read subject to the effect of the 1925 legislation. This has done two things in this context: it has, as to instruments taking effect after 1925—(i) abolished the rule in *Shelley's Case*[39] and (ii) removed the necessity for words of limitation for the creation of a fee simple.[40] But the distinction must still be borne in mind because of the continuing necessity for words of limitation for the creation of entailed interests.[41]

3. *A Modern Illustration*

Marriage articles are rare today presumably because, in so far as marriage settlements are still created, they are highly likely to have been set up at least partly for the purpose of tax avoidance, something which necessitates that all the documents involved should have been carefully thought out and prepared in advance. However, modern examples of executory trusts do exist, an illustration being a pension scheme established by an interim deed of trust which provides for the

---

[37] *Jervoise* v. *Duke of Northumberland* (1820) 1 Jac. & W. 559 at p. 574; *Trevor* v. *Trevor* (1720) 1 P.Wms. 622.
[38] (1706) 2 Vern. 536.
[39] Law of Property 1925, s.131.
[40] *Ibid.* s.60.
[41] *Ibid.* s.130.

subsequent execution of a definitive deed of trust. In *Davis* v. *Richards & Wallington Industries*,[42] the definitive deed of trust was duly executed but its validity was challenged when questions arose as to the entitlement to surplus funds. Scott J. in fact found the definitive deed valid but stated that, had he not done so, the interim deed would have been upheld as a valid executory trust capable of being executed by a court order; this would have had the effect of providing rules corresponding to those in the definitive deed by means of which the questions as to the surplus funds would have been able to be resolved. This interesting illustration shows that the distinction between executed and executory trust can still be important in the field of construction.

4. *Distinction from Completely and Incompletely Constituted Trusts*

It is important to notice that in the case both of an executed and of an executory trust, the trust itself is completely constituted. This is so because *ex hypothesi* the trust property will be vested in the trustees in both cases. In an executory trust the trustees may have duties to perform with regard to the definition of the trust but the trust itself will be perfectly created. Indeed, the question whether a trust is executed or executory will only arise if this is so.

IV. COMPLETELY AND INCOMPLETELY CONSTITUTED TRUSTS

An express trust is completely constituted either by an effective transfer of the trust property to trustees or by an effective declaration of trust. The implications of this principle were clearly brought out by Turner L.J. in his classic judgment in *Milroy* v. *Lord*[43] when he said:

"In order to render a voluntary settlement valid and effectual, the settlor must have done everything which according to the nature of the property comprised in the settlement was necessary to be done in order to render the settlement binding upon him. He may, of course, do this by actually transferring the property to the persons for whom he intends to provide and the provision will then be effectual and it will be equally effectual if he transfers the property to a trustee for the purposes of the settlement, or declares that he himself holds it on trust for those purposes; and if the property is personal, the trust may, as I apprehend, be declared either in writing or parol; but, in order to render the settlement binding, one or other of these modes must, as I understand the law of this court, be resorted to, for there is no equity in this court to perfect an imperfect gift."

---

[42] [1990] 1 W.L.R. 1511.
[43] (1862) 4 De G.F. & J. 264, at p. 274, cited and applied by Upjohn J. in *Re Wale* [1956] 1 W.L.R. 1346.

The latter part of this passage emphasises the crucial difference between a completely constituted trust and an incompletely constituted trust. Only when a trust is completely constituted is it binding on the settlor; in other words, only in such circumstances is a trust enforceable by the beneficiaries, whose equitable proprietary interest in the trust property will then be binding not only upon the settlor but also against any third party into whose hands the interest therein for value without notice. When, on the other hand, a trust has not been completely constituted, there is in effect no trust enforceable by the beneficiaries, who therefore have no equitable proprietary interest whatever. As the equitable maxim states, "Equity will not perfect an imperfect gift"; if the settlor has failed to constitute the trust completely, equity will not do so for him. In such circumstances, the incompletely constituted trust can only be enforced under the law of contract; the rights of the beneficiaries depend on the existence of a binding contract enforceable by them or on their behalf. In the absence of such a contract, they have no rights whatsoever and are described as volunteers. As another equitable maxim states, "Equity will not assist a volunteer".

Consequently the discussion of this topic involves the consideration of two questions: (i) when will a trust be completely constituted? (ii) If a trust is incompletely constituted, when will the beneficiaries have a contractual remedy?

1. *When will a Trust be Completely Constituted?*

(1) Transfer of the Trust Property

(a) **Legal interests.** If the subject matter of the trust is a legal estate or interest, the transfer must be effective to vest such estate in the trustees. This has the consequence that the settlor must comply with all the formalities required for a complete transfer of the property in order that the trustees may have full legal title to it. Exactly the same rule applies where the transfer is made with the intention of making a gift; the donor must comply with all the formalities required for a complete transfer of the property in order that the donee may have full legal title to it. Thus if the subject matter of the trust or gift is land, a deed is necessary[44] followed, in the case of registered land, by registration of the transfer on the Land Register[45]; if it is a copyright, then writing is necessary[46]; if it is a bill of exchange or other negotiable instrument, then whether it is payable to the bearer or to the holder, delivery and the appropriate form of indorsement are necessary[47]; if it is shares in a company, the correct form of transfer is necessary followed, in the case of all shares other than bearer shares,[48] by registration of the transfer in

---

[44] Law of Property Act 1925, s.52.
[45] Land Registration Act 1925 s.19.
[46] Copyright Act 1956, s.5(2).
[47] See *Antrobus* v. *Smith* (1806) 12 Ves. 39; *Jones* v. *Lock* (1865) 1 Ch. App. 25.
[48] The rights attached to bearer shares vest in whoever has physical possession of the share certificates.

the Share Register of the company in question[49]; if it is the benefit of a right of action, writing is necessary, followed by notice in writing to the other party[50]; and, finally, if it is a chattel, either a deed of gift[51] or an intention to give together with a delivery of possession is necessary, although any such personal delivery must be effectual. This last point is illustrated by the decision of the Court of Appeal in *Re Cole*[52] where the facts of the case, which concerned an alleged delivery of furniture by a husband to his wife when the two were living together in a common establishment, did not unequivocally establish either a change in possession or a delivery of the furniture and accordingly there was no effected or perfected gift to her. The court rejected a contention to the effect that a perfect gift of chattels is constituted simply by showing them to the donee and speaking the appropriate words of gift.

The propositions are illustrated by a number of modern cases involving the transfer of shares in a company. In *Re Fry*,[53] the intending donor, who was domiciled in the United States of America, executed transfers of shares in a limited company, partly by way of gift to his son and partly to a trust. The company were unable to register the transfers because the consent of the Treasury had not been obtained under the Defence Regulations then operative. The forms required for obtaining this consent were sent to him and he signed and returned them but died before the consent was given. Romer J. held that the trust was not completely constituted and so the shares did not pass either to the son or to the trust but instead formed part of his residuary estate. It appeared that in order to perfect the transaction it would have been necessary for the donor to effect confirmatory transfers after the consent had been given.[54] The principle which emerges from this case is that if something remains to be done by the transferor in order to render the voluntary transfer effective, then it will remain abortive.[55] However, as will be seen shortly,[56] if the transferor has done everything which it is necessary for him to do to render the transfer effectual but something has yet to be done by a third party, the transfer will be valid *in equity*. In *Re Rose*[57] a settlor executed transfers of shares in a company, partly by way of gift to his wife and partly to a trust. These transfers were not actually registered until six months later. The Court of Appeal held that, since there was nothing more than the transferor could do to divest

---

[49] *Milroy* v. *Lord* (1862) 4 De G.F. & J. 264; *Re Wale* [1956] 1 W.L.R. 1346, see also *post*, p. 61. The relevant Act is the Stock Transfer Act 1963, s.1.

[50] Law of Property Act 1925, s.136.

[51] *Jaffa* v. *Taylor Gallery, The Times*, March 21, 1990 (a trust of a painting was held to have been completely constituted without physical delivery to the trustees (one of whom was abroad) on the grounds that the formal declaration of trust contained in the deed transferred title to the painting to the trustees).

[52] [1964] Ch. 175.

[53] [1946] Ch. 312.

[54] *Ibid.* at p. 316.

[55] See also *Letts* v. *I.R.C.* [1951] 1 W.L.R. 201 (direction by father to company to allot shares direct to children).

[56] See *post*, p. 64.

[57] [1952] Ch. 499, following *Re Rose* [1949] 1 Ch. 78.

himself of the shares in favour of the transferees, the transfer was effective in equity. This meant that, until the registration was effected by the company, the transferor held the shares on trust for the transferees; when it was effected, the transfers would then be effective at law. The principle established in this case is known as the Rule in *Re Rose*.

It is, however, questionable whether it is possible to reconcile the authorities already discussed with *Re Vandervell's Trusts (No. 2)*,[58] the facts of which have already been considered. Lord Denning M.R., as an alternative ground for his decision that the shares in the products company were held on trust for the children's settlement, was of the opinion[59] that Vandervell had made a perfect gift to the trustee company of the dividends on the shares "so far as they were handed over or treated by him as belonging to the trustee company for the benefit of the children". In reaching this conclusion, he purported to follow *Milroy* v. *Lord*.[60] In that case bank shares had not been formally transferred to the trustee and so the transfer was ineffective and the bank shares formed part of the settlor's estate. However, dividends had been paid by the bank to the trustee by virtue of a Power of Attorney executed for this purpose; he paid the dividends to the beneficiary who in turn used them to purchase other shares in a company. It was held that the settlor should be treated as having made a gift of the dividends to the beneficiary; therefore, his executors had no claim to the shares which had been purchased with the dividends. The two cases seem eminently distinguishable. The settlor in *Milroy* v. *Lord* had given the trustee a Power of Attorney to collect the dividends and so must clearly have intended them to be held for the beneficiary, whereas Vandervell had not even been aware that he still retained an equitable interest in the option relating to the shares of his products company at the time when he had made this supposedly perfect gift. It is therefore not easy to justify the conclusion reached by Lord Denning M.R.

(b) Equitable interests. The foregoing cases are illustrations of the important principle that if the subject matter of the trust or gift is a legal interest the transferor must do everything that he can to vest the legal title to the property in the trustee or donee. The same principle applies to the transfer of an equitable interest. It is not, of course, necessary for the transferor to procure a conveyance of the legal interest (which will be held by the trustees); all that is necessary is that he should make a perfect assignment of his interest, which in this case will be necessarily and universally required to be in writing by section 53(1)(c) of the Law of Property Act.[61] This assignment will, where a trust is being

---

[58] [1974] Ch. 269. See *ante*, pp. 39–41.

[59] *Ibid* at p. 321.

[60] (1862) 4 De G.F. & J. 264.

[61] See *Kekewich* v. *Manning* (1851) De G.M. & G. 176 (assignment of equitable reversionary interest in shares); *Gilbert* v. *Overton* (1864) 2 H. & M. 110 (assignment of agreement for lease); and see *ante*, p. 35. *et seq.*

constituted, be followed by a direction to the trustees to hold it for the future upon trust for the assignee.[62] This is as much as the transferor of an equitable interest is able to do. However, the fact that this at least must be done is shown by the decision of the Court of Appeal in *Re McArdle*.[63] In this case, some siblings were entitled under the will of their father to a house after the death of their mother, who lived in the house with one brother and his wife. After the wife had effected various improvements to the house, all the siblings signed a document addressed to her, stating that "in consideration of your carrying out certain alterations to the property . . . we . . . hereby agree that the executors . . . shall repay to you from the estate when distributed the sum of £488" in settlement of the amount spent on improvements. The court held, in effect, that this document was neither one thing nor the other. If it was contractual, it lacked consideration (the only consideration being past). If it was an attempted gift, it was imperfect because the donors had not done all that lay in their power to make the gift complete: it was still necessary for them to authorise the executors to pay and until this was done it was ineffectual.

(2) Declaration of trust

An effective transfer to trustees is the first means by which a trust may be completely constituted. The second means is by a declaration of trust by the settlor, although in fact it is much more common for a settlor to transfer property to trustees than to declare himself to be a trustee. It is not necessary, however, in order to amount to an effective declaration that the settlor should say, in terms, "I hereby declare myself to be a trustee". Any words which clearly express the intention to create a present irrevocable trust are effectual. At the same time, this intention must be satisfactorily shown. This was not the case in *Jones* v. *Lock*.[64] A father put a cheque into the hands of his infant son, saying: "Look you here, I give this to baby; it is for himself." Then he took back the cheque and put it away. He subsequently reiterated his intention of giving the amount of the cheque to his son. Shortly afterwards the father died and the cheque was found among his effects. Lord Cranworth L.C. held that there was neither an effective transfer by way of gift nor a valid declaration of trust. It was quite impossible to regard the somewhat theatrical exercise enacted by the father as a delivery of the moneys represented by the cheque. To effect a perfect transfer, he should have paid the cheque into a bank account opened in the name of his son or in the name of trustees on behalf of his son. Nor had he made a valid declaration of trust; the inference that he had made himself a trustee could not be deduced from his words and actions. In such cases, it is a question of construction whether the words used, taking into account the surrounding circumstances, amount to a clear declaration of trust. So in

---

[62] See *Grey* v. *I.R.C.* [1960] A.C. 1 (direction to trustees to hold on trust may take effect as an assignment), discussed *ante*, p. 36.

[63] [1951] Ch. 669.

[64] (1865) 1 Ch. App. 25.

Paul v. *Constance*,[65] acknowledged[66] to be a "borderline case", the words used by the deceased were, "The money is as much yours as mine", often repeated to the plaintiff, a woman with whom he had lived for a number of years. He was referring to money in a bank account. It was held, distinguishing *Jones* v. *Lock*, that the words, taken with the use of the account, conveyed a present declaration that the plaintiff was entitled to half of the existing balance.

The foregoing appears to be reasonably clear but the requirements, it seems, were materially relaxed in *Re Vandervell's Trusts (No. 2)*.[67] The Court of Appeal managed to find an effective declaration of trust by the trustee company of shares in favour of a settlement for the benefit of Vandervell's children from the following facts: (1) the trustee company had used £5,000 from the children's settlement for the purposes of exercising an option to re-purchase the shares; (2) that thereafter all dividends received by the trustee company were paid by them to the children's settlement and treated as part of the funds of that settlement; and (3) that the solicitors for the trustee company had written to the Inland Revenue stating that the shares would be held on the trusts of the settlement. None of these facts, least of all the third, would seem to indicate a present irrevocable declaration of trust[68]; in addition, as Stephenson L.J. indicated, there may be difficulties in a limited company (as the trustee company was) declaring a trust by parol or conduct and without a resolution of the board of directors.[69] There also remains the problem, which has already been considered, of how Vandervell could have disposed of the equitable interest which the House of Lords had held to be outstanding in him[70] given that he had failed to transfer that interest to the trustees to hold on trust in writing in the manner required by section 53(1)(c) of the Law of Property Act 1925.[71]

Finally, it will be recalled that a declaration of trust must be evidenced in writing if its subject matter includes land.[72]

(3) Ineffective transfer as declaration of trust

Where it is clear that the settlor intended to create a trust by *transfer* but has used an ineffectual method of transfer, the general rule is that this ineffectual transfer will not be interpreted as an effectual declaration of trust. In *Milroy* v. *Lord*[73] Turner L.J., immediately after the passage from his judgment which has already been cited,[74] continued[75]: "The cases, I think, go further to this extent: that if the settlement is intended to be

[65] [1977] 1 W.L.R. 527.
[66] *Ibid.* at p. 532, *per* Scarman L.J.
[67] [1974] Ch. 269. The facts are stated in detail *ante*, at p. 38. *et seq.*
[68] The question was not argued before Megarry J. at first instance.
[69] *Ibid.* at p. 323.
[70] In *Vandervell* v. *I.R.C.* [1967] 2 A.C. 291; see *ante*, pp. 38. *et seq.*
[71] See *ante*, p. 35.
[72] Law of Property Act 1925, s.53(1)(b); see *ante*, p. 34.
[73] (1862) 4 De G.F. & J. 264.
[74] See *ante*, p. 58.
[75] (1862) 4 De G.F. & J. 264 at p. 275.

effectuated by one of the modes to which I have referred, the court will not give effect to it by applying another of these modes. If it is intended to take effect by transfer, the court will not hold the intended transfer to operate as a declaration of trust, for then every imperfect instrument would be made effectual by being converted into a perfect trust." This principle was applied in *Richards* v. *Delbridge*.[76] The deceased, the owner of certain leasehold premises, indorsed and signed on the lease the following memorandum: "This deed and all thereto I give to [the intended transferee] from this time forth, with all the stock-in-trade." The Court of Appeal held that there was no perfected transfer, since the indorsement had not been made with the formalities necessary for a deed and so was ineffective to transfer the leasehold interest. Nor in the circumstances could it take effect as a declaration of trust.

The existence of this principle does not, however, mean that a settlor who intends to create a trust by transfer cannot expressly declare himself to be trustee of the subject matter pending transfer. If he does so, he will himself be the trustee of a completely constituted trust of the subject matter unless and until he transfers that property to the intended trustees. Thus in *Re Ralli's Will Trusts*,[77] a settlor entered into a covenant to transfer any existing or after-acquired property to the trustees of her marriage settlement; it was stated that it was "the intention" of the parties that all such property "shall become subject in equity to the settlement". The settlor failed to transfer to the trustees existing property which was caught by the covenant. Buckley J. held that, although no completely constituted trust of the property had arisen by transfer, the settlor had declared herself to be a trustee of any such property pending transfer and that this completely constituted trust could be enforced by the beneficiaries of the marriage settlement.

Further, in one situation, where the transferor has done everything which it is necessary for him to do to render the transfer effectual but something has yet to be done by a third party, the transfer will become effective *in equity* and, contrary to the general principle, the transferor will be regarded as a trustee of the property for the transferee pending the intervention of the third party.[78] This rule was established by the Court of Appeal in *Re Rose*[79] and for this reason is generally known as the Rule in *Re Rose*.

In *Re Rose*, a settlor executed transfers of shares in a company, partly by way of gift to his wife and partly to a trustee. These transfers were not actually registered until three months later. The transferor subsequently died more than five years after the execution of the transfers but less than five years after their registration. At this time no estate

---

[76] (1874) L.R. 18 Eq. 11.
[77] [1964] Ch. 288. See also *Middleton* v. *Pollock* (1876) 2 Ch.D. 194, where effective declarations of trust were made.
[78] Since this trust does not arise out of any intention of the parties thereto, it must therefore necessarily be brought into existence by operation of law and should therefore be classified as a constructive trust (see *post*, p. 294).
[79] [1952] Ch. 499.

duty was payable on property disposed of more than five years before death.[80] Were the transfers effective upon execution or upon registration? The Court of Appeal held that, once he had executed the transfers in the appropriate form, the transferor had done everything in his power which was necessary to vest the legal interest in the shares in the transferees. Consequently, from that moment the transfers were effective in equity and the transferor consequently held the legal title to the shares on trust for the transferees until they subsequently acquired legal title thereto upon registration of the transfers.

This conclusion is not easy to reconcile either with the judgment of Turner L.J. in *Milroy* v. *Lord*[81] which has already been cited or with the decision in *Re Fry*[82] which has already been considered.[83] The Court of Appeal held that the statement of Turner L.J. only applied where the transfer in question had not been carried out in the appropriate way (admittedly this was the situation under consideration in *Milroy* v. *Lord*[84] but no such restriction is actually mentioned by Turner L.J.). *Re Fry* was distinguished on the basis that there the transferor had not done all in his power to vest the property in the transferees, apparently because the transferor, in order to perfect the transaction, would have had to effect confirmatory transfers after the consent had been given. Neither of these distinctions is particularly convincing. Difficulties also arise in relation to the role of the third party. Some third parties have a merely formal role in that they have no effective discretion to refuse to act—those responsible for registering a transfer of registered land or the transfer of shares in a public company presumably fall within this category. Is the Rule in *Re Rose* limited to situations such as these or does it also operate where the third party in question is able to decline to act? In *Re Rose* itself, because of the nature of the company in question, its directors had the right to refuse to register the share transfers. This suggests that the rule will indeed operate even where the third party in question is entitled to decline to act. However on this point it is once again difficult to reconcile *Re Rose* with *Re Fry*.

Despite the doubts expressed in the previous paragraph, the Rule in *Re Rose* is clearly English law at the present time. The rule was applied by Lord Wilberforce in *Vandervell* v. *I.R.C.*[85] in order to justify his conclusion as to the scope of section 53(1)(c) of the Law of Property Act

---

[80] The necessary period was subsequently increased to seven years but this particular exemption disappeared with the abolition of Estate Duty and the introduction of Capital Transfer Tax in 1974. However, the replacement of Capital Transfer Tax by Inheritance Tax in 1986 brought about the return of the exemption so that the Rule in *Re Rose* is once again extremely significant.

[81] (1862) 4 De G.F. & J. 264 at pp. 274–275.

[82] [1946] Ch. 312.

[83] See *ante*, p. 60.

[84] The settlor had covenanted to transfer bank shares to the defendant on trust for the plaintiff. The defendant already held a general Power of Attorney to transfer shares of the settlor so the settlor merely handed over the share certificates to him. However, neither he nor the settlor ever procured the entry in the books of the bank which was necessary for the transfer of the legal title.

[85] [1967] 2 A.C. 271, see *ante*, p. 38.

1925[86] and more recently in *Mascall* v. *Mascall*[87] it was held that delivery by the transferor of registered land to the transferee of a duly executed transfer form and the land certificate will bring the rule into operation so that, pending the registration of the transferee's title, the transferor will hold the land in question on trust for the transferee. The Rule in *Re Rose* therefore constitutes an exception to the principle that equity will not perfect an imperfect gift.

(4) Other exceptions to the rule that equity will not perfect an imperfect gift

Quite apart from the Rule in *Re Rose*, there are a number of other exceptions to the general rule that equity will not perfect an imperfect gift which will now be considered.

    (a) The rule in *Strong* v. *Bird*.[88] The principle established by this case is that the intention to release a debt or to make a gift is effected by making the debtor or the donee an executor. A complete gift involves two elements: an intention to make the gift and the transfer of the legal title to the donee. The principle underlying *Strong* v. *Bird* is that where there is a continuing intention to make a gift the other requirement for a complete gift is fulfilled when the legal title vests in the executor by operation of law on the death of the donor. The appointment of the intended donee as executor perfects the intention of the donor and completes the gift. The equity of the beneficiaries (if any) under the will is said to be displaced by the donee's prior equity.

    The rule was originally limited to debts. In *Strong* v. *Bird* itself, the defendant had borrowed £1,000 from his stepmother who lived in his house, paying £200 a quarter for board. It was agreed that the debt should be paid off by the deduction of £100 from each quarter's payment. Deductions for this amount were made for two quarters, but on the third quarter-day the stepmother generously refused to hold to the agreement any longer and paid the full £200 board due on each quarter-day; subsequently, until her death four years later, she continued to pay this amount each quarter. The defendant was the sole executor of her will and he proved the will. The next-of-kin then claimed that the defendant still owed the balance of the debt to her estate. At common law it had long been established that a debt owed to a deceased person was extinguished by the appointment of the debtor as executor.[89] *Strong* v. *Bird* decided that equity would in this respect follow the common law and deny any claim by the beneficiaries claiming under the will provided that there was evidence that, up until the moment of his death, the creditor had had a continuing intention to release the debt (this was easily demonstrated in *Strong* v. *Bird* by the fact that the stepmother had continued to pay £200 per quarter).

---

[86] This argument actually begged the question being considered by the House of Lords (see G.H. Jones (1966) 24 C.L.J. 19) but that does not alter the fact that he applied the Rule in *Re Rose*.

[87] (1984) 50 P. & C.R. 119.

[88] (1874) 18 Eq. 315.

[89] At least since *Wankford* v. *Wankford* (1704) 1 Salk. 299.

However, the rule has since been extended very considerably. In *Re Stewart*[90] it was held that an ineffectual gift made *inter vivos* to the person who later became the donor's executor was perfected by his appointment as such. However, it is essential to show that the donor had a continuing intention to make an immediate gift *inter vivos*. In *Re Freeland*[91] a testatrix promised to give the plaintiff a motorcar at a future date but never did so. On the testatrix's death the plaintiff became her executrix and claimed that the imperfect gift had thereby been perfected. However, the Court of Appeal refused to apply the Rule in *Strong* v. *Bird* because the gift had never become absolute. Similarly, in *Re Wale*,[92] the testatrix, having overlooked the need to transfer part of the intended trust property to the trustees, subsequently forgot all about the trust and treated the property as her own. It was held that the Rule in *Strong* v. *Bird* did not apply. It has also been established that the rule is restricted to specific existing property[93]; thus a continuing unfulfilled intention to make a gift of a sum of money will not be perfected if the intended donee subsequently becomes the donor's executor.

Thus far it is possible to justify the existence of the rule. Even though the vast majority of testators will necessarily be unaware of its existence, an executor is at least expressly nominated by his testator. However, it is less easy to justify the subsequent extension of the rule to administrators. This extension occurred in *Re James*[94] where the deceased had, on the death of his father, handed over the title deeds of his father's house to his father's housekeeper. This was of course insufficient to vest the legal title to the house in the housekeeper—this would have necessitated a deed—but she continued to live there until the son died and it was clear that he had at all times intended her to have the house. When he died intestate, she obtained appointment as his administratrix so that the legal title to the house became vested in her by operation of law. It was held that this fortuitous occurence brought the rule in *Strong* v. *Bird* into operation and thus perfected the incomplete gift to her. No administrator is ever nominated by his testator and it is often a matter of pure chance which of the beneficiaries entitled under a will or an intestacy ends up as administrator. It therefore seems unreasonable that that person should obtain an advantage over the other beneficiaries by reason of his appointment. Indeed, for precisely this reason, the original common law rule was never applied to administrators. These points were made forcefully by Walton J. in *Re Gonin (deceased)*,[95] where the decision in *Re James* was doubted. However, since both counsel had accepted its correctness, Walton J. nevertheless applied that decision to an ineffectual gift *inter vivos* of a house and its furniture by a mother to the daughter who had

---

[90] [1908] 2 Ch. 251.
[91] [1952] Ch. 110.
[92] [1956] 1 W.L.R. 1346. See also *Re Eiser's Will Trusts* [1937] 1 All E.R. 244 (donor subsequently took security for the debt given).
[93] *Re Innes* [1952] 1 Ch. 188.
[94] [1935] Ch. 449.
[95] [1964] Ch. 288.

devoted her life to caring for her parents; on the facts, he held that sufficient continuing intention had been made out in respect only of the furniture and not of the house.

Other uncertainties remain. It is probable that, like the original common law rule, the rule in *Strong* v. *Bird* gives the executor or administrator priority only over those beneficially entitled to the estate and not over its creditors but this has never been the subject of judicial comment in this jurisdiction.[96] Nor does it appear to have been expressly decided whether the rule applies where the imperfect gift is in favour of the executor or administrator as trustee rather than beneficially; if so, in such circumstances the operation of the rule will completely constitute the trust in question. However, in *Re Wale*,[97] where the rule was not in fact applied, no objection was made on the grounds that the executors would have taken as trustees. This was also the situation in *Re Ralli's Will Trusts*[98] which appears to extend the Rule in *Strong* v. *Bird* still further.

In this case, a settlor entered into a covenant to transfer any existing or after-acquired property to the trustees of her marriage settlement. She failed to transfer to the trustees existing property which was caught by the covenant but on her death this property vested by operation of law in the sole trustee of her will, who was also the sole trustee of the marriage settlement. As has already been seen,[99] Buckley J. actually held, as a matter of construction, that the settlor had declared herself to be a trustee of any such property pending transfer and that this completely constituted trust could be enforced by the beneficiaries of the marriage settlement. However, he also upheld an alternative argument that, since the property had by operation of law come into the hands of the person to whom it should have been transferred *inter vivos*, the trust of that property in favour of the beneficiaries of the marriage settlement had by this means also become completely constituted by transfer. Buckley J. stated that it was irrelevant how the property had come into the hands of the person to whom it should have been transferred. The mere fact, fortuitous though it was, that the property had reached his hands had completely constituted the trust. It is not clear whether these statements amount to a secondary ratio or are merely obiter d¡cta. Either way, they amount to a very considerable extension of the Rule in *Strong* v. *Bird*. It is of no great significance that the person whose hands the property had reached had no beneficial interest therein—it has never been held that the Rule in *Strong* v. *Bird* is limited to beneficial gifts to executors and administrators. What is significant is that the trustee does not appear to have been either the executor or the administrator of the settlor. What is more, no evidence was either given or required that the settlor had had any continuing intention of transferring the property in question to the trustees of her

---

[96] The question has been considered in Australia; see *Bone* v. *Stamp Duty Commissioner* (1974) 132 C.L.R. 38, 53 (High Court of Australia).
[97] [1956] 1 W.L.R. 1346.
[98] [1964] Ch. 288.
[99] See *ante*, p. 64.

marriage settlement at any time during the thirty-two years which had elapsed between the creation of the settlement and her death.

Given that virtually none of the requirements of the Rule in *Strong* v. *Bird* is actually satisfied by the principle enunciated by Buckley J. in *Re Ralli's Will Trusts*, it therefore seems more appropriate to regard this as a wholly distinct rule. As such, it appears to be inconsistent with the earlier decision of *Re Brooks's Settlement Trusts*[1] (not cited to Buckley J.). In this case, under the terms of a voluntary settlement the settlor had covenanted to transfer to the trustees any property which he might acquire under his parents' marriage settlement. A bank was trustee of both settlements so that, when a sum was subsequently appointed to the settlor under the marriage settlement, it was already in the hands of the trustees to whom he had covenanted to transfer it. For reasons which will be considered later in this section,[2] neither the trustees nor the beneficiaries of the voluntary settlement could have enforced the covenant against the settlor. Consequently Farwell J. held that, despite the coincidence of trustees, the settlor was entitled to receive the sum appointed to him. In the light of this decision, it must be questionable whether *Re Ralli's Will Trusts* was correctly decided on this second ground; it remains to be seen whether it is ever followed.

(b) Donationes mortis causa. These gifts provide a further exception to the maxim that equity will not perfect an imperfect gift. For an effectual *donatio mortis causa*, however, four elements must be present.

(A) The gift must have been made in contemplation of death. Here it is necessary only that the donor contemplated death at the time of the gift. Although the point has never been expressly decided in England[3]; the test would seem to be subjective and not objective. It is the donor's own state of mind, not the actual circumstances, which is material. Moreover, the title of the donee will not be invalidated if the donor dies from some other cause than, for example, the disease from which he is suffering.[4] So, in *Wilkes* v. *Allington*,[5] the donor was suffering from an incurable disease and made the gift knowing that he had not long to live. As things turned out, he lived an even shorter time than he thought, because he died two months later from pneumonia. The gift, however, remained valid.

(B) The gift must have been made under circumstances indicating that it is conditional on the death of the donor. In this respect it is

---

[1] [1939] 1 Ch. 993.

[2] See *post*, p. 88. *et seq.*

[3] It appears that an objective test has been adopted in Canada: see the Canadian cases cited in n. 4, *post*; and see 81 L.Q.R. (1965) 21.

[4] It need not, perhaps, necessarily be illness, though it normally is. Nor apparently need the donor be *in extremis*. The contrary suggestion is made in *Thomson* v. *Meechan* [1958] D.L.R. 103, but this seems incorrect. For a similar suggestion, see *Canada Trust Co.* v. *Labrador* [1962] O.R. 151. See also 81 L.Q.R. (1965) 21.

[5] [1931] 2 Ch. 104 and see *Mills* v. *Shields* [1948] I.R. 367 (death from suicide); cf. *Re Dudman* [1925] Ch. 553 (contemplation of suicide insufficient) but this last case was decided before the Suicide Act 1961, under which suicide is no longer a crime; it is possibly arguable that such a gift may now be valid.

different from a gift *inter vivos* in that that is absolute, whereas a *donatio mortis causa* is necessarily conditional on death. The condition is not usually expressed but an inference to this effect will usually be made from the illness of the donor.[6] This means that the subject matter will revert to the donor if he recovers from his illness and also that it can at any time be revoked by the donor during his lifetime.[7]

Express revocation by the donor will essentially take the form of resuming dominion over it,[8] though there is some authority for the proposition that it is sufficient if the donor simply informs the donee of the revocation.[9] But a purported revocation by will is not enough because obviously the will cannot take effect until the death of the testator and at that time the donee will have become unconditionally entitled.[10]

Nevertheless, although conditional in this sense, it must be a *present* gift and not a gift to take effect in the future.[11]

(C) The donor must have delivered the subject matter of the gift to the donee or alternatively the means or part of the means of getting at the subject matter. It is, of course, a precondition, whatever the subject matter may be, that the donor intended to part with dominion[12] and this will be a matter of fact.

No difficulties will normally arise in the case of ordinary chattels. Delivery[13] will be effected either by delivery of the chattel itself or a means of getting at the chattel, for example, the keys of a wardrobe containing it.[14] At the same time it must also be made in such circumstances as to demonstrate that the donor can no longer interfere with the subject matter.[15]

However, some choses in action, for example, a bank account, are incapable of physical delivery[16] and the question will arise whether the donee can compel the personal representative to complete the gift to him of the chose. The essential condition that must be satisfied is, according to the conventional formulation, that the donor must have delivered to the donee a document which is the essential evidence of his title to the chose in question. This test was applied in *Re Weston*,[17] where a dying man had handed over to his fiancée his Post Office Savings Bank book and this action was held sufficient to constitute an

---

[6] *Re Lillingston* [1952] 2 All ER 184.
[7] *Staniland* v. *Willott* (1850) 3 Mac. & G. 664.
[8] *Bunn* v. *Markham* (1816) 7 Taunt. 224 at 231.
[9] *Jones* v. *Selby* (1710) Prec. Ch. 300 at p. 303. Resuming mere *possession* (for example for safe custody) is not enough: *Re Hawkins* [1924] 2 Ch. 47.
[10] *Jones* v. *Selby, supra.*
[11] *Re Ward* [1946] 2 All E.R. 206.
[12] *Birch* v. *Treasury Solicitor* [1951] Ch. 298.
[13] See *Re Cole* [1964] Ch. 175.
[14] *Re Mustapha* (1891) 8 T.L.R. 160 and see *Re Lillingston* [1952] 2 All E.R. 184.
[15] *Re Craven's Estates (No. 1)* [1937] Ch. 423 at 427, delivery of one of two keys is insufficient.
[16] A chose in action *may* be transferable by delivery, for example bearer bonds. Delivery of such bonds will be sufficient to constitute an effective *donatio mortis causa*; see *Re Wasserberg* [1915] 1 Ch. 195. So also will, for example, delivery of a key of a box containing such choses: *Re Wasserberg, supra.*
[17] [1902] 1 Ch. 680.

effective *donatio mortis causa* of the savings set out in it. It was in this last case that Byrne J. expressed the opinion that the document in question must contain all the essential terms on which the subject matter of the chose in action was held. But this view has now been expressly disapproved by the Court of Appeal in *Birch* v. *Treasury Solicitor*.[18] It is easy to visualise circumstances where a strict application of the test would work injustice, although it did not do so in *Re Weston*. The correct approach now, in the words of Sir Raymond Evershed M.R. in *Birch* v. *Treasury Solicitor*, is that delivery must be made of the "essential indicia . . . of title, possession or production of which entitles the possessor to the money or property, purported to be given".[19] The principle was applied by the Court of Appeal in *Sen* v. *Headley*,[20] where the authorities on *donationes mortis causa* of choses in action are reviewed particularly fully. In this case, three days before his death the deceased had, with the necessary intention, delivered to the donee the only key to the steel box which contained the title deeds to his unregistered house and land. Although in *Duffield* v. *Elwes*,[21] Lord Eldon L.C. had appeared to suggest that land is not capable of being the subject matter of a *donatio mortis causa*, the Court of Appeal stated that anomalies do not justify anomalous exceptions, that to make a distinction in the case of land would be to make just such an exception, and that a *donatio mortis causa* of land was "neither more nor less anomalous than any other".[22] Consequently, since *Birch* v. *Treasury Solicitor* had extended rather than restricted the operation of the doctrine, the court held that land is capable of passing by way of a *donatio mortis causa*.

It must, however, be emphasised that a legal title to the chose in action will not be automatically acquired by the donee on delivery in the manner prescribed. The gift of the moneys or other property represented by the document will still be imperfect. This is even more evident in the case of a *donatio mortis causa* of land. But in this context the important point is that the donor's personal representative will be compelled to perfect the gift.[23] It is therefore in the case of *donationes mortis causa* of choses in action and of land that an exception is made to the general rule that equity will not perfect an imperfect gift.

(D) The final requirement for an effective *donatio mortis causa* is that the property is capable of being the subject matter of such a gift. It has been seen that there can be a valid *donatio* by delivery if the property can pass by that means or, if it cannot, by the handing over of an appropriate document. In general it seems that most property is eligible, particularly now that *Sen* v. *Headley* has upheld the validity of a *donatio mortis causa* of land. However, the handing over to the donee by the donor of his own duly executed cheque is clearly not sufficient to take effect as a *donatio mortis causa* because such a cheque is not property at

[18] [1951] Ch. 298.
[19] *Ibid.* at p. 311.
[20] [1991] 2 W.L.R. 1308.
[21] (1827) 1 Bli. (N.S.) 497.
[22] [1991] 2 W.L.R. 1308 at p. 1319.
[23] *Re Dillon* (1890) 44 Ch.D. 76 at pp. 82–83.

all but simply a revocable order to the bank to make payment to the payee.[24]

(c) **Proprietary estoppel.**[25]   If the doctrine of estoppel were still limited to the sense in which it has traditionally been generally applied, it would barely be worthy of mention here since the traditional form of the doctrine operated only defensively so as to prevent a party from asserting his rights; as such, it obviously could not operate so as to perfect an imperfect gift or complete an incompletely constituted trust.[26] However, the modern principle of proprietary estoppel can be used *offensively*, "as a sword" as it is sometimes described, in order that an imperfect gift can be perfected if the donor has stood by and watched the donee improve property or do other acts to his detriment on the supposition that there has been or will be an effective gift. The doctrine appears to be of early origin[27] but until recently has evolved in the form of three separate overlapping categories of cases: firstly, cases concerning imperfect gifts; secondly, cases concerning common expectations, where parties have consistently dealt with one another in such a way as to cause one of them to rely on a shared supposition that he would acquire rights of some kind in the land of the other; and, thirdly, cases of unilateral mistake, where the owner of land has stood by and allowed another person to act to his detriment on a mistaken belief that he has a legally enforceable interest in the land in question. The principles established by these three groups of authorities have now been synthesised into the modern principle of proprietary estoppel. The key decision in this process seems to have been *Taylor Fashions* v. *Liverpool Victoria Trustees Company*.[28] In this case, Oliver J., although denying that the principle of proprietary estoppel operated on the facts of the case before him, rejected the notion that the principle was narrowly confined to the three categories of cases already mentioned. Instead his lordship found support in these three groups of cases for "a much wider jurisdiction to interfere in cases where the assertion of strict legal rights is found by the courts to be unconscionable".[29]

As a result of this synthesis, it is now clear that a successful claim of proprietary estoppel involves three elements: an assurance, a reliance and a detriment. Such an assurance will occur where the owner of land, expressly or by necessary implication, raises in another person an expectation that that person will obtain some interest or entitlement in land which he would not otherwise have. The assurance can range from

---

[24] *Re Leaper* [1916] 1 Ch. 579.

[25] See K. J. Gray: *Elements of Land Law* (2nd ed. (1993)) Chap. 13.

[26] This is so in a case of so-called promissory estoppel. The latter, unlike proprietary estoppel, is also not permanent in its effect, for the promisor can resile from his position if he gives of the promisee notice which provides him with a reasonable opportunity of resuming his former position: see *Re Vandervell's Trusts (No. 2)* [1964] Ch. 269 at p. 301, *per* Megarry J.

[27] See *Foxcroft* v. *Lester* (1703) 2 Vern. 456.

[28] [1982] Q.B. 133 (Note).

[29] *Ibid.* at p. 147.

an express request to incur expenditure through encouragement or incitement so to do to silent abstention from the assertion of rights, although in the last case the owner of the land obviously has to be shown to have at least some knowledge of the mistaken belief of the other party. Where such an assurance has been made, the other person must then show that he has acted in reliance upon that assurance to his detriment. This involves him showing both that he has changed his position and that this change of position is a direct consequence of the assurance given. Where such a proprietary estoppel has arisen, the court enjoys very considerable flexibility in that a remedy can be provided appropriate to the circumstances of each individual case. Such remedies range from the grant of an unqualified estate in fee simple or lesser interest in or over land such as a lease or an easement through the grant of a right to occupy the land to the grant of monetary compensation; it is also possible for a grant of a right in or a right to occupy land to be combined with a grant of monetary compensation. The doctrine is of course still developing and, as will be seen later,[30] there is an increasing overlap between the doctrine of proprietary estoppel and the "common intention constructive trust". However, although the terminology employed in the majority of the cases decided prior to *Taylor Fashions* v. *Liverpool Victoria Trustees Company* would be very different if those cases were to recur today, there is no doubt whatsoever that they would still be decided in the same way. Consequently, they remain important as illustrations of the situations, formerly quite distinct, which today fall within the doctrine of proprietary estoppel.

For present purposes, what is important is the cases concerning imperfect gifts. A useful starting point is *Dillwyn* v. *Llewelyn*[31] where a father put his son into possession of land without a conveyance. It was intended that the son should build a house on the land. The son successfully claimed that the land should be formally conveyed to him. Lord Westbury L.C. said: "If A puts B in possession of a piece of land and tells him 'I give it to you that you may build a house on it', and B, on the strength of that promise, with the knowledge of A, expends a large sum of money in building a house accordingly, I cannot doubt that the donee acquires a right from the subsequent transaction to call on the donor to perform that contract, and complete the imperfect donation which was made." In other words, the subsequent acts of the donor gave the donee a right which he did not acquire from the original gift.

As has already been mentioned, what estate or interest the donee takes depends on the circumstances of the case. In *Dillwyn* v. *Llewelyn* the donee took the fee simple. This was also the result more recently in *Pascoe* v. *Turner*[32] where the parties had lived together in a house as man and wife and the man had encouraged or acquiesced in the mistress improving the house in the belief that it belonged to her. He was ordered to execute a conveyance of the house to her. But the facts may indicate a lesser estate or some other right. Thus, in *Inwards* v.

---

[30] See *post*, p. 284.
[31] (1862) 4 De G.F. & J. 517.
[32] [1979] 1 W.L.R. 431, C.A.

Baker[33] the donee was held entitled to remain in occupation as long as he wished. And in *E.R. Ives Investments Ltd.* v. *High*[34] the defendant was allowed a right of way so long as the plaintiff and his successors in title maintained the foundations of a building on the defendant's land, because the plaintiff's predecessors by licensing the defendant to use the yard in question had encouraged him to build a garage on his own adjoining land and this created an estoppel. Moreover the equitable interest which thus arose was not subject to the rules regarding the registration of land charges.[35]

Such cases were applied in *Crabb* v. *Arun District Council*[36] where there was an agreement "in principle" (not amount to a contract) that the plaintiff should have a right of access, and relying on it he sold the front portion of his land without reserving a right of way over it in order to reach the back portion. It was held by the Court of Appeal that it was a case of proprietary estoppel entitling him to an easement or licence.[37] He had been encouraged to act to his detriment by the defendant's conduct.[38] Similarly, in *Jones* v. *Jones*,[39] a father had led his son to believe that a house would be his home for the rest of his life, and the son had given up his job and moved on the basis of that expectation. It was held that he could pray in aid the doctrine of estoppel, and both the father and his administratrix were estopped from turning the son out during his life. Again, in *Re Sharpe*,[40] where an aged aunt lent money for the purchase of a house by her nephew so that she could live with him and his wife in it, it was held that an irrevocable licence to occupy the house arose in favour of the aunt until the loan was repaid.

Moreover, the burden of proof is on the plaintiff to show that the defendant has not acted to his detriment or prejudice where the latter relies upon estoppel. So, in *Greasley* v. *Cooke*[41] assurances had been given that the defendant could remain in a house, where not only had she been employed as a maid from 1938 but also had lived with one of the children of the family as man and wife. It was held that these assurances raised an equity in her favour and it was to be presumed that she had acted on the faith of those assurances. The plaintiffs failed to rebut the presumption.[42]

---

[33] [1965] 2 Q.B. 29, C.A. See also *Ward* v. *Kirkland* [1967] Ch. 194, where a perpetual easement of drainage was granted.

[34] [1967] 2 Q.B. 289, C.A.

[35] Under what is now the Land Charges Act 1972.

[36] [1976] Ch. 179.

[37] An easement (according to Lord Denning M.R. and Lawton L.J.); an easement or licence (according to Scarman L.J.).

[38] One of the acts to his detriment was the sale of land separate from the land over which the access was to be granted. Normally, the acts involve expenditure in relation to the actual land intended to be disposed of.

[39] [1977] 1 W.L.R. 438, C.A.

[40] [1980] 1 W.L.R. 219.

[41] [1980] 1 W.L.R. 1306, C.A.

[42] Lord Denning M.R. said (at p. 1311) that the incurring of expenditure of money or other prejudice was not a necessary element. However, this appears to be far too wide a generalisation. *cf.* Dunn L.J. at p. 1313.

The fact that it is essential for a case of proprietary estoppel that a party acted as he did to his detriment in the expectation of acquiring a right to or over somebody else's land is illustrated by *Western Fish Products* v. *Penwith District Council*.[43] It was held on the facts that even if the plaintiffs had to their detriment spent money on their land at the encouragement of the Council, they had not done so in the expectation of acquiring any rights over the Council's or any other land and could not therefore rely on proprietary estoppel.[44]

Given that to raise an estoppel of this kind, the conduct of the owner of the property must give rise in some degree to inequitable consequences, it is conjectural whether this basic principle was correctly applied in *Re Vandervell's Trusts (No. 2)*[45] although it is fair to say that this was not the sole ground on which the Court of Appeal reached its decision.[46] The court was of opinion that if Vandervell, who had concurred in the dealings with the moneys and shares carried out by the trustee company,[47] had been alive, he would have been estopped from denying the existence of the beneficial interest for the children, and his executors could be in no better position. However, as Megarry J. pointed out at first instance,[48] the company had not been able to show that, when the option was exercised, Vandervell knew that he was the beneficial owner of it and, therefore, he was not guilty of any unconscionable behaviour, such behaviour being an element in establishing proprietary estoppel.[49] This argument which is based on the necessity for knowledge on the part of the person alleged to be estopped is attractive and would appear to be difficult to avoid, but Oliver J. appeared to reject it in *Taylors Fashions Ltd.* v. *Liverpool Victoria Trustees Co. Ltd.*[50] in holding that knowledge of the true position by the party alleged to be estopped was merely one of the relevant factors in the overall inquiry. The essential question was whether, in the particular circumstances, it would be unconscionable for a party to be permitted to deny that which, knowingly or unknowingly, he had allowed or encouraged another to assume to his detriment. Accordingly, it was held that the principle could apply where, at the time the expectation was encouraged, both parties (not just the

---

[43] [1981] 2 All E.R. 204, C.A.; see also *Hastlemere Estates* v. *Baker* [1982] 3 All E.R. 525 (there was no legitimate hope or expectation of obtaining any interest in the land).

[44] It was also held that any event an estoppel could not be raised to prevent a statutory body exercising its statutory discretion or performing a statutory duty; see also *Rootkin* v. *Kent County Council* [1981] 1 W.L.R. 1186 as to the exercise of a statutory discretion relating to the payment of travelling expenses of a school pupil.

[45] [1974] Ch. 269. The question was not fully argued before Megarry J. (whose decision was reversed) at first instance.

[46] See *ante*, p. 39.

[47] These dealings are referred to *ante*, p. 40.

[48] *Ibid.* at p. 301.

[49] This is assuming that the court relied on proprietary estoppel. If the estoppel relied on was promissory (see *supra*, n. 26), Megarry J. said (at p. 302) that there would appear to be difficulty in establishing such an estoppel where the person making representations did not know his rights: but *cf. Amalgamated Investment & Property Co. Ltd.* v. *Texas Commerce International Bank Ltd.* [1982] Q.B. 84; leave to appeal dismissed, [1982] 1 W.L.R. 1 H.L.

[50] [1982] Q.B. 133n.

representee) were acting under a mistake of law as to their rights.[51] This case which, as has already been seen, set the doctrine of proprietary estoppel on its present course did not involve the law of trusts but must have an effect on it.

So far as the law of trusts is concerned, particularly in a tax case like *Re Rose*,[52] the doctrine may give rise to further difficulty. One question could be whether a gift or trust perfected by estoppel is to be regarded as being constituted at the making of the gift, or on the happening of the subsequent events which created the estoppel. The latter seems clearly to be the correct approach.[53] In other respects, however, the position is more doubtful. Thus, in *Williams* v. *Staite*,[54] Cumming-Bruce L.J. considered, without finding it necessary to decide the question, that the rights of an equitable licensee for life did not necessarily crystallise when his rights came into existence but when the court came to determine his interest (if any) in the property. Lord Denning M.R. also thought that in an extreme case an equitable licence might be revoked,[55] but the conduct of the licensees, involving excessive user and bad behaviour, was not of a kind to bring the equity established in their favour to an end; their behaviour could be remedied by damages. It may be debatable whether an established equity can be forfeited in this way, but at least it seems clear that, when a person is asserting a right to an equity for the first time, his conduct may be taken into account in deciding whether to implement it, thereby applying the basic maxim that "he who comes to equity must come with clean hands."[56] Indeed, very much must depend on the facts of the case. In some cases, such as *Re Sharpe*[57] where the licensee was not in any way guilty of misconduct, it is essential that the rights must have arisen at the time of the transaction in order that the licensee can have any rights the breach of which can be remedied, in which case the equity must predate any order of the course.[58] The distinction, it seems, is between the pre-existence of an equity and the manner in which the court may choose, in the exercise of its discretion on the facts, to implement it.

It should also be mentioned that the conveyancing implications of proprietary estoppel have not been fully worked out. In *Dodsworth* v. *Dodsworth*[59] the Court of Appeal held that if the equity were implemented by giving the claimant the right to occupy a house for his life, the result would be to create a tenancy for life within the Settled Land Act 1925, with the consequence that he would get more than it had ever been represented that he should have, because he would receive

---

[51] See also *Thomas Bates & Son Ltd.* v. *Wyndhams (Lingerie) Ltd.* [1981] 1 W.L.R. 505: estoppel applied where the mistake was a unilateral rather than a common mistake.

[52] [1952] Ch. 499, discussed *ante*, p. 64.

[53] See generally on the subject, Jackson (1965) 81 L.Q.R. 84, 223; Poole (1968) 38 Conv. (N.S.) 96; Sunnucks (1968) 118 New L.J. 769.

[54] [1979] Ch. 291, C.A.

[55] *Ibid.* at p. 297.

[56] Goff L.J. was of this opinion in *Williams* v. *Staite (supra)*, at p. 299.

[57] [1980] 1 W.L.R. 219. The facts are stated *ante* p. 74.

[58] *Ibid.* at p. 225.

[59] (1973) 228 E.G. 1115.

the statutory powers of a tenant for life under that Act, powers which include the rights to sell, lease and mortgage the property. But, as Goff L.J. indicated in *Griffiths* v. *Williams*,[60] the court did not seem to have considered what might be in such circumstances a difficult problem: what was the "settlement" within section 1(1) of the Settled Land Act 1925? It was not easy, he said, where an equity was being set up by these means, to see how that could be within the terms of the section. The question did not, however, arise for decision.[61]

Many aspects of the scope of the doctrine of proprietary estoppel and the consequences of its utilisation in fiscal and conveyancing terms have still to be clarified. Nevertheless, the doctrine has been described[62] as "one of the most significant movements occurring in the contemporary law of real property". The extent to which its development will increase the scope of this exception to the rule that equity will not perfect an imperfect gift remains to be seen. Nevertheless, there can be no doubt that the development of the doctrine has increased both the importance of this particular exception and the possibilities of a trust becoming completely constituted thereby.

(d) Statutory exceptions. There are also two statutory exceptions to the rule that equity will not perfect an imperfect gift.

First, a minor cannot hold a legal estate in land.[63] But a conveyance of such an estate to him will (under section 19(6) of the Law of Property Act 1925 and under section 27(1) of the Settled Land Act 1925) operate as an agreement for valuable consideration by the grantor to execute a settlement in the minor's favour and in the meantime to hold the legal estate in trust for him. Secondly, it is not possible to create a proper settlement of the legal estate in land without two documents—a trust instrument and a vesting deed or assent.[64] An instrument other than a vesting deed or assent will not pass the legal estate. However, under section 9 of the Settled Land Act 1925 such a document will operate as a trust instrument and, therefore, take effect as an enforceable trust. The trustees may then execute the appropriate vesting deed and they are indeed compelled to do so if the beneficiary who holds the estate in possession for the time being (the person described in the Settled Land Act 1925 as the tenant for life) so requests.

2. *If a Trust is Incompletely Constituted, When Will the Beneficiaries have a Contractual Remedy?*

Where no completely constituted trust has arisen either as a result of the effectual transfer of the intended trust property to the trustees or as a result of a declaration of trust by the settlor and where the beneficiaries

---

[60] (1977) 74 *Guardian Gazette* 1130, 21 December 1977 (C.A.).

[61] Analogous conveyancing problems arise where a constructive trust is imposed as a result of the unconscionable conduct of the trustee in attempting to go back on an undertaking or agreement. See *post*, p. 277.

[62] By K. J. Gray in *Elements of Land Law* (2nd ed. (1993)) p. 312.

[63] Law of Property Act 1925, s.1 (6).

[64] Settled Land Act 1925, s.4.

are unable to rely on any of the exceptions to the rule that equity will not perfect an imperfect gift, the only possibility open to them will be to rely on the law of contract. There are a number of situations where a contractual remedy will enable the beneficiaries either to bring about the complete constitution of the trust or, in default, obtain common law damages. However, this is obviously not always possible and where no contractual remedy is available to the beneficiaries either, the trust in question is said to be voluntary and the beneficiaries are said to be volunteers. It is a long-established equitable maxim that "equity will not assist a volunteer".[65] Although this maxim is invariably relied on by the courts whenever a beneficiary is denied a remedy, its utilisation adds nothing and is a source of potential confusion. The maxim neither denies a remedy to a beneficiary who already has one nor provides a remedy to a beneficiary who does not have one. Consequently, it does no more than state the obvious: namely that, if a beneficiary can point neither to the existence of a completely constituted trust nor to the existence of any form of contract enforceable either by him or on his behalf, then equity will not assist him. More significantly, the existence of the maxim has hindered the development of the law since, unfortunately but predictably, the courts have tended to utilise it as a substitute for reasoned analysis of whether or not in any particular case any contractual remedy is actually available to the beneficiary.

The contractual remedies available to the beneficiaries of an incompletely constituted trust may arise either under a simple contract (a contract constituted as a result of the existence of offer and acceptance, intention to create legal relations, and consideration) or under a specialty contract (a contract constituted by virtue of being contained in a deed, often also described as a covenant). The contract entered into by the settlor may be a straightforward contract to settle some of his existing property, that is to say property of which he is already able to dispose.[66] However, there is normally little reason for a settlor to enter into such a contract in respect of existing property.[67] Such property can be the subject of a valid assignment, of a valid declaration of a trust, and of a valid contract to assign or declare a trust. Consequently, if the subject matter of a proposed trust is existing property, the settlor can just as easily constitute the trust immediately by transfer to trustees or by declaration as enter into a contract so to do. For this reason, most contracts of this type (and most of the cases which have come before the courts) have concerned property which has not yet come into existence; such property is generally known as after-acquired property. Such property cannot be the subject of a valid assignment,

---

[65] Ellison v. Ellison (1802) 6 Ves.Jun. 656 at p. 662 per Lord Eldon L.C.; see also Jefferys v. Jefferys (1841) Cr. & Ph. 138.

[66] Such cases were Williamson v. Codrington (1750) 1 Ves.Sen. 511 (covenant to settle a plantation), Fletcher v. Fletcher (1844) 4 Hare 167 (covenant to settle £60,000), and Re Cavendish Browne's Settlement Trusts [1916] W.N. 341 (covenant to settle property to which the settlor was entitled under the wills of persons who had already died).

[67] In both Williamson v. Codrington and Fletcher v. Fletcher, the reason was undoubtedly the fact that the beneficiaries were the illegitimate children of the settlors, who clearly wished to avoid embarrassing publicity until after their deaths.

which is at law wholly void,[68] although equity will treat the assignment of after-acquired property made in exchange for valuable consideration as a contract to assign or declare a trust if and when the property is acquired.[69] Nor can after-acquired property be the subject of a valid declaration of trust,[70] although equity will enforce this declaration of trust in favour of anyone who has provided valuable consideration if and when the property is acquired.[71] Further, an express contract to assign or declare a trust if and when the property is acquired[71] will be enforced both in equity and at common law[72] if it is a simple contract and is consequently supported by valuable consideration[73] and will be enforced at common law,[74] but not in equity,[75] if it is merely a specialty contract. All this means that if the subject matter of a proposed trust is after-acquired property, the settlor will have no option but to enter into what either is or is deemed by equity to be a contract to settle the property in question if and when it is acquired.

Because of this significant distinction between existing and after-acquired property, it is important to note that for this purpose existing property is not confined to property which has already vested in possession and is thus available for the immediate enjoyment of the person entitled thereto. Existing property also includes property which has not yet come into possession, either because the interest is vested in interest, in other words awaiting the determination of some prior interest (an example is the interest of a person who is absolutely entitled in remainder during a preceding life tenancy) or contingent (an example is the interest of a person entitled to property at the age of thirty when he has not yet attained that age). Further, existing property includes existing choses in action (an example is the right to recover book-debts arising in the course of a business[76]) and the right to exercise an existing power of appointment only at some future time (an example is an already granted power of appointment which is exercise-able only by will). After-acquired property, on the other hand, is property in respect of which only the future will determine whether or not the person in question ever acquires any rights at all (examples are the possibility of receiving property (including the right to exercise a

---

[68] *Holroyd* v. *Marshall* (1862) 10 H.L.C. 191 (assignment by way of mortgage of machinery which in the future might be substituted for existing machinery), *Re Tilt* (1896) 40 Sol.Jo. 224 (assignment of an expectancy under the intestacy of a person who was still alive), *Re Ellenborough* [1903] 1 Ch. 697 (assignment of an expectancy under the will of a person who was still alive).

[69] *Holroyd* v. *Marshall* (1862) 10 H.L.C. 191 at pp. 211, 220.

[70] *Williams* v. *C.I.R.* [1965] N.Z.L.R. 395 (Court of Appeal of New Zealand) (declaration of trust of the first £500 of the net income arising under a life interest in each of four future years).

[71] *Ellison* v. *Ellison* (1802) 6 Ves.Jun.656 at p. 662, *Williams* v. *C.I.R. supra.*

[72] The simple contract will not be enforceable at common law if the valuable consideration in question is marriage, which is not regarded as valuable consideration at law.

[73] *Pullan* v. *Koe* [1913] 1 Ch. 9, see *post*, p. 82.

[74] *Cannon* v. *Hartley* [1949] Ch. 213, see *post*, p. 87.

[75] *Jefferys* v. *Jefferys* (1841) Cr. & P. 138.

[76] As in *Barclays Bank* v. *Willowbrook International* [1987] 1 F.T.L.R. 386.

power of appointment[77]) under the will[78] or intestacy[79] of someone who is still alive or under an as yet unexercised power of appointment, the possibility of receiving royalties payable in respect of a copyright or a mining operation,[80] and the possibility of acquiring future book-debts arising in the course of a business[81]). Consequently, while a settlor may assign an equitable remainder to trustees on trust, declare a trust[82] thereof, or enter into either a simple or a specialty contract to make such an assignment or declaration of trust, his possible courses of action in respect of the payments which he hopes to receive as the royalties on a book are much more restricted; he cannot validly either assign or declare a trust of such payments, although a purported assignment or declaration of trust will be regarded by equity as a contract to assign or declare a trust if and when the property is acquired, but can enter into either a simple contract (enforceable both at law[83] and in equity) or a specialty contract (enforceable only at law) to make such an assignment or declaration of trust.

(1) Simple contract to create the trust

If the settlor and the beneficiary have entered into a simple contract for the creation by the settlor of a completely constituted trust in favour of the beneficiary, then both parties to the contract will be entitled to the appropriate contractual remedies.

(a) Simple contract recognised both at common law and in equity.

Where the consideration provided by the beneficiary is money or money's worth, then the existence of the contract will be recognised both at common law and in equity. Consequently both settlor and beneficiary will be able to obtain damages for breach of contract or, if the contract in question is capable of being specifically enforced, a decree for specific performance. The availability of specific performance means that in equity the property immediately becomes subject to the trust. Thus, if the settlor contracts with the beneficiary for money or money's worth to transfer land to trustees to hold on trust for him, in equity the land will immediately become subject to the trust and the beneficiary will be able to obtain a decree for specific performance of this contract; thus he will be able to oblige the settlor to transfer the land to the trustees in exchange for the money or money's worth in question. This remedy will also be available to the beneficiary where the subject matter of the intended trust is pure personalty for whose loss equity regards damages as an inadequate remedy; this will be the case where the subject matter is a chattel not readily available on the open market, such as a rare painting, a rare antique, a vintage motor

---

[77] *Re Ellenborough* [1903] 1 Ch. 697.
[78] *Re Tilt* (1896) 40 Sol.Jo. 224.
[79] *Re Parkin* [1892] 3 Ch. 510.
[80] *Coulls* v. *Bagot's Trustee* [1967] 40 A.L.J.R. 471.
[81] *Tailby* v. *Official Receiver* (1888) 13 App.Cas. 523.
[82] Strictly speaking, a sub-trust, see *ante*, p. 35.
[83] Provided that the consideration is money or money's worth rather than marriage consideration.

vehicle, or shares in a private company. Where, on the other hand, the contract in question is not capable of being specifically enforced because damages are an adequate remedy for the loss of the subject matter of the intended trust, the beneficiary will be limited to common law damages for breach of contract. These damages will be payable directly to the beneficiary rather than to the intended trustees, although there will obviously be nothing to prevent the beneficiary from himself paying the sum in question on to the trustees and thus creating a completely constituted trust of the money.

These principles apply not only to existing property but also to after-acquired property if and when it is acquired. In *Holroyd* v. *Marshall*[84] following the sale of machinery in a mill the purchaser assigned the machinery to a trustee on trust for the vendor if he should pay £5,000 to the purchaser and if not on trust for the purchaser. The deed of assignment included both the existing machinery and any after-acquired machinery which might be added to or substituted for the original machinery. The House of Lords held that as soon as any further machinery was acquired it vested immediately in equity in the trustee on these trusts and thus could not be the subject of execution by the creditors of the vendor. It has been established by subsequent authorities that this will occur even in the case of property in respect of which specific performance would not normally be decreed provided that the valuable consideration has already been furnished by the beneficiary.[85] Thus in *Re Gillott's Settlement*[86] debtors agreed with their creditors that any income which they received should within three days of receipt be paid to a trustee on various trusts for both debtors and creditors. It was held that an equitable interest in each payment received by the debtors vested immediately in the trustee so that the trust of each payment was immediately completely constituted. The majority of the decided cases, however, concern marriage consideration, a type of valuable consideration which is not recognised by the common law, and so will be discussed in the following section.[87]

(b) Simple contract recognised only in equity. In one particular situation not recognised by the common law, equity will imply both a contract for the creation by the settlor of a completely constituted trust in favour of the beneficiary and the necessary consideration therefor on the part of the beneficiary. This occurs where the beneficiary can bring himself within a marriage consideration. Where a settlement in consideration of marriage is made either before the marriage or contemporaneously with the celebration of the marriage or subsequent to the marriage pursuant to an agreement made prior to the marriage, equity implies that the settlor, the spouses, and the children and more remote descendants of the marriage are parties to a contract in respect of which

[84] (1862) 10 H.L.C. 191.
[85] Principally by the House of Lords in *Tailby* v. *Official Receiver* (1888) 13 App.Cas. 523 (a case concerning an assignment by way of mortgage rather than an assignment to trustees on trust).
[86] [1934] Ch. 97. See also *Re Lind* [1915] 2 Ch. 345 and *Re Haynes' Will Trusts* [1949] Ch. 5.
[87] See *post.*

they have given consideration. Any of the persons thus deemed to be a party to this implied contract can enforce any of the obligations arising thereunder, not only the original obligation of the settlor to create the settlement in question but also any obligations of the spouses to transfer any of their existing or after-acquired property to the trustees to be held on the trusts of the settlement. Any such obligation is capable of being specifically enforced even where damages would normally be an adequate remedy for the loss of the property in question. In the case of a marriage settlement, common law damages are never an adequate remedy for the simple reason that they are not available in an action by the beneficiaries[88]—the common law does not recognise marriage consideration.

These principles are illustrated by the case of *Pullan* v. *Koe*.[89] A wife was given a sum of money which was caught by a covenant to settle after-acquired property into which both she and her husband had entered in their marriage settlement. Part of the money was eventually invested in bonds which were held at a bank in the name of the husband. Following his death, the bonds came into the hands of his executor. Any action by the trustees on the covenants had by then become statute barred. However, it was held that the money received by the wife had been subject to the trusts of the marriage settlement from the moment of its receipt. Consequently, the children of the marriage could specifically enforce the simple contract implied by equity and thus bring about the transfer of the bonds by the executor to the trustees.

Normally the only persons within the marriage consideration are the spouses, the children and the more remote descendants of the marriage.[90] However, there is some authority that, in certain circumstances, illegitimate children and children of an earlier or subsequent marriage of one of the spouses may be brought within the marriage consideration if their interests are so "interwoven" with the interests of the children of the marriage in consideration of which the settlement was made that the interests of the latter cannot be enforced without also enforcing the interests of the former. This was suggested in *Attorney-General* v. *Jacobs-Smith*[91] and was supported by Buckley J. in *Re Cook's Settlement Trusts*.[92] However, this extension, which is in any case somewhat ambiguous, appears to go only thus far and will apparently not be extended further. In *Re Cook's Settlement Trusts*[93] an attempt was made to establish a similar principle to enable an intended beneficiary who is specially an object of the intended trust or is within the consideration of the deed of settlement to enforce any obligations

---

[88] Common law damages will of course be available in an action by the trustees to enforce any covenants entered into by either the settlor or the spouses.

[89] [1913] 1 Ch. 9.

[90] *MacDonald* v. *Scott* [1893] A.C. 642 at p. 650 establishes that "issue" includes both children and grandchildren.

[91] [1895] 2 Q.B. 341 at p. 354, *per* Kay L.J.

[92] [1965] Ch. 902. See also *Re D'Avigdor-Goldsmid* [1951] Ch. 1038 at p. 1053 (overruled on other grounds: [1953] A.C. 347).

[93] [1965] Ch. 902.

contained therein. (This alleged principle bears some resemblance to the former doctrine of "meritorious consideration", a principle analogous to marriage consideration which existed at least until the end of the Eighteenth Century[94]; this principle was based on the natural love and affection between parent and child and consequently could be utilised by the latter to enforce settlements made by the former.) In this case, Sir Francis Cook had entered into a settlement which was not in consideration of marriage in which he had covenanted with his father and with the trustees that in the event that he sold certain valuable paintings which had been transferred to him by his father, he would pay over the proceeds of sale to the trustees to be held on the trusts of the settlement, ultimately for the benefit of his children. He subsequently purported to give one of the paintings to his then wife who wished to sell it. Buckley J. refused to accept the alleged principle, holding that the equitable exception to the rule that equity will not assist a volunteer is confined to persons within the marriage consideration. Having consequently held that the children could not enforce the covenant against Sir Francis, he then went on to hold, for reasons that will be considered later,[95] that the trustees ought not to enforce the covenant against him either.

Because at the time when a marriage settlement is entered into, it is not normally known whether or not there will actually be any issue of the marriage, it is usual to insert an ultimate remainder in favour of the statutory next-of-kin of one of the spouses. Such persons are not within the marriage consideration and cannot enforce any of the obligations arising under the marriage settlement. This is illustrated by *Re Plumptre's Settlement*.[96] The husband and wife, on their marriage, covenanted with their trustees to settle the wife's after-acquired property for the benefit of herself and her husband successively for life, then for the issue of the marriage, and then for the wife's next-of-kin. The husband bought certain stock in the wife's name and the wife afterwards sold it and invested the proceeds of sale in other stock. She then died without issue, leaving her husband as her administrator. It was held that the next-of-kin, because they were volunteers, could not enforce the wife's covenant against her husband as administrator. Nor (it was also held) could the trustees sue for damages for breach of covenant because the claim was statute-barred.[97]

Finally, it should be noted that if the settlement is made after marriage and not in pursuance of an ante-nuptial agreement, it is wholly voluntary. This is because, although there may be consideration between husband and wife, that consideration would not be their

---

[94] This is generally thought to be the basis on which a covenant to settle a plantation on illegitimate children was enforced in *Williamson* v. *Codrington* (1750) 1 Ves.Sen. 511 and is one of the possible explanations of the decision in *Fletcher* v. *Fletcher* (1844) 6 Hare 67 (see G. H. Jones (1965) 24 C.L.J. 46 at p. 49).

[95] See *post*, p. 89.

[96] [1910] 1 Ch. 609. See also to a like effect *Re D'Angibau* (1880) 15 Ch.D. 228.

[97] Any such action, even if not statute-barred, would probably now be impossible because of the decisions in *Re Pryce* [1917] 1 Ch. 234, *Re Kay's Settlement* [1939] Ch. 329 and *Re Cook's Settlement Trusts* [1965] Ch. 902, see *post*, p. 88.

marriage—such being past—but consideration of some other kind to which their children would be strangers.[98] This was expressly held in *Green* v. *Paterson*,[99] which was applied in *Re Cook's Settlement Trusts*.

(2) Specialty contract or covenant to create the trust

Specialty contracts or covenants to settle property on trust have traditionally played an important role in settlements of all types. Not only have settlors commonly entered into covenants to create entirely new trusts by transferring existing or after-acquired property to trustees on trust; trusts which have already been completely constituted have regularly included covenants by the beneficiaries to transfer their existing or after-acquired property to the trustees to be held on the trusts of the settlement. This is illustrated by the cases which have already been discussed in this section. When a covenant to create a trust is entered into in exchange for valuable consideration, it will be enforceable in accordance with the principles which were considered in the immediately preceding part of this section. This part of this section is concerned with the situation where a covenant has been entered into other than for valuable consideration. In such circumstances, the beneficiaries are inevitably in a weaker position. Their only possibilities are as follows: to show that there is a completely constituted trust in their favour of the benefit of the covenant, to show that they are parties to the covenant, and to attempt to enforce the covenant indirectly by means of an action by the trustees on the covenant at common law against the settlor.[1]

(a) **Completely constituted trust of the benefit of the covenant.** There is no reason in principle why there should not be a completely constituted trust of the benefit of a covenant to settle. Any chose in action can be the subject matter of a trust and so a settlor is certainly capable of declaring that the right which, by means of his covenant, he has conferred upon the trustees to enforce the covenant against him should be held on trust for the beneficiaries of the intended trust. If such a trust can be found to have been created, then, although the trust of the property which the settlor covenanted to settle will remain incompletely constituted unless and until he transfers that property to the trustees, the beneficiaries will nevertheless be entitled to enforce the completely constituted trust of the benefit of the covenant. This trust will be enforceable just like any other trust: the beneficiaries can request the trustee to enforce the covenant against the settlor[2] and, if he declines so to do, they can either bring an action to compel him to do so or sue the settlor directly on the covenant joining the trustees as a co-

---

[98] Such as the consideration provided in *Re Cook's Settlement Trusts*.

[99] (1886) 32 Ch.D. 95.

[1] These possibilities have been the subject of an immense body of periodical literature, of which the principal articles are (in chronological order): D.W. Elliott, (1960) 76 L.Q.R. 100; J.A. Hornby, (1962) 78 L.Q.R. 228; W.A. Lee, (1969) 85 L.Q.R. 213; J.L. Barton, (1976) 91 L.Q.R. 236; R.P. Meagher & J.R.F. Lehane, (1976) 92 L.Q.R. 427; C.E.F. Rickett, (1979) 32 C.L.P. 1 & (1981) 34 C.L.P. 189; M.W. Friend, [1982] Conv. 280.

[2] *Lloyd's* v. *Harper* (1880) 16 Ch.D. 290.

defendant to the action.[3] The principal difficulty lies in determining exactly when such a trust will arise.

In *Fletcher* v. *Fletcher*[4] a settlor covenanted with trustees that, if either or both of his two illegitimate sons survived him, his executors should, within twelve months of his death, pay to the trustees £60,000 which was to be held on trust for such of the two as reached the age of twenty-one. The existence of the deed was never revealed by the settlor either to the trustees or to his sons; he retained the deed in his possession until his death and it was only discovered some years later among his papers. Only one of the sons both survived the settlor and reached the age of twenty-one; he sought to enforce the covenant against the executors. Wigram V.C. held that the settlor had clearly vested in the trustees the right to sue his executors for £60,000. He held that this was sufficient to produce a completely constituted trust of the benefit of the covenant, which could be enforced by the son. This decision, which is supported by other contemporaneous authorities,[5] has been interpreted in a variety of ways. However, it has to be seen against the background of the rules which at that time governed certainty of intention (the question of when a settlor will be held to have had sufficient intention to constitute a trust[6]). Until the middle of the Nineteenth Century, the courts tended to take the view that any expression of desire or hope or the like on the part of the settlor was imperative and therefore created a binding trust. Given that the settlor had clearly intended his sons to receive the benefit of the covenant after his death, it was perhaps not unreasonable, in the light of the view then habitually adopted as to certainty of intention, for Wigram V.C. to find a completely constituted trust of the benefit of the covenant. However, following the modification of the rules governing certainty of intention which took place towards the end of the Nineteenth Century,[7] it is difficult to see how any such intention could today be deduced from the facts of *Fletcher* v. *Fletcher*. Certainly no such trust has been upheld in any of the cases subsequent to the change in the certainty of intention rule in which arguments based on *Fletcher* v. *Fletcher* have been raised. Admittedly in one of those cases, *Re Cook's Settlement Trusts*,[8] Buckley J. distinguished *Fletcher* v. *Fletcher* not on this ground but on the basis that the covenant which he was considering related to after-acquired property, something which was also the case in three other decisions in which *Fletcher* v.

---

[3] *Les Affréteurs Réunis* v. *Leopold Walford* [1919] A.C. 801.

[4] (1844) 4 Hare 67.

[5] None of these authorities contains as clear a statement of principle as that contained in *Fletcher* v. *Fletcher*; consequently all have been the subject of different explanations. Wigram V.-C. himself relied on *Clough* v. *Lambert* (1839) 10 Sim. 74 and *Williamson* v. *Codrington* (1750) 1 Ves.Sen. 511 (although this decision is equally explicable as based on "meritorious consideration" (see *supra*, n. 94)). *Watson* v. *Barker* (1843) 6 Beav. 283 and *Cox* v. *Barnard* (1850) 8 Hare 310 have also been described as cases of this type, although the better explanation for the latter, as for the much later inadequately reported *Re Cavendish-Browne's Settlement Trusts* [1916] W.N. 341 may well be the presence of a covenant for further assurance.

[6] See *post*, p. 90. *et seq.*

[7] See *post*, *ibid.*

[8] [1965] Ch. 902. The facts were considered *ante*, p. 82.

Fletcher was not applied.[9] Given that after-acquired property can undoubtedly form the subject matter of a covenant,[10] there seems no good reason for this distinction[11]; nor is it consistent with other authorities. In *Davenport* v. *Bishopp*,[12] Knight-Bruce V.C. indicated that it was possible for there to be a completely constituted trust of the benefit of a covenant to settle after-acquired property, a view which is confirmed by other authorities in which promises to pay uncertain sums on uncertain future dates arising under simple contracts have been held capable of forming the subject matter of a trust.[13] Consequently, the distinction of *Fletcher* v. *Fletcher* on the grounds of lack of certainty of intention seems clearly preferable to the distinction adopted by Buckley J. in *Re Cook's Settlement Trusts*, which is better explained on the grounds that there was no intention to create a trust of the benefit of Sir Francis Cook's covenant in favour of his children but merely an intention to create a trust if and when its subject matter came into existence and was duly transferred to the trustees. On this basis, a completely constituted trust of the benefit of a covenant to settle either existing or after-acquired property must certainly be capable of being found today if the settlor has clearly manifested the appropriate intention[14] by, for example, stating expressly that, pending transfer of the intended trust property, "the benefit of the covenant to settle shall be held by the trustees on the trusts of the settlement".

While all the commentators would be likely to agree that the use of this wording would give rise to a completely constituted trust of the benefit of the covenant in question, there is no general agreement as to what, if any, other situations should be found to give rise to such a trust. On the one hand, it has been contended that such a trust should never be found in the absence of some clear indication of the type exemplified above that this was indeed the intention of the settlor.[15] This view has the merit of being consistent with the modern rule as to certainty of intention and with all the modern authorities; however, it involves distinguishing *Fletcher* v. *Fletcher* in one of the ways mentioned above and undoubtedly enables settlors to go back on voluntary covenants to settle.[16] On the other hand, it has been

---

[9] *Re Plumptre's Settlement* [1910] 1 Ch. 609, *Re Pryce* [1917] 1 Ch. 234, *Re Kay's Settlement* [1939] Ch. 329.

[10] See *ante*, p. 78.

[11] See J. L. Barton and R. P. Meagher & J. R. F. Lehane: *op.cit.*

[12] (1843) 2 Y. & C.C.C. 451 at p. 460.

[13] *Lloyd's* v. *Harper* (1880) 16 Ch.Div. 290 (Lloyd's was held to be entitled to sue as trustee for the benefit of all those with whom an underwriter entered into contracts of insurance), *Royal Exchange Assurance* v. *Tomlin* [1928] Ch. 179 (trust of the benefit of a promise to pay a sum only in the event of a person's death before a certain date upheld).

[14] It has been questioned whether the relevant intention should be that of the settlor or of the trustees, since it is the latter who hold the chose in action which is the subject matter of the trust. However, in the case of a covenant to settle other than for value, the better view is that the relevant intention should be that of the settlor (see *The Restatement of Trusts* (2nd ed.) para. 26, C. E. F. Rickett (1979) 32 C.L.P. 1, and J. D. Feltham (1982) 98 L.Q.R. 17).

[15] This view has been adopted in successive editions of this work, of Hanbury & Martin: *Modern Equity*, and of Pettit: *Equity and the Law of Trusts*.

[16] See J. D. Feltham: *op.cit.*

contended that such a trust should be implied into every covenant to settle.[17] This view is clearly inconsistent with the vast majority of the decided cases[18] but does prevent voluntary covenants to settle becoming unenforceable and, therefore, meaningless.[19] Between these two extreme views, various intermediate positions have been suggested. It has been argued[20] that such a trust should be implied where the covenant in question gives rise to a debt[21] but not otherwise.[22] It has also been argued[23] that such a trust should be implied where the deed in question merely consists of one covenant, on the basis that, since the deed would otherwise be futile, this must be taken to be the intention of the settlor, but should not be implied in the case of lengthy settlements,[24] where the intention of the settlor in relation to individual covenants is necessarily unclear.[25] However, despite the bewildering variety of views which have been expressed,[26] there is absolutely no doubt that at present, for whatever reason, a completely constituted trust of the benefit of a covenant will not be found in the absence of some clear manifestation of the appropriate intention of the settlor; it certainly has to be admitted that only this view seems to be consistent with the modern rule as to certainty of intention.

(b) Beneficiary party to the covenant. The beneficiaries may be able to maintain an action at common law against the settlor on the covenant to settle. This will be the case if the covenant to settle purports to be made with the beneficiaries as covenantees and is either a deed poll (a deed to which only the settlor is a party) or a deed *inter partes* (a deed to which the settlor and others are parties) to which the beneficiaries are either parties or are made parties by section 56 of the Law of Property Act 1925 (which applies only where the subject matter is land).[27] In *Cannon* v. *Hartley*[28] a husband, wife and daughter were all parties to a deed of separation in which the father covenanted to settle on himself, the wife and the daughter one half of any property which he might receive under the will of either of his parents. Having received such property, he refused to settle it. The daughter was held to be entitled to maintain against him an action for damages for breach of covenant.

---

[17] See D. W. Elliott & J. A. Hornby: *op.cit.*

[18] Other than *Fletcher* v. *Fletcher* and the other cases referred to in n. 5 *supra*.

[19] See *The Restatement of Trusts* (2nd ed.) para. 26 and J.D. Feltham: *op.cit.*

[20] By M.W. Friend: *op.cit.*

[21] Which will be the case where the subject matter of the covenant is existing money.

[22] In other words, where the subject matter of the covenant is either specific and presently existing property other than money or after-acquired property.

[23] By D. J. Hayton in Hayton & Marshall: *Cases and Commentary on the Law of Trusts* (9th ed., 1991) pp. 225–226.

[24] Such as marriage settlements, where covenants to settle are invariably made in favour both of persons within the marriage consideration and of persons outside it.

[25] The settlor cannot be taken to have intended to create such a trust in favour of persons outside the marriage consideration.

[26] Those mentioned in the text are only a sample.

[27] See the review of the authorities by Lord Upjohn in *Beswick* v. *Beswick* [1968] A.C. 98 at pp. 102–105.

[28] [1949] Ch. 213.

Since she had given no value, she was clearly unable to obtain specific performance. However, the fact that, because she was a volunteer, equity declined to assist her did not mean that equity would frustrate her right at common law to enforce a covenant to which she was a party. She consequently recovered, by way of damages, the value of the interest which she should have received under the settlement. Thus, while this remedy will not enable the trust to be completely constituted, the beneficiaries will be able to recover compensation for the loss of the interest which they would have obtained thereunder.

(c) **Action by the trustees on the covenant.** Where the beneficiaries are unable to enforce the covenant in either of the two ways already discussed, either in equity by virtue of the existence of a completely constituted trust of the benefit of the covenant or at common law by means of an action on the covenant for damages, they will clearly have no direct means of enforcing it. This somewhat obvious proposition was confirmed by the Court of Appeal in *Re d'Angibau*,[29] where the eventual beneficiaries under a marriage settlement, the wife's next-of-kin, who were of course not within the marriage consideration, were held unable to enforce a covenant by the wife to transfer an equitable remainder to the trustees of the settlement. In such circumstances, the only remaining option of the beneficiaries will be to attempt to enforce the covenant indirectly by means of an action by the trustees on the covenant at law against the settlor.

It is clear that the beneficiaries cannot compel the trusts to bring such an action. In the absence of any completely constituted trust and of any simple or specialty contract to which they are parties, they are clearly in no position to compel anyone to do anything and are undoubtedly volunteers. However, given that the trustees have an undoubted right of action at law against the settlor, it might be thought that they would be entitled to exercise that right of action if they so chose and hold any damages recovered from the settlor on trust for the beneficiaries. This is not in fact the case. It has long been established that, if the trustees seek the directions of the court,[30] they will be directed not to sue the settlor on the covenant. Indeed, this rule is so well established that there is now no need for the trustees to trouble to obtain any directions—the present authorities provide them with a complete defence to any action for breach of trust.[31]

In *Re Pryce*[32] the trustees of a marriage settlement sought directions from the court as to whether they were bound to enforce in favour of the wife's next-of-kin (who were the only persons beneficially entitled other than the wife) a covenant by the wife to settle after-acquired property. Eve J. held that the next-of-kin could not obtain relief

---

[29] (1880) 15 Ch.D. 228.
[30] Something which trustees habitually do before embarking on legal proceedings to avoid any risk of being made personally responsible for the costs in the event that they were subsequently held not to have been properly incurred.
[31] See *Re Ralli's Will Trusts* [1964] Ch. 288 at pp. 301–302.
[32] [1917] 1 Ch. 234.

directly[33]; consequently there was no reason for equity to give them relief indirectly by an order to the trustees to enforce the covenant. He then went on to hold, without further discussion, that they were bound not to enforce the covenant.[34] This decision was followed and applied in *Re Kay's Settlement*,[35] in which the trustees of a voluntary settlement sought directions whether they should or should not take proceedings in favour of the ultimate beneficiaries against the settlor on her covenant to settle after-acquired property and were directed by Simonds J. not to do so.[36] The same conclusion was reached by Buckley J. in *Re Cook's Settlement Trusts*.[37]

None of these cases contains any reasoned discussion of exactly why the trustees must not enforce the covenant. It has been argued[38] that there is no reason for equity thus to restrain parties to a covenant from exercising their legal rights thereunder if they wish to do so.[39] However, it seems that the consequences of such an action would not ultimately favour the beneficiaries. Even on the assumption that the trustees would be able to obtain substantial damages for breach of covenant (an assumption which, although it has been doubted,[40] is in fact supported both by principle[41] and by precedent[42]), there is no reason why these damages should be held on the trusts of the settlement. In a situation where, *a fortiori*, there is not a completely constituted trust of the benefit of the covenant (if there were, the beneficiaries would of course be able to compel the trustees to enforce the covenant), it appears that any damages arising from any action thereon would be held by the trustees not on trust for the beneficiaries but on resulting trust for the settlor.[43] Since any action brought by the trustees against the settlor would thus result in the damages payable being held on resulting trust for the person paying them, equity is clearly correct to prohibit such a circuitous action. Consequently, for this reason *Re*

---

[33] His reasons for reaching this conclusion were in fact erroneous, being based on a misunderstanding of the effect of the Judicature Acts of 1873 and 1875, but the conclusion is nevertheless clearly correct for the reasons already stated in the text.

[34] This conclusion was not in fact necessary, since the negative answer to the question which Eve J. was asked was, strictly speaking, "the trustees are not bound to sue" rather than "the trustees are bound not to sue". This is one of the grounds on which the decision has been criticised; see D.W. Elliott, *op.cit.*

[35] [1939] Ch. 329.

[36] The question put to Simonds J. envisaged three possible answers: "the trustees must sue", "the trustees may sue", "the trustees must not sue". Consequently, his direction to the trustees not to sue clearly constitutes his *ratio decidendi*.

[37] [1965] Ch. 902.

[38] Particularly by D.W. Elliott, *op.cit.*

[39] Because of the risk of being held personally liable for the costs, no trustee would be likely to do so unless the beneficiaries were members of his family or had agreed to indemnify him fully.

[40] See O.R. Marshall, (1950) 3 C.L.P. 30.

[41] The fact that a party to an action at law is a trustee cannot be a ground for limiting him to nominal damages for the simple reason that the common law does not recognise trusts. For this reason, it should not matter that the trust is in fact incompletely constituted or that the property to be settled is after-acquired.

[42] *Re Cavendish-Browne's Settlement Trusts* [1916] W.N. 341. An analogous authority involving a trust of the benefit of a simple contract is *Lloyd's v. Harper* (1880) 16 Ch.D.

[43] See Underhill & Hayton: *Law of Trusts and Trustees* (14th ed., 1987), pp. 130–132.

Pryce, Re Kay's Settlement and *Re Cook's Settlement Trusts* were correctly decided.

It thus follows that the beneficiaries will not be able to enforce a covenant to settle indirectly by means of an action by the trustees on the covenant at law against the settlor and thus, in the absence of a completely constituted trust and of any simple or specialty contract to which they are parties, they will have no means either of bringing about the complete constitution of the trust of the benefit of the covenant or of obtaining any compensation for the settlor's failure to comply with his covenant to settle. In this situation, equity indeed declines to assist volunteers. However, it may be that the recent Law Commission Consultation Paper on Privity of Contract: Contracts for the Benefit of Third Parties[44] will eventually give such beneficiaries the right to enforce covenants entered into for their benefit. The Consultation Paper proposes that third parties should be allowed to enforce contractual provisions made in their favour. If these proposals are ever enacted, then beneficiaries will have a direct action at common law to enforce covenants to settle property on trust for them and the decisions in *Re Pryce, Re Kay's Settlement* and *Re Cook's Settlement Trust* will then become obsolete.

V. CERTAINTY

In the leading case of *Knight* v. *Knight*[45] Lord Langdale laid down that three certainties are required for the creation of a trust:

    (1) The words used must be so couched that, taken as a whole, they may be deemed to be imperative;
    (2) The subject matter of the trust must be certain;
    (3) The persons or objects intended to be benefited must also be certain.

(1) Certainty of intention

Equity looks to the intent rather than the form. No particular form of words is required for the creation of a trust: the use of the word "trust" is not essential, though, of course, highly desirable. It is possible, therefore, that words expressing desire, belief, recommendation or hope (known as precatory words) may create a trust. And if an intention to create a trust can be clearly deduced from the expressions used by the settlor, even though these are in precatory form, the court will give effect to that intention.

It is in connection with this subject that an important change in outlook has occurred. Before the middle of the nineteenth century, the courts tended to take the view that any expression of desire or hope or the like on the part of the testator was imperative and, therefore, created a binding trust. Indeed, it may be said that in the older cases on

---

[44] The Law Commission: Consultation Paper No. 212 (1991).

[45] (1840) 3 Beav. 148 at p. 173. It is not normally possible to introduce extrinsic evidence in order to aid the process of construction (see *Rubin* v. *Gerson Berger Association* [1986] 1 W.L.R. 526).

precatory trusts it is possible to see an intention attributed to a testator which made for an artificial certainty where no certainty really existed. This practice derived from a rule relating to executors. Until 1858 the estates of deceased persons were administered by the ecclesiastical courts and, until the passing of the Executors Act 1830, an executor was permitted to take the residue of the estate (if any) which had been undisposed of by the will. This was obviously unsatisfactory and so the Court of Chancery endeavoured to make the executor a *trustee* of the undisposed-of residue. This had the accidental consequence that the rules relating to certainty of words became confused with the equitable practice in respect of executors. Just as the Court of Chancery was anxious to make the executor a trustee of the undisposed-of residue for the next-of-kin so the court would seize on any expression of hope or desire to negative the presumption that the executor was intended to take beneficially. But the court also went so far as to regard any precatory words in the same light and so as sufficient to create a trust even though the alleged trustee was not an executor and even though there was no undisposed-of residue.

Thus the confusion apparently arose. However, when in 1830 the Executors Act was passed providing that the executor should hold any undisposed-of residue for the next-of-kin unless the testator had shown an intention that the executor should take beneficially, it was no longer necessary or desirable to create a trust in cases where precatory words were used. And during the nineteenth century the change took place. Words such as "desire," "wish," "have full confidence" and so on received fresh consideration.[46] Thus, to take one of many cases, in *Re Adams and Kensington Vestry*,[47] a testator gave all his real and personal estate to his wife "in full confidence that she would do what was right as to the disposal thereof between my children." It was held that under these words the widow took an absolute interest in the property unfettered by any trust in favour of the children. It was also said that some cases had gone very far and unjustifiably imposed upon words a meaning beyond that which they would bear if looked at alone. It is perhaps true to say that by the time this well-known case was decided the wind had already changed direction and beneficiaries were no longer to be made into trustees unless this was clearly intended by the testator.

(a) The modern test. The intention of the testator became all-important. The use of precatory words can still create a trust in an appropriate case, but the intention to create it has to be established upon a construction of the instrument. The question what is an appropriate case can be peculiarly difficult in practice. It cannot be considered *in vacuo* and can only be answered by examining carefully the words

---

[46] Perhaps the earliest case illustrating the new doctrine is *Lambe* v. *Eames* (1871) L.R. 6 Ch. 597 (property to be at disposal of widow "in any way she may think best for the benefit of herself and family").

[47] (1884) 27 Ch.D. 394.

used in the instrument in question.[48] This fact might be thought to be self-evident. It was indeed stated as follows by Lindley L.J. in *Re Hamilton*[49]:

"You must take the will which you have to construe and see what it means, and if you come to the conclusion that no trust was intended you say so, although previous judges have said the contrary on some wills more or less similar to the one you have to construe."

But perhaps some doubts were cast on this impeccable principle by *Re Steele's Will Trusts*[50] for Wynn-Parry J.'s judgment is capable of meaning that if in fact identical words to those before the court had been held to create a trust in a previous case that case should be followed unless it was clearly wrongly decided. Such an approach is rather different from a construction of the instrument on its merits, albeit taking other earlier decisions into account.[51]

└ **(b) Illustrations of the modern rule.** It would be a difficult—and probably also a fruitless—exercise to consider even a small number of the many cases on this topic. But at the risk of making the subject seem easier than it is, two cases, one on each side of the line, may be considered. On the one hand there is *Re Diggles*[52] where a testatrix gave all her property to her daughter, her heirs and assigns and said "And it is my *desire*[53] that she allows to A.G. an annuity of £25 during her life." The Court of Appeal held that no trust to pay this money had been imposed on the daughter.[54] On the other hand, in *Comiskey* v. *Bowring-Hanbury*,[55] which may also be usefully compared with the decision in

---

[48] It is now provided by Administration of Justice Act 1982, s.21, that extrinsic evidence, including evidence of the testator's intention, may be admitted to assist in the interpretation of a will (a) in so far as any part of it is meaningless; (b) in so far as the language used in any part of it is ambiguous on the face of it; (c) in so far as evidence, other than evidence of the testator's intention, shows that the language used in any part of it is ambiguous in the light of the surrounding circumstances. It is also provided (*ibid.* s.20) that the court has jurisdiction to rectify a will if satisfied that it is so expressed that it fails to carry out the testator's intention in consequence of a clerical error or of a failure to understand his instructions.

[49] [1895] 2 Ch. 370 at p. 373. See also *Re Williams* [1897] 2 Ch. 12, at p. 14; *Comiskey* v. *Bowring-Hambury* [1905] A.C. 84 at p. 89.

[50] [1948] Ch. 603, following *Shelley* v. *Shelley* (1868) L.R. 6 Eq. 540.

[51] *Cf.* Langan (1968) 32 Conv. (N.S.) 361.

[52] (1888) 39 Ch.D. 253.

[53] Italics added.

[54] No trust was created in the following cases: *Lambe* v. *Eames, supra*; *Re Hutchinson and Tenant* (1878) 8 Ch.D. 540 ("have confidence"); *Mussoorie Bank* v. *Raynor* (1882) 7 App.Cas. 321, P.C. ("feeling confident"); *Re Hamilton* [1895] 2 Ch. 370 ("wish"); *Hill* v. *Hill* [1897] 1 Q.B. 483 ("request"); *Re Williams* [1897] 2 Ch. 12 ("fullest trust and confidence"); *Re Connolly* [1910] 1 Ch. 219 ("specially desire"); *Re Johnson* [1939] 2 All E.R. 458 ("request"); *Swain* v. *The Law Society* [1982] 3 W.L.R. 261, H.L. ("on behalf of").

[55] [1905] A.C. 84.

Re Adams and Kensington Vestry,[56] the testator gave all his property to his wife "absolutely *in full confidence*[57] that she will make such use of it as I would have made myself and that at her death she will devise it to such one or more of my nieces as she may think fit." The House of Lords held that, on a true construction of the whole will, the words "in full confidence" created a trust. Whatever doubts there may be about the correctness of the actual decision—the significance of the word "absolutely" not being perhaps fully appreciated—it nevertheless, because it is of the highest authority, underlines the rule that in the last analysis the problem should be one of construing the whole instrument.[58]

A modern illustration of some interest, involving the winding-up of a company, is *Re Kayford*[59] which involved rather different considerations. The company carried on a mail order business, and the customers paid the full price in advance or paid a deposit. Difficulties arose over supply and delivery of goods, and a separate bank account was opened by the company called a "Customers' Trust Deposit Account," with the object that all further moneys paid by customers for goods should be paid into that account and withdrawn only when the goods had been delivered. Its purpose was that if the company had to go into liquidation, the money could be refunded to those who had paid it. The company subsequently went into liquidation, and the question before the court was whether the money in the bank account was held in trust for those who paid, or whether it formed part of the general assets of the company. Megarry J. had no doubt on the facts that a trust was created, the facts showing that the moneys remained in the beneficial ownership of those who sent them until the goods were delivered.[60]

It will therefore be seen that what is meant by "certainty of words" is certainty of intention to create a trust appearing from the words in the instrument.[61] It should be noted, moreover, that the legal effect of the wording is relevant not simply in deciding whether a trust proper has been created, or a mere moral obligation. Other possibilities are that a power of appointment has been created,[62] or if the Crown holds property, it may be administering it in the exercise of its governmental

---

[56] *Supra*; see also *Re Williams, supra.*

[57] Italics added.

[58] A trust *was* created in the following cases: *Re Steele's Will Trusts* [1948] Ch. 603, *ante* ("request"); *Re Endacott* [1960] Ch. 232 ("for the purpose of").

[59] [1975] 1 W.L.R. 279, see *ante*, p. 18.

[60] Megarry J. made it clear that the general rule was that if money is sent to a company for goods which are not delivered, the sender is merely a creditor of the company unless a trust has been created. In this case, however, there was a trust whereupon "the obligations in respect of the money are transformed from contract to property, from debt to trust": *ibid.* at p. 282. The judge also indicated that a trust of this kind might not be effective in favour of trade creditors, but in this case the court was only concerned with members of the public.

[61] The question whether a trust or a power has been created is considered *post*, p. 137. *et seq.*

[62] *Ibid.*

functions without creating a trust,[63] and the mere fact that the word "trust" is used in relation to the Crown is not decisive.[64]

The cases cited in the text involved private trusts. If the intention of the instrument is to create a charitable trust but there is an ambiguity in the wording, it was confirmed by the House of Lords in *I.R.C.* v. *McMullen*[65] that a "benignant" construction should be given if possible.[66] It was not, however, necessary to resort to such a construction in that case.

If an intention to create a trust cannot be derived from the words used in the instrument, but at most a mere moral obligation, then the effect of such uncertainty of words is that there is no trust; consequently, the donee will take the property beneficially,[67] unless the words are construed as giving rise to a power of appointment.[68]

(2) Certainty of subject matter

This also is an essential ingredient for the effectual creation of a trust. The property subject to the trust must either be clearly defined or be capable of ascertainment. This requirement has a number of aspects.

It must be possible to establish exactly what property is subject to the trust. In *Palmer* v. *Simmonds*,[69] a testatrix left her residuary estate to her husband "for his own use and benefit" but subject to a trust on his death "to leave the bulk of my residuary estate" to four named relatives. This trust was held to fail for uncertainty of subject-matter so the husband took the property absolutely. A similar result occurred in *Sprange* v. *Barnard;*[70] the testatrix left stock to her husband "for his sole use, and all that is remaining in the stock, that he has not necessary use for, to be equally divided between" her brothers and sisters. In both of these cases, the husband took the property in question absolutely by virtue of the rule in *Hancock* v. *Watson*[71] which establishes that, where there is an absolute gift of property in the first instance and trusts are subsequently imposed on that property, then if the trusts fail for any reason the property is not held on a resulting trust for the settlor or his estate but will vest absolutely in the person to whom the property was first given.

In both *Palmer* v. *Simmonds* and *Sprange* v. *Barnard* the conclusion was reached that the testator had intended the donee to receive an absolute interest on which the failed trusts were subsequently to be engrafted. However, apparently absolute gifts have sometimes been construed as

---

[63] As a "trust in the higher sense": see *Tito* v. *Waddell (No. 2)* [1977] Ch. 106 at p. 216; see *ante*, p. 9.

[64] *Ibid.* at p. 212. The Crown *can* be a trustee but only if it deliberately chooses to do so: *Civilian War Claimants Association Ltd.* v. *The King* [1932] A.C. 14, at p. 27; *Nissan* v. *Att.-Gen.* [1970] A.C. 179 at p. 223; *Tito* v. *Waddell (No. 2) supra* at p. 212.

[65] [1981] A.C. 1. The facts are stated *post*, p. 325.

[66] *Ibid.* at p. 14.

[67] See the cases cited in footnote 54, *supra*.

[68] See *post*, p. 137. *et seq.*

[69] (1854) 2 Drew 221; *cf. Bromley* v. *Tryon* [1952] A.C. 265.

[70] (1789) 2 Bro.C.C. 585.

[71] [1902] A.C. 14 (formerly known as the Rule in *Lassence* v. *Tierney* (1849) 1 Mac. & G. 551).

conferring only a limited interest on the initial beneficiary; such a construction avoids uncertainty of subject matter in respect of the subsequent trusts. In *Re Last*[72] the testatrix left all her property to her brother, providing that "at his death anything that is left, that came from me" was to pass to certain other specified persons. This limitation is very similar to that in *Sprange* v. *Barnard* but it was in fact construed as conferring merely a life interest on the brother; consequently, on his death, *all* the property was held on the trusts specified by the testatrix. Similarly, in the earlier case of *Re Thomson's Estate*[73] a testator left all his property to his widow "to be disposed of as she may think proper for her own use and benefit" but "should there be anything remaining of the said property or any part thereof" on her death, it was to be held on various trusts. Hall V.C. held that the widow had a life interest together with a power to dispose of the property *inter vivos* but no testamentary power; consequently, any property not disposed of during her lifetime was held on the further specified trusts. These decisions are only justifiable on the basis that the intention of the testator was indeed to confer no more than a limited interest on the initial beneficiary. Another method of avoiding uncertainty of subject matter is for the court to find some way of ascertaining what the subject matter of a potentially uncertain trust actually is. In *Re Golay's Will Trusts*[74] the testator directed his trustees to permit a beneficiary to "enjoy one of my flats during her lifetime and to receive a reasonable income from my other properties". Ungoed-Thomas J. upheld the gift, holding that the yardstick of "reasonable income" indicated by the testator was not what he or some other person *subjectively* considered to be reasonable but what he identified *objectively* as "reasonable income", something which the court could therefore quantify. This conclusion was undoubtedly inconsistent with other contemporaneous decisions on certainty[75] but does seem to be consistent with the more recent practice of the courts in trying to avoid, if at all possible, holding dispositions to be void for uncertainty, particularly in respect of expressions such as "reasonable" or "satisfactory".[76]

Problems have also arisen in connection with attempts to declare trusts of some certain but unidentified part of a larger holding. In *Re London Wine Company*,[77] wine dealers sent letters to purchasers of wine confirming that they were the sole beneficial owners of the wine which they had bought and paid for; however, no steps were taken to segregate the wine in question from the general mass of stock held by the dealers. It was held that no trust had arisen so that the purchasers had no proprietary rights in the wine as against the holders of a floating

---

[72] [1958] P. 137.

[73] (1879) 13 Ch.D. 144.

[74] [1965] 1 W.L.R. 969.

[75] Such as *Re Kolb's Will Trusts* [1962] Ch. 531 (reference to "blue-chip" securities held to be uncertain and consequently to render an investment clause void for uncertainty).

[76] See particularly *McPhail* v. *Doulton* [1971] A.C. 424, *post*, p. 98, *et seq*, and, in relation to expressions such as "reasonable" or "satisfactory", *Sudbrook Trading Estates* v. *Eggleton* [1982] 3 W.L.R. 315 and *Graham* v. *Pitkin* [1992] 1 W.L.R. 403.

[77] [1986] Palmer's Company Cases 123.

charge which the dealers had granted over their entire assets. However, this decision was subsequently distinguished in *Hunter* v. *Moss*,[78] where a declaration of trust in respect of fifty shares in a company in which the settlor held nine hundred and fifty shares was upheld on the basis that any identification of the particular fifty shares held on trust was unnecessary and irrelevant. At first instance, the principle enunciated in *Re London Wine Company* was confined to tangible property, since "ostensibly similar or identical assets may in fact have characteristics which distinguish them from other assets in the class"[79]—as the judge[80] said, some of the wine may have become corked or may have deteriorated in some other way. He then went on to state that a declaration of trust in respect of £1,000 in a bank account with a current balance superior to £1,000 would also be effectual. Although the principle thus enunciated must clearly be confined to intangible property similar to the choses in action held by the settlor in respect of the shares and the imaginary bank account, it nevertheless caused some surprise. It has hitherto been thought that trusts of such choses in action would only be valid if the settlor declared a trust either of his entire interest in the chose in action or of a fixed proportion thereof[81] (in other words, on the facts of *Hunter* v. *Moss*, a trust of one-nineteenth of the shares held in the company in question) so that thereafter they would be held on trust for the settlor and the beneficiary in the appropriate proportions. In the Court of Appeal, Dillon L.J.[81A] simply held that *Re London Wine Company* was "a long way from the present" case and concluded that "[j]ust as a person can give by will a specified number of his shares in a certain company, so equally, in my judgment, he can declare himself a trustee of 50 of his ordinary shares . . . and that is effective to give a beneficial proprietary interest to the beneficiary under the trust." This analogy between a bequest and a declaration of trust has been the subject of fierce criticism.[81B] The effect of a will is to vest the whole estate of the testator in his executors to be administered; consequently, a legatee acquires merely an equitable chose in action until the administration has been completed, at which point he will receive whatever shares are allocated to him by the executors. The effect of a declaration of trust, on the other hand, is to vest an immediate proprietary interest in the beneficiary; this necessitates some immediate means of determining which shares are subject to the trust. How otherwise can it be determined, in the event that the trustee subsequently deals with the shares by, for example, selling fifty of them, with whose shares he has actually dealt—his own, those of the beneficiary, or a rateable proportion of the shares of each of them? Whether or not these criticisms are actually justified, there can be no doubt that the decision in *Hunter* v. *Moss* has left the law in a somewhat uncertain

---

[78] [1994] 1 W.L.R. 452.
[79] [1993] 1 W.L.R. 934 at p. 940.
[80] Colin Rimer Q.C. sitting as a Deputy High Court Judge.
[81] See Underhill & Hayton: *Law of Trusts and Trustees* (14th ed., 1987) p. 105
[81A] [1994] 1 W.L.R. 452 at pp. 458, 459. This was an unreserved judgment with which the other two members of the court simply agreed.
[81B] By D. J. Hayton in 110 L.Q.R. (1994).

state. Dillon L.J. made no reference whatever to the distinction between tangible and intangible property adopted at first instance. Is this indeed the distinction between *Re London Wine Company* and *Hunter* v. *Moss*? If not, what is? Since leave to appeal to the House of Lords was refused in *Hunter* v. *Moss*, only future litigation is likely to provide the answer to this question and, consequently, determine whether, as suggested at first instance, it is now possible to declare a trust of a fixed sum in a bank account with a balance superior to that amount.[81C]

Another aspect of uncertainty of subject matter arises where it is clear what property is intended to be subject to the trust but some or all of the beneficial interests are unascertained in the sense that it is not clear what property is held on trust for which beneficiary. In *Curtis* v. *Rippon*[82] the testator left all his property to his wife "trusting that she should, in fear of God, and in love of the children committed to her care, make such use of it as should be for her own and their spiritual and temporal good, remembering always, according to circumstances, the Church of God and the poor". There was no doubt what property was subject to the trust but the beneficial interest was to be taken by an ascertained beneficiary, subject to the right of others to unascertained portions of it. The rights of the latter were held to fail and the ascertained beneficiary took the entirety under the rule in *Hancock* v. *Watson*. Where, on the other hand, all the beneficial interests are unascertained, the trust will fail completely. Thus, in *Boyce* v. *Boyce*[83] a testator devised two houses to trustees on trust to convey to Maria "whichever house she may think proper to choose or select" and to convey the other house to Charlotte. Maria died in the lifetime of the testator and was thus of course unable to make her choice. The court held that it was impossible to establish which house was held on trust for Charlotte and so the houses were held on resulting trust for the testator's residuary estate (the rule in *Hancock* v. *Watson* did not apply since there had been no absolute gift of the houses to the trustees in the first instance). On the other hand, in *Re Steel*,[84] the testator directed that his residue was to be divided between legatees who had only received "small amounts"; Megarry V.-C. held that this gift was valid on the basis that the words were merely explaining the testator's motives and ordered the residue to be divided between all the legatees equally whatever the size of their legacies.

When a trust fails for uncertainty of subject matter, assuming that there is certainty of intention a trust will clearly have been intended and its failure on the grounds of uncertainty of subject matter will not enable the potential trustees to take beneficially unless the Rule in

---

[81C] In *Mac-Jordan Construction* v. *Brookmount Erosion* (1991) 56 B.L.R. 1, retention money was to be held on trust for sub-contractors but was not set aside as a separate fund. The Court of Appeal held that there were no identifiable assets impressed with the trust. However, this case is not decisive of the question posed in the text since no trust of the retained funds was ever actually declared.

[82] (1820) 5 Madd. 434.

[83] (1849) 6 Sim. 476.

[84] [1979] 1 Ch. 218.

Hancock v. *Watson* applies. This Rule, as has already been seen,[85] applies where there is an absolute gift of property in the first instance on which trusts are subsequently imposed; if the trusts fail for any reason the property will vest absolutely in the person to whom the property was first given. In every other case, the property is in principle held on resulting trust for the settlor or (if he is dead) for the residuary legatee or devisee under his will, or, if there is no gift of residue, on trust for the persons entitled to his estate on intestacy. However, there is some authority for the proposition that the court may apply the maxim "equality is equity" and divide the entirety of the beneficial interest equally between the beneficiaries.[86] The best known mode of application of the maxim is to be found in cases involving joint bank accounts held by husband and wife where, after dissolution of the marriage, it is found impracticable to divide the fund meticulously between them.[87] However convenient and "equitable" this may be, it is somewhat difficult to justify in principle the application of the maxim in a case involving uncertainty of the actual beneficial interest taken by trust objects and the position therefore remains doubtful.

(3) Certainty of objects

It is also an essential ingredient for the effectual creation of a trust that its objects should be certain or be capable of being rendered certain. When this is not the case, the consequences are exactly the same as in the case of uncertainty of subject matter: unless the Rule in *Hancock* v. *Watson* applies, in which case the potential trustees will be entitled to take the trust property beneficially, that property will be held on resulting trust for the settlor or his estate. However, it should be observed that there is an important exception to the rule that the objects be certain. This is in the case of charitable trusts where, provided that a paramount intention of charity is manifested, certainty in the charitable objects is not essential to validity.[88] In such a case a *cy-près* scheme may be made enabling the funds to be devoted to definite charitable purposes.

Until the decision of the House of Lords in *McPhail* v. *Doulton* in 1990,[89] the objects of a trust were only certain if it was possible to draw up a complete list of those objects. This rule was originally laid down in *Morice* v. *Bishop of Durham*[90] early in the Nineteenth Century. At this time virtually all trusts were fixed trusts, that is to say trusts in favour of pre-determined beneficiaries or classes of beneficiaries.[91] However, following the subsequent development of discretionary trusts, under which the trustees determine in what proportions, if any, the trust property is to be divided among members of a pre-determined class and sometimes even decide the membership of the class itself, it was

---

[85] See *ante*, p. 94.
[86] See *Doyley* v. *Attorney-General* (1735) 2 Eq.Cas.Abr. 194.
[87] See *Jones* v. *Maynard* [1951] Ch. 572, *Rimmer* v. *Rimmer* [1953] 1 Q.B. 63.
[88] See *post*, p. 297.
[89] [1971] A.C. 424.
[90] (1804) 9 Ves.Jr. 399, affirmed (1805) 10 Ves.Jr. 522.
[91] See *ante*.

confirmed in *I.R.C.* v. *Broadway Cottages Trust*[92] that the same rule applied also to such trusts. In this case the trustees held the funds upon trust to apply the income for the benefit of all or any of a class of beneficiaries as the trustees might think fit. It was held, upon a true construction of the instrument, that this created a trust in favour of the specified class and was void for uncertainty on the ground that the class was unascertainable at any given time; the whole range of objects eligible for selection had to be ascertained or be capable of ascertainment. The basis of the decision was that the court, if called upon to execute the trust, could only do so on the basis of equal division, and there could not be equal division unless all the members of the class were known. This decision established a crucial difference between, on the one hand, discretionary trusts, which would be void for uncertainty unless the trustees could at any given time draw up a complete list of all the potential beneficiaries, and, on the other hand, powers which, as will be seen shortly,[93] had a different test for certainty of objects in that it was and is simply necessary to be able to say with certainty of any individual whether he is or is not one of the persons in whose favour the power is capable of being exercised.

I.R.C. v. *Broadway Cottages Trust* was, however, overruled by the majority of the House of Lords in *McPhail* v. *Doulton*[94] in 1990. The case for rigid rules for trusts was admittedly a persuasive one and had been stated earlier by Lord Upjohn, namely that the imperative nature of trusts should entail the consequence that all the objects should be known.[95] But, as Lord Wilberforce indicated in *McPhail* v. *Doulton*, the law should take account of practicalities, particularly the narrow distinction between discretionary trusts (often also known as trust powers) and mere powers. The theory specifically postulated in *I.R.C.* v. *Broadway Cottages Trust* that the court can only execute a trust by ordering equal distribution in which every beneficiary shares was rejected as inappropriate: "equal division among all may, probably would, produce a result beneficial to none", being "surely the last thing the settlor ever intended".[96] Lord Wilberforce stated that, if the trustees failed to execute the trust, the court would do so "in the manner best calculated to give effect to the settlor's . . . intentions" in one of three ways: either by appointing new trustees, or by directing persons representative of the classes of beneficiaries to prepare a scheme of distribution, or, should the proper basis for distribution be apparent, by directing the trustees how to distribute the fund.[97] (This does not of course mean that equal distribution will never again be ordered; in the case of a small class of beneficiaries whose entire membership is known, it is almost inevitable that equal distribution will still be ordered. It is therefore likely that the novel powers of the court outlined

---

[92] [1955] Ch. 20; see also *Re Sayer* [1957] Ch. 423.
[93] See *infra*.
[94] [1971] A.C. 424.
[95] In *Re Gulbenkian's Settlement* [1970] A.C. 508. The point was restated by Lord Hodson (dissenting) in *McPhail* v. *Doulton* [1971] A.C. 424 at p. 442.
[96] [1971] A.C. 424 at p. 451.
[97] *Ibid.* at p. 457.

by Lord Wilberforce will only in fact be used where it is not possible to ascertain the entire membership of the class of beneficiaries in question, that is to say in the case of discretionary trusts which would be void for uncertainty but for the decision in *McPhail* v. *Doulton*). This fundamental change in judicial attitudes enabled the rules of certainty for discretionary trusts and for powers to be equated: in both cases, the requirements for certainty of objects will now be satisfied if it can be said of "any given postulant" that he is or is not a member of the class of potential beneficiaries.

This rule was originally formulated for powers by Harman J. in *Re Gestetner Settlement*.[98] In this case capital was held in trust for such member or members of a specified class as the trustees might think fit. The specified class comprised certain named individuals; any person living or thereafter born who was a descendant of the settlor's father or uncle; any spouse, widow or widower of any such person; five charitable bodies; any former employee of the settlor or his wife and the widow or widower of any such employee; and any director or employee of a named company. Harman J. held that it was unnecessary in a power of this kind to establish that the objects themselves were all capable of ascertainment. It was simply necessary to be able to say of any given person that he was, or was not, an object of the power. The trustees did not have "to worry their heads to survey the world from China to Peru"[99] to find out who was within the designated class. There was no difficulty in ascertaining whether or not any given postulant was a member of the class. Consequently, the power in question was held to be valid.

Subsequently, there was some uncertainty as to precisely how this test should be applied. Essentially the question was whether it should be applied strictly so that if it was impossible to ascertain whether or not a given individual was within the power, that power would fail even though other classes of persons were clearly within it. Or, alternatively, whether an even more diluted test should be adopted with the result that difficulty in saying whether a person was or was not within the catagory should not be fatal, provided that *somebody* was clearly within it. This latter test was only used on isolated occasions, notably by Lord Denning M.R.[1] The stricter test was supported by a preponderance of authority[2] and it was finally confirmed definitively by the House

---

[98] [1953] Ch. 673.

[99] *Ibid.* at pp. 688–689; an expression incorrectly attributed by Harman J. to Alexander Pope (see, *per* Harman L.J. in *Re Baden's Trust Deeds* [1969] 2 Ch. 388 at p. 397). In fact, the words are those of Samuel Johnson.

[1] In *Re Gulbenkian's Settlement Trusts* [1968] 1 Ch. 126 at p. 134, and see also *per* Winn L.J. at p. 138. For similar formulations, see *Re Gibbard* [1967] 1 W.L.R. 42 ("old friends"), at pp. 47–48 *per* Plowman J.; and *Re Leek* [1967] Ch. 1061 (persons having a "moral claim"), at p. 1073 *per* Buckley J.; affirmed on different grounds [1969] 1 Ch. 563. However, this test applies where there are individual gifts subject to the donee satisfying a condition precedent or answering a particular description; see *post*, p. 104.

[2] *Re Coates* [1955] Ch. 495 (for any friends his wife might feel that he had forgotten); *Re Sayer Trust* [1957] Ch. 423 (power in favour of employees, ex-employees, widow, children and "dependants") (in these cases the power was held valid).

of Lords in *Re Gulbenkian's Settlement*.[3] This case involved the construction of a clause in a work of precedents used by the profession. The
clause was to the effect that a special power of appointment could be
exercised for the maintenance and personal support of all or any one or
more of the following persons as the trustees should in their absolute
discretion think fit: the settlor's son, any wife, children or remoter issue
of the son, and any persons in whose house or apartments or in whose
company or under whose care and control or by whom the husband
might from time to time be employed or residing. The clause had been
considered before in *Re Gresham's Settlement*,[4] where Harman J. held it
void for uncertainty on the grounds that there might be a number of
persons of whom it could not be determined whether they were or were
not within the dragnet of this unusually constructed clause; he
distinguished his own decision in *Re Gestetner Settlement* because there,
although not all the persons within the specified class were actually
known, it could be said whether *any given person* was within the class or
not. However, in *Re Gulbenkian's Settlement* the House of Lords
overruled *Re Gresham's Settlement* and held that the clause was sufficiently certain to satisfy the test laid down in *Re Gestetner Settlement*.
Lord Upjohn, in affirming the latter test, was unable to accept the more
diluted test, which had been put forward by Lord Denning M.R. in the
Court of Appeal.[5] It was the rule thus established as to the certainty of
objects in powers which was subsequently adopted for discretionary
trusts as well in *McPhail* v. *Doulton*.

The fact that the test for certainty of objects in powers and discretionary trusts has now been assimilated does not, however, mean that
powers and discretionary trusts have themselves been assimilated. As
will be seen in a later chapter,[6] there remains the basic distinction that
in the case of a power the court will not normally compel its exercise
and will only interfere where the trustees exceed their power or
possibly if they act capriciously. On the other hand, in the case of a discretionary trust, if the trustees do not exercise their discretion, the court
will do so in the manner thought most appropriate to carry out the
settlor's intentions. Moreover, because of this distinction, "a wider and
more comprehensive range of inquiry"[7] as to the range of objects is
called for in the case of discretionary trusts than in the case of powers.

The test which now applies both to discretionary trusts and to powers
has a number of outstanding problems.

(a) The scope of the test.   *McPhail* v. *Doulton* has affirmed that the
"given postulant" test is the appropriate test both for powers and for

---

[3] [1970] A.C. 508; applied in *Re Denley's Trust Deed* [1968] Ch. 373.
[4] [1956] 1 W.L.R. 573, followed in *Re Allan* [1958] 1 W.L.R. 220; the same clause was in operation.
[5] Lord Donovan reserved his opinion on this point.
[6] See *post*, p. 130.
[7] *McPhail* v. *Doulton* [1971] A.C. 424, *per* Lord Wilberforce at p. 457.

discretionary trusts. In other respects, there may be room for debate as to the applicability of the test.

(i) *Fixed trusts.*   Does the decision in *McPhail* v. *Doulton* only apply to the type of trust in question in that case, namely to discretionary trusts, or does it also apply to fixed trusts? In previous editions of this work,[8] it has been contended that there seems to be no reason in principle why it should not do so. Just as an order for distribution (not necessarily, as has been seen, on the basis of equal division) can be made by the court in the case of a discretionary trust, so also, it might be thought, could such an order be made in the case of a fixed trust where one or more of the beneficiaries are not ascertainable.[9] (The point is conceded to be "more academic than real", arising only in the almost inconceivable case of a trust for objects which could not be fully ascertained also containing a provision for distribution to them in equal or some other definite shares.) However, the more general view, which is shared by the editor of this edition, is that the "given postulant" test does not apply to fixed trusts, in respect of which it is still necessary to be able to draw up a complete list of the objects.[10] It is generally thought, contrary to the view already considered, that if the trust property is to be divided among a class of beneficiaries in fixed shares it would be wholly contrary to the intention of the settlor for the court to order any other form of division; on this basis, it is essential that all the possible beneficiaries should be capable of being ascertained by the time at which any distribution of capital or income has to be made. The description of the beneficiaries must be both conceptually and evidentially certain. Objects will be conceptually uncertain if the exact meaning of the definition used contains any linguistic or semantic uncertainty. Thus, a trust for the settlor's "old friends" in equal shares would be likely to be conceptually uncertain,[11] simply because the expression used is capable of so many different interpretations.[12] On the other hand, objects will be evidentially uncertain if it is impossible to list all the members of the class at the appropriate time. There is no difficulty about a trust for one person for life followed by a gift in remainder to his children in equal shares since, even if the life tenant has no children at the time at which the trust is constituted, it will become clear whether or not he has any children and, if so, how many

---

[8] See, for example, the Fifth Edition (1983) at p. 79.

[9] The authors' reading of Lord Wilberforce's speech was that the new test applies to *all* trusts. Furthermore, it was contended that it would be regrettable if this were not so, because a discretionary trust is a *trust*, although having close affinities with powers.

[10] See, for example, Hanbury & Martin: Modern Equity (14th ed., 1993) at pp. 100–101; Underhill & Hayton: *Law of Trusts and Trustees* (14th ed., 1987) pp. 46–47.

[11] This was stated by Browne-Wilkinson J. in *Re Barlow's Will Trusts* [1970] 1 W.L.R. 278 at pp. 281–282.

[12] However, such an expression would satisfy the more diluted test advocated by Lord Denning M.R. (see *ante*, fn. 1). provided that one "old friend" of the settlor could be clearly identified—this was specifically held by Browne-Wilkinson J. in *Re Barlow's Will Trusts* [1979] 1 W.L.R. 278 in respect of a series of individual gifts with a condition precedent or description attached, to which the more diluted test was held to be applicable.

not later than nine months after the determination of his life interest upon his death.[13] However, the sort of classes of beneficiaries which were established in *Re Gestetner Settlement*,[14] *Re Gulbenkian's Settlement*[15] and *McPhail* v. *Doulton*[16] cannot conceivably be the objects of a fixed trust because of the impossibility of determining between how many persons the capital or income has to be divided. However, provided that it is possible to establish the maximum number of possible beneficiaries, it does not matter that the continued existence or present whereabouts of some of the possible members of the class cannot be discovered since the shares payable to any such beneficiaries can be paid into court to await either their appearance or definitive proof that they did not in fact qualify.[17] All that is necessary is that the list which is able to be drawn up at the appropriate time is, on a balance of probabilities, complete.

(ii) *"Powers in the nature of a trust"*. It has already been seen that discretionary trusts are today often known as trust powers. However, the same name is also used to denote powers whose donees are under an obligation to exercise them. Such powers are also known as "powers in the nature of a trust".[18] Where such a power is found to exist, the court will execute the power in the event that its donee fails to exercise it. Such a case was *Burrough* v. *Philcox*.[19] The testator left property on trust for his two children for life and, subject thereto, to their issue but further declared that, if both his children should die without issue, the surviving child should have the power to dispose by will of the property "among my nephews and nieces or their children, either all to one of them or to as many as my surviving child shall think proper". The surviving child died without so appointing. Lord Cottenham L.C. held that, "when there appears a general intention in favour of a class, and a particular intention in favour of individuals of a class to be selected by another person, and the particular intention fails from that selection not being made, the Court will carry into effect the general intention in favour of the class".[20] He held that the words used evinced a general intention of this type; consequently the court could execute the power on behalf of its donee by dividing the property equally

---

[13] The point at which the children's interest would vest in possession (each child having acquired a vested interest in interest on his birth); the nine month extension is made so that any posthumous children can be included.

[14] *Supra.*

[15] *Supra.*

[16] *Supra.*

[17] See C. T. Emery, (1982) 98 L.Q.R. 551.

[18] The terminological confusion caused by the fact that the expression "trust power" is now used to describe two factually similar but legally quite distinct types of gift has already been mentioned (see *ante*, p. 25). Hanbury & Martin: *Modern Equity* (14th ed., (1993)) at p. 111 suggests that it may have been the two meanings of "trust power" which caused the discrepancy between the majority and the minority in *McPhail* v. *Doulton*, the majority having in mind the modern discretionary trust and the minority the old style power in the nature of a trust.

[19] (1840) 5 Myl. & Cr. 72.

[20] *Ibid.*

among all the members of the class. (Had he not found a general intention of this type, the property would have passed on a resulting trust for those entitled to the residuary estate of the testator.) With which test for certainty of objects do such powers in the nature of a trust have to comply? If it is still the case that the court would automatically execute such a power by dividing the property equally between all the members of the class, then the test must surely be the same as that for fixed trusts; in this case, according to the general view,[21] it must be possible to draw up a complete list of the members of the class at the appropriate time. On the other hand, if the remarks of Lord Wilberforce in *McPhail* v. *Doulton* as to the ways in which the court can now execute a discretionary trust[22] also apply to powers in the nature of a trust, then there will be no need for the "complete list" test to apply and such limitations will presumably also be governed by the "given postulant" test. This question is in fact somewhat academic since powers in the nature of a trust are almost invariably in favour of small groups of beneficiaries, usually, as in *Burrough* v. *Philcox*, the members of a family. Gifts of this type will inevitably satisfy either test for certainty of objects and in practice, the court would almost inevitably order equal distribution quite irrelevant of whether or not this was actually obligatory. It has been argued that powers in the nature of a trust should be regarded as fixed trusts subject to defeasance by exercise of the power of selection and, as a result, must still be governed by the test appropriate to fixed trusts.[23] However, because of the factual similarity between powers in the nature of a trust and discretionary trusts, it seems as a matter of principle to be more appropriate that such powers should today also be governed by the "given postulant" test on the already mentioned assumption that, whenever the entire membership of the class is known, equal division will in fact be ordered.

(iii) *Gifts subject to a condition precedent.* The more diluted rule to the effect that a formulation will be valid provided that one person is clearly within it (specifically rejected in respect of powers in *Re Gulbenkian's Settlement*[24]) does apply to individual gifts subject to the donee satisfying a condition precedent or answering a particular description.[25] For these purposes, conceptual certainty is completely irrelevant. Thus in *Re Allen*[26] a testator left property to the eldest of his nephews "who shall be a member of the Church of England and an adherent to the doctrine of that Church"; this gift was held to be valid on the basis that, whatever the precise meaning of the conditions, it

---

[21] The contrary view has been adopted in previous editions of this work (see *ante*, text to fn. 8).
[22] See *ante*, p. 99.
[23] In Hanbury & Martin: *Modern Equity* (14th ed. (1993)), p. 111.
[24] [1970] A.C. 508, see *ante*, p. 101.
[25] Conditions subsequent are subject to a stricter test; the situations in which such a condition will operate must be wholly clear from the outset; for a recent discussion, see *Re Tepper's Will Trusts* [1987] Ch. 49.
[26] [1953] Ch. 810.

was perfectly possible for a claimant to show that he fell within them. Similarly, in *Re Tuck's Settlement Trusts*,[27] conditions precedent in a settlement that the principal beneficiary for the time being had to be of the Jewish faith and married to an approved Jewish wife were held to be valid. The same principle was applied in *Re Barlow's Will Trust*[28] to a limitation which, although not expressed in the form of a condition precedent, amounted to a series of gifts to any individuals who answered a particular specified description. The testatrix provided that "any friends of mine who may wish to do so" might purchase any of her paintings at their probate valuation. Browne-Wilkinson J. held that, had this been a gift to a class and therefore had had to satisfy the "given postulant" test, it would have been void for conceptual uncertainty. However, he regarded the limitation as creating a series of individual gifts in the form of options exerciseable by any person who qualified as a "friend"; since there might be persons who could, on any conceivable test, prove that they were friends, the limitation was valid. While the applicability of this "one person" test to conditions precedent and other analogous gifts is clearly established, it would certainly not be easy for the court to decide whether any individual did in fact qualify; in such circumstances any doubts as to qualification would presumably lead to the automatic disqualification of the claimant. However, this is not necessarily an objection to the existence of the rule since, as will be seen in the next section, this is now arguably also the case with the "given postulant" rule.

(b) Conceptual uncertainty and evidential uncertainty. In *Re Gulbenkian's Settlement*[29] Lord Upjohn posed the already mentioned distinction between conceptual (linguistic or semantic) uncertainty which, if the court cannot resolve it, renders the gift wholly void, and evidential uncertainty, which the court can deal with on an application for directions. This distinction was adopted in *McPhail* v. *Doulton*[30] and had to be considered in *Re Baden's Deed Trusts (No. 2)*,[31] the sequel to *McPhail* v. *Doulton* in which the test laid down by the House of Lords therein had to be applied to the terms of the trust in question. The trustees were directed to apply the net income of the fund in making at their absolute discretion grants to or for the benefit of any of the officers and employees or ex-officers or ex-employees of a specified company or to any relatives or dependants of any such persons. The Court of Appeal held that this class satisfied the "given postulant" test but the members of the court agreed neither as to the correct interpretation of the test nor, consequently, as to the conceptually certain meaning of the two problematic words, "relatives" and "dependants".

Stamp L.J. interpreted the "given postulant" test strictly, holding that

---

[27] [1978] Ch. 49.
[28] [1978] 1 W.L.R. 278.
[29] [1970] A.C. 508 at p. 524.
[30] [1971] A.C. 424 at p. 457.
[31] [1972] 3 W.L.R. 250.

the test would only be satisfied if it was possible to say either "yes" or "no" to any person who could conceivably present himself to the trustees.[32] On the other hand, both Sachs L.J. and Megaw L.J. seemed to broaden the test laid down by the House of Lords. Sachs L.J. held that, provided that the class was conceptually certain, the gift could never fail for evidential uncertainty; the burden of proof was on the postulant and, if he could not positively prove that he was within the class, then he was outside it.[33] Megaw L.J. held that, if it could be said with certainty that a substantial number of objects did fall within the class, then it did not matter that, as regards a substantial number of other persons, the answer had to be 'it is not proven whether they are in or out".[34] All these views are capable of criticism. The interpretation advocated by Stamp L.J. in practice does not fall far short of a return to the "complete list" test expressly rejected in *McPhail* v. *Doulton*; while there is no need for the trustees actually to draw up a list, it has to be admitted that by virtue of this interpretation those otherwise entitled to the property subject to a discretionary trust will be able to upset that trust whenever they can come up with one person whose claim to be a member of the class cannot be proven one way or the other. On the other hand, the interpretations adopted by both Sachs L.J. and Megaw L.J. move some considerable way towards the more diluted rule specifically rejected in *Re Gulbenkian's Settlement Trusts* that all that is necessary is to find one person clearly within the class; the interpretation adopted by Sachs L.J. could clearly lead to there being only one beneficiary within the class but only if the expression used was conceptually certain, something which is not actually required in the case of gifts subject to the "one person" rule[35]; the interpretation adopted by Megaw L.J. would require a substantial number of persons rather than just one to fall within the class but it is unclear whether or not conceptual certainty would also be required.

Having expressed these differing views as to the interpretation of the "given postulant" test, the members of the Court of Appeal accepted that, no matter what meaning was given to "dependants", the trust would be both conceptually and evidentially certain.[36] Sachs and Megaw L.JJ. held that the trust would be conceptually certain even if the widest possible meaning, "descendants from a common ancestor", was attributed to "relatives" and that there was no evidential difficulty about ascertaining whether any given postulant was a relative.[37] Stamp L.J., on the other hand, held that, if such a meaning was given to "relatives", the trust would fail because of the impossibility of saying that any given postulant was *not* a relative of a past or present officer or employee of the company; he consequently interpreted "relatives" as

---

[32] *Ibid.* at p. 262.
[33] *Ibid.* at p. 255.
[34] *Ibid.* at p. 259.
[35] See *ante*, p. 104.
[36] [1972] 3 W.L.R. 250 at pp. 256–257, 257–258, 264–265.
[37] *Ibid.* at pp. 257, 258.

meaning "statutory next-of-kin", an expression which is on any view both conceptually and evidentially certain.[38]

It is not easy to determine the precise effect of *Re Baden's Deed Trusts (No. 2)* so far as conceptual uncertainty is concerned. There has been little or no subsequent judicial discussion of this aspect of the interpretation of the test laid down in *Re Gulbenkian's Settlements* and *McPhail* v. *Doulton*. The limitation in *Re Baden's Deed Trusts (No. 2)* was, of course, complex and it must not be thought that problems of this kind will often arise. More straightforward illustrations of conceptual uncertainty are to be found in earlier cases where it was plain that there was, and would still be, conceptual uncertainty in the objects of the trust. Thus, in *Re Astor's Settlement Trusts*,[39] which concerned the *Observer* newspaper, a settlement provided for income to be applied to a number of non-charitable purposes including the "maintenance of good understanding, sympathy and co-operation between nations" and "the preservation of the independence and integrity of newspapers" and other such purposes for the protection of newspapers. Roxburgh J. held the trusts to be void because (*inter alia*) they included objects such as those above which were void for uncertainty. Purposes must be stated in phrases which embody definite concepts and, moreover, the means by which the trustees are to attain them must be prescribed with a sufficient degree of certainty. Similarly, in *Re Endacott*[40] it was held by the Court of Appeal that a trust which was in essence for "useful" purposes failed because it was not clear what was meant by "utility". It is generally thought that a discretionary trust in favour of "persons having a moral claim" on the settlor would also be void for uncertainty, although in *Re Leek*[41] a limitation in favour of "such persons as the [trustee] may consider to have a moral claim" on the settlor was held by Buckley J. to be sufficiently certain.[42]

This last decision raises a question of general importance as to the extent to which conceptual uncertainty can be cured by a provision that the matter is to be settled by the decision of either the trustees or of some third party. The orthodox view is that a question of fact can be delegated for resolution in this way[43] but not a question of law, since the jurisdiction of the court to decide matters of law cannot be ousted.[44]

---

[38] *Ibid.* at pp. 262–264. "Relatives" has traditionally been construed as "statutory next-of-kin" if this is necessary to save a gift; however, an appointment by the trustees in favour of relatives who are not statutory next-of-kin is nevertheless valid, which signifies that, in the event that the court is called upon to execute the trust because of a default by the trustees, distribution is necessarily among a narrower class than that available to the trustees (see *Re Poulton's Will Trusts* [1987] 1 W.L.R. 795).

[39] [1952] Ch. 534. See also *post*, p. 112.

[40] [1960] Ch. 232.

[41] [1967] 3 W.L.R. 576.

[42] Buckley J. actually held that this limitation had created a power; at that time powers alone were subject to the "given postulant" test; on appeal, the Court of Appeal found that the limitation had created a trust power which, under the then law, was void for uncertainty (such a trust power would now also be subject to the "given postulant" test).

[43] *Re Coxon* [1948] Ch. 747.

[44] *Re Wynn* [1952] Ch. 747.

For present purposes, this suggests that, while an issue of evidential uncertainty could be delegated by the settlor to the trustees or to some third party for resolution, an issue of conceptual uncertainty could not be so delegated. However, in *Dundee General Hospital Board of Management* v. *Walker*,[45] the House of Lords held, on a Scottish appeal, that a proviso that a legacy was only to be paid to a hospital if the trustees of the will "were in their sole and absolute discretion" satisfied that the hospital had not been placed under state control made the trustees the sole judges of this question and that there could be no appeal to the courts from their decision unless they had considered the wrong question or failed to consider the right question in a proper manner. This decision suggests that a question of law can now be referred to a third party for decision, in which case there seems no reason why an issue of conceptual uncertainty should not similarly be delegated. This impression is confirmed by some remarks of Lord Denning M.R. in *Re Tuck's Settlement Trusts*,[46] which concerned conditions precedent in a settlement that the principal beneficiary for the time being had to be of the Jewish faith and married to an approved Jewish wife, it being provided that any dispute was to be referred to the Chief Rabbi for decision. The majority of the Court of Appeal found that these conditions were conditions precedent and so were sufficiently certain.[47] Lord Denning M.R., however, held that, in the event that there was any conceptual uncertainty in the conditions, this was cured by the reference to the Chief Rabbi.[48] This matter cannot yet be regarded as settled but there is clearly considerably more possibility than hitherto that issues of conceptual uncertainty can now be cured in this way.

(c) **Administrative unworkability.** In *McPhail* v. *Doulton*,[49] Lord Wilberforce added a third class of potential uncertainty, where "the meaning of the words used is clear but the definition of beneficiaries is so hopelessly wide as not to form 'anything like a class' so that the trust is administratively unworkable" (he gave as an example "all the residents of Greater London"). A discretionary trust was indeed struck down for this reason in *R.* v. *District Auditor, ex p. West Yorkshire Metropolitan County Council*,[50] where the local authority resolved to create a trust "for the benefit of any or all or some of the inhabitants of the County of West Yorkshire" for various specific purposes.[51] Given that there were 2,500,000 potential beneficiaries, the court, while prepared to assume without deciding that "inhabitant" was sufficiently conceptually certain, held that the trust was void for administrative unworkability on the grounds that the class was much too large.

While the concept of administrative unworkability thus clearly applies to discretionary trusts, there has been some debate over

[45] [1952] 1 All E.R. 896.
[46] [1978] 2 W.L.R. 411.
[47] *Ibid.*, *per* Lord Russell of Killowen at pp. 420–421, *per* Eveleigh L.J. at pp. 421–422.
[48] *Ibid.* at pp. 417–419.
[49] [1971] A.C. 424 at p. 457.
[50] (1986) 26 R.V.R. 24; see C. Harpum, (1986) 45 C.L.J. 391.
[51] See *post*, p. 110.

whether or not it also applies to powers. In *Blausten* v. *I.R.C.*,[52] the trustees had power to introduce to the class of beneficiaries any person other than the settlor. An argument that this power was void for administrative unworkability was rejected on the ground that although the trustees had this admittedly wide power it could only be exercised with the written consent of the settlor and hence only during his lifetime. Therefore, it could not be said that the settlor had failed to set "metes and bounds" to the beneficial interests which he intended to create or to permit to be created under the settlement. Buckley L.J. clearly assumed, admittedly only by way of dicta, that the concept of administrative unworkability did not apply to powers. This reasoning is, however, difficult to reconcile with the subsequent decision of Templeman J. in *Re Manisty's Settlement*.[53] In this case the trustees had the power to add beneficiaries and to benefit the persons so added, and the power was exerciseable in favour of anyone in the world except the settlor, his wife and some other persons. It was held that this power did not fail for administrative unworkability even though there were no expressed restrictions on its operation by the trustees, Templeman J. preferring the view that a power could not be void on the grounds of breadth of numbers but only if its terms were capricious. Megarry V.C. in *Re Hay's Settlement Trusts*,[54] also took the view that a power would not be administratively unworkable on the grounds of mere numbers since this should neither inhibit the trustees in its exercise nor prevent the courts from controlling them. He did however state that a discretionary trust as broad as the power in that case ("to or for the benefit of any person or persons whatsoever or to any charity" with only the settlor, her husband, and the trustees excluded) would have been void as administratively unworkable. Subsequently, in *Re Beatty's Will Trusts*[55] a power given to trustees in favour of "such person or persons as they think fit" was held valid without any mention of the possibility of it being administratively unworkable. At this stage, it seemed tolerably clear that the concept of administrative unworkability did not apply to powers. However, as will be seen in a later Chapter,[56] the duties of the donee of a power and the remedies available to the objects of a power have now been the subject of an important review in *Mettoy Pensions Trustees* v. *Evans*[57]; this decision envisages the adaption of the remedies available for the enforcement of discretionary trusts for the purpose of enforcing powers. It has therefore been suggested[58] that this may cause the concept of administrative unworkability to be applied to at least some types of powers. It obviously remains to be seen whether this is yet another consequence of this important decision.

---

[52] [1972] Ch. 256.
[53] [1973] 3 W.L.R. 341.
[54] [1982] 1 W.L.R. 202.
[55] [1990] 1 W.L.R. 1503.
[56] See *post*, p. 130.
[57] [1990] 1 W.L.R. 1587.
[58] By S. Gardner, (1991) 107 L.Q.R. 214.

(d) Capriciousness. Another possible ground of potential uncertainty is capriciousness, a concept developed by Templeman J. in *Re Manisty's Settlement*,[59] in which he upheld a power of very considerable breadth. He held that the exercise of the process of selection by discretionary trustees and by the donees of powers may be rendered practically impossible if the terms of the discretionary trusts and powers in question are capricious. He gave as an example of a capricious power one in favour of "the residents of Greater London", not because of the number of donees but "because the terms of the power negative any sensible intention on the part of the settlor" and any "sensible consideration by the trustees of the exercise of the power". "If the settlor intended and expected the trustees would have regard to persons with some claim on his bounty or some interest in an institution favoured by the settlor, or if the settlor had any other sensible intention or expectation, he would not have required the trustees to consider only an accidental conglomeration of persons who have no discernible link with the settlor or with any institution".[60]

Because the example given by Templeman J. of a capricious power was exactly the same as the example given by Lord Wilberforce in *McPhail* v. *Doulton* of an administratively unworkable discretionary trust, it was originally thought that the two concepts were the same,[61] the former being applicable only to powers and the latter being applicable only to discretionary trusts. However, it is now clear that the concept of capriciousness applies both to discretionary trusts and to powers. In *R.* v. *District Auditor, ex p. West Yorkshire Metropolitan County Council*,[62] the discretionary trust held void for administrative unworkability because the 2,500,000 inhabitants of West Yorkshire constituted too large a class was held not to be capricious since the County Council had every reason for wishing to benefit the inhabitants of West Yorkshire. The concepts of administrative unworkability and capriciousness are therefore apparently distinct, the former but not the latter being limited to breadth of numbers. No discretionary trust or power has yet been set aside on the grounds of capriciousness; it will be interesting to see whether this ever occurs.

(e) Duty to survey the field. Given that, save in the case of a fixed trust, the identity of all the objects will not necessarily be known, the trustees of a discretionary trust and those entitled to exercise a power in the nature of a trust or a mere power cannot be obliged to consider the claims of every possible object. In *McPhail* v. *Doulton*[63] Lord Wilberforce stated that the trustees of a discretionary trust "ought to make such a survey of the range of objects or possible beneficiaries as will enable them to carry out their fiduciary duty" and emphasised that a "wider and more comprehensive range of enquiry is called for" in the case of discretionary trusts than in the case of powers. Where the

---

[59] [1973] 3 W.L.R. 341.
[60] *Ibid.* at p. 349.
[61] See C.T. Emery, (1982) 98 L.Q.R. 551.
[62] (1986) 26 R.V.R. 24.
[63] [1971] A.C. 424.

possible objects number thousands or hundreds of thousands, the trustees must assess "the size of the problem" in a businesslike manner.[64] A more detailed account of the duties of discretionary trustees was provided by Megarry V.C. in *Re Hay's Settlement Trusts*[65] in the following passage.

> "The trustee must not simply proceed to exercise the power in favour of such of the objects as happen to be at hand or claim his attention. He must first consider what persons or classes of persons are objects of the power . . . : what is needed is an appreciation of the width of the field, and thus whether a selection is to be made merely from a dozen or, instead, from thousands or millions. . . .
> Only when the trustee has applied his mind to the 'size of the problem' should he then consider in individual cases whether, in relation to other possible claimants, a particular grant is appropriate. In doing this, no doubt he should not prefer the undeserving to the deserving; but he is not required to make an exact calculation whether, as between deserving claimants, A is more deserving than B."

This duty, considerably broader than had hitherto been thought,[66] has so far been applied only to trustees of discretionary trusts but would presumably also be applied to the donees of powers in the nature of a trust. The duties of a donee of a mere power "cannot be more stringent than those for a discretionary trust".[67] A non-fiduciary donee of a mere power is clearly under no obligation to do anything at all and so cannot possibly have any duty to survey the field. On the other hand, in *Mettoy Pension Trustees* v. *Evans*,[68] it was stated that a fiduciary donee of a mere power must consider periodically whether or not he should exercise the power, the range of objects of the power, and the appropriateness of individual appointments. As will be seen in a later chapter,[69] a fiduciary donee of a power is consequently "to some extent subject to the control of the courts in relation to its exercise"[70]; as a result, powers held by fiduciaries may well in some respects have been assimilated to discretionary trusts. However, the precise scope of the duties which were enunciated in *Mettoy Pension Trustees* v. *Evans* must await further clarification.

Moffatt: pp.188-197
pp 590-603

VI. THE BENEFICIARY PRINCIPLE

A further essential ingredient for the effectual creation of a trust is that there should be some beneficiary capable of enforcing it. As Grant M.R.

---

[64] *Re Baden's Deed Trusts (No. 2)* [1973] Ch. 9 at p. 20, (*per* Sachs L.J.).

[65] [1982] 1 W.L.R. 202 at pp. 209–210.

[66] In *Re Gestetner* [1953] Ch. 672 at p. 688 Harman J. had stated that "there is no obligation on the trustees to do more than consider from time to time the merits of such persons of the specified class as are known to them".

[67] *Re Hay's Settlement Trusts* [1982] 1 W.L.R. 202 at pp. 209–210.

[68] [1990] 1 W.L.R. 1587.

[69] See *post*, p. 141.

[70] *Mettoy Pension Trustees* v. *Evans* [1990] 1 W.L.R. 1587 at p. 1614.

stated in *Morice* v. *Bishop of Durham*,[71] "there must be someone in whose favour the court can decree performance". This requirement does not apply to charitable trusts, which can be enforced by the Attorney-General. However, private trusts which do not satisfy the beneficiary requirement will not generally be enforced; "a court of equity does not recognise as valid a trust which it cannot both enforce and control".[72] Nevertheless, there are a number of anomalous cases in which non-charitable purpose trusts have been upheld even though there has been no human beneficiary capable of enforcing them. Such trusts are often described as trusts of imperfect obligation on the grounds that, although they will not be enforced, the courts will not forbid their performance if the trustees wish to carry them out. In *Re Endacott*[73] these cases were said to fall into the following categories: trusts for the erection or maintenance of monuments or graves, trusts for the saying of masses in jurisdictions where such trusts are not regarded as charitable, trusts for the maintenance of particular animals, trusts for the benefit of unincorporated associations, and miscellaneous cases (a few further cases which do not fit into any of the other categories). The decisions which have established these anomalous exceptions have been described as "concessions to human weakness or sentiment"[74] and will not now be extended.[75]

1. *The General Rule*

Trusts for non-charitable purposes are generally void for two different reasons: first, because there is no one who can enforce them and, secondly, because the courts are unable to control the execution of such trusts. This rule was originally established in *Morice* v. *Bishop* of Durham,[76] which concerned a gift of residue to the Bishop of Durham to be applied by him "for such objects of benevolence and liberality as [he] in his own discretion shall most approve of". Grant M.R. held that this gift failed, saying[77] that "there can be no trust, over the exercise of which this Court will not assume a control, for an uncontrollable power of disposition would be ownership, and not trust". On appeal, Lord Eldon L.C. added[78] that the court had to be in a position both to execute the trust if the trustees for any reason did not do so and to prevent mal-administration of the trust. This decision, which was approved by the House of Lords in *Chichester Diocesan Fund and Board of Finance* v. *Simpson*[79] unquestionably represents English law.

The first in a line of important decisions which reconsidered the whole question of trusts of imperfect obligation was *Re Astor's*

---

[71] (1804) 9 Ves. 399 at p. 405.
[72] *Re Astor's Settlement Trusts* [1952] Ch. 534 at p. 549.
[73] [1960] Ch. 232.
[74] *Re Astor's Settlement Trusts* [1952] Ch. 534 at p. 547.
[75] *Re Endacott* [1960] Ch. 232 at pp. 250–251.
[76] (1804) 9 Ves. 399, (1805) 10 Ves. 522.
[77] (1804) 9 Ves. 399 at pp. 404–405.
[78] (1805) 10 Ves. 522 at pp. 539–540.
[79] [1944] A.C. 341.

Settlement Trusts[80] (the *Observer* trust case), whose objects included "the establishment, maintenance and improvement of good understanding, sympathy and co-operation between nations", "the preservation of the independence and integrity of newspapers" and "the promotion of freedom of the press". This case has already been considered on the question of certainty of objects, in which respect it was held, but only as a secondary ground of the decision, that the objects of the trusts were too uncertain; this was clearly correct because they were not defined in terms of concepts capable of clear ascertainment. However, the question which first suggested itself was whether, if the objects had been certain, the arrangement would have been valid as a trust of imperfect obligation. Roxburgh J. reached the conclusion—and this was the primary ground of his decision—that the general principle was that gifts on trust must have a beneficiary or *cestui que trust* and said that the anomalous cases already referred to provided an exception. These cases he suggested should (following Underhill's view[81]), be regarded as concessions to human weakness or sentiment, but they could not be used to justify a proposition that a court of equity would recognise as an equitable obligation a direction to apply funds in furtherance of enumerated non-charitable purposes in a manner no court could control.[82]

The views of Roxburgh J. were applied in another decision at first instance, *Re Shaw*,[83] where the main question was whether George Bernard Shaw's testamentary trusts of residue for 21 years for experimentation in the possible reform of the English alphabet of 26 letters by its substitution for a phonetic alphabet of 40 letters were valid charitable trusts. In the event they were held not to be so. The question then arose whether they could be valid, in effect, as trusts of imperfect obligation. Harman J. held that, since they lacked a *cestui que trust*, they were invalid.

It might have been thought that the compass of these trusts had been firmly confined by the decision of the Court of Appeal in *Re Endacott*,[84] where the testator had given his residuary estate to the North Tawton Parish Council "for the purpose of providing some useful memorial to myself." The court held that this trust did not fall within the "anomalous" class of trusts of imperfect obligation. It was of too wide and uncertain a nature to qualify. Harman L.J. affirmed the views on this class of trust expressed by Roxburgh J. in *Re Astor's Settlement Trusts*. He said[85]: "I applaud the orthodox sentiments expressed by Roxburgh J. and I think as I think he does, that though one knows there have been decisions which are not satisfactorily classified but are merely occasions when Homer has nodded, yet the cases stand by themselves and ought not to be increased in number nor indeed followed except where the one is exactly like the other." And he added

---

[80] [1952] Ch. 534.
[81] See now Underhill & Hayton: *Law of Trusts and Trustees* (14th ed. (1987)) pp. 75–86.
[82] [1952] Ch. 534 at p. 547.
[83] [1957] 1 W.L.R. 729.
[84] [1960] Ch. 232.
[85] *Ibid.* at pp. 250–251.

that he could not think that a case of this kind, that of providing outside a church an unspecified and unidentified memorial, was the kind of instance which should be added to these "troublesome, anomalous and aberrant" cases. Similarly, one of the reasons why the Court of Appeal held in *R* v. *District Auditor ex p. West Yorkshire Metropolitan Council*[86] that a discretionary trust to apply £400,000 for one of four purposes "for the benefit of any or some of the inhabitants of" West Yorkshire was void was because it was a non-charitable purpose trust.

As will be seen later on,[87] in a number of cases involving trusts for unincorporated associations it has been held that, where the subject matter of the gift was to be held on trust for the purposes of the association as a quasi-corporate entity, it would tend to a perpetuity and would be void on that ground. Such cases are primarily concerned with perpetuity and it is thought appropriate to consider them under that head. However, in one of the leading cases, *Leahy* v. *Attorney-General for New South Wales*,[88] although the actual decision was that the gift was void for perpetuity, Viscount Simonds seemed clearly to be of the opinion that such a purpose trust would in any event (apart from perpetuity) be void because there was no *cestui que trust* to enforce it. He said[89]: "If the words 'for the general purposes of the association' were held to import a trust, the question would have to be asked, what is the trust and who are the beneficiaries? A gift can be made to persons (including a corporation) but it cannot be made to a purpose or to an object; so also a trust may be created for the benefit of persons as *cestuis que trust* but not for a purpose or object unless the purpose or object be charitable. For a purpose or object cannot sue but, if it be charitable, the Attorney-General can sue to enforce it".[90]

Cases such as *Re Astor's Settlement Trusts* and *Re Shaw* in particular raised the problem whether the categories of trusts of imperfect obligation could be extended to other non-charitable purposes provided, of course, that they were stated in terms embodying certainty. The answer, in view of what was said in *Re Endacott* as well as in *Leahy* v. *Attorney-General for New South Wales*, seems to be in the negative. The reasoning, that is to say the lack of a *cestui que trust* to enforce them, thereby putting the execution of the trust outside the control of the court, appears to be unimpeachable. And yet it might still be said that the position is not entirely satisfactory. In the present state of law, a person can give his money to human beings, whether good or bad. He can give it to charity. He can even set up trusts for the various anomalous purposes recognised by the law, such as for his dogs and cats or to promote foxhunting. But it seems that *as a general rule* a person cannot give his money for a social experiment falling outside the

---

[86] [1986] R.V.R. 24.

[87] See *post*, p. 124.

[88] [1959] A.C. 457.

[89] *Ibid.* at p. 478.

[90] In *Re Lipinski's Will Trusts* [1976] Ch. 235, Oliver J. argued (at p. 246) that this was not intended as an exhaustive statement or to do more than indicate the broad division of trusts into those where there are ascertainable beneficiaries (whether for particular purposes or not) and trusts where there are none.

confines of the law of charity if it is defined in terms of purposes, no matter how certain those purposes maybe.[91] This proposition of course assumes that it is only possible to construe the gift in terms of purposes; if it is possible instead to construe it as an outright gift to a named person or persons, with the purpose merely an expression of the motive for the gift, it will of course be valid.[92]

The qualification "as a general rule" has been added because, according to the decision of Goff J. in *Re Denley's Trust Deed*,[93] there may in certain circumstances be a way out of these difficulties. For he held that this rule was confined to purpose trusts which were "abstract or impersonal"; but that a trust, even though expressed as a purpose, which directly or indirectly was for the benefit of an individual or individuals was valid, provided that the individuals were ascertainable and the trust was not otherwise void for uncertainty. Here the expressed purpose of the trust was the maintenance of a sports ground primarily for the benefit of such other persons as the trustees allowed to use it. No question of perpetuity was involved. The judge held that the trust was valid on the basis that this was an express private trust in favour of ascertainable beneficiaries who *ex hypothesi* could enforce it. But whether this approach is correct, however commendable as an attempt to "liberalise" the law, seems doubtful. The reason is that if a provision is framed as a *purpose* which, as a matter of construction, plainly seemed to be the position in *Re Denley's Trust Deed*, even though it is for the benefit of individuals, it is the purpose which is the dominant factor and if it is non-charitable it should fail unless it falls within the recognised exceptions.

Nevertheless, *Re Denley's Trust Deed* was followed in *Re Lipinski's Will Trusts*,[94] where the testator left his residuary estate to trustees for an unincorporated recreational association (which was not charitable) to be used for constructing and improving buildings for the association. Oliver J. held that this was a valid purpose trust, principally because the beneficiaries (the members of the association) were ascertainable and could enforce the purpose. As a matter of construction, *Re Lipinski's Will Trusts* may be a stronger case than *Re Denley's Trust Deed* because, as it was held, the gift was to an unincorporated association and was also upheld on that basis[95]; this was not the case in *Re Denley's Trust Deed*. Megarry V.C. also accepted the conclusion arrived at in *Re Denley's Trust Deed* in *Re Northern Developments (Holdings)*.[96] Subsequently, however, in *Re Grant's Will Trusts*[97] Vinelott J. expressed the view that *Re Denley's Trust Deed* did not involve a purpose trust at all but rather a

---

[91] O.R. Marshall (1953) 6 C.L.P. 151. See also, generally, on the subject: A. Kiralfy (1950) 14 Conv. (N.S.) 374; L. Sheridan (1953) 17 Conv. (N.S.). 46.

[92] *Re Sanderson's Trust* (1857) 3 K. & J. 497 at p. 503, *Re Andrew's Trust* [1905] 2 Ch. 48, *Re Osoba* [1979] 1 W.L.R. 247.

[93] [1969] 1 Ch. 373.

[94] [1976] Ch. 235.

[95] It was held that it was valid as a gift in favour of an unincorporated association with a superadded discretion; see *post*, p.126.

[96] (1978) unreported; see (1985) 101 L.Q.R. 280.

[97] [1980] 1 W.L.R. 360.

discretionary trust. This view is not really consistent either with the lengthy discussion of purpose trusts in *Re Denley's Trust Deed* or with the interpretation put on that case by Oliver J. and Megarry V.C. and consequently does not appear to be an acceptable explanation of that decision.

If the view expressed in *Re Grant's Will Trusts* is discounted, these cases, all first instance decisions, indicate that this type of purpose trust may be treated as a valid express private trust for the incidental benefit of ascertainable beneficiaries, albeit for a particular purpose. Such trusts may well, however, have to comply with the rule against inalienability (discussed in the next section) and be limited to take effect only within the perpetuity period. *N.B. : Purposes last longer than people.*

It seems to be necessary to distinguish between these examples of purpose trusts which incidentally benefit persons who have no right to call for the trust property and trusts by virtue of which particular persons are to be benefitted in a particular way. Thus in *Re Osoba*[98] a trust "for the training of my daughter Abiola up to university grade" was construed as an absolute gift made for a particular motive; such a trust automatically satisfies the beneficiary principle and does not have to comply with the rule against inalienability. It is also important to emphasise that a valid power cannot be deduced from what is intended to be a trust, a rule which applies just as much to non-charitable purpose trusts as to other trusts.[99] If a trust is intended, it cannot be treated as a power.[1] There is of course nothing to prevent the express creation of powers for non-charitable purposes but this imposes no obligation on the donees of such powers to exercise them.

But if not express, get round it

Finally, it must be emphasised that, despite the decision in *Re Denley's Trust Deed*, it is nevertheless from a practical point of view inadviseable to endeavour to provide expressly for a non-charitable purpose trust, other than one falling within the existing anomalous exceptions, in the hope that it may be declared valid for other reasons. The simplest solution is to form a company, the objects of which do not need to be charitable, and make gifts by will or *inter vivos* to the company.[2]

2.   *The Anomalous Cases*

As has already been mentioned, the situations in which non-charitable purpose trusts have been upheld even though there has been no human beneficiary capable of enforcing them have been said[3] to fall into the following categories: trusts for the erection or maintenance of

---

[98] [1979] 1 W.L.R. 247. See also *Re Sanderson's Trust* (1857) 3 K. & J. 497 *per* Page-Wood V.C. at p. 503 and *Re Andrew's Trust* [1905] 2 Ch. 48.

[99] *I.R.C.* v. *Broadway Cottages Trust* [1955] Ch. 20 at p. 36; *Re Endacott* [1960] Ch. 232 at p. 246. This principle is not affected by *McPhail* v. *Doulton* [1971] A.C. 424 (see *ante*).

[1] Compare Morris & Leach, *The Rule Against Perpetuities* (2nd ed), pp. 319, *et seq.*

[2] The Goodman Committee on Charity and Law and Voluntary Organisations (see *post*, Chapter 9), recommended that trusts for non-charitable purposes should be valid but no steps have been taken to enact this part of their proposals.

[3] In *Re Endacott* [1960] Ch. 232; the classification adopted was put forward in Morris & Leach: *The Rule against Perpetuities* (2nd ed.) pp. 306 *et seq.*

monuments or graves, trusts for the saying of masses in jurisdictions where such trusts are not regarded as charitable, trusts for the maintenance of particular animals, trusts for the benefit of unincorporated associations, and miscellaneous cases (a few further cases which do not fit into any of the other categories). It also seems that these exceptions will only be upheld if the trust in question is contained in a will; indeed, it has been said that the will must be drafted in such a way that any of the property not expended on the non-charitable purpose will fall into residue.[4] In such circumstances, an order can be made whereby the trustees undertake to carry out the non-charitable purpose with the residuary legatees being given leave to apply to the court if the trustees fail to do so; this makes the trust in question indirectly enforceable in that the trustees have a choice between carrying out the specified purpose and transferring the property to the residuary legatees. However, the residuary legatees or intestate successors can clearly be given such leave to apply even if the will is not drafted in this way; consequently, there seems no reason in principle why such a provision should be necessary or why the subject matter of the trust should not be the residue itself.[5]

The existence of these anomalous cases, particularly the miscellaneous cases, contrasts markedly with the willingness of the courts to strike down as capricious trusts for the management of property in a manner which confers no obvious benefit on anyone. Such a case was *Brown* v. *Burdett*[6] where a gift of a house on trust to block up its windows and doors for twenty years was held to be void. There is no possible justification for this difference in attitude; its explanation may be that the anomalous exceptions are regarded as "concessions to human weakness or sentiment".[7] The present state of the authorities really requires a review by the House of Lords or by the legislature.

These non-charitable purpose trusts are subject to a further requirement, namely that the property subject to the trust must not be rendered inalienable.[8] This principle is one of the aspects of the rule against perpetuities, which will be considered in a later Chapter.[9] If at the time when the trust comes into effect there is any possibility that it is capable of continuing for longer than the appropriate perpetuity period, it will be void. The settlor may specify a perpetuity period consisting of a specified life or lives in being plus 21 years or any fixed period of years up to 21 years.[10] The lives in question can be those of the persons related in some way to the trust or its purposes; it is also common to use what is known a a "royal lives clause", specifying the perpetuity period as, for example, "the period ending at the expiration of 21 years from the death of the last survivor of all the lineal

---

[4] *Re Thompson* [1934] Ch. 342 at p. 344, *Re Astor's Settlement Trusts* [1952] Ch. 534 at p. 546.
[5] See *Re Endacott* [1960] Ch. 232 at p. 240.
[6] (1882) 21 Ch.D. 667.
[7] *Re Astor's Settlement Trusts* [1952] Ch. 534 at p. 547.
[8] *Carne* v. *Long* (1860) 2 De G.F. & J. 75 at p. 80.
[9] See *post* p. 163.
[10] *Re Dean* (1899) 41 Ch. D. 552 at p. 557.

descendants of his late Majesty King George VI[11] who shall be living at the time" when the trust comes into effect. Only human lives can be specified,[12] for otherwise it would be open to an eccentric settlor to tie up property indefinitely by settling it on trusts limited to the lives of tortoises or other animals noted for their longevity. Alternatively, the settlor may prefer to specify "such period as the law allows" in which case, assuming that there are no relevant lives, the perpetuity period will be 21 years. If no period is specified at all, the trust will be void unless it must necessarily determine before the end of the perpetuity period, which in most cases will mean within 21 years. It is thought that any non-charitable purpose trusts which are upheld in accordance with the decision in *Re Denley's Trust Deed*[13] must also comply with the rule against inalienability but this has not yet actually had to be decided since in *Re Denley's Trust Deed* the trust was expressly limited to a 21 year period.

(1) Trusts for the erection or maintenance of monuments or graves
A trust for the erection of a particular monument or for the maintenance of a particular grave is not charitable, but it has been held that it may be valid as a trust of imperfect obligation. Thus in *Trimmer* v. *Danby*[14] a legacy of £1,000 left by the painter Turner to his executors "to erect a monument to my memory in St. Paul's Cathedral" was upheld. There is no requirement that the monument or tombstone be for the testator himself. In *Musset* v. *Bingle*[15] a somewhat bizarre gift for the erection of a monument to the testator's widow's first husband was also upheld. It does, however, seem that the monument must be of a funerary nature if it is to fall within the scope of this exception.[16] The question of perpetuity has not been raised in any of the cases involving the construction of monuments on the basis that it will inevitably be carried out as soon as is reasonably practicable after the testator's death and thus well within the perpetuity period. Perpetuity is, however, an issue in relation to trusts for the maintenance of monuments and graves. Thus in *Re Hooper*[17] a gift to trustees for the upkeep of graves and monuments "so long as they can legally do so" was held to be valid for 21 years but would clearly have been void for perpetuity if it had not been so restricted. Indeed in *Musset* v. *Bingle*[18] a perpetual trust to maintain the monument which was to be erected was agreed to be void

---

[11] The father of the present Queen. Consequently, the royal lives in question are those of H.M. Queen Elizabeth II, H.R.H. Princess Margaret, and their descendants. It is also probably still possible to use King George V (the grandfather of the present Queen), although the number of his descendants is now very considerable. It is certainly unsafe to specify the descendants of any previous sovereign.

[12] *Re Kelly* [1932] I.R. 255.

[13] [1969] 1 Ch. 373.

[14] (1856) 25 L.J.Ch. 424.

[15] [1876] W.N. 171.

[16] See *Re Endacott* [1960] Ch. 232.

[17] [1932] 1 Ch. 38, following *Pirbright* v. *Salwey* [1896] W.N. 86 (a gift of consols for application "so long as law permitted" to keep up a burial enclosure was held valid for 21 years).

[18] [1876] W.N. 171.

for perpetuity. However, as will be seen in the next section,[19] there are certain other methods whereby the maintenance of monuments and graves for longer periods can be achieved.

In the case just discussed and in others deciding the same principle, it was made clear that the trustees could not be compelled to erect the monument or keep up the grave in question but that if they decided to do so they would not be prevented. At the same time, if the trustees are unwilling to perform the trust or if there is a surplus after the purpose has been carried out, they will hold the property or the surplus on a resulting trust for the settlor's estate. It will also "result" on the determination of the period stipulated in the instrument for the duration of the trust or of the perpetuity period, as the case may be.

(2) Trusts for the saying of masses

It was long uncertain whether or not trusts for the saying of masses were charitable but this point was finally settled in *Re Hetherington*[20] where such trusts were held to be charitable provided that the masses are open to the public. However, in the event that this condition is not satisfied in any individual case, as would occur where the masses were to be celebrated for the members of a cloistered and contemplative religious order,[21] the trust in question will clearly be valid as a non-charitable purpose trust, provided that it complies with the rule against inalienability and is limited to take effect only within the perpetuity period.[22]

(3) Trusts for the maintenance of particular animals

Gifts for the maintenance of animals in general are charitable.[23] However, gifts for the maintenance of a *particular* animal or particular animals are not: they can only take effect, if at all, as trusts of imperfect obligation. Thus in *Pettingall* v. *Pettingall*,[24] the testator bequeathed £50 a year to the executor to provide for the testator's favourite black mare. It was held that he could perform the testator's wishes and might keep the surplus for his own purposes. But it was also indicated that if the executor failed to look after the mare the beneficiaries could apply to the court to reconsider the arrangement, but subject to that the trust was to last during the animal's life. There is also the case of *Re Dean*,[25] where there was a bequest of an annual sum for the maintenance of the testator's horses and hounds for a period of 50 years, if any of the horses and hounds should so long live. This was held valid: the trustees were clearly at liberty to carry out the terms of the gift, although the beneficiaries, being dumb, could not compel them to do so. *Re Dean* is an explicit authority—not all the early cases in this area of the law are particularly explicit—that a trust of imperfect obligation for the upkeep of a

---

[19] See *post*, p. 121.
[20] [1990] Ch. 1.
[21] Trusts for such orders are not regarded as charitable; *Gilmour* v. *Coats* [1949] A.C. 426.
[22] *Bourne* v. *Keane* [1919] A.C. 815 at pp. 874–875.
[23] See *post*, p. 323.
[24] (1842) 11 L.J.Ch. 176.
[25] (1889) 41 Ch.D. 552.

given animal may be valid notwithstanding the fact that by its nature it is not enforceable by the beneficiary. Few of the cases on animals deal adequately with the question of perpetuity. Judicial notice is sometimes taken of the fact that the expected life of the animal in question is less than the 21 year period.[26] In a large number of cases, animals will live for a time much shorter than this period and it would seem convenient and not at all improper that, if a period is not stipulated in the trust instrument, the contemplated duration of the life of the animal in question should be taken and if it falls short of the 21 year period, the trust should not fail. However, this does not justify either of the cases mentioned above. Horses can certainly live for more than twenty-one years and so the decision in *Pettingall* v. *Pettingall* that the trust was to last during the animal's life could clearly have contravened the rule against inalienability. Further, the fixed period of 50 years in *Re Dean* certainly does not satisfy the rule and the horses, if not the hounds, could certainly have survived for more than twenty-one years. The only correct (and safe) approach is therefore to limit the duration of the trust by reference to nominated lives in being.

(4) Trusts for the benefit of unincorporated associations

The existence of this category has always been regarded as somewhat doubtful.[27] It was formerly thought in some quarters that some types of trusts for the benefit of unincorporated associations[28] depended for their validity on the existence of a further anomalous exception to the beneficiary principle. Where such a trust is held to have been made by way of endowment (one of a number of ways in which gifts in favour of unincorporated associations can be construed), that endowment is likely to have been intended to be perpetual; consequently the adoption of this construction will generally lead to the gift being held to be void for perpetuity.[29] However, if a trust has been established which satisfies the rule against perpetuities (because, for example, it is held to have been intended to benefit only the existing members[30]), it will undoubtedly be valid. It appears that such a trust would now satisfy the beneficiary principle by virtue of the decision in *Re Denley's Trust Deed*.[31] However, prior to that decision it was sometimes thought that such a trust constituted one of the anomalous exceptions to that principle. It seems clear that any need for the existence of this particular exception to the beneficiary principle has now disappeared.

(5) Miscellaneous cases

There have been from time to time a few further anomalous cases which do not fit into any of the other categories. Of these cases, the Court of

---

[26] *Re Haines* (1925) *The Times*, November 7, 1952 (life of cat approximately 16 years); but this may be wrong—see Morris & Leach: *The Rule against Perpetuities* (2nd ed.) p. 323, and *cf. Re Kelly* [1932] I.R. 255 at pp. 260–261.

[27] Morris & Leach: *op. cit.* in their classification comment that "this group is more doubtful".

[28] Discussed more fully *post*, p. 123.

[29] As in *Leahy* v. *Attorney-General for New South Wales* [1959] A.C. 457.

[30] As in *Re Drummond* [1914] 2 Ch. 90.

[31] [1969] 1 Ch. 393.

Appeal in *Re Endacott*[32] referred only to *Re Catherall*,[33] where Roxburgh J. upheld a gift to a vicar and churchwardens for a suitable memorial to the testator's parents and sisters whether or not it was charitable; the Court of Appeal held that this decision could be justified on the grounds that the purposes were charitable. However, this certainly cannot be said of the best known of these miscellaneous cases, *Re Thompson*,[34] one of a number of such cases reviewed by Roxburgh J. in *Re Astor's Settlement Trusts*.[35] *Re Thompson* concerned a gift of £1,000 to be applied towards the promotion and furtherance of fox-hunting. The residuary legatee, Trinity Hall Cambridge, wished to carry out the testator's wishes in so far as this was legally possible but, as a charity, felt obliged to object to the enforcement of this trust. The gift, which complied with the rule against inalienability, was nevertheless upheld by analogy with *Pettingall* v. *Pettingall*.[36] This decision cannot be supported and, like most of the other miscellaneous cases, is most unlikely to be followed; in this sense the miscellaneous cases are distinct from those in the other categories, which will be applied but not extended.[37]

3. *Maintenance of Monuments and Tombs for longer than the Perpetuity Period*

It has already been seen that a trust for the maintenance of monuments and graves will be valid as a trust of imperfect obligation if its duration is limited to the perpetuity period. It may, however, be possible for a testator to ensure that a trust of perpetual duration for this purpose is valid.[38] But the ways in which this may be achieved are, as will be seen, somewhat complex and heavy-handed.

First, a gift for the maintenance of the whole of the churchyard containing the monument or tomb in question is a valid charitable gift[39] and so, if the gift is made in this way, the maintenance of the monument or tomb for ever will be successfully achieved.

Secondly, a gift to one charity with a gift over to another if the monument or tomb is not kept in repair may also be successful. But it is most important to ensure that no actual trust is imposed on the first charity for its upkeep. A comparison of two cases may be instructive in underlining this rule. In *Re Tyler*[40] a sum of stock was given to the trustees of the London Missionary Society with a gift over to the Blue

---

[32] [1960] Ch. 232.

[33] (June 3 1959) (*unreported*).

[34] [1934] Ch. 342.

[35] [1952] Ch. 534.

[36] (1842) 11 L.J.Ch. 176.

[37] *Re Endacott* [1960] Ch. 232 at pp. 250–251.

[38] It may also be possible to take advantage of Parish Councils and Burial Authorities (Miscellaneous Provisions) Act 1970 s.1, which authorises local authorities and burial authorities to make an agreement to maintain graves *et cetera* for a period not exceeding 99 years. The text is, however, only concerned with the use of trust machinery for this purpose.

[39] *Re Pardoe* [1906] 2 Ch. 184.

[40] [1891] 3 Ch. 252.

Coat School if the Society failed to keep a tomb in repair. Since both the donees were charitable bodies the perpetuity rule did not apply to them[41] but the question still remained whether the *condition* in question (that is to say, for the maintenance of the tomb) contravened the rule. It was held by the Court of Appeal that, since the testator had not actually required the Society to maintain the tomb, the condition was valid. On the other hand, in *Re Dalzeil*[42] the testator gave to the governors of St. Bartholomew's Hospital the sum of £20,000 "upon and subject to the condition" that they should use the income so far as necessary for the upkeep of a certain mausoleum; if they failed to carry out this purpose, there was a gift over to such other charities as the trustees might select on the same conditions. In this case, the condition, on its true construction, amounted to a positive direction that the income was to be applied in the first instance to the maintenance of the mausoleum; it did not—as, conversely, was the case in *Re Tyler*—simply impose a moral obligation. Accordingly, Cohen J. held that the trust failed.

Thirdly, a highly controversial method, which will now apparently no longer work, was to rely on the decision in *Re Chardon*.[43] The testator gave to his trustees £200 to invest and to pay income to a cemetery company "during such period as they shall continue to maintain and keep the graves of my great grandfather and . . . Priscilla Navone in good order and condition." He further provided that, if the graves were not maintained, the income was to go into residue. Romer J. held this gift to be valid. Very great difficulty has been found with the meaning of this case but perhaps the best view, although this does not emerge clearly from the judgment, is that it could be justified at the time it was decided on the ground that a determinable interest such as that given to the cemetery company capable of determining at any time in the future was not then subject to the rule against perpetuities. *Re Chardon* was followed by Wynn-Parry J. on virtually identical facts in *Re Chambers Will Trusts*[44] but was distinguished by the same judge in *Re Wightwick's Will Trusts*.[45] The distinction in the latter case was made on the ground that there the gift contained a *trust* of income for an indefinite period for a non-charitable purpose and was, therefore, void as tending to a perpetuity, whereas there was no actual trust in *Re Chardon*. *Re Wightwick's Will Trusts* showed that there may have been yet another facet of the case—namely, whether or not there was a trust—which had to be taken into account. In view of the uncertain state of the law, even before the passing of the Perpetuities and Accumulations Act 1964, he was a brave man who relied on *Re Chardon*.[46] But this Act appears to have rendered this discussion academic by providing that a determinable interest is now to be subject to the perpetuity rule,[47] that is to say

---

[41] See *post*, p. 297.
[42] [1943] Ch. 277.
[43] [1928] Ch. 464.
[44] [1950] Ch. 267.
[45] [1950] Ch. 260.
[46] See generally W. O. Hart: (1937) 53 L.Q.R. 24; M. J. Albery: (1938) 54 L.Q.R. 258.
[47] Perpetuities and Accumulations Act 1964, s.12.

that the determining event must now take place no later than the end of the perpetuity period. While this provision would not render the gift void *ab initio*, any disposition of the income, whether express or implied, to take effect on the occurrence of the determining event would become void at the end of the perpetuity period. Consequently, by maintaining the graves until the end of the perpetuity period, the cemetery company would then acquire an absolute interest in the fund without any further obligations.[48]

4. *Gifts for the Benefit of Unincorporated Associations*

An unincorporated association has been defined as "two or more persons bound together for one or more common purposes, not being business purposes, by mutual undertakings each having mutual duties and obligations, in an organisation which has rules which identify in whom control of it and its funds rests and on what terms and which can be joined or left at will".[49] Because an unincorporated association is not a legal person, its property necessarily has to be vested in some or all of its members as trustees. Where its purposes are charitable, such trusts do not give rise to any difficulties. Charitable trusts have to comply neither with the requirement of certainty of objects, nor with the beneficiary principle, nor with the rule against perpetuities. All these requirements have to be satisfied, however, when the purposes of an unincorporated association are not charitable, giving rise to very considerable theoretical difficulties.

It was formerly thought that a gift of property to a non-charitable unincorporated association could only be construed in two possible ways. Both these constructions are still possible but have become uncommon; virtually all such gifts are now construed in accordance with a third possible construction enunciated by Cross J. in *Neville Estates* v. *Madden*[50] which has been considerably developed in subsequent decisions.

The first possibility was and is that the gift may be made to the members of the association at the date in question. Such a gift may be outright, in that title to the property in question passes immediately to the members as tenants in common or joint tenants, or may vest the property in trustees for the members as beneficial tenants in common or joint tenants. Either way, if they are tenants in common they can take their share while, if they are joint tenants, any member can sever his share and then claim it, whether or not he remains a member. Where such a trust exists, its objects must be sufficiently certain but it will

---

[48] See Underhill & Hayton: *Law of Trusts and Trustees* (14th ed. (1987) pp. 77–78.

[49] *Conservative and Unionist Central Office* v. *Burrell* [1982] 1 W.L.R. 522, *per* Lawton L.J. at p. 525. The case was concerned with the meaning of "unincorporated association" for the purposes of taxation legislation but this definition seems to be of general application. Underhill & Hayton, *Law of Trusts & Trustees*) (14th ed., (1987) at p. 80 questions whether it is in fact necessary that the association should be able to be joined and left at will on the basis that the existence of rules restricting membership should not negative the existence of an unincorporated association.

[50] [1962] Ch. 832.

clearly comply with the beneficiary principle and will not offend against the rule against perpetuities.[51] However, this construction is not without theoretical difficulties; any member who subsequently leaves will retain his share unless he assigns it to the other members with the appropriate formalities,[52] no member who subsequently joins will acquire any interest in the property in question and, where the members are tenants in common, the share of any member who dies will devolve according to his will or intestacy. In practice, these theoretical difficulties have generally been ignored.

The second possibility was and is that the gift is made by way of endowment for the unincorporated association. Such a gift necessarily has to take effect by way of trust. Any such endowment is likely to have been intended to be perpetual; consequently, the adoption of this construction will generally lead to the gift being held to be void for perpetuity.[53] However, if a trust has been established which satisfies the rule against perpetuities, it will undoubtedly be valid provided that its objects are sufficiently certain; such a trust will clearly satisfy the beneficiary principle by virtue of the decision in *Re Denley's Trust Deed*[54] (prior to that decision, it was sometimes thought that such trusts constituted one of the anomalous exceptions to the beneficiary principle[55]). Some trusts have been held to satisfy the rule against perpetuities on the grounds that they were intended to benefit only the existing members of the unincorporated association.[56] In principle, it must also be possible to satisfy the rule against perpetuities by expressly providing that the property is to be held on trust for the benefit of the unincorporated association until the end of the perpetuity period and then be held for some ascertained person (such as the estate of the donor) or some charitable purpose.

Apart from such exceptional cases, however, prior to the decision in *Neville Estates* v. *Madden* gifts to unincorporated associations were in practice only valid if the first possible construction was adopted; consequently, there was a presumption in favour of this construction. Where there was a gift "for the general purposes of the association", although those words appeared to seek to impose a perpetual trust which would consequently be void they could be disregarded by the court as having virtually no meaning so as to enable the first construction to be adopted.

---

[51] It is not particularly likely that a trust will be utilised if the intention of the donor is really only to benefit the existing members. The intention to exclude future members has been far from clear in some of the decided cases such as *Re Drummond* [1914] 2 Ch. 90, *Re Prevost* [1930] 2 Ch. 383 and *Re Turkington* [1937] 4 All E.R. 501; such cases would today probably be regarded as falling within the more recently developed third possible construction.

[52] Where a trust exists, writing will be required by virtue of Law of Property Act 1925, s.53(1)(*c*).

[53] *Re Macaulay's Estate* (1933) [1943] Ch. 435, *Leahy* v. *Attorney-General for New South Wales* [1959] A.C. 457.

[54] [1969] 1 Ch. 393.

[55] See *ante*, p. 120.

[56] *Re Drummond* [1914] 2 Ch. 90 was a case of this kind. These trusts might equally well be classified as falling within the first possible construction and, like such trusts, would today probably be regarded as falling within the third possible construction.

This was not, however, always possible. In *Leahy* v. *Attorney-General for New South Wales*[57] a ranch was left "upon trust for such order of nuns of the Catholic Church or the Christian Brothers as my executors and trustees shall select". This gift was prima facie valid as a gift to the individual members of the order chosen. However, the Privy Council held that the presumption was rebutted because of the improbability of a beneficial gift to the members of the order who happened to be alive at the date of the death of the testator and because of the nature of the property. As an intended endowment for the benefit of the order as a continuing society, the trust would therefore have been void for perpetuity but for a saving provision in a New South Wales statute.

The absence of any effective method of making gifts for the present and future members of unincorporated associations was hardly satisfactory and was eventually remedied by the enunciation in *Neville Estates* v. *Madden*[58] of a third possible construction. This is that there may be "a gift to the existing members not as joint tenants, but subject to their respective contractual rights and liabilities towards one another as members of the association. In such a case a member cannot sever his share. It will accrue to the other members on his death or resignation, even though such members include persons who became members after the gift took effect. If this is the effect of the gift, it will not now be open to objection on the score of perpetuity or uncertainty unless there is something in its terms or circumstances or in the rules of the association which precludes the members at any given time from dividing the subject of the gift between them on the footing that they are solely entitled to it in equity".[59] Thus the members of an unincorporated association have the possibility of enjoying rights in property in a new manner distinct from the traditional joint tenancy and tenancy in common (whether this is, strictly speaking, a form of co-ownership is not entirely clear). Where a gift to an unincorporated association is construed in this way, the property in question is held by some or all of the individual members (or, of course, by independent trustees) on trust to be applied in accordance with the contract between the members contained in the rules of the association. This apparently resolves the technical difficulties caused by the adoption of the first possible construction in that any member who leaves or dies will lose his share in the property of the association without any need for any formal disposition and any new member of the association will be able to enjoy the benefit of its property without any need for any transfer thereof (precisely how the statutory formal requirements of the Law of Property Act 1925 and the Wills Act 1837 are actually satisfied has never been made entirely clear; signed acceptance by each member of rules drafted in an appropriate form would presumably satisfy Section 53(1)(c) of the Law of Property Act 1925 but certainly would not satisfy the Wills Act 1837—the answer may be that by entering into the contract contained in the rules each member estops himself (and, after

---

[57] [1959] A.C. 457.
[58] [1962] Ch. 832.
[59] *Ibid.* at p. 849 (*per* Cross J.).

his death, his personal representatives) from relying on the absence of the statutory formalities to claim his proportion of the property of the association). The objects of trusts of this type must of course be sufficiently certain[60] but such trusts will clearly satisfy the beneficiary principle and will satisfy the rule against perpetuities provided that the members are entitled under the rules (if necessary as a result of exercising a power in the rules to change them) to bring the association to an end and to divide its property between themselves.

This construction has been adopted and developed on a number of occasions. In *Re Recher's Will Trusts*,[61] the testatrix left part of her residuary estate to a specified "Anti-Vivisection Society" (a non-charitable unincorporated association). Had the society not ceased to exist before her death, the gift would have been upheld as a non-charitable purpose trust. Brightman J. stated that, where the subscriptions of the members of an unincorporated association are held as an accretion to its funds to be applied in accordance with its rules, any gifts or legacies to the association will, in the absence of any words purporting to impose a trust, be held on the same basis. The rules of the association could be changed by the unanimous agreement of the members; therefore, it was irrelevant that it existed for the promotion of some purpose rather than for the benefit of the members themselves, since they could nevertheless vote to change the rules in order to abandon this purpose and to divide the assets between themselves. *Re Lipinski's Will Trusts*[62] concerned a gift to an unincorporated association "in memory of my late wife to be used solely in the work of constructing the new buildings for the association and/or improvement to the said buildings". The purpose specified was within the powers of the association and, despite the fact that the gift was to be used "solely" for this purpose, Oliver J. held that the members would not thereby be prevented from abandoning the specified purpose and instead dividing the assets between themselves. Consequently, the gift was valid as a non-charitable purpose trust for the benefit of the members of the association. In *News Group Newspapers* v. *SOGAT 82*[63] the local branches of the union were held to be unincorporated associations capable of seceding from the union and dissolving themselves; consequently, a sequestration order issued against the union did not apply to funds held by the local branches. Finally, in *Universe Tankships Inc of Morovia* v. *International Transport Workers Federation*,[64] it was held that a payment by shipowners into the Federation fund took effect as an accretion to that fund by way of outright gift rather than a contribution on trust (which would have been void); in the Court of Appeal,[65] Megaw L.J. emphasised that, even if there is no provision for the

---

[60] The trusts in question will almost inevitably be discretionary trusts and so will be governed by *McPhail* v. *Doulton* [1971] A.C. 424.
[61] [1972] Ch. 526.
[62] [1976] Ch. 235.
[63] [1986] I.C.R. 716.
[64] [1983] 1 A.C. 366.
[65] [1981] I.C.R. 129 at p. 159.

amendment of the rules of an association, they can nevertheless be "altered at will by the unanimous agreement of the contracting parties".

There is now a strong presumption that an unincorporated association holds its property in this way; gifts to unincorporated associations will now not normally be construed either as gifts to the members[66] or as gifts for the purposes of endowment. However, this third possible construction is not all-embracing. It can only be applied where there is a set of rules to provide the necessary contract between the members. This was emphasised by Lawton L.J. in *Conservative and Unionist Central Office* v. *Burrell*.[67] No such contract existed between the members of the religious orders in *Leahy* v. *Attorney-General for New South Wales*[68]; consequently, this construction could not have been adopted in that case so that the gift would clearly still be held to be an intended endowment and, but for statute, void for perpetuity. Further, the inability of the members to divide the assets between themselves will also prevent this construction from being adopted. In *Re Grant's Will Trusts*,[69] Vinelott J. held that a gift to "the Labour Party Property Committee for the benefit of the Chertsey Headquarters of the Chertsey and Walton Constituency Labour Party" could not be construed as a gift to the members of the Constituency Party. They did not have the power to alter their rules, which were under the control of the National Labour Party. Although this did not of itself give rise to any problems of perpetuity (because the rules provided, in the last resort, for a resulting trust for the original subscribers), the members were clearly unable to dispose of the property among themselves.[70] Consequently, and in any event, he held that the gift amounted to a trust for the purposes specified and not, as in *Re Lipinski's Will Trusts*,[71] a gift for the members of the Constituency Party for those purposes and for this reason was void for perpetuity. It has been suggested that the requirement that the members should be able to divide the property between themselves is unnecessary provided that they have the right "to ensure that the funds are used to pay for general expenses benefitting them as members".[72] However, the requirement clearly exists at present.

It should be noted that the way in which a gift to an unincorporated association is construed can have some effect on what happens to the assets of the association in the event of its dissolution. The general rule, clearly established in *Re Bucks Constabulary Fund Friendly Society (No. 2)*[73] is that the assets should be divided equally between the existing

---

[66] *Re Grant's Will Trusts* [1980] 1 W.L.R. 360 at p. 365.

[67] [1982] 1 W.L.R. 522 at p. 525.

[68] [1959] A.C. 457.

[69] [1980] 1 W.L.R. 360.

[70] The National Labour Party was entitled to alter the rules so as to require the property to be transferred to it.

[71] [1976] Ch. 235.

[72] Underhill & Hayton, *Law of Trusts and Trustees* (14th ed. (1987)) 84.

[73] [1979] 1 W.L.R. 936. This view expressed by Walton J. in this case is inconsistent with but generally regarded as preferable to the view expressed by Goff J. in *Re West Sussex Constabulary's Benevolent Fund Trusts* [1971] Ch. 1. It is also inconsistent with the more recent decision of Scott J. in *Davis* v. *Richards & Wallington Industries*. These cases are discussed *post* p. 202.

members at the time of its dissolution (the only exception to this rule is where the association has become moribund in that all or all but one of the members have resigned or died, in which case the assets go to the Crown as *bona vacantia*). Gifts to the association which, in accordance with *Re Recher's Will Trusts*,[74] have become part of the general assets of the association will clearly be treated in the same way. However, in the unlikely event that a gift to the association has taken effect as a valid trust by way of endowment, such a trust will necessarily be limited to take effect only within the perpetuity period and will therefore inevitably contain some provision as to what is to happen to the property thereafter; in such circumstances, this endowment property will presumably devolve in accordance with this provision in the event of the dissolution of the association.

Finally, where a gift is made to bodies which do not satisfy the definition of an unincorporated association because of the absence of the necessary mutual obligations contained in the rules, the gift will take effect by way of mandate or agency. In *Conservative and Unionist Central Office* v. *Burrell*,[75] where the Court of Appeal held that the Conservative Party was not an unincorporated association for the purposes of taxation legislation because of the absence of any contractual link between a contributor of funds and their recipient, Brightman L.J. characterised the recipient of the funds as the agent of the contributor to deal with the funds in accordance with the purpose or mandate for which the contribution was made. He said this[76]: "So far as the money is used within the scope of the mandate, the recipient discharges himself vis-à-vis the contributor. The contributor can at any time demand the return of his money so far as not spent, unless the mandate is irrevocable, as it might be or become in certain circumstances. But once the money is spent, the contributor can demand nothing back, only an account of the manner of expenditure. No trust arises, except the fiduciary relationship inherent in the relationship of principal and agent. If, however, the recipient were to apply the money for some purpose outside the scope of the mandate, clearly the recipient would not be discharged. The recipient could be restrained, like any other agent, from a threatened misapplication of the money entrusted to him, and like any other agent could be required to replace any money misapplied." This analysis is not without difficulties. Precisely who is the beneficial owner of the money until it is spent? Presumably the contributor unless and until the mandate becomes irrevocable by, for example, the money being mixed in the larger fund administered by the recipient. What happens if the mandate thereafter cannot be carried out or is carried out leaving a surplus? At first instance[77] Vinelott J. took the view that in such circumstances there would be an implied obligation to return the fund to the subscribers in proportion to their original contributions (anonymous gifts and contributions to raffles would

---

[74] [1972] Ch. 526.
[75] [1982] 1 W.L.R. 522.
[76] *Ibid.* at p. 529.
[77] [1980] 3 All E.R. 42 at pp. 63–64.

devolve as *bona vacantia*). Do the rights of the contributor survive a change in the identity of the person administering the fund? Finally, how can testamentary gifts be brought within the framework of mandate or agency when "no agency could be set up at the moment of death between a testator and his chosen agent"?[78] Whatever the answers to these questions, it is clear that there are considerable differences between the mandate or agency analysis and the treatment of gifts to unincorporated associations. It has been suggested that it might be appropriate for the mandate or agency theory to be extended to gifts to unincorporated associations which, according to the rules which have already been discussed, are void.[79] Whether the theory is extended in this, or indeed in any other, way obviously remains to be seen.

---

[78] [1982] 1 W.L.R. 522 at p. 530. Brightman L.J. thought that the answer to this problem was not difficult to find but no one else has yet succeeded in finding it (see P.St.J. Smart, [1987] Conv. 415).
[79] See P. Creighton, [1983] Conv. 150.

CHAPTER 4

DISCRETIONARY TRUSTS AND POWERS

I. THE CREATION OF DISCRETIONARY TRUSTS AND POWERS

1. *Generally*

ALMOST all trusts involve the exercise of a power or discretion by the trustees. In many cases this does not affect beneficial entitlement. So, depending on the circumstances of the particular trust, trustees will often have powers which include those to vary the investments of the trust[1]; to grant a lease of property which is subject to the trust[2]; to settle claims[3]; to apply income for the support of an infant beneficiary or to accumulate it[4]; to apply to the court for guidance as to the execution of the trust[5]; and to insure trust property.[6] Trustees or any other person designated in the trust instrument for this purpose may have other powers, such as those to remove trustees and to appoint new ones.[7] Indeed it is of the fundamental nature of a trust that a trustee is not a puppet at the end of a wire pulled by the settlor or the beneficiaries,[8] but is a person who is to exercise an independent judgment over a wide field.

The trustees' discretion need not, however, be limited to the administrative and other matters just indicated, but can extend to beneficial entitlement. Trustees can be given a power to select which of a group of persons shall receive any benefit at all from the trust. Alternatively, while the trust instrument may provide that each member of a class of

---

[1] See *post*, p. 431.
[2] Law of Property Act 1925, s.28; Settled Land Act 1925, s.41.
[3] Trustee Act 1925, s.15.
[4] See *post*, p. 483.
[5] See *post*, p. 393.
[6] Trustee Act 1925, s.19. The position is surprising. Trustees are under no duty to insure (*Re McEacharn* (1911) 103 L.T. 900) and the statutory power is only to insure for a sum up to three-quarters of the value of the property. Express powers of insuring usually allow the cover to be effected in the full reinstatement value.
[7] See *post*, p. 360.
[8] It is in this respect that the position of a trustee differs from that of a nominee, who is often under an express or implied contractual obligation to comply in all respects with the beneficiary's directions.

beneficiaries is to receive some benefit, the trustees may be given the power to determine how much each beneficiary will receive. Further, the trustees may have the power to decide whether to distribute income, or to accumulate it.[9] This chapter is generally concerned with considerations affecting the exercise of powers or discretions as to beneficial entitlements, but most of the principles will apply to the other powers and discretions which trustees are given.

2. *Reasons for Creating Discretionary Trusts and Powers*

Some of the reasons for creating trusts with discretionary provisions as to beneficial entitlement have already been mentioned.[10] A settlor or testator often wishes to make a present disposition but to confer a benefit at some time in the future according to circumstances. It may be that a person who is creating a trust for his children or grandchildren wishes the amount, if any, which each receives to depend on their conduct; their financial need; or their success. A much larger payment may be justified to a beneficiary who is an undergraduate or who is training for entry into a profession or vocation than his brother who is already well established in business. Or it may be that a person wishes to devote funds to charitable causes, but to allow the particular recipient to be selected according to the social or other need which seems most pressing at the time.

Apart from this, there are two general considerations. First, there is no suggestion that where there is a discretionary trust the objects *must* be treated unequally. So the father who creates a trust for his children leaves the trustees free to treat them all alike unless some special circumstance occurs. Secondly, the settlor is likely to be able to exercise *de facto* control over the exercise of the discretion. He has no legal rights as settlor[11] but he may have appointed himself to be one of the trustees. Even if he did not do so, he himself will usually have appointed the trustees, and they are likely to listen to his views. A discretionary trust is in practice often used as a method of divesting oneself of the ownership of property while still being able in practice to control its ultimate devolution.

3. *Taxation Considerations*

At the present time, tax reasons are often the most important for the creation of discretionary trusts. Income tax and capital gains tax are so-called "progressive taxes" in that they are imposed on the "slices" of a person's taxable income or capital gains at a progressively increasing

---

[9] See *post*, p. 483.

[10] *Ante*, p. 3.

[11] Generally, once a trust is created, the function of a settlor as such is fulfilled. Occasionally, however, in the case of the variation of a trust, his wishes will be taken into account: see *post*, p. 541.

rate. Each person is entitled to receive the first "slice" of his income free of tax.[12] The next "slice" is taxable at 20 per cent, the next "slice" at the basic rate of 25 per cent, and the residue at the higher rate of 40 per cent.[13] Capital gains tax is imposed at the same rate as income tax on such part of a person's taxable capital gains in each year as exceeds his annual exemption.[14] Inheritance tax, on the other hand, is imposed at a fixed rate of 40 per cent on such part of a person's estate (which for this purpose includes any property disposed of other than for value during the seven years immediately prior to his death) as exceeds his lifetime allowance.[15]

In terms of tax planning, a discretionary trust has three main advantages. First, the terms of the trust instrument usually allow the trustees to decide whether to distribute or withhold income. They can therefore distribute income to a beneficiary in a year when his total income is low, so that his total liability to tax is kept down, and withhold income when the beneficiary's total income is high. Secondly, the trust instrument usually allows the trustees to accumulate income, so that it becomes converted into capital.[16] Thirdly, a discretionary trust allows income and capital to be spread among members of a family, rather than being bunched in the hands of one member. Take a simple example. Suppose that Andrew, Basil and Colin are brothers and suppose, also, that Andrew's top rate of income tax is 40 per cent, that Basil's top rate of income tax is 25 per cent and that Colin, as a student, has no taxable income whatsoever. In principle,[17] if Andrew receives £1,000 of investment income, he would have to pay £400 income tax on it and be left with £600 in his pocket. If, however, the investment income arises in a discretionary trust and the trustees elect to pay £400 to Basil and £600 to Colin, Basil will pay £100 income tax and Colin will pay nothing (assuming in each case, of course, that the investment

---

[12] The amount of this "slice" is calculated by means of personal allowances, which vary according to the personal circumstances of the individual. For the year 1994–95, a single person is entitled to a personal allowance of £3,445; additional allowances are available to married persons, to single parents, to widows and widowers and to pensioners, in respect of dependant relatives and in certain other circumstances. The amounts of these allowances are reviewed annually in each Budget and listed in the Finance Act by means of which each Budget is brought into effect. Income tax is governed by the Income and Corporation Taxes Act 1988.

[13] In 1994–95, the first £3,000 of taxable income was taxed at 20 per cent, taxable income between £3,001 and £23,700 was taxed at 25 per cent and taxable income in excess of £23,700 at 40 per cent. The width of the bands and their thresholds are also reviewed annually in each Budget and listed in each Finance Act.

[14] In 1994–95, £5,800. There are many other exemptions, including the tax payer's main residence, chattels worth less than £6,000, and certain securities. Capital gains tax is governed by the Taxation of Chargeable Gains Act 1992.

[15] In 1994–95, £150,000. Further exemptions include small gifts of up to £3,000 per annum, gifts between spouses, gifts in consideration of marriage, gifts to charities and gifts of agricultural or business property. Inheritance Tax is governed by the Inheritance Tax Act 1984.

[16] See *post*, p. 487.

[17] This example is only given to illustrate the principle. The result is modified by a number of provisions of the income tax legislation.

income does not move his total taxable income into a higher "slice"). The family as a whole, therefore, now pays only £100 in tax, a reduction of £300.[18]

As a result of the widespread use of discretionary trusts in order to preserve income and capital for the benefit of the family, discretionary trusts in general have come under increasing fiscal attack. In relation to income tax, the income arising to a discretionary trust is in general taxed at a flat rate of 35 per cent rather than the lower rate applicable to trusts other than accumulation and discretionary trusts (20 per cent on income from company distributions, 25 per cent on income from other sources.[19] However, in the event that this income is distributed to the beneficiaries rather than accumulated, any beneficiary whose top rate of income tax is 25 per cent or less can recover the excess tax paid by the trust (thus a beneficiary with a top rate of 25 per cent can recover 10 per cent of the income tax paid on the sum distributed to him while a beneficiary with no taxable income at all can recover the whole of the 35 per cent tax paid on the sum distributed to him[20]). In relation to capital gains tax, any transfer *inter vivos* of property (other than cash or the settlor's main residence) to a discretionary trust is regarded as a disposal by the settlor.[21] It is therefore subject to capital gains tax on the difference between its acquisition cost[22] and its market value at the date of transfer in so far as the settlor's total capital gains for that year exceed his annual exemption; however, in certain limited circumstances[23] the settlor can elect to have the capital gain held over so that the trust takes over the property at its original acquisition cost, thus obviously increasing the capital gains tax paid later by the trust on any subsequent disposal[24] (at a flat rate of 35 per cent[25]). On the assumption that most settlors will have to pay capital gains tax at the higher rate of 40 per cent, the transfer of property to a discretionary trust is unlikely significantly to increase the total capital gains tax payable, which can in fact be substantially reduced if the settlor takes full advantage of his annual exemptions. In relation to inheritance tax, any transfer, whether *inter vivos* or testamentary, of any property to a discretionary trust is

---

[18] However, in practice, the administration expenses of the discretionary trust must also be taken into account.

[19] Income and Corporation Taxes Act 1988, s.686 (as amended by Finance Act 1993).

[20] This will not necessarily enable the recovery of all the income tax paid by the trust because any income expended on administration expenses will not be able to be distributed and so the tax paid in respect of these expenses will not be able to be recovered (see *post*, p. 411).

[21] Taxation of Chargeable Gains Act 1992, s.70.

[22] Its market value on March 31, 1982 or, if acquired subsequently, its original acquisition cost.

[23] If the assets settled comprise business property (Taxation of Chargeable Gains Act 1992, s.75) or if the creation of the trust involves a chargeable transfer for the purposes of inheritance tax.

[24] The exemption for trusts is one half of that of individuals, thus £2,900 in 1993–94.

[25] The rate of income tax paid by accumulation and discretionary trusts (other trusts pay 20 per cent on income from company distributions and 25 per cent on income from other sources).

subject to inheritance tax[26] (paid at 20 per cent rather than the usual 40 per cent in the case of transfers *inter vivos*) if the total transfers of property in the previous seven years exceed the settlor's lifetime allowance. A further charge to inheritance tax is made on every tenth anniversary of the creation of the discretionary trust at 30 per cent of the inheritance tax which would have been payable had the property been transferred at that time,[27] the appropriate proportion of this ten-yearly charge being payable when any property is disposed of.[28] However, no additional inheritance tax will in fact be payable by virtue of these provisions if the settlor settles no more than the total amount of his lifetime allowance in each seven year period.

There is no doubt that discretionary trusts are treated more harshly than other settlements but the overall tax payable in respect of a discretionary trust still remains less than that payable by a tax payer with a top rate of 40 per cent and will be considerably less if full advantage is taken of the annual capital gains tax exemption and the amount settled is limited to each settlor's lifetime allowance. Further, the legislature has given privileged treatment to a special type of discretionary trust, known as an accumulation and maintenance settlement.[29] Such a settlement must be for the benefit of one or more children, usually the children or grandchildren of the settlor, who must be entitled to the trust property or to an immediate vested interest in its income upon reaching an age not exceeding 25; in the meantime, the income can either be accumulated or be applied for the maintenance, education or benefit of the children. Such trusts are not liable to any of the additional charges to inheritance tax outlined above; inheritance tax will therefore only be payable in the normal way on the death of the settlor in so far as his estate (including any property disposed of other than for value in the preceding seven years) exceeds his lifetime allowance. Further, save in the case of minor children of the settlor, income applied for the maintenance, education or benefit of the children is taxed at the top rate of the beneficiary in question. However, such trusts can only last for 25 years unless all the beneficiaries have a common grandparent.

Man goes to considerable lengths to preserve his wealth and the device of a discretionary trust remains a popular way of doing so, particularly if full advantage is taken of all exemptions and allowances. However, where the property to be settled very greatly exceeds the settlor's lifetime allowance, there has been an increasing use of discretionary trusts formed in other jurisdictions whose trust law is either based on English law[30] or has been specifically adapted to embrace the English concept of a trust.[31] The problems which the creation of a non-

---

[26] Inheritance Tax Act 1984, ss.2, 3 (1).

[27] Inheritance Tax Act 1984, ss.61, 64.

[28] Inheritance Tax Act 1984, s.65.

[29] Inheritance Tax Act 1984, s.71.

[30] Such as the Channel Islands, the Isle of Man, Bermuda, the Bahamas, the Cayman Islands, and a number of other Caribbean tax havens.

[31] Such as Liechtenstein.

resident settlement involves for a person domiciled and resident in some part of the United Kingdom are discussed in a later Chapter.[32]

II. THE BASIC TOOLS: TRUSTS AND POWERS

1. *Generally*

Where it is left to the trustees or indeed to some other person to decide whether a particular individual shall receive a benefit from the trust at all, or to decide the extent of the benefit of any particular beneficiary, the discretion vested in the trustees or other person will be one of two broad types, depending on whether or not they are under an obligation to exercise it.

If they are under an obligation to exercise it, then they are said to hold a trust power, or a power in the nature of a trust. It is important to note that these terms have traditionally been used to denote two quite distinct situations: first, where the person subject to the obligation has the property in question vested in him as a trustee, in which case the term trust power or power in the nature of a trust is virtually indistinguishable from the term discretionary trust—indeed in the leading case of *McPhail* v. *Doulton*,[33] the two terms were used interchangeably; secondly, where the person subject to the obligation is not himself a trustee of the property in question so that his only role is that of exercising the discretion, in which case, although he may be described as the donee of a trust power or a power in the nature of a trust, he certainly cannot be described as a discretionary trustee since he is not a trustee of anything. If a person is holding property on trust for such of the members of a defined class and in such proportions as *he* shall in his absolute discretion appoint, then he is likely to be held to hold a trust power or a power in the nature of a trust in the former sense; he is in effect a discretionary trustee. If, on the other hand, a person is holding property on trust for such of the members of a defined class and in such proportions as *a third party* shall in his absolute discretion appoint, the third party is likely to be held to have a trust power or a power in the nature of a trust in the latter sense; he is not a trustee of anything and no discretion whatsoever is vested in the person who is holding the property on trust. There is no practical significance in this distinction. In each of the two cases, the holder of the trust power is under an obligation to exercise it and, in the event that he fails to do so, the court will exercise it instead. All that is important is to remember that there is no requirement that the holder of a trust power should himself be a trustee of the property in question.

If the trustees or other person are not under any obligation to exercise the discretion vested in them, then they are said to hold a mere power or, less commonly, a power collateral.[34] Once again these terms cover

---

[32] See *post*, p. 559.

[33] [1971] A.C. 424.

[34] See *Vestey* v. *I.R.C. (No. 2)* [1979] Ch. 198 *per* Megarry J. at p. 206 (affirmed on other grounds in *Vestey* v. *I.R.C. (Nos. 1&2)* [1979] A.C. 1148) and *Re Hay's Settlement Trusts* [1982] 1 W.L.R. 202 *per* Megarry V.C. at p. 210.

two quite distinct situations, identified much more recently[35]: first, where the donee of the mere power holds that power in his capacity as a trustee (either because he is a trustee of the property which is to be appointed or where this is not the case but it is nevertheless apparent that the power has been given to him as a trustee[36]), in which case he is said to be a fiduciary donee; secondly, where the donee of the mere power is not a trustee in any sense, in which case he is said to be a non-fiduciary donee. If a person is holding property on trust for such of the members of a class and in such proportions as *he* may in his absolute discretion appoint and, in default of any such appointment, on trust for an identified beneficiary, he is likely to be held to be a fiduciary donee of a mere power. If, on the other hand, a person is holding property on trust for such of the members of a class and in such proportions as *a third party* may in his absolute discretion appoint and, in default of any such appointment, on trust for an identified beneficiary, the third party is likely to be held to be a non-fiduciary donee of a mere power. This distinction is extremely significant. Although a fiduciary donee of a mere power is under no obligation to exercise it, he does owe certain obligations towards the objects of the power (as well as a duty to those entitled in default of appointment not to misuse the power) and is "to some extent subject to the control of the courts in relation to its exercise".[37] In particular, he must consider periodically whether or not he should exercise the power (in default, the court may direct him to do so and, in the last resort, may remove or replace him), consider the range of objects of the power, consider the appropriateness of individual appointments and, above all, is not entitled to release the power so as to cause the property to pass to those entitled in default of appointment. On the other hand, a non-fiduciary donee of a mere power owes no obligations whatever to the objects of the power (his only duty, owed to those entitled in default of appointment, is not to misuse the power); in particular, he does not even have to consider whether to exercise the power and may release it at any time and consequently cause the property to pass to those entitled in default of appointment.

Thus, the first and crucial question is whether the trustees or other person are obliged to exercise the power in question. If the answer to that question is affirmative, then the only remaining matter is in whose favour it should be exercised, either by the donee of the power or, if he fails to do so, by the court. If, on the other hand, the answer to that question is negative, it is necessary to consider whether the donee of

---

[35] In *Mettoy Pension Trustees* v. *Evans* [1990] 1 W.L.R. 1587 at p. 1614 (not the first enunciation of the distinction but the first fully developed statement of the remedies available against a fiduciary donee of a mere power). See generally S. Gardner, 107 L.Q.R. (1991) 214.

[36] In *Mettoy Pension Trustees* v. *Evans supra*, a company held a power to appoint any surplus in its pension fund, which was actually vested in a separate trustee company, in favour of the pensioners with a gift over in default of appointment to itself. The liquidators of the company wished to release this power and so enable the surplus to become available for its creditors. Warner J. held that it was a fiduciary power and so could not be released.

[37] *Mettoy Pension Trustees* v. *Evans* [1990] 1 W.LR. 1587 at p. 1614.

the power is a fiduciary or a non-fiduciary; only in the former case is there any possibility of the court intervening in the event that the donee himself fails to exercise his power and even then the role of the court will be limited to ensuring that the fiduciary has complied with his duty to consider periodically whether or not to exercise the power.

2. *The Distinction between Trust Powers and Mere Powers*

It is now proposed to consider the distinction between trust powers and mere powers more closely. While powers are most frequently found as provisions in trust instruments, they can exist outside a trust, and it is therefore necessary to consider a power as a separate concept. A power can be said to be the right to exercise, in respect of property belonging to another, one or more of the rights which are the normal incidents of ownership. Some differences are immediately apparent. For example, a trust is necessarily equitable: a power may or may not be. Thus a power of attorney to convey the legal estate is legal. So is a power of sale of the legal estate exercisable by a mortgagee. On the other hand a power affecting beneficial entitlement is now necessarily equitable.[38] But, as has been said, the primary basis of the distinction is that a trust is imperative; a power is not. The distinction is shown by contrasting a trust for sale and a power of sale. If land is given by will to trustees on *express trust* for sale, then, because there is a binding obligation to sell, the land will be converted, in the eyes of the law (even if not in fact converted), into money as soon as the will takes effect, *i.e.* on the testator's death. This is still the position even if a power to postpone sale is contained in the trust instrument and the power of postponement is exercised: the duty to convert is nevertheless regarded as an imperative one. The same considerations apply to an express trust for sale created in a deed *inter vivos*, in which case the land will be treated as money as soon as the deed is executed. On the other hand, if there is merely a *power* of sale, whether in a will or a deed, the land will only be converted into money when the power itself is exercised, and the person in whom the power is vested will not be compelled to exercise it.

The question whether or not a trust or a power has been created is essentially one of construction of the instrument. The distinction may be a fine one in any individual case, because the trust instrument may give what on the face of it appears to be a mere power, but which is in fact a trust power. Although trust powers appear as powers, they are construed and take effect as trusts.

The question, therefore, is, when is a power a trust power? The question is ultimately decided, as will be seen, by extracting, from the actual words used, the real intention of the settlor. But although it is, in the last analysis, a question of construction, certain preliminary general principles are clear:

(A) A *general* power of appointment is incapable by its nature of being a trust power. A general power confers on the donee of the power a power to appoint amongst whomsoever he pleases, including the

---

[38] L.P.A. 1925, s.1(7).

donee himself. Since the donee can appoint to himself beneficially, the court cannot compel an appointment elsewhere or indeed at all. A *special* power of appointment (that is, a power to appoint among designated persons or classes of persons) is, however, capable of taking effect as a trust power. The much more recently developed *hybrid* or intermediate power, that is a power "betwixt and between,"[39] neither strictly general nor special, such as a power to appoint to anybody other than the donee himself,[40] is regarded as a general power for some purposes and a special power for others[41]; it is, however, difficult to see how such a power could possibly take effect as a trust power since, as in the case of a general power, there is no one in whose favour the court can compel appointment.

(B) If there is a gift over in default of appointment (that is, if there is an alternative gift in the event of the donee of the power failing to exercise it), the "power" cannot be a trust power. A gift over is incompatible with the imperative duties of a trust and operates as a denial of its existence. For example, in *Re Mills*,[42] a power was given to appoint among children and remoter issue who in the opinion of the donee of the power should evidence a desire to maintain the family fortune. There then followed a gift elsewhere in default of appointment. The Court of Appeal held that because there was a gift over, the power did not operate as a trust.

However, a residuary gift (that is, a gift of that part of the testator's property which has not been specifically devised or bequeathed) is not a gift over for this purpose, so the presence of a residuary gift will not of necessity deprive the power of the character of a trust. Accordingly, in *Re Brierley*[43] a testator gave his wife a life interest in £50,000. He also gave her the power to bequeath or appoint amongst such of her relatives or next-of-kin as she thought proper. She was also given the residue of her husband's estate absolutely. The wife released and thereby purported to extinguish the power of appointment and claimed the whole £50,000 as her own beneficially under the gift of residue. The court held that this was not possible: a gift of residue was totally different from a gift over of *specific* property which is the subject of the power of appointment.

The gift over must also be *in default of appointment*, in order to prevent a trust power being deduced. If, therefore, the gift over is to take effect in the event of failure of the appointees or their not attaining a specific age, the power is still capable of being a trust power.[44]

---

[39] *Re Gestetner Settlement* [1953] Ch. 672 at p. 685.
[40] As in *Re Park* [1932] 1 Ch. 580. See also *Re Jones* [1945] Ch. 105 (power to appoint to anybody being a person and not a corporation); *Blausten* v. *I.R.C.* [1972] Ch. 256; *Re Manisty's Settlement* [1974] Ch. 17; *Re Hay's Settlement Trusts* [1982] 1 W.L.R. 202. In such cases there may be a power to introduce members to a class of beneficiaries, with certain exceptions.
[41] Such a power is a special power for the purposes of the Wills Act 1837, s.21 and the Perpetuities and Accumulations Act 1964, s.7.
[42] [1930] 1 Ch. 654.
[43] (1894) 43 W.R. 36.
[44] *Re Llewellyn's Settlement* [1921] 2 Ch. 281.

(C) If there is no gift over in default of appointment, there may or may not be a trust power. It is entirely a question of construction whether or not it is: it depends on the real intention of the settlor extracted from the words used in the instrument,[45] as the following cases show. For example, on one side of the line, in *Burrough* v. *Philcox*,[46] the testator directed that, after certain contingencies had been fulfilled, property was to be held in trust for his two children for life, with remainder to their issue, and declared that if they should both die without issue, the survivor should have power to dispose by will of the property among his nephews, nieces and children as he should think fit. The testator's children in fact died without issue and without any appointment having been made by the survivor. It was held that a *trust* was created in favour of the testator's nephews and nieces and their children: the trust was simply subject to a power of selection vested in the surviving child. Lord Cottenham stated the principle in these words: "Where there appears a general intention in favour of a class, and a particular intention in favour of individuals of a class to be selected by another person, and the particular intention fails from that selection not having been made, the court will carry into effect the general intention in favour of the class."[47] And, assuming the power is not exercised, if it is in favour of his relations generally and a *trust* is deduced in their favour, the trust takes effect in favour of the settlor's statutory next-of-kin.[48]

Burrough v. *Philcox* was a case where there was no gift over in default of appointment. But it must be emphasised that it does not necessarily follow from the absence of a gift over that the implication of a trust is automatically to be made. It is evident from other decisions that a trust will not be implied unless there is, upon a true construction, an indication in the instrument of a clear intention to benefit the designated person or class or in any event with only a mere power of selection conferred. Thus, in *Re Weekes' Settlement*,[49] there was a gift to the testatrix's husband for life in certain real property, with "power to dispose of all such property by will amongst our children." There was no gift over in default of appointment, and the power of appointment was not exercised in favour of the children. Romer J. held that the power gave to the husband a mere power, not one coupled with a trust, and accordingly there was no gift to the children by implication. The judge pointed out that there was no gift to such of the class as the husband might appoint—as there was, in effect, in *Burrough* v. *Philcox*[50]—but merely a bare power to appoint amongst a class. Similarly, in *Re Combe*[51] a life interest in property was given to the son of the testator and, after his death, the property was to be held "in trust for such

---

[45] Extrinsic evidence, including that of the testator's intention, may be admitted in certain cases: see A.J.A. 1982, s.21; and see *ante*, p. 92, n. 48.

[46] (1840) 5 Myl. & Cr. 72.

[47] *Ibid.* at p. 92.

[48] *Re Scarisbrick's Will Trusts* [1951] Ch. 622, C.A.; *Re Baden's Deed Trusts (No. 2)* [1973] Ch. 9 at p. 30, *per* Stamp L.J.

[49] [1897] 1 Ch. 289.

[50] *Supra.*

[51] [1925] Ch. 21.0.

person or persons as my said son shall appoint but . . . such appointment must be confined to any relation of mine of the whole blood." Again there was no gift over in default of appointment. It was held that the words quoted created a mere power and not a trust. There was nothing in the words of the will, according to Tomlin J., for importing into it something that was not there. The principle of both these cases was applied in the more recent decision in *Re Perowne*.[52] Here the testratrix gave all her estate to her husband for life and also added these words: "Knowing that he will make arrangements for the disposal of my estate, according to my wishes, for the benefit of my family." The husband did in fact make an appointment but this was void; and the question arose whether, since the power had not been effectively exercised, a trust in favour of the family or a mere power to appoint in their favour had been created. Harman J. refused to spell a trust out of the words used and held they gave a mere power to distribute among the large and indefinite class in question.

It can be seen from these cases that the question is one of construction, whether or not the settlor has shown an intention to benefit the objects of the power. And the absence of a gift over in default of appointment is an argument, and no more, that that was the settlor's intention: it does not raise a necessary inference that a trust was intended. And because it is a question of construction the solution of the problem may depend on "a few words" and "mere straws in the wind."[53]

That this is inescapable in matters of construction is demonstrated by the leading case of *McPhail* v. *Doulton*.[54] The deed in question in this case provided that the trustees should apply the net income in making payments at their absolute discretion "to or for the benefit of any of the officers and employees or ex-officers or ex-employees of the company or to any relatives or dependants of any such persons in such amounts or on such conditions (if any) as they think fit." One question was whether the clause prescribed a trust power or a mere power. At first instance Goff J.[55] held that it created a mere power; the Court of Appeal[56] by a majority held likewise; but the House of Lords[57] unanimously held that it was a trust power and accordingly took effect as a trust: the clearly expressed scheme of the deed pointed to a mandatory construction. But bearing in mind, no doubt, the differing judicial opinions expressed in the various stages of the case, Lord Wilberforce said[58]:

"It is striking how narrow and in a sense artifical is the distinction, in cases such as the present, between trusts, or as the particular

---

[52] [1951] Ch. 785.
[53] *Re Baden's Deed Trusts* [1969] 2 Ch. 388 at p. 398, *per* Harman L.J. For a formulation of rules for construction, see *Re Leek* [1967] Ch. 1061 at p. 1073, *per* Buckley J.
[54] [1971] A.C. 424.
[55] [1967] 1 W.L.R. 1457.
[56] [1969] 2 Ch. 126. Russell L.J. dissented.
[57] [1971] A.C. 424.
[58] *Ibid.* at p. 448.

type of trust is called, trust powers, and powers. It is only necessary to read the learned judgments in the Court of Appeal to see that what to one mind may appear as a power of distribution coupled with a trust to dispose of the undistributed surplus, by accumulation or otherwise, may to another appear as a trust for distribution coupled with a power to withhold a portion and accumulate or otherwise dispose of it. A layman and, I suspect, also a logician would find it hard to understand what difference there is."

In the Court of Appeal in *McPhail* v. *Doulton*,[59] the majority held that in cases where the considerations were evenly balanced in arriving at one or other construction, the court was at liberty to lean towards the construction which might effectuate rather than frustrate the settlor's intentions.[60] In other words, the court could take account of the legal consequences of any given interpretation; in particular if, according to the rules of certainty which were then thought to apply, the instrument was construed as a trust it might fail, but if it was construed as a power it might prevail, then the court would lean in favour of a power. This approach did not fall to be considered in the House of Lords in *McPhail* v. *Doulton*,[61] because it was there held that the same test of certainty applies to trust powers as to mere powers. But the point could still possibly be significant because trust powers and mere powers were not assimilated for other purposes.

3. *The Distinction between Fiduciary and Non-Fiduciary Donees of Mere Powers*

The recently consolidated distinction between fiduciary and non-fiduciary donees of mere powers is certainly not new[62] but its earlier enunciations clearly did not commend themselves to Lord Upjohn who, as recently as 1969, felt able in *Re Gulbenkian's Settlement Trusts*[63] to deny that the donees of mere powers of appointment ever owed any duties to the objects of those powers. However, in *McPhail* v. *Doulton*[64] Lord Wilberforce remarked, foreshadowing the subsequent decision in *Mettoy Pension Trustees* v. *Evans*,[65] that a "trustee of an employees' benefit fund, whether given a power or a trust power, is still a trustee and he would surely consider in either case that he has a fiduciary duty", adding that it would be "a complete misdescription of his position to say that, if what he has is a power unaccompanied by an imperative trust to distribute, he cannot be controlled by the court unless he exercised it capriciously, or outside the field permitted by the trust". These remarks set the scene for the authoritative statement of the

---

[59] [1969] 2 Ch. 126 (*sub nom. Re Baden's Deed Trusts*).
[60] On the principle of *ut res magis valeat quam pereat*.
[61] [1971] A.C. 424.
[62] See the authorities cited by S. Gardner, 107 L.Q.R. (1991) 214.
[63] [1970] A.C. 508 at pp. 521, 524–525.
[64] [1971] A.C. 424 at p. 449.
[65] [1990] 1 W.L.R. 1587.

distinction by Megarry V.C. in *Re Hay's Settlement Trusts*.[66] Having
stated that normally a trustee is not bound to exercise a mere power and
that the court will not compel him to do it, he continued: "That,
however, does not mean that he can simply fold his hands and ignore it,
for normally he must from time to time consider whether or not to
exercise the power, and the court may direct him to do this. . . .
Whereas a person who is not in a fiduciary position is free to exercise
the power in any way that he wishes, unhampered by fiduciary duties,
a trustee to whom, as such, a power is given is bound by the duties of
his office in exercising that power to do so in a responsible manner
according to its purpose. It is not enough for him to refrain from acting
capriciously; he must do more. He must 'make such a survey of the
range of objects or possible beneficiaries' as will enable him to carry out
his fiduciary duty. He must find out 'the permissible area of selection
and then consider responsibly, in individual cases, whether a
contemplated beneficiary was within the power and whether, in
relation to the possible claimants, a particular grant was appropriate'".[67]

This statement established a clear distinction between a mere power
held by the trustees of the property in question and a mere power held
by a third party. It also established that there was some significance in
the distinction in that the court could direct the trustees to consider
whether or not to exercise their power; this in turn leads to the further
conclusion, already enunciated in two earlier judgments,[68] that a refusal
to follow such a direction from the court might well lead to the replacement of the existing trustees. It has now been established that a donee
of a mere power may be classified as fiduciary even if he is not a trustee
of the property in question. In *Mettoy Pension Trustees* v. *Evans*,[68A] a
company held a power to appoint any surplus in its pension fund,
which was actually vested in a separate trustee company, in favour of
the pensioners with a gift over in default of appointment to itself. The
company having become insolvent, its liquidators sought to release this
power so that the surplus could immediately vest in the company and
be made available for the general creditors. Warner J. held that the
company held this mere power as a fiduciary; consequently, as will be
seen later in this Chapter,[69] he held that not only could the power not be
released but all the remedies available to the court to enforce discretionary trusts were also available in the case of mere powers held by
fiduciary donees. For what reasons did he conclude that the company
held this power as a fiduciary?

Two main reasons were adduced in support of this conclusion. First,
that the inclusion of the power in the rules of the pension fund was
quite pointless unless its donee was a fiduciary—since the company
could have made such payments to its pensioners even if it had been

---

[66] [1982] 1 W.L.R. 202 at pp. 209–210.
[67] The quotations come from the speech of Lord Wilberforce in *McPhail* v. *Doulton* [1971]
A.C. 424 at pp. 449, 457.
[68] *Re Gestetner* [1953] Ch. 672 at p. 688, *Re Manisty's Settlement* [1974] Ch. 17 at p. 25.
[68A] [1990] 1 W.L.R. 1587.
[69] See *post*, p. 151.

absolutely entitled to the surplus, a non-fiduciary power would have added nothing. Secondly, that the pensioners were not volunteers, in that it was unlikely that the surplus had arisen solely as a result of over-contribution on the part of the company and, in any event, the existence of the power and the expectation that its utilisation in their favour would be the subject of proper consideration had undoubtedly formed part of the overall scheme which the employees had contracted to obtain. This conclusion has been described as "not overwhelming" and "perhaps swayed by a deeper-lying consideration", namely that, if the donees of such powers are not held to be fiduciaries, "the surpluses to which they apply will in practice fall to companies' creditors and successful take-over predators".[70]

Whether or not the basis of the classification adopted in *Mettoy Pension Trustees* v. *Evans* was indeed the special nature of pension funds and the recent public concern about the security of pension schemes, there seems little doubt, particularly in the light of the wholly novel remedies which that decision has made available to the court, that there will be many future attempts to classify as fiduciaries donees of mere powers who are not trustees of the property in question. It remains to be seen whether powers relating to pension funds come to be regarded as a special case or whether the classification and the remedies adopted in *Mettoy Pension Trustees* v. *Evans* are extended more generally. If they are, the traditional distinctions between trust powers and mere powers may require some reconsideration.

4. *The Requirement of Certainty*

As has already been seen in the previous Chapter,[71] the basic test for certainty of objects is now the same for discretionary trusts, trust powers, powers in the nature of a trust, and mere powers. The only possible continuing distinction relates to the question of the applicability of the requirement of administrative unworkability to mere powers. Prior to the decision in *Mettoy Pension Trustees* v. *Evans*,[72] it seemed tolerably clear that the concept of administrative unworkability did not apply to mere powers.[73] However, now that that decision has upheld the adaption of the remedies available for the enforcement of discretionary trusts, trust powers and powers in the nature of a trust to mere powers held by fiduciaries, it has been suggested[74] that this may cause the concept of administrative unworkability also to be applied to this type of mere power. It obviously remains to be seen whether this is yet another consequence of this important decision.

---

[70] S. Gardner, 107 L.Q.R. [1991] 214 at pp. 215–216, also citing *Re Courage Group's Pension Schemes* [1987] 1 W.L.R. 495 and *Imperial Group Pension Trust* v. *Imperial Tobacco* [1991] 1 W.L.R. 589. Now see also *Re William Makin & Sons* [1993] B.C.C. 435.

[71] See *ante*, p. 98.

[72] [1990] 1 W.L.R. 1587.

[73] See *ante*, p. 108.

[74] By S. Gardner, 107 L.Q.R. (1991) 214 at pp. 218–219.

III. Powers of Appointment, and Other Powers and Discretions

Having considered the conceptual distinction between a trust and a power, it is now possible to consider certain practical aspects of the distinction. The types of device which may be encountered are:

    (*a*) powers of appointment;
    (*b*) other powers and discretions; and
    (*c*) discretionary trusts.

The distinction between, on the one hand, powers of appointment and, on the other hand, other powers and discretions, will be considered in this section (discretionary trusts will be dealt with later[75]).

In some cases, the classification is not straightforward. For example, in *Bond* v *Pickford*[76] the trustees were given power to "apply capital for the benefit of any one or more of the beneficiaries . . . by . . . allocating or appropriating to such beneficiary such sum or sums out of or investments forming part of the capital of the trust fund" as they thought fit. Nourse J held that this power of "allocation or appropriation" was akin to a limited special power of appointment.

Where there exists a power to decide which of the members of a group shall derive benefit from a fund, that power may be a power of appointment; or it may be another type of power, usually called a discretion. This distinction has nothing to do with that between trust powers and mere powers, and, in principle, both powers of appointment and discretions may be either trust powers or mere powers. Nevertheless, there are three important differences between powers of appointment and discretions:

    (*a*) With regard to income a power of appointment governs, strictly, money to arise or to become payable in the future, whereas a discretion deals with funds which are already in hand. The analogy is that of the railway where each wagon represents a payment. The exercise of a power of appointment in favour of a beneficiary is like setting the points towards a particular track. In itself, that does not cause a wagon to pass down the track, but when the trains come then so long as the points remain set in that direction (or while the appointment remains unrevoked), all trains (or income) will go to that destination (or beneficiary) automatically, and without any further action, or decision, being taken. The exercise of a discretion on the other hand is like the operation of a marshalling yard, where the wagons are already under the control of the marshaller, and he has to make a separate decision in respect of each wagon, by deciding to which of the several tracks it will go.

        This distinction is particularly important in respect of income.

---

[75] *Post*, p. 150.
[76] [1982] STC 403; (*The Times*, C.A., May 24, 1983).

If income is subject to a power of appointment, then, once the appointment is made, all income will go to the appointee without any further decision being necessary. In the case of a discretion, however, a separate decision must be taken every time any income is available for distribution. This was shown clearly in *Wilson v Turner.*[77] In that case the trustees had a power to pay or apply income arising from the trusts to or for the maintenance of an infant beneficiary.[78] They did not make a conscious decision on each occasion but merely handed over the income to the infant's father. The Court of Appeal held that the money should be repaid to the trust fund. If, however, the trustees had from time to time actively considered the merits of the case, and had consciously decided to apply the income for the maintenance of that infant, their decision would have been valid.[79]

The distinction as it applies to income is of crucial importance in respect of inheritance tax. It will be seen[80] that the charge to inheritance tax on settled property depends on whether or not a beneficiary has an interest in possession in that property. Where there is an appointment of income in favour of a beneficiary, that beneficiary has an interest in possession, even if the appointment is revocable. A beneficiary who is only entitled to income on the exercise of the trustees' discretion does not have an interest in possession.

(b) The second difference between a power of appointment and a discretion is in relation to formalities. Although in principle no formality is necessary for the exercise of a power of appointment, in practice some formality is almost always prescribed in the instrument by which the power is conferred. Where this is so, considerable importance is placed on the formal requisites. So, if a power of appointment is to be exercised by deed, it cannot be exercised by will,[81] and a power to be exercised by will cannot be exercised by any instrument which is not a will.[82] If however, the donor not only specifies the type of instrument by which the power is to be exercised, such as a deed or will, but specifies particular formalities to be observed in the execution of that instrument, such as requiring six witnesses, these stipulations are sometimes modified by statute. Section 159 of the Law of Property Act 1925 provides that in the case of a power to be exercised by deed, the exercise will be formally valid if the deed is executed in the presence of at least two witnesses, while, in the case of a power to be exercised by will, the exercise will be

---

[77] (1883) 22 Ch.D. 521.

[78] As to the statutory power of maintenance, see *post*, p. 490.

[79] A further example of the same principle is *Re Greenwood* ((1911) 105 L.T. 509), considered *post*, p. 390.

[80] See *post*, p. 420.

[81] *Lord Darlington* v. *Pulteney* (1797) 3 Ves.Jr. 384; *Lady Cavan* v. *Doe* (1795) 6 Bro.P.C. 175; *Re Phillips* (1884) 41 Ch.D. 417.

[82] *Reid* v *Shergold* (1805) 10 Ves.Jr. 370; *Re Evered* [1910] 2 Ch. 147.

formally valid if it complies with the provisions of the Wills
Acts.[83]

As a further exception to the general principle that formal
requirements must be strictly observed, just as equity will in
certain cases perfect an imperfect gift[84] so in somewhat similar
cases equity will perfect an imperfect exercise of a power. These
will be, broadly, where the donee of the power intended to
exercise it, and the exercise was to satisfy a moral obligation.[85]

By contrast, no formality is required for the exercise of a
discretion, for the discretion is exercised at the moment when
those exercising it reach their decision.[86] In general, therefore,
the exercise of a power of appointment requires a physical act,
while the exercise of a discretion is a metaphysical act.

Questions of formality are not to be confused, however, with
any requirement to obtain the consent of any person. The
exercise both of a power of appointment and of a discretion can
be made subject to consents being obtained, and any purported
exercise without those consents will be ineffective.

(c) The third difference between powers of appointment and
discretions relates to revocability. When a discretion is exercised,
its effect is to confer upon the beneficiary a right to a sum which
is in hand. The beneficiary has the right to demand payment, and
payment is in fact usually made to him promptly. It is then too
late for the person exercising his discretion to seek to change his
mind, and to recall the money.[87] On the other hand, because a
power of appointment looks towards the future, it can be
expressed to be revocable, and, subject to the terms of the
instrument by which it was conferred, the appointment can be
revoked and a new appointment made without limit.[88]

It will be appreciated that a discretion and a revocable power
of appointment can both be used to achieve the same general
effect. For example, suppose there is a fund of income which for
the year 1995 is to go to Charles; for 1996 to go to Douglas; and for
1997 to go to Edward. If there is a revocable power of appointment, at the beginning of 1995 the income can be appointed to
Charles; at the beginning of 1996 the appointment can be
revoked, and a new appointment made in favour of Douglas; and
at the beginning of 1997 the appointment can again be revoked
and a new appointment made in favour of Edward. On the other

---

[83] Wills Act 1837, s.10; Wills Act 1963, s.2.

[84] See *ante*, p. 66.

[85] *Chapman* v. *Gibson* (1791) 3 Bro.C.C. 229; *Garth* v. *Townsend* (1869) L.R. 7 Eq. 220;
Kennard v. *Kennard* (1872) L.R. 8 Ch.App. 227.

[86] It would in theory be possible for the donor of the power to prescribe some formal
requirement, but it is most unlikely that this would be done.

[87] Again in theory it would be possible for the donor of the power to provide that the
trustees could change their mind before the sum was actually paid over to the beneficiary, but it is also most unlikely that this would be done.

[88] There appears to be a presumption that an appointment is to be irrevocable, and that
this will apply until it can be shown that there is an express or implied intention that it
shall be revocable.

hand if the matter is dealt with by discretion, a decision can be made at or after the end of 1995 in favour of Charles; or at after the end of 1996 in favour of Douglas; and at or after the end of 1997 in favour of Edward. The result so far as the beneficiaries are concerned is the same in both cases. If under the trust instrument the trustees can take either course of action, they will usually be influenced by the taxation implications.

IV. FACTORS AFFECTING THE EXERCISE OF POWERS AND DISCRETIONS

1. *Delegation*

There is no doubt that a settlor or testator can give a power of appointment to a trustee—even a general power of appointment given by a testator to his trustees cannot be impugned as a delegation of testamentary disposition.[89] However, there is some uncertainty as to the extent to which trustees or others can delegate their powers and discretions. The basic position is that matters involving a decision on a matter of policy, or importance, which would include whether a person is to benefit, and, if so, to what extent, cannot be delegated,[90] but that ancillary decisions taken in order to give effect to the trustees' decision can be delegated.[91] So, if the trustees in the exercise of their discretion decide to give a beneficiary £5, they could leave it to their solicitor to decide whether to pay that sum by cheque or in cash.

The instrument by which a power is conferred can expressly authorise delegation of its exercise, and, occasionally, by express provision statutory powers can be delegated.[92] Where there is no express authority, it seems that delegation can only be made effectively where there is an implied power to this effect in the instrument creating the power. So far as beneficial entitlements are concerned, the question most often arises where there is a power to appoint a fund among a group, and in making the appointment, the appointor seeks to appoint the fund not absolutely, but on certain trusts. Unless there is an express or implied power in the trust instrument, the appointor cannot appoint the fund upon discretionary trusts, because in so doing he is delegating to others, namely the trustees of the new trust, the power of deciding what the beneficiary shall in fact receive.[93] Similarly, if an appointment is made on protective trusts[94] the fixed interest part of the appointment is valid, even though the discretionary trusts which would arise on the determination of the life interest are void.[95] On the other hand, where,

---

[89] *Re Beatty's Will Trusts* (1990) 1 W.L.R. 1503 (see J. D. Davies, 107 L.Q.R. (1991)211).

[90] *Re May* [1926] 1 Ch. 136; *Re Mewburn* [1934] Ch. 112; *Re Wills' Will Trusts* [1959] Ch. 1.

[91] *Att.-Gen.* v. *Scott* (1750) 1 Ves.Sen. 413; *Re Hetling and Merton's Contract* [1893] 3 Ch. 269.

[92] An example of statutory authority to delegate is that conferred by s.29 of the Law of Property Act 1925, enabling trustees for sale to delegate their powers of management; and see also *post*, pp. 389, 400.

[93] *Re Morris' Settlement* [1951] 2 All E.R. 528. *Re Hay's Settlement Trusts* [1982] 1 W.L.R. 202.

[94] See *post*, p. 182.

[95] *Re Boulton's Settlement Trusts* [1928] Ch. 703; *Re Morris' Settlement*, *supra*; *Re Hunter* [1963] Ch. 372.

under the terms of the power, an appointment is validly made upon trust for a life tenant, with remainders over, it is implied that the appointor can include a provision for advancement.[96]

The extent to which trustees can delegate their powers of management and administration, and to appoint agents, is considered in later chapters.[97]

2. *Improper Exercise of Powers and Discretions*

Certain principles have been evolved governing the exercise of powers and discretions. These are:

(a) As well as complying with any formal requirement,[98] a power or discretion is only validly exercised by a positive mental act, and not by allowing a situation to arise merely by inaction. The decision in *Wilson* v *Turner*[99] has already been mentioned.[1] In *Turner* v *Turner*,[2] the exercise of a power of appointment was invalid when the trustees left all the decisions to the settlor (who was not a trustee) and signed the necessary documents without reading them. The position is considered further in a later chapter.[3]

(b) Unless they choose to do so, the trustees cannot be compelled to give reasons for their decisions. This is also considered later.[4]

(c) Where the power has been exercised honestly, the court will support it, even if it would itself have reached a contrary decision.[5]

(d) Where the power has not been exercised honestly, it will be invalid. In this case there is said to be a "fraud on a power." The word "fraud" in equity denotes only improper motive and the expression "fraud on a power" is used both in connection with the exercise of a power, and the exercise of a discretion. In this discussion the word power includes discretion. Various attempts have been made to categorise the circumstances in which there is a fraud on a power,[6] but the most common situations are where a power is exercised in favour of an object where there is a prior agreement with him that he will apply the funds in whole or in part in favour of a non-object[7]; and where, even without such a prior agreement, the power is exercised with

---

[96] *Re Wills' Will Trusts* [1959] Ch. 1; *Pilkington* v. *I.R.C.* (1964) A.C. 612.
[97] *Post,* pp. 389, 400.
[98] *Ante,* p. 34.
[99] (1883) 22 Ch.D. 521.
[1] *Ante,* p. 145.
[2] (1984) Ch. 100.
[3] *Post,* p. 390.
[4] *Post,* p. 391.
[5] See *e.g. R.* v. *Archbishop of Canterbury and Bishop of London* [1903] 1 K.B. 289. See also *Re Hastings-Bass* (1975) Ch. 25, C.A., where the exercise of a discretion by trustees was held valid even though made under a mistake of law; and see *post,* p. 514.
[6] See *Vatcher* v. *Paull* (1915) A.C. 372.
[7] *Ibid.*

the intention of benefiting someone outside the scope of the power.[8] From the cases four points emerge:

(i) The fact that a power is exercised in such a way as to defeat the intention of the donor does not automatically make the exercise void.[9] This is comparable to the fact that beneficiaries may in some cases join together to bring a trust to an end even although the settlor intended that it should continue.[10] Once a power is conferred, or a trust created, the donor or settlor ceases to have any control as such, although the donor of a power could provide at the time of creation of the power that his consent should be obtained to its exercise.

(ii) In each case it is necessary to identify who would be entitled in default of the exercise of the power. The persons to take in default may be specified in the trust instrument, or there may be a resulting trust in their favour. These are the persons who lose by an improper exercise of the power, and, if they agree to it, knowing all relevant facts, the exercise is valid.[11]

(iii) The essential feature which makes the exercise of a power improper is the intention of the person exercising it. If it is exercised with the intention of benefiting some non-object of the power, whether it be the appointor or someone else, the exercise is void. If it is not done with this intention, but the exercise does in fact benefit a non-object, it is valid. Take the situation where a father has a power to appoint in favour of his child. In general, such an appointment is valid[12] but if it is exercised when the child is very ill, with the intention that the appointor will benefit by taking the child's estate on its death, the exercise is invalid[13]; and this is strictly the position even if the child subsequently recovers. If as part of a tax-saving scheme it is desired to bring the trust to an end by exercising the power, and the appointment is made with the intention of benefiting the object, the appointment is valid even although the appointment brings some incidental benefit on the appointor or others.[14]

(iv) Where a power is to be exercised in favour of an object of it, but there is the hope that the recipient will benefit a non-object, the validity of the exercise will depend upon whether the person in whose favour the power was exercised had legal and moral freedom of action.[15] Suppose that a power is exercisable in favour of a person who makes it known that if the power is in fact exercised in his favour he will give part

[8] *Portland* v. *Topham* (1867) 11 H.L.Cas. 32; *Vatcher* v. *Paull, supra.*
[9] *Lee* v. *Ferrie* (1839) 1 B. 483.
[10] See *post*, p. 159.
[11] *Re Turner's Settled Estates* [1884] 28 Ch.D. 205; *Re Greaves* [1954] Ch. 434.
[12] *Henty* v. *Wrey* (1882) 21 Ch.D. 332.
[13] *Lord Hinchinbroke* v. *Seymour* (1789) 1 Bro.C.C. 395.
[14] *Re Merton* [1953] 1 W.L.R. 1096; *Re Robertson's Will Trusts* [1960] 1 W.L.R. 1050.
[15] *Birley* v. *Birley* (1858) 25 B. 299.

of the fund to his parents, who are not objects. If the intention of the appointment is to benefit the parents, the exercise is invalid under the previous paragraph. If the object of the power is under great pressure to benefit the parents, the exercise is also invalid.[16] If, however, the object of the power has genuine freedom of action, but wishes to give his parents a benefit, the exercise of the power is good.[17]

3. *Effects of Invalid Exercise of a Power or Discretion*

In principle, where the exercise of a power is improper, it is totally invalid.[18] This can work harshly on the objects. If the appointor reaches an agreement with an object that the appointor will appoint the object £1,000, provided the object pays £500 to a non-object, then, in principle, the whole appointment is invalid, and the object receives nothing. Accordingly, in an attempt to help objects, in some cases the court will try to sever the improper element in the appointment from the remainder.[19] Clearly, if there is no intent to benefit the object of the power at all, the exercise is entirely invalid.[20] If, however, there is an intent to benefit the object to some extent, and the improper element is in the form of a condition attached to the appointment, the court will delete the condition to leave the object free to take unconditionally.[21]

V. SOME PROVISIONS OF DISCRETIONARY TRUSTS

The expression "discretionary trust" is used in two senses. The first is in the sense of a discretion of the nature considered previously, where there is an obligation to exercise it. But more commonly, it is used to denote the total provisions of the trust instrument, which will probably contain a combination of powers of appointment, discretionary and other powers, both of the nature of mere powers and of trust powers. Two aspects of the provisions commonly found will now be considered.

1. *Time for Exercise*

Trustees must exercise any discretion within a reasonable time. What is reasonable depends on the facts of each case. In *Re Gulbenkian's Settlement Trusts (No. 2)*[22] trustees learned in April 1957 of a decision[23] which cast doubt on the validity of a provision as to the accumulation of income. They therefore retained the income without accumulating it. The doubt was not resolved until the decision of the House of Lords in

---

[16] *Re Crawshay* [1948] Ch. 123; *Re Dick* [1953] Ch. 343.
[17] *Re Marsden's Trusts* (1859) 4 Drew. 594.
[18] *Daubeney* v. *Cockburn* (1816) 1 Mer. 626.
[19] *Topham* v. *Duke of Portland* (1858) 1 D.J. & S. 517.
[20] *Re Cohen* [1911] 1 Ch. 37.
[21] *Hay* v. *Watkins* (1850) 3 Dr. & War. 339.
[22] [1970] Ch. 408.
[23] *Re Gresham's Settlement* [1956] 1 W.L.R. 573, subsequently overruled.

Re Gulbenkian's Settlement Trusts (No. 1)[24] in October 1968. Plowman J. held that their retention of the income was not unreasonable in the circumstances and they could still exercise their discretion in respect of the income which had accrued since 1957. It therefore follows that if the circumstances are reasonable, trustees can retain income for some time, as income, and then accumulate it.

If the trustees do not exercise their discretion within a reasonable time, the result depends on whether their discretion was permissive or obligatory. If the discretion was permissive, that is, while the trustees were under a duty to consider whether to exercise this discretion, they were not under a duty to exercise it, the discretion is lost if it is not exercised within a reasonable time.[25] If, however, the trustees were under an obligation to exercise their discretion, the discretion is not extinguished by lapse of time. Accordingly, the trustees can exercise it much later, and, if they do not do so, the court will direct them to do so.[26]

2. *Modifying the Class of Beneficiaries*

There has been a general trend towards making trusts more and more flexible, so that the discretionary trust has become much more popular than the trust with fixed interests. Two recent developments have been to include powers to alter the class of beneficiaries, or even to revoke all the trusts and declare new ones. The latter provision is considered elsewhere but it is now established that the former is valid. In principle it seems that there is no objection either to giving trustees power to add persons to a class; or to declare a very wide class, and merely give the trustees power to exclude particular persons, usually as a result of new legislation. The practice was approved in *Re Manisty's Settlement*.[27] In that case there was a discretionary trust for the benefit of the children and remoter issue of the settlor. The settlement conferred upon the trustees power to bring other persons into the class, and they purported to exercise this power by bringing in the settlor's mother, and any person who should be a widow of the settlor. Templeman J. held that such a power could be validly conferred on trustees, and that their exercise of it was therefore valid.[28]

VI. RELEASE OF POWERS

1. *Reasons*

Those entitled to exercise powers are sometimes asked to release them. This can be as a result of changes in taxation law. For example, until

---

[24] [1970] A.C. 508; and see *ante*, p. 101.

[25] *Re Gourju's Will Trusts* [1943] Ch. 24; *Re Wise* [1896] 1 Ch. 281; *Re Allen-Meyrick's Will Trusts* [1966] 1. W.L.R. 499.

[26] *Re Locker's Settlement Trusts* [1978] 1 All E.R. 216; see *post*, p. 389, 488.

[27] [1974] Ch. 17; and see *Blausten* v. *I.R.C.* [1982] Ch. 256 and *Re Hay's Settlement Trusts* [1982] 1 W.L.R. 202, discussed *ante*, p. 109.

[28] The decision is in line with the approval of a power of delegation by resettlement in *Pilkington* v. *I.R.C.* [1964] A.C. 612, discussed *post*, p. 513.

April 5, 1973, all income of a trust was taxable in the hands of the trustees at the same rate. With effect from April 6, 1973, however, an additional charge to tax was imposed on income which could be accumulated.[29] In the case of a pre-existing trust under which the trustees had a power to accumulate but, subject thereto, could pay the income to a named person, a possible way of avoiding the additional charge of tax would have been to ask the trustees to release their power to accumulate so that the named beneficiary became entitled to the whole of the income. It is, however, more likely that trustees will be asked to release powers in order to create indefeasible interests. Suppose that trustees hold a fund upon trust for such of Michael, Norman and Oliver as they may appoint and, in default of appointment, for all three equally. As long as the power of appointment is exerciseable, none of the beneficiaries can be sure that he will receive any benefit, since the power may be exercised in favour of the others. Thus, if Michael wishes to raise money by selling or mortgaging his interest, he may ask the trustees to release the power, in order to give him a fixed interest with which he can then deal. Other reasons for releasing powers also arise; in *Re Wills' Trust Deeds*[30] there was a power to appoint between charitable and non-charitable objects and it was wished to release the latter power in order to convert the trust into one which was entirely charitable.

In considering this issue, two questions arise: whether a power can properly be released and the extent to which any release made is effective.

2. *Propriety of Release*

The circumstances in which a power can be effectively released were considered in *Re Wills' Trust Deeds*[31] where Buckley J. formulated the following general propositions on the subject.[32]

    (i) If a power is granted to appoint among a class of objects and in default of appointment there is a trust, either express or implied, in favour of the members of that class, the donee cannot defeat the interest of the members of the class by releasing the power or, which comes to the same thing, by refusing to appoint. (This proposition is self-evident, as Buckley J. himself stated.)

    (ii) A power of the kind just mentioned cannot be released, for the donee is under a duty to exercise it, notwithstanding the fact that the court may not be able to compel him personally to perform that duty. (This proposition seems somewhat

---

[29] Finance Act 1973, s.16; see *ante*, p. 131.

[30] [1964] Ch. 219.

[31] [1964] Ch. 219.

[32] *Ibid.* at pp. 236, 237. In cases of doubt whether a release should be effected, it seems possible to apply to the court for directions (see *Re Allen-Meyrick's Will Trusts* [1966] 1 W.L.R. 499); alternatively, in cases where a variation of trusts is sought, an application to the court on the question may be made under the Variation of Trusts Act 1958 (see *post*, p. 546).

debateable in the form in which it is stated; the donee of such a power will not always be under a duty to exercise it and, if he is not, he can surely release it; however, in practice, in view of the trust in default of appointment, any release would in most cases be ineffectual.)

(iii) Where a power is conferred on trustees *virtute officii* in relation to their trust property, they cannot release it or bind themselves not to exercise it. (This proposition envisages the now established distinction between fiduciary and non-fiduciary donees of mere powers.)

(iv) The same is true if the power is conferred on persons who are trustees of a settlement but is conferred on them by name and not by reference to their office if on the facts they were selected as donees of the power because they were trustees. (This proposition also envisages the now established distinction between fiduciary and non-fiduciary donees of mere powers.)

(v) Where a power is conferred on someone who is not a trustee of property to which the power relates or if he be a trustee is not conferred on him in that capacity then, in the absence of a trust in favour of the object of the power in default of appointment, the donee is not under any duty recognised by the court to exercise the power such as to disable him from releasing it. (This proposition, also described by Buckley J. as self-evident, now requires some reformulation in the light of the fact that it has now been held that a person other than a trustee can be classified as a fiduciary donee of a mere power.)

How do these propositions apply to the different types of powers which have already been discussed?

(1) Trust powers or powers in the nature of a trust

It is clear that there is no possibility of a trust power or a power in the nature of a trust being released. The very essence of such a power is that the person entitled to exercise it is under an obligation so to do and, if he fails to do so, it will be exercised by the court. Such powers fall within the first two propositions enunciated by Buckley J. (because of the existence, in default of appointment, of an implied trust in favour of the members of the class).

(2) Mere powers held by a fiduciary donee

Where such powers are held by trustees, they will fall within the third and fourth propositions enunciated by Buckley J. Where a power is conferred upon a trustee *virtute officii*, it is clearly established that he cannot release that power *"in the absence of words in the trust deed authorising [him] so to do"*.[33] Despite the fact that the donee cannot be obliged to exercise the power, he cannot ignore it since, as has already

---

[33] *Muir* v. *I.R.C.* [1966] 1 W.L.R. 1269 *per* Harman L.J. at p. 1283 (original emphasis).

been seen,[34] he must consider periodically whether or not he should exercise the power, and range and objects of the power and the appropriateness of individual appointments. This is the case both where the power is expressed to be vested in the trustees as such (the third proposition) and where the power is expressed to have been conferred on the trustees by name if they were selected because they were the trustees (the fourth proposition). Thus in *Re Courage Group's Pension Schemes*,[35] it was held that a committee which had been established to manage a pension scheme could not deprive their successors of the right to exercise their powers even if (which was not decided) they were themselves entitled to release, fetter or agree not to exercise these powers.

Where a power is held by a person other than a trustee, the propositions enunciated by Buckley J. would suggest that, save where there is, in default of appointment, an express or implied trust in favour of the members of the class, the power can be released (this follows from the first, second and fifth propositions). However, in *Mettoy Pension Trustees* v *Evans*,[36] a mere power held by a person other than the trustee of the property in question was held to be fiduciary and, consequently, incapable of release. Assuming that the donee of the power was correctly classified as a fiduciary (as has already been seen, this conclusion has been described as "not overwhelming"),[37] this decision is clearly correct and therefore necessitates an additional proposition, immediately after the existing fourth one, to the effect that "the same is true if the power is conferred on persons who are not trustees of the property in question but who are nevertheless held to be fiduciary donees of the power" and the additional exclusion from the existing fifth proposition of fiduciary donees.

However, it must be emphasised that a mere power held by a fiduciary donee can be released if the instrument which created it so authorises. The wording of the relevant clause was held to authorise such a release in *Muir* v *I.R.C.*[38] This was in effect also the position in *Blausten* v *I.R.C.*,[39] where the Court of Appeal came to the conclusion that a resettlement of the trust fund upon trusts identical with the existing trusts, but excluding a particular power vested in the trustees, was a good exercise of the power of appointment (the immediate effect of the appointment was simply to exclude the wife of the settlor from the objects of the discretionary trusts of income and that was held to be within the terms of the power of appointment).

(3) Mere powers held by a non-fiduciary donee

Such powers fall within the first, second and fifth propositions enunciated by Buckley J. This suggests that such powers can be released save where there is, in default of appointment, an express or implied

---

[34] See *ante*, p. 136.

[35] [1987] 1 W.L.R. 495.

[36] [1990] 1 W.L.R. 1587.

[37] See *ante*, p. 143.

[38] [1966] 1 W.L.R. 1269.

[39] [1972] Ch. 256.

trust in favour of the members of the class. There is no doubt that such powers can be released where this exception does not apply. However, as has already been mentioned, given that the donee of such a power will not be under a duty to exercise it, he should surely be able to release it; such a conclusion was indeed reached in *Re Radcliffe*,[40] where the release by a father of a mere power in order that the shares of his sons (who were entitled in default) might become absolute was upheld even though the release also benefited the father, in that he thereby received the share of a deceased son (this is one of the relatively rare cases where a release in such circumstances served a useful purpose). Another question which is not entirely clear is whether it is still possible, as the fifth proposition states, for a trustee of the property, whose power was not conferred on him in that capacity, to be held to be a non-fiduciary donee. The only other point which should be noted is that it has been held that the doctrine of fraud on a power does not apply to the release of a power, since the release benefits those entitled in default.[41]

3. *Effectiveness of Release*

In *Re Wills' Trust Deeds* it was actually held that the power of appointment in question was not coupled with a duty or trust and was capable of being released accordingly. But Buckley J. also raised a fresh point— on which there appeared to be no prior direct authority—in holding that, although the present trustees, by releasing the power, had precluded themselves from exercising it, that would not prevent their successors in title from exercising it. "A power granted to successive holders of an office", he said, "is unlike trust property, the entire ownership of which is vested in the trustees for the time being of the settlement and devolves on each change of trustee by succession. Where a power is granted to successive holders of an office all that is vested in the incumbent for the time being of the office is the capacity to exercise the power while he holds that office".[42] A similar view was taken, although in that case it was not actually decided whether or not the existing donees were entitled to release their power, in *Re Courage Group's Pension Schemes*.[43]

4. *Failure to Exercise Power*

Until such time, if at all, as the power is effectively released, it remains with the trustees and they alone must exercise it. In *Re Allen-Meyrick's Will Trusts*[44] the trustees of a will held the trust fund upon trust to pay so much of the income as they thought fit to the husband of the testatrix and, subject to the exercise of their discretion in his favour, upon trust for her god-daughters. The husband was an undischarged bankrupt

---

[40] [1892] 1 Ch. 227.
[41] *Re Somes* [1896] 1 Ch. 250.
[42] [1964] Ch. 219 at p. 238.
[43] [1987] 1 W.L.R. 495.
[44] [1966] 1 W.L.R. 499.

and the trustees had, in the exercise of their discretion, paid the rent of the house in which he lived but, apart from this, they could not agree on whether to make a further payment to him. They asked the court to accept a surrender of their discretion but Buckley J. refused. It is open to the trustees of any trust to seek the directions of the court in any particular circumstances and the court was prepared to give directions as to what should be done with the income which had accrued but it would not accept a surrender of the trustees' discretion for the future. This seems to have been largely for procedural reasons; had the court accepted that surrender, there would have been no ready way in which it could have been informed of the actual circumstances of the beneficiaries each time that a decision had to be made. It is, however, possible that, although this would not have been welcomed by the court, the trustees could have sought the directions of the court on a new application each year or so.

VII. THE POSITION OF THE POTENTIAL BENEFICIARIES

1. The Potential Beneficiaries Themselves

What is the position of a person who is one of the objects of a power pending its exercise? There are two aspects.

(1) The individual rights of an object of a power

(a) **When can application be made to the court?** A person who is one of the objects of a power can require the donee of the power to consider exercising the power in his favour, or in favour of any of the other objects.[45] Accordingly, if he can show that the donee of the power has refused to consider him as a possible object, he can apply to the court. This is, however, subject to any contrary provision in the instrument by which the power was created (some modern deeds authorise the donees of powers to exercise their discretion in favour of some of the objects of the power without even considering its other objects).

A person who is one of the objects of a power can also apply to the court if, despite giving due consideration to his own position, the donee of the power has acted capriciously in other respects. In *Re Manisty's Settlement*,[46] Templeman J. stated[47] that donees of a power would be acting capriciously if they acted "for reasons which I apprehend could be said to be irrational, perverse or irrelevant to any sensible expectation of the settlor; for example, if they chose a beneficiary by height or complexion or by the irrelevant fact that he was a resident of Greater London."

In other respects, a person who is one of the objects of a power is in a curious position. On the one hand, it seems clear that the donees of the

---

[45] *Re Gestetner* [1953] Ch. 672 *per* Harman J. at p. 688; *Re Manisty's Settlement* [1974] Ch. 17, *per* Templeman J. at p. 25.

[46] [1974] Ch. 17.

[47] *Ibid.* at p. 25.

power are not in any way obliged to inform him that he is an object of the power.[48] On the other hand, if he knows that he is an object of the power, it seems that he is entitled to apply to the court in the event that the trustees in whom the property subject to the power is vested are guilty of any acts of improper administration or in the event that the donee of the power either exercises it improperly or purports to release it in circumstances when this is improper. In order to establish whether any such improper activity has occured, it seems that he is entitled to obtain the same information as a beneficiary under a fixed trust.[49] The existence of these rights provides a good reason for keeping the class of objects of a power as narrow as possible.

The persons entitled to the property in default of appointment are similarly entitled to apply to the court in the event that the trustees in whom the property subject to the power is vested are guilty of any acts of improper administration or in the event that the donee of the power exercises it improperly.

(b) Remedies where the power is not exercised. Where the power in question is a trust power in any of the senses in which the expression is used (whether, in other words, the power is vested in the trustees, in which case it will in effect be a discretionary trust, or in third parties, in which case it will in effect be an old fashioned power in the nature of a trust), the donee of the power will be under an obligation to exercise it; therefore, he can be directed to do so by the court. Where the power is vested in the trustees, the court will additionally have all the powers enunciated by Lord Wilberforce in *McPhail* v *Doulton*.[50] Prior to that decision, a trust power was only valid for certainty of objects if a complete list of all its objects could be drawn up; consequently, in the event that the power was not exercised, the court would invariably order that the property should be divided equally between all the objects of the power. However, the new test for certainty of objects established by *McPhail* v *Doulton* inevitably means that, in the case of trust powers validated by the decision, not all the objects will be known either to the trustees or to the court. Consequently, Lord Wilberforce held that, in such circumstances, the court can either appoint new trustees or direct persons representative of the classes of beneficiaries to prepare a scheme of distribution or, should the proper basis for distribution be apparent, direct the trustees how to distribute the fund (this does not, of course, mean that equal distribution will never again be ordered; in the case of a small class of beneficiaries whose entire membership is known, it is almost inevitable that equal distribution will still be ordered). Where, on the other hand, the power is vested in third parties, there does not seem any basis on which the court can replace those third parties. Consequently, the court can presumably only either direct persons representative of the classes of beneficiaries to prepare a scheme for distribution or, should the proper basis for

---

[48] *Ibid.*
[49] See *post,* pp. 391, 522.
[50] [1971] A.C. 424 at p. 457.

distribution be apparent (normally the case in old fashioned powers in the nature of a trust, which tend to be in favour of reduced groups), direct the trustees how to distribute the fund (in the case of a reduced group, inevitably in equal shares).

Where, on the other hand, the power in question is a mere power, the court is unable to direct its exercise. Where the power is held by a non-fiduciary donee, the court can do nothing at all. Where, however, the power is held by a fiduciary donee, the court can direct the donee to consider whether or not to exercise the power; it has been stated on several occasions[51] that a refusal to follow such a direction from the court might well lead to the replacement of the fiduciary in question. More controversially, it has now been held, in *Mettoy Pension Trustees* v *Evans*[52] that all the remedies available to the court to enforce trust powers are also available in the case of mere powers held by fiduciary donees. This was the case in which a company held a power to appoint any surplus in its pension fund, which was actually vested in a separate trustee company, in favour of the pensioners with a gift over in default of appointment to itself. Warner J. held that the company was unable to release the power and thus make the surplus available for its general creditors. It was obviously impossible to leave the liquidators of the company to exercise the power since their duty to the creditors would have conflicted with and presumably prevailed over their duty to consider the claims of the pensioners. No application had been made for the appointment of new fiduciaries (had there been, the obvious remedy would have been to vest the power in the trustee company, which had been the donee of the power at an earlier stage). Warner J. therefore held that he was entitled to approve or dictate a scheme himself and invited further argument as to what scheme was appropriate.[53] This decision has been criticised[54] on the grounds that judicial exercise of fiduciary discretions is inappropriate, even "as regards quasi-public trusts such as pension funds" and that the judge should have confined himself to appointing suitable new fiduciaries. It remains to be seen whether the novel remedies enunciated in *Mettoy Pension Trustees* v *Evans* for the non-exercise of a mere power by a fiduciary donee are ever actually put into effect.

(c) **Remedies where the power is exercised improperly.** Any improper exercise of any power will be set aside, both where the donees "exceed their power, and possibly if they are proved to have exercised it capriciously".[55] Thus in *Turner* v. *Turner*,[56] where the trustees had left all the decisions to the settlor (who was not a trustee) and had made a series of appointments without reading the necessary documents before signing them, all the appointments were held to be null and void

---

[51] *Re Gestetner* [1953] Ch. 672 at p. 688, *Re Manisty's Settlement* (1974) Ch. 17 at p. 25.
[52] [1990] 1 W.L.R. 1587.
[53] This part of the case was adjourned pending an appeal, which seems subsequently to have been settled.
[54] By S Gardner, 107 L.Q.R. (1991) 214 at pp. 217–218.
[55] *McPhail* v. *Doulton* [1971] A.C. 424 *per* Lord Wilberforce at p. 456.
[56] [1984] Ch. 100.

other than one concerning land which had been effective to transfer the legal title, which the appointee therefore held on trust for the settlement. If the person to whom the property was improperly appointed has dealt with it in favour of a third party, save in the relatively unlikely situation in which the third party has acquired the legal title to the property in question (in which case he may be able to claim to be a bona fide purchaser for value without notice), he will not be able to claim to have taken free of the interests of those otherwise entitled under the power and so will be bound by their interests.[57] The only exception of this is the limited defence provided by Section 157 of the Law of Property Act 1925 which rather curiously is available only when the appointee was at least 25 years old at the time of the transaction and only to the extent that he was presumptively entitled in default of appointment.

(2) The collective rights of the objects of a power
There is one respect in which the objects of a power have a more direct interest in the property subject to the power. It will be seen later that, where a beneficiary of a trust is of full age and *sui juris* and he alone is entitled to the trust fund, he may bring the trust to an end.[58] Somewhat similarly, where all the objects of a trust power combine, then they together may deal with the beneficial interest. In *Re Smith*[59] a fund was held on discretionary trust as to income and capital for Lilian and after her death for her children. Lilian and her three children, who were between them the only persons entitled to benefit under the trust, together assigned all their interest therein to an insurance company. The assignee was held entitled to demand the whole of the income. Romer J. said that in such a case "you treat all the people put together as though they formed one person, for whose benefit the trustees were directed to apply the whole of a particular fund".[60]

(3) The right to release interests
Just as a man cannot be forced to accept a gift,[61] so a man cannot be forced to remain an object of a trust power or a mere power and he can, if he so wishes, release his rights thereunder. In that event, the trust power or mere power is administered as if his name did not appear among the class of those entitled to be considered as objects of the exercise of the donee's discretion.[62]

2. *Assignees and Trustees in Bankruptcy*

An assignee or trustee in bankruptcy is, in principle, in the same position as the potential beneficiary himself. So in *Re Coleman*[63] the

---

[57] *Cloutte* v. *Storey* [1911] 1 Ch. 18.
[58] *See post*, p. 524.
[59] [1928] Ch. 915.
[60] See also *Re Nelson* [1928] Ch. 920n.
[61] *Thompson* v. *Leach* (1690) 2 Vent. 198; *Re Stratton's Deed of Disclaimer* [1958] 2 Ch. 42.
[62] *Re Gulbenkian's Settlement Trusts (No. 2)* [1970] Ch. 408.
[63] (1889) 39 Ch.D. 443.

Court of Appeal held that where the discretionary beneficiary had assigned his beneficial interest the trustees were compelled to pay to the assignee the amount which they had allotted to the beneficiary. *Re Smith*,[64] which was mentioned above, is to the same effect. In principle, the position of a trustee in bankruptcy is the same but this is subject to the general principle of bankruptcy law that a bankrupt is entitled to retain sufficient funds for his own support, the trustee in bankruptcy being entitled only to the balance. This principle was applied by Vaughan Williams J. in *Re Ashby*.[65] In that case a discretionary beneficiary became bankrupt and the trustees continued to make payments to him. The beneficiary was held to be entitled to retain what was necessary for his basic support and his trustee in bankruptcy was held to be able to claim the excess.

The terms of the trust instrument may require payment to be made to the beneficiary personally but, on the other hand, the trustees may be entitled either to pay the beneficiary or to make payments for his benefit. In *Re Bullock*,[66] which was concerned with a discretionary trust of the latter type, Kekewich J. held that, when a discretionary beneficiary became bankrupt, the trustees could continue to pay income for his benefit. The scope of this decision is a matter of some doubt and it has been suggested that the power is restricted so that the trustees can only pay to the bankrupt sufficient for his necessaries. However, this is probably not correct. It seems that, so far as the trustees are concerned, they may continue to apply funds for the benefit of the beneficiary in the same way as they could have done before the bankruptcy. If as a result assets come into the hands of the beneficiary which are not required for his necessaries, as where the trustees apply the money in providing a luxury holiday for the beneficiary, it seems that the trustee in bankruptcy is powerless to intervene. Of course, the trustees must exercise their discretion in good faith and must make the decision to benefit the beneficiary and not to spite the trustee in bankruptcy.

---

[64] [1928] Ch. 915.
[65] [1892] 1 Q.B. 872.
[66] [1891] 64 L.T. 736.

CHAPTER 5

LEGALITY OF A TRUST

I. GENERALLY

IT is an elementary principle that a trust which is *wholly* illegal or contrary to public policy will not be enforced. The court indeed will not only prevent the illegal trust taking effect but will generally go so far as to refuse its assistance to the settlor in recovering the property. "Those who violate the law," said Lord Truro L.C., "must not apply to the law for protection."[1] The principle will not, however, be stretched to its uttermost limit. A settlor is entitled to recover the property where the illegal purpose is merely *contemplated*; in these circumstances there is what is described as a *locus poenitentiae*.[2]

The consequences of a *partially* unlawful trust may be rather different. Strictly, it appears that if part of the trust funds is to be devoted in the first instance to an unlawful purpose and the remainder to a lawful purpose, but the first part cannot be ascertained, the whole trust will fail, for it would be impossible to ascertain the residue.[3]

But there must be a true impossibility of ascertainment and it does appear that the court will, if it is practicable, strive to ascertain it and uphold the remainder of the gift.[4] Indeed there is some—admittedly indecisive—authority[5] for the proposition that the whole of the property will go to the lawful purpose if that is charitable and that the trust for the illegal purpose will be completely disregarded; but in view of the confused state of the case-law it is by no means certain that this truly represents the law, however convenient it may be.

The law relating to bankruptcy and perpetuity is of the utmost importance in any discussion of the legality of a trust, and these subjects are dealt with later in the chapter. But it is beyond the scope of this book to deal exhaustively with the many other classes of illegality and the like which will vitiate a trust as they will vitiate any other trans-

---

[1] *Benyon* v. *Nettlefold* (1850) 3 Mac. & G. 94 at 102. And see *Ayerst* v. *Jenkins* (1873) L.R. 16 Eq. 275, *cf. Phillips* v. *Probyn* [1899] 1 Ch. 811.

[2] *Symes* v. *Hughes* (1870) L.R. 9 Eq. 475.

[3] See *Chapman* v. *Brown* (1801) 6 Ves. 404.

[4] See *Mitford* v. *Reynolds* (1842) 1 Ph. 185.

[5] See *Fisk* v. *Att.-Gen.* (1867) L.R. 4 Eq. 521; *Hunter* v. *Bullock* (1872) L.R. 14 Eq. 45; *Dawson* v *Small* (1874) L.R. 18 Eq. 114; *Re Williams* (1877) 5 Ch.D. 735; *Re Birkett* (1878) 9 Ch.D. 576 (all trusts for maintenance of tombs with surplus for a charitable purpose); see also *Re Rogerson* [1901] 1 Ch. 715.

action. Only a few examples will be briefly considered to indicate in what circumstances a trust will be rendered bad on this basis.

(1) Restraints on alienation

A restraint on alienation of property given to a beneficiary absolutely is contrary to public policy and void.[6]

(2) Illegitimate children

In certain circumstances trusts coming into force before 1970, whether by deed[7] or will,[8] in favour of illegitimate children yet to be born were void on the ground that they promoted immorality, and so were contrary to public policy. The test of public policy was whether or not future immorality was promoted. However, this does not apply in the case of an *inter vivos* gift made, or a will of a person dying, after 1969.[9]

(3) Restraint of marriage

If a condition, or a gift over to take effect upon such condition, is contained in a settlement, and it tends to restrain marriage altogether, the condition and gift over are void.[10] But this rule does not apply to a gift over in the event of a second marriage.[11] Nor does it apply to a *partial* restraint operating against designated persons only.[12]

On the other hand, a limitation of property *until* marriage—as opposed to a limitation to a person *on condition* that he does not marry—is perfectly good.[13] The question whether or not a limitation of this sort will be valid will depend on whether it is construed as creating a determinable interest or an interest upon condition. The distinction is perhaps an unnecessarily fine one, but it is well established.

The same difficulties, curiously enough, do not attach to a *condition* requiring *consent* to marriage. It is, of course, easy to see that if consent is withheld it will effectively bar marriage. But despite the apparent illogicality, it seems to be clearly established that the condition will be valid.[14]

(4) Trusts separating parent and child

If a trust is designed to separate a parent (even if he or she has been divorced[15]) from his or her child, that, too, will be void as contrary to public policy.[16] Yet again a trust will fail if it tends to interfere with parental duties: such duties should be discharged solely with a view to

---

[6] See, *e.g. Floyer* v. *Bankes* (1869) L.R. 8 Eq. 115.
[7] *Blodwell* v. *Edwards* (1596) Cro.Eliz. 509; and see *Occleston* v. *Fullalove* (1874) 9 Ch.App. 147, *per* Mellish L.J.
[8] *Metham* v. *Duke of Devonshire* (1718) 1 P.Wms. 529.
[9] Family Law Reform Act 1969, s.15(7).
[10] *Lloyd* v. *Lloyd* (1852) 2 Sim. (N.S.) 255.
[11] *Allen* v. *Jackson* (1842) 1 Ch.D. 399, C.A.
[12] *Jenner* v. *Turner* (1880) 16 Ch.D. 188.
[13] *Re Lovell* [1920] 1 Ch. 122.
[14] *Re Whiting's Settlement* [1905] 1 Ch. 96.
[15] *Re Piper* [1946] 2 All E.R. 503.
[16] *Re Boulter* [1922] 1 Ch. 75; *Re Sandbrook* [1912] 2 Ch. 471.

the moral and spiritual welfare of the child and without being influenced by mercenary considerations.[17]

(5) Name and arms clauses

A number of decisions were overruled by the Court of Appeal in *Re Neeld*[18] to produce the unexceptionable principle that a name and arms clause (which many people would regard as harmless if anachronistic), requiring a husband to whom a woman may be married to change his name on marriage, is neither contrary to public policy nor uncertain.

II. PERPETUITIES AND ACCUMULATIONS

Since medieval times, English law has been subject to the tension between two conflicting influences. Land and other property owners have desired to tie up their property indefinitely, usually for the benefit of their family or for some institution or cause, while the courts and the legislature have always felt that it is in the interest of the nation as a whole that wealth should circulate freely and that property should not be made inalienable. The result has been a compromise. Property may be tied up indefinitely for a purpose which the law wishes to advance, namely, a charity.[19] Otherwise property may be tied up but only for a comparatively short period. The rule which governs this is known as the rule against perpetuities.

1. *The Rule against Remoteness*

This rule provides that property must vest in the recipient within the period of a life or lives in being at the time when the gift is made and 21 years thereafter (with allowance being made where appropriate for any period of gestation).[20]

The rule has, however, been bedevilled by an excess of zeal on the part of the judges. Starting from the basis that property *must* vest within the perpetuity period, the judges have striven to find some possibility, no matter how remote, whereby it might not vest within that period. If they were able to envisage any such possibility, the gift was bad. In so doing, common sense went out of the window, and Alice walked in the front door. The almost unbelievable nonsense which ensued is illustrated by *Re Dawson*.[21] There a testator gave property to trustees to hold upon trust for his daughter for life, with remainder to such of her children as should attain the age of 21, with a provision that if any of her children should die under the age of 21, but should themselves leave issue, such issue on attaining the age of 21 would take the share of their parent. When the will came into operation, the testator's daughter was aged over 60, and all her children were over 21. Nevertheless, the court managed to hold this gift to be bad. With blithe disregard for the

---

[17] *Re Borwick* [1933] Ch. 657.
[18] [1962] Ch. 643.
[19] See *post*, p. 296.
[20] *Cadell* v. *Palmer* (1833) 1 Cl. & Fin. 372; *Re Wilmer's Trusts* [1903] 2 Ch. 411.
[21] (1888) 39 Ch.D. 155.

principles of biology, it was held that the daughter was still capable of giving birth to a child who might himself have died before reaching the age of 21, but leaving issue. The child was not alive at the death of the testator, so that the relevant life in being was the testator's daughter. In such circumstances the issue of the child would not attain his vested interest within 21 years from the death of the daughter. As it was possible that one of the persons entitled in remainder might not obtain a vested interest within the perpetuity period, the remainder was therefore void for perpetuity. Similarly, in *Re Gaite*[22] the judicial reasoning solemnly proceeded on the basis that a girl aged less than five could give birth to a child. In the apt expression of Morris and Leach[23] the judicial world would seem to be populated by fertile octogenarians, precocious toddlers and so forth.

To overcome some of the traps, and generally to restore some semblance of sanity, Parliament has intervened on two occasions. Small amendments were made by the Law of Property Act 1925 and large scale alterations were made by the Perpetuities and Accumulations Act 1964. With only a few exceptions[24] the latter Act applies only to instruments coming into effect after July 15, 1964.[25]

The rule may be stated as follows: where a future gift is made, it must be seen from the instrument by which it is created that if it will vest at all, then it must vest within the period prescribed by law; but in the case of post-1964 instruments, if it appears that the gift might or might not vest within the prescribed period, the gift is treated as if it does not offend against the rule until such time, if at all, as it becomes clear that it cannot vest within that period.

The elements of this definition must now be examined and expanded.

(1) The rule concerns vesting

The rule requires that a gift must vest within the perpetuity period. The aspect of the rule now being considered—as contrasted with the rule against inalienability which is considered later[26]—has no application to the length of time for which property may be enjoyed. Accordingly, if an outright gift is made to a limited company so that the gift vests immediately, the company may hold the property for over a thousand years without the rule having any operation.[27]

It is, therefore, essential to know what is meant by "vesting". A future gift may be either vested or contingent. A gift is vested if:

(a) the person or persons entitled to the gift are in existence and are ascertained;

(b) the size of the beneficiaries' interests is ascertained[28]; and

---

[22] [1949] 1 All E.R. 459.
[23] *The Rule Against Perpetuities* (2nd ed.), p. 89.
[24] See s.8(2).
[25] The date of the Royal Assent (s.15(5)).
[26] *Post*, p. 172.
[27] See, however, *post*, p. 172.
[28] *Pearks* v. *Moseley* (1880) 5 App. Cas. 714. This requirement for vesting applies only to the rule against perpetuities.

(c) any conditions attached to the gift are satisfied.

If, therefore, property is left upon trust for Romeo for life, with remainder to Juliet, the interest of Juliet is vested even if Romeo is still alive. Juliet's interest is vested because she herself is alive and is an ascertained person; the extent of her interest, namely, in the whole fund, is ascertained; and no conditions have to be satisfied before she becomes entitled. On the other hand, if the gift was to Romeo for life, with remainder to Juliet provided she has danced on the moon, her gift does not become vested until that condition is fulfilled.

A vested interest, therefore, may or may not carry the right to present enjoyment.[29] To show this distinction, vested interests are classified as being:

(a) vested in possession, where the interest does carry the right to present possession or enjoyment; and
(b) vested in interest, where the interest only carries the right to future possession or enjoyment.

The relevance of this for the purpose of the rule against perpetuities is that the rule is satisfied if the gift is only vested in interest. Thus, it was held in *Re Hargreaves*[30] that a gift to a person for life, with remainder to any woman who may become his widow for life, with remainder to his children who attain the age of 21, was good. It is true that the person who might become his wife need not be alive at the date of the settlement, but at the end of the perpetuity period (21 years after the death of the life tenant) it will be possible to say that his widow (if any) and his children who have attained 21 are between them the absolute owners of the property.

(2) The scope of the rule

The general principle is that the rule applies to all future gifts. In particular, for the purposes of the law of trusts, it applies to future gifts arising under an *inter vivos* settlement or trust, and to trusts created by will. To this general principle there are three exceptions:

(a) a gift to charity is exempt from the rule if the prior interests are also given to charity. This is considered in further detail in a later Chapter[30A]
(b) rights of redemption under mortgages are not within the rule, so that a mortgagor's right to redeem can be exercisable outside the perpetuity period.[31] Likewise certain provisions of leases, such as options to renew[32] and options to purchase the reversion,[33] are not within the rule; and

---

[29] It is a question of construction whether an interest is contingent or is vested liable to be divested: *Brotherton* v. *I.R.C.* [1978] 1 W.L.R. 610.
[30] (1889) 43 Ch.D. 401.
[30A] See *post*, p. 296.
[31] *Knightsbridge Estates Trust* v. *Byrne* [1939] Ch. 441.
[32] *Woodall* v. *Clifton* [1905] 2 Ch. 257 at 265, 268.
[33] Perpetuities and Accumulations Act 1964, s.9(1).

(c) future personal obligations are not within the rule. An example would be a covenant to pay mining royalties.[34]

(3) The perpetuity period

The maximum period for which vesting may be postponed is either:

(a) the period of a life or lives in being, and a further period of 21 years; or

(b) where there is no life in being, a period of 21 years; or

(c) in the case of post-1964 gifts, a period not exceeding 80 years which is specified in the instrument creating the gift as the perpetuity period.

In certain circumstances, the statutory period of 80 years may be shorter than the common law period, but the use of the statutory period has the advantage of simplicity and certainty.

One of the more difficult questions affecting perpetuities is to identify the life or lives in being. It is clear that the life or lives chosen need take no benefit. Thus, it is common to use a "royal lives clause," that is, a clause which specifies the perpetuity period as for example, "the period ending at the expiration of 21 years from the death of the last survivor of all the lineal descendants of his late Majesty King George VI[35] who shall be living at the time when the gift comes into effect". In principle, there is no limit to the number of lives which may be selected, provided they can be identified. In *Re Moore*[36] the settlor specified as the lives in being all persons then living, but the gift was void on the ground that it was impossible to identify the survivor.

In the royal lives and similar clauses, it is apparent from the words of the instrument that they are intended as the lives in being for the purposes of the rule. In other cases it may be far more difficult to decide whether a person is to be taken as a life in being. The principle may be stated that every person who is living at the date of the gift and is mentioned in it or is implied by it, is a life in being. Thus, a gift by a testator to "my grandchildren" presupposes the existence of his children, and if they are in fact alive, they will be taken as lives in being for the purpose of the rule.

A child *en ventre sa mère* is treated as a child who is alive if this is necessary to save a gift. Accordingly, if Susan is pregnant, a gift to the children of the child *en ventre* will be valid, for that child will be impli-

---

[34] *Witham* v. *Vane* (1883) Challis R.P. 440.

[35] The father of the present Queen. Consequently, the royal lives in question are those of H.M. Queen Elizabeth II, H.R.H. Princess Margaret, and their descendants. It is also probably still possible to use King George V (the grandfather of the present Queen), although the number of his descendants is now very considerable. It is certainly unsafe to specify the descendants of any previous sovereign (see the doubts cast, as early as 1901, on the validity of using the lives of descendants of Queen Victoria (then still alive) in *Re Moore* [1901] 1 Ch. 936).

[36] [1901] 1 Ch. 936.

cation be regarded as a life in being.[37] Similarly, the perpetuity period itself may be extended where there is a pregnancy. If, therefore, a period of 80 years is prescribed, and at the end of that time a woman is pregnant with a child who would, if alive, take, subject to being born alive that child will in fact take.[38]

There is a dictum in the Irish decision, *Re Kelly*[39] that the life chosen must be that of a human and not of an animal—an obvious if amusing proposition. It appears that only an Irish court has seen fit to pronounce formally upon it.

In the case of post-1964 instruments where advantage is not taken of specifying a period of not more than 80 years, section 3(4) of the 1964 Act prescribes rules for identifying the lives in being. The Act provides that such of the following who are alive and ascertainable at the date of the gift, and no other person, shall constitute the lives in being:

(a) the person who made the disposition. This clearly has no relevance to will trusts;

(b) in the case of a contingent gift to an individual or individuals, any person who may in time satisfy the conditions; or his parent or grandparent;

(c) in the case of a class gift, any member or potential member of the class; or his parent or grandparent;

(d) any person who is given any power, option, or other right in connection with the gift; and

(e) where the interest is to arise only if the prior interest of some person determines, that person having the prior interest.

There are further provisions which apply where there is a special power of appointment.[40]

The lives of persons in categories (b), (c) and (d) are disregarded if the number of those persons is so large as to render it impossible to ascertain the date of death of the survivor.

(4) "Possibilities not probabilities"

The general principle is that any possibility of the gift not vesting within the perpetuity period makes the gift void. This can be expressed by saying that the rule is concerned with "possibilities not probabilities," subject to the "wait and see" rule considered below.[41] Illustrations of this are provided by the decisions in *Re Dawson* and *Re Gaite* which were mentioned above, but the advances in biological knowledge now enable the court, when considering gifts to which the 1964 Act applies, to make certain presumptions.[42] These are that a male

---

[37] *Long* v. *Blackall* (1797) 7 T.R. 100.
[38] See *Cadell* v. *Palmer* (1833) 1 Cl. & F. 372, especially at pp. 421, 422.
[39] [1932] I.R. 255 at 260, 261.
[40] See *post*, para. (9).
[41] See *post*, para. (5).
[42] Perpetuities and Accumulations Act 1964.

cannot have a child at an age less than 14, and that a female can have a child between the ages of 12 and 55, but not outside that age-span.

(5) "Wait and see"

As regards pre-1964 gifts, it is necessary to construe the instrument creating the gift at the date when it comes into operation. So that if a gift is made to a person for life, with remainder to his eldest son to go to Canada, and at the date when the gift comes into force that person has no children, the gift to the eldest son would be void for remoteness: the life tenant is the only life in being, and his eldest son *may* not go to Canada within 21 years from his death. Under the rules, relating to pre-1964 gifts, it is not possible to wait and see whether in fact he does have a son who goes to Canada within 21 years from his death.

Section 3 of the 1964 Act, however, provides that in some cases the court may "wait and see" if a particular gift will offend against the rule. The first and most important case is that where a gift may or may not become vested within the perpetuity period—and this means either the common law period or the statutory period of up to 80 years whichever is relevant—the gift is to be treated as if it does not offend against the rule until it can be definitely shown that the gift *must* vest, if at all, after the end of the period. Thus, if an instrument coming into operation after July 15, 1964, contains a gift to a person who does not as yet have any children for life, with remainder to his eldest son to go to Canada, and if the life tenant leaves a son, it is possible to wait and see whether the son does, in fact, go to Canada within 21 years of the death of the life tenant and his parents.[43] If he does, the gift is valid.

(6) Age-reducing provisions

Section 163(1) of the Law of Property Act 1925 provides that where the vesting of property is made to depend on the attainment by the beneficiary of an age greater than 21, and that by virtue of that condition the gift would be void for remoteness, the age of 21 is to be substituted for the age stated in the instrument. The section applies only when the gift would have been void for remoteness and only to instruments coming into operation before July 16, 1964.

As regards instruments coming into operation after July 15, 1964, section 4 of the 1964 Act replaces section 163. By this section the age substituted is not that of 21, but the age nearest to the age which would have prevented the disposition from being void. Under the 1964 Act, therefore, the instrument is altered only to the extent necessary to save the disposition from offending against the rule.

Before applying section 4 of the 1964 Act, it is necessary to apply the "wait and see" rule. Suppose, therefore, that there is a gift to the first child of William to attain the age of 30. Suppose also that William has no children when the testator dies. As William is a life in being, it is necessary to wait until the death of him and his parents and see the

---

[43] For the purposes of wait and see, the life tenant's parents are also lives in being (under s.3) so it is possible to wait and see until 21 years after the death of the survivor of him and his parents.

position then. If by then all his children have reached the age of 10, the gift must vest if at all within the period. If, however, his only child is then five, the vesting age will be reduced to 25, so that the vesting takes place within 21 years from the death of William and his parents.[44]

A similar provision of the 1964 Act which has no equivalent in the 1925 Act, enables gifts to children to be saved in other situations. Suppose there is a gift to such of the children of Andrew who should be living at the date of death of the survivor of Andrew and his wife. This gift is void at common law, because Andrew might subsequently marry a woman who was not born at the date of the gift. Accordingly, Andrew, and not his wife, would be the life in being, and as his wife might survive him for more than 21 years, the interest of the children might vest outside the perpetuity period. Again the "wait and see" rule is applied. If this does not save the gift, then by virtue of section 5 of the Act the gift vests in interest immediately before the end of the perpetuity period. Accordingly, the gift would vest in interest 21 years from the death of Andrew and his parents.[44]

(7) Class gifts

Special provisions relate to "class gifts." For this purpose, a class is a number of persons who "come within a certain category or description defined by a general or collective formula, and who, if they take at all, are to take one divisible subject in certain proportionate shares."[45] As regards gifts in pre-1964 instruments, for the gift to be valid every member of the class must have fulfilled any necessary conditions within the perpetuity period: if any member has not fulfilled the conditions, the whole gift is void.[46]

Where the 1964 Act applies, however, many class gifts will in any case be saved by the wait and see provisions. But where these do not assist, the gift may still be saved by section 4(4). Under this subsection, if some members of the class have fulfilled the condition, but others have not, the class closes at the end of the perpetuity period to the exclusion of the others. Suppose, then, that there is a gift to a person for life with remainder to such of his children as shall marry, and at the date of the gift he has no children. It is possible to use the wait and see provisions to ascertain whether at the end of the perpetuity period—21 years after the death of him and his parents if no period is specified—he has had any children who have married. If at that time there are three children, and two have married, the class will then close, to the exclusion of the unmarried child, and the two married children will between them take the whole of the property comprised in the gift.

---

[44] Who are also lives in being for the purposes of wait and see.

[45] Per Lord Selborne L.C. in Pearkes v. Mosely (1880) 5 App.Cas. 714 at p. 723.

[46] Pearks v. Moseley (1880) 5 App.Cas. 714; Re Hooper's Settlement Trust [1948] Ch. 586. The effect has been alleviated to some extent by the class closing rules: see the so-called Rule in Andrews v. Partington (1791) 3 Bro.C.C. 401; for recent illustrations of the working of the Rule, see Re Chapman's Settlement Trusts [1977] 1 W.L.R. 1163, C.A.; Re Clifford's Settlement Trusts [1981] Ch. 63.

(8) Dependent limitations

The rule of common law is that where a gift follows and is dependent upon prior limitations which are void, that gift is also void.[47] In order to apply the rule, however, it was necessary to distinguish between a gift which merely followed a prior void gift, and a gift which both followed and was dependent upon that prior void gift.[48] In practice it is difficult to decide whether a gift is dependent in this sense[49] and, in broad terms, a gift must have its own independent date of vesting if it is not to be regarded as dependent.[50]

(9) Powers of appointment

(a) **Classification of powers.** The classification of powers has been discussed earlier.[51] Whether for the purpose of the perpetuity rule hybrid powers should be classified at common law as general or special is doubtful, but it is suggested that the rules prescribed by the 1964 Act for post-1964 instruments should be followed for common law purposes. In any event, by virtue of section 7 of the 1964 Act a general power is a power exercisable by one person only, which can be exercised by the donee of the power to transfer property to himself without the consent of any other person.[52] A power may be general even if it is exercisable by will only, and not *inter vivos*.[53] For the purposes of the perpetuity rule it follows that depending on its terms a hybrid power may be either general or special. If there is a power to appoint to anyone except Sanders, this will be a general power unless the donee of the power is Sanders himself.

(b) **Validity of powers.** There are two questions to be considered:

(*a*) is the power itself valid?
(*b*) is the appointment under the power valid?

(a) *Validity of Power*

(i) **Special powers.** A special power is void if it is capable of being exercised outside the perpetuity period.[54] However, for post-1964 instruments, the wait and see rule may be applied, to see whether it is in fact fully exercised within the period. Where it is exercised within the period, but only partially, the power is only void to the extent that it was not exercised within the period.[55]

---

[47] *Re Hubbard* [1963] Ch. 275; *Re Buckton* [1964] Ch. 497; *cf. Re Robinson* [1963] 1 W.L.R. 628.
[48] *Re Coleman* [1936] Ch. 528.
[49] *Re Backhouse* [1921] 2 Ch. 51.
[50] *Re Coleman, ante.*
[51] *Ante*, p. 135.
[52] Except where consent is required as to the mode of exercise of the power.
[53] This is also the position at common law—*Rous* v. *Jackson* (1885) 29 Ch.D. 521.
[54] *Re Abbot* [1893] 1 Ch. 54.
[55] Perpetuities and Accumulations Act 1964.

(ii) General powers. Because the donee of the power may appoint to himself, property subject to a general power is regarded for most purposes as property belonging to the donee. Therefore, so far as the validity of the power is concerned, it is necessary only that the power should be acquired within the perpetuity period: it is not necessary for it to be exercised within that period.[56] However, where the general power is *exercisable by will*, the same rule applies as for special powers.[57]

(b) *Validity of Appointments*

(i) Special powers. Because the disposition of property subject to a special power is restricted, the perpetuity period commences with the date when the power is created, not when it is exercised. In principle, therefore, it is necessary at common law to consider the position as at the date of creation of the power; assume that the appointment is then made; and then see whether the gift vests within the perpetuity period. Even at common law, however, it is permissible to take into account the circumstances prevailing at the time when the power is exercised. If, therefore, by the terms of the appointment the gift could vest outside the perpetuity period, but when related to the circumstances existing at the time of the appointment it is seen that the vesting must occur within the period, if at all, the appointment is valid. This may be shown by an example. Suppose Charles by will gives property to Desmond for life, and that he also gives Desmond a power to appoint that property to his children. Suppose also that Desmond has a son Fergus who is born after the death of Charles. When Fergus reaches the age of 10, Desmond appoints the property to Fergus "as and when he attains the age of 30." Looking at the situation at the date of creation of the power, on the death of Charles, the gift and appointment are read together as if they provided: "to Desmond for life, with remainder to Fergus as and when he attains the age of 30." As Fergus is not then alive, it is clear that Fergus may take after 21 years from the death of Desmond, and the gift would prima facie be void. However, the modified wait and see rule is applied so that in the light of the circumstances existing when the power was exercised, it is seen that the gift must vest within 20 years of the death of Desmond, with the result that the appointment is valid.

The general wait and see provisions of the 1964 Act apply to powers which are both created and exercised after July 15, 1964.[58]

(ii) General powers. The perpetuity period runs from the date of exercise of the power, and not from the date of its creation. The rules in respect of property comprised in a general power are the same as for property comprised in an absolute gift. However, if a power is general in its terms, but is only exercisable by more than one donee, it is treated as a special power.[59]

---

[56] *Re Fane* [1913] 1 Ch. 404.
[57] *Woolaston* v. *King* (1868) L.R. 8 Eq. 165.
[58] Perpetuities and Accumulations Act 1964.
[59] *Re the Earl of Coventry's Indentures* [1974] Ch. 77.

(10) General effect of the Act

The 1964 Act, which, it is repeated, applies only to gifts coming into force after July 15, 1964,[60] therefore contains provisions which in the long term are welcome[61] but which in the short term create a duality.

If a limitation in a trust instrument infringes the perpetuity rule, that interest will be held upon a resulting trust[62] for the settlor. Where the void limitation is contained in a will, that property will fall into residue, or will be distributed as on intestacy.

2. *The Rule Against Inalienability*

(1) Generally

The corollary to the rule that a gift must vest, if at all, within the perpetuity period is the principle that property must not be rendered inalienable.[63] The reason for this principle is to keep land and other property freely marketable and in circulation among members of the community. A gift is inalienable if there is some provision which prevents the property being disposed of. This provision may be either a term of the gift itself,[64] or, in the case of a gift to a club or association, a rule of that club or association.[65]

To this general principle there are two exceptions. First, by analogy with the perpetuity rule, it seems that property may validly be made inalienable during the lifetime or times of persons in being at the time of the gift, and for 21 years thereafter.[66] Secondly, property may be made inalienable in the hands of a charity.[67]

A gift to a body corporate, which is not a charity, will in general not offend against the rule against inalienability. Even though the company may, if it so wishes, retain the property indefinitely for the benefit of its shareholders, if the gift is absolute, it will not be under any obligation to retain it. If, however, a condition is imposed on the gift prohibiting the company from disposing of it, the gift does offend against the rule and is void.[68]

The rule is principally applicable to non-charitable purpose trusts and to gifts to unincorporated associations. These have already been considered in Chapter 3.[69] It should be noted that Section 15(4) of the 1964 Act provides that a donor of property for these purposes cannot use the statutory period of up to 80 years for the duration of the trust by

---

[60] With the minor exception of s.7.

[61] Except s.10, they represent the recommendations of the Law Reform Committee. Cmnd. 18 (November 1956).

[62] See *post*, p. 201.

[63] *Carne* v. *Long* (1860) 2 De G.F. & J. 75 at p. 80.

[64] *Re Patten* [1929] 2 Ch. 276.

[65] *Rickard* v. *Robson* (1862) 31 Beav. 244; *Re Nottage* [1895] 2 Ch. 649; *Re Drummond* [1914] 2 Ch. 90.

[66] *Carne* v. *Long* (1860) 2 De G.F. & J. 75; *Re Dean* (1889) 41 Ch.D. 552 at p. 557.

[67] *Chamberlayne* v. *Brockett* (1872) 8 Ch.App. 206 at 211.

[68] A further reason for it being void is that no person could enforce the trust: *Morice* v. *Bishop of Durham* (1805) 10 Ves. 521 at p. 539; *Bowman* v. *Secular Society Ltd.* [1917] A.C. 406 at p. 441; *Re Wood* [1949] Ch. 498.

[69] See *ante* p. 112 *et seq.*

analogy with the provision of section 1, and in this respect the pre-1964 position remains unaltered.[70]

As will be explained later[71] a gift to charity is not void even if it is made inalienable, and a gift over from one charity to another charity is not void although the vesting in the second charity may take place at any time in the future.[72] The normal perpetuity provisions apply, however, in the case of a gift from a non-charity to a charity or from a charity to a non-charity.

3. *The Rule Against Accumulations*

Another result of the policy of the law that property and wealth generally should be free to circulate has been the statutory control of accumulations. This resulted from the decision in *Thellusson* v. *Woodford*[73] where Thellusson directed that the income from his property should be accumulated for the perpetuity period, which in his case was somewhat over 70 years.

Parliament intervened and passed the Thellusson Act in 1800 to restrict accumulations to a fairly short period, and the position is now governed by sections 164 to 166 of the Law of Property Act 1925, as amended by section 13 of the Perpetuities and Accumulations Act 1964.[74]

Section 164 of the Law of Property Act 1925 lays down the general rule that income may not be accumulated for longer than any one of the following periods:

(a) the life of the settlor (this is the period adopted in the case of gifts *inter vivos* where no other period is specified);

(b) 21 years from the death of the testator or settlor (this is the period adopted in the case of gifts by will where no other period is specified);

(c) the duration of the minority or minorities of any persons living at the death of the testator or settlor (this period begins from the death of the settlor or testator);

(d) the duration of the minority or minorities of any persons entitled under the settlement (in this case the beneficiary need not be alive at the death of the testator or settlor and the accumulation period will commence at the birth of that beneficiary).

The 1964 Act added, in respect of instruments coming into operation after July 15, 1964,

(e) the period of 21 years from the date of making the disposition; and

---

[70] The provision appears to be clearly to this effect, but see R. H. Maudsley, *The Modern Law of Perpetuities*, p. 177, in which the opposite is argued.

[71] *Post*, p. 297.

[72] *Re Tyler* [1891] 3 Ch. 252; and see *ante*, p. 297.

[73] (1798) 4 Ves.Jun. 227.

[74] As further amended by Family Law Reform Act 1969, Sched. 3, para. 7.

(*f*) the duration of the minority or minorities of any person in being at the date of making an *inter vivos* disposition.

A direction to accumulate for a period longer than one of the foregoing makes the whole gift void if the accumulation is directed for longer than the perpetuity period, but if the accumulation is not directed for longer than the perpetuity period, the direction is invalid only as to the excess over the authorised period.[75]

Section 165 of the Law of Property Act 1925 expressly declares to be valid the case where income is directed to be accumulated for one of the authorised periods, and at the end of that period, the income has to be accumulated under the general law, or under some other statutory provision. As will be noted in due course[76] where by virtue of section 31 of the Trustee Act 1925 money is held upon trust for an infant, such of the income from that money as is not applied for the infant's benefit is to be accumulated until he reaches the age of majority. Thus, suppose a testator gives property to a person for life, with remainder to his eldest son, and there is a direction to accumulate for a period of 21 years from the death of the testator. In the event of the eldest son being a minor at the death of his father, accumulations will arise under the gift for the first 21 years, and thereafter until the eldest son attains his majority by virtue of section 31 of the Trustee Act 1925.[77]

There are certain exceptions from the general restrictions on accumulations, and in these cases any period of accumulation may be specified. These cases are:

(*a*) accumulations for the payment of the debts of any person;
(*b*) accumulations for the purpose of raising portions[78] for children or issue of the settlor, or any person entitled under the settlement; and
(*c*) accumulations of the produce of timber or wood.[79]

4. *Possible future reforms*

In 1993 the Law Commission issued a Consultation Paper on Perpetuities and Accumulations.[79A] This Paper contains a detailed examination of the present law, which is criticised on a number of grounds, including complexity, uncertainty and inconsistency.

So far as concerns the Rule against Perpetuities, the Law Commission suggests four options: first, to do nothing; secondly, to abolish the rule without replacement; thirdly, to replace the rule with a new rule, either a general rule limiting the duration of trusts or the conferral on the courts of a wide discretion to vary trusts; and, fourthly, to reform the

---

[75] *Re Jefferies* [1936] 2 All E.R. 626.
[76] Chap. 17, section 2.
[77] And see *Re Maber* [1928] Ch. 88.
[78] *Re Bourne* (1946) 115 L.J.Ch. 152.
[79] L.P.A., s.164 (2).
[79A] "The Law of Trusts. The Rules against Perpetuities and Excessive Accumulations." Consultation Paper No. 133. October 19, 1993. Responses requested by June 30, 1994.

rule in one or more of five possible ways: removing the need to apply the common law before "wait and see", making a fixed period of years the only perpetuity period, introducing a *cy-près* power for the court to reform dispositions, making provisions for advancements in reproductive technology, and introducing new exceptions to the rule. Their provisional choice is between abolishing the rule without replacement and reforming the rule in one or more of the five ways mentioned.

So far as concerns the Rule against Accumulations, the Law Commission suggests three options: first, to do nothing, secondly, to abolish the rule without replacement; and, thirdly, to reform the rule in one of the following possible ways: changing the accumulation period to a fixed period of, say, 80 years, reducing all existing periods of 21 years to 18 years, codifying all the relevant law in one statute, or introducing new exceptions to the rule. Their provisional choice is between abolishing the rule without replacement and reforming the rule in one of the ways mentioned.

This Consultation Paper will undoubtedly produce considerable comment, both from a technical[79B] and from a comparative[79C] point of view. It is obviously premature to speculate on the likely contents of the future Law Commission Report which will follow the consultation process but they will undoubtedly require discussion in future editions of this work.

III. SAFEGUARDING PROPERTY FROM CREDITORS

For almost as long as the trust has been invented, it has repeatedly been used in an attempt to achieve protection from their creditors by those who contemplate the actual or potential threat of financial ruin. If a man effectively transfers his property to another upon trust for his wife, or other friend or relative, and goes bankrupt, on general principles that man's trustee in bankruptcy will not be able to claim the property subject to the trust. Thus it is and has been common for a man to give his property upon trust for his wife, with the intention that should bankruptcy occur, as the property is in his wife's name, it cannot be taken away, yet he will nevertheless be able to enjoy it. Alternatively, a man may wish to give his property upon trust for his wife or to some other close relative or friend in the hope that they will derive the benefit from it rather than his creditors. Not surprisingly statutory restrictions have long been placed on the use of the trust for this purpose, and it is with these that this section is concerned but nevertheless the basic principle remains true that where the statutory provisions do not operate the trust may be an effective means of preventing creditors from laying their hands upon a person's property.[80]

The relevant statutory provisions were until recently found in two Acts. Section 172 of the Law of Property Act 1925 enabled dispositions of property made with intent to defraud creditors to be set aside,

---

[79B] See H. W. Wilkinson, [1994] Conv. 92; C. T. Emery, 57 M.L.R. (1994).
[79C] See D. Brownbill, [1994] 1 JIntP 1.
[80] See *post*, p. 182.

whether or not the person who made the disposition was bankrupt, while Section 42 of the Bankruptcy Act 1914 enabled various dispositions to be set aside when the person who had made them had become bankrupt. These sections were, however, repealed by the Insolvency Act 1985. The present law is contained in the Insolvency Act 1986.

1. *Transactions Defrauding Creditors*

Section 423 of the Insolvency Act 1986 enables the court to intervene where it is satisfied that any person, whether a natural person or a body corporate,[81] has entered into a transaction at an undervalue for the purpose of putting assets beyond the reach of anyone who is making or may at some time make a claim against him or of otherwise prejudicing the interests of such a person in relation to the claim which he is making or may make.

As in the case of all previous provisions of this type, there is no requirement that the person entering into the transaction should be bankrupt or even that he should be in debt. As Jessel M.R. said in *Re Butterworth*,[82] where a settlement made by a prosperous baker immediately before purchasing a grocer's business, of which he had no experience, was set aside under the predecessor of Section 172 of the Law of Property Act 1925: "a man is not entitled to go into a hazardous business, and immediately before doing so, settle all his property voluntarily, the object being this: 'If I succeed in business, I make a fortune for myself. If I fail, I leave my creditors unpaid. They will bear the loss.' That is the very thing which the Statute of Elizabeth was meant to prevent". It is somewhat ironic that, at about the time when this observation was made, legislation was being introduced permitting for the first time the incorporation of companies with limited liability, which makes it entirely legitimate, subject to certain minimum requirements as to membership, for the shareholders to adopt exactly the policy so stringently condemned by Jessel M.R.. However, despite the fact that the legislature has accepted that an appropriate way for an investor to limit his possible losses in hazardous ventures is to carry them out in the name of a limited company, it has continued to prohibit the use of trusts and settlements for the same purpose. Consequently, a transaction which has been entered into at an undervalue can still be impeached whenever the court is satisfied that it was entered into for one of the purposes mentioned above. Hence Section 423 was successfully invoked in *Moon* v. *Franklin*[83] when a husband used the substantial proceeds of sale of his practice to make substantial gifts to his wife at a time when he was threatened with legal proceedings which he knew might not be covered by sufficient insurance.

A person enters into a transaction at an undervalue in the following circumstances: first, if he makes a gift or enters into a transaction on

---

[81] See also Insolvency Act 1986 s.207.
[82] (1882) 19 Ch.D. 588 at p. 598.
[83] (1990) *The Independent,* June 22, 1990.

terms which provide for him to receive no consideration; secondly, if he enters into a transaction in consideration of marriage; or, thirdly, if he enters into a transaction for a consideration whose value, in money or money's worth, is significantly less than the value, in money or money's worth, of the consideration provided by himself. These requirements were clearly satisfied in *Moon* v. *Franklin*[84] where a husband purchased property in the joint names of himself and his wife without any financial contribution from her, transferred to her his interest in their matrimonial home, and gave her a sum of money. On the other hand, a transaction made for full value cannot be impeached under this section even where there was a clear intention to prejudice creditors.[85] The precise meaning of undervalue was considered in *Re M.C. Bacon*.[86] A company which created a floating charge over its assets in favour of a bank to secure its overdraft in consideration of the bank making further advances, continuing to honour cheques and, consequently, not calling in the overdraft was held not to have entered into a transaction at an undervalue. The assets of the company had not been reduced by the creation of the floating charge and so it had not provided any consideration in money or money's worth. Since no value in money or money's worth could be attributed to the consideration provided by the bank either, there was no imbalance between the consideration provided by the two parties.

Under Section 424, application to the court can be made by anyone prejudiced by the transaction; however, where the person entering into the transaction has become insolvent (bankrupt, in the case of a natural person, wound up or the subject of an administration order[87] in the case of a body corporate), any such application requires the leave of the court—in such circumstances, it is the official receiver, the trustee in bankruptcy, or the liquidator who has the primary right to apply. Where a voluntary arrangement has been approved,[88] the supervisor of the voluntary arrangement can also apply. Any application made is treated as being made on behalf of everyone prejudiced by the transaction.

On application, the court can, under Section 423 (2), make such order as it thinks fit for restoring the position to what it would have been if the transaction had not been entered into and protecting the interests of the persons prejudiced by the transaction. More specifically, Section 425 (1) enables the court to require the vesting in whoever it may direct, for the benefit of everyone in respect of whom the application is treated to be made, of the following: any property transferred, any property representing the application of the proceeds of sale of the property transferred or of any money transferred, and any sum which the court

---

[84] (1990) *The Independent*, June 22, 1990.

[85] This was not the case under Law of Property Act 1925, s.172; see *Lloyds Bank* v. *Marcan* [1973] 1 W.L.R. 1387.

[86] [1990] B.C.L.C. 324 (actually a decision on s.239 (preferences); see *post*, p. 178). See also *In re Kumar (a bankrupt)* [1993] 1 W.L.R. 224.

[87] Under Part II of the Insolvency Act 1986.

[88] Under Part I of the Insolvency Act 1986 in the case of bodies corporate and under Part VIII in the case of natural persons.

decides should be payable in respect of any benefit received as a result of the transaction. Thus, in *Moon* v. *Franklin*,[89] an order was made restraining any dealing with the land and requiring the return of the unspent part of the monetary gift. Such orders are obviously capable of prejudicing third parties; however, Section 425 (2) provides that no such order shall prejudice any interest in property acquired from a person other than the original transferor in good faith for value without notice nor require any person who was not a party to the original transaction to pay any sum in respect of any benefit received in good faith for value without notice.

2. *Transactions Capable of being Impeached on Bankruptcy*

The Insolvency Act 1986 has replaced Section 42 of the Bankruptcy Act 1914 with a series of provisions which enable transactions at an undervalue and by way of preference entered into by natural persons and by bodies corporate to be set aside in the event that they occurred during stipulated periods of time prior to their bankruptcy.

(1) Transactions entered into by natural persons

(a) **Transactions at an undervalue.** Section 339 enables the trustee in bankruptcy to apply to the court for an order where a natural person has entered into a transaction at an undervalue (which has the same meaning as in Section 423[90]) within the periods of time set out in Section 341. The court may make such order as it thinks fit to restore the position to what it would have been if the transaction had not been entered into. The available orders, set out in section 342, are similar to those which may be made under section 425[91]; no order may either prejudice any interest in property which was acquired from a person other than the bankrupt in good faith for value without notice of the relevant circumstances or require a person who was not a party to the transaction to make any payment in respect of any benefit which he received as a result of the transaction in good faith for value without notice of the relevant circumstances.

A trustee in bankruptcy can therefore claim a spouse's share in the matrimonial home to the extent that the beneficial interest held exceeds the contributions made to its acquisition during the appropriate period. The fact that that beneficial interest has been acquired as the result of a property adjustment order on divorce makes no difference since the order can be set aside[92]; particular problems may arise where the matrimonial proceedings were compromised since if the compromise reached cannot be assessed in terms of money or money's worth the section will apply.[93]

Section 341 provides that the basic period is two years prior to the

---

[89] (1990) *The Independent*, June 22, 1990.
[90] See *ante*, p. 176.
[91] See *ante*, p. 177.
[92] Insolvency Act 1986, 14th Schedule.
[93] *In re Kumar (a bankrupt)* [1993] 1 W.L.R. 224.

date of the presentation of the bankruptcy petition but this period is increased to five years if the person later to become bankrupt was insolvent at the time of the transaction or became insolvent as a result of carrying it out. A person is insolvent for this purpose if at the time of the transaction he was unable to pay his debts as they fell due or if the value of his assets was less than the value of his liabilities, taking into account both contingent and prospective liabilities. There is a rebuttable presumption that a person was insolvent in this sense in the event that the other party to the transaction was an associate of his, defined by Section 435 as including relatives of the bankrupt or of his spouse, his partners, his employers, his employees and any companies with which he was at the time related.

The length of this period, the rebuttable presumption of insolvency in the case of transactions between associates, and the very wide definition of associate pose very considerable potential problems, not only because of the difficulty of rebutting the presumption of insolvency but also because of the difficulty of proving five years after the event that the transaction was not at an undervalue. Consequently the only safe way to proceed when entering into a transaction between persons who fall within the definition of associates is to obtain affidavit evidence at the time from suitably qualified persons that the transaction was not at an undervalue and/or from the accountants of the parties that neither of them was insolvent at the time of or in consequence of the transaction. This will obviously involve a certain amount of expense but will avoid any possibility of future problems if any of the parties becomes bankrupt in the next five years.

Even greater problems arise in the case of gifts of unregistered land. Since any subsequent purchaser will see the deed of gift in the course of his investigation of title, he will necessarily have notice of the relevant circumstances that the land was acquired at an undervalue. Consequently, any gift of unregistered land will render the donee's title thereto bad for two years because of the possibility of the transferor becoming bankrupt during that period; the donee will therefore effectively be prevented from making any disposition of it for value for that period. Further, if the donor and donee fall within the definition of associates, something which is in practice highly likely in view of the width of that definition, the period will increase to five years unless the donee can affirmatively prove, presumably by affidavit evidence from the donor's accountants, that the donor was insolvent neither at the time of nor in consequence of the transaction. Even where the donor and donee are not associates, a purchaser will nevertheless be at risk if he acquires notice that the donor was insolvent at the time of or in consequence of the transaction and may be understandably reluctant to proceed in case notice is subsequently attributed to him. Representations have been made with a view to some amendment of Section 339 to deal with this problem.[94]

---

[94] See (1992) 89/5 L.S. Gaz., p. 13.

(b) Transactions by way of preference. Section 340 enables the trustee in bankruptcy to apply to the court for an order where a natural person has given a preference to any person within the periods of time set out in Section 341. The court may make such order as it thinks fit to restore the position to what it would have been if the preference had not been given—the available orders are set out in section 342.[95] Such a preference will have been given if the effect of the transaction is to improve the position of a creditor, surety or guarantor in the event of bankruptcy. An order can only be made if the transaction was influenced by a desire to bring about this result, although such a desire will be presumed where the other person is an associate. However, it has been held that, where the transaction has been entered into as a matter of commercial necessity, it was not influenced by any desire to give a preference.[96]

Section 341 provides that the basic period is six months prior to the date of presentation of the bankruptcy petition but this period is increased to two years if the person to whom the preference was given was an associate. However, if the transaction was not only by way of preference but also at an undervalue, the longer periods which apply to transactions at an undervalue will be applicable instead.

(2) Transactions entered into by bodies corporate

The provisions of the Insolvency Act 1986 which govern transactions entered into by bodies corporate are broadly similar to those which apply to natural persons; only the differences will be mentioned here.

Section 238 deals with transactions at an undervalue (defined in the same way but without any reference to marriage consideration); no order will be made if the court is satisfied that the company entered into the transaction in good faith for the purpose of carrying on its business and there were at the time reasonable grounds for believing that the company would be benefitted thereby. The period of time is two years prior to the onset of insolvency but a transaction will only be set aside if the company was unable to pay its debts at the time of the transaction or became unable to do so as a result of it.

Section 239 deals with transactions by way of preference. In *Re M.C. Bacon*,[97] a company which could not have continued trading without its bank's support created a floating charge over its assets in favour of the bank to secure its overdraft shortly before becoming insolvent; it was held that, since the granting of the floating charge had been made for reasons of commercial necessity and not with any desire to improve the position of the bank in the event of insolvency, no preference had been given. The basic period is six months prior to the onset of insolvency but this period is increased to two years if the transaction by way of preference is in favour of a person connected with the company or at an undervalue. Once again, a transaction will only be set aside if the

---

[95] See *ante*, p. 178.
[96] *Re M.C. Bacon* [1990] B.C.L.C. 324.
[97] [1990] B.C.L.C. 324.

company was unable to pay its debts at the time of the transaction or became unable to do so as a result of it.

IV. SAFEGUARDING PROPERTY FROM CLAIMS BY DEPENDANTS

The development of statutory obligations to maintain dependants has inevitably led to attempts being made to avoid these obligations by the use of trusts and, equally inevitably, to the introduction of statutory restrictions on the use of the trust to defect claims for maintenance and for financial provision out of estates.

1. *Claims made in the Course of Matrimonial Proceedings*

Section 37 of the Matrimonial Causes Act 1973 enables a spouse to apply to the court for an order where the other spouse is about to make or has made some disposition of property with the intention of reducing the assets available for the provision of financial relief in matrimonial proceedings. Such an intention is presumed if the disposition was made within the three year period prior to the date of the application for financial relief; otherwise, it must be proved affirmatively. If the disposition has not yet been made, the court may make such order as it thinks fit; if the disposition has already been made, it may be set aside.

2. *Claims for Financial Provision out of Estates*

Under the Inheritance (Provision for Family and Dependants) Act 1975, the ability of a testator to freely dispose of his assets is made subject to an obligation to provide for his surviving spouse and other dependants, who can apply to the court for a share of the estate if reasonable financial provision for them has not been made. In order to prevent a testator defeating such claims by disposing of all his property *inter vivos*, Sections 10–13 of the Act provide that any person who, during the last six years of the deceased's life, has benefitted from a disposition made other than for value "with the intention of defeating an application for financial provision under this Act" can be required to provide sums of money up to but not exceeding the value of the property received so that appropriate financial provision can be made. It should be noted that the necessary intention has to be determined on a balance of probabilities and does not have to constitute the only motive of the deceased for the making of the disposition.

CHAPTER 6

PROTECTIVE TRUSTS

It has been seen that a trust which contravenes the policy of the bankruptcy laws will be invalid,[1] but there are indirect means available by which this result can be avoided. It is, however, essential to make two points clear at the outset:

(i) that a *proviso* or *condition* contained in a trust of property in favour of a *third party* that it is not to be subject to the claims of creditors will be void[2]; and

(ii) that a trust set up by a person in favour of *himself until* bankruptcy, with remainders over may also be ineffective.[3] If he goes bankrupt the property will generally vest in his trustee in bankruptcy. But the fact that this will not always be the position in illustrated by *Re Detmold*.[4] A husband had settled his own property on trust for himself for life or until alienation, either voluntary or involuntary by process of law in favour of a particular creditor, and then over to his wife and children. North J. held that the gift over in favour of the wife and children was valid and effective on an involuntary alienation. It operated in any event other than the settlor's bankruptcy, which took place afterwards. In other words, if a person goes bankrupt after the gift over has taken effect, as in *Re Detmold*, the trustee in bankruptcy can take nothing. It will be seen, therefore, that the provision for determination will be effective in the happening of events other than the bankruptcy of the settlor.

But it is true to say that if a settlor wishes to achieve his purpose in protecting the estate against a spendthrift or reckless beneficiary and thereby guard against alienation or bankruptcy he must use more sophisticated machinery. Essentially this will take the form of the creation of a determinable interest in favour of a third party coupled, if necessary, with protective and discretionary trusts.

---

[1] See *ante*, p. 175.
[2] *Younghusband* v. *Gisborne* (1844) 1 Coll.C.C. 400, affirmed (1846) 15 L.J. Ch. 355; *Re Sanderson's Trust* (1857) 3 Kay & J. 497.
[3] *Re Burroughs-Fowler* [1916] 2 Ch. 251.
[4] (1889) 40 Ch.D. 585; and see *Re Johnson* [1904] 1 K.B. 134.

I. DETERMINABLE INTERESTS

It may be thought somewhat surprising that, although a settlor cannot settle property on a beneficiary subject to a condition or proviso that it will not be available to his creditors on bankruptcy, he can grant a determinable interest in favour of that beneficiary (if this is not the settlor himself) *until* bankruptcy, which will be perfectly effective.[5] The distinction between a conditional and determinable interest is fundamentally a logical one, however outmoded. A *condition* of its nature cuts down an interest already granted; provision for a *determining* event merely delimits the interest to be granted. The existence of this distinction makes it essential for a draftsman to be careful not to create a conditional interest by accident and, thereby, defeat the intentions of the settlor.

II. PROTECTIVE TRUSTS[6]

These trusts provide a highly effective means of restraining spendthrift beneficiaries. They combine a determinable life interest with a discretionary trust. The beneficiary's life interest will normally be made determinable on alienation or bankruptcy and will be followed in such an event by a discretionary trust in favour of the former life tenant and/or members of his family.

(1) Trustee Act 1925, s. 33

It was formerly the practice to set out protective trusts *in extenso*. But with a view to shortening the length of settlements, section 33 of the Trustee Act 1925 provides that a mere reference to "protective trusts" will bring into play the protective trusts set forth in that section.

This section provides that where *income*, including an annuity or other periodical payment, is directed to be held on protective trusts for the benefit of any person for his life or any less period[7] (such person being described in the section as "the principal beneficiary") then during that period the income is held on the following trusts, although this must be without prejudice to any prior interests:

1. Upon trust for the principal beneficiary during the trust period *or* until he does or attempts to do any act or thing, or any event happens (other than an advance under any statutory or express power) whereby, if the income were payable during the trust period to the principal beneficiary absolutely during that period, he would be deprived of the right to receive the same or any part thereof;
2. If the trust fails or determines during the trust period, then for the

---

[5] *Billson* v. *Crofts* (1873) L.R. 15 Eq. 314; *Re Aylwin's Trusts* (1873) L.R. 16 Eq. 585.
[6] See Sheridan (1957) 21 Conv. (N.S.) 110.
[7] For an illustration of protective trusts designed to last until remarriage and the effect of a nullity decree on the second marriage: see *D'Altroy's Will Trusts* [1968] 1 W.L.R. 120; and see Matrimonial Causes Act 1973, ss.11, 12, 16.

residue of that period, the income is to be held upon trust to be applied as the trustees in their absolute discretion (without being liable to account for the exercise of such discretion) think fit, for the maintenance or support or otherwise for the benefit of all or any of the following persons:

(*a*) The principal beneficiary and his or her wife or husband, if any, and his or her children or more remote issue,[8] if any, *or*

(*b*) the principal beneficiary and the persons who would, if he were dead, be entitled to the trust property or the income where there is no wife or husband or issue in existence.[9]

The section does not apply to trusts coming into operation before the commencement of the Act, and, moreover, it is subject to any variations which may be made in the trust instrument.[10] It is also provided that nothing in the section operates to validate any trust which, if contained in the trust instrument, would be liable to be set aside.[11]

(2) "On protective trusts"

The purpose of the section is to avoid the necessity to set out the trusts expressly in the trust instrument. But protective trusts can, and often still are, expressly created, and in any case there is, as has been seen, provision for modification of the statutory provisions[12] to suit the circumstances of the individual trust. Furthermore, whether the statutory form is used or its essence is set out in terms, its effect is only to engraft trusts on the life interest. Accordingly, it was held by Vaisey J. in *Re Allsopp's Marriage Settlement*[13] that if the life interest is extinguished, as it was in that case by an order of the Divorce Court, the engrafted protective trusts, being incapable of any separate existence, are also extinguished.

(3) Determining events

The question of what events will be sufficient to cause a forfeiture of a protected life interest (as the interest of the principal beneficiary is described) and bring the discretionary trusts into operation has been considered in a large number of cases. The point will be of importance not only where the trusts contained in section 33 are employed but also where there is an express protective trust. Many of the cases to be considered involved express protective trusts, but it is thought that the principles laid down have equal application to the statutory trusts.

It is self-evident that the bankruptcy of or an alienation by the

---

[8] Including illegitimate children and issue: Family Law Reform Act 1969, s.15(3).

[9] s.33(1).

[10] s.33(2).

[11] s.33(3). Accordingly, a settlement made on the settlor himself until bankruptcy and then on discretionary trusts may be ineffective: *Re Burroughs-Fowler* [1916] 2 Ch. 251. See *ante*, p. 183.

[12] See note 10, *ante*.

[13] [1959] Ch. 81.

principal beneficiary will bring about a forfeiture of the protected life interest. But it is not perhaps so obvious (but it was nevertheless so held by Luxmoore L.J. in *Re Walker*[14]) that this will still be the case if the bankruptcy has already occurred when the trust comes into operation. In other cases the determining events have taken the most diverse forms as the following illustrations show.

In *Re Balfour's Settlement*,[15] for example, various sums had in breach of trust been advanced by the trustees to the principal beneficiary. The trustees then asserted their right to retain the income of the fund in order to make good the breach of trust. The principal beneficiary then went bankrupt. Farwell J. held that, since the trustees had asserted their right to the income before the date of bankruptcy, the life interest had determined and the discretionary trust had come into operation and, therefore, nothing passed to the trustee in bankruptcy. Again, in *Re Baring's Settlement Trusts*,[16] the principal beneficiary had failed to bring her children within the jurisdiction and a writ of sequestration was thereupon issued empowering the sequestrators to take possession of all her real and personal estate until she did so. The sequestrators also gave the trustees notice not to pay further money to her and required that income be paid to them. Morton J. held that since the trusts were designed to confer continuous enjoyment of the income on the principal beneficiary, the sequestration was effective to determine her life interest. Yet again, in *Re Dennis' Settlement Trusts*,[17] Farwell J. held that the execution of a deed of variation of the protective trusts contained in the principal deed—the variation providing for payment of part of the income to another person—brought the forfeiture clause into operation.

But there are also many other cases where the events in question have been held *not* to determine the protected life interest. Again, they take a diversity of forms. Not surprisingly, for example, in *Re Tancred's Settlement*,[18] Buckley J. held that an appointment of the trustees as his attorneys to receive the income of the settled funds did not cause the beneficiary's life interest to be forfeited. The same result occurred in *Re Oppenheim's Will Trusts*[19] on the effect of the appointment of a receiver to a principal beneficiary who had been certified as a person of unsound mind. It was similarly held by the Court of Appeal in *Re Westby's Settlement*[20] that a statutory charge, namely the expenses of a receiver in such circumstances, was not the kind of charge intended to be aimed at by forfeiture clauses. All these cases tend to show, in Farwell J.'s words, that "we must bear in mind that the courts do not construe gifts on forfeitures so as to extend their limits beyond the fair meaning of the

---

[14] [1939] Ch. 974.
[15] [1938] Ch. 928.
[16] [1940] Ch. 737.
[17] [1942] Ch. 283.
[18] [1903] 1 Ch. 715.
[19] [1950] Ch. 633.
[20] [1950] Ch. 296.

words unless they are actually driven to it. Forfeitures are not regarded with favour."[21]

The effect of an order of the court on a forfeiture clause has also come into question. Thus in *Re Mair*[22] Farwell J. held that an order of the court under section 57 of the Trustee Act 1925,[23] giving power to trustees to raise capital moneys for the benefit of life tenants, would not cause a forfeiture of protected life interests because the section is an overriding one, the provisions of which are deemed to be read into every settlement. But this decision should be compared with that of Eve J. in *Re Salting*[24] where the result was that, if the scheme sanctioned by the court under section 57 involved an agreement by the life tenant to pay premiums on insurance policies with a promise that if they were not duly paid the trustees were to pay them out of income, the failure by the life tenant to pay would create a forfeiture. In such a case it is plain that it will be the act or omission of the life tenant which creates the forfeiture and not the exercise by the court of its overriding power.

The principles established by the last two decisions are clear enough. But otherwise the position is by no means straightforward. Especial difficulty arises from other cases involving orders in matrimonial proceedings varying protective trusts. The Court of Appeal in *General Accident, Fire and Life Assurance Corporation Ltd.* v. *Inland Revenue Commissioners*[25] were in no doubt that an order in matrimonial proceedings to pay an annual sum of money to the wife during her life did not bring about a forfeiture of the husband's protected life interest under section 33 and, accordingly, the discretionary trusts under this section did not arise. This was so because the court order overrode the settlement trusts, was an event to which both life tenant and trustee had to bow and, moreover, was not such an event as was contemplated by the section, which was intended as a protection to spendthrift or improvident or weak life tenants.[26] But if the principle adumbrated by the Court of Appeal is to be applied generally, it is by no means easy to reconcile the earlier decision of Danckwerts J. in *Re Richardson's Will Trusts*[27] where an order had been made in matrimonial proceedings for payment of an annual sum for the wife of the protected life tenant to be charged on his life interest, and it was also ordered that a deed be settled to give effect to the charge. It was held that, because the order was not complied with by the execution of a deed, its effect was to create an equitable charge on the interest; this involved forfeiture of that interest; and the discretion-

---

[21] *Re Greenwood* [1901] 1 Ch. 887, 891 (assignment of income accrued due in the hands of trustees: no forfeiture). See also *Re Longman* [1955] 1 W.L.R. 197 (authority given by beneficiary for payment of debts out of a future dividend: dividend never declared: no forfeiture). For other cases involving the application of the Trading with the Enemy Act 1939, see *Re Gourju's Will Trusts* [1943] Ch. 24; *Re Hall* [1944] Ch. 46; *Re Wittke* [1944] 1 All E.R. 383; *Re Furness* [1944] 1 All E.R. 575; *Re Harris* [1945] Ch. 316; *Re Pozot's Settlement Trusts* [1952] Ch. 427.

[22] [1935] Ch. 562.

[23] See *post*, p. 542.

[24] [1932] 2 Ch. 57.

[25] [1963] 1 W.L.R. 1207.

[26] *Ibid.* at p. 1218, *per* Donovan L.J.

[27] [1958] Ch. 504.

ary trusts under section 33 came into operation. In some ways no doubt this was a convenient result because the life tenant had later been adjudicated bankrupt; and the antecedent forfeiture meant that the income escaped the hands of his trustee in bankruptcy. However, it would seem a rather curious result if a failure to comply with an order of the court to settle the deed of variation will result in a forfeiture of such an interest, but compliance with such an order will not.

It is considered that the policy behind the decision of the Court of Appeal in *General Accident, Fire and Life Assurance Corporation Ltd.* v. *I.R.C.*[28] is undoubtedly desirable: it is only doubted whether the principle applied is the correct one. The effect of an order of the Family Division—whether or not it is to be implemented by a deed—is to deprive the life tenant of some or all of his income; and this would surely be caught by the terms of section 33 and, probably, by most express protective trusts. On the other hand different considerations may apply to an order of the court under section 57 of the Trustee Act 1925 because that section is to be read into every settlement.

(4) Advances

Section 33 expressly exempts advances under any express or statutory[29] power from causing a forfeiture and bringing the discretionary trusts into play.[30] The question, however, that may be asked is whether the *absence* of exempting words such as these in an *express* protective trust will of necessity mean that the protected life interest will determine if an advancement is made.

The authorities are only in slight disarray, and the general consensus of judicial opinion is that an advancement made under an express or statutory power will not bring about a forfeiture. In *Re Hodgson*[31] Neville J. held that an advance under an express power did not produce a forfeiture. The reasoning which appealed to the judge was that the forfeiture clause "should be read as though there had been inserted at the end of the clause 'But this provision is not to affect any steps taken by the husband to enable the advances by the trustees hereinafter provided for to take effect' ". And in *Re Shaw's Settlement*,[32] Harman J. came to the same conclusion on similar facts. Finally, in *Re Rees*,[33] Upjohn J. held that the same applied to a statutory power of advancement under section 32 of the Trustee Act 1925. Only in *Re Stimpson's Trusts*,[34] where there was again no express advancement clause and reliance was put on the statutory power, was it held that a life tenant forfeited his interest on consenting to an advancement under section 32. There is a factual distinction between the last two cases. It is that in *Re Stimpson* the will was *made* in 1906 (although it did not come into effect until 1929) and the draftsman obviously could not have had in mind the

---

[28] *Supra.*
[29] Under T.A. 1925, s.32, *post*, p. 504.
[30] s.33(1).
[31] [1913] 1 Ch. 34, at p. 40.
[32] [1951] Ch. 833.
[33] [1954] Ch. 202.
[34] [1931] 2 Ch. 77.

section (section 32) of an Act to be enacted nearly 20 years later, whereas in *Re Rees* the will was made in 1935 and the draftsman must be taken to have been well aware of the section.

It is therefore, a possibility (admittedly a remote one) that in the unlikely event that a case like *Re Stimpson* came before the court today, that is to say where a will made before 1926 contains no express advancement clause but the life tenant after 1925 consents to an advancement under the statutory power, then it would be decided in the same way. Although the validity of the decision has been doubted,[35] it appears to apply the correct principle. For the statutory power can be ousted by a contrary intention[36] and the fact that the will is made before 1926 may be such a contrary intention for this purpose.

---

[35] See *per* Upjohn J. in *Re Rees* [1954] Ch. 202 at p. 209.
[36] T.A. 1925, s.69.

CHAPTER 7

IMPLIED OR RESULTING TRUSTS

In all the following cases, the beneficial interest "results" to the settlor or his estate, and for this reason trusts of this type are often described as "resulting trusts." But they are also traditionally described as *implied* trusts because they arise or are presumed to arise from the *implied* intention of the settlor.

It is possible to argue that this basis is at times unreal. For example, in *Vandervell* v. *I.R.C.*[1] it could be said that it was far from Vandervell's intention that he should retain a beneficial interest in an option to re-purchase shares which he had ineffectually disposed of, and yet it was held that the option was to be held on a resulting trust for him. It is therefore noteworthy that Megarry J., in *Re Vandervell's Trusts (No. 2)*,[2] made a distinction between an "automatic" and a "presumed" resulting trust. In the former, as in *Vandervell* v. *I.R.C.*, the resulting trust does not depend upon any intention or presumption but is an automatic consequence of a settlor's failure to dispose of what is vested in him. If, however, a purchase of property is made in another person's name, this is a case of a "presumed" resulting trust, for there can fairly be said to be a presumption or intention that the property is to be held on a resulting trust for the true purchaser. The question to what extent this should be treated as an appropriate redefinition has already been discussed.[3]

I. PURCHASE IN ANOTHER'S NAME

This is one of the most important and common forms of resulting trust. The rule is that where real[4] or personal[5] property is vested in a purchaser jointly with others or in another or other persons alone, a resulting trust will be presumed in favour of the person who is proved to have paid the purchase-money[6]; the beneficial interest in the

---

[1] [1967] 2 A.C. 291, applied in *Re Vandervell's Trusts (No. 2)* [1974] Ch. 269, as between different parties; see *ante*, p. 38.
[2] *Supra.*
[3] *Ante*, p. 30.
[4] *Dyer* v. *Dyer* (1788) 2 Cox Eq. 92.
[5] *Re Scottish Equitable Life Assurance Society* [1902] Ch. 282, in respect of personal property.
[6] *Supra.*

property "results" to the true purchaser. The general principle of such trusts was established as long ago as 1788 in *Dyer* v. *Dyer*[7] by Eyre C.B., and may nowadays be relevant in deciding on the destination of the matrimonial home on breakdown of marriage.

There may be other variations on this theme. Thus if the purchase-money is paid partly by the person in whose favour the property is vested and partly by another, and if they advance it in equal shares, they will prima facie take jointly. But if the payment is made in *unequal* shares then a trust will result to each of them in proportion to the amount of his payment.[8]

But the principle will not be applied arbitrarily. It is essential that a *purchase* be made. Thus, if the payment is made at the request of and by way of loan to a person in whose name the property is vested, there will be no resulting trust, because in such circumstances the lender did not advance the purchase-money as purchaser but merely as lender.[9] And in any case there will be no resulting trust if it would be contrary to the law or to public policy to allow the presumption to arise. So, in an early case it was decided that if a person purchased an estate in the name of another so as to give him a vote at a parliamentary election the other will take beneficially even if there was no intention to give it to him.[10]

It has already been stated that this kind of resulting trust is based upon presumed intention. Accordingly, where no such intention can be implied, the trust will not arise. So, in *Savage* v. *Dunningham*[11] it was held that, where there was an informal flat-sharing arrangement under which contributions were made to the rent, there would not be a resulting trust in favour of the others when one of the flat-sharers purchased the flat. Plowman J. held that an income payment such as rent did not indicate an intention in respect of the subsequent acqui-sition of the capital asset. The facts were different in *Dewar* v. *Dewar*.[12] In this case the plaintiff and the defendant, who were brothers, and their mother, bought a house, the plaintiff and the mother each providing £500, and the defendant raising £3,250 on mortgage. The house was conveyed to the defendant. Goff J. held that the plaintiff's £500 was not a loan; the presumption of a resulting trust applied; and, therefore, he was entitled to an aliquot share in the house. The mother's £500 was held on the facts to be a gift and there was no resulting trust in her favour.

---

[7] (1788) 2 Cox Eq. 92 at p. 93.

[8] *Wray* v. *Steele* (1814) 2 V. & B. 388.

[9] *Aveling* v. *Knipe* (1815) 19 Ves. 441. The opinion of Phillimore L.J. in *Hussey* v. *Palmer* [1972] 1 W.L.R. 1286 at p. 1291, which appears to be to the opposite effect, would seem to be erroneous. Different considerations apply where money is lent for a particular purpose which fails. In such a case the money is held on trust for the lender: see *Barclays Bank Ltd.* v. *Quistclose Investments Ltd.* [1970] A.C. 567; and see *ante*, p. 17, *post*, p. 201.

[10] *Groves v Groves* (1829) 3 Y. & J. 163 at p. 175 and see *Gascoigne* v. *Gascoigne* [1918] 1 K.B. 223; *Re Emery's Investment Trusts* [1959] Ch. 410; *Chettiar* v. *Chettiar (No. 2)* [1962] A.C. 294.

[11] [1974] Ch. 181.

[12] [1975] 1 W.L.R. 1532.

Rebuttable nature of the presumption

The presumption which thus arises on a purchase in the name of another is also rebuttable by parol or other evidence that the purchaser intended to benefit the other. Further, in certain circumstances there is a presumption the other way, namely, that there is no resulting trust. This applies where the person in whom the property is vested is the lawful wife or child of the purchaser or was a person to whom he stood *in loco parentis*. In these cases, the donor is presumed to have intended to "advance" the donee. It should also be remembered in this connection that section 53(1)(*b*) of the Law of Property Act 1925 (that a declaration of trust as to land must be manifested and proved by writing) does not apply to implied, resulting or constructive trusts. This means that oral evidence is admissible to show what was the true nature of the transaction.[13]

1. *Intention to Benefit*

This is entirely a matter of evidence. If it can be shown that there was an intention to benefit the donee, no resulting trust can arise. Thus in *Standing* v. *Bowring*[14] the plaintiff transferred £6,000 Consols into the joint names of herself and her godson. She did this with the express intention that the godson, in the event of his surviving her, should have them but that she herself should retain the dividends during her life. She had been told that her act was irrevocable. The Court of Appeal held that the presumption of a resulting trust had been rebutted. There was ample evidence that at the time of the transfer and for some time previously the plaintiff intended to confer a benefit by the transfer on her godson. Similarly, in *Dewar* v. *Dewar*[15] the presumption of a resulting trust in favour of a mother who had made a contribution to the purchase of property in her son's name was rebutted by evidence of her intention to make a gift.

(1) Joint banking accounts

An intention to benefit has been presumed in cases where a bank balance has been transferred into joint names.[16] It may well be thought, however, that if the donor maintained the right to use the substance of the gift during his lifetime, the gift of the balance of the account to the other would be in the nature of a testamentary provision and, not being made in accordance with the Wills Act 1837,[17] would be ineffective. This argument indeed appealed to Romer J. in *Young* v. *Sealey*[18] but he declined to apply it because of the disturbing effect it would have on

---

[13] L.P.A. 1925, s.53(2).

[14] (1885) 31 Ch.D. 282.

[15] [1975] 1 W.L.R. 1532.

[16] See *Marshal* v. *Crutwell* (1875) L.R. 20 Eq. 328 at p. 330, *per* Jessel M.R. In that case the presumption of advancement was rebutted on the ground that the joint account was opened for convenience. However, in *Re Figgis* [1969] 1 Ch. 123 it was held that the presumption was not rebutted by the available evidence: the "convenience" principle did not apply.

[17] s.9 (as substituted by Administration of Justice Act 1982, s.17).

[18] [1949] Ch. 278.

existing titles. The point is still open for adjudication by the Court of Appeal.

(2) Joint banking accounts of husband and wife

A variant upon the foregoing will arise in cases where husband and wife have maintained a joint bank account into which their mutual resources have been pooled. It will be difficult, and in many cases impossible, to dissect the balance by ascertaining how much was paid in by each. It has, therefore, been held that, in the event of dissolution of the marriage, each will be entitled to one-half. The same principle will apply to investments which have been made by the husband in his own name out of moneys belonging to such a joint banking account.[19] But it should be noted that if such investments were made in the name of the wife the ordinary presumption of advancement may apply and, if so, she would prima facie taken them beneficially.[20]

2. *Presumption of Advancement*

This is the second case in which the presumption of a resulting trust does not operate. It only applies, however, where the real purchaser is the husband or father of or person standing *in loco parentis* to the nominal purchaser. In these cases the presumption is that the transferor intended to advance the transferee, in fact to give the property to him or her, and so there is no resulting trust. Once the presumption has arisen and is not rebutted, it will not be upset by any subsequent event. This can be illustrated by the old case of *Crabb* v. *Crabb*,[21] where a father transferred stock from his own name into the name of the son and a broker. He also told the broker to carry the dividends to the son's account. The father by a codicil made subsequently then bequeathed the stock to another. It was held, however, that the son took absolutely.

(a) **Wife.** The presumption of advancement by a husband in favour of his wife now has an extremely limited application, particularly when the marriage has broken down. This is a result of the following restatement of the law elaborated by Lord Diplock in *Pettitt* v. *Pettitt*.[22]

"The consensus of judicial opinion which gave rise to the presumptions of 'advancement' and 'resulting trust' in transactions between husband and wife is to be found in cases relating to the propertied classes of the nineteenth century and the first quarter of the twentieth century among whom marriage settlements were common, and it was unusual for the wife to contribute her earnings to the family income. It was not until after World War II that the

---

[19] *Jones* v. *Maynard* [1951] Ch. 572; *Rimmer* v. *Rimmer* [1953] 1 Q.B. 63; *cf. Re Cohen* [1953] Ch. 88 where a bundle of notes found hidden in the matrimonial home after the death of both spouses, who died within a few months of each other, was held to be the property of the wife to whom the residue belonged.

[20] See *infra*.

[21] (1834) 1 Myl. & K. 511.

[22] [1970] A.C. 777 at p. 783.

courts were required to consider the proprietary rights in family
assets of a different social class. The advent of legal aid, the wider
employment of married women in industry, commerce and the
professions, and the emergence of a property-owning, particularly a
real-property-mortgaged-to-a-building-society-owning democracy
has compelled the courts to direct their attention to this during the
last 20 years. It would, in my view, be an abuse of the legal
technique for ascertaining or imputing intention to apply to transactions between the post-war generations of married couples 'presumptions' which are based on inferences of fact which an earlier
generation of judges drew as to the most likely intentions of earlier
generations of spouses belonging to the propertied classes of a
different social era."

Notwithstanding these remarks of Lord Diplock, the doctrine of
advancement can still have some application where for some reason,
such as death, one or both of the parties are unable to give evidence.
Where both parties are available to give evidence, the court much
prefers to hear them and to form its own view of their intention. Where
this is done, it is highly unlikely that the presumption of advancement
will ever have any effect.

In so far, if at all, as the presumption may still be operative, it is
immaterial that the marriage is later dissolved or indeed if a decree of
nullity is made where the marriage is regarded as voidable.[23] However,
if the marriage is void *ab initio*, it appears that the presumption of
advancement does not apply because the marriage is treated as never
having had any existence at all.[24] The essential point is that the wife
should be the lawful wife of the transferor. So the presumption does not
apply in favour of the transferor's mistress.[25]

Nor does it apply if the wife purchases property in her husband's
name: a resulting trust will prima facie arise.[26] It used to be the position
that a resulting trust would only be deduced in this event if the
property was purchased with the wife's *capital*, not where it was
purchased with income. But in *Mercier v. Mercier*[27] the Court of Appeal
held that there was no fundamental distinction between capital and
income except in degree, although Romer L.J. made it clear that the fact
could be of importance when he said[28]: "No doubt in certain cases, in
considering whether a gift was intended, the fact of the money having
been income received by him with her consent may be material in

---

[23] *Dunbar v. Dunbar* [1909] 2 Ch. 639. A nullity decree in respect of a *voidable* marriage
now has a prospective, not a retrospective effect; accordingly the marriage is to be
treated as if it had existed until the decree: Matrimonial Causes Act 1973, s.16. For the
grounds on which a marriage is regarded as void or voidable, see *ibid.* ss.11, 12.

[24] See *Re Ames' Settlement* [1946] Ch. 217. See also *Re D'Altroy's Will Trusts* [1968] 1 W.L.R.
120.

[25] *Soar v. Foster* (1858) 4 K. & J. 152.

[26] Although if the property is part of the matrimonial assets the court may apply the
maxim that equality is equity: see, *e.g.* *Jones v. Maynard* [1951] Ch. 572; *Rimmer v.
Rimmer* [1953] 1 Q.B. 63; and see *ante,* p. 192, *post,* p. 280.

[27] [1903] 2 Ch. 98.

[28] *Ibid.* at p. 101.

respect of the weight of evidence but there is no other distinction, so far as I am aware, between capital and income." It is indisputable that the effect of this decision was to upset the previous law, and the fact that income has been applied will only be material evidentially in deciding whether or not there was an intention to benefit the husband and thereby rebut the presumption of a resulting trust in favour of the wife.

(b) Child. The reference here is to a legitimate child. The rule is that if a *father* purchases a property in the name of his child the presumption of advancement applies.[29] But if a mother does the same thing it appears that it will not apply.[30] But the position is by no means clear-cut and the case law is in some degree conflicting. In the first place, in *Re De Visme*[31] it was held that the presumption of advancement would not arise because a married woman was under no obligation to maintain her children. Secondly, in *Sayre* v. *Hughes*,[32] Stuart V.C. appeared to hold that the mere motive of benefit on the mother's part was the most material thing. This is a wide conception and, if accepted, could work an advancement in favour of the child. Thirdly, in *Bennet* v. *Bennet*[33] Jessel M.R. held essentially that the presumption of advancement applied only to the father but this was so, not because—as was held, in effect, in *Re De Visme*—the mother was under no liability to maintain her children, but because the father alone was under a *moral* obligation to make provision for his child; the mother was under no such obligation. The National Assistance Act 1948[34] imposed a *statutory* duty on the mother to care for her children. But this statutory duty will not affect the position if Jessel M.R. was right in postulating the test of a moral obligation. Finally, most recently, the Court of Appeal held in *Gross* v. *French*[35] that, even if the presumption of advancement does apply, there was sufficient evidence to rebut it while in *Sekhon* v. *Alissa*[36] Hoffmann J. presumed a resulting trust in favour of the mother which her daughter failed to rebut.

The position revealed is unsatisfactory. It is particularly difficult to see why a mother, especially if she has money, is not under the same moral obligation as the father is said to be. It should, however, be borne in mind that the presumption of a resulting trust in favour of the mother, if it does in fact follow, can be rebutted in the usual way by showing an intention on her part to benefit the child,[37] and it is quite probable that this will not be difficult to achieve.

(c) Persons in loco parentis. This expression applies to a person standing in the position of a parent, that is to say, in the situation of a person described as the lawful father of the child. A person *in loco*

---

[29] *Dyer* v. *Dyer* (1788) 2 Cox Eq. 92.

[30] *Bennet* v. *Bennet* (1879) 10 Ch.D. 474; *Sekhon* v. *Alissa* [1989] 2 F.L.R. 94.

[31] (1863) 2 De G.J. & S. 17.

[32] (1868) L.R. 5 Eq. 376.

[33] *Supra*.

[34] ss.42(1), 64(1).

[35] (1976) 238 E.G. 376.

[36] [1989] 2 F.L.R. 94.

[37] See *Beecher* v. *Major* (1865) 2 Drew. & Sm. 431.

parentis is, according to Jessel M.R. in *Bennet* v.*Bennet*,[38] a person taking upon himself the duty of a father of a child to make provision for that child. For example, an uncle or grandfather may, in the particular circumstances of the case, put himself *in loco parentis* to a child, for example after the death of his father.[39] Again, a father of an illegitimate child may, in the circumstances, be *in loco parentis* to that child.[40] Yet, if he is to be *in loco parentis* a person must place himself in the situation of the father: for example, simply to pay an illegitimate child's school fees would not be enough in itself to raise the presumption.[41]

Rebuttable nature of the presumption
However, just as the presumption of a resulting trust may be rebutted, so also may the presumption of advancement be rebutted; and it may be done in the same way by evidence of actual intention.

3. *Admissibility of evidence in rebuttal of presumptions*

(a) **What sort of evidence is admissible?** The important question is *how* a presumption can be rebutted, that is to say, what sort of evidence is admissible for this purpose. The leading case on admissibility is *Shephard* v. *Cartwright*.[42] In this case the deceased had been a successful businessman. He had at various times formed a number of private companies. These had succeeded so well that he had amalgamated them into a public company. At varying times he had shares in this company allotted to his three children. There was no evidence that any share certificates had been issued. In any case, the father continued to deal in these shares: at various times he sold them and received the proceeds of sale. Subsequently, he placed to the credit of the children in separate deposit accounts the exact amount of the cash consideration for the shares he had sold. Later still he obtained the children's signature to documents (as to the contents of which the children were ignorant) authorising him to withdraw money from these accounts and, indeed, without their knowledge, he drew on them; by the end of 1936 the accounts were exhausted. The deceased died in 1949. His children brought an action against the father's executors claiming an account of money due to them. They were met with the defence, which succeeded in the Court of Appeal, that the presumption of advancement was rebutted by the control continually exercised by the father over the shares. The House of Lords, however, held (reversing the Court of Appeal) that the shares registered in the name of the children were an advancement and that presumption had not been rebutted. The law on the admissibility of evidence in rebuttal was made quite explicit by

---

[38] (1879) 10 Ch.D. 474 at p. 477.
[39] *Ebrand* v. *Dancer* (1680) 2 Ch. Cas. 26 (grandchild whose father was dead); *Currant* v. *Jago* (1844) 1 Coll.C.C. 261 (nephew of wife maintained by her husband).
[40] *Beckford* v. *Beckford* (1774) Lofft 490.
[41] *Tucker* v. *Burrow* (1865) 2 Hem. & M. 515.
[42] [1955] A.C. 431.

Viscount Simonds. He adopted[43] a passage from Snell's *Principles of Equity*.[44]

> "The acts and declarations of the parties before or at the time of the purchase, or so immediately after it as to constitute a part of the transaction, are admissible in evidence either for or against the party who did the act or made the declaration; subsequent acts and declarations are only admissible as evidence against the party who made them, and not in his favour."

There are numerous cases of high authority,[45] as Viscount Simonds said, on which this passage is founded. Therefore, the applicable law—after having been somewhat disturbed by the Court of Appeal, which appeared to hold that subsequent acts were admissible in favour of the parties who did them—is no longer in doubt.[46] There is not, perhaps, too much difficulty in stating these principles in the abstract. They will mean, in the context of the presumption of advancement, (i) that a father's declaration at the date of the transaction will be admissible in his favour to rebut the presumption, but if made after that date will not be admissible in his favour but only against him by the son in order to support the presumption,[47] and (ii) that subsequent acts and declarations by the son will be admissible against him by the father to rebut the presumption.[48] But in practice difficulties may well be found in applying these general rules. Thus one question in particular may be whether a subsequent act is part of the same transaction as the original purchase or transfer and this may make for problems. For there is no universal criterion by which a link can, for this purpose, be found between one event and another but it is essential that a link is able to be found.[49] In *Shephard* v. *Cartwright* itself Viscount Simonds pointed out that the events which happened after the allotment of shares to the children did not form part of the original transaction, *viz.* the allotment. Those events were independent of that transaction and, so far from flowing inevitably from it, they would never have happened but for the phenomenal success of the testator's business.

A second practical problem is whether, and if so what, subsequent acts and declarations will rebut the presumption. An early case which shows that there may be difficulty in rebutting the presumption on this basis is *Lord Grey* v. *Lady Grey*[50] where Lord Finch L.C., in considering the fact that the son permitted his father to receive the profits of the property, said that that fact was insufficient to rebut the presumption

---

[43] *Ibid.* at p. 445.
[44] (28th ed.) at p. 185.
[45] See, for example, the cases cited in notes 47 and 48, *infra.*
[46] Evidence of subsequent *declarations* may now be admissible as a result of Civil Evidence Act 1968, s.2, which relates to hearsay evidence.
[47] *Stock* v. *McAvoy* (1872) L.R. 15 Eq. 55; *Redington* v. *Redington* (1794) 3 Ridg.P.R. 106 at p. 177; *Sidmouth* v. *Sidmouth* (1840) 2 Beav. 447.
[48] *Scawin* v. *Scawin* (1841) 1 Y. & C.C.C. 65.
[49] [1955] A.C. 431 at pp. 448–449, *per* Viscount Simonds.
[50] (1677) 2 Swans. 594.

because it was an "act of reverence and good manners."[51] But there are, of course, circumstances which will go to rebut it. Thus, it was held in *Warren* v. *Gurney*[52] that if a father retained the title deeds, although that was not itself conclusive, it was of great significance when coupled with contemporaneous declarations by the father. Moreover, the fact that the son is the father's solicitor is another circumstance which assists in rebutting it.[53]

Yet, as Viscount Simonds said in *Shephard* v. *Cartwright*,[54] any such evidence of subsequent acts is regarded jealously. A question which arose in this case was whether, if the events which happened after the allotments could not be admitted as part of the original transaction, they could nevertheless be admitted as an admission against interest. It is, however, an indispensable condition of such conduct being admissible that it should be performed with knowledge of the material facts. But the undisputed fact in *Shephard* v. *Cartwright* itself was that the children, under their father's guidance, did what they were told without inquiry or knowledge, and this fact precluded the admission in evidence of their conduct as constituting an admission against their own interest and if it were admitted would deprive it of all probative value.

(b) Illegal and fraudulent conduct. There is a further restriction on the ability to adduce evidence in rebuttal. This is that the presumption cannot be rebutted by evidence that the transfer was made for a fraudulent or illegal purpose and intended to retain the beneficial interest. Accordingly, in *Gascoigne* v. *Gascoigne*[55] a husband put money into his wife's name but it was held that he could not adduce evidence to show that he did so for the purpose of defeating his creditors. The point was given an interesting application in the Privy Council decision in *Chettiar* v. *Chettiar* (*No. 2*).[56] Certain regulations governed the holding of rubber plantations in Malaya. The material regulations differentiated between holdings of more than 100 acres on the one hand and less than that number on the other. If more were held the permissible production was controlled by an assessment committee. The father owned 99 acres and then acquired a further 40. In order to avoid having to disclose to the authorities that he held more than 100 acres he transferred the 40 acres into the name of his son. He had no intention of giving them. He now claimed that the son held the land in trust for him. The Judicial Committee in an opinion delivered by Lord Denning held that to make out his claim he had to rebut the presumption of advancement. In so doing, he necessarily had to disclose his own illegality in making the transfer, namely, his deceit of the public administration. The court was bound to take notice of the illegality: it would not

---

[51] *Ibid.* at p. 600.
[52] [1944] 2 All E.R. 472.
[53] *Garrett* v. *Wilkinson* (1848) 2 De G. & Sm. 244.
[54] [1955] A.C. 431 at p. 449.
[55] [1918] 1 K.B. 223 and see *Re Emery's Investment Trusts* [1959] Ch. 410 (avoiding payment of taxes).
[56] [1962] A.C. 294.

therefore lend its aid to the father and would let the legal estate lie where it fell.

The principle of such cases was applied in *Tinker* v. *Tinker*[57] to a case where the husband's intention in putting property into his wife's name was apparently *honest*. The husband in this case was, as Lord Denning M.R. said, on the horns of a dilemma. He could not say that the house was his own, and at one and the same time, say that it was his wife's. As against his wife he wanted to say that it belonged to *him*. As against his creditors, that it belonged to *her*. That, however, was not possible. Either it was conveyed to her for her own use absolutely; or it was conveyed to her as trustee for her husband. It had to be one or the other. The presumption was that it was conveyed to her for her own use, and the husband did not rebut the presumption by saying that he only did it to defeat his creditors.

However, the fact that the transfer was made for a fraudulent or illegal purpose will not prevent a property right from being claimed if the claimant can demonstrate his right without having to rely on evidence of the fraudulent or illegal purpose. In *Tinsley* v. *Milligan*,[58] two female lovers agreed to put a house which they were purchasing into the sole name of the plaintiff in order to enable the defendant to make fraudulent claims for housing benefit. After this fraud had been practised for a number of years, the two quarrelled and the plaintiff left. Subsequently, at a time when the defendant had discontinued her fraudulent claims and "made her peace" with the authorities, the plaintiff sought her eviction; the defendant counterclaimed for a declaration that the property was held on trust for both of them in equal shares. In the Court of Appeal[59] it was held that a more flexible approach should be adopted in cases of fraudulent or illegal conduct on the basis that "the underlying principle is the so-called public conscience test. The court must weigh, or balance, the adverse consequences of granting relief against the adverse consequences of refusing relief. The ultimate decision calls for a value judgment."[60] However, this new principle was unanimously rejected by the House of Lords, who confirmed that evidence of a fraudulent or illegal purpose is not admissible to rebut a presumption of resulting trust or of advancement. However, the House held, by a bare majority,[61] that the transaction between the parties had given rise to a presumption of resulting trust in favour of the defendant. Since she could assert her claim to this

---

[57] [1970] P. 136. *Gascoigne* v. *Gascoigne* and *Tinker* v. *Tinker* were distinguished in *Griffiths* v. *Griffiths* [1973] 1 W.L.R. 1454 where a husband's false representation as to ownership formed no part of the legal proceedings between him and his wife (varied by the C.A. on other grounds [1974] 1 All E.R. 932). *Cf.* also *Heseltine* v. *Heseltine* [1972] 1 W.L.R. 342 (where there was no ulterior or improper purpose in making the transfer to the husband, but it was held that property was held on a resulting trust for the wife).

[58] [1993] 3 W.L.R. 126.

[59] [1992] Ch. 310.

[60] *Ibid.* at p. 319, *per* Nicholls L.J.

[61] It had long been established that the legal owner of property can rely on his title despite the fact that it was acquired as a result of an illegal transaction (*Bowmakers* v. *Barnet Instruments* [1945] K.B. 65). The disagreement between the members of the House of Lords was as to whether this principle was also applicable to an equitable owner.

equitable proprietary right without having to produce any evidence as to why the property had been conveyed into the sole name of the plaintiff, she was entitled to her beneficial interest therein. The principle thus enunciated is also applicable to and explains the earlier decision in *Sekhon* v. *Alissa*,[62] where a property purchased by a mother and daughter was conveyed into the sole name of the daughter with a view to evading capital gains tax. Hoffmann J., having concluded that there was no presumption of advancement between mother and daughter, held that, since the illegal purpose had not been carried out, the mother could rely on the unrealised illegal purpose. However, if the principle enunciated by the majority of the House of Lords in *Tinsley* v. *Milligan* is applied to these facts, it can be seen that the absence of any presumption of advancement meant that there was a presumption of resulting trust in favour of the mother, on which she could rely without having to adduce evidence of her illegal purpose. Any attempt by the daughter to rebut the presumption of resulting trust would have required evidence of the illegal purpose, which would not have been admissible. Had, on the other hand, the parties instead been father and daughter, the father would not have been able to rebut the consequential presumption of advancement because the necessary evidence of the illegal purpose would have been inadmissible and the daughter would have been entitled to the property absolutely.

II. JOINT PURCHASES AND VESTING

It has already been seen that where property has been purchased in the name of another it will prima facie result to the person or persons (who may include the nominal purchaser) in proportion to the money actually contributed by each. The situation now being considered arises where the money is contributed by two or more persons and the property is vested in them all. And the question is, to what shares are the purchasers beneficially entitled? The answer will depend essentially on whether the money has been contributed in *equal* or *unequal* shares. If the purchase is made in unequal shares and the conveyance is made to the contributors jointly, then on the death of the first to die, the survivor will become legally entitled to the whole of the property, but, in the absence of an express contrary provision in the conveyance, he will hold the deceased's share on trust for his estate. The reason for this is that, in many cases, equity leans against a joint tenancy with its attendant consequence that the survivor is entitled to the entirety, *i.e.* the right of survivorship. Inequality in contributions to the purchase price is considered to be incompatible with this right and equity accordingly imposes a trust on the survivor.

But if the moneys are contributed equally, no such considerations will come into play; the purchasers will prima facie be deemed, if the property is conveyed to them jointly, to have purchased with a view to the right of survivorship.[63] But this will not apply to partners; here,

---

[62] [1989] 2 F.L.R. 94.
[63] *Lake* v. *Gibson* (1729) 1 Eq. Cas. Abr. 290; *Lake* v. *Craddock* (1732) 3 P.Wms. 158.

even in the event of equality of contributions, the right of survivorship will not arise because in a commercial enterprise such as a partnership an intention to this effect cannot be attributed to them.[64]

III. Joint Mortgages

The position in a case of joint mortgages should be contrasted with that of joint purchases. If two persons advance money on mortgage and take a mortgage in their own favour jointly the survivor is deemed—and this is so whether or not the money is advanced in equal shares—to hold the deceased mortgagee's share as a trustee for the deceased's estate. The reason is stated to be that a mortgage is a commercial undertaking and therefore there cannot be an intention that an interest in it should survive.[65]

IV. Voluntary Conveyance or Transfer

This situation envisages a direct gift without consideration, and to answer the question whether the presumption of a resulting trust applies it is necessary to consider land and pure personalty separately.

1. *Land*

Before 1926, where a conveyance was intended to be voluntary, it would usually be expressed to be made for the use or benefit of the grantee, for in the absence of words such as these, the grantor would have had a resulting trust of the equitable interest, and the legal estate would have been carried back to the grantor by virtue of the Statute of Uses 1535. The Statute of Uses was repealed by the Law of Property Act 1925, and as a consequential provision, section 60(3) of that Act provides that in a voluntary conveyance of land (including leaseholds) a resulting trust for the grantor shall not be implied *merely* by reason that the property is not expressed to be conveyed for the use or benefit of the grantee. There appears to be nothing in section 60(3) which prevents a resulting trust from being implied for other reasons, particularly by the operation of general equitable principles, and to prevent such a resulting trust express words are almost invariably inserted into a voluntary conveyance to rebut the equitable presumption.[66] However, the matter has yet to be finally decided.

2. *Pure Personalty*

It appears that a transferee of pure personalty on a voluntary transfer will prima facie hold the property upon a resulting trust for the

---

[64] *Lake* v. *Gibson, supra.*

[65] *Morley* v. *Bird* (1798) 3 Ves. 628.

[66] Some writers are of a different opinion: see, Underhill & Hayton: *Law of Trusts and Trustees* (14th ed. (1987)) 290. It may be relevant that in *Hodgson* v. *Marks* [1971] Ch. 892, Russell L.J. said that the question was "debatable."

transferor.[67] Thus, in *Re Vinogradoff*,[68] WarLoan Stock was transferred into the joint names of the transferor and her granddaughter who was then four years old, but to whom she was not *in loco parentis*. A resulting trust was held by Farwell J. to arise. The counter-presumption of advancement will, of course, arise if the transferor is the husband or father of, or *in loco parentis* to, the transferee.

V. FAILURE OF THE TRUST OR BENEFICIAL INTEREST

1. *Trust Failing*

Where the trusts fail there is a resulting trust of the trust property for the settlor or his estate. Thus in *Re Ames' Settlement*,[69] the funds of a marriage settlement were held on a resulting trust for the settlor's estate after the marriage had been declared void on a decree of nullity made by a Kenyan court. The settlement of which the marriage had been the consideration completely failed because the legal effect of the decree was that the parties not only were no longer married but never had been.[70] And likewise if property is given to a person on trust and not beneficially, but no effective trusts are ever established, the property will be held on a resulting trust for the grantor.[71]

The same basic principle applies if a loan is made for a particular purpose which fails: the money is held on a secondary[72] trust for the lender. So, in *Barclays Bank* v. *Quistclose Investments*,[73] which concerned the collapse of Rolls Razor, an arrangement had been made whereby Quistclose agreed to lend money to the company but only for the purpose of paying a dividend on the company's shares. Before the dividend was paid the company went into liquidation, and it could not then be paid. It was held that Quistclose was entitled to the repayment of the money on the basis of a secondary trust, the purpose for which it was lent having failed. The money had been paid into an account at the company's bank. It was further held that the bank had notice of the trust and could not retain it against Quistclose so as to reduce the company's overdraft; the bank was a constructive trustee. Although there is some controversy as to the precise nature of this secondary trust, which has variously been classified as an express trust, a resulting trust, and a

---

[67] See also *Fowkes* v. *Pascoe* (1875) 10 Ch.App. 343 at pp. 345–348.

[68] [1935] W.N. 68.

[69] [1946] Ch. 217.

[70] In this case the marriage was voidable, but the effect of the nullity decree was that the marriage was void *ab initio*. Since the Nullity of Marriage Act 1971, s.5 (now Matrimonial Causes Act 1973, s.16), this will no longer be the position in England, for it is thereby provided that a nullity decree in respect of a voidable marriage has a prospective, not a retrospective, effect. If however, the marriage were "void" the marriage is treated as never having taken place at all. For a list of the grounds on which a marriage will be void or voidable, see Matrimonial Causes Act 1973, ss.11, 12.

[71] *Re Vandervell's Trusts (No. 2)* [1974] Ch. 269.

[72] This trust has variously been classified as express, resulting and constructive. See *ante*, p. 18 fn 91.

[73] [1970] A.C. 567.

constructive trust,[74] *Barclays Bank* v. *Quistclose Investments* has been consistently applied.[75]

2. *Beneficial Interest Unexhausted*

The same principle will be applied where the beneficial interest is not wholly disposed of but not, as will be seen, in all cases. A modern illustration is *Re Gillingham Bus Disaster Fund*.[76] In 1951 24 cadets were killed when a motor-vehicle ran into them. The mayors of several boroughs in the area wrote a letter to the *Daily Telegraph* to the following effect: "The Mayors have decided to promote a Royal Marine Cadet Memorial Fund to be devoted . . . to defraying funeral expenses, caring for the boys who may be disabled and then to such worthy cause or causes in memory of the boys who lost their lives as the Mayors may determine." This appeal resulted in subscriptions amounting to nearly £9,000 contributed partly by known persons but mainly anonymously as a result of street collections and the like. The trustees spent about £2,500 and then took out a summons to decide what to do with the surplus. Harman J. held that, because the trust failed as a charity, the surplus should be held on a resulting trust for the donors, even though many of them were in fact anonymous. This followed naturally from the principle that where money was held upon trust and the trust declared did not exhaust the fund it would revert to the donor or settlor upon a resulting trust. The reasoning behind this principle, as applied to the facts, was that a donor did not part with the money out and out, but only *sub modo* to the intent that his wishes as declared by the declaration of trust should be carried into effect. It is important to observe, as Harman J. duly observed, that this doctrine did not rest on any evidence of the state of mind of the donor for no doubt in the vast majority of cases such as this he would not expect to get his money back in any case. A resulting trust would still arise even where the expectation was cheated on fruition for some unknown reason: it might well be, as it was here, an inference of law based on after-knowledge of the event.

The basis of *Re Gillingham Bus Disaster Fund* must be emphasised, that is to say that there was no intention on the part of the donors to part with their money out and out when they contributed it. More particularly, such an intention should no more be attributed to the anonymous contributor who had made his gift in a street collection than it should to a contributor who was identifiable. As Harman J. said,[77] "I see no reason myself to suppose that the small giver who is anonymous has any wider intention than the large giver who is named. They all give for the one object. If they can be found by inquiry the resulting trust can be

---

[74] See *ante*, p. 18 fn 91.

[75] See *ante*, p. 17.

[76] [1958] Ch. 300 (affirmed on points not affecting the decision [1959] Ch. 62, C.A.: see also *post*, p. 336; Atiyah (1958) 74 L.Q.R. 190. For charitable gifts the position is otherwise; see *post*, p. 348.

[77] [1958] Ch. 300 at p. 314.

executed in their favour. If they cannot I do not see how the money could then . . . change its destination and become *bona vacantia*."[78]

This last remark indicates the problem, for if it can be shown that the donor made his gift out and out with no intention of reclaiming it whatever the fate of the appeal might be, the money will belong to the Crown as *bona vacantia*. There is also no doubt that with regard to, for example, the proceeds of collecting boxes, the latter solution would be more practicable because it would be likely to be a fruitless exercise to try to establish, by way of a resulting trust, who in fact contributed their pennies to the collection; and in the result the money would have to be paid into court.[79] The question, however, is whether Harman J.'s decision on the question is correct as a matter of law. In *Re West Sussex Constabulary's Benevolent Fund Trusts*[80] Goff J. declined to follow *Re Gillingham Bus Disaster Fund*, at any rate with regard to the proceeds of collecting boxes. It was held that persons who put money into collecting boxes should be taken to have intended to part with the money out and out absolutely in all circumstances. Therefore, the Crown was entitled to it as *bona vacantia* on later failure of the trusts. There are admittedly dicta in favour of this view,[81] but they are not very weighty. They are all concerned with the question whether the fact that contributions were made by unidentifiable donors to an appeal for *charitable* purposes indicated an intention to make the gifts outright, so that funds could be applied *cy-près*, that is to say to other analagous charitable purposes.[82] The question of whether the proceeds of the collecting boxes were held on resulting trust or were *bona vacantia* is accordingly not settled by either of these two decisions and while, on the one hand, it seems highly artificial to make a distinction between the intention of unidentified donors and that of identified donors, it is equally true that the consequences of the existence of a resulting trust are highly inconvenient.

There is, however, another essential distinction between the two decisions. *Re Gillingham Bus Disaster Fund* concerned a fund raised to deal with one particular tragedy, a fund in which none of the contributors had any direct or indirect financial interest (other, of course, than the possibility of recovering any unspent surplus in the event that that surplus was indeed held on resulting trust). *Re West Sussex Constabulary's Benevolent Fund Trusts*, on the other hand, concerned a fund for the benefit of the dependants of the members of an unincorporated association. Consequently, the fund included not only the proceeds of

---

[78] In similar circumstances a resulting trust was held to arise in *Re Hobourn Aero Components Ltd.'s Air Raid Distress Fund* [1946] Ch. 86, but in that case there was no argument for *bona vacantia*. Cf. *Re Hillier's Trusts* [1954] 1 W.L.R. 9, where Upjohn J. held in these circumstances for *bona vacantia* (affirmed [1954] 1 W.L.R. 700; in C.A. Denning L.J. approved Upjohn J.'s formulation).

[79] Under T.A. 1925, s.63.

[80] [1971] Ch. 1.

[81] *Re Hillier's Trusts* [1954] 1 W.L.R. 700 at p. 715, *per* Denning L.J.; *Re Welsh Hospital (Netley) Fund* [1921] 1 Ch. 655 at pp. 659, 660, *per* P.O. Lawrence J.; *Re North Devon and Somerset Relief Fund Trusts* [1953] 1 W.L.R. 260 at pp. 1266, 1267, *per* Wynn-Parry J.

[82] *See post*, p. 348.

collecting boxes, the proceeds of entertainments, raffles and sweepstakes, and donations and legacies but also the contributions of past and present members. In relation to the proceeds of entertainments, raffles and sweepstakes, Goff J. held that it was not appropriate to apply the doctrine of resulting trusts for two reasons: first, the relationship was one of contract, not of trust (a contributor paid his money as the price of what was offered and that was what he received), and, secondly, there was no direct contribution to the fund at all—it was only the profit, if any, which was ultimately received. The distinction between trust and contract seems to be a sound one in respect of these sources of collection. He then held that, since it was not appropriate to apply the doctrine of resulting trusts, these proceeds must also be held as *bona vacantia*. On the other hand, he held that the donations and legacies were indeed held on resulting trust. The question of the contributions of past and present members was, however, more complex.

Where the funds of an unincorporated association contain a surplus on its dissolution, that surplus can be dealt with in a number of ways. It can be regarded as being held on resulting trust for the members of the association in proportion to their contributions to its funds. This was the view taken in *Re Printers' and Transferrer's Society*[83] where the surplus of the funds of a society which had collected weekly contributions from its members to provide defence and support, and in particular strike and lock-out benefits, for them was divided between those who were members at the time of its dissolution in proportion to their contributions. Similarly, in *Re Holbourn Aero Components Air Raid Distress Fund*,[84] a fund established for employees who were on war service or who suffered loss in air raids which was financed by voluntary subscriptions from the employees was divided up between all contributors in proportion to the amount contributed. Alternatively, the funds can be regarded as being subject to the contractual rights and liabilities of the members towards one another as members of the association. This was the view taken in *Cunnack* v. *Edwards*,[85] where it was held that the personal representatives of members of a society founded to provide funds for the widows of the members could not claim a share when the purposes of the society came to an end. The members, in making their contributions to the society, had received all that they had contracted for in the form of pensions for the widows. Consequently, the Crown took the surplus as *bona vacantia*. Goff J. followed and applied this decision in *Re West Sussex Constabulary's Benevolent Fund Trusts* and therefore held that the contributions of the past and present members were also held as *bona vacantia*.

It is now generally accepted that the resulting trust approach is no longer appropriate; consequently, all the modern authorities have accepted that the funds of an unincorporated association should be regarded as being subject to the contractual rights and liabilities of the

---

[83] [1899] 2 Ch. 184.
[84] [1946] Ch. 86 & 194.
[85] [1896] 2 Ch. 679.

members towards one another as members of the association. However, in *Re Bucks Constabulary Fund Friendly Society (No. 2)*,[86] Walton J. held that only where the association has become moribund, in that all or all but one of the members have resigned or died, will the assets of the association be held as *bona vacantia* and that in all other circumstances they will be divided equally between the existing members at the time of its dissolution, save where the rules of the association provide for division in some other way. He therefore divided equally between the members alive at the date of dissolution the surplus of a fund established to provide benefits for the members and the dependants of the members of a police force which had been amalgamated with other constabularies. Given that the association in question was a friendly society, this decision can be distinguished from that in *Re West Sussex Constabulary's Benevolent Fund Trusts*. However, Walton J. criticised that case and it is tolerably clear that he would have decided it differently, dividing all the funds held by Goff J. to be *bona vacantia* (and possibly even the donations and legacies as well) equally between the members of the association.

It is generally thought that the view adopted by Walton J. in *Re Bucks Constabulary Fund Friendly Society (No. 2)* (which has been followed[87]) is the most appropriate of the various possibilities, principally because it is the view which fits most easily with the modern attitude to unincorporated associations in general.[88] However, this approach is not yet universal. In *Davis v. Richards & Wallington Industries*[89] Scott J. took a different view in relation to a hypothetical surplus in a pension fund, opining that such part of the surplus as represented the employer's contributions would be held on resulting trust while such part as represented the employees' contributions would be held as *bona vacantia*. He reached this latter conclusion only because no intention could be imputed to the employees that they should receive any surplus and because a resulting trust of their contributions would have been unworkable; had this not been the case, neither the contractual relationship between employer and employees nor the fact that they had obtained everything for which they had contracted would necessarily have prevented a resulting trust in their favour as well. This decision seems out of line with the other modern authorities (*Re Bucks Constabulary Fund Friendly Society (No. 2)* was cited but not discussed) but clearly indicates that this particular question is unlikely to be finally settled until the matter is considered by the Court of Appeal.

Thus, while the resulting trust analysis is generally discredited in relation to the surplus funds of an unincorporated association on its dissolution, this analysis has certainly not as yet been completely eradicated. Further, whether surplus funds of the type considered in *Re Gillingham Bus Disaster Fund*, where no unincorporated association was

---

[86] [1979] 1 W.L.R. 936.

[87] In *Re G.K.N. Bolts & Nuts Ltd. (Automotive Division) Birmingham Works, Sports and Social Club* [1982] 1 W.L.R. 774.

[88] See *ante*, p. 123; see also S. Gardner, [1992] Conv. 41.

[89] [1990] 1 W.L.R. 1511; see S. Gardner, *op. cit.*

involved, are held on resulting trust or as *bona vacantia* has still to be clarified in the light of the opposing attitudes adopted in that case and in *Re West Sussex Constabulary's Benevolent Fund Trusts* in this respect.

Incomplete trust

A resulting trust solution will also generally follow where the instrument is silent as to the way in which the beneficial interest is to be applied. Thus if property is settled upon trust to pay the income to a life tenant and the instrument makes no provision for the destination of the property on the death of the life tenant, the trustee will prima facie hold the property on a resulting trust for the settlor or his estate (as in *Re Cochrane*[90] where apparently, as a result of the draftsman's blunder, a provision was left out of the instrument, so that the funds were not effectively disposed of), for in such a situation there is no doubt that the nominated trustee cannot take beneficially, and moreover, he cannot adduce evidence to that effect.[91] Yet it must be emphasised that this is a prima facie implication and it may, as a matter of construction of the instrument, be overridden. The court may be still able to construe the instrument in such a way that the trustee takes beneficially subject to the fulfilment of the trust in favour of the life tenant. So, in *Re Foord*[92] property was given by will to the testator's sister absolutely on trust to pay his wife an annuity. The income was more than sufficient to meet the annuity; and, upon a true construction of the will, the sister was held entitled to the balance. A similar conclusion was arrived at in *Re Andrew's Trust*[93] where a fund had been subscribed for the education of the children of a distressed clergyman and "not for equal division between them." Kekewich J. held that after completion of the education the children were entitled to the balance equally: there was no resulting trust. However, it may be somewhat difficult to reconcile this decision with *Re The Trusts of the Abbott Fund*[94] where a fund had been subscribed for the maintenance of two distressed ladies and Stirling J. held that on the death of the survivor the balance was held on a resulting trust for the donors. Kekewich J. justified his decision in *Re Andrew's Trust* on the ground that education was merely the motive of the gift and the subscribers parted with the money out and out when they gave it. The distinction between these two cases is a very fine one. It is, nevertheless, a question of construction in every case, and it is possible that both *Re Andrew* and *Re Abbott* may have been right on their particular facts. The point was made in *Re Osoba*,[95] where gifts had been made to the mother, wife, and daughter of the testator for various purposes which had failed or become exhausted. The Court of Appeal

---

[90] [1955] Ch. 309.

[91] *Re Rees' Will Trusts* [1949] Ch. 541.

[92] [1922] 2 Ch. 519.

[93] [1905] 2 Ch. 48.

[94] [1900] 2 Ch. 326. In *Re West Sussex Constabulary's Benevolent Fund Trusts* [1971] Ch. 1, it was held that *Re Abbott* was indistinguishable with regard to funds derived from donations and legacies from *identified* persons. For discussion of other aspects of *Re West Sussex*, see *ante*, p. 203.

[95] [1979] 1 W.L.R. 247, C.A.

held, on a construction of the will, that these created trusts for the benefit of the beneficiaries and the respective purposes were to be disregarded as no more than expressions of the testator's motives in making the gifts.

Failure of a common purpose

In most cases the parties have the same purpose, but this is not necessarily so. The question is, where two or more persons acquire property each for a separate purpose and only one of those purposes (uncommunicated to the other persons) fails, whether a resulting trust arises. It appears that it does not. The question was considered in *Burgess* v. *Rawnsley*.[96] An elderly widowed couple met and became friendly.[97] The man was the tenant of a house in which he lived in the downstairs flat, the upstairs flat being vacant. Subsequently, they agreed to purchase the house, each of them providing half of the purchase price, and it was conveyed to them as joint tenants. The man bought the house as a matrimonial home in contemplation of marriage, but the woman said that she had intended to live in the upstairs flat and that he had never mentioned marriage to her. In fact they did not marry and she never moved into the house. Later she orally agreed to sell her share in the house to him, but later refused to sell. He then died, and his daughter, as administratrix of his estate, claimed that there was a resulting trust of his share in favour of his estate or, alternatively, that the joint tenancy had been severed by the oral agreement to sell. The woman claimed that the house was hers by survivorship. The Court of Appeal unanimously held that the joint tenancy had been severed, and that was sufficient to dispose of the case; but there was a difference of opinion in deciding whether there was also a resulting trust. Browne L.J. and Sir John Pennycuick held that, since the man alone had entered into the conveyance in contemplation of marriage and he had not communicated that purpose to the woman, there was no common purpose which had failed so as to give rise to a resulting trust. Lord Denning M.R. considered, however, that where parties contemplate different objects which both fail, the position is the same as where their common object fails, and there is a resulting trust proportionate to their payments. The view of the majority seems to be the more logical.

Termination

It has been seen that a resulting trust comes into existence whenever there is a gap in the beneficial ownership. Accordingly, as was held in *Re Vandervell's Trusts (No. 2)*,[98] when that gap is filled by someone becoming beneficially entitled, or where a trust is expressly declared, the resulting trust comes to an end.[99]

---

[96] [1975] Ch. 429.

[97] Apparently despite the fact that, according to her evidence, "he looked like a tramp" and "had been picking up fag-ends."

[98] [1974] Ch. 269. The facts are stated *ante*, p. 38.

[99] *Ibid.* at p. 320. *Sed quaere*, whether the equitable interest under the resulting trust should be disposed of by writing under L.P.A. 1925, s.53(1)(c): see *ante*, p. 40.

3. *Bona Vacantia*

It has been seen[1] that in some circumstances funds will be applied as *bona vacantia* rather than upon a resulting trust. It is also useful to consider under this head the case where a beneficiary is entitled to property but he later dies intestate in whole or part. It was formerly necessary to distinguish between two classes of case: (i) where the property is vested in *trustees*; and (ii) where it is vested in *executors*.

(1) Trustees

If, for example, property is vested in trustees upon trust absolutely for a beneficiary who is living when the interest takes effect and the beneficiary then dies intestate and leaves nobody in whom his interest can vest, there cannot be a resulting trust because the beneficial interest will have effectively vested in the beneficiary. It is clearly established that if the property is personalty the rule was and is that the interest in such circumstances belongs to the Crown as *bona vacantia*: it has no owner and must devolve accordingly.

But if the property is realty the position was at one time different. The law used to be that the trustee took it beneficially. This was so because the Chancery Court did not apply the law of escheat to interests in realty. The law was changed first by the Intestates Estates Act 1884[2] and then by the Administration of Estates Act 1925 so that now, if a person dies without testate or intestate successors after 1925, his real estate, like his personal estate, will go as *bona vacantia* to the Crown.[3]

(2) Executors

So far as vesting in an executor is concerned, the position at law at one time was that, if a testator died without disposing of the residue, the executor was entitled to it if the residue was personal estate or to the extent to which it consisted of personalty. And equity followed the rule at law unless it was shown, upon a true construction of the will, that the testator intended to exclude the executor from taking a benefit. If such an intention could be shown he would, of course, hold as trustee for the next-of-kin.[4]

The law was changed by statute, namely, the Executors Act 1830, which laid down that an executor should hold as trustee for the next-of-kin unless it could be shown from the will that he was intended to take beneficially. This in effect shifted the burden of proof. But he still, pausing at this date, remained entitled beneficially if there were no next-of-kin. This last loophole was closed, although not until the Administration of Estates Act 1925, when it was provided that even in the absence of persons entitled on intestacy, the executor will hold the property as *bona vacantia*, and this rule will only be overridden if the will clearly shows that he is to take beneficially.[5]

---

[1] See *supra*.
[2] ss.4 and 7.
[3] A.E.A. 1925, ss.45, 46.
[4] See *ante*, p. 90: "Certainty of intention."
[5] ss.46, 49.

CHAPTER 8

CONSTRUCTIVE TRUSTS

I. Introduction[1]

1. *The Nature of Constructive Trusts*

Constructive trusts arise by operation of law. Unlike all other trusts, a constructive trust is imposed by the court as a result of the conduct of the trustee and therefore arises quite independently of the intention of any of the parties. Constructive trusts therefore form a residual category of trusts incapable of precise definition. As Edmund Davies L.J. remarked in *Carl-Zeiss Stiftung* v. *Herbert Smith (No. 2)*,[2] "English law provides no clear and all-embracing definition of a constructive trust. its boundaries have been left perhaps deliberately vague, so as not to restrict the court by technicalities in deciding what the justice of a particular case may demand." Judges have preferred to describe constructive trusts rather than to define them; thus Deane J. in *Muschinski* v. *Dodds*[3] described the constructive trust as "a remedial institution which equity imposes regardless of actual or presumed agreement or intention (and subsequently protects) to preclude the retention or assertion of beneficial ownership to property to the extent that such retention or assertion would be contrary to equitable principle".

The lack of a precise definition makes it difficult to determine precisely what trusts may properly be classified as constructive trusts. The line of distinction between express and constructive trusts has been blurred by the fact that, until the enactment of the Limitation Act 1939, express trustees were unable to rely on the Statutes of Limitation as against the beneficiaries whereas the limitation period ran in favour of potential constructive trustees; this encouraged the courts to classify as express trusts certain trusts which were clearly nothing of the sort.[4] There has also been, historically, some confusion between resulting

---

[1] This chapter is a shortened and updated version of A.J. Oakley: *Constructive Trusts* (2nd ed., 1987). See also A.W. Scott: (1955) 71 L.Q.R. 39, D.W.M. Waters: *The Constructive Trust* (1965), G. Elias: *Explaining Constructive Trusts* (1990), M. Cope: *Constructive Trusts* (1992), Goff & Jones: *The Law of Restitution* (4th ed., 1993), Ch. 2, Ford & Lee: *Principles of the Law of Trusts* (2nd ed.), Ch. 22, Hayton & Marshall: *Cases and Commentary on the Law of Trusts* (9th ed., 1991), Ch. 7.

[2] (1969) 2 Ch. 276, 300.

[3] (1985) 62 A.L.R. 429, 451 (High Court of Australia).

[4] See *Soar* v. *Ashwell* (1893) 2 Q.B. 390.

trusts and constructive trusts and, as has already been seen,[5] some judges have continued to use the terms almost interchangeably when endeavouring to establish the existence and extent of beneficial ownership of residential family property.[6] However, some classifications are well established, long settled, and generally agreed. All the commentators accept that the following three situations give rise to the imposition of a constructive trust: first, where advantages have been obtained by fiduciaries breaching their duty of loyalty[7]; secondly, where strangers have intermeddled with property subject to a trust[8]; and, thirdly, where advantages have been obtained by fraudulent or unconscionable conduct.[9] However, there are certain other types of trust whose classification is more controversial. Such trusts include secret trusts,[10] mutual wills,[11] and the trusts which arise as a result of the creation of contracts of sale which are specifically enforceable,[12] as a result of the exercise by mortgagees of their powers under their mortgage,[13] and in order to give effect in equity to transfers of property which are at law incomplete.[14] These types of trust are extremely difficult to classify and have been classified in many different ways by different commentators. It is, however, suggested that all these trusts other than secret trusts should in fact properly be classified as constructive trusts.

The imposition of a constructive trust potentially produces liabilities both of a proprietary and of a personal nature for the constructive trustee. Given the inherent nature of a trust as a relationship in respect of property, the imposition of a constructive trust necessarily confers on the beneficiary proprietary rights in the subject matter of the constructive trust, while the constructive trustee is necessarily subject to the liability which is imposed on every trustee to account personally to his beneficiary for his actions as trustee. However, the court is able to specify the precise moment at which the constructive trust takes effect and, consequently, the moment at which these proprietary rights and fiduciary obligations come into existence. As Millett J. observed in *Lonhro Plc.* v. *Fayed (No. 2)*,[15] "[i]t is a mistake to suppose that in every situation in which a constructive trust arises the legal owner is necessarily subject to all the fiduciary obligations and disabilities of an express trustee".

It might be expected to follow from the inherent nature of a trust that a constructive trust can only be imposed if there is some identifiable property upon which to impose it, in other words that the property

---

[5] *Ante*, p. 31.
[6] See *Hussey* v. *Palmer* (1972) 1 W.L.R. 1286, 1289.
[7] See s.II of this Chapter, *post*, p. 221.
[8] See s.III of this Chapter, *post*, p. 251.
[9] See s.IV of this Chapter, *post*, p. 272.
[10] See *ante*, p. 45.
[11] See s.V of this Chapter, *post*, p. 285.
[12] See s.VI of this Chapter, *post*, p. 292.
[13] See s.VII of this Chapter, *post*, p. 294.
[14] See *ante*, p. 64 and s.VIII of this Chapter, *post*, p. 294.
[15] (1992) 1 W.L.R. 1, 12.

which is the subject matter of the trust must be able to be identified in the hands of the constructive trustee, either at the time when the matter is brought before the courts or at some earlier stage. There is indeed authority for this proposition.[16] However, there are a number of decided cases in which constructive trusts have been imposed where there has been no obviously identifiable property subject to the trust; in all of these cases, the person upon whom the constructive trust was imposed had in one way or another knowingly assisted in bringing about a misapplication of property subject to a trust.[17] The existence of these authorities has led some commentators to contend that there is a second type of constructive trust which can arise without any necessity for there to be any identifiable trust property.[18] This suggested second type of constructive trust obviously does not confer any proprietary rights on the beneficiary thereunder but merely imposes on the constructive trustee a personal liability to account to the beneficiary for his actions. For this reason, the constructive trust so imposed has been described as "a fiction which provides a useful remedy where no remedy is available in contract or in tort".[19] It has to be admitted that it is virtually impossible to justify some of the existing authorities without accepting the argument that there is indeed such a second kind of constructive trust; nevertheless, it is not easy to see how an obligation which is not imposed in respect of any identifiable property can properly be classified as a trust. Indeed Ungoed-Thomas J. stated in *Selangor United Rubber Estates* v. *Cradock (No. 3)*[20] that this type of constructive trust "is nothing more than a formula for equitable relief. The court of equity says that the defendant shall be liable in equity, as though he were a trustee". In accordance with this reasoning, it seems more appropriate to regard these decisions not as examples of the imposition of a constructive trust but rather as examples of equity imposing a quite distinct remedy—a personal liability to account in the same manner as a trustee. This was confirmed by Millett J. in *Agip (Africa)* v. *Jackson*.[21]

2. *The Effect of the Imposition of a Constructive Trust*[22]

(a) When and how does a constructive trust take effect?
It is important to know at precisely what moment a constructive trust takes effect for a number of reasons. The moment at which the constructive trust takes effect will determine the extent to which the rights of the constructive beneficiary will be binding upon third parties, whether the general creditors of the constructive trustee or any person to whom the property which forms the subject matter of the constructive trust has been transferred. Further, as from the moment at which the constructive

---

[16] *Re Barney* [1892] 2 Ch. 265, 273.
[17] See s.III of this Chapter, *post*, p. 251.
[18] See Hayton & Marshall and Ford & Lee.
[19] D. J. Hayton: (1985) 27 Malaya Law Review 313, 314.
[20] [1968] 1 W.L.R. 1555, 1582.
[21] [1989] 3 W.L.R. 1367, 1389.
[22] See *Equity and Contemporary Legal Developments* (1992) (ed. Goldstein) 427.

trust takes effect, the constructive beneficiary will be entitled to any income or other fruits produced by the property which forms the subject matter of the constructive trust. It seems to be generally accepted that, in the absence of any judicial order to the contrary, a constructive trust will take effect from the moment at which the conduct which has given rise to its imposition occurs. This was specifically held by Browne-Wilkinson J. in *In re Sharpe (a Bankrupt)*[23] and has been assumed without discussion on many other occasions. It is for this reason that the interest of a beneficiary under a constructive trust is binding on the trustee in bankruptcy of the constructive trustee and takes priority over the claims of his general creditors[24]; such an interest is also capable of taking priority over third party purchasers of the property or interests therein[25] provided that the third party in question has not taken free of the beneficial interest in question.[26] Further, any order that the constructive trustee should account for income or profits has effect as from the date upon which the constructive trust took effect.[27] Since the vast majority of constructive trusts are imposed because of the circumstances in which the constructive trustee has acquired the property which forms the subject matter of the constructive trust, that trust will therefore normally take effect from the moment at which the constructive trustee acquires the property in question. However, this is not an absolute rule; there are circumstances in which the conduct which has given rise to the imposition of a constructive trust occurs only some time after the acquisition of the property by the constructive trustee.[28] In this case, consistent with the general rule, the constructive trust will obviously only take effect from the moment at which that conduct occurred.

Despite this universal agreement as to the moment at which a constructive trust takes effect, there is, however, some disagreement between the commentators as to whether or not this can only occur as the result of a court order imposing the constructive trust in question.[29] This question was considered in *Chase Manhattan Bank* v. *Israel (British) Bank*[30] by Goulding J., who held that, at least under American law (with which the case was primarily concerned), a court order is not necessary. This view was also adopted by a bare majority of the Supreme Court of Canada in *Rawluk* v. *Rawluk*.[31] As will be seen later in this section, both these jurisdictions recognise the constructive trust as a general equitable remedy, something which English law has so far rightly declined to do. Consequently, it is suggested that, at least in this jurisdiction, the better view is that a constructive trust should be able to

---

[23] [1980] 1 W.L.R. 219, 225.
[24] As was held in *In re Sharpe (a Bankrupt)* [1980] 1 W.L.R. 219, 225.
[25] As in *Belmont Finance Corporation* v. *William Furniture (No. 2)* [1980] 1 All E.R. 393.
[26] As in *Thompson's Trustee* v. *Heaton* [1974] 1 W.L.R. 605.
[27] As in *Boardman* v. *Phipps* [1967] 2 A.C. 46.
[28] As in *Bannister* v. *Bannister* [1948] W.N. 261, *Lyus* v. *Prowsa* [1982] 2 All E.R. 953 and *Ungurian* v. *Lesnoff* [1989] 3 W.L.R. 840.
[29] Between *Scott on Trusts* and Bogert: *Trusts and Trustees*.
[30] [1980] 2 W.L.R. 202 *passim*.
[31] [1990] 65 D.L.R. (4th) 161.

take effect only as the result of a court order. The manner in which this question is resolved does not in any way affect priorities as between the beneficiary and third parties but may affect the fiscal position of the beneficiary; if a constructive trust can take effect without any need for a court order, the beneficiary may find himself liable to income tax and capital gains tax on an interest arising under a constructive trust which he has never claimed and never enjoyed. It is therefore very much to the advantage of the beneficiary that a constructive trust should not be able to take effect without a court order. Whatever view is taken in this respect, however, it is clear that the general rule is capable of being varied by the court in any individual case. The court is free to specify the precise moment at which the constructive trust takes effect and can therefore modify the effect of its imposition both on third parties and on the constructive trustee himself. Thus, in *Muschinski* v. *Dodds*[32] the High Court of Australia imposed a constructive trust to give effect to a variation in the beneficial interests in property purchased by an unmarried couple but expressly held that, in order to avoid any possible prejudice to third parties, the constructive trust imposed in that case would take effect only as from the date of the publication of the judgments. In the same sort of way, in *Lonhro* v. *Fayed (No. 2)*.[33] Millett J. stated that, in the event that the victim of a fraudulent misrepresentation elects to avoid the contract, the representor thereafter holds its subject matter on constructive trust for him but is not retrospectively subject to all the fiduciary obligations of an express trustee in respect of the period before the contract was avoided.

(b) The position of the constructive beneficiary

(i) The distinct proprietary and personal liabilities of the constructive trustee. The position of the constructive beneficiary who chooses to rely on his proprietary rights will obviously primarily depend on the precise nature of the constructive trust which has been imposed; he will clearly have the rights appropriate to the interest in the trust property to which he has been held to be entitled, which may be either an absolute interest,[34] or a concurrent interest,[35] or a limited interest,[36] or merely an interest by way of lien or charge.[37] Illustrations of all these different types of interest arising as a result of the imposition of a constructive trust will be found in the later sections of this chapter. In the event that the beneficiary is held to have an absolute interest in the property which forms the subject matter of the constructive trust, he will

---

[32] [1986] 160 C.L.R. 583.

[33] [1992] 1 W.L.R. 1, 11–12.

[34] See *Re Duke of Marlborough* [1894] 2 Ch. 133, *Re Macadam* [1946] Ch. 73, discussed *post*, p 537, *Williams* v. *Barton* [1927] 2 Ch. 9, discussed *post*, p. 229 *Lyell* v. *Kennedy* (1889) 14 App.Cas. 437, discussed *post*, p. 253, *Belmont Finance Corporation* v. *Williams Furniture (No. 2)* [1980] 1 All E.R. 393, discussed *post*, p. 266.

[35] See *Burns* v. *Burns* [1984] Ch. 317, *Grant* v. *Edwards* (1986) Ch. 638, discussed in text to p. 282, fn. 35.

[36] See *Bannister* v. *Bannister* [1948] W.N. 261, *Ungurian* v. *Lesnoff* [1989] 3 W.L.R. 840, discussed *post*, p. 277.

[37] See *Phipps* v. *Boardman* [1964] 1 W.L.R. 993 (Ch.Div.), discussed *post*, p. 248.

obviously be entitled to call for the transfer of the property to him together with any income or other fruits which the property has produced since the moment at which the constructive trust took effect. In the event that the beneficiary is held to have any of the other types of interest, his position, at least in relation to the property, will be exactly the same as if the interest in question had been expressly created; thus whether the beneficiary of a constructive trust who has been held to have a concurrent interest in the property which forms its subject matter will be able to enforce that interest against a third party or obtain an order for sale of the property against the wishes of the other co-owners will be determined by exactly the same criteria as apply to a co-ownership which has arisen as the result of an express or statutory trust for sale.[38]

If the beneficiary chooses instead to rely on the personal liability of the constructive trustee to account, he will in effect be claiming damages for breach of trust from the constructive trustee. He will thus recover the value of whatever interest he is held to have in the subject matter of the constructive trust, valued as at the moment at which the constructive trust took effect, together with interest thereon. (This is also the measure of recovery in the alleged second type of constructive trusts, better regarded as examples of equity imposing a personal liability to account in the same manner as a trustee.[39]) Since such reliance on the personal liability of the constructive trustee to account is normally[40] alternative to reliance on the proprietary rights held by the beneficiary in the subject matter of the constructive trust, payment by the constructive trustee of the appropriate sum will have the effect of discharging those proprietary rights; consequently, the constructive trustee will thereafter be absolutely beneficially entitled to the property upon which the constructive trust was imposed.

(ii) The choice of remedy when the property is still in the hands of the constructive trustee.   When the property upon which the constructive trust is imposed is still identifiable in the hands of the constructive trustee, the beneficiary will be able to choose either to exercise his proprietary rights in the subject matter of the constructive trust, or to rely on the personal liability of the constructive trustee to account or, in rare circumstances, to exercise both of these remedies. Where the constructive trustee is solvent, the election between these two remedies will not normally have any particularly significant effects on the measure of the recovery of the beneficiary. As has already been seen, reliance on his proprietary rights will entitle the beneficiary to recover the appropriate interest in the property together with any income or other fruits which the property has produced since the moment at which the constructive trust took effect, while reliance on the personal liability of the constructive trustee to account will entitle the beneficiary to recover the value of

---

[38] See K. J. Gray: *Elements of Land Law* (2nd ed., 1993), Ch. 14.

[39] See *ante*, p. 211 and *post*, p. 252.

[40] Save in the unusual situation where the beneficiary seeks to rely on both the remedies available to him. See the next paragraph.

the appropriate interest at the moment at which the constructive trust took effect together with interest thereon. Consequently, if any increase in the value of the property plus the value of any income or other fruits which it has produced is more or less the same as the interest payable on the value of the property since the moment at which the constructive trust took effect, there will be no financial advantage in the beneficiary electing for one remedy rather than for the other. This is only likely not to be the case in the event of a substantial rise or a substantial fall in the value of the property, when it will obviously be to the advantage of the beneficiary to opt respectively for his proprietary rights or for the personal liability of the constructive trustee to account. The only exception to this will be where it can be shown that any fall in the value of the property was the responsibility of the constructive trustee. In this event, there seems no reason why the beneficiary should not alternatively seek to rely on both the remedies available to him; if this is indeed possible, he will be able both to claim the appropriate interest in the property in question and, by relying on the personal liability of the constructive trustee to account, to obtain damages for the fall in value of the property. While this will not of course increase the total measure of recovery, it will enable the beneficiary to recover the property itself. There seems no reason whatsoever why such a process should not be possible in an appropriate case.

Where, on the other hand, the constructive trustee is insolvent, the election between the two remedies will be immensely significant. If the beneficiary chooses to rely on his proprietary rights, he will take priority over the general creditors of the insolvent constructive trustee, whereas if he instead chooses to rely on the personal liability of the constructive trustee to account, he will rank with, rather than ahead of, the general creditors. Consequently, the only situation in which the beneficiary is likely to choose to rely on the personal liability of the constructive trustee to account will be where the property which is the subject matter of the constructive trust has fallen in value to a percentage of its original value smaller than the percentage which is likely to be paid out by the trustee in bankruptcy to the general creditors. In such circumstances, in the event that it can be shown that the constructive trustee was responsible for the fall in value of the property, it will always be in the interest of the beneficiary to take advantage of the possibility of relying on both the remedies available to him in order both to recover the appropriate interest in the property in question and to claim damages for the fall in its value; this is because such a double claim will give him both the property and the same percentage of the claim for damages as is paid out to the general creditors. However, except in the extremely unlikely situation which has just been considered, the beneficiary will, in the event of the insolvency of the constructive trustee, inevitably choose to rely on his proprietary rights so as to obtain priority over the general creditors. This will in turn diminish the mass of general assets available for distribution among the general creditors of the insolvent trustee so that each general creditor will therefore obtain a smaller proportion of the sum owed to him. Thus, the imposition of a constructive trust upon a person who is, or subsequently becomes, bankrupt will almost inevitably prejudice the interests of his general creditors, who will *ex hypothesi* not be before the court to object to the imposition of the constructive trust in question. In such circumstances, the only possibility of avoiding the consequent prejudice to the interests of the general creditors will be for the trustee in bankruptcy of the constructive trustee to go to the court under s.340 of the Insolvency Act 1986[41] in order to seek an order setting aside the constructive trust on the grounds that its imposition has given a preference to the beneficiary. Such a claim was successfully made in *Re Densham (A Bankrupt)*[42] but, as that case demonstrates, it is often a matter of pure chance whether the legislation is applicable and so this possibility cannot be regarded as a substantial safeguard for the interests of the general creditors.

(iii) The choice of remedy when the property is no longer in the hands of the constructive trustee. When the property upon which the constructive trust is imposed is no longer identifiable in the hands of the constructive trustee, the property may nevertheless still be identifiable in the hands of a third party. In such circumstances, it will be possible to recover the property by tracing it in equity into the hands of that third party, unless the latter is able to establish one of the accepted defences to such equitable proprietary claims; these include bona fide purchase for value of a legal interest in the property without notice of the adverse claim of the beneficiary under the constructive trust (or, in the case of property not subject to the equitable doctrine of notice, the statutory equivalent thereof) and change of position. Such an equitable tracing claim is possible because the imposition of a constructive trust gives rise to the relationship of trustee and beneficiary which, on any view, is sufficient to satisfy the prerequisites of such a claim.[43] Where the trust property can be followed in this way into the hands of a third party, the situation will differ very little from that which has already been discussed. The beneficiary will have a choice between, on the one hand, exercising his proprietary rights in the subject matter of the constructive trust by following that property into the hands of the third party and, on the other hand, relying on the personal liability of the constructive trustee to account. The election between the two remedies will be dependant on exactly the same factors as have already been discussed. Where both the third party and the constructive trustee are solvent, the only relevant factors will be any changes in the value of the property, the presence or absence of income and other fruits, and the amount of interest payable by the constructive trustee. Where, on the other hand, the constructive trustee is insolvent, the beneficiary will almost always choose to rely on his proprietary rights and pursue his equitable tracing claim against the third party.

It may, on the other hand, not be possible to recover the property

---

[41] See p. 180.
[42] [1975] 1 W.L.R. 1519 (this case concerned the previous statutory provision, Bankruptcy Act 1914 s.42).
[43] See p. 608.

upon which the constructive trust has been imposed. This will be the case where the property either has disappeared as the result of casual expenditure or dissipation by the constructive trustee or a third party, or has reached the hands of a third party against whom it is not possible to maintain an equitable tracing claim because he is able to establish one of the accepted defences to such claims. Consequently the only remedy available to him will be to rely on the personal liability of the constructive trustee to account. Where the constructive trustee is solvent, this will not normally produce any particularly significant disadvantage. Where, on the other hand, the constructive trustee is insolvent, the absence of any proprietary rights will prevent the beneficiary from being able to claim priority over the general creditors of the constructive trustee since the liability of the constructive trustee to account will rank with, rather than ahead of, the claims of the general creditors.[44] Exactly the same situation occurs with the alleged second type of constructive trusts, better regarded as examples of equity imposing a personal liability to account in the same manner as a trustee; such a liability will also rank with, rather than ahead of, the claims of the general creditors of the person held liable to account.

3. When and on what Grounds will a Constructive Trust be Imposed?

The most important single factor that will determine when, and on what grounds, a constructive trust will be imposed is the role which the courts consider that the constructive trust occupies in the legal system as a whole. Their perception of this role must inevitably take into account the various possible consequences of the imposition of a constructive trust which have just been considered. In this respect, the different common law jurisdictions adopt different attitudes.

(a) The attitude of the North American jurisdictions

American law has long adopted the attitude that the constructive trust is an instrument for remedying unjust enrichment. Thus a constructive trust may be imposed whenever the constructive trustee has been unjustly enriched at the expense of the constructive beneficiary. In other words, all that has to be shown is that the constructive trustee has received some benefit which, as against the constructive beneficiary, he cannot justly retain. Paragraph 160 of the American Restatement of the Law of Restitution provides: "Where a person holding title to property is subject to an equitable duty to convey it to another on the ground that he would be unjustly enriched if he were permitted to retain it, a constructive trust arises." This provision unquestionably represents the attitude of American judges. As Cardozo J. has remarked[45]: "A constructive trust is the formula through which the conscience of equity finds expression. When property has been acquired in such circumstances that the holder of the legal title may not in good

---

[44] See *Selangor United Rubber Estates* v. *Cradock (No. 3)* [1968] 1 W.L.R. 1555.
[45] In *Beatty* v. *Guggenheim Exploration Co.* (1919) 225 N.Y. 380, 386.

conscience retain the beneficial interest, equity converts him into a trustee." The principle of unjust enrichment is, in America, the underlying basis of the "principal types of situations in which a constructive trust is imposed"[46]; whether a constructive trust is imposed therefore depends on the presence or absence of unjust enrichment, not on whether the case can be brought within one of the distinct situations which English law recognises as giving rise to the imposition of a constructive trust. Much more recently,[47] the Supreme Court of Canada has also recognised the principle of unjust enrichment as a basis for the imposition of a constructive trust. However, in Canada the principle of unjust enrichment has not yet become all-embracing; this new type of remedial constructive trust appears for the moment to exist alongside the more traditional situations in which constructive trusts are imposed.[48]

(b) The attitude of the remaining common law jurisdictions

The remaining common law jurisdictions have not as yet accepted that the unjust enrichment of the constructive trustee is, without more, a sufficient ground for the imposition of a constructive trust. At one time, in the years immediately before and after 1970, it did appear that English law might be moving towards an approach similar to that which was subsequently adopted in Canada. At that time, a number of decisions emanating from the Court of Appeal suggested that a constructive trust "is a trust imposed by law whenever justice and good conscience require it . . . it is an equitable remedy by which the court can enable an aggrieved party to obtain restitution".[49] However, subsequent decisions have rejected the approach manifested in this series of cases and English law seems for the moment to have reverted to its traditional attitude towards the constructive trust, an attitude which has perhaps been most accurately described by the statement that in England "the constructive trust continues to be seen as an institutional obligation attaching to property in certain specified circumstances".[50] However, there are now some signs that English law may be about to make some further move, of a more limited nature than that made in the years immediately before and after 1970, towards a more remedial approach. The Court of Appeal has recently stated[51] that "there is a good arguable case" that circumstances may arise in which "the court will be prepared to impose a constructive trust *de novo* as a foundation for the grant of equitable remedy by way of account or otherwise", classifying such a trust as a "remedial constructive trust".

---

[46] W. A. Seavey & A. W. Scott: (1938) 54 L.Q.R. 29, 42.

[47] In *Pettkus* v. *Becker* (1980) 117 D.L.R. (3d.) 257.

[48] *Lac Minerals* v. *International Corona Resources* (1989) 61 D.L.R. (4th) 14, *Rawluk* v. *Rawluk* (1990) 65 D.L.R. (4th) 161. See D.W.M. Waters in *Equity and Contemporary Legal Developments* (1992) (ed. Goldstein) 457.

[49] *Hussey* v. *Palmer* [1972] 1 W.L.R. 1286, 1290.

[50] *Metall und Rohstoff A.G.* v. *Donaldson Lufkin & Jenrette* [1989] 3 W.L.R. 563, 621.

[51] D. W. M. Waters in *Equity and Contemporary Legal Developments* (1992) (ed. Goldstein) 457.

Similar sentiments have been voiced in Australia and New Zealand,[52] where judicial changes of attitude towards the constructive trust are now very evident. Nevertheless in England, in Australia and in New Zealand, the courts have, generally speaking, only been prepared to impose a constructive trust where some cause of action against the constructive trustee has arisen independently. It is not enough to say, as in America, that a constructive trustee "is not compelled to convey the property because he is a constructive trustee; it is because he can be compelled to convey that he is a constructive trustee".[53] In order to obtain the imposition of a constructive trust, the beneficiary must be able to demonstrate some legal or equitable wrong by the constructive trustee, be it breach of fiduciary duty, participation in a breach of trust, or fraudulent or unconscionable conduct. Such developments in the law as have occurred have been brought about by the enlargement of the concepts of fiduciary relationship[54] and unconscionable conduct[55] rather than by recourse to the principle of unjust enrichment. For the moment, therefore, the unjust enrichment of the constructive trustee is still not in itself sufficient.

(c) What should be the attitude of English law?

It has long been argued that the English courts should adopt the American approach, now also adopted in Canada, and impose constructive trusts in order to prevent unjust enrichment. "What English law needs," wrote Professor D.W.M. Waters in 1964, "is a practical, down to earth remedy, as vivid as specific performance and injunction, and within which the courts are brought immediately face to face with the policy decisions or the equities that the courts must and do already make or weigh".[56] There is, in principle, as is implicit in the recent remarks of the Court of Appeal,[57] no reason why the categories of situations in which English courts will impose a constructive trust should be regarded as closed. However, the liabilities which arise as the result of the imposition of a constructive trust provide a strong argument against its use as a general equitable remedy to do justice in the instant case in the way in which it is used in America. The proprietary nature of these liabilities affects the existing property rights both of the constructive trustee and, in the event of his bankruptcy, of his general creditors. As a matter of principle, such alterations of existing property rights should not be able to ensue merely from the desire of a court to do justice in the instant case. It has never been the practice of English courts to alter existing property rights merely in order to do justice *inter partes*. The House of Lords has repeatedly stated

---

[52] *Muschinski* v. *Dodds* (1985) 160 C.L.R. 583, 615 (Deane J.) (High Court of Australia), *Gillies* v. *Keogh* [1989] 2 N.Z.L.R. 327, 330 (Turner P.) (Court of Appeal of New Zealand).
[53] *Scott on Trusts* (4th ed. 1987), para. 462, p. 306.
[54] See s.II of this Chapter, *post* p. 221.
[55] See s.IV of this Chapter, *post* p. 272.
[56] *The Constructive Trust* (1964) p. 73.
[57] See *ante*, n. 51.

that rights of property are not to be determined according to what is reasonable and fair or just in all the circumstances,[58] a principle which is crucial for the maintenance of that certainty which should be the hallmark of every system of law. The imposition of a constructive trust in order to bring a dispute to a conclusion which appears to be just and equitable in the way that the Court of Appeal did immediately before and after 1970 is inevitably contrary to such a principle. The consequences of the imposition of a constructive trust thus constitute powerful arguments against the use of the constructive trust as a means of doing justice *inter partes*. These important considerations bear no weight in America simply because American law is much more ready to interfere with existing third party rights than is the law of England. In America a claimant is permitted to trace his property in equity whenever he can show that that property has been wrongfully disposed of with knowledge of the wrongful nature of the disposition[59] (the existence of a trust is not, as in English law, a prerequisite of such a claim). A litigant thus permitted to trace will inevitably obtain priority over the third party creditors of the other party. (Now that Canada has espoused the American concept of the remedial constructive trust based on the prevention of unjust enrichment, it must only be a question of time before the adoption of this attitude towards the constructive trust leads the Canadian courts also to adopt the American attitude towards proprietary claims.[60]) Since the rights of third party creditors can thus so readily be altered, the fact that the imposition of a constructive trust brings about such an alteration of priorities is not a particularly significant consideration; there is therefore no reason why this should be specifically taken into account in deciding whether or not a constructive trust should be imposed. In England, on the other hand, the courts are extremely reluctant either to interfere with existing property rights or to grant priority over the general creditors of a bankrupt. Therefore, the fact that the imposition of a constructive trust has both these effects should be a much more significant consideration in England than in America.

Since the imposition of a constructive trust has far-reaching ramifications not only for the person upon whom it is imposed but also for third parties, its indiscriminate invocation and imposition is, at least in England, therefore highly undesirable. The constructive trust should not be invoked in the way that the Court of Appeal did immediately before and after 1970 as some sort of instant remedy to prevent what the court regards as an unjust result in an individual case. Thus, in this sense at least, constructive trusts should not be imposed merely in order to prevent unjust enrichment. This does not mean that the present process whereby the principle of unjust enrichment is gradually being

---

[58] *Pettitt* v. *Pettitt* [1970] A.C. 777, *Gissing* v. *Gissing* [1971] A.C. 886, *Lloyds Bank Plc* v. *Rosset* [1991] 2 W.L.R. 867.

[59] *The American Restatement of the Law of Restitution* (1937) para. 202. See also A. W. Scott: (1955) 71 L.Q.R. 39, 48.

[60] D. W. M. Waters: *Law of Trusts in Canada* (2nd ed. 1984) 386–388.

incorporated into English law[61] should not continue, merely that the constructive trust is not an appropriate instrument for dealing out justice *inter partes*. Although the categories of situations in which English courts will impose constructive trusts should not be regarded as closed, these categories should be extended only where the courts are prepared to lay down some new principle which will apply generally, as the House of Lords has done on occasions in the past.[62] No such principle should be established without the fullest consideration of its probable effects on the interests of third parties and of the possibility of reducing these effects by varying the normal consequences of the imposition of a constructive trust in the way which was done in *Muschinski* v. *Dodds*[63] and envisaged in *Lonhro* v. *Fayed (No. 2)*.[64] Finally, any principle laid down must above all be capable of being applied with sufficient certainty to enable litigants to be safely advised as to the probable outcome of legal proceedings.

II. ADVANTAGES OBTAINED BY FIDUCIARIES BREACHING THEIR DUTY OF LOYALTY

One of the best known situations in which constructive trusts are imposed is where a fiduciary has obtained a benefit as a result of a breach of the duty of loyalty which he owes to his principal.[65]

1. *What Relationships will be Classified as Fiduciary?*

No comprehensive definition of the expression fiduciary has ever been attempted. As Deane J. observed in *Chan* v. *Zacharia*,[66] "[f]iduciary relationships may take a wide variety of forms and may give rise to a wide variety of obligations". The use of the expression "fiduciary" "has generally been descriptive, providing a veil behind which individual rules and principles have been developed".[67] In simple terms, a fiduciary "is, simply, someone who undertakes to act for or on behalf of another in some particular matter or matters. That undertaking may be of a general character. It may be specific and limited. It is immaterial whether the undertaking is gratuitous. And the undertaking may be

---

[61] Most recently in *Lipkin Gorman* v. *Karpnale* [1991] 3 W.L.R. 10 (in relation to the defence of change of position) *post*, p. 628 and in *Woolwich Equitable Building Society* v. *I.R.C.* [1992] 3 W.L.R. 366 (in relation to the recovery of overpayments of taxes made under statutory instruments subsequently held to be *ultra vires*).

[62] As in *Pettitt* v. *Pettitt* [1970] A.C. 777 and *Gissing* v. *Gissing* [1971] A.C. 886, *post*, p. 281.

[63] [1985] 160 C.L.R. 583, *ante*, p. 213.

[64] [1992] 1 W.L.R. 1.

[65] The vast literature on this subject includes: Goff & Jones: Ch. 34, G. H. Jones (1968) 84 L.Q.R. 472, P.D. Finn: *Fiduciary Obligations* (1977) and in *Equity, Fiduciaries and Trusts* (ed. Youdan 1989)) 1, J. C. Shepherd: *The Law of Fiduciaries* (1981) and (1981) 97 L.Q.R. 51, T. Frankel: (1983) 71 Calif.L.Rev. 795 and in *Equity Fiduciaries and Trusts 1993* (ed. Waters (1993)) 173.

[66] (1984) 53 A.L.R. 417, 430 (High Court of Australia).

[67] P. D. Finn: *Fiduciary Obligations* (1977) 1, adopting the view propounded by L.S. Sealy: [1963] C.L.J. 119.

officiously assumed without request".[68] A fiduciary is expected "to act in the interests of the other—to act selflessly and with undivided loyalty".[69] This obligation to act selflessly is what distinguishes a person who owes fiduciary obligations from a person who owes merely contractual obligations; the latter is permitted to act in his own self interest, provided that he does not engage in conduct which the courts are prepared to classify as unconscionable.[70]

The "category of cases in which fiduciary obligations and duties arise from the circumstances of the case and the relationship of the parties is no more closed than the categories of negligence at common law".[71] The majority of the decided cases have concerned four relationships: trustee and beneficiary, agent and principal, director and company, and partner and co-partner (either intentionally created or arising as a result of the officious conduct of the fiduciary). Such relationships are inevitably classified as fiduciary and the full range of fiduciary obligations and prohibitions is normally imposed on such fiduciaries, although this does not mean that the position of each is actually identical. Solicitors, accountants, guardians, promoters and receivers have also been held, in certain circumstances and in respect of specific transactions, to be fiduciaries. This has invariably been because it has been possible for the conclusion to be reached that, as a matter of fact, the person held to be a fiduciary has, or can be presumed to have, scope for the exercise of some discretion or power, which he can unilaterally exercise so as to affect the legal or practical interests of the other party, who is peculiarly vulnerable to or at the mercy of the holder of the discretion or power.[72] Other jurisdictions have reached similar conclusions in respect of doctors[73] and child-abusers[74] and are confidently expected to do the same in respect of priests.[75] In *Reading* v. *Attorney-General*,[76] the House of Lords even held that a member of the armed forces of the Crown was a fiduciary in respect of the use of his uniform and the opportunities and facilities attached to it. On the other hand, in *Tito* v. *Waddell (No. 2)*[77] Megarry V.C. held that a duty imposed by statute to perform certain functions does not, as a general rule, impose fiduciary obligations and that the presumption is, in the absence of indications to the contrary in the statute, that no such

---

[68] *Ibid.* 201.

[69] P. D. Finn in *Equity, Fiduciaries and Trusts* (ed. Youdan (1989)) 1, 4.

[70] *Ibid.* The author argues that there should be an intermediate obligation of good faith, under which a party owing merely contractual obligations is permitted to act in his own self interest, provided that "in his decision and action [he has] regard to the legitimate interests therein of the other".

[71] *Ibid.*

[72] *Ibid.* pp. 41, *et seq.* The formulation in the text comes from the judgment of Wilson J. in *Frame* v. *Smith* (1987) 42 D.L.R.(4th) 81 (Supreme Court of Canada).

[73] *Norberg* v. *Wynrib* (1992) 92 D.L.R.(4th) 449 (two members of the Supreme Court of Canada), *S.E.C.* v. *Willis* (1992) 787 F.Supp. 58 (United States District Court, S.D.N.Y.) and other authorities cited by T. Frankel: *op.cit.*

[74] *K.M.* v. *H.M.* (1993) 96 D.L.R.(4th) 449 (Supreme Court of Canada).

[75] See T. Frankel: *op.cit.*

[76] [1951] A.C. 507. See *post*, p. 228.

[77] [1977] Ch. 106, 235.

obligations are imposed. This also follows from *Swain* v. *The Law Society*,[78] where the House of Lords held that the Law Society was not in a fiduciary relationship with respect to the members of the solicitors' profession. It was also held in *Tito* v. *Waddell (No. 2)*[79] that the Crown will only become a fiduciary if it deliberately chooses so to do.

A more general question, which has been the subject of considerable discussion in recent years, is the extent to which fiduciary obligations should be held to arise under commercial relationships entered into at arm's length and on an equal footing. Many commercial transactions expressly create fiduciary relationships; this will be the case where it is expressly provided that one or more of the parties is subject to fiduciary obligations or where the transaction has expressly created a relationship which is always classified as fiduciary. Where this is not the case, the English courts have, generally speaking, been "mindful of the stern warnings uttered by Lindley L.J.[80] and Atkin L.J.[81] of the dangers of applying equitable doctrines to commercial transactions. To do so . . . would paralyse the trade of the country and fundamentally affect the security of business transactions".[82] These warnings were specifically heeded by the Court of Appeal in *Polly Peck International* v. *Nadir (No. 2)*[83] in 1992. "There has been a natural reluctance to impose upon parties in a commercial relationship who are in a relatively equal position of strength the higher standards of conduct which equity prescribes. One manifestation of this reluctance is the disinclination of judges to find a fiduciary relationship when the arrangement between the parties is of a purely commercial kind and they have dealt with each other at arm's length and on an equal footing".[84] This was undoubtedly the attitude adopted by the Privy Council in relation to an estate agency contract in *Kelly* v. *Cooper*,[85] also in 1992. This attitude has also persisted in other jurisdictions[86]; however, the courts now appear to be much more ready to hold that the parties have not been dealing on an equal footing. In such cases, the "fiduciary relationship has been the spearhead of equity's incursions into the area of commerce".[87] In Australia and in New Zealand, joint venture arrangements have very readily been held to give rise to fiduciary obligations[88] and the Chief Justice of Australia has stated that "a fiduciary relationship will arise out of a commercial arrangement when one party undertakes to act in the interests of the other party rather than in his or her own interests in

---

[78] [1982] 3 W.L.R. 261 (H.L.).

[79] [1977] Ch. 106, 212.

[80] In *Manchester Trust* v. *Furness* [1895] 2 Q.B. 539, 545.

[81] In *Re Wait* [1927] 1 Ch. 606, 634 *et seq.*, especially 639–640.

[82] Sir Anthony Mason (Chief Justice of Australia) extra-judicially, 110 L.Q.R. (1994) 238, 245.

[83] [1992] 4 All E.R. 769, 782, *per* Scott L.J.

[84] Sir Anthony Mason: *op.cit.* 245.

[85] [1992] 3 W.L.R. 936.

[86] *Jirna* v. *Master Donut of Canada* (1973) 40 D.L.R. (3d) 303 (Supreme Court of Canada); *United States Surgical Corporation* v. *Hospital Products International* (1984) 156 C.L.R. 41 (High Court of Australia).

[87] Sir Anthony Mason: *op.cit.* 245.

[88] *United Dominion Corporation* v. *Brian* (1985) 157 C.L.R. 1.

relation to a particular matter or aspect of their arrangement and that other party, being unable to look after his or her interests in that matter or aspect of the arrangement, is basically dependent upon the first party acting in conformity with his or her undertaking".[89] In Canada, an even greater willingness has been shown to impose fiduciary obligations, even where the only vulnerability of the other party has arisen by virtue of the relative sizes and resources of the two commercial enterprises involved.[90]

What are the possibilities of English law adopting similar attitudes? The consequences of the imposition of fiduciary obligations both for the fiduciary himself and for his general creditors constitute strong arguments against the adoption of the Canadian approach in England and any thoughts that English law might be about to develop along the lines of the Australian and New Zealand decisions were rapidly disabused by the recent opinion of the Privy Council in *In re Goldcorp Exchange*.[90A] This, curiously enough, was an appeal from the decision which constituted the principal authority cited by the Chief Justice of Australia in support of the proposition set out in the previous paragraph. The Court of Appeal of New Zealand[90B] had imposed fiduciary obligations on a gold-dealer which had offered its purchasers the option of leaving their bullion in its custody on the purchasers' behalf as "non-allocated bullion". Purchasers who did so were issued with a certificate of ownership and were entitled to take physical possession of their bullion on seven days' notice. The conclusion that the company was a fiduciary was based on two propositions: first, that it was bound to protect the interests of the purchasers and, secondly, that it was, for all practical purposes, free from control and supervision by the purchasers.[90C] The Privy Council, however, heeded the warnings of Lindley L.J. and Atkin L.J. Lord Mustill said this:

"But what kind of fiduciary duties did the company owe to the customer? None have been suggested beyond those which the company assumed under the contracts of sale read with the collateral promises; ... No doubt the fact that one person is placed in a particular position vis-à-vis another through the medium of a contract does not necessarily mean that he does not also owe fiduciary duties to that other by virtue of being in that position. But the essence of a fiduciary relationship is that it creates obligations of a different character from those deriving from the

---

[89] Sir Anthony Mason: *op.cit.* 245–246, citing *Liggett* v. *Kensington* [1993] 3 N.Z.L.R. 257, where the Court of Appeal of New Zealand imposed fiduciary obligations upon a gold trader who had offered purchasers the option of leaving their bullion in the custody of the trader on the purchasers' behalf as "non-allocated bullion". This decision was subsequently reversed by the Privy Council (*In re Goldcorp Exchange* [1994] 3 W.L.R. 199—see *infra*).

[90] *Lac Minerals* v. *International Corona Resources* (1989) 61 D.L.R.(4th) 14 (Supreme Court of Canada).

[90A] [1994] 3 W.L.R. 199.

[90B] [1993] 1 N.Z.L.R. 257.

[90C] *Ibid., per* Cooke P. at pp. 583, 584; *per* Gault J. at pp. 596, 597. Compare the view of the dissentient, McKay J. at pp. 604, 605.

contract itself. . . . Many commercial relationships involve just such a reliance by one party on the other, and to introduce the whole new dimension into such relationships which would flow from giving them a fiduciary character would (as it seems to their Lordships) have adverse consequences far exceeding those foreseen by Atkin L.J. in *In re Wait*.[90D] It is possible without misuse of language to say that the customers put faith in the company, and that their trust has not been repaid. But the vocabulary is misleading; high expectations do not necessarily lead to equitable remedies."

These observations seem to rule out, at least for the present, any possibility of English law developing along the lines of the Australian and New Zealand decisions even in respect of joint venture arrangements, never mind in accordance with the wider principle enunciated by the Chief Justice of Australia. The attitude manifested by the Privy Council does have the great advantage that the interests of third parties cannot be prejudiced by the conversion of a general creditor into a preferential creditor as the result of the imposition of fiduciary obligations on a bankrupt. For this reason, it is hoped that, in the event that English law does one day develop along the lines of the Australian and New Zealand decisions, the courts will not lose sight of the interests of third parties but will take them into account in the manner envisaged in the Introductory Section of this Chapter.

2. *The Nature of the Liability of Fiduciaries*

In *Bray* v. *Ford*[91] Lord Herschell laid down two overlapping principles: a fiduciary cannot be permitted to profit from his fiduciary position and a fiduciary must not allow his personal interest to prevail over his duty of loyalty to his principal. The precise relationship between these two rules has been expressed in a number of ways. In *Swain* v. *The Law Society*[92] Stephenson L.J. regarded the first of these principles as merely one of the many examples of the second principle. However, it is clear that a fiduciary cannot profit from his fiduciary position even when there is no real conflict of interest and duty. Consequently, it is perhaps preferable to adopt the view of Deane J.[93] that the two principles "while overlapping, are distinct".

Within these principles, the attitude of English law towards fiduciaries is relatively consistent. Of course, as is only to be expected, the law differs from fiduciary relationship to fiduciary relationship.[94] This is the case even as between the four main fiduciary relationships—

[90D] [1927] 1 Ch. 606, 634 *et seq.*, especially at pp. 639–640.
[91] [1896] A.C. 44, 51–52.
[92] [1982] 1 W.L.R. 17, 29 (C.A.).
[93] In *Chan* v. *Zacharia* (1984) 53 A.L.R. 417, 433 (High Court of Australia).
[94] See Millett J. in *Lonrho* v. *Fayed (No. 2)* [1992] 1 W.L.R. 1, 11–12.

a director is in a more favourable position with regard to property transactions with his company than is a trustee with regard to property transactions with his trust. This apart, however, the attitude of English law towards fiduciaries is, generally speaking, a harsh one. As James L.J. remarked in *Parker* v. *McKenna*,[95] the rule that a fiduciary may not profit from his position without the knowledge and consent of his principal "is an inexorable rule, and must be applied inexorably by this court, which is not entitled, in my judgment, to receive evidence, or suggestion, or argument as to whether the principal did or did not suffer any injury in fact by reason of the dealing of the [fiduciary]". Not only is it thus irrelevant that the principal has suffered no loss; it is also irrelevant that the fiduciary acted in the utmost good faith and that his actions in fact benefitted his principal. This inexorable rule exists for reasons of policy, namely to avoid the remotest risk of a fiduciary being swayed from his duty of loyalty to his principal by his own self interest. However, the decided cases provide innumerable examples of courts penalising fiduciaries (particularly trustees) totally irrespective of whether there was any serious conflict between their duty of loyalty and their self interest. Only where the making of the profit in question has been authorised in advance in the instrument by which the fiduciary obligation was created or has received the fully informed prior consent or subsequent ratification of the principal is the fiduciary allowed to retain it.[96] Lord Herschell remarked in *Bray* v. *Ford*[97] that this harsh rule "might be departed from in many cases, without any breach of morality, without any wrong being inflicted, and without any consciousness of wrongdoing". However, English law has shown few signs of being disposed to relax its strict penal rule in favour of a more flexible rule that fiduciaries should only be penalised where there has been a serious conflict of interest and duty.

If this strict rule is ever relaxed, as it has been in other jurisdictions, it will have to be decided whether the conflict of interest and duty is to be measured prospectively or retrospectively, whether, in other words, the question of whether there was a real sensible possibility of conflict has to be considered in the light of the facts existing at the time when the course of conduct complained of commenced or in the light of the facts existing at the time when that course of conduct ended. No clear answer to this question has been given in any of the decided cases, perhaps because the adoption of the strict penal rule has rendered it irrelevant. It is, however, suggested that the retrospective approach is preferable.

The many authorities have been classified in a number of different ways. It is proposed to consider them in this order: first, cases where a fiduciary has as a result of his position obtained unauthorised remuneration; secondly, cases where a fiduciary has entered into a transaction in a double capacity in that he has purported to represent the interests both of his principal and himself; and, thirdly, cases where a fiduciary

---

[95] (1874) L.R. 10 Ch. 96.
[96] *Sergeant* v. *National Westminster Bank* (1990) 61 P. & C.R. 518.
[97] [1896] A.C. 44, 51.

has as a result of his position obtained a benefit to the exclusion of his principal.

3. Unauthorised Remuneration Obtained by a Fiduciary as a Result of his Position

(a) When is a fiduciary entitled to claim remuneration?

The detailed rules governing the extent to which a trustee is entitled to claim and retain remuneration and benefits are discussed in Chapter 20.[98] For present purposes, it is merely necessary to state that a trustee is, prima facie, under a duty to act without remuneration, even where he devotes a considerable amount of time and trouble to managing the trust business. Further, if by virtue of his position as trustee, he holds an office of profit, such as a directorship in a company in which the trust has a shareholding, he will prima facie be liable to account to the trust for any remuneration which he receives as a result of holding that office. The position of other express fiduciaries is more favourable; while they are in principle, like trustees, expected to act without remuneration,[99] it is in practice highly unlikely that they will have agreed to do so without first having provided for the payment of the appropriate remuneration. Thus the Articles of Association of a company generally provide for the payment of remuneration to the directors,[1] a Partnership Deed will normally provide for the payment of remuneration to the partners, and a contract of agency will normally make provision for the payment of the appropriate remuneration to the agent. Thus, in normal circumstances, a director of a company who is appointed by the board to a directorship of a subsidiary may undoubtedly retain both sets of directors' fees and a partner who is appointed by his partners to a directorship in a company in which the partnership holds shares may similarly retain his director's fees. However, in the event that the payment of remuneration has not been authorised, or the formula by which authorisation has to be obtained has not been complied with,[2] the fiduciary will not be entitled either to remuneration or to the benefits of any other office to which he has been appointed by virtue of his fiduciary position and will be liable to account to his principal for any sums received.[3] Further, the House of Lords has held that, where the formula by which authorisation has to be obtained has not been complied with, the court has no inherent jurisdiction to award remuneration to the fiduciary in question.[4]

---

[98] *Post*, p. 527.

[99] *Guinness v. Saunders* [1990] 2 W.L.R. 324, 332–333.

[1] The Table A Articles of Association recommended by statute reserve to the company in general meeting the right to determine the remuneration of the directors of the company.

[2] In *Guinness v. Saunders* [1990] 2 W.L.R. 324, the remuneration of the director in question had not, as required by the Articles of Association, been approved by the board of directors.

[3] *Guinness v. Saunders* [1990] 2 W.L.R. 324.

[4] *Ibid.* 335–336, 341–342.

(b) Liability in respect of unauthorised remuneration

Where a fiduciary is liable to account for remuneration received as such, he will in principle clearly be liable as a constructive trustee in respect of the remuneration so obtained. However, only where the remuneration in question is still identifiable at the date of action (as will be the case where the remuneration takes the form of shares) will there be any purpose in imposing such a trust. Where the remuneration has already passed into the general funds of the fiduciary (as will obviously be more usual), then the fiduciary will be liable merely to account to his principal for its value. In this situation there will obviously be no need for the imposition of a constructive trust, since any fiduciary liable to account for remuneration of this kind will inevitably be an express fiduciary.

(c) Liability in respect of secret profits

A fiduciary will also be liable to account for any other payments which he may receive as a result of his position. Such payments are generally known as secret profits. It is clearly established that no fiduciary who receives a secret profit may retain it as against his principal unless its retention was either authorised in advance or subsequently ratified by the principal with full knowledge of all relevant facts.

(i) **Who is regarded as a fiduciary for these purposes?** For the purposes of the application of this principle, the courts take a particularly broad view of what constitutes a fiduciary relationship. In *Attorney-General* v. *Goddard*[5] the principle was applied to a police officer who had been bribed not to report brothel keepers; in *Reading* v. *Attorney-General*[6] it was applied to an ex-R.A.M.C Sergeant who had obtained large sums from smugglers for riding in his uniform through Cairo in lorries in which smuggled goods were being transported, thus enabling the lorries to pass the civil police without search; and in modern conditions it would presumably be applied to a security guard who was bribed to switch off the alarm system, thus facilitating the entrance of thieves.[7] It is arguable whether it is appropriate for relationships of this kind to be classified as fiduciary. In *Reading* v. *Attorney-General*, the Sergeant was claiming by petition of right the return of some £19,000 which had been found in his possession and confiscated when he was eventually apprehended. For this action to fail, some basis for the Crown's right to confiscate the money had to be found. At first instance[8] Denning J. held that there was no fiduciary relationship between the suppliant and the Crown but that no such relationship was in fact necessary. However, in the Court of Appeal[9] Asquith L.J. took a

---

[5] [1929] L.J.(K.B.) 743.
[6] [1951] A.C. 507.
[7] This illustration is provided by Sir Peter Millett extra-judicially in [1993] R.L.R. 7.
[8] [1948] 2 K.B. 268.
[9] [1949] 2 K.B. 232.

different view, holding that, assuming a fiduciary relationship to be necessary, such a relationship arose from the use by the suppliant of his uniform and the opportunities attached to it. He admitted that this was using the concept of fiduciary relationship "in a very loose . . . sense" but this did not stop the House of Lords from confirming his view. It is possible to criticise his reasoning on the grounds that the relationship between Sergeant Reading and the Crown does not appear to satisfy any of the criteria for the existence of a fiduciary relationship; in particular, it is not easy to see what scope he had for the unilateral exercise of any discretion or power so as to effect the legal or practical interests of the Crown or in what sense the Crown was peculiarly vulnerable. That is not to say that *Reading* v. *Attorney-General* was wrongly decided since its result can certainly be justified on other grounds.[10] However, the decision undoubtedly demonstrates how widely the courts are prepared to construe the concept of fiduciary relationship in order to permit the recovery of secret profits.[11]

(ii) **The nature of the liability.** In principle, a fiduciary who is liable to account for secret profits will be liable as a constructive trustee in respect of the secret profit in question. In *Williams* v. *Barton*[12] a trustee used a firm of which he was a member to value trust securities. His action was completely bona fide but he was nevertheless held liable to account to the trust as a constructive trustee for the commission which he had made out of the introduction of the trust business. This decision means that a solicitor who receives a commission for introducing a client to a broker will be liable to account to the client for this commission unless the latter has expressly authorised the retention of the payment in question. The inconsistency of this rule with normal commercial practices is particularly emphasised by the fact that, since the liability imposed is a constructive trust, the principal is therefore entitled to follow the payment into its product in the admittedly unlikely event that it can be shown to have been invested in assets which have appreciated in value.

Until the decision of the Privy Council in *Attorney-General for Hong Kong* v. *Reid*,[13] the decided cases appeared to draw a distinction between bribes and other secret profits. When a fiduciary has received a bribe, which may be defined as an undisclosed payment made to a person known by the payer to be a fiduciary in circumstances in which it could induce the fiduciary to favour the payer in some way in his

---

[10] By virtue of the principle that no criminal may benefit from his crime. See Section IV of this Chapter, *post*, p. 272.

[11] *Reading* v. *Attorney-General* was approved and applied in the equally extreme case of *Jersey City* v. *Hague* (1955) 155 At.(2d) 8, which concerned a successful attempt to recover from the Mayor of Jersey City the percentages of the salaries of each employee of the city which he had extorted over a period of thirty years in consideration of continued employment.

[12] [1927] 2 Ch. 9.

[13] [1993] 3 W.L.R. 1143.

dealings with the fiduciary or with the fiduciary's principal,[14] the principal has a choice of remedies. He can rescind any transaction entered into as a result of the bribe,[15] provided of course that he can still make *restitutio in integrum*, and, additionally or alternatively, sue either the briber[16] or the fiduciary[17] for the amount of the bribe. It is the last of these remedies which is relevant for present purposes. In *Lister & Co.* v. *Stubbs*[18] the defendant was the plaintiff's foreman and was responsible for buying in whatever was needed in his employer's business. He regularly gave orders to a third party in return for a large commission. In an action to recover this bribe, the plaintiff sought an order restraining the defendant from dealing with certain investments purchased with the money received on the basis that the defendant was a constructive trustee of the bribes and so the plaintiff would be entitled to follow the money into its product and recover the investments. However, the Court of Appeal declined to grant this order, holding that the only obligation of the defendant was to pay over the sums received to the plaintiff; the relationship between them was held to be that of debtor-creditor rather than trustee-beneficiary. Although this decision was consistently followed,[19] it seemed quite extraordinary that the defendant in *Williams* v. *Barton* should have been held to have been a constructive trustee of a commission which he had earned in good faith if the defendant in *Lister & Co.* v. *Stubbs* was held not to have been a constructive trustee of an illicitly earned bribe. All the commentators agreed that both cases should have been decided in the same way. Some thought that a constructive trust should not have been imposed in either case on the grounds that proprietary remedies should be limited to situations where the claimant can show that he has lost property which, but for the conduct of the fiduciary, he would have obtained.[20] Others thought that a constructive trust should have been imposed in both cases on the grounds that a fiduciary should never be allowed to retain any advantage from the violation of his fiduciary obligations,

---

[14] *Hovenden and Sons* v. *Milhoff* (1900) 83 L.T. 41, 43; *Industries and General Mortgage Co.* v. *Lewis* [1949] 2 All E.R. 573, 575.

[15] *Logicrose* v. *Southend United F.C.* [1988] 1 W.L.R. 1256.

[16] *Hovenden and Sons* v. *Milhoff* (1900) 83 L.T. 41; *Mahesan* v. *Malaysian Government Officers' Co-operative Housing Society* [1979] A.C. 374, 383.

[17] These claims were held to be alternative rather than cumulative in *Mahesan* v. *Malaysian Government Officers' Co-operative Housing Society* [1979] A.C. 374.

[18] (1890) 45 Ch.D. 1.

[19] In *Att.-Gen. Ref. (No. 1 of 1985)* [1986] 2 All E.R. 219 and in *Islamic Republic of Iran Shipping Line* v. *Denby* [1987] 1 F.T.L.R. 30. In Australia, the view had been expressed that the decision in *Lister & Co.* v. *Stubbs* was anomalous and should be confined to its own facts (*Consul Development* v. *D.P.C. Estates* [1974] 1 N.S.W.L.R. 443 (New South Wales Court of Appeal); the question was left open on the further appeal to the High Court of Australia ((1975) 132 C.L.R. 373)). Subsequently, the reasoning in *Lister & Co.* v. *Stubbs* was described as impeccable when applied to cases in which the person claiming the money had simply made what was described as an outright loan to the fiduciary (*Daly* v. *The Sydney Stock Exchange* (1986) 160 C.L.R. 371 (High Court of Australia)). This restricted the effect of *Lister & Co.* v. *Stubbs* in Australia to cases where a bribe was paid over to a fiduciary in the form of money.

[20] P. B. H. Birks: *An Introduction to the Law of Restitution* (1985): 388; R. M. Goode: (1987) 103 L.Q.R. 433, 422–445, *Essays on the Law of Restitution* (1991) 216.

something which can only be achieved by the imposition of a proprietary remedy.[21] This issue was resolved by the Privy Council in *Attorney-General for Hong Kong* v. *Reid*.[22]

This case concerned a Hong Kong Public Prosecutor, who was convicted of having accepted bribes as an inducement to him to exploit his official position to obstruct the prosecution of certain criminals. He was ordered to pay the Crown the sum of $HK12,400,000, the value of assets then controlled by him which could only have been derived from the bribes. No payments having been made, the Attorney-General for Hong Kong brought proceedings in New Zealand claiming that three freehold houses which the bribes had been used to purchase were held on constructive trust for the Crown. The Court of Appeal of New Zealand applied *Lister & Co* v. *Stubbs* and dismissed this claim.[23] The Privy Council reversed this decision, holding that *Lister & Co.* v. *Stubbs* had been wrongly decided. Lord Templeman's opinion did not directly consider the important issue of policy on which the commentators were divided. Lord Templeman held that, as soon as any bribe is received, the fiduciary becomes in equity the debtor of his principal for the amount of the bribe, which should immediately be transferred to his principal. Because equity considers as done that which ought to have been done, the bribe therefore becomes subject to a constructive trust in favour of the principal as soon as it is received. Although this analysis is questionable in a number of respects,[24] it provided a basis for an examination of the case law, from which Lord Templeman concluded that *Lister & Co* v. *Stubbs* was consistent neither with prior authority nor "with the principles that a fiduciary must not be allowed to benefit from his own breach of duty, that the fiduciary should account for the bribe as soon as he receives it and that equity regards as done that which ought to be done".[24A] Although this decision is not, of course, formally binding on English courts, it will undoubtedly be followed. Whatever its shortcomings, it has removed a glaring inconsistency in the treatment of secret profits and has established that the liability of a fiduciary who receives a bribe will be exactly the same as that of a fiduciary who receives any other type of secret profit.

4. *Transactions into which a Fiduciary has entered in a Double Capacity*

This second group of cases concerns transactions in which a fiduciary has purported to represent the interests of both his principal and himself. Such situations produce an obvious conflict between the

---

[21] Underhill & Hayton: 305; Goff & Jones: 657; Pettit: *Equity and the Law of Trusts* (7th ed., (1993)), 152; Meagher, Gummow & Lehane: Equity Doctrines and Remedies (2nd ed., (1984)), Para. 1323; P. D. Finn: *Fiduciary Obligations* (1977) Para. 513; Sir Anthony Mason extra-judicially in *Essays in Equity* (1985): 246, Sir Peter Millett extra-judicially in [1993] R.L.R. 7.

[22] [1993]3 W.L.R. 1143.

[23] [1992] 2 N.Z.L.R. 385.

[24] See [1994] C.L.J. 31.

[24A] [1993] 3 W.L.R. 1143 at p. 1151.

personal interest of the fiduciary in the transaction and his duty of loyalty towards his principal. Consequently, no matter how fair the transaction, the principal has the right to have the transaction set aside unless he was fully aware of the facts.

(a) Purchases of property by a fiduciary from his principal

Such purchases are regulated by two rules, which have become known as the self-dealing rule and the fair-dealing rule.[25] The self-dealing rule applies to purchases by trustees from their trusts[26] and, at least in theory, to purchases by directors from their companies[27] (although in practice the Articles of Association of virtually all companies expressly permit such purchases provided that appropriate disclosure is made). The fair-dealing rule applies to purchases by trustees of the interests of their beneficiaries[28] and to purchases by other fiduciaries (such as agents) from their principals.[29]

(i) **The self-dealing rule.**   The rationale of the self-dealing rule was laid down by Lord Eldon L.C. in *Ex p. Lacey*.[30] Since in such a purchase the fiduciary is both vendor and purchaser, it is impossible to determine from the evidence whether or not he has obtained an advantage from the purchase; hence, the court has no option but to set aside the sale at the instance of the principal. The many cases in which this rule has been applied have illustrated that it is quite irrelevant that the fiduciary was honest, the sale open and the price fair. In *Wright* v. *Morgan*[31] property was devised to two trustees on trust for sale for one of them. The will stated that the trustees were required to offer the trustee-beneficiary the land at a price to be fixed by independent valuers. The trustee-beneficiary assigned his beneficial interest to the other trustee, who bought the property at the price fixed by the independent valuers in accordance with the terms of the will. The Privy Council held that this sale had to be set aside, since only a sale to the trustee-beneficiary had been authorised by the will. The fact that the price was to be fixed independently was not sufficient, for the trustees could themselves fix the *time* at which the property was to be sold and this could clearly have had a substantial effect on the price ultimately received. Similarly, it has been held in an Eighteenth Century case[32] that a trustee must not purchase trust property which is put up for auction as he is in a position to discourage bidders.

Wright v. *Morgan* demonstrates that a trustee is entitled to purchase the trust property if he is authorised so to do by the trust instrument. This has recently been specifically held in *Sargeant* v. *National*

---

[25] See *Tito* v. *Waddell (No. 2)* [1977] 2 W.L.R. 496, 604–605, 619–622 (Megarry V.C.).

[26] *Ex p. Lacey* (1802) 6 Ves. 625.

[27] *Aberdeen Railway Co.* v. *Blaikie Brothers* (1854) 1 Macq. 461, 472; *Movitex* v. *Bullfield* [1988] B.C.L.C. 104.

[28] *Chalmer* v. *Bradley* (1819) 1 J. & W. 51.

[29] *Edwards* v. *Meyrick* [1842] 2 Hare 60.

[30] (1802) 6 Ves. 625.

[31] [1926] A.C. 788.

[32] *Whelpdale* v. *Cookson* (1747) 1 Ves.Sen. 9.

Westminster Bank.[33] As has already been mentioned, the Articles of Association of virtually all companies also expressly permit purchases by directors provided that disclosure of their interest is made in whatever way is required by the provision in question.[34] It is also clear that a trustee may be authorised to purchase trust property by the court. Such authorisation is obviously necessary in cases where some of the beneficiaries are not *sui juris* or are unborn or unascertained and, for the reasons set out below, is highly prudent in almost all other cases. The court requires to be satisfied that the sale is in the interests of all the beneficiaries before it will grant its approval and the evidence on this point must be very clear.[35] In principle, there seems no reason why a trustee should not purchase trust property without such authorisation if all the beneficiaries agree, provided that they are all *sui juris* and are between them absolutely entitled to the whole of the beneficial interest in the property. The court will not upset a sale where the beneficiaries have genuinely agreed to it. For such agreement to be effective, the trustees would have to disclose to the beneficiaries *all* the information which they have about the property. Nevertheless, although it is theoretically possible for an unimpeachable sale to take place in this way, there are two serious practical objections to it. First, the onus will lie on the trustee-purchaser to show that the beneficiaries were given all the relevant information and that they all freely gave their consent, a very difficult burden of proof to discharge. Secondly, the property may be virtually unmarketable thereafter. The liability to have a sale set aside affects subsequent purchasers with notice; consequently, in most cases it is almost impossible to sell land where the title shows that the vendor formerly held it as a trustee. Even if the trustee can produce a written agreement showing that the beneficiaries have consented, a subsequent purchaser cannot be sure that the trustee gave to the beneficiaries all the information in his possession before they entered into the agreement. Only in highly exceptional circumstances, therefore, would a subsequent purchaser complete his purchase.

Only in most extraordinary circumstances will the court refuse to set aside a purchase of trust property by a trustee at the instance of the beneficiary, other than in the case where the trustee can successfully raise against the beneficiary a defence of delay, or laches.[36] However, the court did refuse to upset a transaction in *Holder* v. *Holder*.[37] One of the executors of a will renounced his executorship after carrying out

---

[33] (1990) 61 P. & C.R. 518.

[34] The Companies Acts have long contained a provision requiring directors who are in any way, ~~whether~~ directly or indirectly, interested in a contract or proposed contract with the company to declare the nature of their interest at a meeting of the directors of the company. The present provision is Companies Act 1985 s.317. The Table A Articles of Association recommended by statute provide that directors will not be liable to account for benefits resulting from transactions with the company which have been duly disclosed in accordance with the section. Many Articles of Association additionally provide that such directors should neither vote nor be counted in the quorum on any matter in which they are interested. See *Movitex* v. *Bullfield* [1988] B.C.L.C. 625.

[35] *Farmer* v. *Dean* (1863) 32 Beav. 327, *Campbell* v. *Walker* (1800) 5 Ves. 678.

[36] See *Tito* v. *Waddell (No. 2)* [1977] 2 W.L.R. 496, 627–628.

[37] [1968] Ch. 353.

certain acts which, it was conceded, amounted to intermeddling. He was the tenant of certain farms which the other executors offered for sale by auction subject to his tenancy. At the auction he purchased the farms at a good price, probably higher than would have been paid by anyone other than a sitting tenant and well above the reserve price (which had been fixed by an independent valuer). One of the beneficiaries subsequently sought to have the sale set aside. The Court of Appeal refused to do so. Harman L.J. held that the rule in *Ex p. Lacey* was based on the principle that no man may be both vendor and purchaser. Here the purchaser had played no real part in the administration of the estate and renounced his executorship long before the sale. All the beneficiaries were aware of this and so could not have been looking to him to protect their interests. Thus the mischief which the rule was intended to prevent did not arise and there was no reason to set aside the sale. Such an attitude, while quite different from that adopted in *Wright* v. *Morgan*, does not in any way affect the principle in *Ex p. Lacey*. But both the other members of the court declined to accept the principle of that decision. Danckwerts L.J. said that Chancery judges were daily engaged in ascertaining the knowledge and intentions of parties to proceedings; the court could unquestionably sanction such a purchase and so the rule in *Ex p. Lacey* could be no more than a rule of practice. So, he held, this type of issue was a matter for the discretion of the judge. Sachs L.J. took very much the same view. All three members of the court then went on to hold that, in any event, the beneficiaries had acquiesced in the purchase and could not now seek to set it aside. The approach taken in this case by Danckwerts and Sachs L.JJ. suggested that the courts might be about to move away from the automatic application of the self-dealing rule and instead apply the fair-dealing rule to purchases of property by a trustee from his trust, a flexible approach which would undoubtedly have been preferable. However, this has not proved to be the case. In *Re Thompson's Settlement*,[38] Vinelott J. took the view that the decision in *Holder* v. *Holder* had been reached for the reasons enunciated by Harman L.J. and held that the self-dealing rule "is applied stringently in cases where a trustee concurs in a transaction which cannot be carried into effect without his concurrence and who also has an interest in or holds a fiduciary duty to another in relation to the same transaction".[39] He therefore held that two leases in favour of a company and a partnership of which the two trustees were respectively a shareholder and a partner were not valid. Thus, the self-dealing rule still retains its full force.

(ii) **The fair-dealing rule.** This rule, which is less stringent, applies to purchases by trustees of the interests of their beneficiaries and to purchases by other fiduciaries (such as agents) from their principals. Where a trustee purchases the beneficial interest of one of the beneficiaries under the trust, the mischief which the rule in *Ex p. Lacey* was intended to solve does not arise since the trustee is not both vendor and

---

[38] [1985] 3 W.L.R. 486.
[39] [1985] 3 W.L.R. 486, 497.

purchaser. Hence the courts have always been prepared to uphold such purchases provided that the trustee is able to establish that he obtained no advantage by reason of his position[40]; in particular, he must be able to show that he did not abuse his position as trustee, that he concealed no material facts, that the price was fair, and that the beneficiary did not rely solely on his advice.[41] This will be an almost impossible burden of proof to discharge when the beneficiary is an infant[42]; in such circumstances, the trustee will need to seek the authorisation of the court. Similarly, where a fiduciary such as an agent purchases property from his principal, he is in practice unlikely to be both sole vendor and purchaser and, even if he is, in comparison with the position of a trustee or a director who is purchasing the property of his principal, he will have far fewer possibilities of taking unfair advantage of his principal. Consequently, such purchases will similarly be upheld provided that the fiduciary is able to show that he did not abuse his position in any way, that he paid a fair price, and that he has made full disclosure of his interest and of any information which he possesses about the property.[43]

(iii) The precise limits of the rules. The self-dealing rule and the fair-dealing rule cannot be evaded by selling to an associate of the fiduciary rather than to the fiduciary himself; the rules have proved strong enough to prevent evasion. Most of the decided cases concern purchases by associates of trustees. In the first place, although a sale to a relative of the trustee is not necessarily bad,[44] a purchase taken in the name of the trustee's children will usually be upset[45] and it is very risky to take a purchase in the name of the trustee's spouse,[46] at least if at the time the two "were living in perfect amity" rather than "separate and in emnity for a dozen years".[47] Nor can the rules be overcome by selling to a limited company of which the trustee is the majority shareholder[48] or of which he has control.[49] It seems that a sale by a trustee to a company of which he is a member, but which he does not control, is not *ipso facto* voidable but, if the beneficiaries seek to upset it, the company may have to show that the trustee had taken all reasonable steps to find a purchaser and that the price paid by the company was at the time adequate.[50] Similar rules presumably apply to partnerships; certainly, a sale to a partnership comprising the trustee and his family will not be valid.[51] It is equally offensive to the rules to sell the property to a third

---

[40] *Chalmer* v. *Bradley* (1819) 1 J. & W. 51.

[41] *Coles* v. *Trecothick* (1804) 9 Ves. 234.

[42] See *Sanderson* v. *Walker* (1807) 13 Ves. 601.

[43] *Edwards* v. *Meyrick* (1842) 2 Hare 60.

[44] *Coles* v. *Trecothick* (1804) 9 Ves. 234.

[45] *Gregory* v. *Gregory* (1821) Jac. 631.

[46] *Ferraby* v. *Hobson* (1847) 2 Ph. 255; *Burrell* v. *Burrell's Trustee* 1915 S.C. 333.

[47] *Tito* v. *Waddell (No. 2)* [1977] 2 W.L.R. 496, 619.

[48] *Silkstone and Haigh Moor Coal Co.* v. *Edey* [1900] 1 Ch. 167, *Movitex* v. *Bullfield* [1988] B.C.L.C. 104.

[49] *Re Thompson's Settlement* [1985] 3 W.L.R. 486, *Movitex* v. *Bullfield* [1988] B.C.L.C. 104.

[50] *Farrar* v. *Farrar's* (1888) 40 Ch.D. 395.

[51] *Re Thompson's Settlement* [1985] 3 W.L.R. 486.

person, with an agreement or understanding for its repurchase.[52] However, it has been held that, where there was no agreement or understanding for repurchase at the time of the sale to the third person, the fact that the trustee had sold the property to that person with the *hope* of being able to repurchase was not a sufficient ground for setting the sale aside.[53] Finally, a sale may be upset if a trustee retires with the intention that the property will be conveyed to him after his retirement.[54] If, however, a sufficient length of time has elapsed between the retirement and the sale for the court to be satisfied that the ex-trustee has not taken any advantage of knowledge about the property gained while he was a trustee, the sale will be uphheld. Such a transaction has been upheld where there was an interval of twelve years between retirement and purchase.[55]

(iv) The consequences of liability. Where a purchase is impeachable under the principles discussed above, it is not void but merely voidable at the instance of the principal. He must therefore avoid the transaction within a reasonable time, otherwise his failure to do so will entitle the fiduciary to invoke the defence of laches.[56] If the sale is so avoided, the consequences will be as follows.

If the property is still in the hands of the fiduciary, then the principal will have a choice. He will be able to recover the property together with any income produced in the meantime provided that he is in a position to make *restitutio in integrum* by returning to the fiduciary the price which he paid therefor. (In the case of beneficiaries under a trust, this option will require the consent of all of them because of the risk that the property may not be able subsequently to be resold at a higher value, in which case "the beneficiaries would be worse off than if the claim had never been made".[57]) Alternatively, the principal can require the property to be put up for sale again under the direction of the court[58]; the fiduciary will not be allowed to bid at this resale if any of his principals objects to him so doing.[59] The reserve price will normally be the price originally paid by the fiduciary with interest thereon, plus the value of any improvements which he has made to the property and interest thereon, less any income produced by the property or, if the fiduciary has himself been in occupation, the appropriate occupation rent.[60] If the sale "realises more than the reserve fixed by the court, the surplus belongs to the [principal], whereas if it realises less [the

---

[52] *Williams* v. *Scott* [1900] A.C. 499.
[53] *Re Postlethwaite* (1888) 37 W.R. 200, 60 L.T. 514.
[54] *Wright* v. *Morgan* [1926] A.C. 788, *Re Mullholland's Will Trusts* [1949] 1 All E.R. 460.
[55] *Re Boles and the British Land Company's Contract* [1902] 1 Ch. 244.
[56] See *Tito* v. *Waddell (No. 2)* [1977] 2 W.L.R. 496, 627–628.
[57] *Holder* v. *Holder* [1968] Ch. 353, 370–371 (Cross J.).
[58] This was what was ordered at first instance in *Holder* v. *Holder* [1968] Ch. 353, where the purchase was set aside.
[59] *Tennant* v. *Trenchard* (1869) 4 Ch.App. 537.
[60] This was the form of order made in *Holder* v. *Holder* at first instance; although the right to add to the reserve price the value of any improvements was conceded in that case, the existence of the right to do so emerges clearly from *O'Sullivan* v. *Management Agency and Music* [1985] Q.B. 428, 466.

fiduciary] will be held to his bargain"[61] and so will lose the difference. It will only be in the interests of the principal to use either of these remedies where the property is worth at least as much as the fiduciary paid for it. If it has fallen in value, avoiding the transaction will give the principal a property worth less than the sum which he has to return to the fiduciary; consequently, it will be in his interests to affirm the transaction.

If, on the other hand, the property is no longer in the hands of the principal, any third party to whom it has been transferred will have acquired legal title thereto because of the fact that the transaction was voidable rather than void. If the third party has not taken free of the right of the principal to have the purchase set aside (a mere equity), he will be in exactly the same position as the fiduciary. If, however, he has taken free of this mere equity because he is a bona fide purchaser for value without notice or a statutory equivalent, then the property will not be able to be recovered by the principal, whose position will be as follows. He will be entitled to recover any profit made by the fiduciary on the resale[62] with interest thereon.[63] In the event of a resale at less than the true value, he will also be able to claim the difference between the price paid and the true value with interest thereon[64]; this will be recoverable by way of compensation for breach of fiduciary duty under the principle laid down by the House of Lords in *Nocton* v. *Lord Ashburton*[65] (such compensation is also available as an alternative to an account of profits[66]). If, on the other hand, the price paid by the third party was less than the price paid by the fiduciary because the property had fallen in value, the fiduciary will have made no profit and the principal will have suffered no loss; consequently, in such circumstances, the principal will neither have nor be entitled to any remedy.

(b) Sales of property by a fiduciary to his principal

Such sales will be set aside at the instance of the principal, unless the fiduciary has fully disclosed the nature of his interest in the transaction, no matter how honest the fiduciary or fair the price.[67] Such a sale may be set aside even where the fiduciary purchased the property in question before he entered into the fiduciary relationship. Thus, in

---

[61] *Holder* v. *Holder* [1968] Ch. 353, 371 (Cross J.).

[62] *Hall* v. *Hallett* (1784) 1 Cox 134, *Ex p. James* (1803) 8 Ves. 337, 351, *Silkstone and Haigh Moor Coal Co.* v. *Edey* [1900] 1 Ch. 167.

[63] Formerly 4% but, following *Bartlett* v. *Barclays Bank Trust Co.* [1980] Ch. 515, 547, it seems that the rate will now be that of the court's short-term investment account (established under the Administration of Justice Act 1965 s.6 (1)).

[64] *Lord Hardwicke* v. *Vernon* (1800) 4 Ves. 411.

[65] [1914] A.C. 932. See I.E. Davidson: (1982) 13 Melbourne U.L.R. 349.

[66] *McKenzie* v. *McDonald* [1927] V.L.R. 134 (Court of Appeal of Victoria). This is one of the possible explanations of *Coleman* v. *Myers* [1977] 2 N.Z.L.R. 225 (Court of Appeal of New Zealand), where minority shareholders recovered compensation from the directors of the company (held, unusually, to owe them fiduciary duties because of the family nature of the company) who had recommended the acceptance of an under-valued takeover bid without disclosing that the offeror was a company controlled by one of them.

[67] *Gillett* v. *Peppercone* (1840) 3 Beav. 78.

Armstrong v. *Jackson*[68] a stockbroker did not disclose to his client that ever since the formation of a company he had owned the shares which he was encouraging the client to buy. Five years later, by which time the shares had fallen in value to less than a fifth of the purchase price, the client discovered the true facts and successfully sought rescission of the sale. If, on the other hand, the property has increased in value, it will not be in the interests of the principal to set aside the transaction. In the event that, for this or any other reason, the principal seeks not to set aside the sale but to recover the profit made by the fiduciary out of the transaction, his right to do so will clearly depend on when the fiduciary purchased the property. In *Bentley* v. *Craven*[69] the defendant was responsible for the purchase of sugar for a partnership of sugar refiners of which he was a member but also carried on an independent business as a sugar dealer. He purchased a quantity of sugar which he later resold to the partnership at a price which, although resulting in a profit to him, was the fair market price of the day. He was held liable to account for his profit to the partnership since he had been a fiduciary at the date of purchase and so should have purchased for the partnership rather than for himself. A similar decision was reached where an investment adviser purchased a property of a type which he knew that his client wished to purchase and subsequently sold it on to her at a substantial profit.[70] On the other hand, in *Re Cape Breton Co.*[71] a director acquiesced in the sale to his company of certain mining claims in which he had a beneficial interest. After discovering the facts, the company elected not to set aside the sale. Subsequently, after the property had been sold on at a loss, the company tried to claim the profit made by the director. This action failed because the director had acquired the property more than two years before the company in question had been formed. This conclusion is clearly correct when the fiduciary has sold at the market value. The Court of Appeal actually held, by a majority, that it made no difference that the director had sold above the market value. However, the House of Lords[72] held that there was no evidence that the sale price was above market value. This point therefore did not have to be decided but Lord Herschell considered that an agent employed to purchase non-specific goods in the market would be liable for the excess if he sold his own goods to the company above market value.[73] Therefore, although the decision of the Court of Appeal clearly constitutes the law at present, this particular point cannot be regarded as finally settled. These authorities show that, when the principal does not seek to rescind the sale or cannot do so because rescission is barred on the grounds of affirmation, laches or bona fide purchase, he will only have a remedy where the fiduciary acquired the property after he entered into the fiduciary relationship in question or, possibly, where

---

[68] [1917] 2 K.B. 822.

[69] (1853) 18 Beav. 75.

[70] *Cook* v. *Evatt (No. 2)* [1992] 1 N.Z.L.R. 676 (High Court of New Zealand).

[71] (1885) 29 Ch.D. 795.

[72] *Cavendish Bentinck* v. *Fenn* (1887) 12 App.Cas. 652.

[73] *Ibid.* 659. The remedy would presumably have been either an account of profits or compensation under *Nocton* v. *Lord Ashburton*.

the sale price was above the market value. None of the authorities discussed actually deals with purchases by trustees of their own property for their trusts. There appears to be no English authority on this point but an American decision[74] and dicta in *Bentley* v. *Craven* suggest that the same rules will apply to such transactions.

(c) Other impugnable transactions

Similar principles will apply to two further situations[75]: where a fiduciary engages in regular trading between his own business and a business which he is managing in a fiduciary capacity and where a fiduciary makes a loan to his principal.

5. *Benefits obtained by a Fiduciary as a result of his Position to the Exclusion of his Principal*

This third group of cases has emerged as the result of the rigorous application by the courts of a decision in 1726[76] which established what was, in the light of the prevailing legal rules and financial circumstances, a wholly understandable prohibition on trustees renewing for their own benefit leases formerly held by their trusts. This decision has had two quite distinct effects. First, it has produced a line of authority concerning the extent to which this prohibition also applies to other fiduciaries and the associated question of whether a fiduciary may purchase for his own benefit the freehold reversion in property of which his principal is lessee. Secondly, and totally unconnected with any question of the renewal of leases or the purchase of reversions, the decision has also had a profound effect on the general question of what opportunities a fiduciary is entitled to utilise for his own benefit.

(a) Speculation by a fiduciary with the property of his principal

This is almost the only situation within this third group of cases which is wholly uncontroversial. Where a fiduciary engages in speculation with the property of his principal, the latter will be entitled to all the profits made by the fiduciary under a constructive trust.[77] Thus in *Reid-Newfoundland Co.* v. *Anglo-American Telegraph Co.*,[78] a railway company had, in direct contravention of a specific contractual provision, utilised for commercial messages a telegraph wire which had been erected by a telegraph company for use only in the operation of the railway. The Privy Council held that, in so doing, it had been acting as the agent of the telegraph company and so held the profits thereby obtained on constructive trust for the telegraph company. In this type of case, where the principal has been owner of the property throughout, and also in cases where the fiduciary is already holding the property in question on trust for his principal, the constructive trust will be imposed merely on the profit. But if the property has instead reached the hands of the

---

[74] *Cornet* v. *Cornet* (1916) 269 No. 298.
[75] These situations are discussed by P.D. Finn: *Fiduciary Obligations* (1977): 228–231.
[76] *Keech* v. *Sandford* (1726) Sel.Cas.Ch. 61.
[77] *Brown* v. *I.R.C.* [1965] A.C. 264.
[78] [1912] A.C. 555.

fiduciary in some other way, both the property and the fiduciary's profit will be subject to a constructive trust. If there is no profit, because the speculation has resulted in a loss, a constructive trust may still be imposed, if necessary, upon any of the property remaining in the hands of the fiduciary and, in the event that the value of the property has fallen as a result of the breach by the fiduciary of his duty of loyalty, the principal will be able to recover compensation for that loss under the principle enunciated by the House of Lords in *Nocton* v. *Lord Ashburton*.[79]

(b) Competition between a fiduciary and the business of his principal

There are certain circumstances in which a fiduciary will not be able to compete with the business of his principal. Different rules apply to the different fiduciary relationships.

Where the trust property includes a business, or the trustees carry on any income earning activity, a trustee must not commence a business or activity on his own account which will compete with that of the trust. Thus, in *Re Thomson*[80] one of the assets of a trust was a yachtbroker's business, which was being carried on by the trustees. One of them sought to set up on his own a similar business in the same town, which would have competed with the trust business, but the court granted an injunction restraining him from doing so. The decision in *Re Thomson* appears to be at variance with that in the earlier Irish case of *Moore* v. *M'Glynn*.[81] There the court had refused an injunction, though it thought that the setting up of a competing business would be a good ground for removing the trustee from his trusteeship. It was said that a breach of trust would only be committed if in carrying on the new business the trustee practised deception, or solicited the customers from the old shop. It is sometimes suggested that this decision can be reconciled with that in *Re Thomson* on the basis that the yachtbroker's business was so specialised that any other yachtbroking business in the town was bound to compete with the trust business, even if the customers were not solicited. This is a possible solution, but it does not appear to have been the basis of the decision in *Re Thomson*. *Re Thomson* seems clearly right in principle and it may well be that *Moore* v. *M'Glynn* would not now be followed. As has been shown, in other circumstances the court has been so astute to find a conflict of interest that it is doubtful if it would stop itself from finding a conflict where the same business was being carried on, at least if it were serving the same locality. Where, however, a person who is carrying on a business is then appointed to be a trustee, the position seems to depend on whether the person making the appointment knew of that business. If he did, the trustee will be entitled to continue his business, but if it then appears that there is an actual conflict of interest, he may be required to resign, or be removed.[82]

---

[79] [1914] A.C. 932.
[80] [1930] 1 Ch. 203.
[81] [1894] 1 Ir.R. 74.
[82] See, by analogy, *Peyton* v. *Robinson* (1823) 1 L.J.(o.s.)Ch. 191, *Moore* v. *M'Glynn* [1894] 1 Ir.R. 74.

It might be expected that, if an unpaid trustee may thus in appropriate circumstances be prevented from competing, the paid director and partner would necessarily be prohibited from so doing. Partners are indeed under a statutory duty not to compete with the partnership business[83] but the position of directors is both obscure and anomalous. At common law, a director is not under any obligation not to compete with his company; this emerges from *London and Mashonaland Exploration Co.* v. *New Mashonaland Exploration Co.*,[84] where it was held that a director cannot be restrained from acting as a director of a rival company, a decision which was approved in *Bell* v. *Lever Bros*[85] by Lord Blanesburgh, who added that "[w]hat he could do for a rival company he could, of course, do for himself". However, in the light of authority that an employee may not compete with the business of his employer,[86] it seems likely that an executive director will be under a similar duty not to compete with his company—this seems to have been recognised by Lord Denning in *Scottish Co-operative Wholesale Society* v. *Meyer*,[87] which concerned an application under what is now section 459 of the Companies Act 1985 to wind a company up on the grounds that the manner in which its affairs were being conducted was unfairly prejudicial to the applicant. In practice, the matter must often be dealt with in the Articles of Association or in the service contract of any individual director. Thus, in *Thomas (Marshall) Exporters* v. *Guinle*,[88] a managing director had specifically agreed in his service contract not to engage in any other business without the company's consent or to disclose confidential information. It was alleged that he had done both as a means of diverting the company's business to himself and that, subsequently, he had repudiated his service contract by resigning half way through a fixed ten year contract. Interim injunctions were granted restraining him from dealing with the company's customers and from disclosing any confidential information. This decision was based primarily on the express contractual stipulation but also, to a lesser extent, on his fiduciary obligations as a director. This suggests that, at least in the case of executive directors, competing with the business of the company will constitute a breach of fiduciary duty. However, it appears that merely to accept directorships in competing companies does not constitute a breach of the duty of loyalty owed by the director to the first company.

The authorities discussed establish that, where a fiduciary has breached his duty of loyalty by competing with the business of his principal, the latter can obtain an injunction restraining such competition. Further, although there does not seem to be any case in which this has actually been held,[89] the fiduciary should be liable to account to

---

[83] By virtue of Partnership Act 1890, s.30.

[84] [1891] 1 W.N. 165.

[85] [1932] A.C. 161, 165.

[86] *Hivac* v. *Park Royal Scientific Instruments* [1946] Ch. 169.

[87] [1959] A.C. 324, 366–367.

[88] [1978] 3 W.L.R. 116.

[89] Such a claim was made, unsuccessfully, in *Moore* v. *M'Glynn* [1894] 1 Ir.R. 74, where the trustee was held to have been entitled to compete with the trust business.

his principal for any profits which he has made out of this competition under a constructive trust.

(c) Renewal by a fiduciary for his own benefit of a lease formerly held by his principal

In *Keech* v. *Sandford*[90] a lease of a market was held on trust for an infant. The trustee sought, unsuccessfully, to renew the lease for the benefit of the trust. However, the landlord, although not prepared to renew the lease to the trust, was prepared to grant a renewal to the trustee in his personal capacity and the trustee duly took up the lease in his own right. Lord King L.C. held that any trustee who abuses his position by entering into a transaction with a third party must account for the benefit of the transaction as a constructive trustee. Consequently the trustee held the benefit of the lease on constructive trust for the infant. The rationale of the rule was stated both simply and cynically: if a trustee on the refusal of a lessor to renew a lease to the trust were permitted to take a lease himself, few leases would ever be renewed in favour of trusts. This prohibition was wholly understandable at that time. Many ecclesiastical, charitable and public bodies were by law restricted as to the length of leases which they were able to grant and leases were therefore renewed more or less as a matter of right. By taking a renewal of a lease for himself, a trustee was therefore in practice depriving the trust of a grant which it had a right to expect. This was also the time of the South Sea Bubble, a period of extravagant financial speculation and even more extravagant financial collapses, when the existence of stringent controls on the activities of fiduciaries was unquestionably necessary. However, the rule laid down in *Keech* v. *Sandford* has continued to be applied despite the relaxation of the rules as to the length of leases and the greater financial stability of the Nineteenth and Twentieth Centuries; indeed it has been extended so as to apply also to other fiduciaries.

The precise limits of the rule were discussed very fully in *Re Biss*.[91] The Court of Appeal held that the rule applies with all its stringency to persons clearly occupying a fiduciary position such as trustees or agents; there is an irrebuttable presumption that such persons cannot retain the benefit of transactions entered into in their personal capacity. On the other hand, persons owing a special but non-fiduciary duty are subject only to a rebuttable presumption. Thus if such a person can show that he did not abuse his position, he can retain the benefit of the transaction. The court considered mortgagees, tenants for life, joint tenants, tenants in common and (rather unexpectedly) partners to be in this category. There seems no good reason why partners, who are quite clearly fiduciaries for all other purposes, should be in the latter rather than the former category and *Thompson's Trustee* v. *Heaton*[92] (which actually concerned the purchase of a freehold reversion) may well have changed the law in this respect. However, this question cannot yet be

---

[90] (1726) Sel.Cas.Ch. 61.
[91] [1903] 2 Ch. 40.
[92] [1974] 1 W.L.R. 605.

regarded as finally settled. On the other hand, it is clear that the rule in *Keech* v. *Sandford* does not apply to a person who owes neither fiduciary obligations nor a special non-fiduciary duty. Thus in *Savage* v. *Dunningham*,[93] where three persons were sharing an unfurnished flat and the rack rent payable therefor, it was held that one of them was perfectly entitled to purchase a long leasehold interest therein for his own benefit.

While the rule in *Keech* v. *Sandford* is certainly a stringent penal rule which it is impossible to justify in modern conditions, there is absolutely no doubt that it remains English law.

(d) Purchase by a fiduciary of the reversion on a lease held by his principal

The rule in *Keech* v. *Sandford* has been extended to cases where the fiduciary has acquired the reversion, normally but obviously not necessarily the freehold reversion, in property of which his principal is lessee. When the fiduciary has acquired the reversion by means of an abuse of his fiduciary position or has only obtained the opportunity to purchase because, as fiduciary, he is the nominal lessee, it is clearly in accordance with principle for a constructive trust to be imposed.[94] Similarly, where the lease in question is renewable by custom, the fiduciary will also hold the reversion on constructive trust for his principal since, otherwise, he would be able to prejudice the interests of his principal by declining to renew the lease.[95] On the other hand, where the lease in question is not renewable by custom or by right, the acquisition of the reversion by the fiduciary can hardly be said to prejudice his principal and until relatively recently it was held that in such circumstances a fiduciary who had not abused his position was entitled to retain the reversion for his own benefit.[96] However, in *Protheroe* v. *Protheroe*,[97] the Court of Appeal, in a short extempore judgment which did not refer to any of the earlier authorities, held that a trustee of leasehold property can never acquire the freehold for himself and imposed a constructive trust. It seems highly likely that the trustee in this case (a husband holding on trust for himself and his separated wife as tenants in common) only acquired the opportunity to purchase the freehold because he was, as trustee, the nominal lessee, in which case discussion and application of the earlier authorities would have made no difference. However, the broad principle thus enunciated was subsequently applied in *Thompson's Trustee* v. *Heaton*[98] where, following the dissolution of a partnership, one of the partners remained in possession of land of which the partners had been and remained joint lessees. After that partner's death fourteen years later, his executors acquired the freehold reversion and subsequently resold the land. It was held that the other partner was entitled to one half of the

---

[93] [1974] Ch. 181.
[94] *Griffith* v. *Owen* [1907] 1 Ch. 105.
[95] *Phillips* v. *Phillips* (1885) 29 Ch.D. 673.
[96] *Randall* v. *Russell* (1817) 3 Mer. 190, *Bevan* v. *Webb* [1905] 1 Ch. 620.
[97] [1968] 1 W.L.R. 519.
[98] [1974] 1 W.L.R. 605.

profit so obtained because, so long as the lease remained an undistributed asset of the partnership, neither partner could acquire the reversion for his sole benefit. This decision obviously casts doubt on the statement by the Court of Appeal in *Re Biss*[99] that partners were only to be caught by the rule in *Keech* v. *Sandford* if it could be shown that an advantage had actually been obtained by virtue of their position (a dictum which has admittedly already been criticised[1]). More significantly, the application of the broad statement in *Protheroe* v. *Protheroe* without reference to the earlier authorities, the application of which might well have led to a different result, indicates that all the earlier distinctions may well now have been swept away; if so, a fiduciary will now never be able to purchase for his own benefit a reversion in property of which his principal is lessee. If this is indeed the case, then only where, as in *Savage* v. *Dunningham*,[2] a purchaser of a reversion is not a fiduciary at all will he be able to acquire it for his own benefit. The principle enunciated in *Protheroe* v. *Protheroe* seems unnecessarily harsh and it is therefore suggested that the approach of the earlier authorities was preferable.

(e) Utilisation by a fiduciary for his own benefit of an opportunity of profit

A fiduciary is obviously entitled to utilise for his own benefit opportunities which have nothing whatever to do with the fiduciary relationship in question. The mere fact that a person is a trustee of an investment fund does not prevent him from purchasing shares in his private capacity—were this not the case, it would be impossible to find anyone prepared to accept a trusteeship. Equally obviously, if such a trustee obtains the opportunity to take up a rights issue by virtue of the fact that the trust is a shareholder in the company in question, then he is not entitled to take up that rights issue in his personal capacity and if he does so the shares in question will be subject to a constructive trust in favour of the fund. A fiduciary will only be in breach of his duty of loyalty to his principal if the transactions into which he enters in his personal capacity fall within the scope of his fiduciary obligations. As Oliver L.J. stated in *Swain* v. *The Law Society*[3]:

> "What one has to do is ascertain first of all whether there was a fiduciary relationship and, if there was, from what it arose and what, if there was any, was the trust property; and then to inquire whether that of which an account is claimed either arose, directly or indirectly, from the trust property itself or was acquired not only in the course of, but by reason of, the fiduciary relationship."

The question of whether a transaction falls within the scope of a fiduciary relationship will sometimes be capable of being resolved by

---

[99] [1903] 2 Ch. 40.
[1] See *supra*.
[2] [1974] Ch. 181.
[3] [1982] 1 W.L.R. 17, 37 (C.A.). This approach was approved by Lord Brightman in the House of Lords ([1983] 1 A.C. 598, 619).

reference to the terms of the agreement between the fiduciary and principal in question. Thus in *Aas* v. *Benham*[4] a member of a ship-broking partnership utilised information which he had received in his capacity as partner to help form a ship-building company of which he became a director. An action by his partners for an account of the benefits received from the company failed on the grounds that the business of the company was quite different from the business of the partnership, the Court of Appeal holding that there was nothing to prevent a partner utilising information obtained in his fiduciary capacity provided that he was not competing with the partnership business.[5] However, it is not often that the scope of a fiduciary obligation is closely defined by the parties thereto and when it is not rather more difficulties can be encountered. Cases of clear misconduct by a fiduciary are of course quite straightforward. In *Cook* v. *Deeks*[6] three of the four directors and shareholders of a company, with the intention of excluding the fourth member, arranged for a contract which they had negotiated on behalf of the company to be made with them in their private capacities. The excluded member claimed successfully that the company was entitled to the benefit of this contract. The Privy Council held that the whole reputation of the three had been obtained with the company; they could have excluded the plaintiff quite legitimately by using their majority shareholding to wind up the company but instead had used their position as directors to deprive the company of any change of obtaining the contract. This was a clear case of abuse of fiduciary position. However, an identical attitude has been adopted where the misconduct of the fiduciary has been much more questionable. The decided cases of this type have generally arisen when the principal in question has been unable or unwilling to utilise an opportunity and the fiduciary has subsequently utilised that opportunity for his own benefit.

In *Regal (Hastings)* v. *Gulliver*[7] the plaintiff company owned a cinema in Hastings and wished to acquire two other local cinemas with the intention of selling the whole enterprise as a package. A subsidiary, with a capital of 5,000 £1 shares, was formed to take leases of these two cinemas. The original scheme was for only 2,000 of these shares to be paid up but the owner of the cinemas declined to grant the leases on this basis. Since the company could not afford to put more than £2,000 into the subsidiary, four of the directors and the company solicitor each subscribed for 500 shares and the fifth director found some outsiders to take up the remaining 500. The combined concern was then sold not as a whole but by way of takeover and each holder of shares in the subsidiary obviously made a profit. The purchasers then brought an action against all five directors and the company solicitor claiming that this profit had been made out of a breach of their fiduciary duty and

---

[4] [1891] 2 Ch. 244.
[5] See also *British American Oil Producing Co.* v. *Midway Oil Company* (1938) 82 P. (2d) 1049 (Supreme Court of Oklahoma).
[6] [1916] A.C. 554.
[7] [1942] 1 All E.R. 378, [1967] 2 A.C. 134n.

therefore had to be accounted for to the company (this claim was wholly unmeritorious; its only objective was to recover part of the price which the purchasers had freely agreed to pay). The action against the director who had not subscribed for any shares obviously failed, for he had made no profit.[8] So too did the action against the company solicitor, for he had subscribed for his shares with the consent of the board of directors as then constituted. But the actions against the other four directors succeeded in the House of Lords, whose decision was based fairly and squarely on *Keech* v. *Sandford*. Lord Russell of Killowen stated that the directors had unquestionably acquired their shares by virtue of their fiduciary position. It made no difference that the company could not itself have subscribed for the shares—the trust in *Keech* v. *Sandford* could not itself have obtained a new lease and that had made no difference. Thus the four directors had to surrender a profit which they would have been able to retain had the transaction been carried out in a different way and so were deprived of any return on their investment, while the purchasers finished up paying less for the cinemas than they had originally bargained to pay.

Given that the company could not afford to put more than £2,000 into the subsidiary, what alternative did the directors have? Lord Russell of Killowen thought that they should have obtained a resolution of the shareholders in general meeting approving the transaction.[9] This view seems to conflict with the decision in *Cook* v. *Deeks*,[10] where such a resolution had been obtained and was held to be ineffective. It was suggested in *Prudential Assurance Co.* v. *Newman Industries (No. 2)* that a ratification by a company in general meeting will only be effective if the directors in question do not control the majority of the votes.[11] It is not clear whether or not the directors of Regal (Hastings) did in fact control the majority[12]; only if they did not is this a valid distinction between *Cook* v. *Deeks* and *Regal (Hastings)* v. *Gulliver*. However, a very much more generous attitude to ratification was subsequently demonstrated by the Privy Council in *Queensland Mines* v. *Hudson*,[13] where the board of the plaintiff company, being fully informed of all relevant facts, decided to renounce all interest in the exploitation of certain mining exploration licences which it had obtained and assented to the venture being taken over by the defendant, a director of the company who had been its managing director until a shortage of finance had prevented the plaintiff from exploiting the licences itself. When the plaintiff subsequently claimed to be entitled to the profit obtained by the defendant, the Privy Council held that the defendant had obtained the opportunity to make this profit by virtue of his position as managing director of the

---

[8] No claim was brought against the outsiders for their profit. Any such claim would have been governed by the principles to be discussed in the next section of this Chapter (*post* p. 251).

[9] [1942] 1 All E.R. 378, 389, [1967] 2 A.C. 134, 150.

[10] [1916] A.C. 554.

[11] [1980] 3 W.L.R. 543, 568 (Vinelott J.).

[12] The Editorial Note in [1942] 1 All E.R. 378, 379 assumed that they did; Vinelott J. in *Prudential Assurance Co.* v. *Newman Industries (No. 2)* (at p. 568) disagreed.

[13] (1977) 18 A.L.R. 1.

plaintiff and was therefore in principle liable under *Regal (Hastings)* v. *Gulliver* to account for his profit; however, the fully-informed decision of the board amounted to sufficient consent to enable him to retain the profit. This conclusion is clearly inconsistent with the decision in *Regal (Hastings)* v. *Gulliver*, where all the members of the board had taken part in the impeached transaction and so must necessarily have consented to it. The approach taken by the Privy Council may be able to be justified on the grounds that the plaintiff had only two shareholders, both of whom were represented on the board, and the shareholder represented by the defendant held only 49% of the shares; the decision of the board can thus be regarded as a decision of the shareholders where the majority was not controlled by the defendant, which satisfies the test suggested in *Prudential Assurance Co.* v. *Newman Industries (No. 2)*. In any event, one commentator has argued that the approach of the Privy Council should now be followed so that "if the board has taken a bona fide decision that the company should reject the opportunity on its merits, it may then permit one (or more) of its members to take it up".[14] It is clear that "a court is likely to take a deal of persuading that the board's decision to reject the opportunity was taken bona fide in the interests of the company rather than in that of their fellow director— especially if he has a powerful personality".[15] In practice, for the moment the only safe option seems to be a decision of the shareholders in general meeting and even this can only be guaranteed to work if the directors in question do not control the majority of the votes.

Leaving on one side the question of ratification, there is no doubt whatsoever that the decisions in *Regal (Hastings)* v. *Gulliver* and *Queensland Mines* v. *Hudson* are entirely consistent on the question of the liability of the directors in question to account and certainly represent English law at present. In both cases it was assumed that, in the absence of the appropriate consent, any director who obtained an opportunity by virtue of his fiduciary position was liable to account to the company for this profit. Thus it is clear that the courts are not prepared to countenance a fiduciary exploiting an opportunity for his own benefit and are more concerned to penalise him for having taken up an opportunity of entering into a profitable transaction on his own behalf than to ascertain whether or not there has been a conflict between his duty of loyalty to his principal and his own self-interest. Other jurisdictions have felt able to adopt a more flexible approach and have permitted directors to take up opportunities for their own benefit without the prior consent or subsequent ratification of their companies where there was no serious conflict of duty and interest.[16] While it is undoubtedly possible to criticise these decisions on the grounds that "[t]o allow directors to decide that the company shall not accept the opportunity and then to accept the opportunity themselves might

---

[14] L. C. B. Gower: *Principles of Modern Company Law* (5th Ed. (1992)) 570.
[15] *Ibid.*
[16] *Peso Silvermines* v. *Cropper* (1966) 56 D.L.R.(2d) 1 (British Columbia Court of Appeal), 58 D.L.R.(2d) 1 (Supreme Court of Canada); *Consul Development* v. *D.P.C. Estates* (1975) 49 A.L.J.R. 74.

impose too great a strain on their impartiality",[17] the sort of attitude adopted by the House of Lords in *Regal (Hastings)* v. *Gulliver* prevents such matters of policy being raised at all; this in itself is an argument for the adoption of a more flexible attitude, even if its adoption does not in the end alter the conclusions actually reached by the courts.

The contrast between the two approaches emerges extremely clearly in the controversial decision of the House of Lords in *Boardman* v. *Phipps*.[18] A testator established a trust for the benefit of his widow and children. Some twelve years after his death, the trust solicitor, Boardman, became concerned about one of the principal assets of the fund—a 27% holding in a private company. After an unsuccessful attempt to bring about the election of one of the testator's sons to the board of the company, Boardman reached the conclusion that the only way of protecting the trust investment was to acquire a majority holding in the company. He suggested this to the managing trustee, who said that it was entirely out of the question for the trust to acquire such a holding. Boardman and the son then decided to purchase the outstanding shares themselves. They duly obtained control of the company and by capitalising some of the assets, were able to make a distribution of capital without reducing the value of the shares. The trust benefitted by this distribution to the tune of £47,000 and Boardman and his colleague made a profit of about £75,000. However, in the course of negotiations leading up to the take-over, Boardman had purported to represent the trust and thereby had incontrovertibly obtained information which would not have been made available to the general public. One of the other sons of the testator, who had not been particularly fully consulted, therefore claimed that this profit of £75,000 had been made by the utilisation of information which had reached Boardman while acting on behalf of the trust and so in a fiduciary capacity. This claim was upheld by the House of Lords, who held that the shares which had been acquired were subject to a constructive trust in favour of the trust. Thus, in effect, the trust obtained the whole of the profit made on the take-over, less an allowance which the House awarded to Boardman under its inherent jurisdiction by way of remuneration for the work which he had done.[19]

All the members of the House of Lords agreed that the defendants had placed themselves in a fiduciary relationship by acting as representatives of the trust for a number of years and that out of this fiduciary relationship they had obtained the opportunity to make a profit and the knowledge that a profit was there to be made. The majority added two inter-connected reasons for going on to hold that the defendants were therefore liable as constructive trustees to account for their profit to the trust. Lord Hodson and Lord Guest both clearly held that, since the only basis on which the defendants had obtained their information was the

---

[17] Gower: *op.cit.* 567. Similar sentiments have been expressed by D. D. Prentice in (1967) 30 M.L.R. 450 and by Swan J. in *Irving Trust Co.* v. *Deutsch* (1934) 73 Fed. (2d) 121, 124 (United States Circuit Court of Appeals).

[18] [1967] 2 A.C. 46.

[19] This aspect of the decision will be discussed in Chapter 20, *post*, p. 527.

fact that they had been purporting to represent the trust, this information was trust property. Therefore, the defendants had, in effect, made a profit out of speculating with trust property and thus were clearly liable. Lord Cohen reached the same conclusion by a slightly different route. He held that information was not property in the strict sense of the word and that it did not necessarily follow that a fiduciary must account for any profit obtained by the use of information acquired in his fiduciary capacity. In this case, however, the information had been acquired while the defendants had been purporting to represent the trust. Thus, the defendants were liable to account for their profit under the principle in *Regal (Hastings)* v. *Gulliver*. Further, all three felt that Boardman had placed himself in a position where his duty and interest might conflict (such a conflict would have arisen, for example, had the trustees sought his advice as to the merits of the trust acquiring a majority holding in the company). No matter how remote the possibility of such a conflict arising, a fiduciary who placed himself in this position was bound to account to his principal for any profit he had made. Since the defendants had accepted that their positions were the same, both were thus liable for their profit. In the opinion of the majority, it was quite immaterial that the defendants had acted honestly and openly in a manner highly beneficial to the trust in a situation where the trust itself could not have utilised the information which they had received. Both the dissentients (Viscount Dilhorne and Lord Upjohn) took the view that the remoteness of the possibility of any conflict of interest arising and the various factors just referred to which the majority had found irrelevant led inescapably to the conclusion that the defendants had not breached their duty of loyalty to the trust. Lord Upjohn said that a conflict of interest only arose where the reasonable man looking at all the relevant circumstances would think that there was a real sensible possibility of conflict and not where the only possibility of conflict arose from events not contemplated as real sensible probabilities by any reasonable person. Boardman knew when he decided to proceed on his own behalf that there was no possibility of the trustees seeking his advice as to the merits of a purchase by the trust—the managing trustee had already told him that this was quite out of the question. Further, Lord Upjohn doubted the classification of the information as trust property. He said that information was not in any sense property; equity would merely restrain its transmission to another in breach of confidence. This was not such a case.

If the information was indeed properly classifiable as trust property, then the defendants had of course made a profit out of speculating with property of the trust and were therefore clearly liable as constructive trustees under the principle laid down in *Reid-Newfoundland Co.* v. *Anglo-American Telegraph Co.*,[20] which was discussed at the beginning of this section.[21] However, it is clear that information cannot be trust property in any normal sense; if it were it could presumably be followed into the hands of the whole world other than a bona fide

[20] [1891] 2 Ch. 244.
[21] See *ante*, p. 239.

purchaser thereof for value without notice. Given the essential nature of information, which can be divulged in its entirety to any number of persons, such a conclusion could lead to quite absurd results.[22] That is not to say that a fiduciary should automatically be entitled to utilise for his own benefit information which has come to him in his fiduciary capacity. A fiduciary who by the utilisation of such information abuses his fiduciary position should clearly be liable as a constructive trustee, but as a result of the application of the principles which have already been discussed, not by the automatic classification of the information as the property of his principal. Such a case was *Industrial Development Consultants* v. *Cooley*.[23] The defendant, who was managing director of the plaintiff company, had been attempting, on behalf of the plaintiff, to obtain a contract to design certain depots for the Eastern Gas Board. These attempts failed because the Gas Board did not like the plaintiff's organisation and were not prepared to deal with the plaintiff in any capacity. The following year, a representative of the Gas Board sought a meeting with the defendant in his private capacity and intimated to him that if he could free himself from his ties with the plaintiff he had a very good chance of obtaining the contract for himself. The defendant therefore secured his release from his contract with the plaintiff by a totally false representation that he was on the verge of a nervous breakdown and accepted an offer from the Gas Board to do substantially the same work which he had unsuccessfully attempted to obtain for the plaintiff the year before. The plaintiff claimed that the defendant was a trustee of that contract for the benefit of the plaintiff and successfully sought an account of the defendant's profits. At the time when the defendant first realised that he had an opportunity of obtaining the contract for himself, the only capacity in which he was carrying on business was as managing director of the plaintiff and as such he was under a fiduciary duty to pass on to the plaintiff any information which reached him while carrying on business in that capacity. His failure to do so and subsequent utilisation of the information for his own benefit was a clear breach of fiduciary duty which made him a trustee of the contract for the plaintiff, who was entitled to all the profit thereunder. Similar decisions have been reached in other jurisdictions.[24] It is thus clear that a constructive trust can be imposed on a fiduciary who has abused his position whether or not the information which he has utilised is classified as the property of his principal.[25] Therefore, given

---

[22] See G. H. Jones: (1968) 84 L.Q.R. 472.

[23] [1972] 1 W.L.R. 443.

[24] *Pre-Cam Exploration Co.* v. *McTavish* [1966] S.C.R. 551, *Canadian Aero Services* v. *O'Malley* (1973) 40 D.L.R.(3d) 371 (both decisions of the Supreme Court of Canada); *Consul Development* v. *D.P.C. Estates* (1975) 49 A.L.J.R. 74 (High Court of Australia).

[25] Quite apart from any question of the imposition of a constructive trust for breach of fiduciary duty, both fiduciaries and non-fiduciaries may be held liable for breach of the equitable obligation of confidence; where a person who has received information in confidence takes unfair advantage of it to the prejudice of the person who disclosed it to him, the courts will consider the whole gamut of remedies open to them and award that which is most appropriate to the situation. See Goff & Jones: *op.cit.* 679–702 and F. Gurry: *Breach of Confidence* (1984).

the absurd consequences of such a classification, there is no good reason why it should ever be adopted.

There has also been considerable criticism of the majority decision in *Boardman* v. *Phipps* that the fiduciaries were not entitled to exploit for their own benefit the opportunity of purchasing a controlling interest in the company.[26] It has been demonstrated not only that the conflict of interest found to exist by the House of Lords is in fact wholly illusory[27] but also that other jurisdictions have felt able to adopt a more flexible approach.[28] There is much to be said for these criticisms but that does not alter the fact that the approach adopted by the majority in *Boardman* v. *Phipps* in relation to the rights of fiduciaries to utilise for their own benefit opportunities of profit is entirely consistent with the earlier authorities such as *Regal (Hastings)* v. *Gulliver* and is undoubtedly representative of the present state of English law.

III. Strangers Intermeddling with Property Subject to a Trust[29]

Equity has always been prepared to impose on any person who has officiously chosen to act as a fiduciary the appropriate fiduciary obligations, by virtue of which he will hold any property which he has received in his assumed capacity on constructive trust for the person on whose behalf he has chosen to act. Such a person is very readily classifiable as an intermeddler but equity is also prepared, in appropriate circumstances, to impose the obligations of trusteeship on other strangers, in particular on anyone who has assisted in bringing about a misapplication of property subject to a trust, on the recipient of any property which has been so misapplied, and on anyone who has dealt inconsistently with property subject to a trust. The growth of corporate fraud has ensured that the courts have had to consider the availability and scope of these remedies on a large number of occasions in recent years. The proceedings which have been brought have, however, generally involved not only claims for the imposition of the obligations of trusteeship but also a considerable number of alternative claims arising out of the same misapplication of property; the possibilities include proprietary claims, both at law and in equity, to trace the misapplied property into the hands of its recipients, personal claims at law for money had and received, and personal claims in equity against whoever was responsible for initiating the misapplication in question.

---

[26] See particularly G. H. Jones: (1968) 84 L.Q.R. 472 and P. D. Finn: *Fiduciary Obligations*: 244–246. Their arguments are summarised in *Constructive Trusts* (2nd ed. (1987)): 81–82.

[27] Had Boardman subsequently been asked to advise the trustees, he could, like any solicitor, have declined to do so or declared his interest.

[28] *Peso Silvermines* v. *Cropper* (1966) 58 D.L.R. (2d) 1 (Supreme Court of Canada), *Manufacturers Trust Co.* v. *Becker* (1949) 338 U.S. 304 (United States Supreme Court).

[29] Virtually every legal periodical has contained a recent article on this subject. See, particularly: C. Harpum: (1986) 102 L.Q.R. 114 & 267 and in *Frontiers of Liability* (ed. Birks (1993)); D. J. Hayton: (1985) 27 Malaya Law Review 313; R. P. Austin in *Essays in Equity* (ed. Finn (1985)) 196; P. L. Loughlin: (1989) 9 O.J.L.S. 260; P. B. H. Birks: [1989] L.M.C.L.Q. 378 & [1993] L.C.M.L.Q. 218; E. McKendrick: [1991] L.M.C.L.Q. 378; P. D. Finn in *Equity, Fiduciaries and Trusts 1993* (ed. Waters (1993)) 195.

The interrelation of all these different claims has made such proceedings extremely complex and commentators have begun to question whether so many different remedies should continue to be available for the same misapplication of property.[30] However, there is no doubt at all that by far the most effective of these claims has been the imposition of the obligations of trusteeship, particularly on strangers who have assisted in bringing about a misapplication of property subject to a trust—this is because such persons tend to be either members of the professions or financial institutions, who are much more likely to be solvent than those who initiated the misapplication or received the property in question. The presumed solvency of persons who have assisted in the misapplication of property subject to a trust is the basic reason why this particular area of the law of trusts is so important today.

1. *Officiously Acting as a Fiduciary*[31]

Any person who takes it upon himself to act as a fiduciary without having been appointed as such will in every respect be treated as if he had been expressly appointed to the office in question and will be held to be a constructive trustee of any property acquired by him in the course of his intervention.

In *Mara* v. *Browne*[32] A. L. Smith L.J. stated that " . . . if one, not being a trustee and not having authority from a trustee, takes upon himself to intermeddle with trust matters or to do acts characteristic of the office of trustee, he may therefore make himself what is called in law a trustee of his own wrong—i.e. a trustee de son tort, or, as it is also termed, a constructive trustee". This occurred in *Blyth* v. *Fladgate*.[33] Trust funds were by direction of the sole trustee, paid to a firm of solicitors and invested in Exchequer Bills, which were deposited in the name of the firm. Subsequently, following the death of the sole trustee and before any new trustees had been appointed, the Exchequer Bills were sold and the proceeds of sale invested in a mortgage, the security for which proved to be insufficient. The partners of the firm were held liable to account to the trust for the sums so lost on the basis that they themselves had been carrying out the functions of the trustees; they were clearly constructive trustees of the proceeds of sale and, as such, responsible for any improper investment. It is entirely proper that the law should impose the office of trustee upon a person who purports to act as such without authority. Such a person should clearly be burdened with all the same responsibilities and liabilities as an express trustee.[34]

---

[30] See particularly Sir Peter Millett, writing extra-judicially: (1991) 107 L.Q.R. 71; Sir Leonard Hoffman, writing extra-judicially, in *Frontiers of Liability* (ed. Birks (1993)); C. Harpum: *ibid.*; P. D. Finn in *Equity, Fiduciaries and Trusts 1993* (ed. Waters (1993)) 195.

[31] C. Harpum in *Frontiers of Liability* (ed. Birks (1993)) describes this as "Primary Liability".

[32] [1896] 1 Ch. 199, 209.

[33] [1891] 1 Ch. 337. The explanation of the decision given in the text is that adopted by Vinelott J. in *Re Bell's Indenture* [1980] 3 All E.R. 425.

[34] *Soar* v. *Ashwell* [1893] 2 Q.B. 390, 394, *per* Lord Esher M.R.

Thus, in addition to being a constructive trustee of any property which he receives, he will also be responsible for any diminution in its value and will be subject to all the rules discussed in the previous section of this Chapter; if an intermeddler obtains a secret profit, he will be in exactly the same position as if he had been an express trustee.

Similar principles apply to fiduciaries other than trustees. Most of the cases have concerned persons who have taken it upon themselves to act as agents. In *Lyell* v. *Kennedy*,[35] during the twenty-two years which it took to determine the identity of the heir at law of a landowner, his manager continued to collect the rents from the tenants without telling them of the death of their landlord. The House of Lords held that, since he had taken it upon himself to receive the rents of property which he knew to belong to another, he held these sums (which had been placed in a separate bank account) on constructive trust for the heir. Lord Selborne emphasised that the motives which induce a person to inter-meddle in the administration of a trust or other fiduciary relationship are totally irrelevant to the imposition of a constructive trust; thus it made no difference whether the manager had intervened with the intention of protecting the interests of the heir at law or with the intention of taking the benefit for himself. The latter was clearly the intention of the prospective purchaser in *English* v. *Dedham Vale Properties*[36] who, purporting without authority to act as agent for the prospective vendors, submitted an application for planning permission in respect of part of the subject matter of the proposed sale and was held liable to account to the vendors for the profits made thereby.[37]

2. *Assistance in Bringing about a Misapplication of Property Subject to a Trust*

(a) Terminology
The vast majority of the decisions in which strangers have been held liable for having assisted in bringing about a misapplication of property subject to a trust describe such strangers as constructive trustees. However, the essential feature of such liability (which is generally known as liability for "knowing assistance"[38]), is the fact that property subject to a trust has, by virtue of the assistance provided, reached the hands of a third party, who may or may not be liable for "knowing receipt" under the rules which will be discussed later on.[39] It is only necessary to attempt to impose liability for "knowing assistance" in respect of misapplied property which has not been received beneficially by the stranger in question; a beneficial recipient of misapplied property will be subject to the different liability for "knowing receipt". If, for example, a bank has permitted a cheque

---

[35] (1889) 14 App.Cas. 437.

[36] [1978] 1 W.L.R. 93.

[37] Had he waited until after exchange of contracts, the equitable interest thereby acquired would have entitled him to make the application for his own benefit.

[38] C. Harpum in *Frontiers of Liability* (ed. Birks (1993)) describes this as "Secondary Liability".

[39] See *post*, p. 262.

drawn on a trust account to be credited in breach of trust to the account of a third party, so long as the bank has merely acted as the conduit by means of which the funds are transferred, its only possible liability will be for "knowing assistance"; but if, on the other hand, the account of the third party was overdrawn at the time of the transfer, the bank may additionally be liable for "knowing receipt" to the extent that it has utilised the funds in reduction of the overdraft. Given that none of the misapplied property has finished up in the hands of a person held liable for "knowing assistance", it is therefore questionable to what extent he can correctly be described as a constructive trustee. As has already been mentioned in the introductory section of this Chapter,[40] some commentators have contended that there is in fact a second type of constructive trust which can arise without any necessity for there to be any identifiable trust property.[41] However, it has already been suggested that it is more appropriate to regard the decisions in which liability for "knowing assistance" has been imposed not as examples of the imposition of a constructive trust but rather as examples of equity imposing a quite distinct remedy—a personal liability to account in the same manner as a trustee. Although this was confirmed by Millett J. in *Agip (Africa)* v. *Jackson*,[42] it must be admitted that the majority of the judges have continued to describe strangers held liable for "knowing assistance" as constructive trustees.[43]

(b) The elements of liability for "knowing assistance"

In *Barnes* v. *Addy*[44] Lord Selborne L.C. stated that "strangers are not to be made constructive trustees merely because they act as the agents of trustees in transactions within their legal powers, transactions, perhaps, of which a Court of Equity may disapprove, unless those agents receive and become chargeable with some part of the trust property, or unless they assist with knowledge in a dishonest and fraudulent design on the part of the trustees". In this passage Lord Selborne was primarily concerned to protect the agents of a trust, such as solicitors or bankers, who as a result of following the instructions of the trustees have assisted in bringing about a misapplication of the trust property. Even though it has been demonstrated that this classic statement of the law was not wholly consistent with the pre-existing authorities,[45] it has been used as the starting point in almost every subsequent decision. What then constitutes assisting with knowledge in a dishonest and fraudulent design on the part of the trustees? In *Baden* v. *Société Générale*[46] Peter Gibson J. isolated four distinct elements: the existence of a trust, the existence of a dishonest and

---

[40] See *ante*, p. 211.

[41] See Hayton & Marshall and Ford & Lee.

[42] [1989] 3 W.L.R. 1367, 1389.

[43] Particularly by the Court of Appeal in *Agip (Africa)* v. *Jackson* [1991] Ch. 547 and in *Polly Peck International* v. *Nadir (No. 2)* [1992] 3 All E.R. 769.

[44] (1874) 9 Ch. App. 244, 251–252.

[45] See C. Harpum in *Frontiers of Liability* (ed. Birks (1993)).

[46] (1983) [1993] 1 W.L.R. 509, 573. The full name of this case is *Baden* v. *Société Générale pour Favoriser le Développement du Commerce et de l'Industrie en France S.A.*

fraudulent design on the part of the trustee of the trust; the assistance by the stranger in that design, and the knowledge of the stranger.

(i) The existence of a trust. "[T]he trust need not be a formal trust. It is sufficient that there should be a fiduciary relationship between the "trustee" and the property of another person."[47] Most of the older cases concerned the situation expressly envisaged by Lord Selborne, where agents of trustees have assisted in bringing about a misapplication of the trust property by following the instructions of the trustees.[48] However, this first requirement is equally satisfied where the misapplication of property occurs as a result of agents following the instructions of any other express fiduciary. The "directors of a company are treated as if they were the trustees of the company's property under their control"[49] and many modern cases have concerned illegal or unauthorised transactions carried out in accordance with the instructions of company directors. There has been a whole series of cases resulting from successful attempts to use the funds of a company to finance its own acquisition,[50] while a number of cases have resulted from directors misapplying a company's funds for their own personal benefit.[51] It is also sufficient if the trust in question is constructive rather than express,[52] even if the constructive trust only arose as a result of the misapplication of the property. Millett J. emphasised in *Agip (Africa)* v. *Jackson*[53] that "the embezzlement of a company's funds almost inevitably involves a breach of fiduciary duty on the part of one of the company's employees or agents" and he went on to hold that "there is a receipt of trust property when a company's funds are misapplied by the director and, in my judgment, this is equally the case where a company's funds are misapplied by any person whose fiduciary position gave him control of them or enabled him to misapply them". This principle is not of course confined to funds but applies to property of any type.[54]

(ii) The existence of a dishonest and fraudulent design on the part of the trustee of the trust. Although this requirement is said "to have

---

[47] *Ibid.*

[48] See *Barnes* v. *Addy* (1874) 9 Ch.App. 214, *Williams* v. *Williams* (1881) 17 Ch.D. 437, *Williams-Ashman* v. *Price & Williams* [1942] 1 Ch. 219.

[49] *Baden* v. *Société Générale* (1983) [1993] 1 W.L.R. 509n, 573.

[50] *Selangor United Rubber Estates* v. *Cradock (No. 3)* [1968] 1 W.L.R. 1555, *Karak Rubber Company* v. *Burden (No. 2)* [1972] 1 W.L.R. 602, *Belmont Finance Corporation* v. *Williams Furniture* [1979] Ch. 250, *(No. 2)* [1980] 1 All E.R. 393, *Eagle Trust Co.* v. *S.B.C. Securities* (1991) [1993] 1 W.L.R. 484.

[51] *Baden* v. *Société Générale* (1983) [1993] 1 W.L.R. 509n, *Eagle Trust Co.* v. *S.B.C. Securities* (1991) [1993] 1 W.L.R. 484, *Cowan de Groot Properties* v. *Eagle Trust* (1991) [1992] 4 All E.R. 700, *Polly Peck International* v. *Nadir (No.2)* [1992] 4 All E.R. 769.

[52] *Competitive Insurance Company* v. *Davies Investments* [1975] 1 W.L.R. 1240.

[53] [1989] 3 W.L.R. 1367, 1387.

[54] Information in respect of which a manager owed a fidiciary duty to his company would have sufficed in *Consul Development* v. *D.P.C. Estates* (1975) 132 C.L.R. 373.

leapt forth fully formed from the brow of Lord Selborne",[55] there is no question that it is at present an essential prerequisite of liability for "knowing assistance".[56] In *Selangor United Rubber Estates* v. *Cradock (No. 2)*[57] Ungoed-Thomas J. held that the adjectives "dishonest" and "reckless" must be understood in accordance with equitable principles for equitable relief and consequently conduct which is morally reprehensible suffices. However, this view was rejected in *Belmont Finance Corporation* v. *Williams Furniture*,[58] where the Court of Appeal held that the two adjectives have the same meaning and signify something more than mere misfeasance or breach of trust. In *Baden* v. *Société Générale*[59] Peter Gibson J. applied these statements of the Court of Appeal and held, quoting *R.* v. *Sinclair*,[60] that what was required was "the taking of a risk to the prejudice of another's rights, which risk is known to be one which there is no right to take". This view has been adopted in all the subsequent decisions.

(iii) **The assistance by the stranger in that design.** It is "a simple question of fact, whether there has been assistance".[61] It makes no difference whether the agent has previously advised against the course of conduct in question,[62] whether he has made the appropriate enquiries and reasonably come to what was in fact an incorrect conclusion,[63] or whether he has simply relied on the instructions given without checking relevant documents in his possession.[64] The fact of assistance in a significant way in a dishonest and fraudulent design is all that matters. In this connection, it should be noted that, although the vast majority of cases of "knowing assistance" inevitably involve agents of trustees or other fiduciaries, liability therefor also extends to strangers who have assisted in some other way in bringing about a misapplication of property subject to a trust. Thus, in *Eaves* v. *Hickson*[65] a father produced a forged marriage certificate to the trustees of a settlement in order to convince them that his children were legitimate[66] and so entitled to the trust property, which was duly distributed to them. When those otherwise entitled to the property sued for its recovery, it

[55] C. Harpum in *Frontiers of Liability* (ed. Birks (1993)). The requirement did not exist earlier in the Nineteenth Century, see *Fyler* v. *Fyler* (1841) 3 Beav. 550, *Attorney-General* v. *The Corporation of Leicester* (1844) 7 Beav. 176.
[56] This was expressly held by the Court of Appeal in *Belmont Finance Corporation* v. *Williams Furniture* [1979] Ch. 250, 267.
[57] [1968] 1 W.L.R. 1555, 1582 & 1590. This remains the law in Australia—see *Consul Development* v. *D.P.C. Estates* (1975) 132 C.L.R. 373, 398, *Equity Corp Finance* v. *Bank of New Zealand* (1993) 32 N.S.W.L.R. 51, 105. This in turn affects the level of knowledge necessary for liability.
[58] [1979] Ch. 250, 267.
[59] (1993) [1993] 1 W.L.R. 509n, 574.
[60] [1968] 1 W.L.R. 1246, 1249.
[61] *Baden* v. *Société Générale* (1983) [1993] 1 W.L.R. 509n, 574–575.
[62] As in *Barnes* v. *Addy* (1874) 9 Ch.App. 214.
[63] As in *Williams* v. *Williams* (1881) 17 Ch.D. 437.
[64] As in *Williams-Ashman* v. *Price & Williams* [1942] 1 Ch. 219.
[65] (1861) 30 Beav. 136.
[66] He had married the mother of the children after their birth but at the time there was no doctrine of legitimation by subsequent marriage.

was held that the father was personally liable to account as a trustee for such of the property as could not be recovered from the children. He was in no sense an agent of the trustees but he had by his conduct induced the misapplication of the trust property and so was clearly liable for "knowing assistance". However, this case was decided before *Barnes* v. *Addy*[67] introduced the requirement for the existence of a dishonest and fraudulent design on the part of the trustee of the trust. This requirement would not have been satisfied in *Eaves* v. *Hickson* and it may therefore be that its absence would now cause the father to escape liability for "knowing assistance"[68]; however, liability for any loss suffered could clearly be imposed on him on other grounds.[69–70]

(iv) The knowledge of the stranger. This is the aspect of liability for "knowing assistance" which has caused most controversy. Discussion of this question in recent years has focused on the five different categories of knowledge identified by Peter Gibson J. in *Baden* v. *Société Générale*[71]: "(i) actual knowledge; (ii) wilfully shutting one's eyes to the obvious; (iii) wilfully and recklessly failing to make such inquiries as an honest and reasonable man would make; (iv) knowledge of circumstances which would indicate the facts to an honest and reasonable man; (v) knowledge of circumstances which would put an honest and reasonable man on inquiry". A person in category (i) obviously has actual knowledge and, "[a]ccording to Peter Gibson J., a person in category (ii) or (iii) will be taken to have actual knowledge, while a person in categories (iv) or (v) has constructive notice only".[72] Warnings have been given "against over refinement or a too ready assumption that categories (iv) or (v) are necessarily cases of constructive notice only. The true distinction is between honesty and dishonesty."[73] Nevertheless, these five categories have been referred to in every single subsequent case. Which of them suffice for the imposition of liability for "knowing assistance"?

Consistent with the expressed primary concern of Lord Selborne in *Barnes* v. *Addy* to protect agents of a trust, the older cases restricted liability for "knowing assistance" to strangers falling within what would later be classified as categories (i), (ii) and (iii). In *Barnes* v. *Addy*[74] itself, solicitors had advised against the appointment as sole trustee of the husband of the tenant for life but nevertheless prepared the requisite deeds; they were exonerated on the grounds that they had had no knowledge or suspicion of any dishonest intention on the part of the trustee. In *Williams* v. *Williams*,[75] a solicitor, who had been

---

[67] (1874) 9 Ch.App. 214.
[68] He could only be held liable if "knowing inducement" was regarded as a head of liability quite distinct from "knowing assistance" or if the requirement for a dishonest and fraudulent design was removed. Both these possibilities have been advocated by C. Harpum in *Frontiers of Liability* (ed. Birks (1993)).
[69–70] He would clearly today be liable for the tort of deceit.
[71] (1983) [1993] 1 W.L.R. 509n, 575–576.
[72] *Per* Millett J. in *Agip (Africa)* v. *Jackson* [1989] 3 W.L.R. 1367, 1389.
[73] By Millett J. in *Agip (Africa)* v. *Jackson* [1989] 3 W.L.R. 1367, 1389–1390.
[74] (1874) 9 Ch.App. 244.
[75] (1881) 17 Ch.D. 437.

instructed to sell lands and use the proceeds of sale to discharge the debts of the vendor, reasonably came to what was in fact an incorrect conclusion that the lands were not subject to any settlement. His conduct was classified as somewhat negligent but his bona fide conviction that there had been no settlement sufficed to avoid liability, although the court stressed that the case would have been very different if he had "wilfully shut his eyes". In *Williams-Ashman* v. *Price & Williams*[76] trust solicitors who, following the instructions of the sole trustee, had paid out part of the trust funds to persons who were not in fact beneficiaries and invested the residue in unauthorised securities without first examining a copy of the trust deed which was in their possession, were similarly exonerated on the basis that they had acted honestly in the course of their agency without actual knowledge of any breach of trust.

However, a different view was taken by Ungoed-Thomas J. in *Selangor United Rubber Estates* v. *Cradock (No. 3)*,[77] the first of a number of cases resulting from successful attempts to use the funds of a company unlawfully[78] to finance its own acquisition. The person promoting the takeover, Cradock, promised his bank manager that the company's account would be transferred to his branch and thus persuaded him to issue a banker's draft for the amount of the purchase price on the basis that it would be taken by a representative of the bank to the meeting at which the takeover was to be completed and exchanged for a draft for a higher sum payable at Cradock. To the meeting the representative of the bank was induced to release the draft without receiving anything in return. The takeover was then completed and the newly-elected board of directors, having duly transferred the company's bank account to Cradock's bank, agreed to lend the company's funds to a third party and drew the appropriate cheque on its new bank account. The third party endorsed this cheque in favour of Cradock, who paid it into his own account and so was able to cover the amount of the draft. Although the bank had clearly acted in good faith without any knowledge of the misapplication of company funds being perpetrated by the directors, Ungoed-Thomas J. held that a reasonable banker would have realised that, by allowing the company's money to be paid into Cradock's account, he was enabling the latter to purchase the company with its own money. He then held that an agent who has assisted in bringing about a misapplication of property subject to a trust will be liable for "knowing assistance" if he either knew or ought to have known of the misapplication in question; consequently, the bank was liable for "knowing assistance". This decision was subsequently followed,[79] most significantly in *Baden* v. *Société Générale*[80] where Peter Gibson J. accepted a concession by counsel that its effect

---

[76] [1942] 1 Ch. 219.

[77] [1968] 1 W.L.R. 1555.

[78] At that time such conduct was unlawful under Companies Act 1948 s.54 (now replaced by Companies Act 1985 ss.151–158).

[79] In cases such as *Karak Rubber Company* v. *Burden (No. 2)* [1972] 1 W.L.R. 602 and *Rowlandson* v. *National Westminster Bank* [1978] 3 All E.R. 370.

[80] (1983) [1993] 1 W.L.R. 509n, 575–582.

was that strangers falling within all five of the categories of knowledge which he had identified would be liable for "knowing assistance". On the other hand, the more traditional approach was adopted in a number of other decisions,[81] most significantly by the Court of Appeal in *Carl-Zeiss Stiftung* v. *Herbert Smith (No. 2)*[82] and in *Belmont Finance Corporation* v. *Williams Furniture.*[83]

Despite the continued existence of these conflicting authorities, it seems now to be generally accepted that the more traditional approach is correct and that a stranger will only be liable for "knowing assistance" if he falls within the first three of the categories of knowledge identified by Peter Gibson J. in *Baden* v. *Société Générale. Agip (Africa)* v. *Jackson*[84] concerned a money-laundering operation whereby funds abstracted from the plaintiff by means of forged payment orders were transferred to a series of dummy companies operated by the defendant accountants, who then immediately transferred the funds on to third parties. Millett J. held that the defendants "were at best indifferent to the possibility of fraud".[85] They were therefore clearly liable for "knowing assistance" on any view of the authorities. However, he considered the five categories of knowledge identified by Peter Gibson J. and held that the concession made by counsel in *Baden* v. *Société Générale* that all five would ground liability for "knowing assistance" "was wrong and should not have been made. . . . In *Belmont Finance Corporation* v. *Williams Furniture*, the Court of Appeal insisted that to hold a stranger liable for "knowing assistance" the breach of trust in question must be a fraudulent and dishonest one.[86] In my judgment it necessarily follows that constructive notice of the fraud is not enough to make him liable. There is no sense in requiring dishonesty on the part of the principal where accepting negligence as sufficient for his assistant. Dishonest furtherance of the dishonest scheme of another is an understandable basis for liability; negligent but honest failure to appreciate that someone else's scheme is dishonest is not."[87] This extremely clear statement of the justification for the more traditional approach appeared to have settled the

---

[81] Such as *Competitive Insurance Company* v. *Davies Investments* [1975] 1 W.L.R. 1240, *Re Montagu's Settlement Trusts* [1987] 2 W.L.R. 1192, and *Lipkin Gorman* v. *Karpnale* [1987] 1 W.L.R. 987 (Alliott J.) (the question did not have to be decided in the Court of Appeal ([1989] 1 W.L.R. 1340) and did not arise in the House of Lords ([1991] 3 W.L.R. 10); this decision is discussed in detail *post*, p. 269.

[82] [1969] 2 Ch. 276. This case principally concerned "knowing receipt" but both Sachs and Edmund Davies L.JJ. stated that an agent cannot be liable for "knowing assistance" unless he has actual knowledge of the misapplication in question.

[83] [1979] 1 All E.R. 118, *(No. 2)* 1 All E.R. 393. This case resulted from another successful attempt to purchase a company with its own money. The Court of Appeal first held, on a pleading issue, that liability for "knowing assistance" is restricted to the first three categories of knowledge later identified by Peter Gibson J. and subsequently held, on the merits, that the agents had throughout genuinely believed that the transaction was a good commercial proposition.

[84] [1989] 3 W.L.R. 1367 (Millett J.), [1991] 3 W.L.R. 116 (C.A.).

[85] [1989] 3 W.L.R. 1367, 1391.

[86] See *ante*, p. 256.

[87] [1989] 3 W.L.R. 1367, 1389.

controversy. Unfortunately, however, in the Court of Appeal[88], where the decision of Millett J. was affirmed, Fox L.J. stated that the degree of knowledge required had been described by Ungoed-Thomas J. in *Selangor United Rubber Estates* v. *Cradock (No. 3)* and by Peter Gibson J. in *Baden* v. *Société Générale*.[89] This reliance on authorities expressly rejected by Millett J. reintroduced considerable confusion. However, in *Eagle Trust* v. *S.B.C. Securities*[90] Vinelott J. said "it is, I think, implicit in his judgment that [Fox L.J.] accepted Millett J.'s conclusion that in a "knowing assistance" case something amounting to dishonesty or want of probity on the part of the defendant must be shown"[91] and held that "constructive notice is not enough".[92] This was confirmed in *Polly Peck International* v. *Nadir (No. 2)*,[93] a case concerning alleged misapplications of the plaintiff's funds by its former chief executive, Asil Nadir, by means of transfers to a London account of the Central Bank of Northern Cyprus controlled by Nadir. In dismissing a claim for a worldwide Mareva Injunction[94] against the Central Bank, Scott L.J. said[95] that "[t]here is a general consensus of opinion that if liability as constructive trustee is sought to be imposed ... on the basis that the defendant has assisted in the misapplication of trust property (knowing assistance), 'something amounting to dishonesty or want of probity on the part of the defendant must be shown' (see per Vinelott J. in *Eagle Trust* v. *S.B.C. Securities*). Vinelott J. described as 'settled law' the proposition that 'a stranger cannot be made liable for knowing assistance in the fraudulent breach of trust unless knowledge of the fraudulent design can be imputed to him ... '. I respectfully agree." It is to be hoped that this clear statement of the law by Scott L.J. has dispersed any confusion caused by the remarks of Fox L.J. in *Agip (Africa)* v. *Jackson* and that it will from now on be generally accepted that a stranger can only be liable for "knowing assistance" if he falls within one of the first three categories of knowledge identified by Peter Gibson J. in *Baden* v. *Société Générale*.

(c) The liability of agents of invalidly appointed trustees

Is the protection conferred by *Barnes* v. *Addy* available to an agent employed by a trustee who has not himself been validly appointed? This issue arose in *Mara* v. *Browne*[96] where it was argued that an agent appointed by such a trustee must act as a principal and so would be deprived of the protection of *Barnes* v. *Addy*—this would mean that the agent in question would be treated as if he were officiously acting as a fiduciary and so, under the principles which have already been

---

[88] [1991] 3 W.L.R. 116.
[89] *Ibid*. 131–132.
[90] (1991) [1993] 1 W.L.R. 484.
[91] *Ibid*. 495.
[92] *Ibid*. 496.
[93] [1992] 4 All E.R. 769.
[94] An injunction issued to prevent dissipation or removal of the assets of a defendant prior to the trial.
[95] [1992] 4 All E.R. 769, 777.
[96] [1896] 1 Ch. 199.

discussed,[97] would inevitably be liable no matter what his motives and his state of knowledge. This argument succeeded at first instance before North J.[98] but the Court of Appeal found that the trustee in question had been validly appointed and so the issue did not have to be decided. However, Lord Herschell stated that the protection of *Barnes* v. *Addy* would be available to such an agent. It is suggested that this latter view, although not clearly established, is preferable since it is unreasonable to expect an agent to carry out a detailed investigation into the status of his principal.

(d) The liability of partners of agents liable for "knowing assistance"
When an agent is held personally liable to account in the same manner as a trustee on the grounds that he has assisted in bringing about a misapplication of property subject to a trust, are his partners subject to the same liability? In *Re Bell's Indenture*[99] liability for "knowing assistance" was imposed on a solicitor who had assisted the trustees of a settlement who were also life tenants thereof to distribute the whole of the trust property to themselves in breach of trust. The remaindermen sought to impose a similar liability on his partners, relying on *Blythe* v. *Fladgate*[1] where, as has already been seen,[2] all the partners of a firm of solicitors who had officiously been acting as trustees were held liable to account to the trust. *Blythe* v. *Fladgate* had been followed at first instance in *Mara* v. *Browne*,[3] where North J. had imposed liability both on the agent employed by the invalidly appointed trustee and on his partner. However, in the Court of Appeal in *Mara* v. *Browne*[4] (where the issue did not arise) all three members of the court had indicated that they would have held the opposite on the grounds that it is not part of the implied authority of a partner to make his co-partners liable for "knowing assistance". In *Re Bell's Indenture* Vinelott J. followed and applied these statements of the Court of Appeal in *Mara* v. *Browne* and exonerated the partners, distinguishing *Blythe* v. *Fladgate* on the grounds that in that case the solicitors had been acting officiously as trustees. However, in *Agip (Africa)* v. *Jackson*[5] both Millett J. and the Court of Appeal, without citation or discussion of any of the previous authorities, imposed liability for "knowing assistance" both on the accountant who had been carrying out the money-laundering and on his partner. This decision of the Court of Appeal must obviously represent the law at present but the matter cannot be regarded as finally settled until the conflicting authorities have been the subject of a reasoned judgment.

---

[97] See *ante*, p. 252.
[98] [1895] 2 Ch. 69.
[99] [1980] 3 All E.R. 425.
[1] [1891] 1 Q.B. 337.
[2] See *ante*, p. 252.
[3] [1895] 2 Ch. 69.
[4] [1896] 1 Ch. 199.
[5] [1989] 3 W.L.R. 1367 (Millett J.), [1991] 3 W.L.R. 116 (C.A.).

(e) What should a suspicious agent do?

If an agent suspects that he may be assisting in a misapplication of property subject to a trust and it is too late for him to withdraw from the transaction (this would be the position of a solicitor or a bank who became suspicious about the provenance of funds being held to the order of a client), he is entitled to apply by originating summons to the High Court under Order 85 of the Rules of the Supreme Court for administration directions. In the event that there are sufficient grounds for his suspicions, any directions given by the court can, if necessary, override any legal or other professional privilege of confidentiality to which the client would normally have been entitled.[6]

3. *Receipt of Property Subject to a Trust which has been Misapplied*

The imposition of the obligations of trusteeship on the recipient of property subject to a trust which has been misapplied (generally known as liability for "knowing receipt"[7]) must be distinguished from, on the one hand, liability for "knowing assistance" and, on the other hand, liability for "inconsistent dealing". Liability for "knowing assistance", which has just been considered, will be imposed on any stranger who, with the requisite level of knowledge, has assisted in bringing about a dishonest and fraudulent misapplication of property subject to a trust. Liability for "knowing receipt" will be imposed on any stranger who, with the requisite level of knowledge, has received for his own benefit misapplied property subject to a trust. Liability for "inconsistent dealing", which will be considered later in this section, will be imposed on any stranger who has received lawfully and not for his own benefit property subject to a trust but who has subsequently either misappropriated it or dealt with it in some other manner which is inconsistent with the trust. Suppose that a bank manager has been duly notified that an account held at his branch in the name of an individual is in fact a trust account. If the bank permits a cheque drawn on that account to be credited in breach of trust to the account of a third party but acts merely as the conduit by means of which the funds are transferred from one account to the other, it will be potentially liable for "knowing assistance"; if the account of the third party is overdrawn at the time of the transfer, the bank may additionally be liable for "knowing receipt" to the extent that it has utilised the funds in reduction of the overdraft; if, on the other hand, the bank itself debits the balance of the account to cover an overdraft created in another account held in the name of the same individual, it will potentially be liable for "inconsistent dealing".

(a) The different remedies available against the recipient

Liability for "knowing receipt" is only one of a number of claims which may be available to the person from whom the property has been abstracted. If the property or its product is still identifiable in the hands

---

[6] *Finers* v. *Miro* [1991] 1 All E.R. 182.

[7] C. Harpum in *Frontiers of Liability* (ed. Birks (1993)) describes this as "Restitutionary Liability".

of the recipient or of any third party to whom it has been subsequently transferred, he will also have the possibility of bringing a proprietary claim, either at law or in equity, to enable him to follow the property into the hands of its present holder,[8] Additionally he may be able to bring a personal action at law for money had and received against the recipient, a personal action in equity against whoever was responsible for initiating the misapplication, and a claim for the imposition of the obligations of trusteeship against anyone who has been guilty of "knowing assistance".[9] For example, in *Agip (Africa)* v. *Jackson*,[10] where funds abstracted from the plaintiff by means of forged payment orders had been transferred to a series of dummy companies operated by the defendant accountants, who then immediately transferred the funds on to third parties, the plaintiff, having already obtained an unsatisfied judgment against the dummy company in question, sought the following relief against the defendants: at law, a proprietary claim to follow the funds into the hands of the defendants and a personal claim for money had and received; and, in equity, a proprietary claim to follow the funds into the hands of the defendants and the imposition of the obligations of trusteeship for "knowing receipt" and "knowing assistance". In *Lipkin Gorman* v. *Karpnale*,[11] where a partner of a firm of solicitors had drawn from the firm's client accounts funds which he subsequently gambled away at a casino, the solicitors claimed that its bank was liable for conversion of cheques, for conversion of a draft, for breach of contract and for "knowing assistance" and that the casino was liable for money had and received, for negligence, for conversion of cheques, for conversion of a draft, and for "knowing receipt" and, additionally, was liable in equity to both proprietary and personal claims as a result of its receipt of the solicitors' funds.

It has already been observed[12] that the interrelation of these different claims makes proceedings of this type extremely complex. The principal difficulty is the existence of what have been described[13] as "arbitrary and anomalous distinctions" between the claims at law and the claims in equity. It is perhaps inevitable that, as will be seen in Chapter 23,[14] the prerequisites of and defences to proprietary claims differ depending on whether the claim is being brought at law or in equity. But there are also distinctions between the different personal claims. An action at law for money had and received will succeed quite irrelevant of the state of mind of the recipient of the money; the only defences available to him will be bona fide purchase for value without notice and change of position.[15] On the other hand, liability in equity for "knowing receipt"

---

[8] See Chap. 23, *post*, p. 601.

[9] See *ante*, p. 253.

[10] [1989] 3 W.L.R. 1367 (Millett J.), [1991] 3 W.L.R. 116 (C.A.).

[11] [1987] 1 W.L.R. 987 (Alliott J.), [1989] 1 W.L.R. 1340 (C.A.), [1991] 3 W.L.R. 10 (H.L.).

[12] See *ante*, p. 253.

[13] By Millett J. in *El Ajou* v. *Dollar Land Holdings* [1993] B.C.L.C. 735, 757. Millett J. contended that these distinctions should not be insisted upon.

[14] See *post*, p 601.

[15] *Lipkin Gorman* v. *Karpnale* [1989] 1 W.L.R. 1340 (C.A.), [1991] 3 W.L.R. 10 (H.L.). See P. B. H. Birks [1991] L.M.C.L.Q. 473.

depends on whether the recipient falls within the appropriate[16] categories of knowledge identified by Peter Gibson J. in *Baden* v. *Société Générale*[17] (this is also true of liability for "knowing assistance"). In other words, liability at law is strict, subject to defences, while liability in equity depends on the state of mind of the recipient. This (and other) distinctions have led commentators to question whether so many different remedies should continue to be available for the same misapplication of property.[18] Indeed Millett J. has recently commented[19] that he does not see "how it would be possible to develop any logical and coherent system of restitution if there were different requirements in respect of knowledge for the common law claim for money had and received, the personal claim for an account in equity against a knowing recipient and the equitable proprietary claim". It is likely that the Law Commission will shortly be considering this whole area of the law with a view to rationalising all the available remedies and it is generally thought that the way forward will be the introduction of a universal principle of strict liability subject to clearly defined defences.[20] For the moment, however, the existing distinctions between the different claims obviously continue.

For present purposes, it is important only to distinguish between, on the one hand, the possibility of following the misapplied property into the hands of its recipient and, on the other hand, the imposition of the obligations of trusteeship upon him. Where property subject to a trust has been misapplied, the interests of the beneficiaries in that property are, in accordance with the basic principles of property law, enforceable against the whole world unless and until the property in question reaches the hands of someone who takes it free of their equitable proprerietary interests therein. Any recipient of misapplied property who is liable to such an equitable tracing claim will of course be a trustee of such property as is in his hands—this is simply because the equitable interests of the beneficiaries therein must necessarily take effect behind a trust of the legal estate. However, the fact that it is thus possible to trace the property into its product does not necessarily mean that the obligations of trusteeship will be imposed on the recipient in respect of all the property originally transferred to him. Indeed, only in three situations will it be necessary to seek the imposition of liability for "knowing receipt": first, where the recipient has dealt with the property in such a way that it can no longer be followed; secondly, where the property has depreciated in value while in the hands of the recipient; and, thirdly, where the recipient has obtained some incidental profit from the property.[21] In these circumstances, the equitable tracing claim will only lead to the recovery of such property, if

---

[16] There is disagreement as to precisely which of the five categories suffice for this purpose.
[17] See *ante*, p 257.
[18] See the articles cited in n. 30, p. 252.
[19] By Millett J. in *El Ajou* v. *Dollar Land Holdings* [June, 12 1992] (unreported) Transcript 40.
[20] See the articles cited in n. 30, p 252.
[21] Such as one of the types of secret profits discussed in the previous section of this Chapter.

any, as remains in the hands of the recipient; the loss caused by any dealing with or reduction in value of the property and any incidental profit obtained will only be recoverable if the recipient is held to have been a constructive trustee of the whole of the property originally transferred to him. In the vast majority of the cases in which the imposition of liability for "knowing receipt" has been sought, the recipient has dealt with the property in such a way that it can no longer be followed.

(b) The elements of liability for "knowing receipt"

Liability for "knowing receipt" is not dependent on the existence of any dishonest or fraudulent design on the part of the person who misapplied the property; it is dependent purely and simply on the receipt, with the requisite level of knowledge, of property subject to a trust which has been misapplied. (The fact of receipt can sometimes be extremely difficult to establish; in such circumstances, it is determined by the application of the rules governing legal and equitable tracing claims[21A].) Further, the existence of the requisite level of knowledge has to be proved by the claimant, not disproved by the recipient. All these points were emphasised by Scott L.J. in *Polly Peck International* v. *Nadir (No. 2).*[22]

It is therefore apparent that a recipient who does not fall within any of the five categories of knowledge identified by Peter Gibson J. in *Baden* v. *Société Générale*[23] will not be liable for "knowing receipt". This is the case whether or not the recipient has given value.[24] In *Re Diplock*,[25] under the provisions of a will subsequently declared to be void for uncertainty, executors distributed large sums of money to various charities who received the property in good faith without the slightest idea that the will would at a later stage be successfully challenged.[26] Although the next of kin were held to be entitled, subject to various defences, to trace the property in equity into the hands of the charities,[27] the Court of Appeal declined to impose "the heavy obligations of trusteeship"[28] upon the charities and held that they were not liable for "knowing receipt". Similarly, in *Cowan de Groot Properties* v. *Eagle Trust*[29] directors of a company which lacked liquid funds sold five properties at a gross undervalue in order to make an urgent payment needed to keep an important company project in existence. Subsequently the company repudiated the sale and claimed that the purchaser was liable for "knowing receipt". Knox J. held that the purchaser did not fall within any of the five categories of knowledge

---

[21A] See *post*, p. 601. A good example is *El Ajou* v. *Dollar Land Holdings* [1993] B.C.L.C. 735.
[22] [1992] 4 All E.R. 769, 777.
[23] See *ante*, p. 257.
[24] Whether or not he has given value will of course be highly relevant in relation to an equitable tracing claim, since only if he has will he be able to make out the defence of bona fide purchase for value without notice.
[25] [1948] Ch. 465.
[26] In the House of Lords in *Chichester Diocesan Fund* v. *Simpson* [1944] A.C. 341.
[27] See Ch. 23, *post*, p. 607.
[28] This was the description utilised by Lord Greene M.R.
[29] [1992] 4 All E.R. 700.

identified by Peter Gibson J. and that the purchaser was consequently not liable for "knowing receipt".

The crucial and controversial question which remains is, therefore, which of the five categories of knowledge identified by Peter Gibson J. in *Baden* v. *Société Générale* suffice for the imposition of liability for "knowing receipt". In this respect, the authorities are in considerable disarray.

A recipient of property subject to a trust who has actual knowledge that it has been misapplied will obviously be liable for "knowing receipt". In *Belmont Finance Corporation* v. *Williams Furniture (No. 2)*[30] the directors of a company had had actual knowledge of a transaction whereby the company had permitted a wholly owned subsidiary to be purchased with its own money; consequently, the purchase price paid to the parent company for its subsidiary was in fact misapplied property subject to a trust. The Court of Appeal held that the parent company was liable for "knowing receipt" and so was a constructive trustee of the purchase moneys. Similarly, in *El Ajou* v. *Dollar Land Holdings*[30A] liability for "knowing receipt" was imposed on a company because it had acquired the interest of a co-venturer at a time when it was aware that the co-venturer had originally acquired its interest with the proceeds of fraud.

Liability for "knowing receipt" is clearly not confined to cases of actual knowledge. In *Nelson* v. *Larholt*[31] an executor drew eight cheques on the estate's bank account, all of which were signed by him as executor of the testator, in favour of the defendant who cashed the cheques in good faith. Denning J. held that the defendant must be taken to have known what any reasonable man would have known. Eight successive requests to cash cheques clearly drawn on the bank account of an estate would have placed a reasonable man on enquiry. Thus the defendant must be taken to have known of the misapplication of the property and so, although he had obtained the cheques for value in good faith, he was held to be liable for "knowing receipt" and was therefore a constructive trustee of the proceeds. The category of knowledge relied on by Denning J. as the basis for this liability for "knowing receipt" appears to fall within the fifth category of knowledge which would subsequently be identified by Peter Gibson J. (knowledge of circumstances which would put an honest and reasonable man on inquiry). Consequently, *Nelson* v. *Larholt*, together with dicta in *Belmont Finance Corporation* v. *Williams Furniture (No. 2)* and various first instance decisions,[32] has been cited[33] as authority for

---

[30] [1980] 1 All E.R. 393.

[30A] [1994] 1 B.C.L.C. 464. At first instance ([1993] B.C.L.C. 735) Millett J. had declined to attribute the knowledge of the chairman to the company but the Court of Appeal took a different view of the role of the chairman in the transaction in which the interest had been originally acquired.

[31] [1948] 1 K.B. 339.

[32] *International Sales and Agencies* v. *Marcus* [1982] 3 All E.R. 551, 558, *Agip (Africa)* v. *Jackson* [1989] 3 W.L.R. 1367, 1388, *Westpac Banking Corp* v. *Savin* [1985] 2 N.Z.L.R. 41, 71 (New Zealand High Court).

[33] In *Cowan de Groot Properties* v. *Eagle Trust* [1992] 4 All E.R. 700.

the proposition that liability for "knowing receipt" will be imposed if the recipient has any of the five categories of knowledge identified by Peter Gibson J.

However, *Nelson* v. *Larholt* was explained in a different way in *Carl-Zeiss Stiftung* v. *Herbert Smith (No. 2).*[34] This was a subsidiary action to a claim brought by an East German company against a West German company, each of whom claimed to be the original Zeiss Foundation. The East German company, which in the main action was claiming that the assets of the West German company were held on trust for it, claimed in the subsidiary action that the solicitors acting for the West German company in the main action were liable for "knowing receipt" of their legal fees. The Court of Appeal dismissed this claim on the somewhat controversial[35] ground that notice of an adverse claim did not amount to notice of a trust and so the solicitors, having no effective notice of any adverse claim, were bona fide purchasers for value without notice. In the course of his judgment,[36] Sachs L.J. described *Nelson* v. *Larholt* as a case where there had been an obvious shutting of eyes as opposed to a mere lack of prudence and suggested that a negligent, if innocent, failure to make inquiry was not sufficient to attract liability for "knowing receipt". This interpretation of the decision appears to place the defendant in *Nelson* v. *Larholt* within the second category of knowledge identified by Peter Gibson J. in *Baden* v. *Société Générale* (knowledge that he would have obtained but for wilfully shutting his eyes to the obvious). This narrower view of liability for "knowing receipt" was adopted by Megarry V.C. in *Re Montagu's Settlement,*[37] where he held that only the first three of the five categories of knowledge identified by Peter Gibson J. in *Baden* v. *Société Générale* should give rise to liability for "knowing receipt". The trustees of a settlement made in 1923 had in 1947 failed to carry out a fiduciary duty to select such of the heirlooms of the Montagu family as they considered suitable for inclusion in the settlement and had instead treated the whole of these heirlooms and not only those which they had not selected, as the absolute property of the Tenth Duke of Manchester. Following his death in 1977, the Eleventh Duke of Manchester sought to recover the heirlooms or their value from his executrix. Megarry V.C. held that such of the selected heirlooms as were still in the hands of the executrix could be traced in equity into her hands but that the Tenth Duke had not been liable for "knowing receipt" and so his executrix was not liable for the value of those heirlooms which had been sold and which could therefore not be traced. Megarry V.C. held that the Tenth Duke did not fall into any of the first three categories of knowledge identified by Peter Gibson J. in *Baden* v. *Société Générale*. Although his solicitor and possibly also the Tenth Duke himself had at one stage been aware of the true position, "a person is not to be taken to have knowledge of a fact that he once knew but has genuinely forgotten: the

---

[34] [1969] 2 Ch. 276.
[35] See D. M. Gordon (1970) 44 A.L.J. 261.
[36] [1969] 2 Ch. 276, 298.
[37] [1987] Ch. 264.

test (or a test) is whether the knowledge continues to operate on that person's mind at the time in question".[38] Nor was any knowledge held by the solicitor to be automatically imputed to his client unless the latter had employed him to investigate the matter in question. This narrower view of liability for "knowing receipt" was subsequently applied by Alliott J. at first instance in *Lipkin Gorman* v. *Karpnale*[39] and by Steyn J. in *Barclays Bank* v. *Quincecare*.[40]

A further refinement was subsequently introduced by Vinelott J. in *Eagle Trust* v. *S.B.C. Securities*.[41] He held that the question of whether the last two categories of knowledge identified by Peter Gibson J. in *Baden* v. *Société Générale* suffice for the imposition of liability for "knowing receipt" only arises in non-commercial transactions.[42] In commercial transactions, on the other hand, "if, in the ordinary course of business, a payment is made in discharge of a liability to the [recipient], the [recipient] cannot be made liable as a constructive trustee merely upon the ground that he knew or had reason to suspect that there had been a breach of trust disentitling the trustee to make the payment. It must be shown that the circumstances are such that knowledge that the payment was improper can be imputed to him".[43] Thus in commercial transactions, liability for "knowing receipt" will be imposed if the recipient has any of the first three categories of knowledge identified by Peter Gibson J. in *Baden* v. *Société Générale* or "if the circumstances are such that, in the absence of any evidence or explanation by the [recipient], that knowledge can be inferred".[44] This statement of principle was subsequently cited with approval by Knox J. in *Cowan de Groot Properties* v. *Eagle Trust*,[45] although in that case the defendant was actually held not to have any relevant knowledge at all.

---

[38] *Ibid.* 285. In *El Ajou* v. *Dollar Land Holdings* [1993] B.C.L.C. 735, 762, Millett J. held that, in the same way, "where the knowledge of a director is attributed to a company, but is not actually imparted to it, the company should not be treated as continuing to possess that knowledge after the director in question has died or left its service. In such circumstances, the company can properly be said to have 'lost its memory'." Although the Court of Appeal reversed Millett J., Nourse L.J. stated ([1994] 1 B.C.L.C. 464, 475) that, while this proposition did not assist the defendant, he "might agree" with it.

[39] [1987] 1 W.L.R. 987 (the question did not have to be decided in the Court of Appeal ([1989] 1 W.L.R. 1340) and did not arise in the House of Lords ([1991] 3 W.L.R. 10); see *post*, p. 269.

[40] (1988) [1992] 4 All E.R. 363.

[41] (1991) [1993] 1 W.L.R. 484.

[42] For such transactions, Vinelott J. appeared to favour the broader view of liability for "knowing receipt" rather than the view expressed in *Re Montagu's Settlement*. A similar view was taken by Millett J. in *El Ajou* v. *Dollar Land Holdings* [1993] B.C.L.C. 735, 758–759, who was "content to assume, without deciding, that dishonesty or want of probity involving actual knowledge (whether proved or inferred) is not a precondition of liability; but that a recipient is not expected to be unduly suspicious and is not to be held liable unless he went ahead without further inquiry in circumstances in which an honest and reasonable man would have realised that the money was probably trust money and was being misapplied".

[43] (1991) [1993] 1 W.L.R. 484, 506.

[44] *Ibid.* Knowledge may be inferred "if the circumstances are such that an honest and reasonable man would have inferred that the moneys were probably trust moneys and were being misapplied".

[45] (1991) [1992] 4 All E.R. 700.

While this further refinement is consistent with the traditional reluctance of equity to extend the doctrine of constructive notice to commercial transactions,[46] to have distinct tests for different types of transactions may well only succeed in confusing the situation even more.

The conflicting lines of authority which have been discussed urgently require a considered review by the Court of Appeal. In *Polly Peck International v. Nadir (No. 2)*[47] Scott L.J. did not consider an interlocutary appeal to be "the right occasion for settling the issue"; however, he left the question open by accepting that the third category of knowledge identified by Peter Gibson J. in *Baden v. Société Générale* would lead to liability for "knowing receipt" while admitting to "some doubts" as to whether the fifth category of knowledge would also do so. It is to be hoped that at least one of the proceedings presently pending in which it is being sought to impose liability for "knowing receipt" reaches the Court of Appeal since any clearly expressed statement of the law would be preferable to the existing confusion.

(c) The way forward

In *Lipkin Gorman v. Karpnale*[48] a partner of a firm of solicitors had drawn from the firm's client accounts funds which he subsequently gambled away at a casino. Liability for "knowing assistance" and "knowing receipt" was considered only at first instance, where Alliott J. held, *inter alia*,[49] that the bank was liable for "knowing assistance" in respect of some of the funds drawn from the client accounts[50] and that the casino was not liable for "knowing receipt". However, the Court of Appeal considered only the potential liability of the bank for breach of contract and the potential liability of the casino principally for money had and received. Both these claims failed and only the liability of the casino was considered (and upheld) in the House of Lords, It has already been observed[51] that an action for money had and received does not depend on the state of mind of the recipient of the money; he will be strictly liable unless he can make out an established defence. The disagreement between the Court of Appeal and the House of Lords was as to whether a casino is a bona fide purchaser for value without notice.[52] The House of Lords denied this defence to the casino but permitted it to invoke a wholly new defence of change of position, under which its liability was restricted to its net winnings from the solicitor. This defence, which will be discussed in detail in Chapter 23[53] is clearly not restricted to actions

---

[46] See *Manchester Trust v. Furness* [1895] 2 Q.B. 539, 545.

[47] [1992] 4 All E.R. 769, 777.

[48] [1987] 1 W.L.R. 987 (Alliott J.), [1989] 1 W.L.R. 1340 (C.A.), [1991] 3 W.L.R. 10 (H.L.).

[49] Alliott J. also held the casino liable for conversion of a draft (this liability was affirmed by both appellate courts) and not liable in an action for money had and received.

[50] For those drawn after the bank manager became aware of the uncontrolled nature of the solicitor's gambling.

[51] *Ante*, p. 263.

[52] This depended on the interpretation of the Gaming Act 1845.

[53] *Post*, p. 628.

for money had and received and is likely to be generally available. It is therefore almost inevitable that any future imposition of liability for "knowing receipt" will be subject to this new defence of change of position. It is therefore generally thought[54] that, when the Law Commission considers this whole area of the law, it is likely to recommend the rationalisation of all the existing remedies by the introduction of a universal principle of strict liability subject only to the defences of bona fide purchase for value without notice and change of position; liability for "knowing receipt" would then no longer depend on the state of mind of the recipient, which would be relevant only in respect of the availability of the defences. Whether and, if so, when such a principle is introduced remains to be seen. For the moment liability for "knowing receipt" clearly still depends on the state of mind of the recipient; what at present remains undecided is the level of knowledge which is necessary.

4. *Inconsistent Dealing with Property Subject to a Trust*

Any person who has received lawfully and not for his own benefit property subject to a trust will be liable to account for that property as a constructive trustee if he subsequently either misappropriates it or deals with it in some other manner which is inconsistent with the trust. The decided cases on what is generally known as liability for "inconsistent dealing"[55] fall into two groups.

The first group of cases concerns agents. It has already been seen[56] that banks enjoy a right of set off between different accounts held by the same customer. If a bank manager has been duly notified that an account held at his branch in the name of an individual is in fact a trust account, the bank will be holding the credit balance of that account wholly lawfully and in no sense for its own benefit. If, however, the bank seeks to debit the credit balance of the trust account by way of set off against an overdraft created in another account held in the name of the same individual, it will potentially be liable for "inconsistent dealing". In *Barclays Bank* v. *Quistclose Investments*,[57] Quistclose Investments made a loan to Rolls Razor for the specific purpose of paying a dividend and the funds were paid into a new account at Barclays Bank opened by Rolls Razor specifically for the purpose. When Rolls Razor went into liquidation prior to the date on which the dividend was due to be paid, Barclays Bank claimed to offset the balance of this new account against the indebtedness of Rolls Razor in other accounts. The House of Lords held that Rolls Razor had been holding the funds in question on trust to pay the dividend and, subject

---

[54] See the articles cited in n. 30, p. 252.
[55] C. Harpum in *Frontiers of Liability* (ed. Birks (1993)): describes this (along with liability for "knowing receipt") as "Restitutionary Liability".
[56] *Ante*, p. 17, n. 88.
[57] [1970] A.C. 567.

thereto, for Quistclose Investments; since the bank had been made aware of the situation but had failed to draw the appropriate inference from facts known to it, it held the funds which it had sought to misapply on trust for Quistclose Investments. Similarly in *Nestlé Oy* v. *Lloyds Bank*[58] the plaintiff shipowner was accustomed whenever one of its vessels entered a United Kingdom port to transfer to the bank account of its agent at Lloyds Bank sufficient funds to enable the agent to discharge all liabilities incurred by the vessel. A number of such payments were made immediately before and immediately after the agent appointed a receiver. Lloyds Bank set off all the payments so made against the indebtedness of the agent. Bingham J. held that there was no express trust of any of the payments and that, even if there had been a trust in respect of any of the payments made before the appointment of the receiver, the bank would have taken free of that trust on the grounds that it did not fall within any of the categories of knowledge identified by Peter Gibson J. in *Baden* v. *Société Générale*. However, he held that the agent had become a trustee of the payment received after the appointment of the receiver; at the time of its arrival, the bank had already known of the appointment of the receiver and had therefore been placed upon enquiry. The bank was consequently bound by this trust and was not subsequently entitled to set off the payment. An agent will thus clearly be liable for "inconsistent dealing" if he knowingly misapplies property subject to a trust; the categories of knowledge which suffice for the imposition of liability for "knowing receipt" should also apply to the imposition of liability for "inconsistent dealing".

The second group of cases concerns strangers who receive property subject to a trust which has been misapplied without sufficient knowledge to be held liable for "knowing receipt". If such a stranger subsequently acquires the necessary knowledge of the misapplication of the property in breach of trust, he will nevertheless be liable as a constructive trustee if he subsequently deals with the property in a manner inconsistent with the trust. In *Sheridan* v. *Joyce*[59] a trustee lent out trust funds in breach of trust. The borrower originally had no knowledge whatever of this breach of trust and so was clearly not liable for "knowing receipt". He subsequently discovered the true facts and thereafter made all the payments of interest to the beneficiary rather than to the trustee. Nevertheless, when the trustee subsequently sought repayment of part of the principal, the borrower made the repayment to him despite the contrary requests of the beneficiary and the money so repaid was lost. The borrower was held liable to repay the sum a second time on the grounds that he had dealt inconsistently with property which he knew to be subject to a trust. Once again the categories of knowledge which suffice for the imposition of liability for "knowing receipt" should also apply to the imposition of liability for "inconsistent dealing".

---

[58] [1983] 2 Lloyd's Rep. 658.
[59] [1844] 1 Jo. & Lat. 41 (Court of Chancery of Ireland).

IV. Advantages Obtained by Fraudulent or Unconscionable Conduct

From its earliest days, equity has always been prepared to grant relief against fraudulent and unconscionable conduct and one aspect of this relief is the imposition of a constructive trust on any person who has obtained an advantage as the result of such conduct.

1. *The Doctrine of Undue Influence:*[60]

In *Barclays Bank* v. *O'Brien*,[61] Lord Browne-Wilkinson said: "A person who has been induced to enter into a transaction by the undue influence of another ("the wrongdoer") is entitled to set that transaction aside as against the wrongdoer. Such undue influence is either actual or presumed". His lordship went on to approve the following classification.[62]

Cases of actual undue influence fall into Class 1. A claimant who alleges this type of undue influence has "to prove affirmatively that the wrongdoer exerted undue influence on the complainant to enter into the particular transaction which is impugned".[63] If he can discharge this burden of proof, the wrongdoer will be unable to retain the benefit of the transaction in question whether or not it was to the manifest disadvantage of the claimant. This was held by the House of Lords in *C.I.B.C. Mortgages* v. *Pitt.*[64] "Actual undue influence is a species of fraud. Like any other victim of fraud, a person who has been induced by undue influence to carry out a transaction which he did not freely and knowingly enter into is entitled to have that transaction set aside as of right.[65]"

On the other hand, cases of presumed undue influence fall into Class 2. In the words of Lord Browne-Wilkinson in *Barclays Bank* v. *O'Brien*[66]:

> "In these cases the complainant only has to show, in the first instance, that there was a relationship of trust and confidence between the complainant and the wrongdoer of such a nature that it is fair to presume that the wrongdoer abused that relationship in procuring the complainant to enter into the impugned transaction. In Class 2 cases therefore there is no need to procure evidence that actual undue influence was exerted in relation to the particular transaction impugned: once a confidential relationship has been proved, the burden then shifts to the wrongdoer to prove that the complainant entered into the impugned transaction freely, for example by showing that the complainant had independent

---

[60] See generally Goff & Jones: *op.cit.* Ch. 10.

[61] [1993] 3 W.L.R. 786 at p. 791.

[62] Originally laid down by the Court of Appeal in *Bank of Credit and Commerce International* v. *Aboody* [1990] 1 Q.B. 923 at p. 953.

[63] [1993] 3 W.L.R. 786 at p. 791.

[64] [1993] 3 W.L.R. 802, overruling on this point the decision of the Court of Appeal in *Bank of Credit and Commerce International* v. *Aboody* [1990] 1 Q.B. 923 at p. 953.

[65] *Ibid.* at p. 808.

[66] [1993] 3 W.L.R. 786 at p. 792.

advice.[67] Such a confidential relationship can be established in two ways, viz.,

Class 2 (A)

Certain relationships (for example solicitor and client, medical advisor and patient) as a matter of law raise the presumption that undue influence has been exercised.[67A]

Class 2 (B)

Even if there is no relationship falling within Class 2 (A), if the complainant proves the de facto existence of a relationship under which the complainant generally reposed trust and confidence in the wrongdoer, the existence of such relationship raises the presumption of undue influence. In a Class 2 (B) case therefore, in the absence of evidence disproving undue influence, the complainant will succeed in setting aside the impugned transaction merely by proof that the complainant reposed trust and confidence in the wrongdoer without having to prove that the wrongdoer exerted actual undue influence or otherwise abused such trust and confidence in relation to the particular transaction impugned."

However, in cases of presumed undue influence, the person who exerted the undue influence will nevertheless be able to retain the benefit of the transaction unless it can be shown to have been wrongful in that, as the House of Lords held in *National Westminster Bank* v. *Morgan*,[67B] it constituted "a disadvantage sufficiently serious to require evidence to rebut the presumption that in the circumstances of the relationship between the parties it was procured by the exercise of undue influence". In the case of a gift, this requirement will be satisfied "if the gift is so large as not to be reasonably accounted for on the ground of friendship, relationship, charity or other ordinary motives on which ordinary men act".[67C] In the case of a bilateral transaction, this requirement will be satisfied by any inadequacy of consideration in favour of the person who has exerted the undue influence; a sale at an undervalue will satisfy this requirement[68] but a short term loan made at a commercial rate of interest to enable the borrower to prevent a mortgagee from going into possession of her home will not.[69]

Where the doctrine of undue influence therefore applies, it is normally sufficient for the courts simply to set aside the transaction by, for example, ordering the return of any property transferred or declaring that a guarantee or mortgage cannot be enforced. In such circumstances, the nature of the interest retained by the person upon whom the undue influence has been exerted does not have to be classified. However, this does become necessary as soon as any third party becomes involved. The right to have a transaction set aside on the

---

[67] This was done in *Inche Noriah* v. *Shaik Allie Bin Omar* [1929] A.C. 127, 135 (P.C.)).

[67A] Other relationships of this type include parent-child, trustee-beneficiary, and, particularly, spiritual adviser-religious devotee (see *Allcard* v. *Skinner* (1887) 36 Ch.D. 145, 183).

[67B] *National Westminster Bank* v. *Morgan* [1985] 2 W.L.R. 588, 597.

[67C] *Allcard* v. *Skinner* (1887) 36 Ch.D. 145, 185.

[68] *Possathurai* v. *Kannappa Chettiar* (1919) L.R. 47 I.A. 1, 3–4 (P.C.).

[69] *National Westminster Bank* v. *Morgan* [1985] 2 W.L.R. 588, 596.

grounds of undue influence can be assigned both *inter vivos*[70] and upon death[71] and will clearly bind the personal representatives or trustee in bankruptcy of the person who exerted the undue influence. This interest is clearly analagous to an interest arising under a trust; consequently, the person who exerted the undue influence and his personal representatives or trustee in bankruptcy are in effect constructive trustees of any property transferred. However, if any property transferred reaches the hands of a third party, the interest of the person upon whom the undue influence has been exerted seems to be regarded as a mere equity rather than a full equitable interest[72] so that the property can be followed in equity (subject, presumably, to the defence of change of position) only into the hands of a third party other than a bona fide purchaser for value without notice of any interest therein.[73] Many of the recent cases have in fact concerned grants of a mortgage by a married couple over their matrimonial home, usually in order to guarantee the indebtedness of the husband's business, as a result of undue influence exerted by the husband over his wife. In such circumstances, the House of Lords has established[73A] that the mortgage will be valid and enforceable against the wife unless either the husband was genuinely acting as the agent of the creditor in procuring the grant of the mortgage or the circumstances were such as to put the creditor on inquiry as to the possibility that the wife agreed to stand surety as a result of the undue influence of (or some misrepresentation by) the husband.[73B]

2. *The Benefits of Crime*[74]

It has long[75] been clear that "no system of jurisprudence can with reason include among the rights which it enforces rights directly resulting to the person asserting them from the crime of that person".[76] Of the two obvious areas where this principle might be expected to operate, where property has been acquired by means of theft or as a result of an unlawful killing, there is in fact little scope[77] for the operation of the principle in the former area since a thief acquires no

---

[70] *Dickinson* v. *Burrell* (1866) L.R. 1 Eq. 337.

[71] *Stump* v. *Gaby* (1852) 2 De G.M. & G. 623.

[72] *Goddard* v. *Carlisle* (1821) 9 Price 169.

[73] *Lancashire Looms* v. *Black* [1934] 1 K.B. 380.

[73A] In *Barclays Bank* v. *O'Brien* [1993] 3 W.L.R. 786.

[73B] Lord Browne-Wilkinson said (*ibid.* at p. 798) that a creditor is put on inquiry where "(a) the transaction is on its face not to the financial advantage of the wife; and (b) there is a substantial risk that, in procuring the wife to act as surety, the husband has committed a legal or equitable wrong that entitles the wife to set aside the transaction". In such circumstances, the creditor will have constructive notice of the wife's rights unless he takes reasonable steps to satisfy himself that the wife's agreement to stand surety has been properly obtained.

[74] See Goff & Jones: *op.cit.* Ch. 37, T. G. Youdan: (1973) 89 L.Q.R. 235, T. K. Earnshaw & P. J. Pace: (1974) 37 M.L.R. 481.

[75] At least since *Bridgman* v. *Green* (1755) 2 Ves.Sen. 627.

[76] *Cleaver* v. *Mutual Reserve Fund Life Association* [1892] 1 Q.B. 147, 156.

[77] Although the principle might have been a preferable ground for the conclusion reached in *Reading* v. *Attorney-General* [1951] A.C. 507 (see *ante*, p. 228).

title to the property which he steals and so is normally[78] unable to pass any title to any third party. There is, however, very considerable scope for the operation of the principle in the latter area. This is well illustrated by *In the Estate of Crippen*[79] where the residuary legatee of the hanged Dr. Crippen (his mistress) was held not to be entitled to the property which Crippen would normally have received as the intestate successor of the wife whom he had murdered.

Some difficulties have arisen as to the precise scope of the operation of the principle. It clearly applies to anyone found to have committed murder, even unsuccessfully[80]; it is not necessary for a conviction to have been secured in criminal proceedings,[81] nor are the results of any criminal proceedings decisive.[82] On the other hand, the principle does not apply to an insane killer (a person found not guilty of murder by reason of insanity or subsequently held by a civil court to have been insane[83]), since a finding of insanity constitutes an acquittal.[84] The extent to which the principle should operate between these two extremes, in particular in relation to manslaughter and to the offence of causing death by reckless driving,[85] is a matter of some controversy. It has been contended[86] that the operation of the principle should be limited to intentional killing and should therefore not apply to a person convicted either of unintentional manslaughter (involuntary manslaughter or voluntary manslaughter on the ground of diminished responsibility) or of causing death by reckless driving. However, although it has been stated that there may be some types of unlawful killing to which the principle does not apply,[87] the courts have so far taken the view that it is not appropriate to draw any distinction between voluntary and involuntary manslaughter and have applied the principle to both[88] (it seems to follow from this approach that the principle would also be applied to the offence of causing death by dangerous driving—rather surprisingly, this question does not yet seem to have been considered).

When applicable, the principle will deprive the unlawful killer of

---

[78] Except where there has been a sale in market overt or the purchaser is protected by the Sale of Goods Act 1979 or the Consumer Credit Act 1974.

[79] [1911] P. 108.

[80] In *Evans* v. *Evans* [1989] 1 F.L.R. 351, a wife convicted of inciting others to murder her former husband, who survived, was deprived of benefits payable under the divorce settlement.

[81] In *Re Sigsworth* [1935] 1 Ch. 89, the murderer committed suicide and so no criminal proceedings could be brought.

[82] *Gray* v. *Barr* [1971] 2 Q.B. 554 (principle applied where the defendant was acquitted of both murder and manslaughter); this is possible because of the different standards of proof, although according to *Halford* v. *Brookes* (1991) *The Times* October 10, 1991 a finding of murder in civil proceedings requires the criminal standard of proof.

[83] *Re Holgate* (1971) (discussed by Earnshaw & Pace: *op.cit.*).

[84] Criminal Procedure (Insanity) Act 1964, s.1.

[85] Synonymous with involuntary manslaughter except in name and maximum sentence (*R.* v. *Seymour (Edward)* [1983] 3 W.L.R. 349).

[86] By Youdan: *op.cit.* 237–238, Earnshaw & Pace: *op.cit.* 492–496.

[87] In *Gray* v. *Barr* [1971] 2 Q.B. 554, 581.

[88] *Re Giles* [1972] Ch. 544, *R.* v. *Chief National Insurance Commissioner, ex p. Connor* [1981] 2 W.L.R. 213, *Re Royce* [1984] 3 W.L.R. 784, *Re K. (deceased)* [1985] 2 W.L.R. 262.

benefits received under his victim's will,[89] his victim's intestacy,[90] the proceeds of a life insurance policy maintained on the life of his victim,[91] and enhanced social security benefits arising out of the death of his victim.[92] In the unlikely event that the property has already reached his hands (normally it will be intercepted), a constructive trust will be imposed for the benefit of those otherwise entitled. In *Re Sigsworth*[93] a murderer was absolutely entitled under the will of his victim, his mother, and was also, with his brother, her intestate successor; her entire estate passed to her other intestate successor, her other son. The courts have never had to decide whether those claiming through an unlawful killer are also disqualified or whether he is treated as having predeceased his victim. This question would have arisen in *Re Sigsworth* had the murderer left issue, who under the intestacy rules would have stood in his shoes had he predeceased his victim. It has been suggested[94] that an unlawful killer should be treated as having predeceased his victim; this view would entitle the notional issue of the murderer in *Re Sigsworth* to take jointly with the other intestate successor. Similar problems arise where the unlawful killer and his victim hold joint or successive interests. Where one of two joint tenants unlawfully kills the other, it has been held that the killer acquires the entire legal title to the property by virtue of the principle of survivorship but holds that legal title on constructive trust for himself and the representatives of his victim in equal shares as tenants in common.[95] Where a person entitled to property in remainder unlawfully kills the life tenant,[96] it has been suggested[97] that the killer's enjoyment should be postponed for as long as mortality tables predict that the victim would have lived, the latter's representatives receiving the income in the meantime under a constructive trust.

The court now has a discretion under the Forfeiture Act 1982 to grant relief against forfeiture to a person guilty of unlawful killing other than murder.[98] Where a court has determined that the principle has operated to bring about a forfeiture, it can modify the effect of the principle where it "is satisfied that, having regard to the conduct of the offender and of the deceased and to such other circumstances as appear to the court to be material, the justice of the case requires the effect of the rule

---

[89] *Re Sigsworth* [1935] 1 Ch. 89.

[90] *In the Estate of Crippen* [1911] P. 108, *Re Sigsworth* [1935] 1 Ch. 89.

[91] *Cleaver* v. *Mutual Reserve Fund Life Association* [1892] 1 Q.B. 147, *Davitt* v. *Titcumb* [1990] 2 W.L.R. 168.

[92] *R.* v. *Chief National Insurance Commissioner, ex p. Connor* [1981] 1 Q.B. 758 (murderess of husband deprived of widow's pension).

[93] [1935] 1 Ch. 89.

[94] In Goff & Jones: *op.cit.* Ch. 37, p. 707.

[95] *Re K. (deceased)* [1985] 2 W.L.R. 262. This conclusion, although supported by Commonwealth authority, is not of course consistent with the view that the unlawful killer is treated as having predeceased his victim since on this hypothesis the representatives of the victim would be entitled to the property absolutely.

[96] The problem has not as yet arisen, although it was postulated in *Re Calloway* [1956] Ch. 559.

[97] By Youdan: *op.cit.* pp. 250–251.

[98] Excluded by Forfeiture Act 1982 s.5.

to be so modified in that case".[99] Such an order was made in *Re K (deceased)*[1] wholly relieving from forfeiture a wife convicted of the manslaughter of her husband, who had for years been violently attacking her; during one such attack, with the intention of frightening him and deterring him from following her out of the room, she picked up a loaded shot gun which went off and killed him. Although the extreme facts of this case made this decision to exercise the discretion wholly uncontroversial, it is questionable whether it is entirely appropriate for judges to be obliged to make moral judgments of the type envisaged by this legislation.

3. *Other Fraudulent and Unconscionable Conduct*

The courts have always been prepared to impose a constructive trust upon a person who has acquired property by other types of fraudulent or unconscionable conduct. The vast majority of such constructive trusts have been imposed in order to prevent a transferee of property from going back on an undertaking or agreement made at the time of acquisition to respect an interest therein which has not been created or protected in the manner required by the law. Such cases are manifestations of the principle that equity will not permit the provisions of a statute to be used as an instrument of fraud.[2]

Of course it is not always fraudulent to rely on a failure to comply with the requirements of the law. Equity will not prevent a party to an oral contract for the sale of land from repudiating it on the grounds that it does not comply with the Law of Property (Miscellaneous Provisions) Act 1989[3] nor prevent a settlor who has made an oral declaration of trust respecting land from raising the absence of the writing required by the Law of Property Act 1925.[4] Similarly, if an incumbrancer has neglected to protect his interest by the appropriate registration, equity will not prevent a third party purchaser of land from relying on a statutory right to take free of the interest in question.[5] Equity will only intervene in the event of an attempt to renege on an undertaking or agreement. Thus in *Bannister v. Bannister*[6] the defendant sold and conveyed two adjoining cottages to the plaintiff on the basis that she could continue to occupy one of them rent free for as long as she wished. When he subsequently sought to evict her on the basis that the conveyance did not mention her right of occupation, she successfully counterclaimed for a declaration that the plaintiff held the cottage on trust for her for her lifetime. The Court of Appeal classified as fraudulent the conduct of the plaintiff in attempting to rely on the absence of the writing which the Law of Property Act 1925 requires for the creation of the interest claimed by the

---

[99] Forfeiture Act 1982 s.2(2).

[1] [1985] 1 W.L.R. 262 (Vinelott J.), [1986] Ch. 180 (C.A.).

[2] *Rochefoucauld v. Boustead* [1897] 1 Ch. 196, 206.

[3] s.2 requires that all the terms of such a contract must be in writing and signed by all the parties.

[4] s.53(1)(*b*). See *ante*, p. 34.

[5] *Midland Bank Trust Company v. Green* [1981] A.C. 513.

[6] [1948] W.N. 261.

defendant and imposed a constructive trust under which he held the property on trust for her for her lifetime.[7] In this case, the informal agreement in question was being enforced by the person in whose favour it had originally been made; however, equity is equally prepared to enforce agreements made for the benefit of third parties. Thus in *Binions* v. *Evans*[8] a cottage was sold at a reduced price on the basis that the purchasers would honour the right of a widow of a former employee of the vendor to occupy the property rent-free for the rest of her life. When they sought to evict her, the majority of the Court of Appeal classified the conduct of the purchasers as unconscionable, applied *Bannister* v. *Bannister* and imposed a constructive trust on the purchasers to give effect to the interest of the widow.[9] Similarly, in *Lyus* v. *Prowsa Developments*[10] a building plot was sold by mortgagees subject to and with the benefit of a building contract between the mortgagor and the plaintiffs. The purchaser subsequently claimed to have taken the land free of this contract because the plaintiffs had failed to protect it in the manner required by the Land Registration Act 1925. It was held that the provision in the contract of sale relating to the building contract had conferred new rights on the plaintiffs, which the purchaser had expressly agreed to honour. Consequently, because of the subsequent attempt to renege on this agreement, the purchaser held the plot on constructive trust to complete the house thereon and convey the plot to the plaintiffs for the price agreed in the original contract.

4. The Legacy of the "new model" Constructive Trust[11]

Until relatively recently the courts limited the imposition of constructive trusts for the purpose of granting relief against fraudulent and unconscionable conduct to the extreme situations which have been considered so far. However, in the years immediately before and after 1970, a series of decisions emanating from the Court of Appeal imposed constructive trusts of this type not only as a result of fraudulent or unconscionable conduct but also as a result of conduct which the individual judges were prepared to classify merely as inequitable. The underlying and indeed often expressed objective of the judges in question was to prevent results which would otherwise have been inequitable. If application of the basic principles of property law led to a result which, in the view of the court in question, was contrary to good conscience, that court acted upon the conscience of the party who would otherwise have obtained this unjust benefit and imposed a constructive trust upon him to bring the result into line with the

---

[7] This caused the imposition of a settlement under the Settled Land Act 1925 and thus potentially involved the reconveyance of the cottage to the defendant, an admittedly odd result but one of which the plaintiff could hardly complain.

[8] [1972] Ch. 359.

[9] Lord Denning M.R. reached the same conclusion by a different route (see *post*, p. 280).

[10] [1982] 1 W.L.R. 1044. This decision has been criticised on the grounds that it casts doubt on the ability of a purchaser to rely on his statutory right to take free of incumbrances of which he is aware but which have not been protected in the appropriate way. However, the decision is explicable for the reasons stated in the text.

[11] This expression was coined by Lord Denning M.R. in *Eves* v. *Eves* [1975] 1 W.L.R. 1338.

requirements of justice. This approach was, of course, much closer to the American attitude to the constructive trust[12] and was thought to be symptomatic of a general change of attitude towards the constructive trust. However, subsequent decisions have rejected the approach manifested in this series of cases and English law seems for the moment to have reverted to its traditional position. The recent acceptance by the Court of Appeal that "there is a good arguable case" for the existence of a "remedial constructive trust"[13] may well indicate the possibility of a move towards a more remedial approach but this is likely to be of a much more limited nature than the attempt made in the years immediately before and after 1970 to convert the constructive trust into a general equitable remedy capable of doing justice in any individual case. This does not mean, however, that the series of decisions handed down at that time can be wholly ignored. While their influence on the law governing contractual licences has, admittedly, been almost wholly negated, their influence on the law governing joint enterprises entered into by the members of a family unit has undoubtedly played some part in the development of what some commentators now call "the common intention constructive trust.[14]

(a) Contractual Licences

Contractual licences have traditionally been regarded more as creatures of the law of contract than of the law of property. While it has long[15] been recognised that a contractual licensee may, in appropriate circumstances, be able to obtain the assistance of equity to force the licensor to perform his contract,[16] until 1952 it had never been suggested that he had any proprietary right in the subject matter of his licence capable of binding a third party, unless the latter had in some way estopped himself from revoking the licence.[17] However, in *Errington* v. *Errington and Woods*,[18] despite the existence of clear House of Lords authority to the contrary,[19] the Court of Appeal held that a contractual licence which could be enforced in this way against the licensor created an interest in land capable of binding third parties. Despite subsequent doubts,[20] Lord Denning M.R. carried this novel

---

[12] See *ante*, p. 217.
[13] In *Metall und Rohstoff A.G.* v. *Donaldson Lufkin & Jenrette* [1989] 3 W.L.R. 563, 621.
[14] See, particularly, D. J. Hayton in [1990] Conv. 370 and in Hayton & Marshall: *op.cit.* pp. 497–510.
[15] Since *Winter Garden Theatre (London)* v. *Millenium Productions* [1948] A.C. 173.
[16] *Foster* v. *Robinson* [1951] 1 K.B. 149 (injunction), *Verrall* v. *Great Yarmouth Borough Council* [1981] Q.B. 202 (specific performance).
[17] *Inwards* v. *Baker* [1965] 2 Q.B. 29, *Greasley* v. *Cooke* [1980] 1 W.L.R. 1306, *Hopgood* v. *Brown* [1955] 1 All E.R. 550, *E.R. Ives Investment* v. *High* [1967] 2 Q.B. 379. In *Re Basham* [1986] 1 W.L.R. 1498 the existence of a proprietary estoppel was held to give rise to the existence of a "floating" constructive trust like that which arises in the case of Mutual Wills (see *post*, p. 285) but this view is generally held to be misconceived.
[18] [1952] 1 K.B. 290.
[19] *King* v. *David Allen and Sons, Billposting* [1916] 2 A.C. 54.
[20] As a result of *National Provincial Bank* v. *Hastings Car Mart* [1965] A.C. 1175, 1239, 1251 (matter left open for future discussion) and *Re Solomon (A Bankrupt)* [1967] Ch. 573, 583 (contrary view preferred).

proposition a stage further in *Binions* v. *Evans*[21] by holding that such a licence could be enforced by the imposition of a constructive trust if it was just and equitable so to do, a view which was subsequently ratified by the whole of the Court of Appeal in *D.H.N. Food Distributors* v. *Tower Hamlets L.B.C.*[22] However, the Court of Appeal subsequently "put the *quietus* to the heresy that a mere licence creates an interest in land"[23] in *Ashburn Anstalt* v. *Arnold*.[24] The court accepted that a third party who attempted to renege on an agreement or undertaking to honour a contractual licence would be liable as a constructive trustee in the manner which has already been discussed.[25] However, in the absence of any such agreement or undertaking, the court held that a contractual licence could bind no third party and that in such circumstances it would not be appropriate for a constructive trust to be imposed. Although the court obviously could not overrule *Errington* v. *Errington and Woods*, it stated that that decision had been made *per incuriam*, which makes it unlikely that anything further will be heard either of the principle enunciated therein or of its subsequent extension in *Binions* v. *Evans*. This legacy of the "new model" constructive trust thus appears to have been nullified.

(b) Joint enterprises by members of a family unit

It has already been seen[26] that where property has been purchased in the name of another it will be presumed to result to whoever actually provided the purchase moneys, including if appropriate the person into whose name the property has been put, in proportion to their respective contributions. Such resulting trusts are just as applicable to joint enterprises by members of a family unit as to any other situation. However, during the last thirty years, the courts have had to grapple with an increasing variety of less direct contributions to the acquisition of property made by members of family units, whose interests have often been protected by what have been described[27] as "common intention constructive trusts" and, more recently, by the principle of equitable proprietary estoppel.

The first cases of this type concerned the devolution of matrimonial property on the breakdown of marriage. The law contained in these cases no longer applies where the marriage has been terminated since the courts have now acquired the absolute discretion to vary matrimonial property rights at the termination of marriage[28] but is still applicable to disputes that arise during marriage concerning the property rights of the spouses, to analogous situations involving unmarried couples and to other types of joint enterprise. The

---

[21] [1972] Ch. 359, see *ante*, p. 278.

[22] [1976] 1 W.L.R. 852.

[23] *I.D.C. Group* v. *Clark* [1992] 1 E.G.L.R. 187, 190.

[24] [1988] 2 W.L.R. 706.

[25] See *ante*, p. 277.

[26] See *ante*, p. 189.

[27] See, particularly, D. J. Hayton in [1990] Conv. 370 and in Hayton & Marshall: *op.cit.* pp. 497–510.

[28] Under what is now Matrimonial Causes Act 1973 s.25.

underlying principle applicable to cases of this type was laid down by
the House of Lords in *Pettitt* v. *Pettitt*[29] and *Gissing* v. *Gissing*,[30] namely
that property rights have to be determined in the light of the intentions
of the parties at the time of acquisition of the property. However, in
Gissing v. *Gissing* Lord Diplock said this[31]:

> "A resulting, implied or constructive trust—and it is unnecessary
> for present purposes to distinguish between these three classes of
> trust—is created by a transaction between the trustee and the *cestui
> que trust* in connection with the acquisition by the trustee of a legal
> estate in land, whenever the trustee has so conducted himself that
> it would be inequitable to deny to the *cestui que trust* a beneficial
> interest in the land acquired. And he will be held so to have
> conducted himself if by his words or conduct he has induced the
> *cestui que trust* to act to his own detriment in the reasonable belief
> that by so acting he was acquiring a beneficial interest in the land."

The first sentence of this passage, when isolated from the qualification subsequently placed thereon, appears to suggest that the courts
may impose a constructive trust to do justice *inter partes* whenever the
result would, otherwise, be inequitable and it was indeed cited as
authority for that proposition in several subsequent cases in the Court
of Appeal,[32] in one of which[33] Lord Denning M.R. stated that
"whenever two parties by their joint efforts acquire property to be used
for their joint benefit, the courts may impose or impute a constructive or
resulting trust".

The two different approaches can be seen side by side in *Eves* v.
Eves.[34] The parties, who were living together as man and wife,
purchased a delapidated house as a home for themselves and their
children, which was conveyed into the sole name of the man because he
pretended to the woman that she was too young to acquire the legal
title. All the purchase price was found by the man but the woman did a
very considerable amount of work on the house. In the Court of Appeal
she was granted a one-quarter share therein under a constructive trust.
Lord Denning M.R. imposed a "new model" constructive trust on the
strength of the first sentence of the passage cited above. But the
majority applied *Pettitt* v. *Pettitt* and *Gissing* v. *Gissing* correctly, holding
that it could be inferred from the circumstances that there had been an
arrangement between the parties whereby the woman was to acquire a
beneficial interest in the house in return for her labour in contributing
to its repair and improvement; this entitled her to an interest under
what was subsequently been called a "common intention constructive

---

[29] [1970] A.C. 777.
[30] [1971] A.C. 886.
[31] *Ibid.* 905.
[32] *Heseltine* v. *Heseltine* [1971] 1 W.L.R. 342 (dispute during marriage concerning the
property rights of the spouses), *Cooke* v. *Head* [1972] 1 W.L.R. 518 (unmarried couple),
Hussey v. *Palmer* [1972] 1 W.L.R. 1286 (joint enterprise between married couple and
parent).
[33] *Cooke* v. *Head* [1972] 1 W.L.R. 518, 520.
[34] [1975] 1 W.L.R. 1338.

trust". Subsequent cases have preferred this latter approach[35] and the scope of the "common intention constructive trust" has now been restated, if anything more narrowly, by the House of Lords in *Lloyds Bank* v. *Rosset*.[36]

In this case Lord Bridge, speaking for the House of Lords, said this[37]:

"The first and fundamental question which must always be resolved is whether, independently of any inference to be drawn from the conduct of the parties in the course of sharing the house as their home and managing their joint affairs, there has at any time prior to acquisition, or exceptionally at some later date, been any agreement, arrangement or understanding reached between them that the property is to be shared beneficially. The finding of an agreement or arrangement to share in this sense can only, I think, be based on evidence of express discussions between the partners, however, imperfectly remembered and however imprecise their terms may have been. Once a finding to this effect is made it will only be necessary for the partner asserting a claim to a beneficial interest against the partner entitled to the legal estate to show that he or she has acted to his or her detriment or significantly altered his or her position in reliance on the agreement in order to give rise to a constructive trust or a proprietary estoppel.

In sharp contrast with this situation is the very different one where there is no evidence to support a finding of an agreement or an arrangement to share, however reasonable it might have been for the parties to reach such an agreement if they had applied their minds to the question, and where the court must rely entirely on the conduct of the parties both as the basis from which to infer a common intention to share the property beneficially and as the conduct relied on to give rise to a constructive trust. In this situation direct contributions to the purchase price by the partner who is not the legal owner, whether initially or by payment of mortgage instalments, will readily justify the inference necessary to the creation of a constructive trust. But, as I read the authorities, it is at least extremely doubtful whether anything less will do."

This admirably succinct statement of the present law establishes that, provided that there has been some express agreement, arrangement or understanding that the property is to be shared beneficially, then any act of detriment, whether or not actually envisaged by the agreement, will be sufficient to give rise to a constructive trust; on the other hand, where an agreement between the parties can only be inferred, only direct financial contributions to the purchase price will justify the inference necessary to give rise to a constructive trust.

---

[35] *Midland Bank* v. *Dobson* [1986] 1 F.L.R. 171 (dispute during marriage concerning the property rights of the spouses), *Burns* v. *Burns* [1984] 2 W.L.R. 582, *Grant* v. *Edwards* [1986] 3 W.L.R. 114 (unmarried couples), *Re Sharpe (a bankrupt)* [1980] 1 W.L.R. 219 (joint enterprise between nephew and aunt).

[36] [1990] 2 W.L.R. 867.

[37] *Ibid.* 877.

The first limb of this test is, if anything, broader than the pre-existing law; where some express agreement can be found, not only the contribution envisaged in that agreement but also any other act of detriment, even if none was envisaged, will give rise to a constructive trust. Thus, if *Eves* v. *Eves* recurred, provided that there had indeed been an express agreement that the woman was to have an interest, it would now be irrelevant whether or not the parties had envisaged that she would do her very considerable amount of work on the house; all that would matter would be that she had actually done so.

On the other hand, the second limb of this test is considerably narrower than the pre-existing law. In the absence of an express agreement, no matter how much work the woman in *Eves* v. *Eves* had done she would not now obtain a beneficial interest simply because she had not made any direct financial contribution to the purchase price. Thus in *Lloyds Bank* v. *Rosset* itself, the wife had supervised builders who were renovating a delapidated building and had herself done a certain amount of preparatory cleaning and some painting and decorating but had made no direct contribution to the purchase price; this was held to be insufficient to justify the inference of any common intention that she should have a beneficial interest. It is of course highly desirable that unsolicited work on the property of another should not, in the absence of express subsequent ratification, lead to the creation of an interest therein. However, the requirement for a direct financial contribution to the purchase price may cause difficulties when substantial indirect financial contributions to, for example, household expenses have been necessary to enable the holder of the legal title to repay the mortgage. There will obviously be no difficulty where there is direct evidence of an express common intention that the contributer is to have a beneficial interest,[38] since this situation will fall within the first limb of the test. In the absence of any such express agreement, prior to *Lloyds Bank* v. *Rosset* such contributions would have caused such a common intention to be inferred.[39] However, it appears that such contributions will now be insufficient to justify the inference necessary to give rise to a constructive trust; the contributer will therefore presumably be limited to claiming what is likely to be a much smaller beneficial interest under a resulting trust proportional to the contributions actually made. This aspect of the present law may well require some reconsideration.

Further difficulties[40] may arise in quantifying the beneficial interests. Where the express common intention of the parties envisaged that the beneficial interest should be held in specific proportions, then this common intention should clearly be upheld provided that the parties have duly made whatever contribution was envisaged. But what is to happen where one of the parties has failed to provide the whole of the

---

[38] This was the situation in *Grant* v. *Edwards* [1986] 3 W.L.R. 114, a decision which was expressly approved by Lord Bridge in *Lloyds Bank* v. *Rosset*.

[39] As in *Burns* v. *Burns* [1984] 2 W.L.R. 582.

[40] Highlighted by D. J. Hayton in [1990] Conv. 370 and in Hayton & Marshall: *op.cit.* pp. 497–510.

contribution which was envisaged?[41] The difficulties are even greater where a common intention envisaging a beneficial interest but no contribution is followed by acts of detriment in reliance on the existence of the beneficial interest. Are the beneficial interests to be quantified in the proportions envisaged quite irrelevant of the scale of the acts of detrimental reliance? These questions have yet to be considered by the courts but it has been suggested[42] that the courts should adopt the flexible approach already utilised in the area of equitable proprietary estoppel and provide a remedy appropriate to the circumstances of each individual case.[43] There is no doubt that in this area of the law there is an increasing overlap between the "common intention constructive trust" and the doctrine of equitable proprietary estoppel[44]; indeed it has been suggested[45] that the distinction between the two is now quite illusory and that it is "time that the courts and counsel moved beyond pigeon-holing circumstances into common intention constructive trusts and equitable estoppels and concentrated upon the basic principle of unconscionability underlying both doctrines".[46] The principle of unconscionability certainly underlies "common intention constructive trusts"; it is only appropriate to classify them as constructive trusts at all because of the fact that in cases of this type the holder of the legal title will almost inevitably have attempted to go back on an express agreement or common intention. Indeed it is precisely for this reason that, when there is no such express agreement or common intention, only direct contributions to the purchase price will do, a proposition which is only another way of saying that in such circumstances the trust which arises is resulting rather than constructive. It is clear that this area of the law has yet to find its final form; however, unless and until the House of Lords chooses to go back on *Lloyds Bank* v. *Rosset*, the principles enunciated in that decision constitute the framework within which the profession and the lower courts must attempt to operate.

The legacy of the "new model" constructive trust in this area of the law has therefore been to produce a line of authority culminating in *Lloyds Bank* v. *Rosset* and, ironically, in a considerable narrowing of the circumstances in which this type of constructive trust will be held to arise. This in turn has thrown into sharper relief the principle of unconscionability which now underlies much more clearly the new "common intention constructive trusts". The short existence of the "new model" constructive trust may therefore in the end lead to the development of a general principle of unconscionability to replace both

---

[41] Hayton & Marshall: *op.cit.* 502 envisages the situation where half of the potential contribution is withheld.

[42] *Ibid.*

[43] Following suggestions made by Browne-Wilkinson V.-C. in *Grant* v. *Edwards* [1986] 3 W.L.R. 114, 129–130.

[44] See particularly *per* Browne-Wilkinson V.-C. in *Grant* v. *Edwards* [1986] 3 W.L.R. 114, 129–130 and *per* Lord Bridge in *Lloyds Bank* v. *Rosset* [1990] 2 W.L.R. 867, 877.

[45] In Hayton & Marshall: *op.cit.* 506–507.

[46] *Ibid.* 507.

the "common intention constructive trusts" and the doctrine of equitable proprietary estoppel.

V. MUTUAL WILLS

Mutual wills arise where two or more persons enter into a legally binding agreement to make wills in a particular form with the intention that the provisions of such wills will be irrevocably binding. As soon as the first of the parties dies leaving a will made in accordance with the agreement, equity regards that agreement as irrevocable so far as the survivor is concerned and gives effect to it by the imposition of a trust. Thus if the survivor ultimately leaves his property other than in accordance with the agreement, his personal representatives will be deemed to hold it on trust for the agreed beneficiary.

This intervention of equity is, on the face of things, directly contrary to the Wills Act 1837 in that the agreement between the parties will normally[47] have to be proved by evidence which does not comply with the formal requirements for wills contained in s.9 thereof. This provision was enacted for an obvious and important reason of policy— to ensure that false claims cannot be generated after the death of a testator when he is in no position to refute them. However, it has long been accepted that the intervention of equity can be justified by the fact that the survivor would otherwise be enabled to benefit by his own fraud.[48] As soon as one of the parties dies leaving a will made in accordance with the agreement, he will irrevocably have disposed of his property in reliance upon the agreement. Therefore any revocation of the mutual will at this stage will be a blatant fraud in that it will enable the survivor to take the benefit for which he contracted—the disposition by the other party of his property in accordance with that agreement—without the corresponding burden. This will be the case not only where the survivor takes some material benefit under the will but also where he disclaims any such benefit and where the agreement gave him no such benefit since in all three situations he will have obtained the benefit which he sought—the disposition of the property under the will. Consequently, equity imposes a trust to prevent the survivor from benefiting by his own fraud.

1. *The Prerequisites of Mutual Wills*

(a) A legally binding agreement between the parties
Evidence must be adduced that the parties intended that the provisions of their wills should be irrevocably binding. The best conceivable evidence is obviously recitals in the wills themselves. In *Re Hagger*[49] a

---

[47] The agreement between the parties may be recited in one or both of the wills in question although this is not usually the case. It will certainly not be mentioned in any will executed in breach of the agreement.

[48] *Dufour* v. *Pereira* (1769) Dick 419, 421 (better reported in 2 Hargrave, *Jurisconsult Exercitations* 100, 104).

[49] [1930] 2 Ch. 190.

husband and wife made a joint will[50] which expressly stated that the parties had agreed to dispose of their property by that will and that there was to be no alteration or revocation except by agreement. Although the mere fact that the parties had made a joint will did not necessarily make it a mutual will, this recital clearly showed that the parties had agreed to bind themselves to make a mutual will. Equally convincing proof will be recitals of this type in the separate wills of the parties to the agreement. However, cases only tend to reach the courts where the survivor has revoked his mutual will in breach of the agreement and in such a situation his will will obviously contain no such recital. A recital in the sole will of the first party to die will be no more than prima facie evidence of an agreement.[51] In such a case and also in situations where there is no mention of any agreement in either will, the agreement will have to be proved by other forms of evidence. No agreement will be inferred merely because two parties make wills in substantially similar forms. In Re Oldham[52] a husband and wife both made wills leaving their property to the other absolutely with the same alternative provisions in the event of the other's predecease. Although it was clear that they had agreed to make substantially identical wills, no evidence could be adduced of any agreement not to revoke and so the judge declined to infer such an agreement, particularly since both had left their property to the other absolutely (although this will clearly be a factor against the implication of such an agreement, there is nothing to prevent parties expressly agreeing to make mutual wills in this form, something which occured both in Re Green[53] and in Re Cleaver[54]). In such circumstances, convincing extrinsic evidence of the intentions of the parties will have to be adduced.

(b) A disposition of property in accordance with the agreement
Equity will only intervene once one of the parties has died leaving a will made in accordance with the agreement. The vast majority of mutual wills involve the parties making a disposition in favour of the other with the same ultimate or substitutionary beneficiary; thus each party may leave property to the other for life and subject thereto to the same third party[55] or to the other absolutely with the same substitutionary provisions in the event of predecease.[56] The property in question is most commonly the residuary estate of each but there is no reason why the agreement should not be for each to leave a specific sum of money or specific assets in this way with no restriction whatever on the disposition of the residue. Even where the agreement in question is for each party to dispose of his residue in this manner, it is common for

---

[50] Such a document takes effect not as one will but as the separate wills of each party and is admitted to probate successively as the will of each testator.

[51] If it is finally found that there is insufficient evidence to prove the existence of mutual wills, it is possible that the equitable doctrine of election may apply.

[52] [1925] Ch. 75.

[53] [1951] Ch. 148.

[54] [1981] 1 W.L.R. 939.

[55] As in Re Haggar [1930] 2 Ch. 190.

[56] As in Re Green [1951] Ch. 148 and Re Cleaver [1981] 1 W.L.R. 939.

each to make individual specific bequests or pecuniary legacies.[57] Until recently it has been unclear whether or not it is a prerequisite of the doctrine of mutual wills that the will of the first to die should, as in all the examples discussed so far, contain some disposition in favour of the survivor; however, it has now been established that this is not actually necessary. In *Re Dale*[58] spouses both made wills which they had agreed should be irrevocable in favour of their two children in equal shares. It was contended that the doctrine of mutual wills could only operate where the survivor obtained a personal financial benefit under the will of the first to die. Morritt J. rejected this argument, holding that it would be no less a fraud on the first to die if the agreement was that each party should leave his property to third parties rather than to the other; in both cases the survivor would have obtained the benefit for which he had contracted—the agreed disposition of property in the will of the first to die. It must follow from this decision that the survivor will be equally bound to dispose of his property in accordance with the agreement if he disclaims any benefit to which he is entitled under the will of the first to die; in this case also he will have obtained the benefit for which he has contracted but will have freely chosen to renounce it.[59] A further question, which has not yet been considered by the courts, is whether the doctrine of mutual wills is limited to agreements which, as in all the examples discussed so far, are in substantially similar form. Will the doctrine also operate if the agreement is that, if the first party leaves property to the second party, the latter will leave that property and other property of his own on to a third party? Such an agreement is obviously subject to two conditions precedent: the first party must die before the second party and must leave the property in question to him; equally obviously, if either of these pre-conditions is not fulfilled, the second party will clearly be under no obligation whatsoever to leave his own property to the third party. On the assumption that the necessary legally binding agreement in this form can be proved, there seems no reason why this situation should not be regarded as falling within the doctrine of mutual wills; if so, once the first party has predeceased the second party having made the appropriate disposition of property in his favour, equity will intervene to prevent the second party from going back on the agreement.

2. *The Effect of Mutual Wills*

(a) Before either party has died

Equity will not intervene until one of the parties has died leaving a will made in accordance with the agreement. Consequently the position before either party has died will be governed by contractual principles. Like any other contract, the agreement between the parties can of course be revoked at any time by mutual agreement. If on the other hand, one party unilaterally revokes his mutual will in breach of the

---

[57] As in *Re Cleaver* [1981] 1 W.L.R. 939.

[58] [1993] 3 W.L.R. 652.

[59] This was stated *obiter* in *Re Haggar* [1930] 2 Ch. 190 and must now clearly have been confirmed by *Re Dale* [1993] 3 W.L.R. 652.

agreement during the lifetime of the other, the latter will be able to recover damages for breach of contract. However, since the only possible loss is loss of the right to receive an unascertained amount at an unascertained time in the future and since the other party still has unrestricted powers to dispose of his own property, it is relatively unlikely that any substantial damages could be recovered. A further bar to any successful action for damages in these circumstances is the fact that it seems that no such action will be available if the mutual will was revoked not by the act of the party but by operation of law (for example by his marriage, divorce or remarriage[60]); it appears that only intentional revocation will ground an action for damages.[61] Thus, while it is clear that revocation of the mutual will during the joint lives of the parties will determine the agreement and release the other party from his obligations thereunder,[62] no effective remedy is likely to result to the other party.

(b) Where the first party to die does not leave a will made in accordance with the agreement

If the other party does not discover that the first party to die has revoked his will until after the latter has died without leaving a will in accordance with the agreement, he will be able to claim damages from the latter's estate. However, although the loss suffered will certainly be able to be quantified in such a case, the other party will not have relinquished his powers over his own property and so may still find difficulty in obtaining substantial damages. The only exception to this seems to be the situation where he himself dies so soon after the first party to die that he does not have any opportunity of changing his own will and so dies leaving a will made in accordance with the agreement; in these circumstances, there seems no reason why his estate should not successfully bring an action for damages for breach of contract against the estate of the first to die for the value of the property which, according to the agreement, should have been disposed of in the will of the first to die. Save in this exceptional situation, however, where the first party to die does not leave a will made in accordance with the agreement, while it is clear that the survivor will be released from his own obligations under the agreement, he is unlikely to have any effective remedy against the estate of the first to die.

(c) Where the first party to die leaves a will made in accordance with the agreement:[63]

Once the first party to die has made the disposition of property envisaged by the agreement, a trust is immediately imposed upon the survivor for the benefit of those entitled under the agreement. This

---

[60] Wills Act 1837 ss.18, 18A.

[61] *Robinson* v. *Ommanney* (1883) 23 Ch.D. 285. See also *Re Marsland* [1939] Ch. 820, where the Court of Appeal reached a similar conclusion in respect of a covenant not to revoke a will contained in a deed of separation.

[62] *Stone* v. *Hoskins* [1905] P. 194.

[63] See J. D. B. Mitchell: (1951) 14 M.L.R. 137.

emerges most clearly from *Re Hagger*[64] where one of the ultimate beneficiaries under the joint mutual will of a husband and wife survived the
wife but predeceased the husband. Clauson J. held that her interest
under the trust imposed by equity arose on the death of the first to die,
the wife, and therefore did not lapse when she predeceased the
husband.

The purpose of the imposition of the trust is to prevent the survivor
from revoking his will in breach of the agreement. However, equity
does not interfere with the fundamental probate principle that no will is
irrevocable. If the survivor revokes his mutual will in breach of the
agreement, his property will pass under his new will or his intestacy to
his personal representatives, who will hold it on trust to give effect to
the agreement.[65] This will be the case even if the will is revoked by
operation of law upon a subsequent marriage, divorce or remarriage.[66]
However, whether or not the survivor revokes his will, difficulties arise
in determining precisely what property is subject to the trust. Of course
this will primarily be determined by the agreement. In *Re Green*[67] the
agreement specifically provided that each party would leave his
property to the other absolutely and, at the death of the survivor, half
his residuary estate was to be treated as his property and the other half
as property received under the will of the first to die. Vaisey J. held that
only the property which was to be treated as the property of the first to
die was subject to the trust. This decision is justifiable as a matter of
construction of the agreement in question but certainly cannot apply
where an agreement contains no such provision. In such a case, there is
absolutely no doubt that the property received by the survivor under
the mutual will is subject to a trust. If the survivor receives a limited
interest, such as a life interest, the property will already be held on an
express trust and so there is no scope for the trust imposed by equity. If,
on the other hand, he receives an absolute interest, a trust will clearly be
imposed but its precise nature is far from clear. In one sense, the
survivor will be holding the property on trust for himself for his lifetime
and then for the benefit of the ultimate beneficiary of the mutual will.
But it is most unclear whether the interest of the survivor is a life
interest in the technical sense (in which case he will have no right to
resort to the capital) or whether the survivor has the right to dispose of
the capital for his own benefit. This problem becomes even more acute
when the survivor's own property is considered. Is this property
subject to a trust from the time the first party dies and, if so, what is the
nature of this trust?

It seems fairly clear from the decision in *Re Hagger*[68] that the
survivor's own property is subject to a trust from the death of the first
party since in that case the beneficiary was held to have an interest in
property which was quite clearly vested in the survivor until his death.

---

[64] [1930] 2 Ch. 190.
[65] *In the Estate of Heys* [1914] P. 192.
[66] *Re Green* [1951] Ch. 148.
[67] [1951] Ch. 148.
[68] [1930] 2 Ch. 190.

But if all the property owned by the survivor at the death of the first party becomes subject to a trust in favour of himself for life and thereafter for the ultimate beneficiary of the mutual will, the survivor will not be able to dispose of his own property for his own benefit without committing a breach of trust. Further, what happens to any property acquired by the survivor after the death of the first party? Does it immediately become subject to the same trust? If so, the effect of the death of the first party will be to make the survivor a life tenant not only of the property which he receives under the will but also of his own property, whether then existing or after acquired. The survivor will therefore have no power during the rest of his life to apply any capital for his own benefit. It could of course on the other hand be argued that the intention of the parties could reasonably be assumed to be that the survivor has the right to deal as he wishes with his own property and perhaps also with the property left to him absolutely under the terms of the agreement. The difficulty about this view is that the trust imposed by equity then becomes so uncertain as to be virtually useless since the survivor can destroy the subject matter of the agreement by alienation or dissipation.

The English courts have been spared the task of considering this problem because most litigation involving mutual wills does not commence until after the death of the survivor—only then will the ultimate beneficiary discover whether or not the survivor has honoured his agreement. Litigation commenced at this stage can in practice only be concerned with the property owned by the survivor at his death and so English courts have generally been content to apply the terms of the agreement to this property. However, in the Australian case of *Birmingham* v. *Renfrew*,[69] Dixon J. considered the issue and said this[70]:

"The purpose of an arrangement for corresponding wills must often be, as in this case, to enable the survivor during his life to deal as absolute owner with the property passing under the will of the party first dying. That is to say, the object of the transaction is to put the survivor in a position to enjoy for his own benefit the full ownership so that, for instance, he may convert it and expend the proceeds if he choose. But when he dies he is to bequeath what is left in the manner agreed upon. It is only by the special doctrines of equity that such a floating obligation, suspended, so to speak, during the lifetime of the survivor can descend upon the assets at his death and crystallise into a trust. No doubt gifts and settlements, *inter vivos*, if calculated to defeat the intention of the compact, could not be made by the survivor and his right of disposition, *inter vivos*, is, therefore, not unqualified. But, substantially, the purpose of the arrangement will often be to allow full enjoyment for the survivor's own benefit and advantage upon condition that at his death the residue shall pass as arranged."

---

[69] (1937) 57 C.L.R. 666 (High Court of Australia).
[70] *Ibid.* p. 689.

A somewhat similar view was expressed by Brightman J. in *Ottaway v. Norman*,[71] a case concerning secret trusts, where he said:

"I am content to assume for present purposes but without so deciding that if property is given to the primary donee on the understanding that the primary donee will dispose by will of such assets, if any, as he may have at his command at his death in favour of the secondary donee, a valid trust is created in favour of the secondary donee which is in suspense during the lifetime of the primary donee, but attaches to the estate of the primary donee at the moment of the latter's death."

Both these views undoubtedly recognise what actually happens in most mutual will cases; the only difference between them is that Dixon J. seems to envisage the possibility of the ultimate beneficiary restraining an *inter vivos* disposition by the survivor whereas Brightman J. instead limits the scope of the trust to the property available to the survivor at this death (this difference may be because Brightman J. was actually dealing with a secret trust rather than with mutual wills). It would be extremely interesting to see how a court reacted to such an attempt to restrain an *inter vivos* disposition by the survivor and, in particular, whether any relief given was limited to the property received under the will of the first to die or extended to the survivor's own property. In any event, it seems hardly satisfactory to describe the suspended obligation referred to by both judges as a trust, since such an obligation lacks the element of certainty of subject matter which is one of the principal requirements of a trust. Perhaps the only answer is to regard the trust imposed to give effect to mutual wills as an entrenched anomaly.

3. *The Nature of the Trust Imposed by Equity*

It is quite clear that the trust imposed to give effect to mutual wills is not an express trust. However, there is a difference of opinion as to whether this trust is an implied or resulting trust or a constructive trust. Nothing turns on the classification adopted. Previous editions of this work have suggested that it should be classified as an "implied, though not a resulting" trust.[72] However, in *Re Cleaver*[73] Nourse J. took the view that it should be classified as a constructive trust. Both views are referred to with apparent approval in different sections of the judgment in *Re Dale*.[74] However, since this trust is imposed to prevent the survivor obtaining a benefit by his own fraudulent conduct, it seems to the editor of the present edition that it is akin to the types of constructive trust described in the previous section of this Chapter and so should be classified as a constructive trust.

---

[71] [1972] Ch. 698, 713.
[72] (5th ed.) 154.
[73] [1981] 1 W.L.R. 939.
[74] [1993] 3 W.L.R. 652.

VI. THE VENDOR AS CONSTRUCTIVE TRUSTEE

When a vendor has entered into a contract of sale which is capable of being specifically enforced, equity in accordance with one of its earliest maxims regards as done that which ought to be done. Consequently, the equitable doctrine of conversion operates and equity regards the purchaser as owner of the subject matter of the contract and the vendor as owner of the purchase money. The operation of this equitable doctrine does not, of course, affect the legal title to the subject matter of the contract, which remains in the vendor pending performance of the contract. Thus the effect of the operation of the doctrine is to separate the legal and beneficial ownership of the property and it is only to be expected that equity therefore regards the vendor as a constructive trustee of the property pending performance of the contract. No corresponding trust of the purchase money will arise simply because such a trust would lack the necessary certainty of subject matter but the vendor acquires a lien or charge on the property for the unpaid purchase money.

The operation of the equitable doctrine of conversion and the consequent constructive trust are important because of the effect that can be produced both upon the devolution of property and upon the liabilities of the parties. Where a party to a contract dies after the equitable doctrine has operated, his property will devolve as if the contract has been performed. Thus, if a vendor or purchaser of freehold land dies after the doctrine of conversion has operated, the interest of the vendor devolves with his personalty and the interest of the purchaser devolves with his realty. However today[75] this is important only in the relatively unlikely case of a testator leaving his realty and his personalty (or his land and pure personalty) to different persons. However, the effect of the operation of the doctrine of conversion on the liabilities of the parties remains as important today as it has ever been because of the fact that the vendor becomes a trustee of the subject matter of the contract. His liability to deal with the property as a trustee can be relied on by the purchaser not only in the event that the vendor fails to take reasonable care to preserve the property in a reasonable state of preservation[76] but also to recover secret profits[77] and to follow the subject matter of the trust into its product[78]; the corollary of this, however, is that the purchaser becomes liable for all the risks attendant upon ownership, in particular that of accidental destruction.[79] Of course, this trusteeship of the vendor is of an extremely unusual nature; the vendor himself retains a substantial interest in the property for the simple reason that, in the event that the contract is not in the end

---

[75] Before 1926, when real and personal property devolved in different ways on intestacy, this effect was of much greater importance.

[76] *Clarke* v. *Ramuz* [1891] 2 Q.B. 456, 459–460.

[77] *English* v. *Dedham Vale Properties* [1978] 1 W.L.R. 95.

[78] *Lake* v. *Bayliss* [1974] 1 W.L.R. 1075.

[79] The Law Commission has proposed that this risk should pass only on completion (Law Commission No. 191 (1990) Para. 2. 25) and a provision to this effect has been inserted in the Standard Conditions of Sale (2nd ed. (1992)) Cond. 5.1.1.

completed, he will once again become absolute legal and beneficial owner; further, he is entitled to receive and retain any income produced by the property until the completion of the sale.[80] However, as soon as the purchase price has been paid in full, the qualified nature of the vendor's trusteeship will disappear since he no longer has any interest to protect and from that moment onwards he will be a bare trustee of the property for the purchaser.

Since the doctrine of conversion will only operate when a contract of sale is capable of being specifically enforced, it is a prerequisite that the failure of the vendor to transfer the subject matter of the contract to the purchaser is incapable of being adequately compensated by an award of damages. Little or no difficulties have been encountered in applying the equitable doctrine to the relatively few contracts for the sale of chattels which satisfy this requirement[81]; such contracts are capable of being specifically enforced from the moment at which they are entered into and so the vendor under such a contract will hold its subject matter on trust for the purchaser from the moment of contract. However, the vast majority of contracts which are capable of being specifically enforced are contracts for the sale of land and the application of the equitable doctrine to contracts of this type has encountered difficulties caused by the nature of title to land and, in particular, by the fact that a contract for the sale of land is not specifically enforceable until the vendor has made title in accordance with the contract or the purchaser has agreed to accept such other title as the vendor actually has. The constructive trusteeship of the vendor does not therefore arise until title has been so made or accepted,[82] when it is generally thought to have retrospective effect to the date of the contract. This is not an appropriate place to consider the various ways in which this basic principle has been developed in the light of the many different situations which can arise under the various types of contracts for the sale of land; these matters are fully discussed in the standard texts on conveyancing.[83]

It has to be admitted that the inevitable self-interest of the vendor in the successful conclusion of the transaction does not sit very easily with his classification as a trustee. For this reason, many doubts have been expressed[84] as to whether it is appropriate for the relationship of vendor and purchaser to be classified as that of trustee and beneficiary. There is no doubt that the classification has led to the development of some anomalous rules but it is by no means certain that different anomalies would not have resulted from basing the relationship entirely on the law of contract. In any event, for the moment there seems little justification for or likelihood of any attempt to recast the relationship between vendor and purchaser on any other basis than that of constructive trustee and beneficiary.

---

[80] *Cuddon* v. *Tite* (1858) 1 Giff. 395.

[81] Such as contracts to sell a rare antique, a rare book, or shares in a private company.

[82] *Lysaght* v. *Edwards* (1876) 2 Ch.D. 499, 506–507, 510, 518.

[83] See D. G. Barnsley: *Conveyancing Law and Practice* (3rd ed. (1988)) 226–241 & J. T. Farrand, *Contract & Conveyance* (4th ed. (1983)) 167–173.

[84] Notably by D. W. M. Waters: *The Constructive Trust* (1964) 141–142.

VII. THE MORTGAGEE AS CONSTRUCTIVE TRUSTEE

At the time[85] when the majority of mortgages of land were effected by means of transfer of the subject matter of the mortgage to the mortgagee subject to a proviso for retransfer upon discharge of the mortgage debt, many judges saw fit to describe the mortgagee as a constructive trustee of the mortgaged property. Even when the courts came to recognise that the mortgagee, as such, was not a trustee at all,[86] it was nevertheless still clearly established that a mortgagee might be held to have become a constructive trustee as a result of the exercise of his powers under the mortgage and that, once the mortgage debt had been fully repaid, the mortgagee became a constructive trustee of the mortgaged property pending its retransfer to the mortgagor. Now[87] that mortgages of land cannot be created by way of transfer of the subject matter, a mortgagee cannot possibly become a constructive trustee of the mortgaged property, which cannot now be vested in him, but only of property which reaches his hands as a result of the exercise of his powers under the mortgage. After some initial uncertainty, it became clear that the mortgagee was not a trustee of his power of sale and therefore could exercise his contractual right quite irrespective of the interests of the mortgagor[88]; however, any surplus produced by the exercise of this power of sale was held by the mortgagee on a constructive trust for the mortgagor.[89] This old constructive trust of the proceeds of sale seems now to have been totally superseded by the creation of a statutory trust.[90] Further, the better view is that a mortgagee in possession is not a constructive trustee of any rents and profits which he has or should have received but is merely under an obligation to account for them to the mortgagor.[91] It thus seems that, so far as the mortgagee is concerned, the constructive trust no longer has any role to play.

VIII. TRANSFERS OF PROPERTY WHICH ARE AT LAW INCOMPLETE

As has already been seen,[92] the formalities necessary for the transfer of the legal title to certain kinds of property cannot all be carried out by the parties themselves. A transfer of registered land is not effective to pass the legal title to that land until the duly executed transfer form is presented to the Land Registry and registered in the Register of Titles. Similarly, a transfer of shares is not effective to pass the legal title to those shares until the transferor has complied with the procedure required by the Articles of Association of the company in question and the transfer is duly registered in the Register of Shareholders. In both

---

[85] Prior to the enactment of the Property Legislation of 1925.
[86] See *Marquis Cholmondeley* v. *Lord Clinton* (1820) 2 Jac. & W. 1.
[87] Law of Property Act 1925 s.85.
[88] *Warner* v. *Jacob* (1882) 20 Ch.D. 220.
[89] *Banner* v. *Berridge* (1881) 18 Ch.D. 254.
[90] Law of Property Act 1925 s.105 (originally Conveyancing Act 1881 s.21(3)).
[91] *Kirkwood* v. *Thompson* (1865) 2 De G.J. & S. 613.
[92] See *ante*, p. 64.

these cases, the intervention of a third party is necessary to enable legal title to pass; consequently the transfer will not be effective at law until the third party in question acts. However, it has been held that once the parties have complied with all the formal requirements capable of being carried out by themselves, the transfer will become effective in equity and the transferor will hold the property in question on trust for the transferee pending the intervention of the third party. This rule was established by the Court of Appeal in *Re Rose*[93] and for this reason is generally known as the Rule in *Re Rose*.

The precise scope of this Rule, which is clearly English law at the present time, has already been considered.[94] It is also clear that the trust which arises as a result of the operation of the Rule in *Re Rose* does not arise out of any intention of the parties thereto; it must therefore necessarily be brought into existence by operation of law and should therefore be classified as a constructive trust.

---

[93] [1952] Ch. 499.
[94] See *ante*, p. 64.

CHAPTER 9

CHARITABLE TRUSTS

I. CHARITIES ACT 1993

THE law and practice of charitable trusts was radically reformed by the Charities Act 1960.[1] This Act achieved the arduous task of renovating the appalling mass of statute law relating to charitable trusts. It cleared a great deal of dead wood from the Statute Book, especially that body of statutes known as the Charitable Trusts Acts 1853–1939. What was not obsolete was extracted from them and conveniently contained in the new statute. It is true to say that this Act contained the whole of the statute law relating to charitable trusts from the sixteenth century to the present day, and also added new provisions in keeping with modern circumstances, although, as will be seen, the Act was not primarily concerned with the legal nature of charity which continues to be governed by the case law. The Act implemented, wholly or in part, many of the recommendations of the Nathan Committee on such trusts which published its report in 1952.[2] Subsequently, further reforms, intended to increase the powers of the Charity Commissioners to control abuse and maladministration by charitable trustees, were enacted in the Charities Act 1992 as a result of the Woodfield Report.[3] The Charities Act 1960 and much of the Charities Act 1992 have now been consolidated in the Charities Act 1993 which, with the exception of some provisions relating to Charity Accounts, Reports, Returns and Investigations, came into force on August 31, 1993. Its effect and scope, where of general interest, is considered in the succeeding pages.

II. DISTINCTIONS FROM PRIVATE TRUSTS

A charitable trust is aimed to benefit society at large or an appreciable part of it. A private trust is aimed to benefit defined persons or defined classes of persons. In general, charitable trusts are subject to the same rules as private trusts, but because of their public nature they enjoy a number of advantages which are not shared by private trusts.

---

[1] For accounts of the Act, see Nathan, *Charities Act* 1960; Maurice, *Charities Act* 1960.
[2] Cmd. 9538. (Its full title is the "Committee on the Law and Practice relating to Charitable Trusts.")
[3] Efficiency Scrutiny of the Supervision of Charities, 1987; National Audit Office Report. House of Commons Paper 380. 1986–87; Annual Report 1987.

(1) Perpetuity[4]

Charitable trusts are not subject to that aspect of the perpetuity rule commonly called the rule against inalienability. The objects of the charity may last for ever, but a gift for such purpose will still be valid.[5] But they are, generally, subject to the perpetuity rule in the sense that the interest must vest in the charity within the perpetuity period. Thus, in *Re Lord Stratheden and Campbell*[6] an annuity of £100 was bequeathed for provision "for the Central London Rangers on the appointment of the next lieutenant-colonel." Since the next lieutenant-colonel might not be appointed within the perpetuity period, the limitation transgressed the rule and the gift was held by Romer J. to be invalid. However, even here there is an exception: provided that the trust in favour of one charity takes effect within the period, a gift over from that charity to another on the happening of an event which may be too remote will still be valid.[7] But this exception will not apply to a *gift over* to a charity after a gift to a non-charity[8]; in such a case the normal rules as to vesting in the second charity within the perpetuity period must be observed. It is as if for this purpose the law regards "charity" as a unity—thus a gift from one charity to another charity is from or to this "unity" so that there is no scope for the operation of the perpetuity rule, while a gift from or to this unity is subject to it in the usual way.

(2) Certainty

A charity will not fail for uncertainty of objects provided that the settlor clearly intended the fund to go exclusively to charity.[9] If this is satisfied the trust will not fail if he omits to specify the objects with particularity. In such circumstances a *cy-près* scheme[10] will be made to render the objects more precise. Again, for this purpose, it seems that the law regards charity as a unity, so that once the gift to this unity is established, it cannot fail.

(3) Construction

In construing instruments the intention of which is to set up a charitable trust but where there is an ambiguity, a "benignant" construction should be given if possible.[11] This was confirmed by the

---

[4] See *ante*, p. 163.

[5] *Chamberlayne* v. *Brockett* (1872) L.R. 8 Ch.App. 206.

[6] [1894] 3 Ch. 265, applying *Chamberlayne* v. *Brockett* (1872) L.R. 8 Ch.App. 206. It is now possible to take advantage of the "wait and see" rule introduced by the Perpetuities and Accumulations Act 1964, s.3, in respect of instruments taking effect after the commencement of the Act.

[7] *Re Tyler* [1891] 3 Ch. 252; *cf. Re Dalziel* [1943] Ch. 277; these cases are discussed at p. 121, *ante*.

[8] *Re Bowen* [1893] 2 Ch. 491 at p. 494; *Re Peel's Release* [1921] 2 Ch. 218; *Re Wightwick's Will Trusts* [1950] Ch. 260; *Re Spensley's Will Trusts* [1954] Ch. 233.

[9] See *Moggridge* v. *Thackwell* (1803) 7 Ves. 36, affirmed (1807) 13 Ves. 416. Provided that the gift has a charitable object, it does not matter that the precise purposes specified are too vague and uncertain to be charitable themselves; *Re Koeppler's Will Trusts* [1986] Ch. 423.

[10] See *post*, p. 338.

[11] See *ante*, p. 94 in relation to construction of private trusts.

House of Lords in *I.R.C.* v. *McMullen*[12] (although it was not necessary to resort to such a construction in that case) and such a construction was adopted by the House of Lords in *Guild* v. *I.R.C.*[13]

(4) Taxation

For taxation purposes, the distinction between a charitable trust and a private trust is seen both in the special taxation privileges which are afforded to a charitable trust, and to the taxation inducements which are offered to individuals for them to confer benefits on charitable trusts.

(a) Income tax and corporation tax　With regard to income tax, it is necessary to distinguish between the *investment* income and the *trading* income of the charity. Its investment income is exempt from income tax provided that it is applied for charitable purposes only.[14] If the charity carries on trade, its profits from the trade are exempt from income tax only if they are applied solely for its purpose and *either* (a) if the purpose or one of the primary purposes of the charity is to carry on that particular trade, *or* (b) if the work in connection with the trade is mainly carried out by the beneficiaries of the charity.[15] Where the charity is incorporated, the same principles as for income tax apply to corporation tax.[16]

The question whether a body is established for charitable purposes is a question of law to be decided in accordance with the usual principles, but the question whether or to what extent income is applied to charitable purposes is one of fact.[17] However, in *I.R.C.* v. *Helen Slater Charitable Trust Ltd.*[18] the Court of Appeal held that one charity "applies" its income for charitable purposes if it pays that income to another charity, albeit that the terms of the instrument governing the second charity are almost identical to those of the instrument governing the first charity.

(b) Deeds of covenant　If a person executes a deed of covenant by which he covenants to pay a part of his income to a charity for a four year period that part of his income is treated as the income of the charity for the purposes of the basic rate of income tax.[19] In practice, the covenantor deducts income tax at the basic rate from his payment, and the charity is entitled to claim a refund of the tax. In 1994/95 the basic rate of income tax is 25 per cent. Accordingly, where an individual is liable to income tax at this rate, the net cost, after income tax, of paying £5,000 p.a. to charity is £3,750.

The same general principles apply to the case of a company which enters into a deed of covenant. It may deduct the gross amount of the

---

[12] [1981] A.C. 1 at p. 16. The facts are stated *post*, p. 328. See also *Re Hetherington (deceased)* [1990] Ch. 1.
[13] [1992] 2 A.C. 310.
[14] Income and Corporation Taxes Act 1988, s.505.
[15] *Ibid.*
[16] *Ibid.* ss.505(1), 506(1).
[17] *See Williams' Trustees* v. *I.R.C.* [1947] A.C. 447.
[18] [1981] 3 All E.R. 98, C.A.
[19] I.C.T.A. 1988, s.660. Finance Act 1989, s.56.

payments from its profits before these are assessed for corporation tax, provided that it deducts income tax at the basic rate from the gross amount before making the payment to the charity and accounts to the Revenue for the tax so deducted.[20]

(c) Capital gains tax   A capital gain accruing to a charity will not attract capital gains tax provided that it is both applicable and is in fact applied to the charitable purposes.[21] If the charity is incorporated, then it is entitled to exemption from corporation tax on its capital gains on the same basis.[22]

There is also a substantial inducement to make gifts *to* a charity. Normally, when a person makes a gift, capital gains tax is payable by him on, broadly, the difference between the value of the asset at the time of the gift, and its value at the time of acquisition.[23] However, no capital gains tax is payable where the disposal is to a charity.[24]

(d) Inheritance tax   Compared with other private persons or bodies, charities enjoy important privileges with regard to inheritance tax:

    (i) gifts made to charities, whether by will or *inter vivos*, are wholly exempt from the tax[25];

   (ii) gifts made to nationally important institutions, such as the National Gallery, the British Museum or the National Trust, are wholly exempt from the tax, whether the gift takes effect on death or *inter vivos*[26];

  (iii) gifts made to a charity by way of a payment from a discretionary trust are entitled to unlimited exemption[27];

  (iv) the Treasury is empowered to exempt, for example, a gift of land of outstanding scenic or historical or scientific interest; gifts of buildings of outstanding historical or architectural or aesthetic interest; property given as a source of income for the upkeep of such land or buildings; and pictures, books, manuscripts, works of art, and so forth, of national or historic or scientific interest.[28]

It is, however, important to emphasise that, as a general rule, the exemptions apply only to gifts to charities which are immediate and absolute.[29] To this general rule there is the qualification that if the donor wishes a charity to benefit only after the death of himself and his spouse, he can leave a life interest in the property to the spouse, and on

---

[20] I.C.T.A. 1988, s.683. Finance Act 1989, s.59.
[21] Taxation of Chargeable Gains Act 1992, s.256.
[22] Capital gains tax applies only to capital gains made by individuals. Capital gains made by corporations are subject to corporation tax.
[23] *Ibid.* s.35.
[24] *Ibid.* s.257.
[25] Inheritance Tax Act 1984, s.23.
[26] *Ibid.*
[27] *Ibid.* s.76.
[28] *Ibid.* s.27.
[29] *Ibid.* s.23.

the latter's death, to the charity absolutely. Inheritance tax is not payable on the death either of the donor or his spouse.[30]

In addition to taking advantage of these immunities which are peculiar to charity, a donor may also take advantage of another exemption which applies generally, namely, that gifts to a total value of £3,000 in any one year are exempt.[31]

There is, therefore, considerable encouragement to make gifts to charity. Moreover, from the charity's point of view, any capital distributions made by it are also exempt.[32]

(e) Stamp duty[33]

Charities are exempt from stamp duty in relation to any conveyance, transfer or letting made or agreed to be made to them.[34]

(f) Value added tax

Although there is no general exemption for charities from value added tax, certain medical charities are, in effect, exempt from the tax,[35] and supplies to such charities are also exempt.[36]

(g) Rating

The general law of rating is governed by the Local Government Finance Act 1933, section 43 of which provides for the rating relief (both mandatory and discretionary) given to charities.

Mandatory relief to the extent of 80 per cent.[37] of the non-domestic rates which would otherwise be chargeable is available in respect of land (i) occupied by or used by trustees for a charity and (ii) wholly or mainly used for charitable purposes. With regard to occupation, it is in most cases clear that the charity or the trustees of the charity are in occupation. More difficult questions may arise where the charity has provided a house or accommodation for servants or staff and whether mandatory relief can be claimed in respect of it. The test appears to be whether the occupation of the servant is required with a view to the more efficient performance of his duties so as to constitute occupation by the charity.[38] Secondly, with regard to the requirement that the land be wholly or mainly used for charitable purposes, it appears to be required that the charity's use of the property be wholly "ancillary to" or "directly facilitates" the carrying out of its main charitable purposes.[39] The meaning of these expressions was considered by the

---

[30] *Ibid.* s.18.

[31] *Ibid.* s.57.

[32] *Ibid.* s.58(1)(*a*).

[33] See *post*, p. 407.

[34] F.A. 1982, s.129.

[35] Value Added Tax Act 1983. Scheds. 5 and 6.

[36] *Ibid.*

[37] Special mandatory relief in the form of total exemption from rates is available in respect of places of public religious worship and buildings ancillary thereto: Local Government Finance Act 1988, Sched. 5. para. 11; and see *Broxtowe Borough Council* v. *Birch* [1983] 1 All E.R. 641, C.A., for the meaning of "public religious worship."

[38] *Glasgow Corporation* v. *Johnstone* [1965] A.C. 609; *Northern Ireland Valuation Court* v. *Fermanagh Protestant Board of Education* [1969] 1 W.L.R. 1708.

[39] *Glasgow Corporation* v. *Johnstone, supra* at p. 622, *per* Lord Reid.

House of Lords in *Oxfam* v. *Birmingham City District Council*,[40] where Oxfam claimed relief from rates in respect of gift shops which it used for the sale of articles, mostly clothing, which had been donated to it, the profits being applied to Oxfam's objects. It was held that the charity gift shops did not "directly facilitate" the main object of the charity, and rating relief could not be claimed. There was a distinction, said Lord Cross of Chelsea,[41] between user for the purpose of getting in, raising or earning money for the charity, as opposed to user for purposes directly related to the achievement of the objects of the charity. The charity gift shops simply raised money for Oxfam and were accordingly excluded from relief.[42]

In addition to this relief, which is obtainable as of right, the rating authority has a discretion to reduce further, or remit entirely, the rates payable by a charity.[43]

III. DEFINITION OF A CHARITY

What is a charity?[44] For the reasons implicit in the distinctions already made between charitable and private trusts, it is essential to know when a trust is charitable and when it is not. The answer to this question is to be found, if at all, almost entirely in the case law. But the answer—in borderline cases, at any rate—may be difficult to find. In fact the whole subject has been condemned in the words of one writer as the "wilderness of legal charity."[45] There is a vast number of cases, and they certainly do not present an orderly picture.

In borderline cases, it may still be necessary to go back to a statute of Elizabeth I (43 Eliz. I, c. 4, 1601) commonly called the Charitable Uses Act 1601, in the preamble of which certain objects are listed. These are as follows:

"The relief of aged, impotent and poor people; the maintenance of sick and maimed soldiers and mariners, schools of learning, free schools and schools in universities; the repair of bridges, ports, havens, causeways, churches, sea-banks and highways; the education and preferment of orphans; the relief, stock or mainten-ance for houses of correction; the marriage of poor maids; the supportation, aid and help of young tradesmen, handicraftsmen and persons decayed; the relief or redemption of prisoners or captives; and the aid or ease of any poor inhabitants concerning payment of fifteens, setting out of soldiers and other taxes."

The statute itself was repealed by the Mortmain and Charitable Uses

---

[40] [1976] A.C. 126; cf. *Aldous* v. *Southwark London B.C.* [1968] 1 W.L.R. 1671.

[41] *Ibid.* at p. 146.

[42] The Rating (Charity Shops) Act 1976 remedied the effect of this decision with regard to charity shops so as to make them eligible for relief, but otherwise the decision remains intact.

[43] Local Government Finance Act 1988, s.47.

[44] See, for general surveys, Brunyate (1945) 61 L.Q.R. 268; Cross (1956) 72 L.Q.R. 187.

[45] Bentwich (1936) 49 L.Q.R. 520.

Act 1888, but in effect the preamble remained alive.[46] Admittedly, the purposes listed in this ancient statute have never been treated as sacrosanct. In many cases they have been extended by the addition of a multitude of analogous objects, analogy upon analogy, and in some cases the analogies are perhaps rather far-fetched. In others, the decision has been based on a more general question whether the purpose is or is not within the "spirit and intendment" or the "equity" or the "mischief" of the statute—with analogy used only as "handmade."[47] Even so, it is still possible to find a number of cases based on a detailed examination of the words of the statute in recent years.[48]

The living preamble. It was commonly thought that section 13(2) of the Mortmain and Charitable Uses Act 1888. although this repealed the Statute of Elizabeth I, had expressly preserved the preamble; and when this subsection was itself repealed by the Charities Act 1960[49] the preamble was thereby destroyed. However, if section 13(2) is considered it seems to fall short of providing that in *all* cases the court must continue to refer to the preamble; it refers specifically only to enactments and documents in which a reference to charity is made, and these do not prima facie include the reported judgments of superior courts. But the main point is that even if section 13(2) had been omitted altogether from the 1888 Act, the court would still have been bound to decide a case with the preamble in mind, because the practice of the courts had developed into a rule of law. And this rule of law—having, as it were, an independent existence irrespective of statute—could not be extinguished without an express statutory provision to that effect. Indeed the Charities Act 1960 made it reasonably clear that no change in the law was intended. The Act repealed section 13(2) but in substitution provided that a reference in any enactment or document to a charity within the preamble should be construed as a reference to charity in the meaning it bears as a legal term according to the law of England and Wales.[50] Thus the Charities Act 1960 itself seemed to make it clear that the law of England and Wales, based on the preamble over a period of 380 years, should remain intact. In other words the repeal of section 13(2) with the substitution of new provisions does not affect the edifice of law built on the foundations of the preamble.[51]

This approach, based on a construction of the relevant statutory provisions, seems reasonably conclusive on its own. The relevance of

---

[46] *Infra.*

[47] *Incorporated Council of Law Reporting for England and Wales* v. *Att.-Gen.* [1972] Ch. 73 at p. 88 *per* Russell L.J.

[48] See for recent examples, *Re Cole* [1958] Ch. 877, C.A.; *Re Sahal's Will Trusts* [1958] 1 W.L.R. 1243.

[49] s.38(1).

[50] s.38(4). See also the definition of "charity" in s.45(1) (now Charities Act 1993, s.96) and "charitable purposes" in s.46(1) (now Charities Act 1993, s.97). For the purposes of the former provision the charity must be subject to control by the High Court in the exercise of the court's jurisdiction with respect to charities: see *Construction Training Board* v. *Att.-Gen.* [1973] Ch. 173; and see *post*, p. 352.

[51] See *Tudor on Charities* (7th ed.), pp. 2 *et seq.*

the preamble has, however, also been affirmed by subsequent authoritative judicial decisions. Thus in *Scottish Burial Reform and Cremation Society* v. *Glasgow City Corporation*,[52] where cremation was held to be a charitable purpose, the House of Lords acknowledged that this was undoubtedly the accepted test, though, as Lord Upjohn said, "in only a very wide and broad sense,"[53] meaning, as Lord Wilberforce put it, "that what must be regarded is not the wording of the preamble, but the effect of decisions given by the courts as to its scope, decisions which have endeavoured to keep the law as to charities moving according as new social needs arise or old ones become obsolete or satisfied."[54] Likewise, in *Incorporated Council of Law Reporting for England and Wales* v. *Att.-Gen.*,[55] the Court of Appeal, in affirming the charitable status of the Council, specifically held that the publication or dissemination of law reports was a purpose beneficial to the community, being within the spirit and intendment of the preamble to the Statute of Elizabeth.

In short, it is still technically necessary today to decide whether a case falls within "the letter or the spirit and intendment" of the preamble. In practice, in most cases, it will be sufficient to refer to the relevant prior case law to dispose of the problem whether a particular trust is charitable or not. Only in a novel case may the court be compelled to refer back to the basic principles or indeed the letter of the preamble.

Reform. The preamble was not, of course, a *definition* of charity. It was simply a catalogue of purposes which in 1601 were regarded as charitable. Indeed at no time has there been a statutory definition, except for the limited one provided for in section 1 of the Recreational Charities Act 1958.[56] Suggestions were made before the Charities Act 1960 was passed that there ought to be a definition of charity in the Act.[57] A similar discussion is contained in the 1989 White Paper "Charities: A Framework For the Future".[57A] But these suggestions have so far been resisted because it was thought to be almost impossible to provide a foolproof definition applicable to all the cases that might arise.[58] If any had been provided it might have proved an erratic or insufficient yardstick. The question is debatable. Many laymen and some lawyers find it extraordinary that the question whether a trust is charitable—with all the fiscal and other privileges enjoyed by legal charity—should depend at the present day on a statutory provision of the early seventeenth century and the welter of case law which has grown up around it.

---

[52] [1968] A.C. 138.
[53] *Ibid.* at p. 151.
[54] *Ibid.* at p. 154.
[55] [1972] Ch. 73.
[56] See *post*, p. 209.
[57] See *e.g.* Nathan Report.
[57A] Cmd. 694.
[58] "There is no limit to the number and diversity of the ways in which man will seek to benefit his fellow men"; *I.R.C.* v. *Baddeley* [1955] A.C. 572 at p. 583, *per* Viscount Simonds.

The point has been judicially recognised. For example, Lord Upjohn once said that the preamble had been "stretched almost to breaking-point."[59] The difficulties are undoubtedly exacerbated by the immunity from taxation which all English charities enjoy. In the words of Lord Cross of Chelsea in *Dingle* v. *Turner*,[60] validity and fiscal immunity march hand in hand. He suggested that one possible solution would be to separate them and say that only some charities should enjoy fiscal privileges. No doubt this would cause a great deal of contention, but might prove to be a practical proposition. Perhaps the membership of this country of the European Economic Community—as well as the growing number of transnational charities—may impel us to embark on a statutory rationalisation of the law.[61]

The problems of definition should not, however, be underestimated and it may be noteworthy that the Goodman Committee[62] was unable to devise one, but instead recommended that the categories of charity should be re-stated in simple and modern language replacing that of the Act of 1601 and extending these to include objects now considered to be within the scope of charity (so called "guide-lines").[63] The case law would not be irrelevant but the court would have more freedom to reconsider it in the light of the new categorisation. On the other hand, the Expenditure Committee of the House of Commons[63A] has recommended that a statutory definition of charity is needed. They do not, however, provide one; they simply emphasise that all charities should be required to satisfy the test of benefit to the community.[64] On this it may be observed that one of the difficulties in this area of the law is to define what is, and what is not, for the "public benefit."[65]

Legislation embodying the Goodman Committee's "guide-lines" would be helpful in modernising the law.

IV. CLASSIFICATION OF CHARITABLE TRUSTS

A leading case in which a classification of charitable trusts was made and on which many succeeding cases have been based is *Commissioners*

---

[59] *Scottish Burial Reform and Cremation Society* v. *Glasgow City Corporation* [1968] A.C. 138 at p. 153, *cf. Incorporated Council of Law Reporting for England and Wales* v. *Att.-Gen.* [1972] Ch. 73 at p. 94, *per* Sachs L.J.: "I appreciate the wisdom of the legislature in refraining from providing a detailed definition of charitable purposes in the 1960 Act. . . . Any statutory definition might well produce a fresh spate of litigation and provide a set of undesirable artifical distinctions."

[60] [1972] A.C. 601 at p. 624; a case involving the relief of poverty, discussed *post*, p. 309.

[61] See Official Report of Debates of the Council of Europe, 1972, Vol. 3, p. 598; Doc. 3052, 1972, of the Council of Europe, Vol. 11. See also *Trusts and Foundations in Europe* (ed. Neuhoff and Pavel); Pomey, *Traité des Fondations D'Utilité Publique*; Boúúaert, *Tax Problems of Cultural Foundations and of Patronage in the European Community*: S. Bright, [1989] Conv. 28 and N. Gravells, 40 M.L.R. (1977) 397.

[62] An independent committee on Charity Law and Voluntary Organisations set up by the National Council of Social Service under the chairmanship of Lord Goodman which reported in 1976.

[63] At p. 16. These "guide-lines" are set out in Appendix 1 to the Report (p. 123).

[63A] 10th Report Session 1974–75.

[64] At p. xiii.

[65] See *post*, p. 305.

for Special Purposes of Income Tax v. *Pemsel.*[66] Here Lord Macnaghten classified the trusts which have been held to be charitable under four heads:

(1) Trusts for the relief of poverty;
(2) Trusts for the advancement of education;
(3) Trusts for the advancement of religion;
(4) Trusts for other purposes beneficial to the community not falling under any of the other three heads.[67]

This is the nearest that there is to a definition in English law. The first three heads do not, generally, present too much difficulty. A case falling within any of those heads will prima facie be assumed to be charitable as being for the benefit of the community, unless the contrary is shown. The fourth head presents, as will be seen, greater difficulty but it seems that the courts prefer the vague and undefined approach based on the "equity" or the "mischief" of the preamble, rather than the stepping-stones approach based on analogy, in determining the question whether a trust falling under this head is charitable.[68]

Before each head is considered, it is necessary to emphasise the requirement, which applies generally, that a charitable trust must have a public character.[69]

1. *Public Element in Charity*

It does not follow from the requirement of a public character that *all* public trusts are charitable. What it means is that a trust is incapable of being charitable in the legal sense unless it is for the benefit of the public, or some section of the public, with the exception only of trusts for the relief of poverty[70]—and whether or not the test is satisfied is decided by the court on the evidence[71] and not on the opinion of the settlor. A number of illustrations, from the many cases on the topic, may be taken. Thus in *Re Compton*[72] a trust for the education of the descendants of three named persons was held not to be a valid charitable trust, because the beneficiaries were defined by reference to a personal relationship and it, therefore, lacked the quality of a public trust. The trust was indeed a family trust and not one for the benefit of a section of the public. Again, in *Re Holbourn Aero Components Air Raid*

---

[66] [1891] A.C. 531 at p. 583. *cf.* the classification in the American *Restatement of Trusts* which specifically refers also to two other purposes: (1) promotion of health and (2) governmental and municipal purposes (Vol. II. p. 1140).

[67] The classification was based on the argument of Sir Samuel Romilly in *Morice* v. *Bishop of Durham* (1805) 10 Ves. 522 at p. 532.

[68] The H.L. preferred it in *Scottish Burial Reform and Cremation Society* v. *Glasgow City Corporation* [1968] A.C. 138 and the C.A. preferred it in *Incorporated Council of Law Reporting for England and Wales* v. *Att.-Gen.* [1972] Ch. 73.

[69] Another requirement to be satisfied is that the trust be exclusively charitable: see *post*, p. 333.

[70] See *post*, p. 309.

[71] *Re Hummeltenberg* [1923] 1 Ch. 237; *National Anti-Vivisection Society* v. *I.R.C.* [1948] A.C. 31; *Re Wootton* [1968] 1 W.L.R. 681.

[72] [1945] Ch. 123.

Distress Fund[73] an emergency fund which had been built up during the last war had been used partly for comforts for ex-employees serving in the Forces, and later for employees who had suffered distress from air-raids. It was held that because of the absence of a public element no charitable trust had been created and the surplus funds, over which the application had been made to the court, should be returned to the contributors.[74]

But perhaps the most important illustration is to be found in *Oppenheim* v. *Tobacco Securities Trust Co. Ltd.*,[75] where *Re Compton*[76] was applied. Here, trustees were directed under a settlement to apply moneys in providing for the education of children of employees or ex-employees of British American Tobacco or any of its subsidiary or allied companies. The employees numbered over 110,000. The House of Lords held (Lord MacDermott dissenting) that, although the group of persons indicated was numerous, the nexus between them was employment by a particular employer and it therefore followed that the trust did not satisfy the test of public benefit which was required to establish it as charitable. It was argued that the court should take into account the number of employees, but this was rejected by the majority. As Lord Normand said,[77] if there is no public element to be found in the bare nexus of common employment all attempts to build up the public element out of circumstances which had no necessary relation with it but were adventitious, accidental or variable must be unavailing where the settlor has chosen to define the selected class solely by the attribute of common employment. Putting this more generally, an aggregate of individuals ascertained by reference to some personal tie (*e.g.* blood or contract), such as the relations of a particular individual, the members of a particular family, the members of a particular association, does not amount to the public or a section thereof for the purpose of the general rule and will not, accordingly, rank as legally charitable.[78]

It has been said that Lord MacDermott dissented in *Oppenheim's* case. He said[79] that he saw "much difficulty in dividing the qualities or attributes, which may serve to bind human beings into classes, into two mutually exclusive groups, the one involving individual status and purely personal, the other disregarding such status and quite impersonal. As a task this seems to me no less baffling and elusive than the problem to which it is directed, namely the determination of what is and what is not a section of the public for the purposes of this branch of

---

[73] [1946] Ch. 194.

[74] On the basis that they were the members of an unincorporated association (see *ante*, p. 204).

[75] [1951] A.C. 297; applied in *I.R.C.* v. *Educational Grants Association Ltd.* [1967] Ch. 993, C.A. (up to 85 per cent, of income of educational trust paid to children of employees of Metal Box Ltd.: income tax not recoverable because income not applied for charitable purposes only).

[76] *Supra.*

[77] *Ibid.* at pp. 310–311.

[78] *Re Scarisbrick* [1951] Ch. 622 at p. 649, *per* Jenkins L.J. See also *Re Compton* [1945] Ch. 123.

[79] [1951] A.C. 297 at p. 317.

the law." More recently, in *Dingle* v. *Turner*[80] Lord Cross of Chelsea was of the same opinion. Moreover, he felt that whether or not the potential beneficiaries of a trust could fairly be said to constitute a section of the public was "a question of degree" and depended on the purpose of the trust. This sort of formulation, however, seems to be no more helpful, perhaps less helpful, in the present state of the law than the old formulation based on the distinction between personal and impersonal relationship.

However, if the trust is construed so as to grant a mere preference to a limited class, such as employees or relations, the trust will succeed as a charity. It succeeded, for example, in *Re Koettgen's Will Trusts*,[81] where a trust was established for the furtherance of the commercial education of British-born persons, with a direction that preference be given to employees of a particular firm. The essential question is whether or not it is a mere expression of preference. If it goes beyond that and amounts to a positive obligation the trust will not be regarded as charitable because the obligation will vitiate the public character of the trust. And it is certainly possible to argue on this basis, as it has been argued,[82] that *Re Koettgen's Will Trusts* was wrongly decided. Its validity was indeed doubted by Lord Radcliffe in *Caffoor* v. *Commission of Income Tax, Colombo*,[83] where it was held by the Privy Council that the trust in question was a family trust and not of a public character for charitable purposes. The doubts were repeated by Walton J. in *Re Martin*[84] where a trust to establish a home for old people, with a right for either or both of the testator's daughters to reside there, was held not to be charitable. In essence the question will always be reduced to one of construction.[85]

Overseas charities. A number of major charities carry on part of their activities in foreign countries, and the question which is still not finally settled is whether or how the requirement of public benefit is satisfied in such a case. The essential question is what is meant by the public or a section thereof. The Charity Commissioners appear to have no doubt that the advancement of religion, the advancement of education and the relief of poverty (the first three heads mentioned in *Pemsel's* case)[86] are charitable purposes in whatever part of the world they are carried out; but, with regard to the fourth head of that classification, *i.e.* for other purposes beneficial to the community, such purposes will only be charitable if of benefit to the community of the United Kingdom.[87] The Commissioners concede that benefit to the United Kingdom, when derived from charities carried out overseas, need not be material or

---

[80] [1972] A.C. 601 at p. 621.

[81] [1954] Ch. 252.

[82] See, *e.g.*, *I.R.C.* v. *Educational Grants Association* [1967] Ch. 123.

[83] [1961] A.C. 584 at p. 604. *cf. Re George Drexler Ofrex Foundation Trustees* v. *I.R.C.* [1966] Ch. 675.

[84] *The Times*, November 16, 1977.

[85] For other aspects of "public benefit," particularly in relation to trusts for the advancement of religion and for other purposes beneficial to the community, see *post*, pp. 207, 208.

[86] [1891] A.C. 531 at p. 583.

[87] Report of the Charity Commissioners for England and Wales for 1963, p. 24.

direct; accordingly, charities with general humanitarian objects (*e.g.* cancer research) can benefit the community of the United Kingdom even if carried on in foreign countries; but where the purposes are for the local provision of public works or development projects such as roads and irrigation, these will only be charitable "if they are a reasonably direct means to the end of relieving poverty in observable cases." Where there is a benefit to the community of the United Kingdom, the court will not ignore the probable results of the trust on the community of the country in question which may well have a wholly distinct history and social structure. One of the reasons why a trust to bring about the abolition of torture and other inhuman punishments was held not to be charitable in *McGovern* v. *Attorney-General*[88] was that the court could not judge the probable effects on the local community of the necessary legislation.

There is ample authority of long standing that overseas charities falling within the first three heads of Lord Macnaghten's classification will be charitable[89]; there is little authority, and that conflicting, as to the fourth head. In *Camille and Henry Dreyfus Foundation Inc.* v. *I.R.C.*,[90] Lord Evershed M.R. expressed the opinion, *obiter*, that there should be a benefit to the United Kingdom, whereas in *Re Jacobs*[91] it was held by Foster J. that a gift for the planting of a grove of trees in Israel was a valid charitable gift.[92] The latter decision is plainly in conflict with the views of the Charity Commissioners, but is not necessarily wrong. It is not easy to distinguish the fourth head of charity from the other preceding heads in this context. Why, for example, should a missionary trust be charitable but not a trust for public works which will raise standards of living? It should be added that a case like *Keren Kayemeth Le Jisroel Ltd.* v. *I.R.C.*,[93] which might seem to support the Commissioners' opinion,[94] is not directly in point. In this case a company had been formed with the main object of purchasing land in Palestine, Syria and other parts of Turkey in Asia, and the peninsula of Sinai, for the purpose of settling Jews in such lands. The House of Lords held that the company's objects were not charitable within Lord Macnaghten's fourth head. The reasons, however, for so holding was that the court could not identify the community either as the community of all Jews throughout the world or as the community of the Jews in the regions prescribed for the settlement. It was on the ground of lack of "identifia-

---

[88] [1982] Ch. 321.
[89] See, *e.g. New* v. *Bonaker* (1867) L.R. 4 Eq. 655 (education); *Re Norman* [1947] Ch. 349 (religion); *Re Robinson* [1931] Ch. 122 (relief of disabled foreign soldiers: to be equated for this purpose with relief of poverty). *Re Niyazi's Will Trusts* [1978] 1 W.L.R. 910 (relief of poverty in Cyprus).
[90] [1954] Ch. 672 at p. 684.
[91] (1970) 114 S.J. 515.
[92] As promoting agriculture: see *I.R.C.* v. *Yorkshire Agricultural Society* [1928] 1 K.B. 61, applied in *Brisbane City Council* v. *Att.-Gen. for Queensland* [1979] A.C. 411, P.C. (showground); and see *Re Hadden* [1932] 1 Ch. 133.
[93] [1932] A.C. 650.
[94] The Commissioners do not, however, cite any authorities for their views.

bility" and not on grounds of overseas benefit that the case was decided.[95]

The Goodman Committee recommended that no distinction should be drawn between charitable activity by English charities at home or abroad; any object which is charitable at home should also be considered as charitable when carried out abroad.[96]

A separate question concerns the status of foreign charities. These cannot acquire charitable status here, for the simple reason that the law of charity in the foreign country may be different from ours.[97]

2. The Poverty Exception

The principle that a trust should have a public element is not of absolutely universal application. There is, as indicated above, one important exception to it. This is that trusts for the relief of poverty have been held to be charitable even though they are not for the benefit of the public or a section of it. The exception may arise where the personal tie is one of blood or contract. In the case of blood, there are the so-called "poor relations" cases. The case of contract may be exemplified by a trust for the relief of poverty amongst employees of a particular firm or company.

This particular exception cannot be accounted for by reference to any principle,[98] but it was established by authorities of long standing which were binding on the Court of Appeal, and were reaffirmed by the House of Lords in *Dingle* v. *Turner*.[99] In that case there was a trust to apply income in paying pensions to poor employees of a company. It was held that the trust was charitable.

The class of persons within the expression "poor relations" is self-evident[1]: but cases such as *Dingle* v. *Turner and Gibson* v. *South American Stores (Gath & Chaves) Ltd.*[2] where a gift to employees of a particular company to whom a poverty qualification was attached was upheld as a

---

[95] See also *Williams' Trustees* v. *I.R.C.* [1947] A.C. 447, which involved an institute for the moral, social and spiritual welfare of Welsh people in London. Lord Simonds held that the difficulty of finding the community of Welsh people was not less than the difficulty of finding the community of Jews in *Keren Kayemeth Le Jisroel* v. *I.R.C.*

[96] The Goodman Committee, however, stated that if the overseas activities of the charity are contrary to the public interest of the U.K., there should be a procedure whereby the Foreign Office could make an order requiring the charity to stop that activity (p. 36).

[97] The Goodman Committee recommended (p. 37) that the law governing foreign charities should remain as it is, but consideration should be given to allowing such charities to register in this country if certain conditions (*e.g.* satisfying the Charity Commissioners that the objects are charitable in English law and filing accounts here) are satisfied and mutual arrangements can be made by international convention. See also the works cited at p. 304 n. 61 *ante*.

[98] It has been tentatively suggested that "the relief of poverty is of so altruistic a character that the public benefit may necessarily be inferred": see *Re Scarisbrick* [1951] Ch. 622 at p. 639, *per* Evershed M.R. But this is not the basis of the case law and in any event seems highly debatable. In *Dingle* v. *Turner* [1972] A.C. 601 it was assumed that the law was anomalous.

[99] [1972] A.C. 601.

[1] See, *e.g. Isaac* v. *Defriez* (1754) Amb. 595; *White* v. *White* (1802) 7 Ves. 423; *Att-Gen* v. *Price* (1810) 17 Ves. 371; *Re Scarisbrick* [1951] Ch. 622; *Re Cohen* [1973] 1 W.L.R. 415.

[2] [1950] Ch. 177. See also *Re Coulthurst* [1951] Ch. 661 (officers and ex-officers of bank).

valid charitable gift illustrate the contractual tie. And the principle was applied in *Re Young*[3] to members of a club and in *Spiller* v. *Maude*[4] to members of a society. It was argued in *Dingle* v. *Turner* that the tests postulated in *Re Compton*[5] and *Oppenheim* v. *Tobacco Securities Trust Ltd.*[6] ought, in principle, to apply to all charitable trusts and that the "poor relations" cases, the "poor members" cases and the "poor employees" cases were all anomalous and should be overruled; or if it were not practicable to overrule the "poor relations" cases because of their antiquity the same could not be said of the "poor employees" cases which dated only from 1900.[7] But it was held that the "poor members" and "poor employees" decisions were a natural development of the "poor relations" cases and to draw a distinction between them would be quite illogical; and, moreover, although not as old as "poor relations" trusts, "poor employees" trusts had been recognised for many years, and there would be a large number of such trusts in operation today.[8] The exception will not, however, be extended to other classes of trusts.[9]

It was also decided by the Court of Appeal in *Re Scarisbrick*[10]—and this did not appear to have been expressly decided before—that the exception was not restricted to perpetual or continuing trusts (to which it will normally apply) but even covered a trust for immediate distribution. Here a gift for poor members of the class of relations of three children of the testatrix was upheld as a valid charitable trust, although the distribution of the property had to be made within the perpetuity period.

3. *Limits of Public Benefit*

It is important to notice that although the general rule is (subject to trusts for the relief of poverty) that every charitable trust should have a public element, it is not essential that everybody should be able to avail himself of its benefits. As Viscount Simonds said in *Inland Revenue Commissioners* v. *Baddeley*,[11] there is a distinction "between a form of relief extended to the whole community, yet by its very nature advantageous only to the few and a form of relief accorded to a selected few out of a larger number equally willing and able to take advantage of it." Thus, to illustrate the first class cited by Viscount Simonds—which will create a valid charitable trust—a gift for the benefit of New South Wales soldiers returning after the 1914–18 war was held by the Privy Council

---

[3] [1955] 1 W.L.R. 1269.
[4] (1881) 32 Ch.D. 158n.
[5] [1945] Ch. 123.
[6] [1951] A.C. 297.
[7] *Re Gosling* [1900] 2 W.R. 300.
[8] The Goodman Committee considered that "poor relations" and "poor employees" trusts are not justifiable and should no longer qualify as charitable (p. 17).
[9] *Re Compton, supra* (education); *Oppenheim* v. *Tobacco Securities Trust Ltd., supra* (education); *Davies* v. *Perpetual Trustee Co.* [1959] A.C. 439 (religion).
[10] [1951] Ch. 622.
[11] [1955] A.C. 572 at p. 592. The case is considered *post*, p. 324.

in *Verge* v. *Somerville*[12] to be valid; so also will a trust for the erection of a sea wall even though this is perhaps of benefit primarily to persons whose houses front the sea.

In illustration of Viscount Simonds' second class—which will fail as a charity—a gift to Presbyterians who could claim a particular descent failed for this reason in the Privy Council decision in *Davies* v. *Perpetual Trustee Co.*[13] A trust in favour of the Methodists in West Ham and Leyton in *I.R.C.* v. *Baddeley*[14] also failed.

4. *Lord Macnaghten's Classification*

(1) Trusts for the relief of poverty

The Act of 1601 included among its objects the relief of "the aged, impotent and poor." But although the word "and" was used it became well-settled that the expression should be read disjunctively.[15] This rule was confirmed in *Re Robinson*[16] where there was a gift to the old over 65 years of a certain district: and in *Re Lewis*,[17] where there was a gift for 20 blind children of another district. Both gifts were upheld. The question was most recently considered in *Joseph Rowntree Memorial Trust Housing Association Ltd* v. *Att.-Gen.*[18] where Peter Gibson J., although confirming the disjunctive reading, added a significant rider, which did not appear from the cases previously cited, namely, that in order to be charitable, the gift to the beneficiaries (the aged or the impotent) had to have as its purpose the relief of a need attributable to their condition. It is hoped that this approach will finally scotch the theory that a trust for the relief of "aged peers" or "impotent millionaires" will be charitable.[19] A gift of money to such persons would not relieve a need of theirs as aged or impotent persons. In the case itself, a charitable housing association wished to build small self-contained dwellings for sale to elderly people on long leases in consideration of a capital payment. It was held that since the provision of special accommodation relieved a particular need of the elderly, whether poor or not, attributable to their aged condition, the proposed housing schemes were charitable. Peter Gibson J., in reaching this conclusion, applied the reasoning of Lord Wilberforce in *Re Resch's Will Trusts*,[20] which concerned a private hospital which charged substantial fees but was not run for the profit of individuals. A gift to the hospital was held to be charitable.

The next question is, what is meant by the words "aged," "impotent"

---

[12] [1924] A.C. 496.
[13] [1959] A.C. 439.
[14] See n. 11.
[15] *Re Fraser* (1883) 22 Ch.D. 827; *Re Elliott* (1910) 102 LT. 528; *Re Glyn* (1950) 66 T.L.R. (Pt. 2) 510; *Re Cottam* [1955] 1 W.L.R. 1299; and see also the cases cited in the text.
[16] [1951] Ch. 198.
[17] [1955] Ch. 104.
[18] [1983] 2 W.L.R. 284.
[19] (1955) 71 L.Q.R. 16 (R.E.M.).
[20] [1969] 1 A.C. 514, P.C.; and see *Re Neal* (1966) 110 Sol. Jo. 549.

and "poor" in this context? First, what is meant by "poverty"? It is clear that the degree of poverty need not be acute. It is unnecessary to show destitution. Accordingly gifts for such objects as "ladies of limited means"[21] or "decayed actors"[22] and similar purposes are well recognised as being charitable. All that seems to be required is that the individuals in question be in straitened circumstances and unable to maintain a modest standard of living.[23] But it is essential that all the objects fall within the designation "poor" if a trust for the relief of poverty is to be upheld. If someone who is not poor is able to benefit, the gift will fail as a gift for the relief of poverty. Thus, in Re Gwyon[24] a fund was directed to be set aside to provide "knickers" (by which was meant a type of short trouser) for the boys of Farnham. The garments were unusual not only in their name but also because there were to be embroidered on the waistband the words "Gwyon's Present." Successful applicants were to be entitled to a new pair of knickers each year provided that on the subsequent application the legend "Gwyon's Present" was still decipherable on the old ones. Whatever may have been the testator's intention none of these conditions *necessarily* imported poverty, and the trust failed as a charity. Moreover it was held in Re Sanders' Will Trusts[25] that a gift for the "working classes" was not a gift for the relief of poverty because this expression did not necessarily indicate poor persons. It is possible, as Harman J. said—and indeed it has been so held[26]—that if the gift had been made to members of the "working classes" who were aged or widows, then the object of relieving poverty might be implied. But in Re Sanders, as Harman J. made plain, there was nothing of this kind. The members of the working class were not old persons, they were not widows, they were simply men working in the docks and their families. It was, therefore, impossible to infer any element of poverty. This case was, however, distinguished in Re Niyazi's Will Trusts[27] where a trust for a working men's hostel in Famagusta, Cyprus, providing modest accommodation for persons of the lower income group, was upheld as charitable, although, in the words of Megarry V.-C., the case was "desperately near the border-line."[28]

There is also no decisive definition of the terms "aged" or "impotent." It has been held that people who are not under the age of 50 are aged.[29] But in view of the advance in medical science this now

---

[21] *Re Gardom* [1914] 1 Ch. 662.

[22] *Spiller* v. *Maude* (1881) 32 Ch.D. 158n.

[23] See *Re Mary Clark Homes* [1904] 2 K.B. 645; *Re Gardom* [1914] 1 Ch. 662; *Shaw* v. *Halifax Corporation* [1915] 2 K.B. 170; *Re Clarke* [1923] 2 Ch. 407; *Re De Carteret* [1933] Ch. 103. See also Cross (1956) 72 L.Q.R. 182 at p. 206.

[24] [1930] 1 Ch. 225.

[25] [1954] Ch. 265 (appeal settled, *The Times*, July 22, 1954).

[26] *Re Glyn* (1950) 66 T.L.R. (Pt. 2) 510; see also *Re Cottam* [1955] 1 W.L.R. 1299 (provision of flats for aged).

[27] [1978] 1 W.L.R. 910.

[28] *Ibid.* at p. 915.

[29] *Re Wall* (1889) 42 Ch.D. 510. See also *Re Payling's Will Trusts* [1969] 1 W.L.R. 1595; *Re Armitage* [1972] Ch. 438.

seems very doubtful. If the settlor wishes to specify an age he may be taking a risk today if the age is lower than 60. The word "impotent" has been generously construed, although never precisely defined. It includes permanent disability,[30] the seriously ill or wounded,[31] and also covers the prevention of cruelty to children.[32]

It is, of course, essential to establish that in the case of relief of poverty there is a trust for the relief of poverty in the proper sense of that expression. The point is that a trust for poor persons may take effect as a private rather than a charitable trust. The distinction is—and this is a matter of construction—whether the gift is for the relief of poverty amongst a particular description of poor people *or* is merely a gift to particular poor persons, the relief of poverty among them being the motive of the gift. In the former case the trust is charitable, in the latter it is private.[33]

Housing Associations. A related question involves housing associations, which provide housing for the "aged, impotent and poor" and which enjoy charitable status because they are within the preamble to the Act of 1601. But it is common to find associations feeling the need to adopt a particular policy of tenant selection, for example, selecting tenants who earn less than the average wage, so as to preserve charitable status. Such a policy may be inconvenient and indeed fail if one or more of the residents are not in fact poor.[34] The Goodman Committee recommended[35] that housing trusts should be charitable even though the trustees take account of the housing need, not merely of the income of the tenant, provided that, to avoid abuse, the association is registered with the Housing Corporation under the Housing Acts and registered with the Charity Commission. Such difficulties now appear to have been alleviated in some degree by the decision in *Joseph Rowntree Memorial Trust Housing Association Ltd.* v. *Att.-Gen.*[36] It was held that it was not essential that a charitable gift be made solely by way of bounty and, accordingly, the beneficiaries could be required to contribute to its cost. The fact that the housing schemes concerned made provision for special housing for the elderly on a contractual basis did not therefore prevent the schemes from being charitable. It was also held that the possibility that a beneficiary might profit by an increase in value of the property on a subsequent sale by him did not alter the fact that the trusts were charitable.

---

[30] *Re Fraser* (1883) 22 Ch.D. 827; *Re Lewis* [1955] Ch. 104.

[31] *Re Hillier* [1944] 1 All E.R. 486.

[32] *C.I.R.* v. *Pemsel* [1891] A.C. 531 at p. 572; *cf. Re Cole* [1958] Ch. 477; *Re Sahal's Will Trusts* [1958] 1 W.L.R. 1243 and see *post.*

[33] *Re Scarisbrick* [1951] Ch. 622, 650, 651 (*per* Jenkins L.J.); *Dingle* v. *Turner* [1972] A.C. 601 at p. 617 (*per* Lord Cross of Chelsea); *Re Cohen* [1973] 1 W.L.R. 415 at p. 423 (*per* Templeman J.).

[34] *Over-Seventies Housing Association* v. *Westminster London Borough Council* (1974) 230 E.G. 1593.

[35] At p. 32.

[36] [1983] 2 W.L.R. 284. The facts are stated *ante,* p. 311.

(2) Trusts for the advancement of education

The general rule is conventionally stated to be that there must be an intention that learning should be imparted, not simply that it should be accumulated. This may now be a somewhat misleading yardstick, because the tendency in many of the cases is to widen the field of "education" in this context. But the conventional meaning appears to have been adopted by Harman J. in *Re Shaw*.[37] Here George Bernard Shaw by his will directed his trustees to use his residuary estate for a number of designated purposes. These included (i) inquiries into how much time per individual scribe would be saved by substituting for the established English alphabet one containing at least 40 letters; (ii) to inquire how many persons were speaking and writing English in the usual form at any moment in the world; (iii) to ascertain the time and labour wasted by the lack of at least 14 unequivocal syllables and estimate the loss of income in British and American currency; and (iv) to employ a phonetic expert to transliterate the testator's play *Androcles and the Lion* into the proposed English alphabet. It was held that the trusts were not charitable for they merely tended to an increase of public knowledge in the advantages of the proposed alternative alphabet: the research and propaganda enjoined by the testator merely tended to the increase of public knowledge in a particular respect, namely, the saving of time and money by the use of the proposed alphabet. There was "no element of teaching or education" combined with this. It was also argued that the trusts were charitable as being in some way beneficial to the community (within the fourth head of Lord Macnaghten's classification). This argument was also rejected because it was highly controversial whether the proposals were in fact beneficial.

The question of the ambit of "education" was given fresh consideration by Wilberforce J. in *Re Hopkins' Will Trusts*.[38] The testatrix had given part of her residuary estate to the "Francis Bacon Society" to be applied towards finding the "Bacon-Shakespeare" manuscripts. One of the main objects of the society was "to encourage the general study of the evidence of Francis Bacon's authorship of plays commonly ascribed to Shakespeare." The terms of the will were, therefore, held to mean that the money was to be used to search for manuscripts of plays commonly ascribed to Shakespeare but believed by the testatrix and the society to have been written by Bacon. The judge held that the purposes of search or research for original manuscripts of England's greatest dramatist were within the law's conception of a charitable purpose on two grounds, (i) as being for education and (ii) as being for other purposes beneficial to the community within the fourth head of Lord Macnaghten's classification, because it was a gift for the improvement of this country's literary heritage. He had something to say about

---

[37] [1957] 1 W.L.R. 729; appeal dismissed by consent on terms that a sum of money should be devoted to these inquiries: [1958] 1 All E.R. 245n.

[38] [1965] Ch. 669. See also *Re Shakespeare Memorial Trust* [1923] 2 Ch. 398 (erection and endowment of a Shakespeare Memorial National Theatre with the object of performing Shakespeare's plays, reviving English classical drama and stimulating the art of acting: good charitable trust).

Harman J.'s dictum in *Re Shaw* that if the object was merely the increase of knowledge that in itself was not a charitable object unless combined with teaching or education. Wilberforce J. was unwilling to treat these words as meaning that the promotion of academic research was not a charitable purpose unless the researchers were engaged in teaching or education in the conventional sense. Many people would agree with the judge's conclusion that the term "education" should be used in a wide sense, certainly as extending beyond teaching.[39] Wilberforce J. also performed the valuable service of spelling out the requirements that must be satisfied by "research" in order to be charitable, though even this formulation was not expressed to be exhaustive: (i) it must be of educational value to the researcher, or (ii) it must be so directed so as to lead to something which will pass into the store of educational material, or (iii) so as to improve the sum of communicable knowledge in an area which education may cover, education in this last context extending to the formation of literary taste and appreciation.[40]

This decision might be said to be part of a trend which has broadened the field of "education," from which *Re Shaw* is arguably an aberration. Among many cases which demonstrate how widely the idea of education has been considered,[41] *Re Dupree's Deed Trusts*[42] where a trust for the encouragement of chess playing among the boys and youths of Portsmouth was upheld as charitable might be instanced. Again, in *Re Delius*[43] the wife of the composer Delius gave her residuary estate for the advancement of her husband's musical work by means of gramophone recordings, publication of his works and financing of public performances of his work. It was held that the purpose of the trust was to spread the knowledge and appreciation of Delius's work throughout the world and constituted an effective educational charity. It seems rather curious that it was found necessary to point out that the fact that pleasure was an incident of that appreciation or that the effect of the trust was to enhance the reputation of Delius did not prevent this result. More conventionally, the promotion of "art" has also been held to be charitable.[44] But perhaps one of the most striking, if not startling, cases in which education was given an extremely and perhaps unjustifiably wide connotation was *Re Shaw's Will Trusts*[45] where the

---

[39] *Ibid* at p. 680.

[40] At p. 680. The Goodman Committee recommended that "research" should be a charitable object in its own right.

[41] See also *Re Mellody* [1918] 1 Ch. 228 (annual school treat); *Re Cranstoun* [1932] 1 Ch. 537 (preservation of ancient buildings); *Re Spence* [1938] Ch. 96 (collection of arms and antiques); *Re Webber* [1954] 1 W.L.R. 1500 (Boy Scouts); *Re Levien* [1955] 1 W.L.R. 964 (raising musical standards); *Re Koettgen's Will Trusts* [1954] Ch. 252 (commercial education); *Royal Choral Society* v. *I.R.C.* (1943) 112 L.J.K.B. 648 (choral society); *Re Royce* [1940] Ch. 514 (church choir).

[42] [1945] Ch. 16.

[43] [1957] Ch. 299.

[44] *Re The Town and Country Planning Act 1947, Crystal Palace* v. *Minister of Town and Country Planning* [1951] Ch. 132. But "artistic" is too vague to be charitable: see *Associated Artists Ltd* v. *I.R.C.* [1956] 1 W.L.R. 752. With regard to "the arts" the Goodman Committee recommended that their promotion should be a proper charitable object in its own right, not merely as a sub-branch of education.

[45] [1952] Ch. 163.

testatrix, who was the wife of George Bernard Shaw and (it is necessary to add) herself of Irish origin bequeathed the residue of her estate upon trusts (*inter alia*) for the teaching, promotion and encouragement in Ireland of self-control, elocution, oratory, deportment, the arts of personal contact, of social intercourse and the other arts of public and private life. It was held that these somewhat eccentric trusts were wholly educational in character and constituted valid charitable trusts. Much less controversial was *Re South Place Ethical Society*[46] where it was held that the cultivation of a rational religious sentiment was for the advancement of education because a rational sentiment could only be cultivated by educational methods.

As might be expected, trusts for the establishment and support of professorships and lectureships are educational in character[47] but it should also be noticed that satellite purposes such as increasing the stipends of university teachers and fellows of colleges will also be upheld.[48] The same principles apply to schools,[49] colleges and universities,[50] and learned societies and institutions.[51]

It was also held in *Incorporated Council of Law Reporting for England and Wales* v. *Att.-Gen.*[52] that the Council was an educational charity[53]: the preparation of law reports was for the advancement of education because their purpose was to record accurately the development and application of judge-made law and thereby disseminate knowledge of that law. The law, it was held by the Court of Appeal, was properly to be regarded as a science and, therefore, books which were produced for the purpose of enabling it to be studied were published for the advancement of education. It was also held that the fact that the reports were used by the legal profession for the purpose of earning fees did not make the purposes non-charitable. It may be observed that, albeit the Council was carrying on a business, its profits could only be applied in pursuit of the Council's objects. If the profits could have enured for the benefit of the individual members it would not have achieved charitable status.[54]

Another case, which may be thought to have given an equally robust interpretation to educational charity, is *London Hospital Medical College*

---

[46] [1980] 1 W.L.R. 1565. For other aspects of the case see *post*, pp. 319, 323, 338.

[47] *Att.-Gen* v. *Margaret and Regius Professors at Cambridge* (1682) 1 Vern. 55.

[48] *Case of Christ's College, Cambridge* (1751) 1 W.B.1. 90.

[49] See *The Abbey Malvern Wells Ltd* v. *Ministry of Local Government and Planning* [1951] Ch. 728, where a girls' school was carried on by a private company, but under a trust deed all dividends were applied for school purposes. The school was held charitable. Danckwerts J. said (at p. 737) that all schools of learning are treated as charitable unless they exist purely as profit-making ventures. *cf. Re Girls Public Day School Trust Ltd.* [1951] Ch. 400 where the school in question was not charitable because shareholders were beneficially interested. See also *post, infra*, 324.

[50] *Case of Christ's College, Cambridge* (1751) 1 W.B.1. 90.

[51] *e.g.* the Royal College of Surgeons: see *Royal College of Surgeons* v. *National Provincial Bank Ltd.* [1952] A.C. 631.

[52] [1972] Ch. 73.

[53] Russell L.J. dissented, so far as the educational aspect was concerned, but all members of the C.A. agreed that it was also charitable as being for the benefit of the community within the fourth head of Lord Macnaghten's classification: see *post*, p. 323.

[54] *cf.* the cases cited in n. 49, *ante*.

v. *I.R.C.*,[55] which involved the students' union of the London Hospital. The union was under the control of the medical college, an educational charity, and its objects were to "promote social, cultural and athletic activities amongst the members and to add to the comfort and enjoyment of the students." The question was whether the predominant object of the union was the furtherance of the purposes of the medical college as a school of learning (in which case it was charitable); or whether its objects were the private and personal benefit of those students who were members of the union (in which case it would not be).[56] Brightman J. held that it had no *raison d'être* except to further the educational purposes of the medical college and it was accordingly charitable. What it did and was intended to do, said the judge, was to assist the teaching of medicine by providing those physical, cultural and social outlets which were needed, or at any rate highly desirable, if the art of teaching was to be efficiently performed at the College.[57]

But although, generally speaking, education has been regarded as a conception of some width for the purposes of charity, there are limits beyond which the courts will not go. There is, in the end, a question of degree to be determined, and it might be argued that the alphabet trust in *Re Shaw* fell on the wrong side of the line. But a case where the trusts were clearly out of order was *Re Pinion*[58] and this was the decision of the Court of Appeal reversing Wilberforce J. A testator gave his studio and pictures, one of which he attributed to Lely and some of which were painted by himself, his antique furniture, silver, china and other things to be offered to the National Trust to be kept intact in the studio and maintained as a collection. If the National Trust declined the trust, as in fact it did, he authorised the appointment of trustees to carry out the trust. It was acknowledged that a gift to found a public museum may be assumed to be charitable if no one questions it. But if the utility of the gift was brought in question, as it was here, it was essential to know something of the quality of the exhibits and for this purpose expert evidence was admissible to assist the court in judging the educational value of the gift.[59] The evidence was to the effect that the collection was of low quality—the Lely was bogus and the testator's own paintings were bad. Among the furniture there were some genuine English and Continental pieces of the seventeenth and eighteenth centuries which might be acceptable as a gift to a minor provincial museum. But, according to the terms of the will, everything had to be exhibited

---

[55] [1976] 1 W.L.R. 613; *cf. Re Bushnell* [1975] 1 W.L.R. 1596 in which a trust for the advancement of "socialised medicine" was held not to be educational: discussed *post*, p. 331. In certain cases trusts for sport may be upheld as educational trusts: see *post*, p. 327.

[56] This was the result in *I.R.C. v. City of Glasgow Police Athletic Association* [1953] A.C. 380, discussed *post*, p. 327.

[57] *Ibid.* at pp. 623, 624. It was apparently thought relevant that the London Hospital is on a site adjoining the Whitechapel and Commercial Roads in the East End of London; this was described as a "somewhat remote part of London": *ibid.* at p. 621.

[58] [1965] Ch. 85.

[59] For another example of expert evidence being admitted, see *Gilmour v. Coats* [1949] A.C. 426 and see *post*, p. 322.

together, and the good things would be stifled by the large number of absolutely valueless pictures and objects. Harman L.J. could conceive of no useful purpose in "foisting on the public this mass of junk."[60] The trust had neither public utility nor educational value and, therefore, failed as a charity.

It is, it might be thought, an elementary proposition that if an institution is devoted to educational purposes (or indeed any other specific charitable purposes) its funds can only be applied to those purposes. Nevertheless the question arose for decision in *Baldry* v. *Feintuck*.[61] In this case the University of Sussex Students Union, which was conceded in argument[62] to be an educational charity, voted to authorise payments to "War on Want," a charitable (but non-educational) organisation and to a campaign of protest against the Government's policy of ending the supply of free milk to schoolchildren, this being political and therefore non-charitable.[63] Brightman J. held that the moneys could not be applied for such purposes. A similar decision was reached in *Webb* v. *O'Doherty*[63A], where expenditure of student union funds on a campaign to end the Gulf War was restrained.

One of the current controversial questions in the field of education, which requires a mention, concerns the charitable status of independent schools[64]; there is no doubt that many are registered charities. The Expenditure Committee has recommended that in order to be charitable, schools should, "manifestly devote the education they provide towards meeting a range of clear educational needs throughout the whole community,[65] thereby indicating that many independent schools should lose their charitable status. The Goodman Committee considered, however, that any decision to curtail independent education would be a political one; that any such policy should be implemented by political decision; and while independent education continues to exist it should, as a general proposition, remain within the ambit of charity.[66]

(3) Trusts for the advancement of religion

As in the criminal law, so in equity there is a large measure of toleration. Indeed a high degree of toleration was recognised over a hundred years ago in *Thornton* v. *Howe*[67] where Sir John Romilly M.R. recognised as charitable a trust for the publication of the work of Joanna Southcott even though he evidently thought her doctrines to be

---

[60] [1965] Ch. 85 at p. 107.
[61] [1972] 1 W.L.R. 552.
[62] See *per* Brightman J. in *London Hospital Medical College* v. *I.R.C.* [1976] 1 W.L.R. 613 at p. 624.
[63] See *post*, p. 330.
[63A] *The Times*, February 11, 1991.
[64] See *ante*, p. 316.
[65] *Loc. cit.* at p. xvi.
[66] Making the point that the present system makes a very considerable contribution to the field of education, p. 25.
[67] (1862) 31 Beav. 14.

ridiculous. It would also appear from this case that the advancement of all religions which are "not subversive of all morality"[68] will be held to be charitable. As it happens, there is not a great deal of authority on non-Christian religions,[69] but there seems no reason why all of them should not be recognised. Yet there may be limits to the court's liberality, for the court appears in this context to have taken account only of monotheistic religion. Thus in *Yeap Cheah Neo* v. *Ong Cheng Neo*[70] the Privy Council held that a trust requiring ancestor worship was not charitable. This case is not, however, decisive, and it could be distinguished on the ground that the religious observances enjoined were not for the public benefit, merely for the alleged advantage of the deceased and his family. It would appear that the time has come to recognise formally the major religions of the world, whatever their forms, although in certain cases a line has to be drawn. Increasingly today "fringe" religious organisations have come into being.[71] Some are so fanciful or freakish that public benefit can justly be said to be lacking, and charitable status should not be accorded to them.[72]

Clearly, however, a gift for rationalist purposes—designed to demonstrate that religious belief is erroneous—would not fall within the ambit of a trust for the advancement of religion.[73] Likewise, gifts for ethical or moral societies not founded on belief in a deity are not for the advancement of religion. Nevertheless, they may be held to be charitable on other grounds. The question arose in *Re South Place Ethical Society*[74] which was established for the study and dissemination of "ethical principles" and the cultivation of a rational religious sentiment, but eschewing all supernatural belief. "Ethical principles" were described by Dillon J. as belief in the excellence of truth, love and beauty, but not belief in anything supernatural. It was held that the Society was not founded for the advancement of religion because, in the words of the judge, "religion . . . is concerned with man's relations

---

[68] *Ibid.* at p. 20. This principle was applied by Plowman J. in *Re Watson* [1973] 1 W.L.R. 1472 in upholding a trust for the publication and distribution of religious writings of no intrinsic merit but which displayed a religious tendency, and by Walton J. in *Holmes* v. *Att.-Gen.* [1981] Ch. Com. Rep. 10 in upholding a trust for the Exclusive Brethren. The correctness of Romilly M.R.'s statement of principle in *Thornton* v. *Howe*, however, still remains open to review by the court. See also *Bowman* v. *Secular Society Ltd.* [1917] A.C. 406.

[69] But see *Straus* v. *Goldsmid* (1837) 8 Sim. 614 (trust for practice of Jewish religion valid); *Neville Estates Ltd.* v. *Madden* [1962] Ch. 832 (trust for Catford synagogue valid); *Dawkins* v. *Gown Suppliers (PSA)* The Times, February 4, 1993 (Rastafarians).

[70] (1875) L.R. 381. See also *Re Hummeltenberg* [1923] 1 Ch. 237 (gift to college for training spiritualistic mediums); *Re Price* [1943] Ch. 422 (gift to the "Anthroposophical Society"). Neither case fell within trusts for the advancement of religion, and could only be considered under the fourth head of Lord Macnaghten's classification. The former was held invalid; the latter valid.

[71] The Unification Church (The "Moonies") has been registered as a Charity (Annual Report 1982, paras. 36–38).

[72] The Goodman Committee considered that religious organisations detrimental to the moral welfare of the community should be excluded (p. 23).

[73] *Bowman* v. *Secular Society Ltd.* [1917] A.C. 406.

[74] [1981] 1 W.L.R. 1565.

with God, and ethics are concerned with man's relations with man."[75] The objects of the Society were, however, upheld as charitable on other grounds, first, they were for the mental and moral improvement of man and were, therefore, beneficial to the community within the fourth head of Lord Macnaghten's classification,[76] and secondly, they were for the advancement of education.[77]

Quite apart from gifts for the advancement of a religion or a religious sect as such, a number of satellite purposes have been recognised as charitable under this head, notably gifts for mission work. Thus in *Re Moon's Will Trusts*[78] a bequest for "mission work" was made. The expression was held on the evidence to connote "Christian mission work" and that was held to be charitable. Similarly, trusts for the maintenance and repair of a church, a stained glass window[79] or vault[80] within the church have been held to be charitable; and the same will apply to the churchyard and burial ground even if restricted to a particular religious sect[81] and also to the graves in it, provided that the maintenance of *all* the graves is the object for the gift.[82] Indeed cremation has also been held to be a charitable purpose.[83]

It is essential that the purpose of a trust should be exclusively charitable, and this rule applies generally in the law, subject to the Charitable Trusts (Validation) Act 1954.[84] In this context, therefore, the purpose of the trust should be exclusively religious. A draftsman may easily say quite unwittingly far too much—even by a word or two—in the trust instrument. The cases on the question whether a trust is exclusively religious are difficult and present several fine distinctions. Normally, a gift will be made to a person holding a religious office, such as a bishop, and the additional words that may permissibly be used to create a valid charitable trust appear to fall into two groups:

(1) They may give an absolute discretion to the donee. In *Re Garrard*,[85] a gift was made "to the vicar and churchwardens of Kingston to be applied by them in such manner as they shall in their sole discretion think fit." Similarly, in *Re Rumball*[86] a gift was made "to the bishop for the time being of the Windward Islands to be applied by him

---

[75] *Ibid.* at p. 571. It was noted (at p. 573) that Buddhism was accepted as a religion although there was no belief in a god, but that question was not explored further.

[76] See *post*, p. 323.

[77] See *ante*, p. 314. The Goodman Committee recommended that ethical and moral societies not founded on belief in a deity should be recognised as charitable on the basis that they promote the moral improvement of the community.

[78] [1948] 1 All E.R. 300.

[79] *Re King* [1923] 1 Ch. 243. See also *Re Royce* [1940] Ch. 514.

[80] *Hoare* v. *Osborne* (1886) L.R. 1 Eq. 585.

[81] *Re Manser* [1905] 1 Ch. 68 (Society of Friends).

[82] *Re Pardoe* [1906] 2 Ch. 184; in this case a gift for a peal of bells on the anniversary of the restoration of the monarchy also held to be charitable: *sed quaere. cf.* Brunyate (1946) 61 L.Q.R. 268, 274; *Re Eighmie* [1935] Ch. 524 (keeping in repair burial ground *and* monument to testator's late husband) and see *ante*, p. 121).

[83] *Scottish Burial Reform and Cremation Society Ltd.* v. *Glasgow Corporation* [1968] A.C. 138.

[84] See *post*, p. 335.

[85] [1907] 1 Ch. 382.

[86] [1956] Ch. 105. The judgment of Jenkins L.J. is a notable exposition of the law.

as he thinks fit in his diocese." In both cases, as in several others,[87] where an absolute discretion was conferred, the gift was upheld as charitable. The reason was the gift was made to a person by his official name whose official status required charitable duties to be performed. Accordingly, the gift was assumed to be made for the charitable purposes inherent in that official status. This principle which arises *virtute officii* applies not merely to religious persons but to the holders of other offices.

(2) The words confine the object of the gift within the ambit of the donee's religious function. For example, in *Re Eastes*[88] there was a gift "to the vicar and churchwardens, to be used by them for any purpose *in connection with the Church*[89] which they shall select." This gift was upheld. But if the testator goes on to invite the donee to take into account the *social* as well as the religious functions of his office, the gift will fail. Here the settlor may unconsciously say too much. This principle—though it may be no more than apparent—is illustrated by the leading case of *Dunne* v. *Byrne*[90] where a gift was made to the Roman Catholic Archbishop of Brisbane and his successors to be used as they *may judge most conducive to the good of religion in the diocese.* The italicised words were held by the Privy Council to be too wide and the gift failed. Perhaps the most notorious words to induce fatality are "parish work": a gift failed for this reason in the well-known decision of the House of Lords in *Farley* v. *Westminster Bank.*[91]

What has been said so far represents an attempt at rationalising some of the case law. But the reader should be warned that these cases are difficult and depend on a close reading of the gift or trust. And at times to recognise the distinction between any two cases decided differently requires hair-splitting which seems excessive.[92]

Public benefit[93]

Like other charitable trusts—with the exception of trusts for the relief of poverty—a religious trust must be for the benefit of the public. It is no doubt a difficult task to assess public benefit in a religious trust. Nevertheless the test has to be satisfied. Thus, in the controversial decision in

---

[87] See *Re Simson* [1946] Ch. 299 ("to the Vicar of St. Luke's Ramsgate, to be used for work in the parish": valid): *cf. Farley* v. *Westminster Bank* [1939] A.C. 430, *infra* ("for parish work": bad): *Re Flinn* [1948] Ch. 241 (to the Archbishop of Westminster Cathedral to be used by him "for such purposes as he shall in his absolute discretion think fit": valid). See also *Re Norman* [1947] Ch. 349 (to the editors of a missionary periodical who were also trustees of a missionary church, to be applied "for such objects as they may think fit": valid).

[88] [1948] Ch. 257. See also *Re Bain* [1930] 1 Ch. 224 (to a vicar "for such objects connected with the church as he shall think fit"); *Re Norton's Will Trusts* [1948] 2 All E.R. 842 ("for the benefit of the parish": *cf. Farley* v. *Westminster Bank, supra*).

[89] Italics added.

[90] [1912] A.C. 407.

[91] [1939] A.C. 430. The words "parochial institutions or purposes" were also fatal in *Re Stratton* [1931] 1 Ch. 197.

[92] See cases cited in nn. 87 and 88, *supra*.

[93] See Newark (1946) 62 L.Q.R. 234.

Gilmour v. *Coats*,[94] the trust fund was to be applied to the purposes of a Carmelite convent. The convent comprised an association of strictly cloistered and purely contemplative nuns who did not engage in any activities for the benefit of people outside the convent. The House of Lords held that (i) the benefit of intercessory prayer could not be proved in law and (ii) the element of edification was too vague and intangible. It might be thought that far too stringent a test of public benefit was applied in this case.[95] However, whether this is so or not, it is distinguishable from a case like *Neville Estates* v. *Madden*.[96] This involved Catford synagogue which was not open to the public as of right, and Cross J. held that a trust in favour of the synagogue was charitable. The distinction is that the enclosed nuns lived apart from the world, whereas the members of the synagogue lived in the world, and a public benefit accrued as a result of their attendance at a place of religious worship.

Rather different considerations have been applied to trusts for masses for the dead.[97] Luxmoore J. in *Re Caus*[98] held that a gift for such purposes was charitable. There was no provision in the testator's will in this case that the masses should be said in public; and the judge did not distinguish between masses said in public and those said in private. Indeed he seemed to indicate that a gift for masses was in all cases charitable. In view of *Gilmour* v. *Coats* this seemed to be wrong. This was confirmed in *Re Hetherington (deceased)*[99] where a gift of £2,000 to the Roman Catholic Bishop of Westminster for "masses for the repose of the souls of my husband and my parents and my sisters and also myself when I die" was held to be charitable on the grounds that sufficient public benefit was conferred by the public celebration of a religious rite and that the provision of stipends for the celebrants endowed the priesthood. It does not, however, seem likely that the latter reason would be sufficient to cause a gift for masses to be said in private to be charitable. Such trusts can however take effect as non-charitable purpose trusts.[1]

---

[94] [1949] A.C. 426. Likewise see *Cocks* v. *Manners* (1871) L.R. 12 Eq. 574 (enclosed Roman Catholic convent); *Hoare* v. *Hoare* (1886) 56 L.T. 147 (private chapel): *Re Joy* (1889) 60 L.T. 175 (to suppress cruelty to animals by prayer); *Re Warre's Will Trusts* [1953] 1 W.L.R. 725 (retreat house; but this case seems to have been wrongly decided: retreatants do mix in the world: they go into retreat only for a few days' contemplation and prayer). *cf. Neville Estates Ltd.* v. *Madden* [1962] Ch. 832 discussed in the text. *cf.* also *Re Banfield* [1968] 1 W.L.R. 846, where the gift was to a religious community ("Pilsdon Community House") and Goff J. held this to be a charitable trust because of its primarily religious character and also because it was for the general public benefit in providing a temporary home of rest for those who need it.

[95] The Goodman Committee suggested that contemplative communities do not normally have proper charitable objects, but a value judgment has to be made in each case.

[96] [1962] Ch. 832; and see *Holmes* v. *Att.-Gen.* (1981) Ch. Com. Rep. 10 (Exclusive Brethren).

[97] It is established that a gift for masses is not void as being for superstitious uses: *Bourne* v. *Kean* [1919] A.C. 815. The question remains however whether it is charitable.

[98] [1934] Ch. 162.

[99] [1990] Ch. 1.

[1] See *ante*, p. 119.

(4) Trusts for other purposes beneficial to the community

This is the residuary class in Lord Macnaghten's classification in *Pemsel's* case. It has been seen that the modern trend appears to be to look to the "equity" or the "mischief" of the preamble to the Statute of Elizabeth I, in order to decide whether a given purpose falls within it, rather than rely on the approach based upon analogy.[2] The class certainly presents a most variegated collection of decisions and the following does not profess to be an exhaustive account, but merely illustrations of a number of the purposes allowed admission into this class.[3]

(a) **Animals.** It is clearly established that a trust for the protection of animals generally is a valid charitable trust.[4] This is so, as it has been held, because it benefits humanity by promoting morality and curbing an inborn tendency to cruelty[5]—a somewhat surprising process of reasoning even in an animal-loving country. But, however surprising, it indicates that the reason for the recognition of these trusts is that they promote the moral or spiritual welfare of the community whereas the basis of most other examples of Lord Macnaghten's fourth head is "public utility."[6]

A second proposition, which arises from the decision of a particular case, *Re Grove-Grady*,[7] is that if the settlor establishes a trust to provide a sanctuary for all kinds of animals from human molestation with no safeguards against the destruction of the weaker animals by the stronger, the trust is not charitable. As Lord Hanworth M.R. pointed out[8] the one characteristic of the trust was that the sanctuary was to be free from molestation by man, while all the fauna within it were to be free to molest and harry one another. And such a purpose did not afford any advantage to animals or any protection from cruelty to animals; nor did it afford any elevating lesson to mankind.[9]

---

[2] See, *e.g. Scottish Burial Reform and Cremation Society* v. *Glasgow City Corporation* [1968] A.C. 138; *Incorporated Council of Law Reporting for England and Wales* v. *Att.-Gen.* [1972] Ch. 73; and see *ante*, p. 316.

[3] For a detailed treatment, see *Tudor on Charities* (7th ed.), pp. 82 *et seq.*

[4] *Re Wedgwood* [1915] 1 Ch. 113 (secret trust for protection and benefit of animals).

[5] *Re Wedgwood, ibid.* at p. 117, *per* Lord Cozens-Hardy M.R.; *Re Moss* [1949] 1 All E.R. 415 at pp. 497–498, *per* Romer J. (cats and kittens); *cf.* earlier cases *e.g. London University* v. *Yarrow* (1857) 1 De G. & J. 72 (animal hospital) and *Re Douglas* (1887) 35 Ch.D. 472 (Home for Lost Dogs): the court emphasised public utility but this is not the modern trend; *cf.* also *ante*, p. 119.

[6] For other examples of "moral or spiritual improvement" see *Re Price* [1943] Ch. 422 (gift to the "Anthroposophical Society"); *Re South Place Ethical Society* [1980] 1 W.L.R. 1565 (society for the study and dissemination of "ethical principles" and the cultivation of a rational religious sentiment: see *ante*, p. 316).

[7] [1929] 1 Ch. 557, compromised on appeal *sub nom. Att.-Gen.* v. *Plowden* [1931] W.N. 89.

[8] *Ibid.* at pp. 573–574.

[9] The main reason for citing this case is to emphasise the importance of careful drafting of the trust instrument, so that the "public benefit" requirement is satisfied. There is no doubt that a competently drawn trust for the preservation of wild life, taking due account of public benefit, will be charitable.

Thirdly, there is the principle established by the House of Lords in *National Anti-Vivisection Society* v. *I.R.C.*[10] that a trust to abolish vivisection is not charitable. It was so held in this case for two reasons, (i) the advantages accruing from the abolition of vivisection did not equal those derived from its retention and (ii) anti-vivisection could not be achieved except by legislation and (so it was said) the law could not stultify itself by holding that it was for the public benefit that the law itself should be changed.[11]

Finally, it should be noticed that although prima facie an animal hospital is a charity[12] it will not be so if it is carried on for private profit as a profession, occupation or trade.[13]

(b) Recreational trusts. The Recreational Charities Act 1958, which came into force on March 3, 1958, regulates recreational trusts. The Act was passed because of the highly inconvenient decision of the House of Lords in *I.R.C.* v. *Baddeley*[14] which concerned certain trusts "for the promotion of the moral, social and physical well-being of persons resident in West Ham and Leyton who for the time being are members or likely to become members of the Methodist Church . . . by the provision of facilities for moral, social and physical training and recreation." It was decided, by a majority, that the trusts failed because they were expressed in language so vague as to permit the property to be used for purposes which the law did not recognise as charitable and also because they did not satisfy the necessary test of public benefit. This case produced a situation where legislation of some kind was essential because as a result of the decision it appeared that there might be grave doubts as to the charitable status of many organisations and trusts, including women's institutes, boys' clubs, miners' welfare trusts and village halls which, it had been assumed, had enjoyed charitable status for a very long time. The legislation that very promptly followed was the Recreational Charities Act of 1958. It provides that it shall be and shall be deemed always to have been charitable to provide, or assist in providing, facilities for recreation or other leisure-time occupations if the facilities are provided in the interest of social welfare.[15] This is subject to the overriding proviso that the trust will not be charitable unless it is for the public benefit.[16] Furthermore the requirement that facilities must be provided in the interest of social welfare is not satisfied unless:

---

[10] [1948] A.C. 31, reversing *Re Foveaux* [1895] 2 Ch. 501. See also *Re Jenkins's Will Trusts* [1966] Ch. 249 (gift to the British Union for the Abolition of Vivisection).

[11] Adopting *Tyssen on Charitable Bequests* (1st ed., 1898), p. 176. See also *Bowman* v. *Secular Society Ltd.* [1917] A.C. 406 at p. 442 (*per* Lord Parker) (Political purposes); and see *post*, p. 330.

[12] *London University* v. *Yarrow* (1857) 1 De G. & J. 72.

[13] See *Re Satterthwaite's Will Trusts* [1966] 1 W.L.R. 277 at p. 284, *per* Russell L.J.

[14] [1955] A.C. 572.

[15] s.1.(1). The expression "social welfare" is used in the Local Government Finance Act 1988.

[16] s.1(1) proviso.

(a) it is provided with the object of improving the conditions of life for the persons for whom the facilities are primarily intended,[17] *and*

(b) either (i) those persons have need of such facilities by reason of their youth, age, infirmity or disablement, poverty or social and economic circumstances[18] or (ii) the facilities are to be available to the members or female members of the public at large.[19]

The composition of this part of the Act seems to be somewhat curious. It will be noted in particular that ingredient (ii) is alternative to ingredient (i) and this will mean that a trust must satisfy one or other of them. Accordingly, it appears that a recreational trust in favour of a limited class of the public will be within the Act if the beneficiaries are youthful, aged, infirm, disabled, or their "social and economic circumstances" are such that they have need of the facilities provided. But if the beneficiaries do not fall into these prescribed classes, the facilities must be available to the whole of the public, and a trust in favour of a limited class would fail. There may well be a case for thus confining the objectives of the Act. But it is perhaps unfortunate that the position is not formulated with more precision.

The effect of these provisions (in particular the terms "social welfare" and "conditions of life") was considered by the Court of Appeal in *I.R.C.* v. *McMullen*[20] which concerned the Football Association Youth Trust. It was held (*inter alia*) by the majority that the recreational facilities provided were primarily intended for pupils in schools and universities but they were not provided with the object of improving the conditions of life of such pupils: they were provided for those of them who were persuaded to, or did, play football or some other game or sport irrespective of their conditions of life. Therefore, the trusts did not fall within the Act. Bridge L.J. dissented on the ground that the provision of recreational facilities for pupils unquestionably improved the pupils' conditions of life and met a social need of youth. This decision was reversed by the House of Lords on other grounds,[21] so the question of the effect of the Act did not fall to be considered. As a matter of statutory interpretation, however, the opinion of Bridge L.J. appears to be highly persuasive and has now been approved by the House of Lords in *Guild* v. *I.R.C.*[22] The case concerned a gift of residue "to the town council of North Berwick for the use in connection with the sports centre in North Berwick or some similar purpose in connection with sport". This gift was held to fall within the Act on the grounds that

---

[17] s.1(2)(*a*).

[18] s.1(2)(*b*)(i).

[19] s.1(2)(*b*)(ii).

[20] [1979] 1 W.L.R. 130; for another aspect of the decision and the facts, see *post*, p. 328. See also Warburton (1980) Conv. 173.

[21] [1981] A.C. 1; see *post*, p. 328.

[22] [1992] 2 W.L.R. 397 (a Scottish Appeal but the English definition of charity is incorporated into Scots law for tax purposes).

"persons in all walks of life and all kinds of social circumstances may have their condition of life improved by the provision of recreational facilities of suitable character"[23] and the facilities of the centre would have this effect.

Subject to the facilities being provided in the interests of social welfare, the Act is specifically applied, in particular, to the "provision of facilities at village halls, community centres and women's institutes and to the provision and maintenance of grounds and buildings to be used for purposes of recreation or leisure-time occupation and extends to the provision of facilities for those purposes by the organising of any activity".[24] But these are simply well-known examples of recreational charity and this provision will not affect the generality of the statutory powers.

Miners' welfare trusts are specially provided for[25]: such trusts as were declared before December 17, 1957,[26] are validated retrospectively though there are certain savings as to past transactions.[27] Indeed this provision appears to be entirely retrospective so that all *new* miners' trusts must fall within the statutory provisions discussed at the outset.[28]

The Act leaves untouched the existing law as to the meaning of charity.[29] It would also seem to leave untouched the other point—that the trusts must be for the public benefit—which came under consideration in *I.R.C.* v. *Baddeley* case. It appeared, certainly in the opinion of Viscount Simonds,[30] that the membership, actual or potential, of the Methodist Church, at least in a defined area, did not amount to a class sufficient to satisfy the test of public benefit, although Lord Reid, who dissented, took a different view.[31] If the opinion of Viscount Simonds is adopted, trusts such as these would still fail. It was that part of the decision that the trusts were too uncertain which aroused apprehension among the women's institutes and other bodies and which the statute was designed to cure. This limited objective may have been successfully achieved, even though the material provisions are somewhat clumsily and ambiguously expressed. It was thought at the time that it would be difficult to apply and probably create more difficulties than it solved,[32] but only occasionally in the reported cases has it arisen for consideration.[33]

---

[23] *Ibid.* at p. 404.
[24] s.1(3).
[25] s.2.
[26] This was the day of the first reading of the Bill in the House of Lords.
[27] s.3(2)(3)(4)(5).
[28] *i.e.* s.1.
[29] s.3(1).
[30] *Supra*, at pp. 589–593.
[31] *Supra*, at p. 606. Lord Somervell of Harrow seemed to agree with Lord Simonds; Lords Porter and Tucker expressed no opinion on the point.
[32] See Maurice (1959) 23 Conv. (N.S.) 15.
[33] See, *e.g. Wynn* v. *Skegness U.D.C.* [1967] 1 W.L.R. 52 where a seaside holiday home for Derbyshire miners was assumed to fall within the 1958 Act as a recreational charity; *I.R.C.* v. *McMullen* [1979] 1 W.L.R. 130 C.A., reversed on other grounds [1981] A.C. 1, H.L.; discussed *supra*, and *post*, p. 328.

(c) National and local defence. All trusts which promote the armed forces of the Crown are charitable[34] and this rule will apply even if the means to the end are indirect.[35] Likewise a trust for the Mercantile Marine, though not strictly part of the armed forces of the Crown, is charitable.[36] A more general purpose of promoting the defence of the United Kingdom from the attack of hostile aircraft has also been upheld.[37]

The same applies to more mundane, but equally important, domestic protection. Thus in *Re Wokingham Fire Brigade Trusts*,[38] Danckwerts J. held that the provision and maintenance of a public fire brigade was a charitable purpose because it was designed to prevent damage to property and loss of life. The promotion of the efficiency of the police is also self-evidently charitable. This was stated in *I.R.C. v. City of Glasgow Police Athletic Association*,[39] but in that case the question was whether the association itself was charitable and it was held not to be so because it was simply a sports club for the benefit of the members.

(d) Trusts for sport. It appears to be settled that a gift for the promotion of any given sport *simpliciter* is not charitable. Accordingly, in *Re Nottage*,[40] where a trust was established to provide annually a cup for the most successful yacht of the season, the testator stating that his object was to encourage the sport of yacht racing, the Court of Appeal held that that was a gift for the encouragement of a mere sport which, though it might be beneficial to the public, was not charitable.[41] But it should be pointed out that trusts for this purpose, if drawn so as to fall within the Recreational Charities Act 1958,[42] will now be effective. In any case, the provision of prizes for sport in a school was held in *Re Mariette*[43] to be valid as advancing that part of the education of students which had to do with their bodily and physical development. And the same result occurred in *Re Gray*,[44] where there was a gift for the promotion of a sport in an army regiment and it was held to be charitable because it increased the army's efficiency; but the validity of this last decision was doubted in *I.R.C. v. City of Glasgow Police Athletic*

---

[34] *Re Stratheden and Campbell* [1894] 3 Ch. 265 (benefit of volunteer corps); *Re Stephens* (1892) 8 T.L.R. 792 (for teaching shooting); *Re Barker* (1909) 25 T.L.R. 753 (for prizes to be competed for by cadets).

[35] *Re Good* [1905] 2 Ch. 60 (providing a library for officers' mess and providing plate for mess); *Re Donald* [1909] 2 Ch. 410 (for the mess of regiment and poor of regiment); *Re Gray* [1925] Ch. 362 (regimental fund for promotion of sport).

[36] *Re Corbyn* [1941] Ch. 400.

[37] *Re Driffill* [1950] Ch. 92.

[38] [1951] Ch. 373.

[39] [1953] A.C. 380 at 391.

[40] [1895] 2 Ch. 649.

[41] See also to the same effect *Re Clifford* (1911) 106 L.T. 14 (angling); *Re Patten* [1929] 2 Ch. 276, 289, 290 (cricket); *Re King* [1931] W.N. 232 (general sport); *I.R.C. v. City of Glasgow Police Athletic Association* [1953] A.C. 380 (athletic sports and general pastimes: discussed *supra.*).

[42] See *infra.*

[43] [1915] 2 Ch. 284. See also *Re Dupree's Deed Trusts* [1945] Ch. 16 (chess: discussed at p. 315, *ante*).

[44] [1925] Ch. 362.

Association.[45] The doubts appear to be unfounded because the army's efficiency is indeed promoted if soldiers are physically fit.[46]

It is clear that the trust instrument has to be construed to decide whether a particular charitable purpose is in fact promoted by the prescribed sporting activity. In *I.R.C.* v. *McMullen,*[47] for example, the legal effect of the Football Association Youth Trust had to be decided. Its object was to organise or provide or assist in the organisation and provision of facilities which would enable and encourage students at schools and universities to play Association Football or other games and sports and thereby to assist in ensuring that due attention was given to the physical education and development of such pupils as well as the occupation of their minds and, with a view to furthering this object, to providing such facilities as playing fields, equipment, and so forth. The House of Lords held (unanimously reversing Walton J. and the Court of Appeal) that the purpose of the deed was not merely to organise the playing of Association Football in schools and universities, but also to promote the physical education and development of students as an addition to their formal education and, therefore, it created a valid charitable trust for the advancement of education,[48] the sporting activities contributing to a balanced education. Lord Hailsham of St. Marylebone L.C.[49] was at pains to reject any idea which would cramp the education of the young within the school or university campus, limit it to formal instruction or render it devoid of pleasure in the exercise of skill.[50] The principle in *Re Mariette*[51] was held to apply.

(e) Locality trusts. A gift to a locality, such as a town or village, will be charitable even if no charitable purposes are specified.[52] A scheme[53] will be made so that the funds can be devoted to such purposes within the locality as are charitable. It has also been decided that the same principle applies to a gift to "my country, England."[54] That such trusts should be valid as charities seems curious[55] but is now established

---

[45] [1953] A.C. 380 at pp. 391, 401.

[46] The Goodman Committee recommended that the encouragement of sport and recreation should be recognised as an independent charitable object, provided that the necessary element of benefit to the community is present, and in so far as the Recreational Charities Act 1958 (see *ante,* p. 324) does not make this clear, then it should be amended.

[47] [1981] A.C. 1.

[48] For consideration of the Recreational Charities Act 1958, see *ante,* p. 324.

[49] A former Secretary of State for Education and Science.

[50] *Ibid.* at p. 18.

[51] *Supra.*

[52] See *Goodman* v. *Saltash Corpn.* (1882) 7 App.Cas. 633; *Re Allen* [1905] 2 Ch. 400; *Re Norton's Will Trusts* [1948] 2 All E.R. 842.

[53] See *post,* p. 338.

[54] *Re Smith* [1932] 1 Ch. 153. See also *Nightingale* v. *Goulbourne* (1847) 5 Hare 484 (gift to "the Queen's Chancellor of the Exchequer for the time being" to be used by him for the benefit of "my beloved country, Great Britain": valid. The case can also be justified on the ground that it was made *virtute officii,* see *ante,* p. 321).

[55] See *Tudor on Charities* (7th ed.), pp. 109 *et seq.* And see *Williams' Trustees* v. *I.R.C.* [1947] A.C. 447 at p. 459, *per* Lord Simonds.

beyond all possible doubt.[56] But it is most important, if a locality trust is to be upheld, to ensure that either exclusively charitable purposes within the locality be specified in the trust instrument, or, alternatively, that no purposes whatsoever be specified. If the settlor uses words which demonstrate in terms that the subject-matter of the gift may be used for non-charitable purposes it will fail. It failed, for example, in *Houston* v. *Burns*,[57] where the trust was for "public, benevolent or charitable purposes" in a Scottish parish. If, therefore, the purposes are not charitable *per se*, the localisation of them will not of itself make them charitable.[58]

(f) Institutional and other charities. A trust which is designed for a village hall, community centre, or other similar institutional purposes if drawn so as to fall within the Recreational Charities Act 1958[59] will create a valid charitable trust. Trusts for hospitals and other kindred purposes have been upheld as charitable as a matter of general law.[60]

Children's homes. The refinements all too evident in the law of charity were brought to the fore in the controversial and unfortunate decision of the Court of Appeal in *Re Cole*,[61] where the majority held that a gift for "the general benefit and general welfare" of children for the time being in a children's home maintained by a local authority was not charitable, Romer L.J. in particular based his decision to this effect on a close reading of the preamble to the Charitable Uses Act 1601 and concluded that the conceivable provision of benefits, and these could

---

[56] The Goodman Committee considered that local and denominational charities should be permitted to continue and be encouraged, and the same general principles should apply to analogous trusts for ethnic or national groups. With regard to the latter, there is a limited exception in favour of charities in the Race Relations Act 1976; it is provided (s.34) that any discrimination necessary to comply with the terms of the governing instrument of a charity which is established to confer a benefit on persons of a particular racial group shall not be unlawful, but it specifically excludes from the exception any provision which restricts the benefits by reference to race or colour. Accordingly, a school for the education of Pakistanis or Spaniards could lawfully be confined to such persons, but any provision *excepting* persons on racial grounds would be in breach of the Act. There is also an exception in favour of charity under the Sex Discrimination Act 1975. It is provided (s.43) that where the trusts contain a provision for conferring benefits on one sex only, anything done by the charity trustees to comply with that provision is not unlawful. This safeguards the position of single sex charities, like the Y.M.C.A., Y.W.C.A., Boy Scouts and Girl Guides, and many small parochial charities restricted to one sex (such as elderly widows). See further, the Reports of the Charity Commissioners for 1975 and 1976.
[57] [1918] A.C. 337; see also *Att.-Gen.* v. *National Provincial and Union Bank of England* [1924] A.C. 262 (patriotic purposes in the British Empire). And see *Re Strakosch* [1949] Ch. 529. The matter is discussed generally at p. 333, *post*.
[58] *Williams' Trustees* v. *I.R.C., supra*, at pp. 459–460, *per* Lord Simonds. This case involved an Institute of Welshmen in London which was not charitable because they were not an identifiable section of the community.
[59] See *ante*, p. 324.
[60] See, *e.g. Re Dean's Will Trusts* [1950] 1 All E.R. 882; *Re White's Will Trusts* [1951] 1 All E.R. 528; *Re Smith's Will Trusts* [1962] 2 All E.R. 563; *Re Adams* [1967] 1 W.L.R. 162; *Le Cras* v. *Perpetual Trustee Co.* [1967] 1 All E.R. 915, P.C.; *Re Resch's Will Trusts* [1969] A.C. 514, P.C.
[61] [1958] Ch. 877.

include such new-fangled devices as television sets, for the children in question (who might be juvenile delinquents) were not within the express terms of the preamble or within its spirit and intendment. The decision was followed by Danckwerts J. in *Re Sahal's Will Trusts*[62] on similar facts. But the dissenting view of Lord Evershed M.R. in *Re Cole* seems the more commendable, by reason of its wider outlook: "that the inference to be drawn from the preamble is that the care and upbringing of children who for any reason have not got the advantage or opportunity of being looked after and brought up by responsible and competent persons, or who could by these or other reasons, properly be regarded as defenceless or 'deprived' are matters which prima facie qualify as charitable purposes."[63]

(g) Political trusts. In *Bowman* v. *Secular Society Ltd.*[64] Lord Parker of Waddington stated the general position as follows:

"A trust for the attainment of political objects has always been held invalid, not because it is illegal, for everyone is at liberty to advocate or promote by any lawful means a change in the law, but because the court has no means of judging whether a proposed change in the law will or will not be for the public benefit, and therefore cannot say that a gift to secure the change is a charitable gift."

This basic principle, as has been seen,[65] was applied by the House of Lords in *National Anti-Vivisection Society* v. *I.R.C.*[66] in rejecting as charitable a trust to abolish vivisection as it would involve legislation to change the law, and it was reaffirmed more recently by Slade J. in *McGovern* v. *Att.-Gen.*[67] which concerned the legal status of Amnesty International. The general object of this unincorporated non-profit making body was expressed to be to secure throughout the world the observance of the provisions of the Universal Declaration of Human Rights in regard to various categories of persons referred to in its constitution as "prisoners of conscience," namely, persons who were imprisoned, detained or restricted because of their political, religious or conscientiously held beliefs or their ethnic origin, sex, colour or language. There were also various specific objects of the association the legal effect of which required to be considered: (1) the release of prisoners of conscience: this was held to be for political purposes and, therefore, not charitable because it involved putting pressure on foreign governments to change their policies; (2) the abolition of torture or inhumane treatment or punishment: this was not charitable because it would involve legislation requiring the abolition of corporal or capital punishment; and (3) providing research into the observance of human

---

[62] [1958] 1 W.L.R. 1243.
[63] [1958] Ch. 877 at p. 892.
[64] [1917] A.C. 406.
[65] See *ante*, p. 324.
[66] [1948] A.C. 31.
[67] [1982] 2 W.L.R. 222.

rights and the dissemination of that research: this would, if it had stood alone, have been charitable; but it did not stand alone: the trusts were required to be exclusively charitable and they were not. Accordingly, they all failed. This decision is an important illustration of the principle that, although a trust for the relief of human suffering or distress may well be capable of being of a charitable nature, it will not qualify if the main object is to secure an alteration in the law or government policy not only of the United Kingdom but also of a foreign country. It is, therefore, established that a trust to advance a political purpose will fail as a charity. Such trusts are often disguised as educational trusts, but such educational character as they may have will not enable them to succeed as charities if the primary object is political.[68] This was in effect the position in *McGovern* v. *Att.-Gen.* The trusts also failed for this reason in *Bonar Law Memorial Trust* v. *I.R.C.*[69] and in *Re Hopkinson*,[70] Conservative and Labour Party trusts respectively.

These last two mentioned cases were applied in *Re Bushnell*,[71] where the testator had directed a fund to be used "for the advancement and propagation of the teaching of socialised medicine", with directions on how the managers of the fund should carry out and foster this purpose. Goulding J. held that the trust could not be supported as an educational trust: the directions with regard to the principles of "socialised medicine" dominated the whole of the trust. It was also held that the trust was not beneficial to the community (within the fourth head of Lord Macnaghten's classification in *Pemsel's* case) since validity or otherwise had to be tested at the date of the testator's death (in this case 1941), and at that date the court could not have decided the question because it involved considering the desirability or otherwise of legislation to bring a state health service into being, which would be a political matter. The fact that a state health service was subsequently introduced was irrelevant; the trust had to stand or fall by the character of the objects at the date of the testator's death.

It should be stressed that the mere existence of some political motive is not necessarily fatal to a good charitable trust. Thus in *Re Koeppler's Will Trust*[72] the organisation of conferences with political themes but without any intention of furthering the interests of any particular political party was held to be an educational charitable purpose. The question is whether its leading purpose is political (*e.g.* promoting legislation to change the law), in which case it fails, or whether the purpose is subsidiary. The point was made by Lord Normand in *I.R.C.* v. *National Anti-Vivisection Society.*[73] In that case the primary purpose of the Society was political—as were the objects of Amnesty International in *McGovern* v. *Att.-Gen.* It is by no means easy to distinguish the

---

[68] See *Bowman* v. *Secular Society Ltd.* [1917] A.C. 406.
[69] (1933) 49 T.L.R. 220.
[70] [1949] 1 All E.R. 346.
[71] [1975] 1 W.L.R. 1596.
[72] [1986] Ch. 423.
[73] [1948] A.C. 31 at p. 76, and see *ante*, p. 324.

earlier decision of Stirling J. in *Re Scowcroft*,[74] where it was held that a gift for the maintenance of a village club and reading-room "to be used for the furtherance of Conservative principles and religious and mental improvement, and to be kept free from intoxicants and dancing" was good. But it may perhaps be distinguishable on the ground on which the case was apparently decided, that all the purposes prescribed were to be carried out simultaneously, and the political purpose was not, therefore, predominant.

A recent development in charity law and administration is, as the Charity Commissioners have pointed out,[75] the increasing desire of charities for "involvement" in the causes with which their work is connected, for example, housing and other services for the under-privileged in society. *McGovern* v. *Att.-Gen.* is an example of the problem in the international arena, but many charities operating in this country also feel that merely to relieve distress in particular cases is not enough. They wish to go further: to draw the attention of the public as forcefully as they can to the need for action to remedy certain social conditions. And the result has been that pressure groups, action groups and lobbies have come into being. The problem is whether such activities are of such a "political" nature as to vitiate the charitable status of the organisation in question. The Charity Commissioners in their Report for 1981 suggested fairly detailed guidelines for charity trustees in these circumstances. These include[76] the following: (i) a charity should undertake only those activities which can reasonably be said to be directed to achieving its purposes and which are within the powers conferred by its governing instrument; (ii) the governing instrument should not include powers to exert political pressure except in a way that is merely ancillary to a charitable purpose; (iii) the powers and purposes of a charity should not include power to bring pressure to bear on the Government to adopt, alter or maintain a particular line of action; (iv) the charity should spend its money on the promotion of public general legislation only if in doing so it is exercising a power which is ancillary to and in furtherance of its charitable purposes; (v) if the objects include the advancement of education, care should be taken not to overstep the boundary between education and propaganda; (vi) if the objects include research, the charity must aim for objectivity and balance; and (vii) charities whether operating in this country or overseas, must avoid (a) seeking to influence or remedy those causes of poverty which lie in the social, economic and political structures of countries or communities,[77] (b) bringing pressure to bear on a government to procure a change in policies or administrative practices and (c) seeking to eliminate social, economic, political or other injustice.

---

[74] [1898] 2 Ch. 638.
[75] Report of the Charity Commissioners for England and Wales for 1969, p. 5; see also Report for 1981, p. 19.
[76] For further details, see the Report for 1981 pp. 19–22 and the Annual Report 1986, App. A. Guidelines had been suggested earlier: see the Report for 1969.
[77] See the Report for 1981 (pp. 22–23) for the Commissioners' criticism of the "political" activities of War on Want.

(h) Trusts for the environment. Trusts for the protection of the environment and the conservation of the national heritage have become increasingly active. Such trusts are analogous to the public works referred to in the preamble to the Act of 1601.[78] They often appear to be involved in the area of politics, but provided that the political activity carried on by the trustees is ancillary to and not the main object of the trust they would appear to be unobjectionable.[79]

V. THE EXCLUSIVE NATURE OF CHARITY

It is essential, subject to the Charitable Trusts (Validation) Act 1954, where it applies, that the trustees be bound to devote the funds to charitable purposes, even if these are expressed not specifically, but in a general way. For example, the settlor may join the word "charitable" with another adjective, such as "benevolent," "patriotic," "philanthropic." It might be thought that if the word "and" is used, *e.g.* "for charitable *and* benevolent purposes," the gift would succeed because it could only be applied to such benevolent purposes as are charitable. It might also be thought that if the word "or" is used, *e.g.* "for charitable *or* benevolent purposes," the gift would fail because the property could be applied to "benevolent" purposes which are not charitable. What is thought in the case of "and" and "or" may well turn out to be correct, but this cannot be relied on. It is entirely a question of construction: the word "and" may have been used disjunctively and the word "or" conjunctively.[80] There is a great deal of authority on "and/or."[81] Two leading cases, both of the House of Lords, may be mentioned briefly to emphasise the rule that a trust fund must be capable of being devoted exclusively to charitable purposes, and in which the word "or" was given its normal disjunctive meaning. In *Houston* v. *Burns*[82] the gift was made for "public benevolent or charitable" purposes in a Scottish parish. The gift failed as not being charitable because the words were wide enough to justify the trustees in disposing of the fund to non-charitable purposes. But the case which brought home the effect of this rule with a vengeance was *Chichester Diocesan Fund and Board of Finance* v.

---

[78] The preamble refers to the repair of bridges, ports, havens, causeways, sea banks and highways.

[79] See *supra*. The Goodman Committee (p. 34) recommended that environmental trusts should continue to enjoy charitable status and that their scope should be widened (*e.g.* so as to deal with the method of development of the environment).

[80] See *Re Sutton* (1885) 28 Ch.D. 464; *Re Best* [1904] 2 Ch. 354 ("charitable and deserving" and "charitable and benevolent" objects respectively were upheld). Contrast *Attorney-General of the Bahamas* v. *Royal Trust Co.* [1986] 1 W.L.R. 1001, where a gift for "education and welfare" was interpreted disjunctively and was held void.

[81] See, in addition to the cases mentioned in the text, *Morice* v. *Bishop of Durham* (1805) 10 Ves. 522; *Hunter* v. *Att.-Gen.* [1899] A.C. 309; *Blair* v. *Duncan* [1902] A.C. 37; *Re Davidson* [1909] 1 Ch. 567; *Re Da Costa* [1912] 1 Ch. 337; *Att.-Gen. for New Zealand* v. *Brown* [1917] A.C. 393; *Re Chapman* [1922] 2 Ch. 479; *Re Davis* [1923] 1 Ch. 225; *Att.-Gen.* v. *National Provincial and Union Bank of England Ltd.* [1924] A.C. 262; *Att.-Gen. for New Zealand* v. *New Zealand Insurance Co.* [1936] 3 All E.R. 888; *Re Atkinson's Will Trusts* [1978] 1 W.L.R. 586 (evidence inadmissible to show that by "worthy" the testator meant "charitable").

[82] [1918] A.C. 337.

Simpson.[83] The words used were "charitable or benevolent" and the same result as in *Houston* v. *Burns* occurred. Here the trustees had paid the money, which was considerable, to various charities, not anticipating litigation by the next-of-kin, which in fact occurred. Their case to recover the money from the charities themselves also went to the House of Lords in the leading case of *Re Diplock.*[84]

1. *Apportionment*

It should be remembered, however, that a settlor may direct an apportionment of the funds between charitable and non-charitable purposes. This class of gift will not fail, even if the trustees fail to make the appointment, because the court will in the last resort apportion the funds equally between the objects. Therefore, if the non-charitable purposes are void, for example, for uncertainty, only that part of the funds devoted to them will fail.[85]

2. *Incidental Non-Charitable Purposes*

It is also important to notice that the fact that a non-charitable purpose is incidental or ancillary to the achievement of a purpose which is, in fact, charitable will not destroy the gift. Thus, in *Royal College of Surgeons* v. *National Provincial Bank*[86] the House of Lords held that the College was in law a charity, since its object, as recited in the Charter, was "the due promotion and encouragement of the study and practice of surgery", the professional protection of its members provided for in its by-laws being merely ancillary to that object. Likewise, in *Incorporated Council of Law Reporting for England and Wales* v. *Att.-Gen.*,[87] it was held that the fact that legal practitioners used law reports in order to earn their professional fees did not have the result that the objects of the Council were not charitable. The same result occurred in *Re Coxen*[88] where a sum of money was given by the testator to the Court of Aldermen of the City for an annual dinner at their meeting on the business of managing a trust in favour of orthopaedic hospitals which the testator had also set up. The dinner was held by Jenkins J. to be purely ancillary to the primary charitable trust and for its better administration. And in *London Hospital Medical College* v. *I.R.C.*[89] it was held that if the students' union existed to further the educational purposes of the College,[90] then it was immaterial that the union also provided a

---

[83] [1944] A.C. 341.
[84] [1948] Ch. 465 (affirmed *sub nom. Ministry of Health* v. *Simpson* [1951] A.C. 251); *post.* p. 601.
[85] *Salusbury* v. *Denton* (1857) 3 K. & J. 529; *Re Clarke* [1923] 2 Ch. 407.
[86] [1952] A.C. 631.
[87] [1972] Ch. 73.
[88] [1948] Ch. 747.
[89] [1976] 1 W.L.R. 613.
[90] This was held to be the position: see *ante*, p. 316.

personal benefit for the individual students who were elected members of the union and chose to make use of its facilities.[91]

3. *Subsidiary Purposes*

Incidental purposes such as those just mentioned must be carefully distinguished from purposes which are *subsidiary* but not merely incidental. A well-known illustration is *Oxford Group* v. *Inland Revenue Commissioners*[92] where the Court of Appeal held that one of the objects set out in the Group's memorandum of association, namely to support "any charitable or benevolent" associations, actually conferred powers which were so wide that they could not be regarded as charitable; they were not merely ancillary to the main objects, admittedly charitable and also set out elsewhere in the memorandum. The Group did not, therefore, constitute a charity.

4. *Charitable Trusts (Validation) Act 1954*

It was as a result of the decision in *Oxford Group* v. *Inland Revenue Commissioners* that the Nathan Committee in its report recommended some amendment of the law because the decision was thought to affect a large number of charities.[93] But they did not go so far as to recommend its complete reversal. The legislative result was the Charitable Trusts (Validation) Act 1954,[94] a brief but, as it has been found, exceptionally difficult, statute to interpret.

First, the Act defines, in section 1(1), as an "imperfect trust provision" any provision declaring the objects and so describing them that consistently with the terms of the provision of the property *could* be used exclusively for charitable purposes but could nevertheless be used for purposes which are not charitable. Secondly, the instrument in which the "imperfect trust provision" is contained must take effect before December 16, 1952[95] (the date of the publication of the Nathan Report). Thirdly, the Act is to apply under section 2(1), to any disposition or covenant to make such a disposition where, apart from the Act, the disposition or covenant is invalid[96] under the law of England and Wales, but would be valid if the objects were exclusively charitable. Fourthly, it will not apply if the property or income from it has been paid or distributed on the basis that the imperfect trust provision was void.[97] Finally, and this emphasises the limited applicability of the Act, the imperfect trust provision takes effect (i) as to the period before the

---

[91] See also, to a similar effect, *Neville Estates Ltd* v. *Madden* [1962] Ch. 852, in which it was held that the social activities of a synagogue were merely ancillary to the strictly religious activities of the synagogue: see also *ante*, p. 322.

[92] [1949] 2 All E.R. 537. See also *Ellis* v. *I.R.C.* (1949) 31 Tax Cas. 178.

[93] 1952 Cmd. 8710, Chap. 12.

[94] Compare the Conveyancing Act 1919–1954 (N.S.W.), discussed in *Leahy* v. *Att.-Gen. for New South Wales* [1959] A.C. 457.

[95] s.1(2).

[96] For example, for perpetuity, uncertainty or other similar reason: *Vernon* v. *I.R.C.* [1956] 1 W.L.R. 1169.

[97] s.2(2).

Act came into force on July 30, 1954, as if the whole of the declared objects were charitable, and (ii) as to the period after the Act came into force as if the provision required the property to be applied for the declared objects only so far as they are charitable.[98]

Very real difficulty, as already indicated, has been found in the interpretation of these provisions: indeed one Lord Justice of Appeal confessed that he was "floored" by them on two occasions.[99] Especial difficulty has been found in reconciling section 1(1) and section 2(1), which are mentioned above. The definition of an imperfect trust provision is limited to a provision declaring the objects for which the property is held and "objects" is synonymous in section 1(1) with purposes. When section 2(1) is considered the question is what to make of it. The argument is—and it seems most forcible—that the definition in section 1(1) would include certain gifts which are already valid by the law of England, for example a gift to certain named purposes for a period limited to the perpetuity period, some of the purposes being charitable and some not (for example "for my dog Fido")—and which would otherwise be valid. Section 2(1)—according to this line of argument—then took this class of bequest outside the mischief of the Act into which section 1 had put it. It is hard to disagree that it is "an odd state of things if Acts of Parliament are passed in such a form that it is necessary to amend the effect of the first section by putting in a second."[1]

Apart from this problem other difficulties have arisen. A leading case on one of these is *Re Gillingham Bus Disaster Fund*,[2] some features of which have had a somewhat mixed reception in later cases of first instance. One question was whether the appeal launched in the *Daily Telegraph* was validated by the Act. This appeal was launched by the mayors of several boroughs, after a number of cadets had been killed and injured in a road accident, "to promote a Royal Marine Cadet Memorial Fund to be devoted . . . to defraying funeral expenses, caring for the boys who may be disabled and then to such worthy cause or causes in memory of the boys who lost their lives as the Mayors may determine". A majority of the Court of Appeal held that an imperfect trust provision was not validated unless the contributions to the fund were *dispositions* to which the Act applied, namely dispositions creating more than one interest in the same property.[3] A contribution was admittedly a disposition but, in view of the terms of the appeal, it did not create *separate* interests in the same property, one for funeral expenses, the second for the care of the disabled and the third for worthy causes, and accordingly it was held not to be validated by the Act.[4]

---

[98] s.1(2)(*a*)(*b*).
[99] *Re Harpur's Will Trusts* [1962] Ch. 78 at p. 95, *per* Harman L.J. See also *Re Gillingham Bus Disaster Fund* [1958] 1 Ch. 300 (Harman J.).
[1] *Re Harpur's Will Trusts, supra* at p. 96, *per* Harman L.J.
[2] [1959] Ch. 62.
[3] s.2(3).
[4] *cf. Re Chitty's Will Trusts* [1970] Ch. 254.

This is also what Harman J. held at first instance and this view would seem to be correct.[5] But he also held *obiter* that section 1(1) of the Act should be construed as applying only to trusts framed in such terms that the objects referred to included some *express* reference to charitable purposes as well as including other non-charitable purposes. It did not apply to purposes stated in a general way (for example for public purposes) which could embrace charitable purposes but contained no expressed reference to charity or any charitable purpose. As has already been shown, the Court of Appeal by a majority decided the point on a ground which rendered this question irrelevant and, although they expressed some sympathy with the view of Harman J., they abstained from expressing any opinion on it. Ormerod L.J. who dissented and to whose decision alone the point was relevant, decided that section 1(1) should not be construed in the restricted manner favoured by Harman J. but in accordance with its language which he considered to be unambiguous.

In these circumstances Buckley J. in *Re Wykes' Will Trusts*[6] felt himself free to adopt the view on this point favoured by Ormerod L.J. and declared that a trust for "benevolent or welfare" purposes was an imperfect trust provision to which the Act applied. This last decision was considered by Cross J. in *Re Mead's Trust Deed.*[7] He said that a benevolent or welfare fund "is closely akin to a trust for the relief of poverty".[8] It was there held that a trust to provide a convalescent home for members of a trade union and a home for poor retired members was validated by the Act and as from the date of the Act the property should be held for those members of the union who were poor persons and, in the case of the home for the aged, for poor retired members. *Re Wykes' Will Trusts* was further considered, again by Cross J., in *Re Saxone Shoe Co. Ltd.'s Trust Deed*[9] and assumed to have been correctly decided, but it was held on the facts that this particular trust was essentially a discretionary private trust and was not, therefore, validated. However, the judge set certain clear limits to the doctrine enunciated by Buckley J. in *Re Wykes.* He said: "In such a phrase as 'welfare purposes' there is at least some flavour of charity which may justify one in saying that the testator was seeking to benefit the public through the relief of a limited class. Here there is nothing of that kind, and if such a trust as this is validated by the Act, I do not see why one should stop short of turning any such invalid private trust into a trust for the relief of such beneficiaries as may from time to time be poor."[10] Nevertheless this problem— which is essentially one of construction of the Act—remains open: it has not been directly adjudicated upon by the Court of Appeal. There seems, however, to be no overriding reason why the restricted appli-

---

[5] Although dissented from by Ormerod L.J. [1959] Ch. 62.
[6] [1961] Ch. 229.
[7] [1961] 1 W.L.R. 1244.
[8] *Ibid.* at p. 1251.
[9] [1962] 1 W.L.R. 943.
[10] *Ibid.* at pp. 958–959.

cation favoured by Harman J. should be adopted: all that seems to be essential is that the expression used has a charitable connotation. Indeed, in *Re South Place Ethical Society*[11] Dillon J. held that the words "for such purposes either religious or civil" as the trustees might appoint constituted an imperfect trust provision within the meaning of the Act; they were to be construed as "such purposes, either religious or civil, being charitable" and the provision was accordingly validated.

The vexed question of the effect of the Act also arose for decision on another matter in *Re Harpur's Will Trusts*.[12] The Court of Appeal had to consider the question whether a trust to divide a trust fund "between such institutions and associations having for their main objects the assistance and care of soldiers, sailors, airmen and other members of H.M. Forces who have been wounded or incapacitated during the recent world war" as the trustees thought fit, had been validated by the Act. It was held that this provision was not within the scope of section 1(1) because that was limited to provisions declaring the objects and so describing them as to enable effect to be given to them by an application to purposes which are exclusively charitable. This has the somewhat surprising result that a gift to institutions, where their *objects* are not described in the instrument, will not be comprehended within the subsection.

It will have been observed that the Act can only apply to instruments taking effect before December 16, 1952. But since the validity of a provision may also arise for consideration on the determination of a life or other limited interest which is still in being, the Act cannot be regarded as merely of academic interest.[13] By now, however, its importance has substantially diminished.

VI. CY-PRÈS DOCTRINE

It is possible that a settlor may select a particular object of charity and that object may fail, or be or become impossible or impracticable[14] to carry out, or may have become illegal,[15] or may not exhaust the whole fund. The question is, what happens to the trust in circumstances such as these? The answer is that it will not necessarily fail. It is here that the *cy-près* doctrine[16] may apply and, if so, the funds will be applied to objects as near as possible to the settlor's intention.

---

[11] [1980] 1 W.L.R. 1565.

[12] [1962] Ch. 78.

[13] If a person has a future interest in property the subject of the provision, he may challenge its validity within one year of the interest vesting in possession: s.3; *Re Chitty's Will Trusts* [1970] Ch. 254.

[14] See cases cited in text, *post*, and also *Att.-Gen.* v. *City of London* (1790) 3 Bro.C.C. 171 (promotion of Christianity among the infidels of Virginia); *Ironmongers Co* v. *Att.-Gen.* (1844) 10 Cl. & F. 908 (redemption of British slaves in Turkey or Barbary).

[15] *e.g.* exceeding the rules of accumulation: *Re Monk* [1927] 2 Ch. 197; *Re Bradwell* [1952] Ch. 575 (income settled on trusts exceeding accumulation periods).

[16] For a full survey of the subject, see Sheridan and Delaney, *The Cy-près Doctrine; Tudor on Charities* (7th ed.), pp. 219 *et seq.*

1. *Conditions for Application of the Doctrine*

There are two conditions to be satisfied, the first involving the requirement of a "general charitable intention," and the second, the doctrine of "impossibility" and the effect on it of section 13 of the Charities Act 1993.[17]

(a) General charitable intention

The settlor must, in general, have shown a *general charitable intention*. But it must be emphasised that this requirement does not apply universally. It will only apply where the original trust has failed *ab initio*. The absence of a general charitable intention will not be fatal to those trusts which have taken effect but have failed later: in such a case (and also in the case of unidentified donors which is considered later)[18] the funds will be applicable *cy-près*. Once money has been effectively and absolutely dedicated to charity, whether in pursuance of a general or a particular charitable intent, the testator's next-of-kin or residuary legatees are for ever excluded.[19] It was indeed held by the Court of Appeal in *Re Wright*[20] that this will hold good even if the failure occurs during the subsistence of a prior life interest and before the charity is entitled in possession to the funds. This will mean that the material date for the purpose of deciding whether the *cy-près* doctrine is applicable is the date when the trust came into effect (that is to say in a will, on the death of the testator). If it has failed then, the question whether a general charitable intention for purposes of *cy-près* has been shown becomes material.

However, it is essential for this purpose that an absolute gift be made. The question is one of construction of the instrument whether (1) an absolute and perpetual gift has been made to charity with a gift over which fails for remoteness or some other reason, but the original gift remains; or (2) whether the gift is to charity for a limited period in which case the undisposed-of interest results to the grantor.[21]

(1) Gifts to charitable purposes

In cases of initial failure the question whether or not a general charitable intention has been shown is entirely one of construction of the instrument. It is necessary to consider, as in all matters of construction, its whole scope and intent. The essential question that has to be decided on such construction, is whether the paramount object of the settlor was to benefit a particular object *simpliciter*, or whether it was to

---

[17] Formerly Charities Act 1960, s.13.

[18] See *post*, p. 348.

[19] *Re Wright* [1954] Ch. 347 at p. 363, *per* Romer L.J. See also *Re Wokingham Fire Brigade* [1951] Ch. 373.

[20] *Ante*; see also to the same effect *Re Moon's Will Trusts* [1948] 1 All E.R. 300.

[21] See *Re Cooper's Conveyance Trusts* [1956] 1 W.L.R. 1096 at p. 1102 (*per* Upjohn J.) *cf. Re Peel's Release* [1921] Ch. 218; *Re Bawden's Settlement* [1954] 1 W.L.R. 33n. The rule in *Hancock v. Watson* [1902] A.C. 14 which was formerly known as the rule in *Lassence* v. *Tierney* (1849) 1 Mac. & G. (gift to donee with superadded directions which do not exhaust the funds: donee may take absolutely) also applies to charitable gifts: *Re Monk* [1927] 2 Ch. 197 at p. 211.

effect a particular mode of charity independently of the given object even though an object is specifically indicated.[22]

Subject to the warning that the cases present by no means a consistent picture, the authorities may perhaps be divided into two classes:

(i) One has a class of case where in form the gift is made for a particular charitable purpose but it is possible, taking the instrument as a whole, to say that, notwithstanding the form of the gift, the paramount intention is to give the property in the first instance for a general charitable purpose rather than a specified purpose: a direction is, as it were, engrafted onto the general gift as to the intention of the settlor relating to the manner in which the general gift is to be carried into effect. In this sort of case, even though it may be impossible to carry out the specified directions, the gift for the general charitable purpose will remain perfectly good, and the court or the Charity Commission will direct a scheme as to how it is to be carried out—a *cy-près* scheme.

(ii) The second class of case will arise, where on the true construction of the instrument the gift is not only in form but also in substance one for a particular purpose only, and if, for example, it proves impossible to carry out that particular purpose, the whole gift will fail: there is no room here for the application of *cy-près*.[23]

The question into which class the gift falls often raises serious problems of construction. The way in which the court sets about its task may be illustrated by the following cases. In *Biscoe* v. *Jackson*[24] money was to be applied towards the establishment of a soup kitchen in Shoreditch and a cottage hospital there. It was not in fact possible to apply the fund in the manner indicated. The Court of Appeal held that there was a sufficient general intention of charity for the benefit of the poor of Shoreditch to entitle the court to execute the trust *cy-près*. It was decided in this case, in effect, that the direction to establish a soup kitchen and cottage hospital was only one means of benefiting the poor of Shoreditch whom there was a *general* intention of benefiting. Another rather more difficult example is *Re Lysaght*.[25] Here the testatrix gave a fund to the Royal College of Surgeons, for the establishment of studentships. She provided (*inter alia*) that Jews and Roman Catholics should be excluded from them. Buckley J. held (1) that this discriminatory provision did not form an essential part of the testatrix's intention; (2) that her paramount intention was that the College should be the trustee of the fund; and (3) that the impracticability of giving effect to this inessential part of her intention (because of the College's refusal to accept subject to it) would not be allowed to defeat her paramount intention. Accordingly a scheme was directed by which the offending provision was deleted. Although the principle behind the decision is clear, it is not, however, easy, as a matter of construction of the will, to

---

[22] See *Re Taylor* (1888) 58 L.T. 538, 543.

[23] The substance of this formulation is borrowed from *Re Wilson* [1913] 1 Ch. 314 at p. 320. For another formulation, see *per* Buckley J. in *Re Lysaght* [1966] Ch. 191 at pp. 201, 202.

[24] (1887) 35 Ch.D. 460.

[25] [1966] Ch. 191, applying *Re Robinson* [1923] 2 Ch. 332 (requirement of wearing a black gown in church held impracticable).

accept the Judge's conclusion that such discrimination was not part of the testatrix's paramount intention.

Another illustration, probably more straightforward from the point of view of construction, is *Re Woodhams*,[26] where the testator gave the residue of his estate to two colleges of music to found scholarships which were to be restricted to boys who were orphans from named children's homes. The colleges refused to accept on these conditions (partly because of the decrease in the number of orphans and partly because of the adequacy of public grants for education), but was prepared to accept if the restrictions were deleted. Vinelott J. held that the testator chose orphans from these homes as those most likely to need assistance, but it was not an essential part of the scheme that the scholarships should be so restricted and accordingly that the trusts could be modified without frustrating his intention.

A case on the other side of the line which affords a contrast with such cases is *Re Good*,[27] where there was a trust to provide rest homes in Hull. There was a detailed scheme of the types of home to be provided, the types of inmates to be admitted and the management powers of the trustees. The scheme was in fact impracticable, because the funds were insufficient. It was held by Wynn-Parry J. that the language of the will and in particular the detailed instructions were inconsistent with the implication of a general charitable intention and, therefore, the *cy-près* doctrine did not apply. Likewise, in *Re Spence*,[28] Megarry V.C. held, on a construction of the will, that a gift to a specified old folk's home was one for a specific charitable purpose which, although possible when the will was made, had become impossible. It was not a gift to the old people of a particular district. Accordingly there was no general charitable intention and the gift failed.

(2) Gift to charitable institutions[29]
The above illustrations generally concerned trusts for charitable *purposes*, rather than trusts for charitable *institutions*. It appears to be necessary to deal with the latter separately since the circumstances of the institution may vary considerably. It will also be seen that the existence of a general charitable intention is not necessarily decisive of the matter.[30]

(i) **Non-existent institutions.** It appears to be relatively easy to infer a general charitable intention where the charity named by the testator has

---

[26] [1981] 1 W.L.R. 493.

[27] [1950] 2 All E.R. 653. See also to the same effect *Re Packe* [1918] 1 Ch. 437 (holiday home for clergymen of Church of England and their wives); *Re White's Trusts* (1886) 33 Ch.D. 449 (almshouses); *Re Wilson* [1913] 1 Ch. 314 (school); *Re Harwood* [1936] Ch. 285; *cf. Re Finger's Will Trusts* [1972] Ch. 286.

[28] [1979] Ch. 483; another gift in the same will to a Blind Home was held to be identifiable with a home for the blind of a different name and address and was valid.

[29] *cf.* the discussion by Hutton (1969) 32 M.L.R. 283.

[30] *cf.* Megarry V.C. in *Re Spence* [1978] [1979] Ch. 483 at p. 491 that the distinction is between particularity and generality; but this is not exhaustive: see *infra*.

never existed. In *Re Harwood*,[31] for example, it was held that a gift to a "peace society" which had never existed indicated a general charitable intention so that the fund could be applied *cy-près* to other existing similar organisations. This construction may, however, be rebutted by the circumstances of the gift. Thus, Harman J. held in *Re Goldschmidt*[32] that the presence in the will of a residuary gift in favour of other charitable purposes into which lapsed funds would fall was a factor against deducing a general charitable intention.

(ii) **Institutions ceasing to exist.** Real difficulty is encountered in reconciling some of the cases in this category; much may depend on the wording of the gift and the circumstances of the institution. The main question, however, is whether the institution has ceased to exist, or whether it has merely changed its form so that the original charity may be identified in its new form.

In *Re Rymer*[33] there was a gift by will to the Rector for the time being of St. Thomas' Seminary for the education of priests in the diocese of Westminster for the purposes of such seminary. The seminary ceased to exist in the testator's lifetime. It was held that the gift had been made to a particular institution and it lapsed. Although the case could have been treated as a *purpose* trust, *viz.* for the purpose of training priests (it was not in fact), presumably it would still have failed because a particular, rather than a general, charitable intention was shown. In some cases, however, the gift may be construed as one for the *purposes* of the institution. If so, the gift will not necessarily lapse if the institution ceases to exist. Thus, in *Re Roberts*,[34] there was a gift of residue for division among six named charitable institutions including the Sheffield Boys Working Home. The home was not in existence at the testator's death: it had been sold. Wilberforce J. held that the bequest in favour of the home was validly given on charitable trusts because (*inter alia*), although the bequest was a gift for the purposes of the institution, it was not so correlated with the physical entity of the institution that the charity ended when the trusts of the Home ceased to exist. The funds of the Home remained subject to charitable trusts. A scheme was therefore appropriate and the gift was applicable in accordance with that scheme.

The question is not, however, merely one of deducing a continuation of the charitable purposes in this way; it appears that there is an additional requirement to be satisfied, namely, that on the closing down of the institution there are still funds (or endowments) available for carrying out its work. This requirement was insisted on by Plowman J. in *Re Slatter's Will Trusts*[35] where the gift had been made to a hospital which had closed down and it was held that its work was not

---

[31] [1936] Ch. 285. See also *Re Davis* [1902] 1 Ch. 876 ("Homes for the Homeless"). See also *Re Satterthwaite's W.T.* [1966] 1 W.L.R. 277, C.A.

[32] [1957] 1 W.L.R. 524 (gift to "Fund for Relief of Distressed German Jews" and no fund of that name existed: failed).

[33] [1895] 1 Ch. 19. See, for a similar result, *Re Goldney* (1946) 115 L.J.Ch. 337.

[34] [1963] 1 W.L.R. 406.

[35] [1964] Ch. 512.

transferred elsewhere because the need for it had gone and because it had no funds available for carrying out that work.

(iii) Amalgamated, absorbed or re-organised institutions. The point made by *Re Slatter's Will Trusts* is also generally relevant in cases where an institution has been amalgamated with, or absorbed in, other institutions, or otherwise re-organised. Such changes may be effected in various ways, most commonly by a scheme made by the court or the Charity Commissioners. Thus, in *Re Faraker*,[36] a scheme had been made by the Commissioners consolidating the endowments of a number of charities with the general purpose of relief of the poor of Rotherhithe. A gift was then made to one of these charities ("Hannah Bayley's Charity") whose object originally was rather more limited. It was held that the gift did not lapse. The principle derived from this case is that an endowed charity cannot be destroyed by alterations made by scheme of the court or the Charity Commissioners and any subsequent accretion to its funds takes effect on the trusts as altered. The case was subsequently applied in similar circumstances in *Re Lucas*.[37]

Alterations to the constitution or objects of the institution in this way may have been made not only by scheme, but by statute,[38] or (improperly) under the terms of the trust deed without the sanction of the court or the Charity Commissioners.[39] Subsequent gifts to an endowed institution will not lapse. Informal changes are sometimes made by trustees (even more improperly) without reference to the terms of the trust deed. The essence of the matter in the case of informal changes of this kind is that just as the court or the Charity Commissioners cannot destroy an endowed charity, neither can the trustees or the governing body destroy it, again with the result that gifts to the original institution will not lapse.[40]

There is, however, a complicating factor, for if an institution has power to dissolve itself and it formally does so, it appears that a subsequent gift to the institution *will* lapse unless a general charitable intention is shown on the part of the donor. This is the effect of *Re Stemson's Will Trusts*[41] where Plowman J. held that a gift to an incorporated institution lapsed when it had previously been dissolved and its funds had been disposed of in accordance with its constitution. In the result, therefore, it appears that a charity which no one has power to terminate retains its existence despite such vicissitudes as schemes, amalgamations or changes of name, so long as it has funds. But if the charity is founded, not as a perpetual charity, but as one liable to

---

[36] [1912] 2 Ch. 488, C.A.

[37] [1948] Ch. 424, C.A.; distinguished in *Re Spence* [1979] Ch. 483.

[38] Many of the cases involved re-organisation of hospitals nationalised and re-organised under the National Health Services Act 1946; see *e.g. Re Morgan's Will Trusts* [1950] Ch. 137; *Re Glass* [1950] Ch. 643n; *Re Hutchinson's Will Trusts* [1953] Ch. 387.

[39] See *Re Bagshawe* [1954] 1 W.L.R. 238, where a scheme was made simply in accordance with the trust machinery, not by an outside body.

[40] See, to this effect, *Re Watt* [1932] Ch. 243n; *Re Withall* [1932] Ch. 236; see also *Re Hutchinson's Will Trusts* [1953] Ch. 387. A scheme is necessary or at any rate desirable where an informal change has been effected: see *Re Roberts* [1963] 1 W.L.R. 406.

[41] [1970] Ch. 16.

termination and its constitution provides for disposal of its funds in that event, then if the organisation ceases to exist, and if a gift is subsequently made to the charity, it lapses in the absence of a general charitable intention.[42]

(iv) Distinction between incorporated and unincorporated institutions. If the law were not already sufficiently involved, it appears that a distinction must also be drawn between bodies which are incorporated and those which are unincorporated. This distinction was made by Buckley J. in *Re Vernon's Will Trusts*[43] and applied by Goff J. in *Re Finger's Will Trusts*[44] which was in turn applied by the Court of Appeal in *Re Koeppler's Will Trust.*[45] The reasoning is that in the case of an unincorporated body the gift is *per se* a purpose trust; provided, therefore, that the work is still being carried on, it will be given effect to by a scheme notwithstanding the disappearance of the donee during the lifetime of the testator *unless* there is something positive to show that the continued existence of the donee is essential to the gift. In the case of a corporation, however, the position is different, as there *has to be* something positive in the will to create a purpose trust at all,[46] on the ground that a gift to a corporate body takes effect prima facie as a gift to that body beneficially.[47]

On analysis, the distinction may be thought to be debatable, for it is arguable that if a gift or trust is made in favour of an incorporated body, it is not for that body *simpliciter*, but for its purposes: companies have objects. *Re Finger's Will Trusts*[48] illustrates the difficulties. There were gifts by will both to an unincorporated association, the National Radium Commission, and to an incorporated body, the National Council for Maternity and Child Welfare. Both had been dissolved before the testator's death. The gift to the Commission was held to be a purpose trust for the work of the Commission which was not dependent on its continuing existence, and the fund could be applied under a scheme.[49] The gift to the Council, however, failed because the testator could not be taken as intending that the gift could be applied for its purposes. Goff J. managed to avoid this apparently anomalous result by holding that, although the gift to the Council failed, the share of the fund applicable to the Council could be applied *cy-près* because the will as a whole showed a general charitable intention.[50]

(v) Institutions ceasing to exist after the gift takes effect. The illustrations above concern cases where the institution has ceased to exist or been otherwise reorganised before the gift takes effect. If the charity ceases to exist after the testator's death it is clear, as was held by the

---

[42] *Ibid.* at p. 26.
[43] [1972] Ch. 300n.
[44] [1986] Ch. 423.
[45] [1972] Ch. 286.
[46] *Ibid.* at p. 295.
[47] See *Re Stemson's Will Trusts* [1970] Ch. 16.
[48] *Supra.*
[49] See also *ante*, p. 343 in respect of re-organisation of charitable institutions.
[50] See also *Re Stemson's Will Trusts* [1970] Ch. 16, *supra.*

Court of Appeal in *Re Slevin*[51], that it is unnecessary to show a general charitable intention for the gift to be upheld. The subject matter of the gift will have already vested in the recipient and since it has ceased to exist it will devolve on the Crown with the rest of the institution's property. The Crown will in practice allow it to be disposed of in favour of charity.

(3) Gifts to a mixture of charitable and non-charitable purposes or institutions

The fact that one gift for a non-charitable purpose is found among a number of gifts for charitable purposes does not permit the inference that the testator intended the non-charitable gift to take effect as a charitable gift when in terms it is not charitable. And this is so even though the non-charitable gift may have a close relation to the purposes for which the charitable gifts were made. This was held to be the position in *Re Jenkins's Will Trusts*[52] where a gift made to an association for anti-vivisection (non-charitable) was coupled with gifts for charitable purposes (preventing cruelty to animals). As Buckley J. said, in rejecting an application for a *cy-près* scheme: "If you meet seven men with black hair and one with red hair you are not entitled to say that there are eight men with black hair."[53]

It has been argued[54] that the previous case of *Re Satterthwaite's Will Trusts*[55] is inconsistent with this decision. In this case a human-hating testatrix gave money to the "London Animal Hospital." No hospital of this name could be identified, but because of other gifts in favour of established animal charities, the gift was held by the Court of Appeal to be applicable *cy-près*. The case is, however, probably distinguishable on the ground that a gift to an (admittedly unidentified) animal hospital had a sufficient charitable "flavour" about it to justify this result.

(b) "Impossibility" and Charities Act 1993, s.13[56]

The second condition for the application of the *cy-près* doctrine used to be that it was or had become "impossible"[57] to carry out the settlor's intention; or alternatively that a surplus remained after fulfilment of the purpose[58]; indeed, so it has been held,[59] the same applies to any surplus which is directed to be accumulated in excess of the statutory rules for accumulation.

The question to be considered is the meaning of "impossibility." It was not—and indeed is still not—possible simply to disregard the

---

[51] [1891] 2 Ch. 236.

[52] [1966] Ch. 249.

[53] *Ibid.* at p. 256.

[54] See *Pettit* (7th ed.), p. 307.

[55] [1966] 1 W.L.R. 277.

[56] Formerly Charities Act 1960, s.13.

[57] See cases cited in text, *infra*, and also *Att.-Gen.* v. *City of London* (1790) 3 Bro.C.C. 171 (the promotion of Christianity among the infidels of Virginia); *Re Ironmongers Co.* v. *Att.-Gen.* (1844) 10 Cl. & F. 908 (redemption of British slaves in Turkey and Barbary).

[58] *Re King* [1923] 1 Ch. 243; *Re North Devon and West Somerset Relief Fund* [1953] 1 W.L.R. 1260; *Re Raine* [1956] Ch. 417.

[59] *e.g. Re Monk* [1927] 2 Ch. 197; *Re Bradwell* [1952] Ch. 575.

wishes of a settlor because they are unpopular or because the moneys could be applied to a more beneficial purpose. Nevertheless the word "impossible" was in general widely construed. Thus in *Re Dominion Students Hall Trust*[60] the charity in question was restricted to Dominion students of European origin, yet the objects were stated to be the promotion of community interest in the Empire. An application was made to the court to delete the words "of European origin". Evershed J. held that the retention of these words amounted to a "colour bar" which would defeat the object of the charity: the word "impossible" should be construed widely and covered the case.

In view of the dilution of the term "impossible" it was clearly desirable to provide a new test to replace it. Section 13 of the Charities Act 1960, now section 13 of the Charities Act 1993, provided a comprehensive treatment of the subject. It is sufficient if the matter can be brought under one of the following heads:

(A) Where the original purposes[61] in whole or in part, (i) have been as far as may be fulfilled, or (ii) cannot be carried out, or not according to the directions given and to the spirit of the gift.[62] This expression "spirit of the gift" appears in four of the five paragraphs. It is not a new phrase, but is apparently borrowed from the Education (Scotland) Act 1946.[63] Although doubts about its meaning have been expressed,[64] it should not create any real difficulties. It has been said that "it is equivalent in meaning to the basic intention underlying the gift, as ascertained from its terms in the light of the admissible evidence."[65] The working of paragraph (A) is illustrated by the decision in *Re Lepton's Charity*.[66] This case concerned the gift by will in 1715 of land to be held on trust to pay out of the rents a sum of £3 a year to the minister of a chapel and the net overplus to the poor and aged of the town. The evidence was to the effect that at the date of the will the total income was £5 a year. The land had now been sold and was represented by investments yielding £791 a year. Pennycuick V.C. held that the basic intention was plainly defeated when, in the conditions of England today, the minister took a derisory £3 out of the total of £791, and made an order by way of scheme to provide for the payment to the minister to be raised from £3 to £100 per annum.

(B) Where the original purposes provide a use for part only of the property.[67] This would be illustrated by the facts of *Re North Devon and West Somerset Relief Fund*[68] where a surplus remained out of funds subscribed for the relief of the flood disaster at Lynmouth.

---

[60] [1947] Ch. 183.
[61] The words "original purposes" appear in all five paragraphs. They are applicable to the trusts of the disposition as a whole, and not severally in relation to its respective parts: *Re Lepton's Charity* [1972] Ch. 276 at p. 285.
[62] Charities Act 1993, s.13(1)(a).
[63] s.116(2).
[64] Viscount Simonds, 221 H.O.L. Official Report 601 (March 1, 1960).
[65] *Re Lepton's Charity* [1972] 276 at p. 285 (*per* Pennycuick V.C.). See also *Re Lysaght* [1966] Ch. 191; discussed *ante*, p. 340.
[66] See also *post*, p. 348.
[67] s.13(1)(b).
[68] [1953] 1 W.L.R. 1260; see also *Re King* [1923] 1 Ch. 243; *Re Raine* [1956] Ch. 417.

(C) Where the property given and other property applicable for similar purposes can be more effectively used in conjunction, and to that end can suitably, regard being had to the spirit of the gift, be made applicable for common purposes.[69] Strictly speaking, this is not a *cy-près* scheme and it was never necessary to show "impossibility" to effect a consolidation of a number of charities.[70]

(D) Where the original purposes were laid down by reference to an area which was then, but has since ceased to be, a unit for some other purpose, or by reference to a class of persons or to an area which has for any reason since ceased to be suitable, regard being had to the spirit of the gift, or to be practical in administering the gift.[71] Common examples of the application of this paragraph would arise where the original area of the charity, because of changes in local government boundaries or the class of beneficiaries, is hard to identify or where the area or class of beneficiaries has dwindled or is otherwise provided for, the result being that no public benefit is substantially conferred by fulfilment of the original purposes. Thus in *Peggs* v. *Lamb*[72] this paragraph was applied to a gift for the benefit of the freemen of the borough of Huntingdon, whose numbers had become substantially reduced; a scheme was directed so as to enlarge the class to cover the inhabitants of the borough as a whole.

(E) Where the original purposes, in whole or in part have, since they were laid down—

(i) been adequately provided for by other means;

(ii) ceased as being useless or harmful to the community, or, for other reasons, to be in law charitable; or

(iii) ceased in any other way to provide a suitable and effective method of using the property given, regard being had to the spirit of the gift.[73]

The jurisdiction created by this paragraph (in particular sub-paragraphs (i) and (iii)) affords the most important relaxation of the old *cy-près* rule and will probably be of the most practical use in enabling funds to be utilised for the maximum benefit of the public. Sub-paragraph (i) may be illustrated by a *cy-près* application where the original benefits of the charity are now provided for by the statutory services of public or local authorities. This would apply, for example, to a charity for the upkeep of a road or bridge[74]: if the original purpose is kept on foot its only real purpose would be to relieve the rates or exchequer and it is now possible to apply the funds *cy-près*. Sub-paragraph (ii) will not often arise; indeed, there does not appear to be a reported case where a valid charitable trust has ceased to be charitable. But the principle may now, since the passing of the Act, possibly be applied more often than may be thought. This is because an institution registered by the Charity Commissioners is conclusively presumed to

---

[69] s.13(1)(*c*).
[70] See *Re Faraker* [1912] 2 Ch. 488.
[71] s.13(1)(*d*).
[72] [1994] 2 W.L.R. 1.
[73] s.13(1)(*e*).
[74] See Charitable Uses Act 1601, *ante*, p. 301.

be a charity while on the register for all purposes other than rectifi-cation of the register.[75] This sub-paragraph will therefore arise for application if a charity is *removed*[76] from the register on the ground that its purposes are not in fact, or (less likely to happen) are no longer charitable. It is sub-paragraph (iii), however, which provides the widest relaxation of all. But although the words are very general it does not have a completely unlimited effect. It is still necessary to take into account the spirit of the gift and this will prevent a *cy-près* scheme being made simply because the original purpose selected by the donor would be less effective than some other application. It is still essential to establish that the mode of application which the donor selected has *ceased* to be suitable or effective.[77] In *Re Lepton's Charity*[78] it was held that the court had jurisdiction under this sub-paragraph (as well as under the wider terms of paragraph (A): "Where the original purposes, in whole or in part . . . cannot be carried out, or not according to the directions given and to the spirit of the gift")[79] to direct an application of the property *cy-près*.

The provisions mentioned above, contained in section 13 of the Charities Act 1993, alter the law only so far as it previously required a failure of the original purposes of a charity before a *cy-près* application could be ordered.[80] This will mean therefore that it is still necessary that a *general charitable intention*, on the lines already discussed, should be manifested, subject to the modifications provided for in respect of unidentified donors.[81] It must also be emphasised the section applies only to alterations of the "original purposes"; only then is a scheme necessary. Proposals which do not involve any such alteration are governed by different principles.[82]

The jurisdiction to make a scheme is exercisable by the court, or almost invariably in practice, by the Charity Commissioners.[83]

2. *Unidentified Donors*

Section 14 of the Charities Act 1960, now section 14 of the Charities Act 1993, introduced reforms which were long overdue. It provides that property given for *specific* charitable purposes which fail are to be applicable *cy-près* as though it had been given for charitable purposes generally, provided that it belongs (a) to donors who, after such adver-

---

[75] Charities Act 1993, s.4(1).

[76] s.4(2).

[77] The Goodman Committee recommended (p. 95) that the *cy-près* doctrine should be amended or clarified to make it clear in appropriate cases that a fundamental change in the objects of the charity can be allowed.

[78] [1972] Ch. 276.

[79] See *ante*, p. 346. Pennycuick V.-C. was of opinion that this sub-paragraph was no more than "a final writing out at large" of paragraph [A]: *ibid.* at p. 285.

[80] s.13(2).

[81] *Infra*.

[82] *Oldham Borough Council* v. *Attorney-General* [1993] 2 W.L.R. 224.

[83] *Post*, p. 350.

tisements and inquiries as are prescribed by regulations made by the Charity Commissioners,[84] cannot be identified or found *or* (b) to a donor who has executed a written disclaimer of his right to have the property returned.[85] It is further provided that, for these purposes, property is to be conclusively presumed, without the necessity for advertisements or inquiries, to belong to donors who cannot be identified if it consists of (a) the proceeds of cash collections made by means of collecting boxes or other means not adapted for distinguishing one gift from another *or* (b) the proceeds of any lottery, competition, entertainment, sale or other such money-raising activity, although, as regards the latter, allowance must be made for prizes or articles for sale to enable the activity to be undertaken.[86] Donors who can be identified or who apply within six months of the making of a scheme are entitled to the return of their property or its proceeds of sale.[87] The court may, by order, direct that property be treated (without advertisement or inquiry) as belonging to donors who cannot be identified whenever it appears to the court *either* (a) that it would be unreasonable, having regard to the amounts likely to be returned to the donor, to incur expense with a view to returning the property, *or* (b) it would be unreasonable, having regard to the nature, circumstances and amount of the gifts, and to the lapse of time since they were made, for the donors to expect the property to be returned.[88] Finally, the section is retrospective: it therefore applies to property given for charitable purposes before the commencement of the Charities Act 1960.[89]

These provisions reversed the previous law. Formerly the law was that unless a *general* charitable intention could be shown in the usual way the trustees were bound to refund the money and if the donors could not be found the money had to be paid into court to await the usually remote possibility that they would reclaim it. This was indeed the result in *Re Ulverston*[90] where an appeal was launched for the building of a new hospital and insufficient funds were given for the purpose. The Court of Appeal held that a *specific*, not a general, charitable intention had been manifested and the funds were therefore to be held on a resulting trust for the contributors. As has been seen, the Act reverses the previous law by the simple expedient of providing that donors in the circumstances indicated—but only in those circumstances—shall be *deemed* to have a general charitable intention.[91] Moreover, the fact that the section is retrospective enables money lodged in court, before the commencement of the Charities Act 1960, now to be applied *cy-près*.

---

[84] Charities Act 1993, s.14(8).
[85] Charities Act 1993, s.14(1).
[86] s.14(3).
[87] s.14(5),(6), (10).
[88] s.14(4).
[89] Charities Act 1993, s.14(10), Charities Act 1960, s.14(7).
[90] [1956] Ch. 622.
[91] The fact that contributions are from anonymous sources may, however, still be relevant in cases where the trust is *not* charitable: see *ante*, p. 202.

VII. ADMINISTRATION OF CHARITIES

1. *Central Authorities*

There is now only one central authority exercising jurisdiction over charities,[92] that is to say the Charity Commissioners for England and Wales.[93] Formerly, the Secretary of State for Education and Science and the Secretary of State for Wales had concurrent jurisdiction with the Charity Commissioners and exercised it in relation to charities of an educational nature.[94] The reason for conferring the exercise of functions under the Charities Act exclusively upon the Commissioners is that these functions are primarily judicial and not, therefore, appropriately exercised by Ministers of the Crown. As to the constitution of the Commission it is provided that there are to be a Chief Charity Commissioner and from two to four other Commissioners,[95] and two at least of them must be barristers or solicitors.[96] They are appointed by the Home Secretary[97] but are quite independent of him in day-to-day administration[98]: they cannot even be compelled to follow any general guidance he may care to give.[99]

2. *Official Custodian for Charities*

Before the Charities Act 1960 there were two officers, one the Official Trustee of Charity Lands and the other the Official Trustee of Charitable Funds. They existed so that the legal title of charity lands and funds respectively could be vested in them. There seemed to be no good reason why there should be two such offices[1] and the Charities Act 1960 combined them into one under the title above.[2] There are advantages in

---

[92] This has been the case since the Education Act 1973 s.1(1)(*a*), which came into force on February 4, 1974.

[93] Charities Act 1993, s1(1) and Sched. 1. The Goodman Committee recommended (p. 120) that in addition an independent Charities Board should be created with a chairman and members independent of the Charity Commission. Its members would come from a wide background and from different parts of the country. Its function would include being consulted by the Charity Commissioners and to advise them on matters of policy and administration.

[94] Charities Act 1960, s.2(1), repealed by Education Act 1973, s.1(1)(*a*).

[95] Charities Act 1993, Sched. 1. paras. 1(1), 1(5). At present there are four other Commissioners.

[96] Sched. 1, para. 1(2).

[97] *Ibid.* para. 1(3).

[98] s.1(3)(4).

[99] *Ibid.* The Expenditure Committee recommended (p. 31) that the Home Secretary should answer questions on charities and on the Charity Commissioners (such questions are at the present time referred to the Commissioners who reply in writing), and that the Home Secretary should have more flexibility where amendments to the law are required and wider powers to make orders and statutory instruments affecting the Commissioners and their work, subject to affirmative resolution of the House of Commons. The Goodman Committee, however, considered (p. 122) that the Commissioners should have the same degree of self-regulation as many other public bodies.

[1] See Nathan Report, para. 228.

[2] Charities Act 1960, s.3(1), now Charities Act 1993, s.2(1). See also Charities Act 1993, ss.21–22 for the vesting of property in the Official Custodian.

vesting property in the Official Custodian as custodian trustee. First, it may render the title more simple and, secondly, and more important, it renders it unnecessary to appoint new trustees on deaths or retirements, thereby saving the expense of new appointments. He is an officer of the Charity Commissioners and ranks as a corporation sole, having perpetual succession and an official seal. Because he is simply a custodian trustee, the actual management and control of the charity remains in the charity trustees. However, by virtue of the Charities Act 1992 the future role of the Official Custodian is to be limited to land[2A] and he is to progressively divest himself of other property by transferring it to the trustees, or to such other persons as they nominate. This reform, which involves the divesting of holdings in excess of £1.25 billion, was carried out in order to increase the responsibility of the trustees. The Official Custodian nevertheless may retain any property vested in him by virtue of an order of the Commissioners made under section 18 of the 1993 Act where they feel that this is necessary for the protection of the charity in question.[2B]

3. Registration

Sections 3 and 4 of the Charities Act 1993[3] provide for a central register of charities. Before the Charities Act 1960 was passed it was an alarming fact that neither the actual number of charities nor the amount of money devoted to charitable purposes had ever been known with any sort of precision. These registration provisions must, since 1960, have gone a long way towards curing this palpable defect of charity administration. There is now a positive duty on charity trustees to apply for registration enforceable by order of the Commissioners.[4] And all charities are registrable[5] unless they are expressly relieved from the requirement.[6] One example of the latter is to be found in the so-called "exempt charities": these are not subject to any of the supervisory powers of the Commissioners because satisfactory arrangements have already been made for carrying out the objects of such trusts and safeguarding the trust property. Examples of exempt charities are certain universities and colleges, the Church Commissioners, industrial and provident societies

---

[2A] s.29.

[2B] See (1992) 142 N.L.J. 541.

[3] These provisions were in 1960 almost entirely new in their effect. Although a statutory obligation to register was imposed by the Charitable Donations Act 1812, this was not observed in practice.

[4] On December 31, 1992, the total number of charities on the register was 170,357. Report of the Charity Commissioners for England and Wales for 1992.

[5] It is necessary that, in order to be a charity, the organisation in question be subject to control by the High Court in the exercise of the court's jurisdiction with respect to charities. If that jurisdiction is wholly ousted by statute in relation to the organisation, then the organisation is not a charity and cannot be registered: see *Construction Training Board* v. *Att.-Gen.* [1973] Ch. 173, C.A. (where, however, the Board was held to be a charity because the provisions of the Industrial Training Act 1964 did not oust the jurisdiction of the court; the court still had control over the Board's functions).

[6] Charities Act 1993, s.3.

and friendly societies.[7] Some charities are also entitled to relief from registration in addition to the "exempt charities" so called. These are charities without any permanent endowment (*i.e.* property which must be retained as capital), without property bringing in an income of more than £1,000 a year and without land which it uses and occupies.[8] Furthermore, any charity excepted by order or regulation is not required to be registered[9]; a number of regulations to this effect covering, for example, voluntary schools,[10] boy scouts and girl guides[11] have been made. A further exemption[12] operates in favour of registered places of worship.[13]

Registration raises a conclusive presumption that the institution is a charity at any time while it is on the register.[14] This accordingly removes a great deal of uncertainty about the status of certain institutions. But provision is necessarily made for a person who is or may be affected by the registration of an institution or trust as a charity to object to its entry on the register or apply for its removal on the ground that it is not in fact a charity, which is a question of general law.[15] This is intended for people, especially next-of-kin, whose interests will be affected by the answer to the question whether the institutions or trusts should be classed accordingly. An appeal against any decision of the Commissioners may be brought in the High Court.[16] The Commissioners also themselves have the positive duty to remove from the register any institution which no longer appears to them to be a charity and also to remove any charity because it ceases to exist or does not operate.[17]

Any registered charity with a gross income of over £5,000 in its last financial year must state the fact of its registration in all documents soliciting donations, and on all bills, invoices and receipts.

---

[7] See Charities Act 1993, s.3(5)(*a*), Sched. 2.

[8] s.3(5)(*c*).

[9] s.3(5)(*b*).

[10] The Charities (Exception of Voluntary Schools from Registration) Regulations 1960 (S.I. 1960 No. 2366).

[11] The Charities (Exception of Certain Charities for Boy Scouts and Girl Guides for Registration) Regulations 1961 (No. 1044).

[12] The Goodman Committee recommended (p. 75) that the Home Secretary should re-examine regularly the validity of exemptions and exceptions.

[13] Charities Act 1993, s.3(5)(*c*); and for definition of "Registered Place of Worship," see Places of Worship Registration Act 1855, s.9.

[14] s.4(1).

[15] s.4(2).

[16] s.4(3)(4). The Goodman Committee recommended that appeals from administrative decisions of the Charity Commissioners should be made to an appellate tribunal; that there should be a right of appeal to the court from the decision of that tribunal on a point of law; and that legal aid should be available for appeals on points of law.

[17] s.3(4). The Goodman Committee recommended (p. 69) that the Charity Commissioners should have power to require such information as they think fit about the proposed activities of the charity with power to refuse registration if it appears appropriate or, alternatively, to grant registration subject to review after three years. A charitable company incorporated under the Companies Acts may also be wound up on an application made by the Attorney-General under C.A. 1993 s.63(1): see *Liverpool and District Hospital for Diseases of the Heart* v. *Att.-Gen.* [1981] Ch. 193.

4. *Co-ordination of Charitable Activities*

Sections 76 to 78 of the 1993 Act, which were entirely new in 1960,[18] have as their aim the foundation of a basis for co-operation between charity and the statutory welfare services. They authorise local authorities to review the working of those charities with that of the statutory services.[19] But no obligation is put on a charity to co-operate. The Act requires mutual agreement between the local authority and the charity.[20] It may lead, as must be hoped, to rationalisation of charitable activities over the country as a whole, but it is fair to say that few reviews have so far been put in hand.[21] Moreover, the review powers relate only to local charities. There are no powers to ensure reviews or co-ordination of national charities.[22]

5. *Scheme-Making and Other Powers*

Section 16 of the 1993 Act empowers the Commissioners to exercise a jurisdiction concurrent with that of the High Court to make schemes relating to the administration of the charity, or orders for the appointment and removal of trustees and with regard to the vesting or transfer of property.[23] Although the court has a scheme-making power, it should be emphasised that in practice the vast majority of such schemes will be made by the Commissioners.[24] A scheme will obviously take a wide diversity of forms: it may, for example, take the drastic form of rewriting the original user trusts or management trusts of the charity or both. Appointments and removals of trustees will not normally require a scheme: they will be made simply by order of the Commissioners. And the same will apply to vesting the property in the Official Custodian.[25]

In the usual way jurisdiction can only be exercised by the Commissioners on an application made by the charity or on a reference by the court[26] or, save in the case of an exempt charity, on the application of the Attorney-General. However, in the case of a non-exempt charity with an annual income of less than £500, they may exercise their

---

[18] Charities Act 1993, s.5(1).

[19] As Charities Act 1960, ss.10–12.

[20] s.78(2).

[21] The Goodman Committee recommended (p. 82) that the review process should be proceeded with as speedily as possible, and that responsibility should be taken from the local authorities and given to the Charity Commissioners. It is also recommended that "neighbourhood trusts," catering for not too large an area, should be set up whenever practicable so as to retain the local character of the trusts. The Expenditure Committee recommended (p. 21) compulsory powers of "municipalisation" of local charities: this was rejected by the Goodman Committee.

[22] The Goodman Committee recommended (p. 99) that co-operation between national charities should be developed and encouraged by persuasion, not by legal means, and that the Charity Commissioners should initiate a review or reviews to determine how this can be done.

[23] s.16(1).

[24] s.16(1), 4.

[25] s.18.

[26] s.16(4).

jurisdiction on the application of any trustee, any person interested in the charity, or of any two inhabitants in the locality where it operates.[27]

Power is also specifically given to the Commissioners to act for the protection of charities where there has been misconduct or mismanagement, or the property of the charity should be protected and properly applied.[28] In these circumstances they are empowered (*inter alia*) to remove or appoint trustees or prevent the operation of any banking account.[29]

A number of miscellaneous powers are also conferred on the Commissioners. Most important perhaps of all is the power to make an order where it appears that the proposed action is in the interests of the charity, authorising dealings or other action to be made or taken, whether or not it is within the administrative powers of the trustees.[30] This power, which is primarily administrative, is akin to the powers conferred by section 57 of the Trustee Act 1925[31] and section 64 of the Settled Land Act 1925.[32] It may, for example, authorise any given transaction, compromise or application of property or may, more specifically, authorise a charity to use common premises, or employ a common staff or otherwise combine, for any administrative purposes, with any other charity—though the latter are purely examples and do not limit the generality of the statutory power.[33]

Other powers include that of advising charity trustees if the latter apply for advice[34]—a most convenient facility in practice—and powers to preserve charity documents.[35]

Finally, the Commissioners may demand accounts with a view to instituting inquiries and as a last resort removing the existing trustees. The duties of trustees of unincorporated charities[36] in this respect have been greatly increased by the Charities Act 1992, now the Charities Act 1993, which requires the preparation and submission of annual reports with duly audited accounts and the auditor's report.[37]

6. *Investment*

The powers and duties of trustees of a charity, with regard to investment of trust funds, are governed, in general, in the same manner as in the case of non-charitable trusts, by the terms of the trust

---

[27] s.16(5).
[28] s.18(1).
[29] s.18(1). For the procedure on appeal against removal (see s.18(7)), see *Jones* v. *Att.-Gen.* [1974] Ch. 148.
[30] s.26(1).
[31] *Post*, pp. 394, 542.
[32] *Post*, p. 543.
[33] s.26(2).
[34] s.29.
[35] s.30.
[36] Corporate charities are bound by the accounting rules of the Companies Act 1985.
[37] Charities Act 1993, ss.41–49. An audit is only required if income exceeds £100,000; if income is less than £25,000, all that is required is statements of income and expenditure and a balance sheet.

instrument (if any) and by the general law of trusts relating to investments.[38]

The Trustee Investments Act 1961[39] enables trustees, subject to a number of safeguards, to invest a proportion, not exceeding one-half of the trust fund, in a wide range of investments including stocks and shares in public companies. But in order to make effective use of the provisions of this Act a substantial fund is necessary so that risk can be spread and management expenses assimilated without difficulty. However, many charities have extremely small trust funds and if special provision had not been made, a large number would not have been able to get effectual benefits from the Act. It was, therefore, desirable to make general provision, by way of common investment schemes, for the joint administration of a number of charitable trust funds for the purposes of investment. Common investment schemes had been made before, but only in particular cases, by statute[40] and the court,[41] and the Charity Commissioners have always had the power to make schemes of a similar nature; but no *general* provisions for the establishment of common investment funds were available until the passing of the Charities Act 1960.

Section 22 of the Charities Act 1960, now section 24 of the Charities Act 1993, enables the court and the Commissioners to make schemes, known as "common investment schemes", for the establishment of common investment funds, providing (a) for property transferred to the fund by or on behalf of a charity participating in the scheme to be invested under the control of trustees appointed to manage the fund; and (b) for the participating charities to be entitled (subject to the provisions of the scheme) to the capital and income of the fund in shares determined by reference to the amount or value of the property transferred to it by or on behalf of each of them and to the value of the fund at the time of the transfers.[42]

It is expressly provided that the court or the Commissioners may make a common investment scheme on the application of two or more charities.[43] In *Re University of London Charitable Trusts*[44] Wilberforce J. held that this provision enabled an application to be made by the trustees of any two or more charitable trusts, notwithstanding the fact

---

[38] *Post*, p. 430; and see also *Soldiers', Sailors' and Airmen's Families Association* v. *Att.-Gen.* [1968] 1 W.L.R. 313, where it was held that a corporation incorporated by royal charter cannot, by the making of rules, confer upon itself powers wider than those conferred upon it by the general law or the royal charter.

[39] *Post*, p. 441.

[40] See Universities and Colleges (Trusts) Act 1943 which enabled the Universities of Oxford and Cambridge and the Colleges in those universities, and also Winchester College, to make schemes providing for funds to be administered as a single fund. (See *Re Freeston's Charity* [1978] 1 W.L.R. 741, C.A.). Private Acts have established common investment schemes for other universities; see *e.g.* Liverpool University Act 1931; Birmingham University Act 1948.

[41] See *e.g. Royal Society's Charitable Trusts* [1956] Ch. 87; *Re University of London Charitable Trusts* [1964] Ch. 282.

[42] s.24(1).

[43] s.24(2).

[44] [1964] Ch. 282.

that, as in this case, the trustees of such trusts are the same. More recently, the creation of common deposit funds has been authorised so as to still any doubts as to whether funds could merely be deposited at interest under the earlier schemes. These are now governed by section 25 of the Charities Act 1993.

Initially, a scheme was made by the Commissioners, known as the Charities Official Investment Fund, in which all charities may participate[45] and in 1976 two further schemes were made.[46]

7. *Dealings with Charity Property*

Here an important reform was effected by section 29 of the Charities Act 1960. It abolished the old restrictions on dealings in charity property, fraught as they were with excessive complexity. It was necessary in the past to decide for this purpose whether a charity was, in the language employed, a plain or an endowed or a mixed charity. But these distinctions—and their attendant difficulties—can now be forgotten except in the increasingly unlikely event that a past transaction appears on the title to property and requires investigation.[47] Under section 29, the question which had to be considered was, what was the class of land in the ownership of the charity? It may be of three kinds: (i) part of the permanent endowment. By "permanent endowment" is meant property held subject to a restriction which prevents its being spent in the same way as income.[47A] It is necessary for this purpose, therefore, that a distinction be made in the trust instrument between the expenditure of capital and the expenditure of income; (ii) it may be "functional land", *i.e.* land which may or may not be part of the permanent endowment but is or has been in the use and occupation of the charity[48]; or (iii) it may be neither of these, but may have been brought as an investment with funds expendable without distinction between capital and income. In cases (i) and (ii) the sanction of the court or the Commissioners was required. In case (iii) it was not[49]; in this case, which is probably the least common of all, a sale would not indicate a radical chance in the character of the charity as would a sale under heads (i) and (ii), and for this reason, presumably, no consent is required.

Section 29 has now been replaced by what is now section 36 of the Charities Act 1993 (originally section 32 of the Charities Act 1992). No land may be sold, leased or otherwise disposed of without an order of the court or of the Commissioners unless the trustees have obtained and considered a written report on the proposed disposition from a qualified surveyor, advertised the proposed disposition for such period

---

[45] It was made on December 4, 1962.
[46] Charinco Charities Narrower-Range Common Investment Fund, and Charibond Charities Narrower-Range Common Investment Fund: see the Report of the Charity Commissioners for 1976.
[47] See *Tudor on Charities* (7th ed.), pp. 418–420, 556 *et seq.*
[47A] s.45(3).
[48] s.29(2).
[49] *Ibid.*

and in such manner as the surveyor has advised, and are satisfied that the terms are the best reasonably obtainable. Leases for seven years are subject to less stringent requirements.[50] Where the land in question is expressly held on trust for the purposes of the charity, it is also required that public notice be given and representations received within one month duly considered, unless the purpose of the transaction is to acquire replacement property. The instrument by which any disposition is effected must certify that these provisions have been complied with; the certificate is conclusive in favour of a purchaser for money or money's worth.[51]

8. *Ex Gratia Payments*

The court and the Attorney-General have the power to authorise charity trustees to make *ex gratia* payments out of funds held on charitable trusts,[52] for example, in pursuance of a moral obligation in favour of relatives of the deceased. This jurisdiction is not, however, exercised lightly: it is necessary to show that if the charity were an individual, it would be morally wrong of him not to make the payment.[53]

9. *Appointment of Charity Trustees*[54]

Generally the rules which apply to private trusts govern appointment of charity trustees.[55] A major general exception is that the restriction on the number of trustees imposed by section 34 of the Trustee Act 1925,[56] does not apply. But there were and still are certain other specific provisions. Under the Trustees Appointment Acts 1850, 1869 and 1890, a convenient mode of appointment was provided. The Acts related to land held on religious or educational trusts where the method of appointment was not prescribed in the trust instrument or had lapsed. All that was required was that the appointment should be made under the hand and seal of the chairman of a meeting of the charity at which the appointment could be made: it was simply to be executed in the presence of the meeting and attested by two witnesses. This was a "conclusive" act of appointment and also operated to vest the property in the new trustees together with the continuing trustees. The Acts were repealed by the Charities Act 1960,[57] but nevertheless the

---

[50] Comparable provisions apply to mortgages; see s.38.

[51] s.37.

[52] *Re Snowden* [1970] Ch. 700.

[53] *Ibid.* at p. 710.

[54] The Goodman Committee recommended (p. 77) (1) that all charities should normally have a provision for rotation of trustees other than *ex officio* trustees; (2) that there should be an age limit of 70 for trustees other than *ex officio* trustees; (3) that charity executives should not be trustees as a general rule. These recommendations were welcome on the grounds that too many charities appear to provide employment (albeit often unpaid) for the very aged members of the community but have not been enacted. For the powers of a receiver and manager appointed for a charity, see *Att.-Gen.* v. *Schonfeld* [1980] 1 W.L.R. 1182.

[55] See *post*, p. 360.

[56] See *post*, p. 374.

[57] s.35(6).

provisions were preserved in relation to land acquired before January 1, 1961.

Apart from this the Charities Act 1960 also provided in what is now section 83 of the Charities Act 1993 that new trustees may be appointed at a meeting, if a memorandum of the appointment is signed at the meeting by the person presiding or in some other manner prescribed by the meeting, and attested by two witnesses: that is then "sufficient" evidence of the appointment. This provision applies to all charities (unlike the Trustees Appointment Acts), but on the other hand it can be made use of only when the trusts permit it; and (most important) it is only "sufficient" (as opposed to "conclusive") evidence of appointment, thus enabling its sufficiency to be checked on investigation of title by a purchaser.

The Charities Act 1992 in what is now section 73 of the Charities Act 1993 provided for the disqualification from holding the office of trustee of a charity of anyone convicted of an offence involving dishonesty or deception, undischarged bankrupts, and those previously removed from such an office on the grounds of misconduct or mismanagement. Any one who acts while so disqualified is guilty of an offence carrying a maximum sentence of two years imprisonment and/or a fine. The Commissioners may remove any trustee if satisfied that there has been misconduct or mismanagement and that this is necessary or desirable for the purpose of protecting the property of the charity or if he has been discharged from bankruptcy during the last five years, is a corporation in liquidation, is mentally incapable, has not acted, is outside England and Wales, or cannot be found.[58]

10. *Mortmain*

The law of mortmain was belatedly repealed by the Charities Act 1960.[59] This law, going back as far as the Thirteenth Century, prevented corporations holding land without a licence from the Crown. Its purpose was to prevent land being tied up in the dead hand (mortmain) of such artificial persons, and it was aimed particularly at religious houses. It had as its underlying purpose the protection of the feudal revenues of the Crown and the mesne lords. The law was extended to gifts to charity by the Charitable Uses Act 1735. This Act, as well as the old law, was re-enacted by the Mortmain and Charitable Uses Act 1888. One of the principal provisions relating to charity in this Act was to require enrolment of every assurance of land in the Central Office of the Supreme Court. It was later replaced by section 29(4) of the Settled Land Act 1925, which required, in place of this, recording with the Commissioners. This subsection, in turn, was repealed and replaced, so far as educational charities were concerned, by section 87(2) of the Education Act 1944, which required assurances of land to be recorded with the Minister of Education.

The registration provisions of the Charities Acts have rendered

---

[58] Charities Act 1993, s.18.
[59] s.38; Sched. 7, Pt. II.

recording unnecessary. But since the whole of the law of mortmain has been abolished, it is not only the field of charity that is affected but the law generally. Moreover, the repeal is retrospective so that the title to property will not be defeated by failure to comply with the Mortmain Acts in the past.[60]

11. *Enforcement of Charitable Trusts*[61]

The Crown has the function of enforcing charitable trusts as *parens patriae*, and the Attorney-General, on behalf of the Crown, will be joined as a party to any proceedings involving charity. However, proceedings may be taken with reference to a charity, not only by the Attorney-General, but also by the charity, by any of the charity trustees, or by any persons interested in the charity, or, if it is a local charity, by any two or more inhabitants of the area of the charity,[62] but not where there is a bona fide dispute as to the existence of a charity; if there is such a dispute the Attorney-General should bring the action.[63] All such persons, other than the Attorney-General, must first obtain an order from the Charity Commissioners or the court authorising the institution of proceedings.[64]

---

[60] *i.e.* before July 29, 1960; s.38(2).
[61] For personal liability of charity trustees, see Hawkins (1979) 75 L.Q.R. 99.
[62] Charities Act 1993, s.33(1).
[63] *Re Belling* [1967] Ch. 425; *Hauxwell* v. *Barton-upon-Humber U.D.C.* [1974] Ch. 432, and see also *Childs* v. *Att.-Gen.* [1973] 1 W.L.R. 497.
[64] Charities Act 1993, s.33(2).

CHAPTER 10

THE APPOINTMENT, RETIREMENT AND REMOVAL OF TRUSTEES

THE appointment and retirement of trustees is a matter of prime concern for everyone connected with the trust. Once the trust has been set up the settlor, unless he has specially reserved powers to himself, he has handed to his trustees complete control over the property made subject to the trust. The interest of the beneficiaries will only be adequately protected if the trustees are scrupulously honest; are prepared to give adequate time to the administration of the trust; have enough common sense and business acumen to do well with the trust property; and are able to treat fairly beneficiaries with possibly conflicting interests, such as tenant for life and remainderman.[1] As far as the trustee himself is concerned, his appointment is not to be considered lightly. Unless there is a provision in the trust instrument to the contrary[2] he will have to devote his time to the administration of the trust entirely without payment or other benefit. He may receive not gratitude from the beneficiaries for his efforts but bitterness,[3] and if he is not very careful and makes a mistake, he may be liable to make good any loss out of his own pocket.[4]

1. TYPES OF TRUSTEE

1. *Ordinary Trustees*

In general, any individual, limited company or other corporation may be appointed a trustee,[5] and a limited company may act as a trustee jointly with an individual.[6] Except in the case of infants[7] there is no statutory prohibition upon the appointment of any person as a trustee, but there are, however, some persons who, while they have the legal capacity to be trustees, may nevertheless be so undesirable as trustees

---

[1] The conflict of interest between tenant for life and remainderman is explained in connection with investments, *post*, p. 430, *et seq.*

[2] *Post*, p. 528 *et seq.*

[3] In *Re Londonderry* [1964] Ch. 594, a discretionary beneficiary who and whose family had received a total of £165,000 showed the reverse of gratitude to the trustees.

[4] *Post*, p. 577.

[5] See *ante*, p. 33.

[6] The Bodies Corporate (Joint Tenancy) Act 1889. See *Re Thompson's Settlement Trusts* [1905] 1 Ch. 229.

[7] *Infra.*

that the court will remove them if appointed. A person may in this sense be undesirable either because of a defect in his character involving financial irresponsibility, as manifested by some circumstances leading to bankruptcy[8]; or by conviction of crimes involving dishonesty[9]; or because by being appointed a trustee he would be placed in a position where his interest as a beneficiary under the trust would conflict with his duty as a trustee. It appears however, that there has been a change in attitude with regard to the appointment of a beneficiary as a trustee. In *Forster* v. *Abraham*,[10] in 1874, where the court upheld the appointment of a life tenant as a trustee, the general undesirability of making such appointments was stressed. By contrast, one of the fundamental bases of the Settled Land Act 1925[11] is to make the beneficiary who is a tenant for life also a trustee: Parliament has given the lie to the old notions. While the appointment of a beneficiary as a *sole* trustee may well be undesirable, the appointment of a beneficiary as one of two or more trustees will often be advantageous, because the beneficiary will be induced to do the best he can for the trust by his financial interest in the property as well as his duty as a trustee.

Infants are in a curious position. It is clear that an infant may *be* a trustee. Thus in *Re Vinogradoff*[12] a woman transferred a holding of War Stock into the joint names of herself and her granddaughter, Laura, aged four. There was no presumption of advancement[13] and the court decided that Laura held that stock as a trustee on a resulting trust.[14] But although an infant may be a trustee, he cannot be expressly appointed to be a trustee. Section 20 of the Law of Property Act 1925 declares void the appointment of an infant as a trustee. If, therefore, an infant is to be a trustee, he will have to become a trustee otherwise than by express appointment.

The general principle is that an ordinary trustee is not entitled to remuneration for his services. This is considered in detail later.[15]

2. *Judicial Trustees*

A judicial trustee is a person or corporation appointed by the court to act as a trustee where it is desired that the administration of the trust shall be subject to close supervision by the court. The appointment is made under the provisions of the Judicial Trustees Act 1896, and is not to be confused with the appointment of a private trustee by the court. The appointment of a judicial trustee is generally made on the application of an existing trustee or beneficiary, but the appointment can also be made at the instance of a person who is intending to create a

---

[8] *Re Barker's Trusts* (1875) 1 Ch.D. 43.
[9] *Coombe* v. *Brookes* (1871) L.R. 12 Eq. 61; *Re Forster* (1886) 55 L.T. 479; *Re Henderson* [1940] Ch. 764; and see *post*, p. 372.
[10] (1874) L.R. 17 Eq. 351.
[11] See s.16.
[12] [1935] W.N. 68.
[13] The woman did not stand *in loco parentis* to Laura.
[14] *Ante*, p. 189.
[15] *Post*, p. 527.

trust.[16] It is also possible to appoint a judicial trustee in respect of the administration of an estate. At one time, when there was no machinery by means of which a personal representative could retire, this provided a means of replacing one who was no longer able to act. However, the court can now appoint a replacement under section 50 of the Administration of Justice Act 1985. In an application under the 1985 Act, the court may proceed as if it were an application under the 1896 Act and vice versa.[16A]

The characteristic features of being a judicial trustee are that the beneficiaries are protected in the event of his defalcation because he is usually required to give security to the court for the proper performance of his duties.[17] He is subject to close supervision by the court, and special provisions govern the auditing of his accounts.[18] In return, a judicial trustee becomes an officer of the court, so that he is able to obtain the directions of the court informally at any time.

In practice it is rare for a judicial trustee to be appointed otherwise than where there is complex litigation,[19] where there has been gross mismanagement of a trust in the past, or where there is a problem of extraordinary complexity or difficulty involved in its administration.[20]

A judicial trustee may always charge for his services[21] and is paid from the trust funds.

3. *Trust Corporations*

(1) Definition

It has been shown[22] that, in principle, any company as well as any individual can be appointed a trustee, but a company which is appointed a trustee is not necessarily a trust corporation. This term is applied to a body corporate, such as a bank or insurance company, which undertakes the business of acting as a trustee, and which fulfils certain conditions.[23] The basic conditions are[24]:

---

[16] Judicial Trustees Act 1896, s.1(1).
[16A] Administration of Justice Act 1985, s.50(4), Judicial Trustees Act 1896, s.1(7).
[17] Judicial Trustees Act 1896, s.4(1); Judicial Trustee Rules 1983, r. 6.
[18] Judicial Trustees Act 1896, ss.1(6), 4(1); Administration of Justice Act 1982, s.57; *Re Ridsdel, Ridsdel* v. *Rawlinson* [1947] Ch. 597.
[19] See *Re Diplock, Diplock* v. *Wintle* [1948] Ch. 465; affirmed *sub nom. Minister of Health* v. *Simpson* [1951] A.C. 251.
[20] *Re Chisholm* (1898) 43 S.J. 43.
[21] Judicial Trustees Act, ss.1(5), 4(1); Judicial Trustee Rules 1983, r. 11.
[22] *Ante*, p. 360.
[23] The path to the definition is tortuous:
(a) certain bodies are entitled to act as custodian trustee (see *post*, p. 365) by virtue of the Public Trustee Rules 1912, as amended.
(b) The Public Trustee Rules 1912 were made under the power conferred by the Public Trustee Act 1906.
(c) s.68(18) of the T.A. 1925, provides that the definition of a "trust corporation" for the purposes of the Act includes any corporation entitled to act as a custodian trustee under the rules made under the Public Trustee Act 1906.
[24] The Public Trustee (Custodian Trustee) Rules 1975 (S.I. 1975 No. 1189). The rules were made to implement the EEC Council Directive 73/183/EEC.

1. Its constitution must authorise it to undertake the business of acting as a trustee, and of acting as a personal representative.
2. It must have an issued capital of not less than £250,000, of which not less than £100,000 must have been paid up in cash.
3. The company must either:
   (a) be incorporated in the United Kingdom or
   (b) be incorporated in any other EEC country.
4. The company must have a place of business in the United Kingdom, wherever it is incorporated.

The second condition, which was intended to afford a considerable measure of protection to beneficiaries, is now totally inadequate to do so. The value of assets in any one trust may exceed by several times the amount of the minimum required paid up capital. Furthermore, the test is as to the amount of the issued share capital of the company, and not as to its asset value. Thus, if a company had issued shares to the extent of £250,000, it would still be eligible to be a trust corporation even if it had by improvidence lost all its shareholders' funds.

In addition to commercial companies which carry on the business of acting as trustees, a number of other bodies also rank as trust corporations. They are given this status so that they can take advantage of the privileges given to trust corporations.[25] The following persons and bodies are included in the definition of trust corporation:

(a) Any body corporate which is appointed by the court to be a trustee in any particular case.[26]
(b) Certain bodies which are incorporated to act as trustees of charitable trusts.[27]
(c) Certain public officers, such as the Public Trustee,[28] the Treasury Solicitor, and the Official Solicitor.[29]
(d) Major local authorities,[30] and certain public authorities, such as the Gas Council and Regional Hospital Boards.[31]

(2) Ability to act

A trust corporation can act in the administration of any trust[32] unless the trust instrument forbids its employment.

(3) Privileges

The general principle is that where statutory provisions require an act to be done by two private trustees, that act can be done by a sole trustee

---

[25] *Post.*
[26] T.A. 1925, s.68(18).
[27] The incorporation must be by Special Act, or Royal Charter, or under the Charitable Trustees Incorporation Act 1872: Public Trustee Rules 1912, r. 30(c)(d), as substituted.
[28] Trustee Act 1925, s.68(18). See also the Public Trustee and Administration of Funds Act 1986, which confers on the Public Trustee all the functions of the Judge of the Court of Protection under the Mental Health Act 1983 Part VII.
[29] Law of Property (Amendment) Act 1926, s.3(1).
[30] The Public Trustee Rules 1912, r. 30(g); Local Government Act 1972, s.241.
[31] The Public Trustee Rules 1912, r. 30(e)(f).
[32] *Re Cherry's Trusts, Robinson* v. *Wesleyan Methodist Chapel Purposes Trustees* [1914] 1 Ch. 83.

where that trustee is a trust corporation. It follows that the main privileges of a trust corporation are as follows:

1. A trust corporation can by itself give a good receipt for capital money under a trust for sale[33] or a settlement.[34]
2. A trust corporation can by itself exercise various powers of management, such as the apportionment of blended funds; accepting compositions; and effective compromises.[35]
3. Where a private trustee acts jointly with a trust corporation and the private trustee wishes to delegate the performance of his duties, he may delegate them to the trust corporation.[36] He cannot, however, delegate his powers to his co-trustee if the co-trustee is a private trustee.
4. A private trustee may be discharged without a fresh trustee being appointed in his place where a trust corporation will be left to perform the trusts.[37]

As a result of these provisions, it is common to find a trust corporation acting as the sole trustee of a trust, although it can act jointly with a private trustee.

(4) Remuneration

A trust corporation is generally in the same position as a private trustee[38]; and is only entitled to remuneration where there is a provision to that effect in the trust instrument. In practice, therefore, a commercial body which is a trust corporation will not agree to act until arrangements are made for its remuneration. Where, however, the court appoints a trust corporation to be a trustee, it may fix its remuneration.[39]

4. The Public Trustee

The Public Trustee is a corporation sole and was established by the Public Trustee Act 1906. His main function is to administer private trusts, particularly small trusts, although he may also be appointed a judicial[40] or custodian trustee,[41] and be appointed to administer the property of a convict.[42] His functions were extended by the Public Trustee and Administration of Funds Act 1986, which confers on him all the functions of the Judge of the Court of Protection in relation to the property and affairs of mental patients under Part VII of the Mental Health Act 1983.[42A] He may not act as the trustee of a religious or

---

[33] Trustee Act 1925, s.14(2).
[34] Settled Land Act 1925, ss.94, 95.
[35] T.A. 1925, s.19.
[36] T.A. 1925, s.25(1)(2), substituted by the Powers of Attorney Act 1971. See *post*, p. 406.
[37] *Post*, p. 377.
[38] See *post*, p. 528.
[39] T.A. 1925, s.42.
[40] *Supra.*
[41] *Infra.*
[42] Public Trustee Act 1906, s.5.
[42A] s.3.

charitable trust[43] and may only carry on a business owned by a trust for the purpose of winding it up.[44] Although the Public Trustee is a public officer, he can only act in the administration of any trust if he has been appointed to do so in the same way as a private individual. Also, he may refuse to accept any trust for any reason other than the smallness of the trust property. He may act either alone or jointly with other trustees.

As he is a corporation sole, the Public Trustee never dies. This means that where he is the sole trustee, it is never necessary for there to be an appointment of new trustees. A further advantage is that if he acts improperly, and loss occurs, the State makes good that loss.[45]

The Public Trustee may always charge for his services,[46] his fees being calculated not on the amount of work done, but on the value of the property administered. This provision is particularly important where persons are trustees of a trust instrument which contains no charging clause. They themselves cannot derive any benefit from the trust, and may find it difficult to persuade private trustees to accept office in their stead, but they can hand over to the Public Trustee.

5. *Custodian Trustees*

The function of a custodian trustee, who may be the Public Trustee or any other trust corporation, is to hold the trust property, leaving the administration of the trust in the hands of managing trustees. A custodian trustee is usually appointed so that once the trust property is vested in his name, it will not be necessary to have any further appointment of new trustees, and so that he may have custody of the trust deeds and securities.

A custodian trustee may always charge for the services which he performs in that capacity.[47]

II. THE APPOINTMENT OF TRUSTEES

1. *Persons who can Appoint*

It is necessary to distinguish the occasions on which trustees are appointed, and the manner in which they are appointed. Trustees may be appointed:

(a) on the creation of a new trust; and
(b) during the continuance of an existing trust, whether in substitution for a trustee who is retiring or who has died, or in addition to the existing trustees.

In both cases, almost always the appointment is made by deed without the court becoming involved in any way, but in exceptional

---

[43] *Re Hampton* (1918) 88 L.J.Ch. 103.
[44] Public Trustee Rules 1912, r. 7(1) and (2).
[45] P.T.A. 1906, s.7.
[46] P.T.A. 1906, s.9, as amended by the Public Trustee (Fees) Act 1957.
[47] P.T.A. 1906, s.2; see *post*, p. 533.

cases, when there is no one else able to do so, the court will make the appointment itself. Thus both appointments made outside the court, and appointments made by the court itself must be considered.

(1) The creation of a new trust

When he creates a trust *inter vivos*, the settlor will usually appoint the first trustees of the settlement himself. If he wishes to appoint people other than himself to be the trustees, he will include a clause appointing them in the original settlement or trust deed. On the other hand, he may wish to appoint himself. He may make a declaration of trust—that is, he may declare that from the time of that declaration he will hold specified property on certain trusts—and he will then be the only trustee of the trust. Or he may appoint himself and another to be the first trustees. But as soon as the trust has come into existence, the settlor has lost his right *qua settlor* to appoint the trustees of the settlement. He may in the trust instrument have given someone the power to nominate future trustees, and he may have nominated himself[48] but if he makes any future appointment under that power, he will do so because he is the person named in the trust instrument, and not because he was the settlor.

Occasionally, there will be no trustees of a new trust. The trustees named in the settlement may be dead, or may refuse to act. Or the settlor may have forgotten to name any. If the trust instrument nominates someone to appoint new trustees, that power can be used: otherwise the appointment will be made by the court.[49] In doing so, the court will give effect to the equitable maxim that "the court will not allow a trust to fail for want of a trustee."

In practice trusts arise most frequently on death. Where the deceased left a will, he may have expressly set up a trust by his will, or a trust may arise by operation of law. Thus, if he left a legacy to a child, the money cannot actually be paid to that child until he reaches the age of eighteen, because an infant cannot give a good receipt for capital money. Until then the money will have to be held upon trust for the child. If the deceased died intestate, the devolution of his property is governed by the Administration of Estates Act 1925, as varied by subsequent statutes and statutory instruments[50] the last being the Family Provision (Intestate Succession) Order 1993. In some circumstances, the intestate's property will have to be held on statutory trusts. For example, if the deceased was worth £200,000 and left a wife and son, the wife will be entitled to £125,000. The remaining £75,000 is divided into two parts: one part goes to the son, and the other part is held upon trust for the wife for life, with remainder after her death for the son.[51]

It is possible where the trust is created by will to designate different persons as trustees and executors but normally the same persons are both executors and trustees. In particular, where there is no appointment of a different person as a trustee, the executor may automatically

---

[48] *Infra.*

[49] *Dodkin* v. *Brunt* (1868) L.R. 6 Eq. 580.

[50] *i.e.* the Intestates Estates Act 1952; the Family Provision Act 1966; and the Inheritance (Provision for Family and Dependents) Act 1975.

[51] The wife would in addition receive the personal chattels of the deceased.

become the trustee. Whether he will in fact do so depends on the function which the person is discharging at the point in time being considered. The rules which govern the time at which an executor becomes a trustee are not considered here,[52] but it is sufficient to say that the functions of an executor (or, in the case of an intestacy, an administrator) are:

(a) in the case of an executor, obtaining probate of the deceased's will, or in the case of an administrator, obtaining letters of administration of his estate;

(b) getting in the deceased's property, and the debts due to him;

(c) paying any inheritance tax, and the deceased's debts;

(d) paying the legacies;

(e) agreeing the distribution account with the beneficiaries; and

(f) distributing all the property which can be immediately distributed, that is to say all the property remaining after the payment of debts and legacies, other than that which is governed by a trust, or which is not payable at once to a beneficiary because he is under eighteen.

When all this has been done, in general, the executor or administrator ceases to be a personal representative and if there is still any of the deceased's property in his name, thenceforth he holds it as a trustee, not as a personal representative. In the case of land, however, an executor or administrator will continue to hold the property as personal representative until he assents to its vesting in himself as trustee.[53] In this case, therefore, the test is not one of function, but whether there has been the formal act of making an assent.

(2) Appointment of a new trustee

Whether the trust was set up *inter vivos* or arose on death, the rules relating to the appointment of new trustees are the same. The trust instrument may make provision for the appointment of new trustees, and if reliance is placed on that power, its terms must be strictly followed. If the trust instrument does not make provision there is a statutory power contained in section 36(1) of the Trustee Act 1925, and if there is conflict between the provisions of the trust instrument and the statutory power, the statutory power prevails. Under the statutory power, the following persons, and in the following order, have the right to appoint new trustees. Only if there is no person in one group, or if they refuse to appoint, can the appointment be made by a person in the subsequent group. These groups are:

Statutory power:

(a) the person or persons nominated in the trust instrument;

(b) the existing trustees;

(c) the personal representatives of the last or only surviving trustee.

---

[52] See further Mellows, *The Law of Succession* (5th ed.), p. 321.
[53] *Re King's Will Trusts* [1964] Ch. 542; see *ante*, p. 19.

Other powers

    (d) the beneficiaries in certain limited cases;
    (e) the court.

This order is strictly followed. Thus, in *Re Higginbottom*[54] the existing trustee had the power to appoint new trustees, and her right to do so was held to prevail against the wishes of a large majority of the beneficiaries who sought to appoint others.[55] Further, where an appointment is made in good faith by the person entitled, the court will not interfere with the appointment even if it would prefer someone else to be appointed.[56]

Where two or more persons have the power of appointing new trustees, they must exercise the power jointly unless there is a provision in the trust instrument to the contrary. If they cannot agree who the new trustee shall be, they are treated as refusing to exercise their power, so that the power becomes exercisable by the persons in the next category. So in *Re Sheppard's Settlement Trusts*[57] the trust instrument gave the power of appointing trustees to two persons. When they could not agree on the appointee, it was held that the power could be exercised by the continuing trustees. The position is the same if the person having the power to appoint cannot be found,[58] or is incapable of making the appointment.[59]

(a) Persons nominated in the trust instrument. As was mentioned above,[60] if a settlor wishes himself to make an appointment of trustees of an existing trust, he must have given himself this power in the trust instrument. Otherwise, he has no power to appoint. In many cases, of course, the settlor will give some other person the power to appoint new trustees.

Where a person is nominated in the trust instrument[61] he is usually given the power to appoint new trustees in all circumstances, but if he is only given power to do so in limited circumstances, that power is strictly construed. In *Re Wheeler*,[62] for example, a person was nominated to appoint a new trustee in the place of any trustee being "incapable" of acting. One trustee became bankrupt, and so became "unfit" to act,[63] but not "incapable" of acting. It was held that the nominated person did not have a power to appoint in those circumstances because the

---

[54] [1892] 3 Ch. 132.
[55] See also *Re Brockbank* [1948] Ch. 206; *infra*.
[56] *Re Gadd, Eastwood v. Clark* (1883) 23 Ch.D. 134, C.A.; *Re Norris, Allen v. Norris* (1884) 27 Ch.D. 333; *Re Sales, Sales v. Sales* (1911) 55 S.J. 838.
[57] [1888] W.N. 234.
[58] *Craddock v. Witham* [1895] W.N. 75.
[59] *Re Blake* [1887] W.N. 75.
[60] *Ante*, p. 366.
[61] See *Re Walker and Hughes* (1883) 24 Ch.D. 698 and *Re Sheppard's Settlement Trusts* [1888] W.N. 234.
[62] [1896] 1 Ch. 315 (a case on s.10(1), Trustee Act 1893, re-enacted in s.36(1), Trustee Act 1925).
[63] As to the distinction, see *post*, pp. 372, 373.

condition was not fulfilled.[64] Further, where a power to appoint is given jointly to two or more persons, it can only be exercised by those persons. Unless, therefore, there is evidence of a contrary intention, the power will not be exercisable at all where one of the donees of the power dies, or becomes incapable of making the appointment.[65]

Where a beneficiary is nominated in the trust instrument as having power to appoint new trustees, the power of appointment is generally treated as being detached from the beneficial interest. Thus, if the beneficiary disposes of his interest then, unless there is a provision in the trust instrument to the contrary, he will still be entitled to appoint new trustees.[66]

An illogical difference exists in respect of the appointment of a new trustee between the position where an existing trustee is retiring, and where an additional trustee is to be appointed without the retirement of an existing trustee. If he is acting solely under the statutory power,[67] a person who is nominated in the trust instrument to appoint new trustees may appoint himself to be a trustee in the place of a retiring trustee but not as an additional trustee. This results from a difference of wording in the Trustee Act. Section 36(1), which applies where a new trustee is being appointed in the place of an outgoing trustee, gives the power to the nominated person to "appoint one or more other persons (whether or not being the persons exercising the power) to be a trustee," while section 36(6), which confers the power to appoint additional trustees, gives the nominated person a power to appoint "*another* person or other persons to be the trustee." This difference was doubtless unintentional on the part of Parliament.

(b) The existing trustees, and the personal representatives of the last surviving trustee. The right of the existing trustees, or if there are none, the personal representatives of the last surviving trustee,[68] to appoint new trustees is one which takes precedence over any wishes of the beneficiaries. In *Re Brockbank*[69] where there was a dispute between the existing trustees and the beneficiaries as to who should be appointed a new trustee, it was held that as long as the trustees wished to make an appointment, they could do so irrespectively of the wishes of the beneficiaries. The appointment of new trustees was a function which Parliament has entrusted to the continuing trustees, and as long as they were willing to exercise it, the beneficiaries could not interfere.

Rather surprisingly, section 36(8) enacts that the provisions of section 36 which relate to a continuing trustee include a refusing or retiring trustee if he is willing to act in exercising the powers of the section. The

---

[64] See also *Turner* v. *Maule* (1850) 15 Jur. 761; *Re Watts' Settlement* (1851) 9 Hare 106; *Re May's Will Trusts* [1941] Ch. 109.

[65] *Re Harding, Harding* v. *Paterson* [1923] 1 Ch. 182.

[66] *Hardaker* v. *Moorhouse* (1884) 26 Ch.D. 417.

[67] *Re Power's Settlement Trust* [1951] Ch. 1074. The Law Reform Committee (23rd Report, 1982) recommended that the person having power to appoint trustees should be able to appoint himself.

[68] *Re Shafto's Trusts* (1885) 29 Ch.D. 247.

[69] [1948] Ch. 206.

result of this is that if a trustee refuses to act as a trustee, or wishes to retire, he must be allowed to join in the appointment of a new trustee if he wishes to do so. But for the purposes of this provision, the expression "refusing or retiring trustee" is narrowly construed. In *Re Stoneham's Settlement Trusts*[70] a new trustee was appointed in the place of another trustee who had remained out of the United Kingdom for longer than twelve months. On his return, the displaced trustee applied to the court to upset the appointment on the ground that he had not participated in it, but Danckwerts J. held that a trustee who is removed compulsorily from the trust is not a "refusing or retiring" trustee but a "removed" trustee, so that his participation is not necessary.

Where there are no existing trustees, the appointment can be made by the personal representative of the last surviving trustee. In this respect it is necessary to distinguish the power of appointment itself on the one hand and the method of proving entitlement to exercise that power on the other hand. An executor has the power of appointing new trustees as soon as the last trustee dies. Accordingly, it is not necessary for the executor to obtain a grant of probate before exercising the power.[71] However, a personal representative can only prove his entitlement to exercise the power by producing a grant of probate or letters of administration.

It is the general practice of the English court only to recognise grants of probate or letters of administration which have been issued in the United Kingdom or, if issued by a court overseas, have been re-sealed by a court in the United Kingdom. The point arose in *Re Crowhurst Park*.[72] In that case, the deceased was the sole trustee of various tenancies of land in England. His widow obtained a grant of probate of his will in Jersey, but she did not obtain a grant in the United Kingdom. The widow executed a deed by which, in her capacity as the personal representative of the deceased, she purported to appoint herself as the new trustee of that trust. It was held that while she was entitled to exercise the power of appointment, she could only prove that entitlement by a grant of probate or letters of administration granted in the United Kingdom. Accordingly, the widow could not take action in respect of the tenancies until she obtained a United Kingdom grant.

Although personal representatives of the last surviving trustee may appoint new trustees, this is a mere power, and they cannot be compelled to do so.[73] They are, however, given statutory encouragement to exercise their power. Thus, even if they intend to renounce their office as personal representatives, they are still entitled to appoint new trustees before they renounce.[74] Without the express statutory provision, the exercise of the power would be sufficient to show an acceptance of the office of personal representative.

The appointment of trustees, whether by a surviving or continuing

---

[70] [1953] Ch. 59.
[71] *Re Parker's Trusts* [1894] 1 Ch. 707; *Re Crowhurst Park, Sims-Hilditch* v. *Simmons* [1974] 1 All E.R. 991, at 1001.
[72] [1974] 1 All E.R. 991.
[73] *Re Knight's Will* (1883) 26 Ch.D. 82, C.A.
[74] T.A. 1925, s.36(5).

trustee, or by personal representatives of the last surviving trustee, must be made *inter vivos*, and cannot be made by will.[75]

(c) Beneficiaries.   Where there is no person nominated in the trust instrument, no existing trustees, and no personal representatives of the last surviving trustee in existence and willing to make an appointment, the beneficiaries may probably do so if they are all *sui juris* and between them absolutely entitled to the whole of the beneficial interest, but in this situation it is preferable to obtain an order of the court appointing the new trustees.[76] As is explained later,[77] where the beneficiaries are unable to make the appointment the court will do so.

2. *When a New Trustee may be Appointed*

Section 36 of the Trustee Act 1925 makes provision for the appointment of new trustees in two types of case:

(1) in the place of an outgoing trustee; and
(2) as an additional trustee, where all existing trustees are remaining.

(1) In place of outgoing trustee
Section 36(1) provides that in certain specified circumstances, the person nominated for the purpose in the trust instrument, or, if there is no such person, the surviving trustees or trustee, or the personal representatives of the last surviving trustee, in that order, may appoint by writing[78] one or more persons to be trustees in the place of an outgoing trustee. The section applies in the case of any outgoing trustee, whether or not he was the original trustee of the trust, and whether or not he was appointed by the court. Section 36(1) applies:

(a) where a trustee is dead;
(b) where he remains out of the United Kingdom for more than twelve months;
(c) where he desires to be discharged;
(d) where he refuses to act;
(e) where he is unfit to act;
 (f) where he is incapable of acting;
(g) where he is an infant; and
(h) by virtue of section 36(3), in the case of a corporation which is a trustee, where that corporation is dissolved.

These provisions require elaboration, but it may be noted at once that these events only give rise to a power to appoint a new trustee: they do not impose a duty to appoint.

---

[75] See *Re Parker's Trust* [1894] 1 Ch. 707.
[76] *Re Brockbank, ante.*
[77] *Post*, p. 375.
[78] The statute only requires the appointment to be in writing and not by deed. It is desirable to make the appointment by deed in most cases, so that s.40, Trustee Act 1925, may operate; *post*, p. 381.

(a) **Trustee dead.** This includes the position where a person nominated as a trustee dies without ever having taken up his office. This would be the case, for example, where a person who is nominated as the trustee of a will trust dies before the death of the testator.

(b) **Remaining out of the United Kingdom.** The residence abroad must be a continuous residence and a break for even a very short time, such as a week, will prevent this provision operating.[79] The motive for the residence is irrelevant,[80] so that even if the trustee has been imprisoned abroad, he can still be removed from his trusteeship.

In some circumstances the trust instrument modifies the statutory provision, and seeks to achieve the same broad effect by different wording. Where this is done, the provision must be carefully construed, but the courts lean towards an interpretation that the period abroad must have an element of permanence. This was satisfied in *Re Earl of Stamford*[81] where the power arose if a trustee should "be abroad," and a trustee lived in France, making only occasional visits to England.[82]

The provision can now be totally inappropriate where a foreign trust is to be established, or where an English trust is to be "exported."[83] In such cases, it is prudent to provide expressly that a trustee shall not be capable of being replaced merely because he is resident abroad.

(c) **Desiring to be discharged.** This statutory provision is wide enough to include the position where the trustee desires to be discharged from only part of the trust.[84] This might occur where part of a trust fund is set aside to provide a life interest for a beneficiary and the trustee wishes to retire as a trustee of the main fund, while remaining a trustee of the appropriated fund.

(d) **Refusal to act.** Logically, this provision should apply only to a person who has accepted the trusteeship, and refuses to act after accepting office. Until that time, it is difficult to see how he could be a "trustee." However, there is old authority on the predecessor of the section to the effect that it also includes a trustee who disclaims.[85]

(e) **Unfit to act.** There is little authority as to the meaning of "unfitness" for the purposes of this provision, but it seems clear that "unfitness" here refers not to medical infirmity but to defects of character. In the absence of authority, it is only possible to deduce the meaning of the expression from some of the circumstances in which the

---

[79] *Re Walker, Summers* v. *Barrow* [1910] 1 Ch. 259.

[80] *Re Stoneham* [1953] Ch. 59.

[81] [1896] 1 Ch. 288.

[82] See also *Re Moravian Society* (1858) 26 Beav. 101.

[83] See *post*, Chap. 22.

[84] If this statutory power is excluded, a trustee cannot be discharged from part only of the fund without the intervention of the court; *Savile* v. *Couper* (1887) 36 Ch.D. 520; *Re Moss's Trusts* (1888) 37 Ch.D. 513.

[85] *Noble* v. *Meymott* (1841) 14 Beav. 471; *Re Hadley, ex p. Hadley,* (1851) 5 De G. & Sm. 67; *Viscountess D'Adhemar* v. *Bertrand* (1865) 35 Beav. 19; *Re Birchall, Birchall* v. *Ashton* (1889) 40 Ch.D. 436.

court will remove trustees.[86] These cases include conviction of a crime involving dishonesty[87] and in certain circumstances bankruptcy. In the case of bankruptcy the court will generally remove a trustee who has become bankrupt,[88] particularly if the beneficiaries request this to be done, if only on the ground that a person who has lost all his own money ought not to be in charge of other people's money. But as an exception to this, the court has refused to remove a trustee whose bankruptcy was due to misfortune and who was entirely free of moral blame.[89]

(f) Incapable of acting. Incapacity refers to physical or mental incapacity to attend, or to attend properly, to the administration of the trust.[90] Special provisions affect mental incapacity where the trustee also has a beneficial interest in the property if he is a person whose mental illness makes him subject to the provisions of the Mental Health Act 1983. In this case, no appointment of a new trustee in his place may be made without the consent of the authority having jurisdiction over him under Part VII of the Mental Health Act 1983.[91]

A person is also incapable of acting if there is any legislation in force which expressly prohibits persons in specified circumstances from holding property or acting as trustees. Such a prohibition has applied to enemy aliens in time of war.[92]

(g) Trustee a minor. As has been seen,[93] a minor cannot validly be expressly appointed a trustee, and the provisions will only apply where the minor is a trustee under a resulting or constructive trust.

(2) Additional trustees: existing trustees remaining

The statutory power of appointing additional trustees is contained in section 36(6). The person nominated in the trust instrument for the purpose of appointing new trustees, or the existing trustee or trustees, in that order, may appoint by writing an additional trustee or additional trustees of the trust where there are not more than three existing trustees. Although more than one additional trustee may be appointed at the same time, the total number of trustees must not be increased beyond four, and this restriction applies to all trusts, and is not confined to trusts affecting land.[94] Additional trustees cannot be

---

[86] *Post,* p. 379.
[87] *Turner* v. *Maule* (1850) 15 Jur. 761; *Re Wheeler and De Rochow* [1896] 1 Ch. 315; *Re Sichel's Settlements, Sichel* v. *Sichel* [1916] 1 Ch. 358.
[88] *Re Barker's Trusts* (1875) 1 Ch.D. 43.
[89] *Re Bridgman* (1860) 1 Drew. & Sm. 164.
[90] *Re Moravian Society* (1858) 26 Beav. 101; *Re Watt's Settlement* (1872) L.R. 7 Ch. 223; *Turner* v. *Maule* (1850) 15 Jur. 761; *Re East* (1873) 8 Ch.App. 735; *Re Lemann's Trusts* (1883) 22 Ch.D. 633; *Re Blake* [1887] W.N. 173, C.A.; *Re Weston's Trusts* [1898] W.N. 151.
[91] Mental Health Act 1983, s.148, Sched. IV para. 4(*a*), replacing Mental Health Act 1959 ss.149(1), 153 & Sched. VII, which in turn replaced T.A. 1925, s.36(9).
[92] *Re Sichel's Settlements, Sichel* v. *Sichel, ante.*
[93] *Ante,* p. 360.
[94] See next section.

appointed under this section if any existing trustee is a trust corporation.[94A]

(3) Trustees of separate property

The person who has the power of appointing new trustees may appoint a separate set of trustees for any part of the trust property which is held on trusts distinct from the remainder of the trust property.[95] If, therefore, trustees hold three quarters of the trust fund upon trust for Andrew and his family, and one quarter for Bernard and his family, separate trustees can be appointed of the quarter held for Bernard. While, however, the appointment is valid for all purposes connected with the administration of the trust, for certain tax purposes the original trustees will continue to be regarded as trustees.[96]

3. *Restrictions on the Numbers of Trustees*

The general principle is that any number of persons may be trustees, and the determining factor is not a legal one, but the practical one of having enough trustees to be able to take advantage of various skills and experience, but not too many to make the working of the trust unwieldly.

Nevertheless, there are certain restrictions on the numbers of trustees:

(a) The maximum number of trustees of a settlement of land or of land held upon trust for sale is four, and if more than four persons are named, the first four named who are able and willing to act are the trustees (Trustee Act 1925, s. 34). This limitation does not apply in the case of land held upon trust for charitable, ecclesiastical or public purposes.[97]

(b) There need only be one trustee to *hold* land, but unless that trustee is a trust corporation two or more trustees are needed to give a valid receipt for capital money,[98] so that two or more trustees are in fact needed to *sell* land.

(c) Where under a will or on intestacy property is to be held for an infant, and no trustees are appointed by any will, the personal representatives of the deceased may appoint trustees to hold that property on trust for the infant, but the number of those trustees must not exceed four.[99] This applies whatever the nature of the property.

(d) Where an additional trustee is being appointed under the statutory power referred to above and all the existing trustees are

---

[94A] The Law Reform Committee (23rd Report, 1982) recommended the abolition of this rule.

[95] T.A. 1925, s.37(1)(*b*).

[96] *Roome* v. *Edwards* [1981] 3 All E.R. 736, H.L.

[97] T.A. 1925, s.34(3). The Law Reform Committee (23rd Report, 1982) recommended that, unless the trust instrument otherwise provides, there should never be more than four trustees of a private trust.

[98] T.A. 1925, s.14(2).

[99] Administration of Estates Act 1925, s.42.

remaining, the number of trustees must not be increased to more than four in any case.

(e) Where a trustee wishes to retire, but it is not proposed to appoint a new trustee in his place, he can only do so if, *inter alia*, at least two trustees will remain (Trustee Act 1925, s. 39).[1]

In any case a minimum of two trustees is usually *desirable*, in order to give the beneficiaries adequate protection. One of the basic safeguards for beneficiaries is that property must usually be under the control of at least two persons, so that it is very much more difficult for one to misappropriate the money.

4. *Assumption of Office by Conduct*

Acceptance of the office of trustee of an *inter vivos* trust is usually signified by the trustee executing the trust deed. But in any case, where a trustee does any act in carrying out the trust, he will be presumed from his conduct to have accepted the office. Any act, even though slight, in carrying out the terms of the trust is sufficient.[2]

5. *Appointment by the Court*

Whenever it is desirable that a new trustee should be appointed, and it is "inexpedient, difficult or impracticable so to do without the assistance of the court" the court may appoint a new trustee either as an additional trustee, or in substitution for an existing trustee.[3] The court will not, in the absence of exceptional circumstances, exercise its power if advantage can be taken of a provision in the trust instrument or of the statutory power.[4] Further, there appears to be no reported decision in which the court has appointed a trustee against the wishes of a person who has the power to appoint and who is prepared to exercise it in good faith. This is so even if the court would prefer to see someone else appointed.[5] Where the court proposes to appoint a new trustee in substitution for an existing trustee, it may do so even against the wishes of the existing trustee.[6]

In practice this power is used mainly (a) where there is doubt whether the statutory power can be exercised, for example, if a trustee is in fact "unfit" to act; (b) where there is no person capable of making an appointment, and (c) where it is desired to increase the number of trustees and the statutory power under section 36 does not apply.

Occasionally an application is made to the court for the appointment

---

[1] *Post*, p. 377.

[2] *Lord Montfort* v. *Lord Cadogan* (1816) 19 Ves. 635; *James* v. *Frearson* (1842) 1 Y. & C.C.C. 370. Thus a person designated a trustee should expressly announce if he does not wish to act.

[3] Trustee Act 1925, s.41. See also *Re Hodson's Settlement* (1851) 9 Hare 118; *Finlay* v. *Howard* (1842) 2 Dru. & War. 490.

[4] *Re Gibbon* (1882) 45 L.T. 756; 30 W.R. 287.

[5] *Re Higginbottom* [1892] 3 Ch. 132; *ante*, p. 368; *Re Brockbank, Ward* v. *Bates* [1948] Ch. 206, *ante*, p. 369.

[6] *Re Henderson* [1940] Ch. 764.

of a new trustee, because if a new trustee is appointed by the court it cannot afterwards be alleged that the trustee was appointed in circumstances which were improper or in order to facilitate a breach of trust.[7] The court will, therefore, only exercise its power where it is clearly in the interest of the beneficiaries for it to make the appointment. An example of a case where the court refused to exercise its power is *Re Weston's Settlement*[8] which is discussed in a later chapter.[9]

The court has a discretion as to whom it will appoint as a trustee, but the principles upon which this discretion will be exercised are:

(a) If the settlor has expressly or by clear implication made known his wishes, the court will have regard to his wishes. This is particularly so if the settlor has indicated whom he does *not* wish to be appointed.

(b) A trustee will not be appointed to promote the interest of some of the beneficiaries in opposition to the interest of other beneficiaries.[10] The attitude of the courts has, however, changed over the last century or so in two important respects. First, it used to be that the court would not appoint a beneficiary to be a trustee.[11] The reason was the fear that the trustee-beneficiary would be tempted to act more in his own interest than that of the other beneficiaries. However, more recently, following the statutory examples,[12] it has been realised that in some circumstances a person who has a beneficial interest may put a greater effort and enthusiasm into the administration of the trust than someone else, and that the appointment of such a person as a trustee may be appropriate, particularly where there is also an independent trustee. The second respect in which the attitude of the courts has changed is with regard to professional advisers. In the middle of the nineteenth century the courts would almost never appoint the family solicitor to be a trustee,[13] but with perhaps greater confidence in the integrity of professional advisers, and realisation of the advantage which detailed knowledge of the family circumstances brings, such persons may now be appointed, particularly where this is desired by the beneficiaries.

(c) The court will have regard to whether the proposed appointment will promote the execution of the trust, or whether it will impede it.[14]

An interesting situation arises where the existing trustees make it known that they will refuse to act with the person whom the court

---

[7] See *post*, p. 577.

[8] [1969] 1 Ch. 223, C.A.

[9] *Post*, p. 573.

[10] *Re Parsons, Barnsdale and Smallman v. Parsons* [1940] Ch. 973.

[11] *e.g. Re Harrop's Trusts* (1883) 24 Ch.D. 717; *Re Knowles' Settled Estates* (1884) 27 Ch.D. 707.

[12] *Ante*, p. 361.

[13] *Re Kemp's Settled Estates* (1883) 24 Ch.D. 485, C.A.; *Re Earl of Stamford, Payne v. Stamford* [1896] 1 Ch. 288; *Re Spencer's Settled Estates* [1903] 1 Ch. 75.

[14] *Re Tempest* (1866) 1 Ch.App. 485.

proposes to appoint. On the one hand the court's dignity is involved. In *Re Tempest*[15] Turner L.J. said: "I think it would be going too far to say that the court ought, on that ground alone, to refuse to appoint the proposed trustee: for this would, as suggested in the argument, be to give the continuing or surviving trustee a veto upon the appointment of the new trustee. In such a case I think it must be the duty of the court to inquire and ascertain whether the objection of the surviving or continuing trustee is well founded or not, and to act or refuse to act upon it accordingly."[16] On the other hand, the basic object of the court's power is to promote the interests of the beneficiaries, and these are not protected if there is serious friction between the trustees. Indeed, on this ground alone the court will sometimes remove a trustee.[17]

Unless, presumably, a trustee has been guilty of serious malpractice, so that his removal is a matter of urgency, the court is reluctant to appoint new trustees in the place of existing trustees if to do so would place the existing trustees in a worse financial position. In *Re Pauling's Settlement (No. 2)*,[18] it was sought to remove trustees against whom an action had been brought for breach of trust.[19] But this was resisted because they might have been able to have impounded the beneficiaries' interests[20] if they were successful in an appeal in the other action. Wilberforce J. held that even if they were removed they could still exercise their right to impound. As it happened the court refused to appoint new trustees in the place of the existing trustees, because, *inter alia*, to have done so would have deprived them of security for the costs which would be payable to them if the appeal were successful.

III. RETIREMENT

1. *Circumstances in Which Trustees May Retire*

A trustee may retire from his office in any of four ways:

(a) by taking advantage of any power in the trust instrument;
(b) by taking advantage of the powers in the Trustee Act 1925, namely,
   (i) section 36, where a new trustee is being appointed in his place; or
   (ii) section 39, where no new trustee is being appointed;
(c) by obtaining the consent of all beneficiaries, who must be *sui juris* and between them absolutely entitled to the whole beneficial interest;
(d) by obtaining the consent of the court.

If there is provision in the trust instrument for a trustee to retire, then

---

[15] (1866) L.R. 1 Ch. App. 485.
[16] (1866) L.R. 1 Ch. App. 485, 490.
[17] *Re Henderson, ante.*
[18] [1963] Ch. 576.
[19] This is the case discussed at pp. 507 and 598.
[20] As to the circumstances in which a beneficiary's interest can be impounded, see *post*, p. 600.

a trustee can take advantage of this power, even though it is wider than the statutory power. But the statutory power in sections 36 and 39 of the Trustee Act 1925 is so wide that specific provisions are not now normally included in trust instruments. Retirement when coupled with the appointment of a new trustee has already been considered, but by section 39 a trustee can retire even where no new trustee is being appointed in his place. Under this section, a trustee may retire if

(a) after his retirement there will remain a minimum of two trustees or a trust corporation; and
(b) he obtains the consent to his retirement of the remaining trustees; and
(c) he obtains the consent of anyone named in the trust instrument as having the power to appoint new trustees; and
(d) the retirement is by deed.

None of these conditions applies, however, if one of the remaining trustees is the Public Trustee.[21] The requirement that two trustees or a trust corporation shall remain applies to all trusts: it has no connection with the requirement for two trustees or a trust corporation to give a receipt for land subject to a trust.[22]

Provided the conditions of section 39 are fulfilled, the retirement will be effective, but if the trustee has retired in order to procure or facilitate a breach of trust, he may nevertheless remain liable for such breach.[23]

As a last resort, if none of these cases applies, a trustee may apply to the court to be discharged as a trustee. The court will usually discharge the trustee if there is at least one other trustee who continues or some suitable new trustee can be found, but the trustee who wishes to retire will usually be ordered to pay the costs of the application unless he can show that the circumstances have materially altered since he accepted the trusteeship.[24]

There is one important difference between the scope of section 36 and that of section 39. As has been seen,[25] under section 36 a trustee can retire from part only of the trusts, but under section 39 the trustee can retire only from the whole of the trusts.

Whether these conditions can be overriden by the express provisions of the settlement is unclear.[25A]

A retirement which does not comply with these requirements is invalid and the trustee in question will consequently remain in office.[25B]

---

[21] Public Trustee Act 1906, s.6.

[22] *Ante*, p. 374.

[23] *Post*, p. 578.

[24] The court has expressed its disapproval of applications being made to the court for the appointment of a new trustee where advantage could be taken of the statutory power, and doubtless it would be equally disapproving if applications were made to it for retirement when advantage could be taken of the statutory power.

[25] *Supra*.

[25A] See *Mettoy Pension Trustees* v. *Evans* [1990] 1 W.L.R. 1587 at p. 1607 and M. Jacobs, (1986) 1 Trust Law & Practice 95.

[25B] *Mettoy Pension Trustees* v. *Evans* [1990] 1 W.L.R. 1587.

2. *Release of Retiring Trustees*

When trustees retire they sometimes request a formal release of any liability arising from the trusteeship. If trustees retire in favour of new trustees, they are not entitled to such a release, but it seems that if they retire upon the winding up of the trust they are so entitled.[26] Such a release is only effective to the extent that the beneficiaries are in possession of all relevant facts.

IV. REMOVAL OF TRUSTEES

A trustee may be removed from his office:

(1) under a power contained in the trust instrument;
(2) under the statutory power contained in section 36 of the Trustee Act; or
(3) by the court.

Powers of removing trustees contained in the trust instrument are strictly construed, so that if it is desired to take advantage of any such power, it must be clear that the circumstances envisaged by such power obtain.[27] The power of removal of trustees under section 36, when a new trustee is being appointed, has been dealt with above. The circumstances are, it will be recalled,

(a) where the trustee remains out of the United Kingdom for more than 12 months consecutively;
(b) where he refuses to act;
(c) where he is unfit to act;
(d) where he is incapable of acting.[28]

Removal by the court presents some difficulty. The court's primary concern is to protect and enhance the interests of the beneficiaries. So that where the trustee is convicted of dishonesty, or by becoming bankrupt or otherwise[29] shows that he is not fit to be in charge of other people's property, the court will remove him.[30] Nevertheless, removal by the court does involve, at least to the outside world, some moral stigma, and difficulties arise where an application is made to remove a trustee, not because he has done anything wrong, but because he cannot agree with or get on with his co-trustees.

The position was considered by the Privy Council in *Letterstedt* v.

---

[26] *Tiger* v. *Barclays Bank Ltd.* [1951] 2 K.B. 556.
[27] *London and County Banking Co.* v. *Goddard* [1897] 1 Ch. 642.
[28] *Re Lemann's Trust* (1883) 22 Ch.D. 633.
[29] *Ibid.*; *Re Phelps' Settlement Trust* (1885) 55 L.J.Ch. 465 (intellectual decay).
[30] See the cases discussed *ante*, p. 372.

Broers.[31] Lord Blackburn observed: "In exercising so delicate a jurisdiction as that of removing trustees, their Lordships do not venture to lay down any general rule beyond the very broad principle . . . that their main guide must be the welfare of the beneficiaries. Probably it is not possible to lay down any more definite rule in a matter so essentially dependent on details often of great nicety. . . ."[32] Mere friction between trustee and beneficiary is not an adequate ground, but if there is a permanent condition of hostility between one trustee and the other trustees, the court probably would remove him. In *Re Wrightson*[33] Warrington J. said: "You must find something which induces the court to think either that the trust property will not be safe or that the trust will not be properly executed in the interests of the beneficiaries." A permanent condition of hostility between trustees would probably be a sufficient deterrent to efficient administration of the trust for the court to exercise its powers.

It is difficult to appeal successfully against an order by an inferior court ordering the removal of a trustee. Thus, in *Re Edwards Will Trusts*,[34] where Megarry V.C., had removed a trustee without giving any reasons for so doing, the Court of Appeal refused to interfere with his decision.

V. DELEGATION OF TRUSTEESHIP

In limited circumstances, a person can delegate his powers as trustee without ceasing to be a trustee. These are considered later.[35]

VI. VESTING OF PROPERTY ON CHANGE OF TRUSTEE

One of the first acts that a person should do on his appointment as a trustee is to secure that the trust property is put in the names of himself and his co-trustees. As soon as he is appointed he becomes responsible with his co-trustees for what happens to the trust property, and if he negligently allows property to remain in the names of others and loss occurs, he may be liable to make good the loss to the beneficiaries out of his own pocket.[36]

The property may be placed in the name of the new trustee, jointly with the continuing trustees, by the mode of transfer appropriate to the type of property.[37] The appropriate mode of transfer in respect of the major types of property is:

---

[31] (1884) 9 App.Cas. 371. And see *Earl of Portsmouth* v. *Fellows* (1820) 5 Madd. 450.

[32] (1884) 9 App.Cas. 371, at p. 382.

[33] [1908] 1 Ch. 789, at p. 803.

[34] [1981] 2 All E.R. 941, C.A.

[35] *Post*, p. 400.

[36] See *post*, p. 577.

[37] The use of the appropriate mode of transfer is also discussed in connection with whether a trust is completely constituted; *ante*, p. 58.

(a) freehold land, where title not registered by H.M. Land Registry	Conveyance
(b) leasehold land, where title not registered by H.M. Land Registry	Assignment
(c) freehold or leasehold land, where title is registered by H.M. Land Registry	Transfer, and registration of transfer at Land Registry
(d) stocks and shares	Transfer, and registration of transfer by company or authority concerned
(e) debts, and other choses in action	Assignment (plus notice to the other party to secure priority)
(f) negotiable instruments payable to bearer	Delivery and indorsement
(g) personal chattels	Either assignment or physical delivery

These formalities can sometimes be avoided, however, by virtue of section 40 of the Trustee Act 1925, when a person is appointed a new trustee, or retires from trusteeship, and the appointment or retirement, as the case may be, is effected by deed. This section provides that unless the deed contains a provision to the contrary, it automatically vests the trust property in the new or remaining trustees as joint tenants. The section applies to all types of trust property except:

(1) mortgages of land, when a formal transfer of mortgage is required;
(2) leasehold land, where the lease provides that before any assignment the permission of the landlord must be obtained, and the landlord's permission has not been obtained before the deed of appointment or retirement has been executed. The reason for this exception is to prevent an unwitting breach of covenant under the lease, so giving rise to a possible claim for forfeiture;
(3) stocks and shares, where a formal transfer has to be registered by the company;
(4) land registered by H.M. Land Registry, where, although no transfer is necessary,[38] the deed of appointment or retirement has to be registered so that the proprietorship register is brought up to date.

The first three exceptions arise by virtue of subsection (4) of section 40, and the fourth by section 47 of the Land Registration Act 1925.

Section 40 only applies where there is an appointment of a new trustee of an existing trust. It does not apply where property is held by a

---

[38] Although a transfer is not essential, for practical purposes it is desirable, as if a transfer is not executed, H.M. Land Registry may insist on retaining the deed of appointment or retirement, or on being supplied with a certified copy of it.

personal representative,[39] because, in this case, there is not an existing trust.

VII. PROTECTION OF PURCHASERS

A useful provision for the protection of purchasers is contained in section 38 of the Trustee Act 1925. It will be remembered that under section 36, some of the grounds for the removal of a trustee and the appointment of a new one are that the trustee has remained out of the United Kingdom for more than 12 months, that he refuses to act, or that he is unfit to act. Some of these grounds can give rise to dispute. Thus a displaced trustee might argue that he was not, in fact, unfit to act, so that his purported removal was ineffective. In the absence of a provision to the contrary, in the event of the purported removal being ineffective a purchaser would not obtain a good title if he bought from the new trustees. However, section 38 provides that a statement in a deed of appointment that a trustee

> (1) has remained out of the United Kingdom for more than 12 months; or
> (2) refuses to act; or
> (3) is incapable of acting; or
> (4) is unfit to act

"shall, in favour of a purchaser of a legal estate, be conclusive evidence of the matter stated." Because it is "conclusive" a purchaser need not look behind the statement.[40] Further, in favour of a purchaser, an appointment of trustees which depends on such a statement being true is valid, and any express or implied vesting declaration is also valid.[41]

Section 38 only applies, however, in the case of land and no protection is conferred by the inclusion of such a statement in other circumstances.

Although the section gives protection to purchasers, it does not affect the position of a person who has not in fact ceased to be a trustee. If, therefore, a person is purportedly removed as a trustee on the ground that he is unfit to act, and another person is purportedly appointed in his stead, the person purportedly removed could apply to the court for a declaration that he continues to be a trustee. Even if such a declaration were to be made, however, it would not prejudice a purchaser of land who had relied on the statement in the instrument of appointment.

---

[39] See *ante*, p. 19.

[40] Contrast the position where enactments provide only for "sufficient" evidence. See, *e.g.* Administration of Estates Act 1925, s.36(7), and *Re Duce and Boots Cash Chemists (Southern), Ltd's Contract* [1937] Ch. 642.

[41] T.A. 1925, s.38(2).

Chapter 11

ACTION ON APPOINTMENT AS TRUSTEE

I. Disclosure Prior to Appointment

It has already been seen in Chapter 8 that a trustee should not, except with the express consent of the person setting up the trust, or of all the beneficiaries, put himself in a position in which his own interests might conflict with his duties of impartiality as a trustee. As a result of this rule, it has been decided that a person who is asked to become a trustee ought before being appointed to disclose any circumstances unknown to the persons appointing him which might bring his interest and duty into conflict. In *Peyton* v. *Robinson*,[1] for example, a beneficiary under a trust was indebted to the trustee personally, but this fact was not known to the settlor. The terms of the trust instrument gave the trustee a discretion to make payments to this beneficiary. In exercise of this discretion, the trustee made payments, but it was held that he could not accept repayment of his debt from the amount paid to the beneficiary. The trustee was placed in a position where his interest, to pay trust money to the beneficiary with a view to being repaid his debt, conflicted with his duty, to exercise his discretion entirely without thought for his own personal advantage.

II. Following Appointment

When a person accepts a trusteeship, he should do four things, and if he fails to do so he may make himself liable for an action for breach of trust. These things are:

- (a) acquaint himself with the terms of the trust;
- (b) inspect the trust instrument and any other trust deeds;
- (c) procure that all the property subject to the trust is vested in the joint names of himself and his co-trustees, and that all title deeds are placed under their joint control; and
- (d) in the case of an appointment as a new trustee of an existing trust, to investigate any suspicious circumstances which indicate a prior breach of trust, and to take action to recoup the trust fund if any breach has in fact taken place.

---

[1] (1823) 1 L.J. (o.s) Ch. 191.

(a) The terms of the trust

The terms of the trust instrument must be known and understood because, as is explained elsewhere,[2] if a trustee pays money to a wrong beneficiary, or pays the right beneficiary too little money, or departs in any other way without authority from the terms of the trust instrument, he thereby commits a breach of trust, however honestly he may act. In certain circumstances he may apply to the court for relief from liability,[3] but even if the court grants total or partial relief, a breach of trust will still have been committed. In *Nestlé* v. *National Westminster Bank*[3A] the trustee bank had doubts as to the precise nature of its investment powers. The Court of Appeal described these doubts as "understandable" but held that it was "inexcusable that the bank took no step at any time to obtain legal advice as to the scope of its powers."[3B] In fact, however, the plaintiff beneficiary was unable to show that she had suffered any loss thereby so no liability was actually imposed.

(b) Inspection of trust instrument

The second duty on appointment, to inspect the trust instrument, is to ascertain whether any notices have previously been given to the trustees of dealings by beneficiaries with their interests in the trust fund. A beneficiary who has an interest under a trust may usually sell, mortgage, give away or in some other manner deal with his interest in the trust fund, just as he may deal with any other property. As far as the trustees are concerned, this disposition is complete when the assignee gives notice of the disposition to the trustees.[4] Once such notice has been given, the trustees must pay to the assignee the trust money to which the beneficiary named in the trust instrument would otherwise have been entitled. If a memorandum of the transaction is endorsed on the trust instrument, this is sufficient to give the persons who are the trustees for the time being notice of the dealing by the beneficiary with his equitable interest.[5]

Furthermore, if a beneficiary should attempt to assign or charge his interest more than once, the assignee or chargee who is the first to give notice of the dealing to the trustees takes priority.[6] If, therefore, a newly appointed trustee finds on inspection of the trust instrument more than one notice of assignment, he must ascertain carefully the order in which such notices were received.

(c) Trust property under joint control

Thirdly, the trustee must ensure that all the trust property is placed in the joint names of the trustees. By virtue of section 40 of the Trustee Act 1925, which has already been considered,[7] where the trustee is

---

[2] *Post*, p. 577.
[3] Under Trustee Act 1925, s.61, discussed *post*, p. 596.
[3A] [1993] 1 W.L.R. 1260.
[3B] *Ibid.* at p. 1265, *per* Dillon L.J.
[4] By virtue of the rule in *Dearle* v. *Hall* (1828) 3 Russ. 1.
[5] LPA 1925, s.137.
[6] *Dearle* v. *Hall* (1828) 3 Russ. 1.
[7] See *ante*, p. 381.

appointed by deed, the trust property may automatically vest in him, but he must ensure that property not covered by this automatic vesting provision is put into his name. A trustee who leaves the trust fund in the sole name, or under the sole control, of his co-trustee or co-trustees will usually be liable if it is lost.[8] Difficulties sometimes arise in connection with "bearer" securities. These are securities issued by companies similar to ordinary securities, but different from them in that they are not registered in the owner's name. The issuing company pays dividends to whoever at the time when the dividend is payable produces to the company the bearer certificate, or any coupons attached to it. By definition bearer securities cannot be placed in the names of the trustees. Section 7 of the Trustee Act 1925, however, provides that bearer securities shall be deposited by the trustees for safe custody and collection of income with a bank, and that the trustees are not responsible for any loss which may result from such deposit. Provided the bank holds the securities to the order of *all* the trustees, they are absolutely protected. But in *Lewis* v. *Nobbs*,[9] where one trustee allowed bearer securities to remain in the hands of his co-trustee, who misappropriated them, it was held that the trustee was guilty of breach of trust in allowing the securities to remain under the control of the other so that they could be so misappropriated. Similarly, all title deeds to trust property should be deposited with a bank or agent to be held to the order of all trustees.[10]

(d) Previous breaches of trust

The last duty on appointment as a trustee of an existing trust is with regard to previous breaches of trust. A new trustee is not expected to act like a bloodhound straining to sniff out some breach of trust; in the absence of suspicious circumstances he may assume that the previous trustees have properly discharged their duties.[11] But the new trustee must inquire into any circumstances which might suggest that a breach of trust has been committed, for if, through not inquiring into such circumstances, the trust fund suffers, the new trustee may be liable. He is liable not because he participated in the original breach of trust, but because he himself has committed a breach of trust in not inquiring.[12] The most obvious circumstances which would put a new trustee on inquiry is if the trust fund is materially less when he is appointed than it has been at some previous time. There may be many bona fide explanations of this, but the new trustee must inquire, and, if appropriate, take action.

---

[8] *Lewis* v. *Nobbs* (1878) 8 Ch.D. 591.
[9] (1878) 8 Ch.D. 591.
[10] See also *Underwood* v. *Stevens* (1816) 1 Mer. 712; *post*, p. 580.
[11] *Re Straham, ex. p. Greaves* (1856) 8 De G.M. & G. 291.
[12] *Harvey* v. *Olliver* (1887) 57 L.T. 239.

CHAPTER 12

THE ADMINISTRATION OF A TRUST

THIS chapter is concerned with the general obligations of the trustees with regard to the trust property, and various specific powers which they are given to facilitate its administration.

I. THE TRUSTEES' STANDARD OF CARE

In the management of a trust, one of the most frequent decisions which trustees are likely to take is in respect of investments, and their duties in this respect are dealt with fully in Chapter 15. It is, however, proposed to deal here with the standard of care which trustees are bound to exercise over the whole field of administration of a trust. In a series of cases[1] the rule has been laid down that unpaid trustees are bound to use only such due diligence and care in the management of the trust as an ordinary prudent man of business would use in the management of his own affairs. There is no doubt about the rule, but its application to particular circumstances can cause great difficulty. No doubt this is due, at least in part, to the fact, as Lord Blackburn pointed out in *Speight* v. *Gaunt,*[2] that judges and lawyers who see brought before them the cases in which losses have been incurred, and do not see the infinitely more numerous cases in which expense and trouble and inconvenience have been avoided, are apt to think men of business rash.

Each case will of course be decided on its own facts, but several decisions can be quoted. Thus, with regard to debts payable to the trust, trustees should obtain payment with all reasonable speed, and if payment is not made within a reasonable time, proceedings should be instituted,[3] for this is the manner in which an ordinary prudent man of business would deal with debts due to him. But in *Ward* v. *Ward*[4] the House of Lords held that a trustee exercised his discretion reasonably in not suing immediately a beneficiary who was also a debtor to the trust, for had proceedings been taken, that beneficiary would have been ruined, and his children, who were also beneficiaries, placed in difficult circumstances.

---

[1] *Brice* v. *Stokes* (1805) 11 Ves.319; *Massey* v. *Banner* (1820) 1 Jac. & W. 241; *Bullock* v. *Bullock* (1886) 56 L.J.Ch. 221; *Speight* v. *Gaunt* (1883) 9 App.Cas. 1.
[2] (1883) 9 App.Cas. 1.
[3] *Re Brogden, Billing* v. *Brogden* (1888) 38 Ch.D. 546; *Millar's Trustees* v. *Polson* (1897) 34 Sc.L.R. 798; *Fenwick* v. *Greenwell* (1847) 10 Bea v. 412; *Grove* v. *Price* (1858) 26 Beav. 103.
[4] (1843) 2 H.L.Cas. 777.

Where trustees hold shares in a private company, they must exercise reasonable care to obtain information about the affairs of the company, and where a trustee is also a director, he may be held liable in an action by a beneficiary as a result of his conduct of the management of the company. In *Re Lucking's Will Trusts*[5] a trustee was a director of a private company, in which the trust held a majority shareholding. The trustee-director allowed another director to overdraw heavily from the company until he was eventually dismissed. This overdrawing was largely possible because the other director sent blank cheques to the trustee-director, which he signed and returned. In due course the dismissed director was adjudicated bankrupt, owing the company about £16,000. The trustee-director was held liable for the reduction in the value of the trust shares as a result of that defalcation.[6]

A trustee does well to bear in mind continually that at some time in the future a disgruntled beneficiary may well seek to question his actions. Thus, where, for example, trustees wish to sell or lease property, they should usually ascertain the true value of the property by employing a valuer, and sell or lease with regard to his figures.[7] In so doing they both comply with the test of the ordinary prudent man of business, and also give themselves protection against subsequent accusations by the beneficiaries that the property was dealt with at too low a figure.[8]

Many of the clearest examples of trustees acting but not complying with the standard of the ordinary prudent man of business are cases of failure to take action. Therefore, if a trustee allows rent to fall into arrears, he may be ordered to make good the loss[9] and a trustee will also be liable if he fails to register any transaction which needs to be registered, such as a transfer of registered land, or of shares, and by failing to do so enables someone else to obtain priority.[10]

Occasionally, however, the rule that a trustee must act like an ordinary prudent man of business conflicts with another rule, that a trustee must do the best he can for the beneficiaries. Suppose, for example, that trustees wish to sell a house and receive and provisionally accept an offer for £100,000. Suppose they then receive an offer for £110,000. The trustees are under an obligation to consider the second offer, even if, had they been dealing with their own property, they would not have entertained it, if only for considerations of ordinary commercial morality. They still retain their discretion, and if there is some reason which genuinely leads them to conclude that the first offer should be accepted, for example, if the sale to the first proposed purchaser would be completed materially earlier, they may conclude that the first offer should be accepted. But their discretion must be exercised generally in the interests of the beneficiaries[11] and, in the

---

[5] [1968] 1 W.L.R. 866.
[6] See also *Re Miller's Deed Trusts*, L.S. Gaz., May 3, 1978.
[7] *Oliver* v. *Court* (1820) 8 Pr. 127.
[8] *Grove* v. *Search* (1906) 22 T.L.R. 290.
[9] *Tebbs* v. *Carpenter* (1816) 1 Madd. 290.
[10] *Macnamara* v. *Carey* (1867) Ir.R. 1 Eq. 9.
[11] *Buttle* v. *Saunders* [1950] 2 All E.R. 193.

example given, they should accept the second offer unless there is some good reason for accepting the first.

The courts appear to recognise that an ordinary prudent man of business does not make a wise decision on every occasion. A trustee is not, therefore, liable merely because he makes an error of judgment. In *Buxton* v. *Buxton*[12] a trustee was directed to sell bonds with all reasonable speed. He decided to delay sale, but the bonds fell in price. It was held that he was not liable to make good the loss. He had actively exercised his discretion, and acted in complete good faith, and was not made liable merely because his decision, as events turned out, was wrong.

What has been said so far applies to the unpaid trustee. Where the trustee is a paid trustee, a higher standard of diligence is required. As Harman J. said in *Re Waterman's Will Trusts*[13] "I do not forget that a paid trustee is expected to exercise a higher standard of diligence and knowledge than an unpaid trustee." The test for the paid trustee may probably be stated to be that he must exercise the degree of diligence and show the degree of knowledge that a specialist in trust administration could be expected to show.

II. JOINT ACTS

Except in rare circumstances, any act or decision to be effective must be the act or decision of all the trustees. There is no question here of a decision of the majority binding all the trustees.[14] The settlor or testator has reposed his trust in all the trustees: the liabilities and responsibilities are those of all the trustees. The acts or decisions in the administration of the trust must therefore be those of all the trustees. It may often happen that one trustee who is more enthusiastic in his duties than his co-trustee will come to be spoken of as the "acting trustee," whose decisions are merely endorsed by the co-trustee. But in this context "acting trustee" is not a concept recognised by law. The trustees must each exercise their discretion, and each is equally liable.[15]

Should a dispute arise, a trustee may be justified in concurring in an action of his co-trustee with which he is not in favour, either because he considers his co-trustee to be more experienced in, or to be more knowledgeable of, the type of transaction in hand,[16] or to prevent a complete deadlock in the administration of the trust. Whether he is being reasonable in deferring to his co-trustee, or whether he should have stood firm and if necessary made an application to the court, will depend on the circumstances of the particular case.

To this general rule that all the trustees must act jointly there are certain exceptions. First, the trust instrument can of course authorise individual action. Secondly, one trustee alone often has power to give a

---

[12] (1835) 1 Myl. & Cr. 80.
[13] *Re Waterman's Will Trusts, Lloyds Bank Ltd.* v. *Sutton* [1952] 2 All E.R. 1054. See also *Re Pauling* [1964] Ch. 303.
[14] *Boardman* v. *Phipps* [1967] 2 A.C. 46.
[15] *Munch* v. *Cockerell* (1840) 5 Myl. & Cr. 178.
[16] *Re Schneider* (1906) 22 T.L.R.

receipt for income, whether rent or dividends from shares. The latter is a necessary provision, because the articles of association of most companies provide that dividends are to be paid to the first-named registered holder of those shares. Thirdly, just as some acts can be delegated to an agent, so most of those acts can be delegated by all the trustees to one of their number. Lastly, in the case of trustees of a private trust, a majority of trustees can pay money into court[17] even if the minority objects.

Although it is not an exception to the theoretical principle, if a provision to this effect is contained in a trust instrument it is possible to achieve the practical result that not all the trustees need agree on a certain course of action. The method of doing this is to impose a primary duty on the trustees to do an act, but to give them a secondary power not to do it, or to do some other act if they all agree. This method was adopted by the Law of Property Act 1925 in the case of land which is held upon trust for sale,[18] so that trustees are under a primary duty to sell the land, but they have a secondary power to postpone sale. To postpone sale, however, all trustees must agree to exercise their power, with the result that if one only wishes to sell, they all have to give effect to the duty to sell.[19] This is a statutory example, but the principle applies equally to provisions of trust instruments to a similar effect.

In some circumstances, the decision of the majority of trustees of a charity can bind them all.[20]

III. THE TRUSTEES' DISCRETION

It is inherent in a trustee's position that he must exercise his discretion,[21] and must do so in a wide variety of circumstances. The trustee may, of course, only exercise his discretion within the limits prescribed by law, or by the trust instrument, so that if trustees are given a discretion to do certain acts with the consent of some person, they must ensure that that consent is obtained. In *Re Massingberd's Settlement*[22] trustees were given power to vary investments with the consent of the tenant for life. They sold Consols, which were an authorised security, and with consent invested in an unauthorised mortgage. Subsequently they realised that unauthorised mortgage, and reinvested in an authorised mortgage, but without the consent of the tenant for life. As this consent had not been obtained, it was held that they had committed a breach of trust, and were liable to purchase for the trust the same number of Consols as had originally been held, credit

---

[17] Trustee Act 1925, s.63.

[18] Law of Property Act 1925, s.25.

[19] *Re Mayo* [1943] Ch. 302; but, exceptionally, in the case of a trust for sale implied by statute as a result of co-ownership the court will not compel a sale, where it is contrary to contractual provisions, or involves sharp dealing; *Re Buchanan-Wollaston's Conveyance* [1939] Ch. 738; or where it would defeat the purpose for which the trust was set up: *Jones* v. *Challenger* [1961] 1 Q.B. 176. See also *Rawlings* v. *Rawlings* [1964] P. 378.

[20] *Re Whiteley* [1910] 1 Ch. 600.

[21] Generally with regard to the trustee's discretion, see, *ante*, Chap. 4.

[22] *Re Massingbred's Settlement, Clark* v. *Trelawney* (1890) 63 L.T. 296.

being given for the investment which they had made in the authorised security.

Assuming that all such limits on the trustee's discretion are observed, it is of paramount importance that the trustees should exercise their discretion as an active mental process, and not allow a situation to result merely through inaction. The decision in *Wilson* v. *Turner*[23] is illustrative.[24] In that case the trustees had a power to pay or apply income arising from the trusts to or for the maintenance of an infant beneficiary. They did not make a conscious decision, but merely handed over the income to the infant's father, and the Court of Appeal held that the money should be repaid to the trust fund. If, however, the trustees had actively considered the merits of the case, and had consciously decided to apply the income for the maintenance of the infant, their decision would have been valid. A further case is *Re Greenwood*.[25] Section 15 of the Trustee Act 1925 gives trustees a power to compound liabilities, and, provided they act in good faith, they are protected against loss. In *Re Greenwood*, however, Eve J. said that this section only protects trustees if they have actively exercised their discretion, and if loss results merely through inaction on the part of the trustees they would not be protected. The test is not therefore the result of the trustees' action, or inaction, but their own mental process.[26]

Where, however, the trustees do consciously exercise their discretion, they derive a large measure of support from the courts. Trustees are not obliged to give reasons for their decisions, and if they do not do so, the court will not interfere with their decision unless they have acted dishonestly. The court will not interfere even if it would itself have come to a different decision. In *Re Beloved Wilkes Charity*[27] Lord Truro said: "It is to the discretion of the trustees that the execution of the trust is confided, that discretion being exercised with an entire absence of indirect motive, with honesty of intention, and with a fair consideration of the subject. The duty of supervision on the part of this court will thus be confined to the question of the honesty, integrity and fairness with which the deliberation has been conducted, and will not be extended to the accuracy of the conclusion arrived at." It has been established that trustees need not give reasons for their decisions[28] but if they do state reasons for their decisions, the court will examine those reasons to see if the trustees have acted in error.[29]

What is the position of trustees who, having a discretion, fail to exercise it? The answer depends on whether the discretion arises under a power which is merely permissive, or whether it is obligatory. If the power is permissive only, that is, the trustees are not under any obligation to exercise it, it will lapse after a reasonable period, and

---

[23] (1883) 22 Ch. D. 521.
[24] See also *ante*, p. 148.
[25] (1911) 105 L.T. 509.
[26] Trustee Act, 1925, s.15 does not make it necessary for all the beneficiaries to consent before the trustees accept the compromise: *Re Earl of Stafford* [1978] 3 W.L.R. 223.
[27] (1851) 3 Mac. & G. 440.
[28] *R.* v. *Archbishop of Canterbury and Bishop of London* [1903] 1 K.B. 298; and *see post*, p. 391.
[29] *Ibid.*

cannot be revived.[30] If, however, the discretion is obligatory, it will not lapse, but will be enforced. In *Re Locker's Settlement Trusts*[31] the trustees of a discretionary trust held income upon a positive obligation to distribute the income among such beneficiaries as they should determine. They failed to distribute income which arose during a period of three years, but some years later wished to do so. They applied to the court for a declaration whether the discretion was still exercisable. It was held that it was still exercisable, as the discretion was of an obligatory nature.

IV. DUTY TO ACCOUNT AND GIVE INFORMATION

A trustee must be prepared at all times to give a beneficiary information as to the state of the trust property, and to dealings with it. This obligation involves

(a) keeping financial accounts; and
(b) providing information, within certain limits, as to action taken in the administration of a trust.[32]

A trustee must therefore, maintain accurate accounts of the trust property. He must allow a beneficiary, or his solicitor, to inspect those accounts, and the vouchers supporting them, and he must be prepared to give full information as to the amount of the trust fund. He is not obliged to supply copies of the accounts, or settlements of account, to the beneficiaries, unless the beneficiaries themselves pay for them. In one case[33] it was held that a trustee who was illiterate, and so could not keep accounts, was justified in employing an agent to keep the accounts. Under the modern law, trustees, whether illiterate or not, will be entitled to employ agents for this purpose.[34]

Where trust money is invested, the trustees must on request supply a beneficiary with details of the investments, and even produce to the beneficiary the stock or share certificates, or other deeds and documents, representing that investment. Where, however, a beneficiary requires information as to his position under a trust, and this information cannot be supplied by the trustees without incurring expense, the trustees can pass on the expense to the beneficiary. Trustees who do not keep proper accounts may be ordered to do so by the court, and may be forced to bear personally the costs of the application to the court.[35] As the trustees may at any time be called upon to give information as to the administration of a trust, it is advisable for them to keep in addition to the trust accounts a trust diary. This is a type of minute book in which decisions taken in the administration of a trust are recorded. In

---

[30] *Re Allen-Mayrick's Will Trusts, Mangnall* v. *Allen-Mayrick* (1966) 1 W.L.R. 499; *Re Gulbenkian's Settlement Trusts (No. 2); Stephens* v. *Maun* [1970] Ch. 408.
[31] [1978] 1 All E.R. 216.
[32] *Tiger* v. *Barclays Bank* [1952] W.N. 38; [1952] 1 All E.R. 85.
[33] *Wroe* v. *Seed* (1863) 4 Giff. 425.
[34] *Post*, p. 400.
[35] See (1936) 52 L.Q.R. 365.

view of the fact that a beneficiary is usually entitled to access to the trust diary and that, as has just been said, if trustees give reasons for their decisions, the court will inquire into the accuracy of their decision but not otherwise, trustees may choose to record their decision but not their reason.

In the same way that a beneficiary is entitled to inspect deeds and documents representing trust investments, he is entitled to inspect most other documents relating to the trust. This is because, just as the beneficiaries are the equitable owners of the trust property, they are also the equitable owners of the documents which have arisen in the course of the trust administration, and often at the expense of the trust. In *O'Rourkey* v. *Darbishire*,[36] for example, Lord Wrenbury observed: "a beneficiary has a right of access to the documents which he desires to inspect upon what has been called in the judgments in this case a pro-prietary right. The beneficiary is entitled to see all trust documents, because they are trust documents, and because he is a beneficiary. They are, in this sense, his own."

In *Re Marquess of Londonderry's Settlement*[37] there was a conflict between the rule just considered, that a beneficiary is entitled to inspect trust documents, and the rule that trustees are not obliged to give reasons for their decisions. In this case the trustees of the settlement were to distribute the trust fund in such proportions as they thought fit among certain named persons. One of these considered that she had received too little[38] and, in order to launch an attack upon the trustees, sought to inspect numerous trust documents which would probably have indicated the reasons which led the trustees to make the distribu-tions that they had made. The disgruntled beneficiary claimed that she had a right to inspect the documents: the trustees claimed that she had not, as they were not to be compelled to give reasons for their decisions and, if the court ordered that the beneficiary was able to see the documents which she wished to see, the rule which enabled the trustees to keep their reasons to themselves would be defeated. The Court of Appeal held, in effect, that the rule enabling a beneficiary to inspect trust documents did not extend to documents which gave reasons for the trustees' decisions, and the court even went so far as to order that if a document was basically in the category of those which the beneficiary is entitled to see, but also contains details of the trustees' reasons, those passages should be covered up when the document is produced to a beneficiary.

The decision is certainly welcome, but the reasons for it are far from clear. This was a case where the court had sympathy with the trustees' contention that if the beneficiary were given access to documents which gave their reasons for dealing with the trust property family strife would result. It may well be that in this case the Court of Appeal decided what answer they wanted to reach, and then strove to find

---

[36] [1920] A.C. 581.

[37] [1964] Ch. 594.

[38] She and her family had in fact received £165,000. The total amount of the trust fund is not recorded.

reasons to support it. Harman L.J. considered, but did not decide, whether the documents were "trust documents" at all, with the implication that if they were not, then the beneficiary would not have a right of access to them. He could not make up his mind about this, but said: "I would hold that, even if documents of this type ought properly to be described as trust documents, they are protected for the special reason which protects the trustees' deliberations on a discretionary matter from disclosure. If necessary, I hold that this principle overrides the ordinary rule."[39] Danckwerts L.J. based his decision firmly on the practical ground that, if the trustees' reasons were not protected from disclosure, it would be impossible for them to do their job. The third member of the Court of Appeal, Salmon L.J., also toyed with the idea of declaring that the documents were not trust documents but he had to admit defeat: "The category of trust documents has never been comprehensively defined. Nor could it be—certainly not by me." There are, then, several possible reasons to explain the rule, but the rule itself is now established that beneficiaries do not have a right of access to documents which the trustees intend to be private and which record the reasons for their decisions.

Re Marquess of Londonderry's Settlement was concerned with a direct application by a beneficiary to inspect trust documents. It was made clear by the Court of Appeal that the decision did not govern the position of disclosure of documents in pending proceedings brought upon some other ground. If, for example, a beneficiary brings proceedings against the trustees for breach of trust, perhaps involving improper motive on the part of the trustees, it may well be that by way of discovery the beneficiary will be entitled to see all the trustees' documents, including those which give reasons for decisions. There is, however, no direct authority on the point.

V. DIRECTIONS OF THE COURT

Where trustees are in doubt as to the manner in which they should act, they may apply to the court by way of summons for its directions. If the trustees place before the court all the relevant facts, and subsequently act in accordance with the court's directions, the principle is that they will be absolutely protected. In *Re Marquess of Londonderry's Settlement*,[40] for example, the trustees applied to the court for its directions, and Plowman J. decided at first instance that the documents ought to have been disclosed. The trustees appealed, successfully as it turned out, but the Court of Appeal nearly refused to hear the appeal. Harman L.J. observed: "This appeal, as it seems to me, is an irregularity. Trustees seeking the protection of the court are protected by the court's order and it is not for them to appeal."[41] There is little doubt that if the trustees had acted under the (erroneous) decision of Plowman J. they would have been protected. But if, as they did, they considered the

---

[39] [1964] Ch. 594, at p. 598.
[40] [1964] Ch. 594.
[41] [1964] Ch. 594, at p. 597.

decision wrong, and adverse to the interests of the beneficiaries, why should they not appeal? It is particularly ironic that this statement[42] on the part of Harman L.J., which tends to reflect a narrow outlook all too often encountered in the Chancery Division, should have been made in a case where, because the trustees did appeal, the law was patently improved—for all trustees. Fortunately Salmon L.J. took a different view: "However, in my view the trustees were fully justified in bringing this appeal. Indeed it was their duty to bring it since they believed, rightly, that an appeal was essential for the protection of the general body of beneficiaries." It is remarkable, not that Salmon L.J. made this statement, but that he had to make it.

Unfortunately, Salmon L.J. introduced a further difficulty. It might have been thought that the rule should have been that if trustees apply to the court, and are given a decision which is wrong, then they *may* appeal. According to Salmon L.J. they *must* appeal: they have a duty to do so. One day it may fall to be decided how far trustees are protected if they act in accordance with the decision of the court, but believe that decision to be wrong.

A further example of an application to the court by the trustees was *Barker* v. *Peile*,[43] where several actions had arisen out of uncertainty as to who were proper beneficiaries, and the trustee wished to be relieved of the liability and annoyance of being a trustee. Special circumstances must, however, exist, before the court will release a trustee from his obligations in this way.

Trustees may also make an application to the court for the construction of words in a will or settlement where the meaning is uncertain.

A useful power in connection with administration which the court has, is contained in section 57 of the Trustee Act 1925. This section is considered in detail later,[44] but for present purposes it may be noted that by virtue of this provision, where the trustees wish to effect any sale, letting, charge, or any other disposition of trust property, or wish to purchase property or make an investment with trust money, and there is no power to do so in the trust instrument or under the general law, the court may sanction that transaction. The court has jurisdiction to impose any conditions it thinks fit when approving such a transaction, but it can only authorise a transaction which is made "in the management or administration" of the trust property. It will be seen that the court has power to give authority under this section:

(1) where the trustees propose to do an act not authorised by the general law or by the trust instrument;
(2) that act is in the management or administration of the trust property; and
(3) the court thinks it expedient to sanction it.

Section 57 is designed to secure that the property shall be

---

[42] See also (1965) 29 Conv. (N.S.) 81.
[43] (1865) 2 Dr. & Sm. 340.
[44] *Post*, p. 542.

administered as advantageously as possible in the interests of the beneficiaries, but the provision must be considered in conjunction with the
general principle that the court will not rewrite a trust. The result is that
the power will only be exercised to authorise specific dealings with
trust property. In *Boardman* v. *Phipps*[45] the trustee held shares in a
private company and had the opportunity to acquire further shares,
although such acquisition was not authorised by the trust instrument.
In subsequent litigation the court said that the acquisition of these
shares was so clearly in the interest of the beneficiaries, the proper
course would have been for the trustees to have applied under section
57 for power to purchase the additional shares.[45A]

Section 57 does not itself authorise rearrangement of beneficial
interests, but this may be effected particularly under the Variation of
Trusts Act 1958, which is dealt with in Chapter 21.

VI. ADMINISTRATIVE POWERS RELATING TO TRUST PROPERTY

Part II of the Trustee Act 1925 confers general powers on trustees, particularly with regard to the administration of property. Under these
powers, trustees may where appropriate raise money by sale or
mortgage, sell trust property at auction and insure the property.
Although not mentioned by statute, trustees are bound to see that trust
property does not fall into decay through want of repair.[46]

The provisions of the Trustee Act 1925 relating to insurance are
somewhat curious. Section 19 gives the trustees power *if they so wish* to
insure the property for an amount not exceeding three-quarters of the
full value of the property. This section seems to envisage a standard
considerably lower than that of the ordinary prudent man of business,
who would at least in present times almost invariably insure, and for
the full re-building cost of the property.[47]

Section 15 confers upon trustees the power to

"(a) accept any property, real or personal, before the time at which it
is made transferable or payable; or
(b) sever and apportion any blended trust funds or property; or
(c) pay or allow any debt or claim on any evidence that he or they
think sufficient; or
(d) accept any composition or any security, real or personal, for any
debt or for any property, real or personal, claimed; or
(e) allow any time for payment of any debt; or
(f) compromise, compound, abandon, submit to arbitration, or
otherwise settle any debt, account, claim, or thing whatever
relating to the testator's or intestate's estate or to the trust."

---

[45] [1967] 2 A.C. 46.
[45A] See *per* Lord Denning M.R. in the Court of Appeal [1965] 2 W.L.R. 839 at p. 861.
[46] *Re Hotchkys, Freke* v. *Calmady* (1886) 32 Ch.D. 408.
[47] See, further, Kenny, "The Underinsured Beneficiary" (1982) 79 L.S.G. 755 (June 16). The
Law Reform Committee (23rd Report, 1982) has recommended that trustees of new
trusts should be placed under a duty to insure against such risks as against which an
ordinary prudent man of business would insure.

A trustee will not be liable for any loss which occurs from the exercise of any of these powers, provided he has acted in good faith.[48] The consent of the beneficiaries is not necessary.[49] An example of the operation of the rule is *Re The Earl of Strafford*.[50] In that case, the settlor had settled valuable chattels, and his wife owned similar chattels. When the wife died, beneficiaries under her will took her chattels, but beneficiaries under the trust claimed that those chattels were trust property. A compromise was proposed under which, broadly, the beneficiaries under the wife's will would take some chattels outright, take a life interest in others, and give up the remainder. The trustees were minded to accept the proposed compromise but one of the beneficiaries under the trust objected. The Court of Appeal held that it was for the trustees to decide whether they considered the compromise was in the interest of all beneficiaries taken together and that, if they did, they had power to accept it despite the opposition of one of the beneficiaries.

Some powers over property can only be exercised on proof of legal ownership, and in respect of trust property these powers can only be exercised by the trustees. In *Schalit* v. *Nadler*[51] a beneficiary who was solely entitled to trust property which was let levied distress for arrears of rent. It was held that only the trustee as legal owner could levy distress, so that the distress actually levied was wrongful. Similarly, only the legal owner can serve a notice to quit.

VII. MORTGAGING THE TRUST PROPERTY

Section 16 of the Trustee Act 1925 applies where trustees are authorised either by the general law or by the trust instrument "to pay or apply capital money subject to the trust for any purpose or in any manner". In these circumstances, section 16 gives the trustees power to raise the requisite money either by mortgaging or selling the trust assets. However, the section is construed narrowly, and is confined to the cases where money is required either to preserve assets or to advance capital. In *Re Suenson-Taylor's Settlement*[52] the trustees, who had very wide powers of investment and who, in accordance with these powers, properly held a large area of land for investment purposes, wished to borrow upon the security of that land in order to buy further land. It was held that this would be outside the power conferred by section 16. The court observed, however, that there could be cases where it was necessary to purchase further land in order to protect existing investments. For example, if trustees own a house, it may be appropriate to buy land which the house overlooks, in order to prevent anyone else building upon it. The point was left open, but it seems that in these

---

[48] *Per* Eve J., *Re Greenwood* (1911) 105 L.T. 509.
[49] *Re Earl of Strafford* [1979] 1 All E.R. 513, C.A.
[50] [1979] 1 All E.R. 513, C.A.
[51] [1933] 2 K.B. 79; and *see ante*, p. 12.
[52] *Re Suenson-Taylor's Settlement, Moores* v. *Moores* [1974] 3 All E.R. 397.

circumstances raising money by mortgage in order to effect the purchase might well be within the statutory power.[52A]

VIII. EXPENSES

It is shown later[53] that except in special cases a trustee is not entitled to be paid for his services. He is, however, entitled to be reimbursed all his expenses which have been properly incurred. This right of reimbursement is in respect both of money actually spent by the trustee, and of liabilities which he has incurred. Thus in *Benett* v. *Wyndham*[54] a trustee of an estate directed woodcutters employed on the estate to fell some trees. The woodcutters were negligent and allowed a bough to fall on a passer-by who was injured. The trustee, as legal owner of the estate, was sued and he was allowed to reimburse himself the damages out of the trust fund. Normally the trustee is not entitled to interest on his expenses. It does not follow that a trustee will be allowed all his expenses: they must be reasonable and proper in all the circumstances. An ingenious trustee in *Malcolm* v. *O'Callaghan*[55] made journeys to Paris to be present at the hearing of a case in the French courts which concerned the trust, but which turned solely on a question of French law and for which the trustee's presence was in no way necessary. He was not allowed his expenses against the trust.

A trustee is entitled to be reimbursed the expenses of properly taking or defending legal proceedings on behalf of the trust in the same way as other expenses. But before taking or defending proceedings a trustee can apply to the court for its approval but, if he does not do so and he is unsuccessful, it will be up to him to prove that he had reasonable grounds for taking or defending proceedings. If he cannot prove this, he will be deprived of his costs.

The trustee's right of indemnity is generally against the trust property,[56] not against the beneficiaries. If, therefore, the trustee's right of indemnity exceeds the value of the trust property, he will not normally be able to claim the balance from the beneficiaries personally. The right of indemnity does, however, extend to the beneficiary personally:

(a) where the beneficiary was the creator of the trust[57];
(b) where the trustee is a bare trustee,[58] and
(c) where the trustee accepted the trust at the request of the beneficiary.[59]

[52A] The Law Reform Committee (23rd Report, 1982) has recommended that trustees should have a general statutory power to purchase a residence for beneficiaries on mortgage.
[53] *Post*, p. 528.
[54] (1862) 4 De G.7. & J. 259.
[55] (1835) 3 Myl. & Cr. 52.
[56] Trustee Act 1925, s.30(2).
[57] *Matthews* v. *Ruggles-Brise* [1911] 1 Ch. 194.
[58] *Hardoon* v. *Belilios* [1901] A.C. 118.
[59] *Jervis* v. *Wolferstan* (1874) L.R. 18 Eq. 18, at p. 24.

IX. PAYMENT TO BENEFICIARIES

The general principle is that a trustee is absolutely responsible for ensuring that the right amount is paid to the right beneficiary. In *Eaves* v. *Hickson*[60] trustees paid trust money to the wrong person in reliance on a forged marriage certificate. They were held liable to make good to the rightful beneficiary so much as could not be recovered from the wrongful recipient. Similarly, where trustees paid trust money to a wrongful beneficiary, on an erroneous but bona fide construction of the trust instrument, they were held liable to make good the loss.[61] Where the trustees have in the particular circumstances acted honestly and reasonably, and ought fairly to be excused, the court has a discretion to grant them relief,[62] but this does not alter the trustees' primary obligation of ensuring payment to the rightful beneficiary.

Where there is any doubt as to who is entitled to trust property, the trustees should apply to the court for directions, and will then be protected if those directions are complied with. If the beneficiary entitled cannot be traced, the trustees may pay the money into court, and so obtain a good discharge for it. And where one of several beneficiaries cannot be traced, the court may authorise the trustees to distribute the trust fund as if the beneficiary who cannot be traced were dead.[63] Nevertheless, the court will discourage trustees from making payment into court of trust money where there is no good reason for doing so by making the trustees personally pay the costs of the application for payment in. The power of payment into court is one of the exceptional cases in which the wishes of the majority of the trustees binds them all.

The court discourages applications by trustees for protection where they incur no practical risk at all. Thus, in *Re Pettifor*[64] Pennycuick J. said that in normal circumstances the court would consider it an unnecessary waste of money for trustees to come to court and ask for liberty to distribute a trust fund on the basis that a woman of 70 would not have a further child.

In most cases of long-standing trusts, there cannot be any debts due from the trust of which the trustees are unaware. Where there is a possibility of outstanding debts, however, advantage should be taken of section 27 of the Trustee Act 1925. Under this section, the trustees may advertise in the *London Gazette*, and usually in another newspaper, their intention of distributing the trust fund and requiring persons interested to send them notice of their claim. Claims must be sent in within the time fixed by the notice, which must not be less than two months after it is published. At the expiration of that time, the trustees are safe in distributing the trust fund after discharging only those claims of which they have notice. If subsequently a creditor comes

---

[60] *Eaves* v. *Hickson* (1861) 30 Beav. 136.
[61] *Hilliard* v. *Fulford* (1876) 4 Ch.D. 389.
[62] Trustee Act 1925, s.61, *post*, p. 596.
[63] The so-called "Benjamin Order": *Re Benjamin* [1902] 1 Ch. 723.
[64] [1966] Ch. 257.

forward, he may be able to follow the trust property into the hands of the beneficiary, but he has no remedy against the trustees themselves.

Trustees must, of course, remember that beneficial interests under the trust can be assigned or charged. Where an assignee makes a claim to trust property, the trustees will, before making payment, have to investigate his title to the interest assigned, and they will be obliged to give effect to effective assignments.

When a trusteeship is completed, the trustee is entitled to put himself into the position in which no further disputes can be raised about payments to the beneficiaries. To achieve this he is entitled to present his final accounts to the beneficiaries and to require them to give him a formal discharge from his trusteeship. If they refuse, he may have the accounts taken in court, that is, examined by an official of the Chancery Division, and in that way obtain confirmation that they are in order.

Chapter 13

DELEGATION: THE EMPLOYMENT OF AGENTS

THE trustees may wish to engage others to assist them in the execution of the trust or the administration of trust property. This may be so, for example, where the trustees consider it appropriate for the trust accounts and records to be kept by a solicitor or accountant; or where particular action requires special skills, such as advising with regard to changes of investment; or where there are particular difficulties in administrations, as where trust property is situated abroad.

Where the trustees appoint any person to act on their behalf in the execution of the trust, he is known as their "agent."

Whenever an agent is appointed there are six questions to be asked:

1. What powers do trustees have for the appointment of agents?
2. Should the power be exercised?
3. In what manner is it to be exercised?
4. What is the extent of the agent's authority?
5. Can agents be paid from the trust fund?
6. If an agent defaults, and loss is occasioned to the trust fund, to what extent are the trustees themselves liable for that loss?

(1) Powers to appoint agents

(a) **The trust instrument.** The trust instrument itself may confer an effective power for the appointment of agents.

(b) **Section 23(1) of the Trustee Act 1925.** This subsection gives the main power for the appointment of agents. It empowers trustees to appoint a solicitor, banker, stockbroker, or any other person to transact any business, or to do any act which is necessary in the execution of the trust, or the administration of the trust property.

It will be appreciated that what must be necessary is the doing of the act, or the transaction of the business, not the appointment of the agent. Accordingly, trustees have the power to appoint an agent to do an act even if they could have done it themselves.[1]

In practice, almost all agents are appointed under this power.

----

[1] See, however, *infra.*

(c) Other powers. Other, narrower, powers are:

(i) Power to appoint agents to deal with property situated abroad[2];
(ii) Power to permit a solicitor to have a deed incorporating a receipt for money signed by the trustees.[3] This is required for an ordinary sale of trust property where a conveyance or transfer incorporating such a receipt will be handed over by the trustees' solicitor in exchange for the purchase money;
(iii) Power to permit a solicitor or banker to have a receipt for insurance monies signed by the trustees, so that the solicitor or banker can obtain the policy monies from the insurers.[4]
(iv) Power to employ a valuer in connection with a proposed loan of trust money which is to be secured by mortgage[5]; and
(v) Power for trustees for the sale of land to delegate revocably their powers of management or leasing the land to the person who is entitled in possession to the net rents and profits.[6]

(2) Should the power be exercised?

The general rule is that trustees must consider the exercise of any power,[7] and, if they do decide to exercise it, that exercise is only good if the trustees consider that it is in the interest of the trust.[8] The power to appoint agents is subject to this general rule. There will usually be no difficulty where the agent is appointed to transact business which requires some special skill which the trustees do not themselves have. Even if an agent is appointed to do an act which the trustees could have done themselves, the appointment will be good if the trustees consider it to be in the interest of the trust.

(3) The manner in which the power is to be exercised

Subject to any provision in the trust instrument to the contrary, all agents must be personally appointed by the trustees, and they must exercise reasonable care in deciding whether to make the appointment.

This is illustrated by *Fry* v. *Tapson*.[9] Trustees were prepared to lend trust money on mortgage, as they were entitled to do. The trustees did not exercise their own judgment as to the valuer to be appointed but relied on the advice of their solicitors. The surveyor chosen in fact was the agent of a mortgagor and had a financial interest in the transaction being completed. The money was lent and, when loss occurred, it was held that the trustees were bound to make good the loss. They would not have been made liable if they had made an independent choice of the agent themselves. This is an example of a decision which the trustees ought themselves to have made, and not an act which could properly be delegated.

---

[2] Trustee Act 1925, s.23(2).
[3] T.A. 1925, s.23(3)(*a*).
[4] T.A. 1925, s.23(3)(*c*).
[5] T.A. 1925, s.8.
[6] Law of Property Act 1925, s.29.
[7] *Klug* v. *Klug* [1918] 2 Ch. 67.
[8] *Re Lofthouse* (1885) 29 Ch.D. 921, at p. 930.
[9] (1884) 28 Ch.D.268.

(4) The extent of the agent's authority

The general principle is clear.

It is that trustees have to take the basic decisions themselves. For example, if there is a discretionary class of beneficiaries under the trust, the trustees must themselves decide the proportions in which the beneficiaries are to receive the trust property; or, if the trust has capital money, how it is to be invested. On the other hand they can employ agents to implement their decisions and to carry out most of the routine administration of the trust. Thus the trustees must make the decisions: they may employ agents to carry them out.[10] And they may employ agents whether or not they could have done the acts themselves.[11] This represents a marked change from the pre-1926 position, when a trustee could not properly appoint an agent unless it was reasonably necessary to do so, or the circumstances were such that a man of ordinary prudence would have appointed an agent had he been dealing with his own affairs.[12] If the trustees purported to delegate to an agent a function that they ought personally to have discharged, such as that relating to the distribution of a discretionary trust fund, the agent's decision would be ineffective.[13] Thus the money would have been distributed without a proper decision being made, and the trustees could be called upon to make good the money to the trust fund out of their own pockets.

There can often be difficulty in determining whether an agent is to be appointed to do a ministerial act, where the appointment is proper, or an act which requires the trustees' own decisions. This is particularly so with regard to investment. Is it necessary for the trustees to take the decision on each sale and purchase or, provided that they have laid down guidelines, can they leave it to investment advisors to make the particular decisions? An actively-managed portfolio of stock exchange investments may require rapid decisions to be made, often within the day, and sometimes within the hour. Accordingly, private individuals may give stockbrokers or merchant bankers authority to deal with investments in whatever way they think fit. The interests of the trust fund may require such agents to have similar powers.

(5) Remuneration of agents

An agent will have been properly appointed if:

    (a) the trustees had power to appoint him to carry out the particular matter for which he has been appointed;

    (b) the trustees considered that the appointment was in the interest of the trust; and

---

[10] It follows that, in making the basic decisions, a trustee should not allow someone who is not a trustee to join in making those decisions: *Salway* v. *Salway* (1831) 2 Russ. & Myl. 215; *White* v. *Baugh* (1835) 3 Cl. & Fin. 44. But although the trustees must themselves make the decision, there is no objection to them *consulting* the beneficiaries: *Fraser* v. *Murdoch* (1881) 6 App.Cas. 855.

[11] *Re Vickery* [1931] 1 Ch. 572.

[12] *Re Weall* (1889) 42 Ch.D. 674; *Ex p. Belchier* (1754) Amb. 218; *Speight* v. *Gaunt* (1883) 22 Ch.D. 727.

[13] See, *e.g.*, *Wilson* v. *Turner* (1883) 22 Ch.D. 521; *post*, p. 493.

(c) the trustees themselves decided to make the appointment.

Where these conditions are satisfied, the trustees are entitled to pay agents their proper remuneration from the trust fund.[14]

(6) Trustees' liability for agent's default

It might have been expected that if an agent is properly appointed,[15] trustees would not be liable for any loss which occurs if the agent defaults. However, because of inconsistency between two statutory provisions, there is some uncertainty as to the extent of the trustees' liability in such circumstances.

These provisions are:

(a) section 23(1), which gives the general power to appoint agents and which concludes by providing that trustees "shall not be responsible for the default of any such agent if employed in good faith"; and

(b) section 30, which provides that a trustee shall be answerable and accountable only for his own acts, receipts, neglects or defaults, and not for those of any other person with whom any trust money or securities may be deposited, or for any other loss "unless the same happens through his own wilful default."

Under the old law, it had been held in *Re Brier*[16] that, where there was a provision exempting a trustee from liability for loss caused by an act of an agent unless the loss occurred through the "wilful default" of the trustee, the trustee was nevertheless liable for the loss because he failed to exercise reasonable supervision over the agent.

It would, therefore, appear at first sight that section 23(1) may be inconsistent with section 30. Suppose that an agent was appointed in good faith, but the trustee failed to exercise reasonable supervision over him, and loss occurred. If section 23(1) is applied, the trustee is not liable, because the test of liability is the *appointment* of the agent, and in this example the agent was appointed in good faith. But if section 30 applies, and the old law is followed, the trustee is liable, because he has been guilty of wilful default in not exercising adequate supervision.

It was against this background that *Re Vickery*[17] was decided in 1931. The executor of a will employed a solicitor to wind up the estate. At the time when he appointed him, he knew nothing about the solicitor which could have suggested that he should not be appointed. Three months after his appointment, one of the beneficiaries under the will told the executor that the solicitor had previously been suspended from practice, and that, although this was the case, he had subsequently been allowed to practice again. The beneficiary asked the executor to employ another solicitor and objected to the executor giving to the solicitor (in accordance with the usual practice) a signed authority so that he could

---

[14] T.A. 1925, s.23(1).
[15] *Supra.*
[16] (1884) 26 Ch.D. 238.
[17] [1931] 1 Ch. 572.

obtain money on behalf of the estate from the Post Office Savings Department. The executor refused to take the matter away from that solicitor, who was then promising to settle it, but he did not do so and ultimately absconded. The beneficiary sued the executor. Maugham J. observed: "It is hardly too much to say that [section 23] revolutionises the position of a trustee or an executor so far as regards the employment of agents. He is no longer required to do any actual work himself, but he may employ a solicitor or other agent to do it, whether there is any real necessity for the employment or not."[18] To this extent there is no quarrel with the decision, but the judge found that the solicitor was undoubtedly appointed in good faith and he also held that the executor was not himself guilty of "wilful default." As the agent was appointed in good faith and the executor had not himself been guilty of wilful default, he was not liable for the money, either under section 23, or under section 30.

"Wilful default," the judge said, means either "a consciousness of negligence or breach of duty, or recklessness."[19] In coming to this conclusion, the judge purported to follow two decisions of the Court of Appeal: *Re Trusts of Leeds City Brewery Ltd.'s Deed*[20] and *Re City Equitable Fire Insurance Co.*[21] In doing so, Maugham J. appears to have altered the previous position as laid down in *Re Brier*.[22]

The decision has been criticised[23] in so far as it appears to decide that a trustee is no longer under an obligation to exercise supervision over his agent. It is possible to criticise the decision on several grounds. In the first place, the Trustee Act 1925 is generally a consolidating Act, and section 30 is a re-enactment of the substance of section 31 of the Law of Property Amendment Act 1859, under which *Re Brier* was decided. The decision in *Re Vickery* is therefore contrary to the presumption that a consolidating Act does not change the law. Secondly, the case of *Re City Equitable Fire Insurance Co.*, which contained the definition of wilful default which Maugham J. followed, was not a case on the law of trusts, and while for cases outside the law of trusts this may be adequate, it is alleged by some that this case ought not to apply to the employment of agents by trustees, because in connection with trusts "wilful default" has had the wider meaning, as in *Re Brier*, of including lack of reasonable care. Thirdly, it is difficult to reconcile this interpretation of section 23(1) with other parts of section 23. Subsections (2) and (3) of section 23, which deal with the power to appoint agents in specific circumstances, appear to be unnecessary. For example, section 23(3)(*a*) expressly empowers a trustee to appoint a solicitor to be his agent to receive trust money yet, in view of section 23(1), there would appear to be no need for this provision.

---

[18] [1931] 1 Ch. 572, at p. 581.
[19] And see *Wyman* v. *Paterson* [1900] A.C. 271; *Re Sheppard* [1911] 1 Ch. 50; *Robinson* v. *Harkin* [1896] 2 Ch. 415.
[20] [1925] Ch. 532.
[21] [1925] Ch. 407.
[22] (1884) 26 Ch.D. 238.
[23] See articles (1931) 47 L.Q.R. 330–332 (Potter); (1931) 47 L.Q.R. 463–465 (Holdsworth); (1959) 22 M.L.R. 381 (Jones).

More importantly, *Re Vickery* does not resolve the apparent inconsistency between section 23(1) and section 30, and their tests of appointment in good faith and wilful default, respectively. Perhaps they are to be reconciled on the basis that a trustee will be liable for any loss which arises through the default of an agent who is *not* appointed in good faith, but that if he is appointed in good faith, the trustee will nevertheless be liable if he is guilty of wilful default in the sense mentioned.[24] It is also possible to argue that section 23(1) excludes only the trustee's vicarious liability for the acts of an agent while his personal liability is governed by section 30.[24A]

The force of the other criticisms remains. There seems little doubt that the decision in *Re Vickery* was technically incorrect on the legal principles previously established. It can, however, be argued that the result of the case is desirable. Due regard must indeed be paid to the fact that a trustee is looking after someone else's money, and must certainly not be flippant in so doing. But regard must also be had to the fact that the trustees may be acting without remuneration, and may derive no benefit whatever from their trusteeship, no matter how much time and trouble they devote to the trust. Surely Maugham J., while admittedly changing the law, introduced a measure of equity where little existed before. A trustee is still plainly liable if he is consciously negligent or reckless: why should he be liable for more?[25]

(7) Delegation of trusteeship

So far this chapter has been concerned with the delegation by a trustee of ministerial acts, while retaining his responsibility to take the fundamental decision himself. In one case, however, a trustee may delegate the power to take the basic decisions. Under section 25 of the Trustee Act 1925[26] a trustee can by power of attorney delegate all or any of his trusts, powers and discretions. The delegation cannot be for a period exceeding one year, although there appears to be no restriction on the number of times on which a delegation can be made.

The delegation is made by power of attorney, and the donor must give written notice of the delegation to each of the other trustees, and to any other person who has a power of appointing new trustees.[27] This

---

[24] *Re Vickery* was distinguished by Cross J. in *Re Lucking's Will Trusts* [1968] 1 W.L.R. 866, on the basis that a person employed by a trustee as managing director of a business owned by the trust was not a person with whom trust money or securities were deposited within the meaning of s.30, and accordingly the test of "wilful default" was irrelevant. The trustee was held liable for the loss caused by the managing director's defalcations on the ground that he had failed in his duty to conduct the business of the trust with the same care that an ordinary prudent businessman would apply to his own affairs. See also *post*, p. 579.

[24A] See G. H. Jones (1959) 22 M.L.R. 381.

[25] *Underwood* v. *Stevens*, discussed *post*, p. 580, is an example of the injustice of the pre-1926 position. The Law Reform Committee (23rd Report, 1982) has recommended that a trustee should be liable for the default of his agent unless:
(i) it was reasonable for him to employ the agent;
(ii) he took reasonable steps to ensure that the agent was competent; and
(iii) he took reasonable steps to ensure that the agent did his work competently

[26] Substituted by Powers of Attorney Act 1971, s.9.

[27] Trustee Act 1925, s.25(4).

notice specifies the date when the power comes into operation, its duration, the donee, the reason why the power is given, and which of the trusts, powers and discretions are delegated. However, if this notice is not given, a person dealing with the donee of the power is not prejudiced.[28] The donee of the power stands in the same position as the donor, except that the donee cannot himself delegate.[29]

The delegation can in principle be to anyone but where there are only two trustees, one trustee cannot delegate to the other, except where that other is a trust corporation.[30]

The section is in practice rarely used. While it is useful in enabling a delegation of discretions, it has a disadvantage for the donor of the power in that the donor is liable for every act or default of the donee. Thus, even if the donee is only doing an act which could have been the subject of a section 23 delegation, the donor will nevertheless be fully liable. The section could work completely unjustly, particularly as the donor may have no control over the acts of the donee.

Since the enactment of the Enduring Powers of Attorney Act 1985, it has been possible to create a power of attorney which will survive the incapacity of the donor. Powers of attorney under section 25 of the Trustee Act cannot be enduring powers of attorney—this is expressly provided by section 2(8) of the 1985 Act. However, section 3(3) provides that the donee of an enduring power of attorney may "execute or exercise all, or any of the trusts, powers or discretions vested in the donor as trustee" and may also give a valid receipt for capital money. On the face of things, this provision seems to have given trustees a quite separate right to delegate their powers by enduring power of attorney not subject either to any time limit or to any obligation to notify anyone. To make matters worse, the execution of any enduring power of attorney will presumably constitute such a delegation, whether or not the donor trustee has considered the matter and so intends. This goes way beyond the intended purpose of the subsection, which was to enable one of two trustees for sale to permit the other to deal with jointly owned properly vested in them in the event of his incapacity. Assuming that the subsection is not at present so limited,[31] it certainly should be. This matter is at present under consideration by the Law Commission.[32]

---

[28] *Ibid.*
[29] s.25(6).
[30] s.25(2).
[31] D. J. Hayton argues that it already is in (1990) 106 L.Q.R. 87 at p. 89.
[32] See Consultation Paper No. 118 (1991): *The Law of Trusts: Delegation by Individual Trustees.*

CHAPTER 14

THE TAXATION OF A TRUST

IN order to appreciate the contemporary significance of a trust, it is necessary to understand the basic principles of taxation which affect trusts. On the one hand, the prime motive for the creation of the trust may be the mitigation of the family's taxation liability.[1] On the other hand, when the trust is in being, taxation considerations will weigh heavily with the trustees. These considerations may influence the way in which the trust fund is invested,[2] how the trustees deal with income,[3] and the manner in which they exercise their discretion in favour of beneficiaries.[4] Trustees are concerned with four main taxes[5]:

1. stamp duty;
2. income tax;
3. capital gains tax; and
4. inheritance tax.

In particular circumstances they are also concerned with other types of taxation. For example, if they own land, they may be subject to council tax, but these other types of taxation are not considered in this chapter.

I. STAMP DUTY

Stamp duty is a once-and-for-all tax payable on a variety of different transactions. Where the transaction is one which gives rise to liability to stamp duty, the duty is paid at a stamping office of the Inland Revenue, and upon payment of the duty a stamp is impressed on the document showing the amount of the duty paid. It follows that if a transaction can be effected without any document, such as a purely oral declaration of trust,[6] no question of stamp duty can arise.

The main inducement to pay stamp duty is that a document which ought to be stamped but is not stamped cannot be admitted in evidence in any legal proceedings.[7] Further no registrar will register a stampable document which is unstamped because if he does so, he renders

---

[1] *Ante*, p. 6.
[2] See, generally, Chap. 15.
[3] See *post*, p. 482.
[4] See *post*, p. 502.
[5] For charitable trusts see *ante*, p. 296. For a more detailed treatment of the problems raised in this chapter, see Mellows, *Taxation for Executors and Trustees*.
[6] See, however, *ante*, p. 35 *et seq.*
[7] Stamp Act 1891, s.14(4). *Ram Rattam* v. *Parma Nand* (1945) L.R. 73 Ind.App. 28.

himself liable to a fine.[8] Trustees will insist that a trust deed is properly stamped, because they may at any time have to justify their position, or their acts as trustees, by production in court of the trust deed.

Technically an instrument should be stamped before execution but in practice the Revenue permit stamping within 30 days of its execution without imposing any penalty.[9] Where it is not stamped within that period, the Revenue are entitled to charge as a condition for stamping the document out of time the amount of the duty, a penalty of up to £10, and interest at 5 per cent. on the unpaid duty up to a maximum of the unpaid duty.[10] In some cases, even though no duty is actually payable, the legislation nevertheless requires the document to be presented for adjudication and in these cases the document is deemed not to have been properly stamped unless it contains a stamp to the effect that it has been adjudicated.[11]

There is no general principle that every document by which every transaction is effected attracts stamp duty: a document is only stampable if it comes within one of the classes of documents specifically mentioned in the Stamp Act 1891. The amount of stamp duty to be paid depends on the class of documents within which it falls; however, the sum payable will be either a fixed duty (usually 50p)[12] or an *ad valorem* duty (usually a percentage of the value of the transaction). Where *ad valorem* duty is payable, in the case of shares and securities it will be charged at 50p per £100 or part of £100 (in effect a rate of 0.5 per cent.); in the case of all other property it will be charged at £1 per £100 or part of £100 of the value of the transaction (in effect a rate of 1 per cent.) unless the value of the transaction does not exceed £60,000 and the instrument contains a certificate of value, in which case the duty is nil.[13] The certificate must state that the transaction effected by the instrument does not form part of a larger transaction or series of transactions in respect of which the amount or value or the aggregate amount or value of the consideration exceeds £60,000.[14]

It is appropriate to consider liability to stamp duty on the inception of the trust, during the continuance of the trust, and upon its termination.

(1) Inception of trust

A conveyance or transfer on sale is subject to *ad valorem* duty.[15] A voluntary disposition executed before March 26, 1985, was also subject to *ad valorem* duty "as if" it were a conveyance or transfer on sale.[16] A declaration of trust which, while not voluntary, was not for full consideration was stated to fall within this provision[17] and a voluntary dec-

---

[8] Stamp Act 1891, s.17.
[9] Stamp Act 1891, s.15.
[10] Stamp Act 1891, s.15 (1).
[11] Stamp Act 1891, s.12.
[12] Stamp Act 1891, s.62.
[13] Finance Act 1986 *passim*.
[14] The £60,000 exemption does not apply to shares and securities because it would be too easy to split larger transactions into £60,000 slices (Finance Act 1963, s.55 (2)).
[15] Stamp Act 1891, Sched. I.
[16] Finance (1909–10) Act 1910, s.74(1).
[17] s.74(5).

laration of trust was held to do so[18]; however, a declaration of trust in consideration of marriage was exempt.[19] Consequently, the creation *inter vivos*[20] in writing of a trust of property which could only be transferred by an instrument, such as land, shares and securities, was subject to *ad valorem* duty, although such a transfer of cash was subject only to the fixed 50p duty. However, this charge to *ad valorem* duty was abolished by the Finance Act 1985.[21] The fixed 50p duty and an adjudication stamp continued to be required until 1987 when these requirements were also removed.[22] The effect of these reforms is that a transfer of property to trustees on trust no longer attracts stamp duty of any kind save in the relatively unlikely case that consideration in money or money's worth is furnished, in which case the transaction will be a transfer on sale and will be subject to the appropriate *ad valorem* duty. However, a declaration in writing by a settlor that he is himself holding property on trust is still subject to the fixed 50p duty. No stamp duty is ever payable in the case of conveyances, transfers or lettings to a charity.[23]

When a transfer *inter vivos* of property to trustees on trust was prima facie subject to *ad valorem* duty, the duty was chargeable on the document by which the beneficial interest was transferred. Many *inter vivos* settlements are created by means of two instruments, one being the trust instrument declaring the terms of the trust and the other being the conveyance or transfer transferring the legal title. In such a case, the former document was chargeable with the *ad valorem* duty and the latter with the fixed 50p duty. If, therefore, the owner of shares wished to create a settlement of them, he might execute a transfer of the shares to the proposed trustees and then execute the trust instrument; only on the execution of the latter instrument was the *ad valorem* duty payable.

This fact caused a number of attempts to be made to avoid the *ad valorem* duty by creating the trust merely by means of an oral declaration. In a trust of any size, however, this was not convenient because a record of the exact terms of any trust is highly desirable. Accordingly, it became common for a settlor to make an oral declaration of trust in his solicitor's office, with one of the solicitor's secretaries taking a shorthand note of what was said. This would provide a permanent record. Although this device was theoretically justifiable, its efficacy became open to some doubt in view of *Cohen and Moore* v. *I.R.C.*[24] In that case settlors orally declared that they would hold certain securities upon the trusts declared by a draft deed. Five weeks later, the draft deed was executed. It was held that the verbal declaration and the later deed formed one transaction, so that duty was payable.

A similar device, less open to this sort of objection, would be for the

---

[18] *Martin* v. *I.R.C.* (1930) 15 A.T.C. 631.

[19] Finance Act 1963, s.64.

[20] No stamp duty is payable on either a will or a grant of representation so that no duty has ever been payable in respect of the creation of testamentary trusts.

[21] s.82.

[22] Stamp Duty (Exempt Instruments) Regulations 1987.

[23] Finance Act 1982, s.129.

[24] [1933] 2 K.B. 126.

settlor to make his declaration of trust by recording it with its complicated provisions on tape and for the tape not to be transcribed for a considerable period. A tape would almost certainly not rank as a document and so *ad valorem* duty would not be exigible.

An extension of the device first described was for the settlor first to transfer the property to the trustees to hold as his nominees, then orally to direct them to hold the property on the trusts of the settlement, and finally for the trustees to execute declarations of their acceptance of the settlor's directions. However, as has already been seen,[25] this device was struck down by the House of Lords in *Grey* v. *I.R.C.*[25A] on the grounds that the oral direction amounted to a disposition of a subsisting equitable interest and so was void under section 53(1)(*c*) of the Law of Property Act 1925; consequently, the written declarations of trust transferred the beneficial interests and so were subject to *ad valorem* duty.

Of course, at present none of these devices is necessary but if *ad valorem* duty is ever reimposed on voluntary dispositions they will once again become extremely important. However, it is questionable whether these devices would in fact survive in the light of the intervening evolution of the much more stringent attitude towards tax avoidance enunciated in *Craven* v. *White*,[25B] where Lord Oliver stated that, if any pre-ordained series of transactions is in practice always likely to and in fact does take place in its pre-ordained order for the sole purpose of tax mitigation, the court can be justified in treating the series as a single composite whole.

Finally, it should be noted that no stamp duty is payable on either a will or a grant of representation so that no duty has ever been payable in respect of the creation of testamentary trusts.

Any stamp duty which is payable on the creation of a trust is the responsibility of the settlor and it is not properly payable out of the trust fund unless the trust instrument contains an express authority for the duty to be paid by the trustees.

(2) During administration of trust

Where a conveyance or transfer is made without causing any change in the beneficial interests, that document prima facie attracts only the fixed 50p duty.[25C] Accordingly a deed of retirement or appointment of new trustees, or some other instrument executed in connection with such retirement or appointment, such as a transfer of shares from an old to a new trustee,[25D] formerly attracted the payment of this fixed duty.[25E] However, by virtue of the Stamp Duty (Exempt) Regulations 1987, the

---

[25] See *ante*, p. 36.
[25A] [1960] A.C. 1.
[25B] [1989] A.C. 398.
[25C] Stamp Act 1891, s.62.
[25D] Stock exchange securities are excluded from the automatic vesting provisions of Trustee Act, s.49; see *ante*, p. 381.
[25E] Stamp Act 1891, ss.23(1), 62.

vesting of property subject to a trust in the trustees on the appointment of a new trustee or in the continuing trustees on the retirement of a trustee is exempted from the fixed 50p duty and does not have to be presented for adjudication; however a certificate should be included in, endorsed on, or attached to the instrument to the effect that the instrument falls within the appropriate category (in the illustration given, category A) of the Schedule to the Regulations.

If the trustees in the course of administration of the trust rearrange the assets, they will be liable to stamp duty on the purchase of assets at the same rate as on a purchase by any individual. This is so notwithstanding that the value of the trust fund is not increased, for stamp duty is payable on each transaction, in this case on the purchase of shares. Stamp duty paid on such purchase documents ranks as part of the cost of the asset for capital gains tax purposes.[25F]

One apparent anomaly is that, by virtue of a Practice Direction,[25G] when an order is made under the Variation of Trusts Act 1958,[25H] an undertaking is given to submit a duplicate of the order for adjudication. At the time when the Practice Direction was made, voluntary dispositions were subject to *ad valorem* duty. Now that this is no longer the case, there seems no good reason for the continuing requirement of adjudication, which should be declared to be redundant.

(3) On termination of trust

In normal circumstances no *ad valorem* duty is payable on the termination of a trust, for by that time the beneficiary has become absolutely entitled beneficially with the result that the termination of the trust produces no change in the beneficial interests. The fixed 50p duty is prima facie payable but this requirement is in fact removed by the Stamp Duty (Exempt Instruments) Regulations 1987. If, however, the termination comes about as the result of a rearrangement of beneficial interests, the rearrangement formerly constituted a voluntary disposition of a beneficial interest and so was subject to *ad valorem* duty. This in *Platt's Trustees* v. *I.R.C.*,[25I] where a life tenant executed a deed releasing his life interest, thereby accelerating the interest in remainder and enabling distribution of the trust fund, *ad valorem* duty was held to be payable on the deed of release. However, this will clearly no longer be the case unless *ad valorem* duty is reimposed on voluntary dispositions.

II. Income Tax

For the purposes of income tax, and for that matter of capital gains tax and of inheritance tax, trustees are treated as a separate and continuing

---

[25F] See *post*, p. 416.
[25G] [1966] 1 W.L.R. 345.
[25H] See *post*, p. 546.
[25I] (1953) 34 A.T.C. 292.

body of persons.[26] Because trustees constitute a separate body, the liability of the trust to tax is computed without taking into account the trustees' personal tax position. Because trustees constitute a continuing body, the tax liability of the trust is unaffected by any changes in the persons who are from time to time the trustees. For most taxation purposes, therefore, a trust is treated almost as if it had its own separate legal personality.

The taxation of the income of trusts is in many ways more simple than the taxation of income of private individuals, because the various allowances and reliefs which affect the computation of an individual's liability do not apply.

The taxation of the income of a trust is based on these principles:

(a) The whole of the income of the trust is taxable, irrespective of its ultimate disposal.[27] Thus, the income of the trust is taxable whether it is paid to beneficiaries, absorbed in administration expenses, or accumulated.

(b) Trust income is generally taxable at the basic rate of income tax. This varies from time to time, but at present[28] it is 25 per cent.,[29] save in the case of company distributions, such as dividends on shares, which are taxable only at 20 per cent.[29A] In the case of a private individual, on the other hand, the effect of personal allowances is to exempt from income tax the first "slice" of his income.[30] The next "slice" is taxable at 20 per cent., the next slice at the basic rate of 25 per cent., and the residue at the higher rate of 40 per cent.[31] (company distributions are taxed at 20 per cent. unless the individual is liable to tax at the higher rate of 40 per cent., in which case they are treated as the top slice of his income and are therefore taxable at 40 per cent.).[32] None of these complications generally applies to trust income. Whether the income is £1 per annum or £100,000 per annum that income is chargeable at the basic rate of 25 per cent. (or, in the case of company distributions, at 20 per cent.).

---

[26] The principle is assumed but not expressly enacted for the purposes of income tax.

[27] The rate at which income tax is paid will vary according to the nature of the income and to whether the trust is discretionary or not; see *infra*.

[28] In 1994–95.

[29] This has been the case since 1988–89.

[29A] Income and Corporation Taxes Act 1988, s.207A (inserted by Finance Act 1993).

[30] In 1994–95, a single person was entitled to a personal allowance of £3,445; additional allowances are available to married persons, to single parents, to widows and widowers and pensioners, in respect of dependant relatives and in certain other circumstances. The amounts of these allowances are reviewed annually in each budget.

[31] In 1994–95, the first £3,000 of taxable income was taxed at 20 per cent, taxable income between £3,001 and £23,700 was taxed at 25 per cent and taxable income in excess of £23,700 at 40 per cent. The width of the bands and their thresholds are also reviewed annually in each Budget.

[32] Assuming that the taxpayer is liable to pay 40 per cent tax even if the company distributions are disregarded; if he still has some part of his 25 per cent band unutilised, the distributions will be taxed at 25 per cent until the threshold of the higher rate is reached.

(c) There is one exception to the above principles. Accumulation and discretionary settlements have long been used as devices to take income away from taxpayers who are liable to pay income tax at the higher rate. In an attempt to counteract this, it is provided that income which is to be accumulated, or which is payable under a discretion,[33] is chargeable at a flat rate of 35 per cent. rather than at the basic rate of 25 per cent. or, in the case of company distributions, 20 per cent.[34] Consequently, the trustees have to pay a further 10 per cent. tax (15 per cent. in the case of company distributions). This does not apply, however, to the extent that the income arises under a charitable trust, or is properly applied in the administration of the trust.[35] The beneficiary is in no worse position where the income is distributed to him as income,[36] for he can make a repayment claim if he is not liable to pay tax at the higher rate of 40 per cent. on the top slice of his income.

It follows from these principles that all payments of income from the trust to the beneficiaries are paid from a fund which has been taxed. Accordingly, with each payment of income, the trustees are bound to issue to the beneficiary a certificate of the tax notionally deducted from that payment.

The gross equivalent of the net payment made to the beneficiary is then regarded as part of the beneficiary's total income, and he may then obtain any repayment which is appropriate having regard to his total income.

An example may illustrate these principles. Suppose that a trust fund has an income of £4,000 per annum gross, £2,000 of which proceeds from company dividends and £2,000 from other sources. The administration expenses are £400 and the trustees are obliged by the trust instrument to accumulate one half of the income and to distribute the other half to a beneficiary who has a fixed interest. The 20 per cent. tax payable on the company dividends will be the subject of a tax credit received from the company in question; consequently, the trustees will not need to take any action in respect of this income except in the case of the part of the settlement which is an accumulation and discretionary settlement, where they will have to pay the further 15 per cent. tax. However, the trustees will be responsible for all the tax payable in respect of the income from other sources, whether it is taxable at 25 per cent. or at 35 per cent. The gross figures of course determine the tax liability of any beneficiary to whom income is distributed.[37] The tax payable is calculated as follows:

---

[33] Income and Corporation Taxes Act 1988, s.686 (as amended by Finance Act 1993).

[34] Income and Corporation Taxes Act 1988, s.207A.

[35] Income and Corporation Taxes Act 1988, s.686(2).

[36] If the income is accumulated and the beneficiary receives a sum from the accumulation, he receives a capital, and not an income sum, and no repayment claim can be made.

[37] For the purposes of the example, the gross figure for dividend income will be used.

Gross income		£4,000
Less: tax at 20% on dividends of £2,000	£400	
tax at 25% on other income of £2,000	£500	
administration expenses[38]	£400	
	———	
	£1,300	£1,300
	———	———
		£2,700
Net income available for distribution (50%)		£1,350
Gross income available for accumulation (50%)	£1,350	———
Less: additional tax to raise to 35%: 35% × £1,800 (income susceptible to 35% rate) less 50% of tax already paid (50% × £900)[39]	£180	
	———	
Net income available for accumulation	£1,170	
	———	

The beneficiary who receives £1,350 net is treated as having received £1,800[40] from which tax of £405 is treated as having been deducted.[41] Suppose that he has no significant income from other sources and, even with the trust income, his income is insufficient to absorb his personal reliefs so that he will not be liable to income tax, not even at the lower rate of 20 per cent. In these circumstances, he can make a repayment claim and recover from the Inland Revenue the £405 tax which he has suffered (in order to do this, he will need to produce a certificate of deduction of tax issued by the trustees). The net benefit to him will therefore be £1,755.[42] If, on the other hand, the beneficiary is already paying income tax at the higher rate of 40 per cent., he will be treated as having received £1,800 from which tax of £405 has been deducted. He is, however, liable to pay tax at the higher rate of 40 per cent. Therefore, his overall tax liability is £720 (40 per cent. of £1,800) and he will consequently have to pay a further £315 (£720 less the £405 treated as having been paid by the trust). The net benefit to him will therefore only be £1,035.

These principles lead to three general results which trustees will wish to bear in mind. First, as the whole income of the trust is taxable,

---

[38] Administration expenses are not liable to the flat rate of 35 per cent.

[39] The total income available for accumulation before tax is £2,000 (half the total) from which half the administration expenses (£200) has to be deducted because these expenses are not liable to the flat rate of 35 per cent. Half the tax already paid is attributable to each half of the fund.

[40] Grossed up by 25 per cent (the basic rate of tax).

[41] The tax credit is of 20 per cent in respect of the half of the income from the dividends and of 25 per cent in respect of the half of the income from other sources; hence 20 per cent x £900 (£180)+25 per cent x £900 (£225).

[42] This figure does not equal the total income attributable to this half of the fund (£2,000) less its half share of the administration expenses (£200) because the tax payable on the administration expenses cannot be recovered.

liability to tax can only be avoided if non-income-producing assets are held by the trust. An example is for trusts to purchase pieces of silver or works of art.[43] A more prosaic example is the purchase of National Savings Certificates, which produce no income but are repayable on maturity with a capital bonus.[44] However, such increments will be of a capital nature for all purposes, so that a life tenant will not, in general, be entitled to any part of the bonus.[45] While a trustee must keep tax considerations in mind, he must also keep in mind his general obligation to balance the interests of tenant for life and remainder-man.[46]

The second result of the basic principles is that, where trustees have a discretion to accumulate income, they can only accumulate out of taxed income. Accordingly, accumulation is not a method of avoiding income tax completely but, as is shown in a later chapter,[47] in some circumstances it may be appropriate to accumulate income as capital and then to make an advancement of capital.

The third result is that trustees will wish to consider the likely taxation result of a distribution of income upon the tax position of the beneficiary. If, as in the example given above, the personal tax position of the beneficiary is such that he can make a repayment claim, a distribution of income to him will be clearly advantageous. If, however, the beneficiary is already paying income tax at the higher rate of 40 per cent., the trustees will know that the beneficiary will also have to pay higher rate income tax on any income paid to him by the trust.

If, instead, the trustees have a discretion as to the payment of income, all the income will be taxable at a flat rate of 35 per cent. Consequently, most tax will be recoverable if the trustees pay as much as possible of the income to the beneficiaries with the lowest personal rate of taxation since they will be able to reclaim at least some of the tax paid by the trust on the sum actually distributed to them.[48] If, on the other hand, all the beneficiaries are paying tax at the higher rate of 40 per cent., no tax will be able to be recovered and the trustees will have to choose between accumulating the income, which will at least restrict their tax liability to the 35 per cent. already paid, with a view to a subsequent capital distribution, or paying the income to one or more of the bene-ficiaries on the basis that they will then be responsible for paying a further 5 per cent. tax on the sum actually distributed to them.

---

[43] Provided that the pieces of silver are sold for a figure not in excess of £6,000, no capital gains tax is payable. Trustees hope, therefore, to dispose of the silver at a profit which will attract liability neither to income tax, because the profit is not of an income nature, nor to capital gains tax.

[44] See *post*, p. 436.

[45] *Re Holder* (1953) Ch. 468. See, however, *post*, p. 480.

[46] In *Nestlé* v. *National Westminster Bank* [1993] 1 W.L.R. 1260, the remainderman accused the trustees of allowing the tax interests of the tenant for life to influence unduly their choice of investments. The judgments contain an important discussion of the criteria which trustees should follow (see *post*, p. 433).

[47] See *post*, p. 502.

[48] The tax paid on any administration expenses will not be able to be recovered since the right of recovery is limited to the income actually received by the beneficiary.

III. CAPITAL GAINS TAX

The object of capital gains tax is to make a charge on capital gains made either by private individuals or by any body of persons such as trustees as a result of any actual or deemed disposal of an asset *inter vivos*, whether by way of sale, exchange or gift; no charge is made on disposals *mortis causa*.[49] Capital gains tax is imposed on any increase in the value of an asset between the date of its acquisition and the date of its disposal; any decrease in the value of an asset can be set off against future capital gains. The value of the asset at the date of its acquisition is adjusted to take account of inflation; however, in the case of an asset acquired before March 31, 1982, its acquisition value is deemed to be its market value on that date[50] so that gains made prior to that date escape tax. The tax is payable at the same rate as income tax[51] on that part of a person's capital gains in each year as exceeds his annual exemption, £5,800 in the case of private individuals and £2,900 in the case of trusts[52] (there are many other exemptions, including a private individual's main residence,[53] chattels worth less than £6,000,[54] and certain securities).[55] Trustees are liable to pay capital gains tax on gains arising on trust assets in the same way as an individual would on gains arising on his personal assets.

(1) Trusts to which the capital gains tax legislation applies

The trust provisions of the capital gains tax legislation only apply where there are not one or more beneficiaries absolutely and concurrently entitled to the whole of the trust property as against the trustees. The basic rule is that property is regarded as "settled property" for the purposes of the capital gains tax legislation whenever it is held on trust.[56] However, there are three situations in which the trust property is treated as if it were vested in the beneficiary[57]: first, where the beneficiary is absolutely entitled to the property as against the trustee; secondly, where the beneficiary would be absolutely entitled to the property as against the trustee were he not an infant; and, thirdly, where the property is held for two or more persons who jointly are or would be absolutely entitled to the property as against the trustee. Such a situation was claimed to arise in *Tomlinson* v. *Glyns Executor and Trustee Company*[58] where trustees held property in trust for such of four

---

[49] The property of a deceased person is deemed to be acquired by his personal representatives for its market value on the date of his death, thus giving the beneficiaries a "tax-free uplift" in the event that this value is superior to its acquisition value.

[50] Taxation of Chargeable Gains Act 1992, s.35. From that date, there is a published indexation allowance.

[51] *Ibid.* s.4. Hence the rate is either 20 per cent, 25 per cent or 40 per cent for private individuals and 25 per cent for trusts other than accumulation and discretionary trusts, whose rate is 35 per cent.

[52] *Ibid.* s.3, Sched. I (these exemptions are index-linked).

[53] *Ibid.* s.222.

[54] *Ibid.* s.262.

[55] *Ibid.* s.115.

[56] *Ibid.* s.68.

[57] *Ibid.* s.60.

[58] [1970] Ch. 112.

infant beneficiaries as attained the age of 21 or married under that age. When the trustees disposed of certain investments at a profit, they claimed that the infant beneficiaries were together absolutely entitled to the investments as against the trustees.[59] The Court of Appeal held that infancy was not the only reason which, at the time of the disposal of the investments, prevented the beneficiaries from being absolutely entitled because they had only a contingent interest until they reached the age of 21 or married under that age.

(2) Capital gains on the creation of a settlement

The creation of a settlement constitutes a disposal of the trust property by the settlor at its market value, even if the settlement is revocable, and whether or not he or his spouse is a beneficiary.[60] If chargeable assets are settled, any chargeable gain will be made by the settlor and capital gains tax will be payable by him thereon at the same rate as that at which he pays income tax; any chargeable loss[60A] will also be made by the settlor but, because he and the trustees are connected persons,[61] that loss will be deductible only from future chargeable gains arising out of subsequent disposals by the settlor to the same settlement. It used to be possible to postpone the payment of the tax until the property was eventually sold[62] but this is now only possible if the assets settled comprise business property[63] or if the creation of the trust involves a chargeable transfer for the purposes of inheritance tax.[64]

(3) Capital Gains on the disposal of assets by the trustees

When a trust is created, the trustees are deemed to acquire the trust property at its market value (or, if acquired before March 31, 1982, at its market value then). When an asset is purchased in a transaction at arm's length, the consideration, together with the expenses associated with the purchase, constitutes the acquisition value.

Apart from assets which are exempt from capital gains tax, not many of which are likely to be held by trustees, any disposition of an asset for a consideration in excess of its acquisition value gives rise to a chargeable gain in respect of the difference. Where the trustees incur expense such as stamp duty, legal costs and registration fees in acquiring an asset and in arranging for its disposal, the total of these costs is added to the acquisition value and only the difference is chargeable. Capital gains made by trusts are taxable at 25 per cent. except for accumulation and discretionary trusts, whose capital gains are taxable at 35 per cent.

---

[59] If the trustees had succeeded in their contention, there would still have been a capital gains tax liability. However, it would have been calculated according to a special basis then in force which was open only to private individuals; see Finance Act 1965, s.21.

[60] Taxation of Chargeable Gains Act 1992, s.70.

[60A] For disposals after November 29, 1993 the indexation allowance cannot create or increase an allowable loss. Consequently losses will be only chargeable if genuinely incurred.

[61] By virtue of Taxation of Chargeable Gains Act 1992, s.18(3).

[62] Under Finance Act 1980, s.79 (repealed in 1989).

[63] Taxation of Chargeable Gains Act 1992, s.165.

[64] See post, p. 420.

A simple transaction, without taking account of any adjustment to the acquisition cost by virtue of inflation, would be:

Proceeds of sale of shares		£10,100
Less: purchase price	£8,000	
broker's commission on purchase	£100	
stamp duty on purchase	£40	
	£8,140	£8,140
		£1,960
Less: expenses of sale		£160
Chargeable gain		£1,800
Capital gains tax payable:		
non accumulation or discretionary trust: 25% of £1,800:		£450
accumulation or discretionary trust: 35% of £1,800:		£630

Of course, if this was the only chargeable gain made by the trust during the year in question, it would be within the annual exemption of, at present, £2,900. The tax shown above would therefore only be payable in full if the annual exemption had already been completely used up.

Clearly, the most usual situation in which trustees will incur this type of liability is where they switch assets in the course of the administration of the trust. Equally clearly, the existence of capital gains tax will have an inhibiting effect on changing assets, particularly in the case of an accumulation or discretionary trust.

(4) The exit charge
When a beneficiary becomes absolutely entitled to the whole or any part of the trust property, the trustees are deemed to have disposed of the assets in question to him at their market value at that date and he is deemed to have acquired them for their market value at that date.[65] A beneficiary will become absolutely entitled in this sense on fulfilling some contingency, such as attaining the age of 21, or on the determination of a prior interest, or when in other circumstances the trustees make a decision to pay or to transfer the asset to him. An immediate liability to capital gains tax will arise which is payable by the trustees; payment of the tax can only be postponed in the limited circumstances already discussed. If after this time the trustees continue to hold the assets in their name, they do so as nominees for the beneficiary. In this case, the trust will no longer be a settlement for the purposes of the capital gains tax legislation; the property will be deemed to be held by the beneficiary so that any future liability for capital gains tax will fall on the beneficiary and not on the trustees.

---

[65] Taxation of Chargeable Gains Act 1992, s.71(1).

Thus if shares worth £100,000 were settled on trust for the settlor's daughter contingent on her reaching the age of 21, a deemed disposal will take place when she attains that age. If the shares are then worth £120,000, capital gains tax of £5,000 (25 per cent. of £20,000) will be payable by the trustees (this trust is not an accumulation or discretionary trust; if instead the shares were held on trust for such of the settlor's children as the trustees might in their absolute discretion determine, then, if the trustees decided to allocate these shares to the settlor's daughter absolutely, there would also be a deemed disposal, this time taxable at 35 per cent.). If the shares are subsequently sold for £130,000, then, whether they have in the meantime been retained by the trustees or transferred to the daughter, the further capital gain of £10,000 will be attributable to the daughter and she will pay capital gains tax thereon at the same rate as that at which she pays income tax.

In principle, one beneficiary can become absolutely entitled as against the trustees even though there are other beneficiaries who do not. If, therefore, property is held on trust for such of the settlor's three children as attain the age of 25 and, if more than one of them, in equal shares, when the eldest child attains the age of 25 the membership of the class will become fixed.[66] If there are then three children, the eldest child will immediately become absolutely entitled to a one third share in the property even though the younger children are still under 25.[66] If the second child dies under the age of 25, the eldest child will then become absolutely entitled to a further one sixth share (one half of the deceased child's presumptive share) and, when the youngest child attains the age of 25, the latter will become absolutely entitled to the remaining half share of the property.[67] However, where the settled property consists of land, it seems that one beneficiary cannot become absolutely entitled if the other beneficiaries do not also do so.[68]

Special rules apply when a beneficiary becomes absolutely entitled as the result of the determination of a prior life interest because of the death of the life tenant. Although there is still a deemed disposal by the trust and a deemed acquisition by the beneficiary, no capital gains tax will be payable because of the basic principle that no charge to capital gains tax is made on disposals *mortis causa*.[69] The absolutely entitled beneficiary will therefore acquire the trust property at its market value on the date of the death of the life tenant. There may, however, be inheritance tax liability.[70] The only exception to this rule is where the settlor has postponed the payment of the capital gains tax payable on the creation of the settlement; in this case, the capital gains tax becomes payable on the death of the life tenant.[71]

---

[66] Under the class closing rules mentioned *ante*, p. 169, fn. 46.
[67] *Stephenson* v. *Barclays Bank Trust Company* [1975] S.T.C. 151, *Pexton* v. *Bell* [1976] 1 W.L.R. 885.
[68] *Crowe* v. *Appleby* [1976] 1 W.L.R. 885.
[69] Taxation of Chargeable Gains Act 1992, s.73.
[70] See *post*, p. 420.
[71] Taxation of Chargeable Gains Act 1992, s.74.

(5) Where a settlement continues

Where on the determination of a prior interest a settlement continues without any beneficiary becoming absolutely entitled, there are no capital gains tax consequences unless the prior interest has determined because of the death of the life tenant, in which case the rules discussed immediately above apply: there will be a deemed disposal and a deemed reacquisition by the trustees but no capital gains tax will be payable unless the settlor has postponed payment of his own capital gains tax.[72] Thus, if property is settled on the settlor's daughter until her marriage and subject thereto to his son if he attains the age of 25, the marriage of the daughter before the son has attained the age of 25 will determine her interest but the son is still not absolutely entitled and so there will be no deemed disposal until he reaches the age of 25, when capital gains tax will be payable. If, on the other hand, the trust is to the daughter for life and subject thereto to the son if he attains the age of 25, the death of the daughter before the son has attained the age of 25 will produce a deemed disposal and reacquisition of the property by the trustees at its market value on the date of the daughter's death but no capital gains tax will be payable.

(6) Resettlements

When property is transferred from one settlement to another, the trustees of the second settlement (even if they are the same persons as the trustees of the original settlement) become absolutely entitled as against the original trustees and a charge to capital gains tax will normally arise.[73] If the resettlement occurs only as the result of the exercise by the trustees of their powers under the original settlement, it seems that the exercise of a special power of appointment will not amount to a resettlement and a consequential deemed disposal of the property in question[74]; on the other hand, while the exercise of a wider power, such as a power of advancement, will not necessarily amount to a resettlement, it will have this effect if the new settlement is complete in itself and is sufficiently separate to require no further reference back for any purpose to the original settlement.[75]

IV. Inheritance Tax

Inheritance tax is imposed at a fixed rate of 40 per cent. on such part of a person's estate (which for this purpose includes any property disposed of by him other than for value during the seven years immediately prior to his death) as exceeds his lifetime allowance of, at present,[76] £150,000.[77] Inheritance tax is governed by what is now known as the

---

[72] *Ibid.* s.72.
[73] *Hoare Trustees* v. *Gardner* [1979] Ch. 1.
[74] *Roome* v. *Edwards* [1981] S.T.C. 96, *Bond* v. *Pickford* [1983] S.T.C. 517.
[75] *Swires* v. *Renton* [1991] S.T.C. 490.
[76] In 1994–95.
[77] There are also a number of further exemptions, including small gifts of up to £3,000 per annum, gifts between spouses, gifts in consideration of marriage, gifts to charities, and gifts of agricultural or business property.

Inheritance Tax Act 1984,[78] which was subsequently substantially modified by the Finance Act 1986.

(1) Exempt, potentially exempt, and chargeable transfers

Inheritance tax focuses around the transfer of value, something which occurs whenever a person makes a disposition as a result of which the value of his estate immediately after the disposition is less than it would have been but for the transfer, the amount by which it is less being the value transferred by the transfer.[79] A transfer of value may be exempt, potentially exempt, or chargeable.

The principal example of an exempt transfer is any transfer of any amount between spouses, whether *inter vivos* or *mortis causa*.[80-81] There are a number of further exemptions. Some are personal, such as gifts of up to £3,000 per donor and £250 per donee per annum, gifts in consideration of marriage of varying amounts up to £5,000, and payments for the maintenance of dependants. Others are institutional, including gifts to charities, to certain bodies concerned with the preservation of the national heritage or of a public nature, and to political parties and gifts of works of art, of agricultural or business property, and of woodlands.

A potentially exempt transfer is any transfer made *inter vivos* by a private individual after March 17, 1986.[82] If the transferor dies within three years of making the transfer, the rate of inheritance tax payable is the same as that chargeable on death; the tax is payable on the value of the property at the time of transfer or the value of the property at the date of death, whichever is the lower. If he dies more than three years but less than seven years after making the transfer, the rate of inheritance tax payable is a proportion of that chargeable on death (there is a reduction of 20 per cent. of the tax for each year or part of a year after the first three that the transferor has survived); as before, the tax is payable on the value of the property at the time of transfer or the value of the property at the date of death, whichever is the lower. If the transferor survives for seven years after making the transfer, it becomes exempt from inheritance tax. However, in certain exceptional circumstances, a transfer made *inter vivos* by a private individual is immediately liable to inheritance tax, at half the rate applicable on death (such a transfer is known as an initially chargeable transfer). The tax so paid forms part of the property transferred; consequently, if the transferor pays the tax himself, the transfer must be "grossed up" for this purpose.[83] In the event that the transferor dies within seven years, additional inheritance tax is payable in the manner already described. The principal example

---

[78] It was originally called the Capital Transfer Tax Act 1984 (the tax was rechristened in 1986) and the Act may be cited in either form; herein it will be cited as the Inheritance Tax Act 1984.

[79] Inheritance Tax Act 1984, s.3.

[80-81] *Ibid*, s.18.

[82] *Ibid*. s.3A (introduced by Finance Act 1986, s.101).

[83] *Ibid*. s.7. Where the transferor pays the inheritance tax on an immediately chargeable transfer of £100,000, the "grossed up" figure will be £125,000 (because 80 per cent of this amount is £100,000), thus producing a tax liability of £25,000.

of a transfer of this type is the creation of an accumulation or discretionary trust.

A chargeable transfer is any transfer made *inter vivos* by a private individual which is either initially chargeable or subsequently becomes chargeable by reason of his failure to survive seven years and any transfer *mortis causa*. Inheritance tax is payable on the value of all chargeable transfers after the first £150,000[84] at 40 per cent. in respect of transfers on death or within three years of death, at the appropriate proportion of 40 per cent. in respect of transfers made within seven years of but more than three years before death, and at 20 per cent. in respect of initially chargeable lifetime transfers. It is therefore necessary to keep a lifetime record of all transfers *inter vivos*; first, because if any potentially exempt transfer becomes chargeable any transfers made during the seven year period preceding that transfer will have to be aggregated with it in order to decide the inheritance tax ultimately payable thereon; secondly, because any transfers made within the seven years preceding death will have to be aggregated with the estate of the transferor to determine the amount of inheritance tax payable in respect of his estate. The presence of potentially exempt transfers makes the calculation of the inheritance tax payable far from straightforward.

A potentially exempt transfer will take effect as a chargeable transfer in the event that the transferor has reserved a benefit thereunder; this is for the somewhat obvious reason that he cannot be permitted to enjoy the advantages of making a potentially exempt transfer if he has retained enjoyment of the property in question. Where there is such a reservation of benefit, the property will be regarded as continuing to form part of the transferor's estate unless and until such time as the benefit in question ceases (from which time the seven year period will start to run) and will be taxed accordingly on his death. The transferor will be treated as having reserved a benefit in two cases[85]: first, where the donee has not, prior to the seven year period preceding the donor's death (or, if the donor has died within seven years of the gift, at the date of the gift), bona fide assumed the possession and enjoyment of the property; secondly, where, at any time during the seven years prior to the donor's death (or, if he dies within seven years of the gift, at any time after the gift), the property is not enjoyed "to the entire exclusion, or virtually to the entire exclusion, of the donor and of any benefit to him by contract or otherwise".

(2) How inheritance tax is calculated

Suppose that a person who has just died, leaving an estate, other than that part which he has left to his spouse and which is therefore exempt from inheritance tax, of £250,000, made the following *inter vivos* transfers: eight years ago, a transfer of £100,000 to his son (a potentially exempt transfer); six and a half years ago, a transfer of £150,000 to trustees on trust for such of his grandchildren as attain the age of 21 (a potentially exempt transfer); four and a half years ago, a transfer of

---

[84] In 1994–95.
[85] Inheritance Tax Act 1984, ss.38, 39.

£200,000 to trustees on discretionary trust for all his descendants (an initially chargeable transfer); and two years ago, a transfer of £100,000 to his daughter (a potentially exempt transfer). Suppose also that throughout this period and at the time of his death the lifetime allowance was £150,000 and the only rate of inheritance tax was 40 per cent. (this is of course totally unrealistic, since the lifetime allowance is raised in line with inflation, but it is the only way to make the example comprehensible). It is necessary to calculate the inheritance tax payable twice: first, transfer by transfer during the deceased's lifetime and, secondly, on his death.

The transfers made eight years ago and six and a half years ago were both potentially exempt so no inheritance tax was payable on either occasion. The transfer made four and a half years ago was, however, initially chargeable so inheritance tax was payable. At that time, the deceased had not used up any of his lifetime allowance of £150,000 (the potentially exempt transfers were assumed not to be chargeable and therefore did not have to be aggregated for that purpose); consequently, the first £150,000 of the £200,000 used up the deceased's lifetime allowance of £150,000 so that inheritance tax was payable at 20 per cent. (half the death rate) on the remaining £50,000, thus requiring the immediate payment of £10,000 (it will be presumed that the tax was paid by the trustees of the settlement—had it been paid by the deceased, the total amount of the transfer would have had to be "grossed up" to take account of the tax). The transfer made two years ago was also potentially exempt so no inheritance tax was payable then either. Thus the total inheritance tax payable during the deceased's lifetime was £10,000.

By the time of the deceased's death, the potentially exempt transfer of £100,000 made eight years ago had become exempt. However, all of the other three transfers and the deceased's estate give rise to inheritance tax liabilities which need to be calculated individually in chronological order. The personal representatives are liable to pay any inheritance tax due in respect of the estate; any liability in respect of the *inter vivos* transfers falls primarily on the individual transferees but in default also passes to the personal representatives.

(a) The potentially exempt transfer of £150,000 made six and a half years ago is not in fact exempt. During the seven years preceding that transfer, the deceased had made one previous transfer, that of £100,000 eight years ago. that used up £100,000 of his lifetime allowance of £150,000. Thus, £50,000 of this allowance remained at that time to offset against the transfer of £150,000. The £100,000 balance is thus liable to inheritance tax. The death rate is 40 per cent. but because the deceased survived for six and a half further years, there is a reduction of 80 per cent. (20 per cent. for each year or part of a year after the first three). Consequently, the inheritance tax payable is 20 per cent. of 40 per cent. of £100,000, thus £8,000.

(b) The initially chargeable transfer of £200,000 made four and a half years ago has already suffered inheritance tax of £10,000. During the seven years preceding that transfer, the deceased had made two previous transfers, that of £100,000 eight years ago and that of £150,000 six and a half years ago. These used up all his lifetime allowance of £150,000. Thus, the whole of the £200,000 is liable to inheritance tax. The death rate is 40 per cent. but because the deceased survived for four and half further years, there is a reduction of 40 per cent. (20 per cent. for each year or part of a year after the first three). Consequently, the inheritance tax payable is 60 per cent. of 40 per cent. of £200,000 less the £10,000 already paid, thus £38,000.

(c) The potentially exempt transfer of £100,000 made two years ago is not in fact exempt. During the seven years preceding that transfer, the deceased had made three previous transfers, that of £100,000 eight years ago, that of £150,000 six and a half years ago, and that of £200,000 four and a half years ago. These used up all his lifetime allowance of £150,000. Thus, the whole of the £100,000 is liable to inheritance tax. The death rate is 40 per cent. and there is no reduction because the deceased did not survive for three years. Consequently, the inheritance tax payable is 40 per cent. of £100,000, thus £40,000.

(d) The deceased's estate of £250,000, other than the part which he left to his spouse, which is therefore exempt from inheritance tax, is liable to inheritance tax. During the seven years preceding his death, the deceased has made three previous transfers, that of £150,000 six and a half years ago, that of £200,000 four and a half years ago, and that of £100,000 two years ago. These used up all his lifetime allowance of £150,000. Thus, the whole of the £250,000 is liable to inheritance tax. The death rate is 40 per cent. Consequently, the inheritance tax payable is 40 per cent. of £250,000, thus £100,000.

As the amount of inheritance tax payable illustrates, this is of course a splendid illustration of how not to do it! In general, the potentially exempt transfers and, preferably, also the initially chargeable transfers during any seven year period should be restricted to the amount of the lifetime allowance because of the risk that the transferor may die before they have become exempt, thus producing the sort of countback and the level of inheritance tax liability evidenced in the example.

(3) The liability to inheritance tax of settlements

When potentially exempt transfers were introduced,[86] only one specific type of trust, an accumulation and maintenance trust, was able to take effect as such a transfer. However, potentially exempt transfers were subsequently enlarged to include settlements in which there is an interest in possession[87]; consequently, when such a settlement is created *inter vivos*, it is capable of taking effect as a potentially exempt transfer, subject of course to the rules about reservation of benefit by

---

[86] By Finance Act 1986.
[87] By Finance (No. 2) Act 1987.

the settlor which have already been discussed. However, discretionary trusts (other than accumulation and maintenance trusts) can still not take effect as potentially exempt transfers and, if created *inter vivos*, are consequently still initially chargeable transfers.

(a) **Settlements in which there is an interest in possession.** A settlement contains an interest in possession for the purposes of the inheritance tax legislation if the beneficiary whose interest is in possession has the right to receive the income of the settlement as it arises. It does not matter that the trustees have power to revoke his entitlement or to appoint the income to someone else; however, the existence of a power to accumulate, whether or not it is being exercised, prevents the settlement from having an interest in possession for this purpose.[88]

A settlement in which there is an interest in possession for the purposes of the inheritance tax legislation can take effect as a potentially exempt transfer, provided that there is no reservation of benefit by the settlor. Consequently, there is no liability to inheritance tax on the creation of the settlement although, in the event that the settlor does not survive for a further seven years, inheritance tax may nevertheless be payable on his death for the reasons and upon the bases illustrated in the previous section.

A beneficiary who has an interest in possession for the purposes of the inheritance tax legislation is regarded as being beneficially entitled to the property which forms the subject matter of the settlement—the fact that he may have no more than a life interest therein is irrelevant for this purpose.[89] Consequently, when an interest in possession comes to an end, its beneficiary is regarded as having made a transfer of the value of his interest whether its determination was the result of his own positive act, such as a disposition or surrender, or the result of reaching its natural limit, such as the occurrence of a determining event or the death of a life tenant.[90] Such a transfer may be exempt, potentially exempt, or chargeable. It will be exempt if it falls within any of the general exemptions already mentioned (other than the small gifts exemption of £250, which does not apply to settlements).[91] (Consequently, if a husband has an interest in possession under a settlement for his life time and the beneficiary next entitled under the settlement is his wife, no inheritance tax will be payable whether it passes to her as a result of a surrender *inter vivos* or as a result of his death.) Such a transfer will be potentially exempt if it occurs *inter vivos*. Consequently, a disposition or surrender of the interest *inter vivos* and a determination as a result of the interest reaching its natural limit will all be potentially exempt transfers. If the beneficiary survives a further seven years, the transfer will become exempt. If he does not do so, the transfer will become chargeable, as will any non-exempt transfer occurring as a

---

[88] The authorities all concern capital transfer tax, where the same criteria applied. See particularly *Pearson v. I.R.C.* [1981] A.C. 753.
[89] Inheritance Tax Act 1984, s.49.
[90] *Ibid.* ss.51, 52.
[91] *Ibid.* s.57.

result of the death of the beneficiary. In these cases, the inheritance tax payable is assessed on the basis of the lifetime transfers made by the beneficiary, not those made by the settlor.[92] However, the tax due is actually payable out of the settled property and the trustees and the beneficiary are jointly responsible for its payment.

There are certain special reliefs: where the settled property reverts to the settlor or his spouse, there is, subject to certain qualifications, total relief[93]; where as a result of the transfer the beneficiary becomes entitled to some other interest in the settled property, there will be partial relief if and to the extent to which his new interest is worth less than his previous interest (there being a potentially exempt transfer to this extent), while if he becomes entitled to the settled property absolutely, there will be a potentially exempt transfer of the amount of any purchase moneys he has paid for the outstanding interests[94]; finally, where tax is payable within five years of a previous chargeable transfer, quick succession relief reduces the rate of tax.[95]

(b) Discretionary Trusts. For the purposes of the inheritance tax legislation, a discretionary trust is any settlement in which there is no interest in possession,[96] with the exception of accumulation and maintenance trusts, which will be considered in the next section, and certain other trusts which are given special treatment (including charitable trusts, newspaper trusts, maintenance funds for historic buildings, superannuation schemes, trusts for the benefit of employees and disabled persons, and protective trusts).[97]

As has already been seen, the creation *inter vivos* of a discretionary trust is an initially chargeable transfer and consequently is subject to an immediate payment of inheritance tax, charged at half the death rate (thus at present[98] charged at 20 per cent. rather than 40 per cent.) if and to the extent that the total of transfers which are neither exempt nor potentially exempt during the seven years preceding the transfer exceed the settlor's lifetime allowance. Further, in the event that the settlor dies within seven years of the transfer, the amount of inheritance tax payable may have to be reassessed if any transfer which was potentially exempt at the time of the original assessment turns out in the end not to be exempt from inheritance tax (see the example discussed in the previous section).

A further charge to inheritance tax is made on every tenth anniversary of the creation of the discretionary trust at 30 per cent. of the inheritance tax which would have been payable if the property subject to the settlement on the day before the tenth anniversary in question had been transferred to the settlement at that time[99]; calculation of the

---

[92] *Ibid.* s.52.
[93] *Ibid.* s.54.
[94] *Ibid.* s.53(2).
[95] *Ibid.* s.141.
[96] *Ibid.* s.58.
[97] *Ibid.* ss.58, 86, 87, 88 and 89.
[98] In 1994–95.
[99] Inheritance Tax Act 1984, ss.64, 66.

inheritance tax due takes into account the state of the settlor's lifetime allowance at the time when the settlement was originally made and any transfers made during the seven years immediately preceding the creation of the settlement. Account is also taken of any settled property which has ceased to be subject to the discretionary trust during the preceding ten years (as will be seen in the next paragraph, inheritance tax will have been payable when that property ceased to be subject to the trust).

If any of the settled property ceases to be subject to the discretionary trust, a further charge to inheritance tax is made.[1] This charge arises not only where a capital payment is made to a beneficiary but also where, in accordance with their discretionary powers, the trustees create a settlement with an interest in possession or an accumulation and maintenance trust. The intention of this charge is to produce the appropriate proportion of the inheritance tax which would have been payable on the next tenth anniversary of the creation of the discretionary trust. If the discretionary trust has already lasted for more than ten years, the further charge is the appropriate fraction of the tax paid on the last ten year anniversary, taking into account the number of quarters which have passed in the current ten year period.[2] (Consequently, if two years have passed since the last ten year anniversary, the appropriate fraction is eight-fortieths so the tax payable on the value of the property taken out is eight-fortieths of the rate of tax payable on the last ten year anniversary, which was of course itself 30 per cent. of the inheritance tax which would have been payable had the property been settled then.) If, on the other hand, the discretionary trust has not yet lasted for ten years, the rate of tax payable is 30 per cent. of the appropriate fraction (calculated in the same way on the basis of the number of quarters in the first ten year period which have already passed) of the rate of tax which would have been payable on a hypothetical chargeable transfer, at the time when the property is taken out of the settlement, of the property originally settled, taking into account as before the state of the settlor's lifetime allowance at the date of the creation of the settlement.[3] A simple illustration of these formulae follows; more complex illustrations are provided in specialist works on taxation.

Suppose that £100,000 is settled on discretionary trust by a settlor who, at the date of the settlement, has already used up all his lifetime allowance in the preceding seven years. Exactly five years after the creation of the settlement, the trustees appoint an interest in possession in £10,000 to one of the beneficiaries. Exactly twelve years after the creation of the settlement, they make a similar appointment of £10,000 to another beneficiary. Suppose also that the only rate of inheritance tax is at all times 40 per cent. Inheritance tax will be payable on the creation of the settlement, on each appointment of £10,000, and on the tenth anniversary of the creation of the settlement (if the settlor fails to survive for seven years after the date of the creation of the settlement,

---

[1] *Ibid.* s.65.
[2] *Ibid.* s.69.
[3] *Ibid.* s.68.

further inheritance tax may also be payable on his death; this possibility is illustrated by the example discussed earlier on pages 422–424).

(a) On the creation of the settlement, inheritance tax is payable
charged at half the death rate (therefore at 20 per cent.). Since the
settlor has at the date of the settlement already used up all his
lifetime allowance in the preceding seven years, this tax is
payable in full. Consequently, £20,000 tax is payable. It will be
assumed that this is paid by the trustees (were it to be paid by
the settlor, the sum settled would have to be "grossed up"). Thus
only £80,000 is actually held on discretionary trust.

(b) On the appointment of £10,000 exactly five years after the
creation of the settlement, twenty quarters have passed. Consequently, the inheritance tax payable is twenty-fortieths (50 per
cent.) of 30 per cent. of the rate of tax payable on a hypothetical
chargeable transfer of the property originally settled taking into
account the state of the settlor's lifetime allowance at the date of
the creation of the settlement. The latter rate is once again 20 per
cent., since the settlor had already used up all his lifetime
allowance at the date of the creation of the settlement. Consequently, the overall rate of tax is 50 per cent. of 30 per cent. of 20
per cent., which is 3 per cent. Therefore the tax payable is 3 per
cent. of £10,000, thus £300. It will be assumed that this is paid by
the beneficiary (were it to be paid by the trustees, the sum
appointed would have to be "grossed up").

(c) On the tenth anniversary of the creation of the settlement,
suppose that the property subject to the settlement is now worth,
due to capital appreciation and some accumulation of income,
£110,000. The hypothetical chargeable transfer is thus of £120,000
(the £110,000 still settled and the £10,000 paid out during the
preceding ten year period). The tax payable on such a hypothetical transfer would once again be 20 per cent., the settlor having
used up all his lifetime allowance at the date of the creation of the
settlement. Consequently, the overall rate of tax is 30 per cent. of
20 per cent., which is 6 per cent. Therefore, the tax payable is 6
per cent. of £120,000, thus £7,200 (this will have to be paid out of
the settled property).

(d) On the appointment of £10,000 exactly twelve years after the
creation of the settlement, eight quarters have passed since the
tenth anniversary of the creation of the settlement. Consequently, the inheritance tax payable is eight-fortieths (20 per
cent.) of the rate of tax paid on the tenth anniversary of the
creation of the settlement, which was 6 per cent. Therefore, the
tax payable is 20 per cent. of 6 per cent., that is 1.2 per cent., of
£10,000, thus £120. It will once again be assumed that this is paid
by the beneficiary (were it to be paid by the trustees, the sum
appointed would have to be "grossed up").

It will be seen from this example that, apart from the inheritance tax
payable on the creation of the settlement, which will be avoided if the

property settled falls within the settlor's lifetime allowance, the incidence of inheritance tax is not substantial. This type of trust therefore retains some attraction for a settlor, particularly if it is limited to the settlor's lifetime allowance.

(c) **Accumulation and maintenance trusts.** An accumulation and maintenance settlement must be for the benefit of one or more children, usually the children or grandchildren of the settlor, who must be entitled to the trust property or to an immediate vested interest in its income upon reaching an age not exceeding 25; in the meantime, the income can either be accumulated or be applied for the maintenance education or benefit of the children.[4] However, such trusts can only last for 25 years unless all the beneficiaries have a common grandparent (if the trust ceases to qualify, inheritance tax becomes payable as if it were a normal discretionary trust). There are no particular fiscal advantages in respect of income tax; the income of the trust is taxed at the flat rate of 35 per cent. and any income applied for the maintenance or education of a beneficiary is, provided that the trust is irrevocable, taxed as the income of the beneficiary (unless he is a minor unmarried child of the settlor, in which case it is aggregated with the income of the latter).[5] The fiscal advantages of such trusts is that they are potentially exempt transfers[6]; consequently, such trusts are not liable to any of the additional charges to inheritance tax outlined in the previous section (this is why inheritance tax is payable if a discretionary trust is converted into an accumulation and maintenance trust). No inheritance tax will be payable at all if the settlor survives a further seven years; even if he fails to do so, inheritance tax will only be payable to the extent that his estate and the transfers made during the last seven years of his life exceed his lifetime allowance.

---

[4] *Ibid.* s.71. For a detailed discussion of the conditions, see *Inglewood (Lord)* v. *I.R.C.* [1983] 1 W.L.R. 366.

[5] Income and Corporation Taxes Act 1988, ss.663–665.

[6] Inheritance Tax Act 1984, s.3A.

CHAPTER 15

INVESTMENT

I. THE GENERAL STANDARD OF CARE

THE duty of a trustee in investing trust funds is to take such care as an ordinary prudent man would take if he were under a duty to make the investment for the benefit of other persons for whom he felt morally bound to provide.[1] Lord Watson in *Learoyd* v. *Whiteley*[2] specified the requirement as follows:

> "As a general rule the law requires of a trustee no higher degree of diligence in the execution of his office than a man of ordinary prudence would exercise in the management of his own private affairs. Yet he is not allowed the same discretion in investing the moneys of the trust as if he were a person *sui juris* dealing with his own estate. Business men of prudence may, and frequently do, select investments which are more or less of a speculative character but it is the duty of a trustee to confine himself to the class of investments which are permitted by the trust and likewise to avoid all investments of that class which are attended with hazard. So long as he acts in the honest observance of these limitations the general rule already stated will apply."

In addition to adhering to this general standard of care, a trustee is also bound to make his investments in such a way that those entitled in possession will obtain a reasonable income and yet the capital will be preserved for those entitled to it in remainder.[3] A balance must be secured so that all beneficiaries are treated equally and fairly.

It follows from the foregoing that even if the trustee invests in securities authorised by the Trustee Investments Act 1961,[4] or by the trust instrument itself,[5] he will not necessarily be protected from attack by the beneficiaries. Even an authorised investment may in the particular circumstances of the case be unjustified and amount to a breach of the trustees' general duties of care and impartiality. But in circumstances such as these the onus would be on the beneficiaries to

---

[1] *Re Whiteley* (1886) 33 Ch.D. 347 at 355, *per* Lindley L.J.; affirmed *sub nom. Learoyd* v. *Whiteley* (1887) 12 App. Cas. 727.

[2] *Ibid.* at p. 733.

[3] *Re Whiteley, ante,* at p. 350, *per* Cotton L.J.

[4] *Post,* p. 441.

[5] See *post,* p. 446.

establish that the investment was imprudent, and not for the trustees to show the converse.[6] Moreover, in addition to these general duties, certain positive duties in relation to investment are now expressly imposed by the Trustee Investments Act 1961,[7] and these will apply to any power of investment, whether it is exercised under or outside the Act.

All the same principles apply to the variation and continuation of investments. The trustees have, as might be expected, the power to vary investments already made,[8] and also to continue these investments even if they have since ceased to be authorised.[9] But these powers are, of course, subject to the general and statutory[10] duties of care and impartiality incumbent on a trustee.

There has recently been some discussion of whether trustees, in reaching their decisions as to the selection and retention of particular investments, are entitled to take into account non-financial consider-ations. In *Cowan* v. *Scargill*,[10A] five of the ten trustees of a mineworkers' pension fund were appointed by the National Union of Miners. They refused to accept an investment plan submitted to the trustees by an advisory panel of experts in so far as it envisaged new or continuing investment overseas and in energies which were in direct competition with coal. Such investments were contrary to the policy of the National Union of Miners, which was understandably primarily interested in preserving the prosperity and, consequently, in ensuring the continued existence of the British coal mining industry. Their arguments were thus ideological in nature. There can be little doubt that most pension funds would indeed be benefited by the maintenance of the prosperity of the industry in question; but, as Sir Robert Megarry V.C. commented, the mineworkers' pension fund was in this respect unusual because of the declining nature of the coal mining industry, there being substantially more pensioners than miners so that the assets of the fund far exceeded the value of the industry. Further, overseas investments can be substantially more risky than home investments because of the possibility of exchange rate variations. However, Sir Robert Megarry V.C. held that the trustees would be in breach of trust unless they accepted the investment plan submitted. Their duty was to act in the best interests of their beneficiaries and, if the purpose of the trust was the provision of financial benefits, a power of investment had to be exercised so that the funds yielded the best return by way of income and capital appreciation.

> "Trustees may have strongly held social or political views. They may be firmly opposed to any investment in South Africa or other countries, or they may object to any form of investment in

---

[6] *Shaw* v. *Cates* [1909] 1 Ch. 389, at p. 395, *per* Parker J.
[7] s.6(1)(*a*)(*b*), discussed *post*, p. 448.
[8] *Hume* v. *Lopes* [1892] A.C. 112.
[9] Trustee Act 1925, s.4, as modified by the Trustee Investments Act 1961, s.3(4), Sched. 3, para. 2, and discussed *post*, p. 448.
[10] T.I.A. 1961, s.6(1)(*a*)(*b*), and see *post*, p. 448.
[10A] [1984] 3 W.L.R. 501.

companies concerned with alcohol, tobacco, armaments or many other things. In the conduct of their own affairs, of course, they are free to abstain from making any such investments. Yet under a trust, if investments of this type would be more beneficial to the beneficiaries than other investments, the trustees must not refrain from making the investments by reason of the views that they hold."[10B]

In exceptional cases, account could be taken of the particular inclinations of the beneficiaries but this was not relevant in the case in hand since many of the beneficiaries no longer had any financial interest in the welfare of the coal industry. The trustees were therefore pursuing union policy at the potential expense of the beneficiaries and, in the last resort, would have to be removed from office.

It is possible that the fact that the trustees so overtly based their case on ideological grounds did not favour their case. There seems no reason why trustees should not limit themselves to investments which they regard as politically and ethically "sound" provided that they have satisfied themselves that these investments are no less financially sound than those which they have rejected. What *Cowan* v. *Scargill* decides is that they must not fetter their discretion by deciding to exclude any particular class of investments irrelevant of their financial merits. This is confirmed by *Martin* v. *City of Edinburgh District Council*,[10C] where a Scottish court held that a breach of duty had been committed by a local authority which, in order to oppose apartheid, had adopted a policy of disinvesting in companies which had interests in South Africa without considering whether this was in the best financial interests of the beneficiaries. It is therefore clear that no investment policy, whether to prefer or whether to avoid particular classes of investments, can be adopted unless the trustees have paid the necessary attention to the financial interests of the beneficiaries.

It has also been contended that trusts for charitable purposes should not make investments in undertakings whose operations are incompatible with those purposes. In *Harris* v. *Church Commissioners*[10D] the Bishop of Oxford sought a declaration that in the management of their assets the Church Commissioners were obliged to have regard to the object of promoting the Christian faith through the established Church of England and were not entitled to act in a manner which would be incompatible with that object. This declaration was denied. Sir Donald Nicholls V.C. held that, where charitable trustees held assets as investments, the discharge of their duty of furthering the purposes of the trust would normally require them to seek the maximum return which was consistent with commercial prudence and they could not property use such assets for non-investment purposes. The Commissioners already had a policy of excluding investments in certain business activities which might be offensive to the Church of England,

---

[10B] *Ibid.* at p. 514.
[10C] [1988] S.L.T. 329.
[10D] [1992] 1 W.L.R. 1241.

such as armaments, gambling, tobacco, newspapers and South Africa. This was entirely proper but it would not be right for them to adopt a still more restrictive policy which would entail taking into account non-financial considerations to an extent which would give rise to a risk of significant financial detriment to the proper object of the trusts.

All the cases which have been discussed concerned trusts of a public nature. While the considerations expressed therein clearly also apply to private trusts, there is of course nothing to stop any settlor, or indeed the totality of the beneficiaries if they are all *sui juris*, from prescribing that the trustees either must make or must refrain from making investments of any particular type.

Finally, it should be noted that, where the beneficial interests of a trust are limited by way of succession, the trustees must also consider the competing interests of the tenant for life and the remaindermen. High income investments are likely to produce little, if any, capital appreciation and thus will generally benefit the tenant for life at the expense of the remaindermen, while low income investments are likely to produce more substantial capital appreciation and thus will generally benefit the remaindermen at the expense of the tenant for life. In *Nestlé* v. *National Westminster Bank*,[10E] the remainderman complained that the fund to which she became entitled when her interest vested in possession would have been worth almost four times as much had it been properly invested. The trustees had erroneously regarded their investment powers as more limited than they actually were and, as a result, had invested in a more restricted range of investments than they were actually obliged to. Further, they had failed to make sufficiently regular reviews of the fund. However, since the remainderman was unable to prove that any loss had been suffered thereby, the Court of Appeal held that she was not entitled to any compensation. The Court also emphasised that trustees are entitled to take into account the taxation position of the beneficiaries; consequently, they had been entitled, where the tenant for life was non-resident, to purchase investments which would not be subject to deduction of income tax at source or to what is now inheritance tax on his death; further, they could take into account the relative wealth of the tenant for life and the remainderman in deciding whether to purchase high income or low income investments. However, the Court did hold that at least half of a trust fund held for persons by way of succession should be invested in equities.

II. Types Of Investment

It has just been indicated that when any investment is contemplated, the trustee will have to give due consideration to the interest of all the beneficiaries, and he will have to hold the balance equally between them. Further, as will be shown later in this chapter, before deciding on an investment, a trustee must generally consider advice—and consider is the operative word: he must not unthinkingly follow such advice—on

---

[10E] [1993] 1 W.L.R. 1260.

whether the contemplated investment will be satisfactory. Again, he must diversify the trust investments, which means not merely that the trust fund must be held in different investments but, so far as is appropriate to the circumstances of the trust, that it must be held in different *types* of investment.

Before he can adequately do any of these things, a trustee must have some knowledge of the characteristics of different types of investment. (Investments are colloquially termed "securities", but that term is somewhat dangerous: a "security" in this sense is not necessarily "secure".) The points to consider with any investment are, *inter alia*.

(a) whether or not that investment is a "fixed-interest" security;
(b) whether or not the capital value will fluctuate; and
(c) if the capital value will fluctuate, in what way such fluctuation is likely.

If a security is a "fixed-interest" security, the amount of interest or dividend which is produced will never alter. The trustee who buys £1,000 Treasury 10.5 per cent. stock 1999 knows that, whatever happens to the economic state of the nation, he will receive £105 per annum income. On the other hand, if he invests in ordinary shares of commercial companies, known as "equities", he does not know what he will receive, for this will depend entirely on the amount of the dividend which the companies in each year decide to pay. In bad years they may pay nothing, but in other years they may pay a larger amount than any fixed-interest security.

As regards capital value, there are only a few types of security where there will be no fluctuation. This will only occur where such securities are purchasable only from the Government or other persons issuing them, and are not bought and sold among private individuals. The best-known examples are National Savings Certificates, which may be bought over the counter of the Post Office or Trustee Savings Bank, and some bonds issued by local authorities.

By contrast, the capital value of all other securities, whether of the Government, local authorities, or commercial undertakings dealt with on a stock exchange, will fluctuate. To understand the terminology used in connection with this fluctuation, it is necessary to distinguish between the nominal price of an investment, and its market price. The nominal price is the value of the investment as named on its face, and at which, usually, it was originally issued. The market price is the price at which that security can for the time being be purchased. Suppose that the Government issued in 1950 a new stock which carries interest at £4 per cent. and that a person purchased from the Government a holding of £100 of the stock for £100 cash. Suppose also that in 1985 someone buys on the Stock Exchange that holding for £80 cash. The purchaser would be described as buying that holding of £100 nominal stock for a market price of £80. The interest, of course, is always calculated on the nominal value, and so however much the market price alters, the amount of interest will always be the same. When a security is bought for the same amount of cash as its nominal value—in the example just given, the purchase in 1950 of £100 nominal stock for £100—that security is said to be bought at "par."

The other term which is used in this context is "yield". This is the amount of income from a security expressed as a percentage of the market price paid for it, and not of its nominal price. So if £80 cash is paid for £100 nominal £4 per cent. stock, as the interest is fixed at £4 p.a., the yield is

$$£\frac{4}{80} \times 100 = £5 \text{ per cent.}$$

More precisely, the "yield" as just described is the "interest only" or "flat" yield. Where an investment is purchased at less than its nominal value, but will be redeemed at its nominal value there may also be calculated its "redemption yield". Very broadly, the redemption yield measures the gain to be expected on the redemption of the security together with the income which will be derived.[11]

It must be stressed that there are many factors which will govern fluctuations of market price, but in the case of Government securities, there are two in particular. First, there is the general level of interest rates obtainable elsewhere. If the normal yield at any time is £10 per cent. from investments which are considered "safe," the market price of Government securities is likely to be adjusted so that that security will produce a yield of about £10 per cent. If the market price were substantially higher, no one would buy them, because they could obtain a safe £10 per cent. yield elsewhere. The second factor is whether and at what pace inflation (and so, depreciation in the purchasing power of money) is likely to occur. If a period of rapid inflation is forecast, most investors will not favour fixed-interest securities, but will choose investments from which the return is likely to increase as inflation occurs; thus lack of demand will force down the market value of the fixed-interest securities. The most notorious example is $3\frac{1}{2}$ per cent. War Loan, which during 1993 had a market value in the region of £38 for each £100 nominal of stock but which has now, at the time of writing,[12] risen to £55 because of the reducing rate of inflation.

In the case of ordinary shares in commercial companies, the yield will also be important, and this may be expected to be rather higher than from Government securities, for a commercial undertaking cannot give the capital guarantee which the Government does and the yield is greater to compensate for this. Companies of national standing can become insolvent. But there are two other important factors which influence the capital value of ordinary shares. First, the anticipated ability of the company to pay dividends in the future at least at the rate which it has paid for them in the past. Secondly, the company's prospects for any increased profits and growth in the future.

With these principles in mind, the major types of investment can be considered as follows:

---

[11] The redemption yield is, strictly, the amount by which the eventual capital sum which will be obtained on the redemption of the security, together with the income which will arise until redemption, has to be discounted to reduce the security to its present value.
[12] January 1994.

(1) Fixed-interest securities

(a) National Savings Income Bonds. The capital value of these securities issued by the Government never changes, and the investor is guaranteed that he will receive back the amount he invested. These bonds are not, strictly, fixed interest securities because the rate of interest paid is adjusted from time to time in line with general changes in sterling interest levels. The interest is paid monthly.

(b) National Savings Certificates. These are also Government securities, but differ from National Savings Income Bonds because the interest is not paid as it accrues, but is added to capital. When the certificates are repaid, the investor therefore receives back the exact amount of his investment, together with the accumulated interest in the form of an addition to capital.[13]

(c) Building society investments. Investments in building societies are of two main kinds: on deposit accounts and on share accounts. The difference is that, should the building society be wound up, the depositors are paid out in full before the shareholders. For this reason, the shareholders receive a slightly larger income than that paid to the depositors, but in practice investments both in deposit accounts and in share accounts in building societies which are recognised as suitable for trustee investments[14] are regarded as absolutely safe, although only investments on deposit account are within the narrower range of "trustee investments."[15] The interest is usually payable twice yearly, or it can be added to capital.

Although dealt with here under the heading of fixed-interest securities, building society investments are not strictly fixed-interest ones because the rate of interest does fluctuate slightly, but not usually by a large amount. There is, however, no variation at all in the capital value of building society investments.

(d) "Gilt-edged" securities. This term, which is a hark-back to days when securities of the British Government were thought of more highly than today, denotes stocks issued or guaranteed by the Government, by the nationalised industries, and by some Commonwealth governments. They are fixed-interest securities, but as they are dealt with on the Stock Exchange[16] their capital value does fluctuate.

There are two categories of gilt-edged securities: dated and undated stock. When stock is dated—for example 35 per cent. Funding Stock 1999—the investor knows that at the stated date the security will be

---

[13] As to the entitlement to the increment, see *post*, p. 480.

[14] Under the provisions of House Purchase and Housing Act 1959, s.1. See also T.I.A. 1961, Sched. 1, Pt. II, para. 12.

[15] *Post*, p. 443.

[16] Persons who have National Savings Bank accounts may purchase "gilts" through the Post Office, and at their option have the dividends, credited to their National Savings Bank account. In this case the Post Office acts as intermediary, and it purchases the security on the Stock Exchange. Thus, although in this case the securities may be purchased through the Post Office, the principle is not altered.

redeemed at its nominal value. If, therefore, trustees buy £100 3. 5 per cent. Funding Stock 1999 in 1992 for £70, they know that in 1999 the Government will in effect buy back the stock from them for £100.

Undated stocks are often never redeemed, and the holders of them can never know how much their holdings will realise on the market at any future time.

Some British Government securities are "index-linked." These are considered later.[17]

(e) Debentures. A "debenture" is an acknowledgment of indebtedness by a company supported by a mortgage or charge created by the company over its assets, or a bond issued by a company unsupported by such a charge.[18] A private individual can only mortgage or charge property which he has at the time when that mortgage or charge is created, and a debenture may likewise be secured by a charge on a specific item of a company's property. But a company has an advantage over individuals in that it may create a "floating charge" which is a general charge over all its assets. Such a charge does not restrict the company from dealing with its assets, but should any liquidation occur, the charge which until then has been "floating" above the company's assets suddenly "descends" upon them, and converts itself into a fixed charge over those assets. This is a convenient way for a company to support its borrowing with security without impeding its dealings with its assets. But there is no need for a debenture to be supported by any security. If it is not, it operates in the same way as an unsecured loan to a private individual. For investment purposes, debentures are frequently equated with preference shares, with which they will be considered further.

(f) Preference shares. Preference shares are shares issued by commercial companies carrying a fixed rate of interest, and in this respect they are similar to debentures. The rate of interest is usually but not necessarily indicated in the title, *e.g.* 6 per cent. Preference Shares. The 6 per cent. is the rate of interest calculated by reference to the nominal value of the stock, and not to its market value. As long as the company makes a profit, or, usually, has reserves of profits from previous years, the holder is paid his dividend.

Debenture holders stand in the position of lenders to the company, and they are entitled to have their interest paid first. Preference shareholders are in the position of investors in the company, and they rank next after the debenture holders. It is only after the debenture and the preference shareholders have been paid that the company can declare a dividend on its ordinary shares.

There is a risk, in some cases more theoretical than real, that the company will not have any money, and in this case, of course, the debenture holder or preference shareholder will receive nothing. To compensate for this risk, the yield on debentures and preference shares

---

[17] *Post*, p. 438.
[18] Companies Act 1985, s.744; T.I.A. 1961, Sched. 1, Pt. IV, para. 4.

is usually higher than on gilt-edged. Frequently both debentures and preference shares are redeemable at a given date in the same way as dated gilt-edged stocks, and sometimes the holder has the option to convert the shares into ordinary shares at a stated time. Both debentures and preference shares may be dealt with on the Stock Exchange,[19] so that their capital value fluctuates.

There are two special classes of preference shares. The first is the *cumulative preference share*. The significance of the word "cumulative" is that if in any year the company does not pay a dividend, the dividend for that year will be paid out of any profits for future years. The other special type of preference share is the *participating preference share*. This type of share combines the characteristics of preference and ordinary shares. The company first pays the shareholders a dividend up to the amount of their preference—say, 6 per cent.; it then pays the ordinary shareholders a dividend of the same amount, and if there is still any money available for distribution, it is divided equally between holders of the participating preference and ordinary shares. Participating preference shares are, therefore, preference shares which are capable, subject to certain conditions, of participating in profits normally reserved for ordinary shareholders. Preference shares which are non-participating do not carry this right.

(2) Inflation-adjusted securities
A relatively recent development has been the issue of British Government securities which carry a low rate of interest, but the capital value of which is adjusted in accordance with increases in the Index of Retail Prices. Most of these securities are dealt in on the Stock Exchange, but there are also index-linked National Savings Certificates.

Index-linked stocks which are dealt in on the Stock Exchange have a base figure determined by the Retail Prices Index in force eight months[20] before the stock was issued. The amount of interest payable, and the amount payable on the redemption of the stock are then both adjusted for movements in the Retail Prices Index.

The amount payable on the redemption of index-linked National Savings Certificates is similarly calculated. In addition, certain bonuses are also payable.

(3) Ordinary shares
Ordinary shares, or "equities," are the basic type of share issued by commercial companies. In each year the company decides the amount available for distribution after paying its expenses and making provision for future requirements. The holders of debentures and preference shares are then paid out, and however much is left is distributed between the ordinary shareholders (with, sometimes, the

---

[19] "May" be dealt with on the Stock Exchange, because private companies, whose securities are not handled by the Stock Exchange, may nevertheless issue debentures and shares. When these securities change hands, the price is a matter for direct negotiation between buyer and seller, unless some provision is made in the articles of association to govern the price.

[20] The eight-month lag is for administrative convenience in making the calculations.

participating preference shareholders also benefiting). The dividend on the ordinary share, therefore, fluctuates with the trading profits of the company. If the company is flourishing, as its trading profits go up so will its ordinary dividends, and as the dividend increases so people will be prepared to pay more for the shares, or, in other words, the capital value goes up as well. But the reverse is the case when the company does badly.

Equities have a distinct advantage in times of inflation, for as inflation goes on, so the price of the company's products will increase, and this will lead to more money being available for dividends. The purchasing power of these dividends may well be no more than before, but at least the investment stands the chance of keeping pace with inflation, and so preserving its purchasing power.

Speaking generally, equities are the least safe of the various types of investment. For this reason their capital value fluctuates more than that of the other types.

Some equity shares produce a fairly small income, because rather than distribute its profits the company may prefer to plough back much of its profits into its business. In this case, although the dividends are small, the value of the company itself may be growing, and this will lead to an increase in the value of the shares. On the other hand, some shares will pay a high dividend but the prospects of the company may be precarious, or the profitability of the company may be unlikely to increase, in which case there is not likely to be much capital appreciation of the shares. And it must be remembered that capital appreciation is likely to benefit the remainderman more than the life-tenant.[21]

(4) Unit and investment trusts[22]

The managers of these trusts buy other Stock Exchange securities and invite the public to invest in the fund. The managers then receive the dividends from the securities, pay the expenses, and themselves a salary, and distribute the remainder to the investors. Such an investor has, therefore, a minimal stake in numerous companies, and thus spreads the risk. But at the same time he receives less than he would have done had he invested directly in the most profitable companies in which the managers invest, and it must be remembered that the managers take out their remuneration before any money is available for the unit holders. One advantage of investing these trusts is that the managers are in a position to keep a day-to-day eye on the investments, and they have the ready opportunity for altering investments at the appropriate time.

Unit and investment trusts are often organised to cope for special needs, *e.g.* low income and high capital appreciation, or high income and low capital appreciation, or something between the two.

---

[21] Although, of course, if the capital appreciation occurs because the dividends are being increased, the tenant for life will benefit by virtue of this increase in the dividends.

[22] See *ante*, p. 5.

(5) Non-income producing investments

The traditional meaning of the word "investment" is an asset which produces income[23] with the connotation that it is likely to produce a surplus on revenue account over the anticipated period of holding of the asset.[24] This is still the legal meaning of the word. However, as a result of fiscal legislation it has become more and more prudent in many situations to reduce or eliminate income, and to seek capital appreciation. Consequently in general and financial usage, the word now implies any asset which will produce a good return, even if that is entirely in the form of capital appreciation.

The fiscal legislation has produced the following results:

   (a) income, when paid to a beneficiary, is taxable in his hands up to a maximum effective rate of 40 per cent.[25] Capital gains realised by trustees are taxable at the maximum rate of 35 per cent., by beneficiaries at the maximum rate of 40 per cent.;

   (b) where trustees receive income in the first instance, and accumulate it, that income is subject to income tax at 25 per cent. or, in the case of accumulation and discretionary settlements, 35 per cent.[26] If they hold an asset which never produces income, their liability is to capital gains tax only, and this is payable only when the asset is disposed of.[27]

As a result, trustees have increasingly sought to lay out trust funds in the acquisition of non-income, or low-income, producing assets. It must be stressed that this can only be done where there is an express power in the trust instrument[28] but, given this power, the following are some of the possibilities which have recently found favour.

   (a) **Split-level shares and units.**   In principle these are either equity shares or units in unit trusts. The device depends on there being two classes of shares or units. One class carries the entitlement to all income, but no capital appreciation. The other class carries entitlement to all capital appreciation, but no income. Shares and units in the former class are usually taken up by bodies which are exempt from income tax, such as charities and pension funds. Shares and units in the latter class are usually taken up by private individuals and trustees. It will be appreciated that in normal circumstances shares and units in the latter class, although paying no dividends, will steadily increase in value, and that value will be realised on disposal.

   (b) **Single-Premium Bonds.**   The essence of this arrangement is that a policy of assurance is effected with an insurance company for the

---

[23] See *Re Power* [1947] Ch. 572; see *infra.*
[24] See the reasoning in *Cooke* v. *Haddock* (1960) 39 T.C. 64; *Johnston* v. *Heath* [1970] 3 All E.R. 915; [1970] 1 W.L.R. 1567.
[25] See *ante*, p. 411.
[26] See *ante*, p. 411.
[27] See *ante*, p. 416.
[28] *Re Power* [1947] Ch. 572.

payment of one premium only, which is paid at the outset. The insurance company invests the funds in an agreed manner, such as in equities or in property. At an agreed date, often after the expiry of 10 years, or on the earlier death of the life assured, the policy matures, and the payee receives a sum equivalent to the original premium paid, together with a profit which depends on the success which the insurance company has had in the investment of its funds. In principle, the total proceeds of the policy are received as capital.[29]

(c) Chattels. A wide variety of chattels have been purchased by trustees as growth investments. Over the last few years trustees have invested in works of art, antique furniture, silver, silver bullion and oriental carpets. Almost invariably these are unsuitable as investments unless one has considerable freedom of choice as to the time of disposal: due to the volatility of the various markets, a period of some years may have to elapse before it becomes a good time to sell.

(d) Loans to beneficiaries. In some circumstances, it may be thought desirable that capital appreciation should accrue to a beneficiary rather than to the trustees. In such circumstances, the trustees may wish to lend trust funds to the beneficiary, interest free, perhaps securing the loan by taking a charge over the assets which the beneficiary purchases with them. On the death of the beneficiary, the loan is repaid from his estate. However, where this is done, the whole of the capital appreciation accrues to the beneficiary, and not to the fund as a whole, so that this could only be proper where it is expressly authorised by the trust instrument, or all other beneficiaries affected agree.

(6) Foreign currency securities
As well as considering the type of investment to be made, trustees will wish to consider the currency of the investment. For example, trustees may wish to invest part of the fund in the stocks of foreign governments or companies, such as United States Treasury Bills, denominated in United States dollars, or Australian equity shares. Most of the types of investment which have so far been described have their counterparts in other countries. In addition, it is possible to invest in "currency funds." In essence, these are shares in companies[30] who apply the whole of their funds in making deposits in the various leading currencies of the world. By this spread, some protection is obtained against a fall in the exchange rate of sterling and those other currencies.

III. Trustee Investments Act 1961

Under the general law trustees are entitled to invest funds only in investments authorised *either* by express terms of their trust instrument *or* by statute. Until the Act was passed the investments authorised by

---

[29] Although, so far as the trustees are concerned, the total proceeds rank as a capital receipt, a charge to income tax may arise.

[30] For taxation reasons, the companies are incorporated outside the U.K., most frequently in Jersey.

statute were extremely limited. They were largely governed by section 1 of the Trustee Act 1925. Generally speaking, the statutory trustee list of investments (the "Statutory List" as it was usually called) was restricted to the following: stock issued by the British Government and governments of Commonwealth countries and colonies; stock guaranteed by the British Government; stock and mortgages issued by British local authorities; mortgages of land in Great Britain, among others. The essential point—on which criticism tended to fasten—was the restricted nature of these investments. Practically all of them carry interest at a fixed rate and are repayable at par. And this took no account of the decline, over the years, in the value of the pound. In the first place, eventual *repayment* of invested capital at its nominal par value would involve a *capital* loss in real values. Secondly, the income received by a life-tenant might remain nominally the same but, again, over the years, it will have become progressively worth in real value less than at the date the trust was established. And these two difficulties would become more and more acute as the trust itself became older. This is, of course, pre-supposing that investments were made in securities authorised by the Statutory List. But until 1961 there was often no alternative, because, unless a wider power of investment was conferred by the trust instrument, the trustees were restricted to the Statutory List. Indeed, many trusts over 60 years of age were drawn so as to comprehend only these investments and the result has been that a large number of trusts have suffered income and capital losses on the lines already mentioned. One striking omission from the List— understandable no doubt in 1925—was that there was no power to invest in equities. From the short-term viewpoint this was fortunate, for in the economic depression from which Britain suffered in the decade after the Act was passed, gilt-edged securities were generally far better investments than equities. But from the longer viewpoint it appears to be the position that those trusts which contained an unrestricted power of investment—thus enabling investment to be made in equities—have fared a great deal better than those restricted to the Statutory List. Accordingly, in the past 50 years or so, settlors have been advised to give their trustees very much wider investment powers than those contained in the List. But this practice left untouched those many trusts which conferred only the statutory investment powers.

It is not surprising, therefore, that many voices were raised against the continuation of this state of affairs. Among others the Nathan Committee in 1952 advocated reform, and in 1955 a White Paper stated that the Government intended to introduce a reform of the law. During the period before the Act was passed some relaxations occurred. For example, charities have long had the power to go to the court for an extension of their investment powers, but it was only as a result of the decision in *Re Royal Society's Charitable Trusts*[31] that this was generally realised. Of more general importance, the power to apply to the court was extended to all trusts—non-charitable trusts as well as charitable

---

[31] [1956] Ch. 87.

trusts—by the Variation of Trusts Act 1958[32]; many applications have been made under the Act for an extension of investment powers as well as for a variation of beneficial interests.

An application to the court, however, cost time and money. What was required was a general reform of the law based on section 1 of the Trustee Act 1925, without any obligation on the trustees to apply to the court. The reform was at long last achieved, but in a linguistically complex form, by the Trustee Investments Act 1961, which came into force on August 3, 1961.[33]

The basic point about this Act is that it replaced the old Statutory List. The new List is set out in the First Schedule to the Act. This is divided into three parts. Parts I and II are concerned with the "narrower-range investments" and Part III with the "wider-range investments" so called.

(1) Narrower-range investments

The investments specified in Part I include Defence Bonds, National Savings Certificates and National Savings Bank deposits are conveniently described as "small savings" investments. In general terms, they are the type of investment which can be made over the counter at a Post Office or Trustee Savings Bank, and advice is not necessary because there is no fluctuation in capital value. They are placed in this separate category because it is unnecessary for a trustee to seek expert advice before investing in this class, whereas it is required for investment in Parts II and III securities.[34] The investments specified in Part II approximate to those in the old Statutory List. But they also include certain securities which did not previously rank as trustee investments, namely (i) fixed-interest securities[35] registered in the United Kingdom issued by local or public authorities[36] in the Commonwealth, in the European Community, or by the World Bank

---

[32] See post, p. 546.

[33] The Law Reform Committee (23rd Report, 1982) considered that the 1961 Act is out of date. They recommended that authorised investments should be divided into those which can be made without advice and those which can only be made with advice; and that the trustees should be free to invest in such proportions as they may choose. The Act is even more out of date today in the light of the many new types of investments which have emerged in the last fifteen years.

[34] s.6(2). The narrower-range investments specified in Pt. I also now include Ulster Development Bonds (Trustee Investments (Additional Powers) (No. 2) Order 1962 (S.I. 1962 No. 2611)); National Development Bonds (Trustee Investments (Additional Powers) Order 1964 (S.I. 1964 No. 703)); British Savings Bonds (Trustee Investment (Additional Powers Order 1968 (S.I. 1968 No. 470)); National Savings Income Bonds (Trustee Investments (Additional Powers) Order 1982 (S.I. 1982 No. 1086)); National Savings Deposit Bonds (Trustee Investments (Additional Powers) (No. 2) Order 1983 (S.I. 1983 No. 1525)); National Savings Indexed-Income Bonds (S.I. 1985 No. 1780); and National Savings Capital Bonds (Trustee Investments (Additional Powers) Order 1988 (S.I. 1988 No. 2554)).

[35] i.e. securities which under the terms of issue bear a fixed rate of interest: Sched. 1, Pt. IV, para. 4. "Securities" includes "shares, debentures, Treasury Bills and Tax Reserve Certificates": ibid. Variable-interest securities have been added by Trustee Investment (Additional Powers) Order 1977 (S.I. No. 831).

[36] Sched. 1, Pt. V, para. 4.

and by regional Development Banks[37]; (ii) debentures[38] of United Kingdom companies which comply with certain prescribed conditions as to paid-up capital and dividend records[39]; and (iii) deposits with most building societies.[40]

(2) Wider-range investments

The narrower range did not excite a great deal of attention; but the new wider range did. This, which is contained in Part III of the First Schedule, includes (i) shares, stock and debentures of certain United Kingdom companies[41]; (ii) shares of certain designated building societies[42]; and (iii) units of authorised unit trusts.[43] It is to be noted in particular—and this is the striking feature—that equities and other securities of the United Kingdom companies are included. But such investments in United Kingdom companies are, as will now be seen, hedged round with restrictions.

(3) Companies eligible for investment

The rules now to be mentioned apply to investment in debentures (Part II securities) and in shares and stock (Part III securities).

In the first place, they will not constitute trustee investments unless they are quoted on a recognised stock exchange.[44] Secondly, shares and debenture stock must be fully paid up or issued on terms that they are to be fully paid up within nine months from the date of issue.[45] And, thirdly—and this is the most stringent test of all—the company must have a total issued or paid-up capital of at least £1 million[46] and also have paid in each of the immediately preceding five years a dividend on all its shares.[47] There is no statutory requirement as to the *amount* of the dividend which has to be paid. In order to ensure that its shares will continue to be trustee investments, when a company experiences bad trading conditions, it will often pay a small dividend on its shares, even if it is as little as 0.01p a share.

(4) Division of the fund

The trustees cannot make or retain investments in the wider range unless the trust fund is divided into two parts, a narrower-range part and a wider-range part.[48] And only the wider-range part can be used for investment in the wider-range investments specified in Part III.[49] This

---

[37] *Ibid.* paras. 5, 5A, 5B.
[38] "Debenture" includes for this purpose debenture stock and bonds whether containing a charge on the assets or not, and loan stock and notes (Sched. 1, Pt. IV, para. 4).
[39] Sched. 1, Pt. II, para. 4; *ibid.* Pt. IV, para. 3. These requirements are the same as for Pt. III investments, *infra.*
[40] Building Societies Act 1986, s.120(1), Sched. 18, Pt. I, para. 4.
[41] Sched. 1, Pt. II, para. 1; *ibid.* Pt. IV, para. 3.
[42] Sched. 1, Pt. III, para. 2.
[43] *Ibid.* para. 3.
[44] Sched. 1, Pt. IV, para. 2(*a*).
[45] Sched. 1, Pt. IV, para. 2(*b*).
[46] Sched. 1, Pt. IV, para. 3(*a*).
[47] Sched. 1, Pt. IV, para. 3(*b*).
[48] s.2(1).
[49] s.2(1)(2).

division, which is perhaps the most important general feature of the Act, is to be made into two equal parts (the "50:50 rule")[50] and once made it is permanent and the two parts of the fund are kept separate.[51] It has the consequence that the wider-range part can be invested in wider-range investments, although there is nothing to prevent the trustee from investing it in the narrower-range investments if he chooses. On the other hand, the narrower-range part *must* be invested in narrower-range investments.

Moreover, in order to make sure that the division is permanent, provision is made for "compensating transfers" if property is transferred from the narrower range to the wider range.[52] Thus if property forming part of the narrower range is invested in a wider-range investment there must be a compensating transfer from the wider range in the opposite direction; or, alternatively, it must be sold and reinvested in narrower-range investments as soon as possible.[53]

(5) Accruals

Again, it may be that property accrues to the trust fund after the division. Some difficulties may arise here. For this purpose a distinction has been made between various classes of accrual. If property accrues to a trust fund in right of ownership of property that is already in their hands (*e.g.* on a bonus issue of shares or on the foreclosure of a mortgage) or was previously in their hands (*e.g.* where trustees have sold shares but retained their right to a bonus issue), then it will accrue to that part of the fund which contains or contained the investment of that generated it.[54] But in any other case the trustees must ensure that the value of each part of the fund is increased proportionately by the same amount, and this may mean that a compensating transfer must be made from one part of the fund to the other.[55] This would prove to be necessary where, for example, dividends or income are received as capital, where an expectancy falls in or the proceeds of sale of an expectancy are received, or where a gift is made to trustees on the trusts of the settlement.

(6) Withdrawals

Although, in general, compensating transfers may be necessary, special provision is made for one class of withdrawal. For it is provided that withdrawals from a trust fund in *the exercise of any power or duty*[56] of the

---

[50] s.2(1). The Treasury may, by order, direct that on any division made during the continuance of the order, the wider-range part shall be such proportion of the whole, being greater than one-half but not more than three-quarters, as may be prescribed by the order, and any such order may be revoked by a subsequent order prescribing a greater proportion: s.13.

[51] *Ibid.*

[52] s.2(1).

[53] s.2(2).

[54] s.2(3)(*a*).

[55] s.2(3)(*b*).

[56] See T.A. 1925, s.10(4).

trustees may be made from either part of the fund at their discretion.[57] In this case there is no need for compensating transfers. For example, if there is £1,000 in the narrower range and £1,000 in the wider range, and the trustees have to raise £500 for taxation or to pay it to a beneficiary absolutely entitled or to appropriate it to a separate trust fund or any other purpose, the £500 can be taken from either part of the fund at the trustees' discretion. This may well mean that the 50:50 rule will be partially abrogated unless, of course, £250 is taken from each part. This breach in the rule is presumably justified by the advantage of giving a certain latitude to trustees in the performance of their powers and duties in this respect.[58]

Moreover, there are certain ancillary provisions governing the trustees' power to appropriate part of the fund to form a separate trust fund. If at the time of appropriation the original fund was divided into a wider-range and a narrower-range part, it will be necessary to make a division of the new fund if it is intended to make use of the new investment powers as to that fund. But this division need not necessarily be 50:50. It is provided that the wider-range and narrower-range parts may be constituted:

(i) on the 50:50 basis; *or*
(ii) so as to bear the same proportion to each other as the two corresponding parts of the original fund bore at the date of appropriation; *or*
(iii) "in some intermediate proportion."[59]

This third alternative requires elucidation. It will presumably apply to a case where at the date of appropriation the 50:50 rule applies to the original fund, but in fact the wider-range part has increased beyond 50 per cent. (*e.g.* 60 per cent. of the whole) so that the proportions are 60:40 and not 50:50. In this case the wider-range and the narrower-range parts of the appropriated funds may be constituted in any proportion between 60:40 and 50:50. It could legitimately, for example, be in the proportion of 55 for the wider-range and 45 for the narrower.

It should also be noticed that no provision is made for compensating transfers between the two parts of the original fund which is not appropriated to form a separate trust fund. Thus if at the date of appropriation £10,000 is comprised in wider-range investments and £8,000 in narrower-range investments and £3,000 is appropriated out of the narrower-range funds, the proportion to which the original fund will now be constituted will be altered to 2:1.

(7) Special range
It is provided that the statutory powers of investment are additional to any special powers, *e.g.* conferred by the will or settlement or by the

---

[57] s.2(4).
[58] See 234 H. of L. Official Report 13, 14.
[59] s.4(3).

court[60] or by Parliament.[61] As a result, provision also had to be made for cases where special powers of investment were contained in the trust instrument which the trustees wish to combine with the powers under the Act. Accordingly, it is enacted that any property (not including narrower-range investments but including wider-range investments) which trustees are entitled to hold pursuant to such special powers must be carried to a separate "special-range" part of the fund.[62] So it may well happen, if the Act is made use of in cases where the trust contains a special power of investment of some sort, that the fund will be divided into three parts—a special-range part, a wider-range part and a narrower-range part.

Difficulties of administration may, however, arise if "special-range" property is converted. If it is, the trustees must ensure that the value of *both* the narrower range and the wider range is increased by the same amount, if necessary, by compensating transfers so that the 50:50 rule is maintained.[63] For example, the trust may confer a special power of investment in land, and the trustees may hold land pursuant to this power. Assume that they also hold gilt-edged securities but wish to take advantage of the Act and invest in equities. The land, if the trustees wish to retain it, is carried to a separate part of the fund, namely the special range. The gilt-edged securities are divided into a narrower-range part and a wider-range part, and the trustees may then invest the wider-range part of these securities in equities. If further land accrues to the trust it will also have to be carried to the special range. But if some of the land is converted into securities authorised by the Act, the proceeds of the conversion will have to be dealt with in such a way that the wider-range part and the narrower range are each increased by the same amount.

There is no doubt that the wider-range part of investments can at any time be used to purchase more land under the special power. Whether the narrower-range part of the investments can be used for this purpose is not at all clear. If indeed it can be so used, it might have the surprising result that the narrower-range investments could be exhausted in exercising the special power so that the trust fund would be constituted of only wider-range investments and land acquired under the special power. This would seem to be contrary to the whole principle of equality as between gilt-edged and equities which in general underlies this legislation, but there does not appear to be anything in the Act to prevent it happening. If this is so an unexpected lacuna in the Act is revealed. However, it would be dangerous for

---

[60] *e.g.* under the Variation of Trusts Act 1958 or Trustee Act 1925 s.57; see *post*, p. 542. See also s.15, which preserves the power of the court to confer investment powers wider than those given by the 1961 Act; and see *Re Cooper's Settlement* [1962] Ch. 826; *Re Kolb's Will Trusts* [1962] Ch. 531; *Re Clarke's Will Trusts* [1961] 1 W.L.R. 1471; *Re University of London Charitable Trusts* [1964] Ch. 282; *Trustees of the British Museum* v. *Attorney General* [1984] 1 W.L.R. 418 (all cases on Variation of Trusts Act 1958); *Anker-Petersen* v. *Anker-Petersen* (1991) 88/16 L.S.Gaz. 32 (Trustee Act 1925 s.57).

[61] s.3(1).

[62] s.3(3), Sched. 2.

[63] Sched. 2, para. 3.

trustees to take advantage of this, for it could perhaps be impugned as a breach of the trustees' general duties of care and of their statutory duties of ensuring diversification.[64]

These provisions relating to special-range property do not apply where the trustees' powers of investment were conferred or varied by an order of the court made within the period of 10 years ending on August 3, 1961, or by an enactment or statutory instrument made within the like period or by a local Act passed within the session 9 & 10 Eliz. 2.[65] If this has happened and the trustees now wish to make use of the Act, the normal rules as to division of the fund into a narrower range and a wider range apply, but the trustees cannot make use of the Act so as to make or hold wider-range investments whilst any wider-range investments are comprised in the narrower-range part of the fund.[66] The rule of general law that a trustee may retain an investment which has ceased to be authorised[67] is thereby overridden for this purpose.[68] To take an example, the trusts may have been varied within the prescribed period by the court to enable the trustees to invest 75 per cent. of the fund in what are now described as wider-range investments (*e.g.* the units of a unit trust scheme). The trust fund would, therefore, have to be divided in the usual way, but because certain wider-range investments would be comprised in the narrower-range part of the fund these would have to be sold for reinvestment in the narrower-range investments, and until this was done the trustees would not be able to make any investment in the units of a unit trust. They would be unable to make use of the statutory powers until a true division had been effected. Because this situation would arise, it is obviously much more likely that an application would be made to the court to seek the extension of investment powers required,[69] and not rely on the Act.

(8) Duties of trustees

Trustees naturally have, as a matter of general law, a duty of care and impartiality in making investments, and this is so whether these are made under the Act or under a special power of investment.[70] But the Act itself imposes certain positive statutory duties in addition. First, they must have regard to the need for securing diversification in so far as is appropriate to the circumstances of the trust.[71] No doubt circumstances legitimately to be taken into account would be smallness of the fund or the life-tenant's paramount need of income. Secondly, they must have regard to the suitability to the trust of investments of the class proposed *and* of the *particular* investment as an investment of that class.[72] The sort of problem with which trustees will be faced here

---

[64] *Infra.*
[65] s.3(4).
[66] Sched. 3, para. 1.
[67] T.A. 1925, s.4; *ante*, p. 431.
[68] Sched. 3, para. 2.
[69] Under V. of T.A. 1958 or T.A. 1925 s.57; *infra* fn. 60.
[70] See *ante*, p. 430.
[71] s.6(1)(*a*).
[72] s.6(1)(*b*).

is whether, and to what extent, for instance, present income should be sacrificed to future growth, and much will depend on arriving at a decision on the actual needs of the beneficiaries, the expected duration of the trust and, most important today, the beneficiaries' tax position.

The way in which these factors have to be considered is shown by taking three examples:

(a) If trustees are holding money for an infant beneficiary when he attains 18 in, say 1999, they might invest not merely in any gilt, nor merely in any dated gilt, but in 10.25 per cent. Conversion Stock 1999. This particular stock will be redeemed in 1999 at its highest value, just in time for the money to be paid to the beneficiary, and it has the added attraction that the increase in its capital value will be exempt from capital gains tax,[73] whereas increases in the capital value of most other investments will be subject to that tax.

(b) If a very small sum is to be held for a fairly short period—say, between five and 10 years—but the beneficiary has adequate income from other sources, National Savings Certificates might be a suitable investment, for although the rate of interest is small, this interest is free of tax[74] and the certificates are also exempt from capital gains tax.[75]

(c) If the beneficiary currently entitled to the income of the trust has a small total income, the trustees might endeavour to invest at least part of the fund in a security which produces a high income, so far as they consider this consistent with their duties to the remainderman. But this will not be *any* security which produces a high income, nor necessarily *any* security which produces a high income and is considered particularly safe. For where a beneficiary's total income is small, he is able to make an income tax repayment claim, but in so far as his income consists of dividends from securities, the repayment claim is limited to the "tax credit" in respect of the dividend. This does not apply, however, where the income is derived from abroad. Accordingly, where the beneficiary can make a repayment claim, the trustees will look for a company which has virtually the whole of its activities in England, so that a full tax credit will be available.

It is in the light of this type of consideration that there becomes apparent the full significance of the requirement for trustees to have regard to the suitability both of the class of investment proposed, and of the particular investment as an investment of that class.

Furthermore, with the exception of investments in the small savings investments listed in Part I, the trustee must, before deciding on an investment, obtain and consider proper written advice as to whether the investment is satisfactory, and here he must take into account the

---

[73] Taxation of Chargeable Gains Act 1992. s.115.
[74] Income and Corporation Taxes Act 1988, s.326.
[75] Taxation of Chargeable Gains Act 1992, s.121.

statutory requirements mentioned above. The operative words are "obtain and consider"; the trustee is not therefore bound to follow the advice. Different considerations apply to a mortgage investment. In this case the advice is not required to extend to the suitability of the loan in question: this is a matter that depends on the valuation required by section 8 of the Trustee Act 1925.[76]

It is also enacted that a trustee retaining any investment which has been made must decide at what intervals the circumstances and particularly the true nature of the investment make it desirable to "obtain and consider" proper written advice as to whether it should be retained, and he must obtain and consider it.[77]

The question now is, what is "proper advice"? It is the advice of a person whom the trustee reasonably believes to be qualified to give it by reason of his financial ability and experience.[78] But these requirements will not apply where one of two or more trustees is himself so qualified: he may well be qualified as a stockbroker or solicitor to give advice and he may properly give it.[79] He is not under a duty to obtain and consider advice from another source. The position is the same where one of the trustees is a trust corporation, such as a bank. If an officer of the corporation gives advice, it will be unnecessary to take further advice.[80]

(9) The fifty-fifty rule

It has already been seen that this rule is not, though of general application, absolute. But, apart from this, provision is made for the new powers to be extended or varied by Order in Council, so the 50:50 rule could conceivably be changed in the future. It is enacted for this purpose that the Treasury may by order direct that the proportion of a trust fund which may be invested in equities shall be increased from one-half to a maximum of 75 per cent.: when such an order is operative trustees who wish to avail themselves of the Act will have to divide it in the proportions prescribed by the order, while trustees who have already made a division must make a further division if they wish to take advantage of the new proportion.[81] As yet no order has been made.

(10) Saving for powers of the court

It is expressly enacted that the extension of investment powers provided for in the Act is not to lessen the court's power to confer wider powers on trustees.[82] This will in particular refer to the Variation of Trusts Act 1958. The interaction between the latter statute and the 1961 Act will be dealt with when the subject of variation of trusts is considered.[83]

---

[76] See *post*, p. 451.
[77] s.6(3)(5).
[78] s.6(4).
[79] s.6(6).
[80] s.6(4)(6).
[81] s.13.
[82] s.15.
[83] See n. 60 and see *post*, p. 541.

(11) Generally

What is the significance of this Act generally? Clearly its most important and controversial feature is the division of the fund into two parts. There is no doubt a case for saying that only a limited and carefully prescribed proportion of the trust fund should be invested in wider-range investments, and the remainder in gilt-edged: at present this proportion is in general on a 50:50 basis. It was thought that the problem of administration in maintaining a division into two parts, or three if special-range property is added, would be a decisive factor in practice, particularly for the smaller private trusts, in deterring the trustees of such trusts from operating the statutory scheme. But despite these difficulties and the complexity of the language of the statute, it seems that many trustees have made use of the Act for old-established trusts. Nevertheless, it would seem that the practice in respect of newly established trusts will remain as it has been for the last 50 years. That is to say, trustees will be given an absolute discretion to invest trust funds as they think fit. There is then no need to rely on the Act or enter into its complicated computations. Admittedly an unrestricted power of investment has its dangers: if the trustees take advantage of it they may well benefit the trust, but they may make an unfortunate investment to the loss of all concerned. But it is likely that the present practice will continue.

IV. Mortgages of Land

(1) General principles

Investment in a mortgage of land will be an authorised investment within the meaning of the Trustee Investments Act 1961 falling within the narrower range requiring advice if made on a mortgage of property in the United Kingdom if it is freehold property or leasehold property where the unexpired term is not less than 60 years.[84] This kind of investment, whether within or outside the statutory limits, may also be expressly authorised by the trust instrument.

But a trustee is not always justified in investing the trust funds on mortgage. He must naturally act in good faith and with reasonable care and impartiality. He should not therefore make this sort of investment simply for the benefit of one of the beneficiaries and certainly not for the benefit of a person who is not even a beneficiary.[85] The rule that a trustee is not necessarily free from responsibility because he invests in an authorised security[86] applies with considerable force to investment on mortgage; and the limitations imposed by both general principles such as these and by statute on the trustee's powers show this clearly.

Certain general propositions have been established by the caselaw. Accordingly a trustee should, in the absence of express authority to do otherwise, invest only in *first legal* mortgages of freehold or leasehold

---

[84] Sched. 1, Pt. II, para. 13.
[85] See *Whitney* v. *Smith* (1869) L.R. 4 Ch. 513 at 521; *Re Walker* (1890) 62 L.T. 449.
[86] See *ante*, p. 430.

land within the limits prescribed. It should be a first mortgage because it is desirable that the mortgage should enjoy priority. He should therefore avoid second mortgages since a first mortgagee may exercise the power of sale in such circumstances as to leave nothing for the second mortgagee.[87] He should obtain a legal interest and, in theory, avoid equitable mortgages because otherwise he might be postponed to a subsequent legal mortgage. In practice, however, the possibility of protecting equitable mortgages[88] under the provisions of the Land Registration Act 1925 and the Land Charges Act 1972 will prevent an equitable mortgage which has been protected in the appropriate way from being postponed to any subsequent mortgage; this would seem to constitute sufficient protection. A trustee should also avoid what is called a contributory mortgage (*i.e.* a joint loan by the trustee and other persons) because in such a case the trustee would not possess complete control.[89] On the other hand, a sub-mortgage, if legal, may be quite proper, for here the mortgagee will mortgage to the trustee and the latter will obtain a legal interest.[90]

However, the Trustee Investments Act 1961 may now have modified the necessity for a first legal mortgage because, having declared that mortgages of freehold property and certain leasehold property are narrower-range investments,[91] it gives "mortgage" the same definition as in the Trustee Act 1925.[92] This definition includes "every estate and interest regarded in equity as merely a security for money,"[93] which will include an equitable mortgage. Lewin suggests that the effect of the Act is to sweep away the old prohibitions on inferior types of mortgage.[94] But it is highly doubtful whether this was the legislative intention and it seems safer for trustees to assume that the old restrictions still apply.

(2) Statutory duties

A trustee should also observe the statutory rules relating to the value of the property.

Various conditions in relation to value which are expressly imposed by the Trustee Act 1925—and which are unaffected by the Act of 1961—should be fulfilled before investment is made in this class of security. It must be emphasised that the rule is that he "should," as a matter of prudence, fulfil these conditions: he is *not bound* to do so.[95] But he would be unwise in ignoring them because they provide cogent

---

[87] *Norris* v. *Wright* (1851) 14 Beav. 291; *Lockhart* v. *Reilly* (1857) 1 De G. & J. 464. The Law Reform Committee (23rd Report, 1982) have recommended that trustees should have power to lend on second mortgage.
[88] *Swaffield* v. *Nelson* [1876] W.N. 255.
[89] *Webb* v. *Jonas* (1888) 39 Ch.D. 660.
[90] *Smethurst* v. *Hastings* (1885) 30 Ch.D. 490.
[91] s.1(1); Sched. 1, Pt. II, para. 13.
[92] s.17(4).
[93] T.A. 1925, s.68(7).
[94] (16th ed.), pp. 370, 371.
[95] *Palmer* v. *Emerson* [1911] 1 Ch. 758.

evidence of the existence of care.[96] The material provisions are found in section 8 of the 1925 Act.

It is here enacted that a trustee lending money on the security of any property will not be chargeable with breach of trust by reason only of the proportion borne by the amount of the loan to the value of the property at the time when the loan was made if it appears to the court that:

(1) In making the loan the trustee was acting upon a report as to the value of the property made by a person whom he reasonably believed to be an able practical surveyor or valuer instructed and employed independently of any owner of the property, whether such surveyor or valuer carries on business in the locality where the property is situated or elsewhere.[97] In interpreting this provision Kekewich J. held in *Re Walker*[98] that the trustee need only believe the surveyor or valuer to be able; but he must in *fact* be employed independently of the owner of the property. The point about employment was doubted by Warrington J. in *Re Solomon*,[99] where he seemed to think that a *belief* of independent employment would be sufficient. But, according to the natural meaning of the words in the section, it seems that Kekewich J. was right. In deciding whether the surveyor or valuer is an able practical man, it would appear that the trustee must still exercise his own judgment: he cannot, for example, trust blindly to the nomination of his solicitor, nor of course to that of the mortgagor's solicitor.[1] He need not, however, necessarily be a local man, nor have specialised local knowledge.[2]

(2) The amount of the loan does not exceed two-thirds of the value of the property as stated in the report.[3] This is the utmost limit, and a trustee ought not to lend more even if the surveyor advises that a greater proportion may be advanced; indeed in many cases, in order to leave a margin for depreciation it will be advisable to lend less. Everything depends on the particular property. If it is liable to deteriorate or is specially subject to fluctuations in value then a prudent trustee will, assuming that the investment is itself a proper one, require a larger margin for protection.[4] The question next arises, what is the position if the trustee lends more than two-thirds? Section 9 provides the answer. It is enacted that if a trustee makes such a loan but the security is otherwise a proper investment—the *amount only* being exceeded—then it will be deemed to be an authorised investment for

---

[96] *Re Stuart* [1897] 2 Ch. 583 at p. 592; *Palmer* v. *Emerson* [1911] 1 Ch. 758 at p. 769. See also *Chapman* v. *Brown* [1902] 1 Ch. 785.
[97] s.8(1)(*a*).
[98] (1890) 62 L.T. 449 at p. 452; and see also *Re Somerset* [1894] 1 Ch. 231 at p. 253, *per* Kekewich J.
[99] [1912] 1 Ch. 261 at p. 281. Compromised on appeal [1913] 1 Ch. 200. See also *Shaw* v. *Cates* [1909] 1 Ch. 389.
[1] *Shaw* v. *Cates* [1909] 1 Ch. 389 at p. 404, *per* Parker J.
[2] There is no such requirement in the Act. However, the trustee should not ignore the importance of local knowledge in arriving at a correct valuation, see *Fry* v. *Tapson* (1884) 28 Ch.D. 268.
[3] s.8(1)(*b*).
[4] See *Shaw* v. *Cates* [1909] 1 Ch. 389 at pp. 398, 399 and also *Palmer* v. *Emerson* [1911] 1 Ch. 758 at pp. 765, 766.

the proper sum and the trustee will only be liable in respect of the excess with interest. Thus in *Shaw* v. *Cates*[5] the trustees had advanced £4,400 on real security. This was held to be a proper investment only for £3,400. The trustees were, therefore, liable only to make good the excess of £1,000 with interest.

(3) The loan is made under the advice of the surveyor or valuer expressed in the report.[6] This means, of course, that he must actually advise the trustee that the investment is a proper one.

(3) Limitations to the statutory provisions
It will be observed that section 8 of the Trustee Act 1925 provides relief from liability "by reason *only of the proportion*[7] borne by the amount of the loan to the value of the property". It also refers to lendings on the security of property "on which he can properly lend". Section 9 refers to a security which is "otherwise proper", the amount only being exceeded. These words would appear clearly to provide protection only in matters of value and will not be of assistance where the nature of the security itself comes into question. The trustee must establish in the first instance the propriety of the investment independently of value.[8] It seems to follow that a trustee would be liable in any case for advancing money on speculative property and particularly on wasting property and his liability would be based on the fact that he should never have lent the money on such a security in any case, not because (even if such is the case) he has lent too much. Yet curiously enough, Warrington J. held in *Re Solomon*[9]—and Parker J.'s general approach in *Shaw* v. *Cates*[10] could also be considered as being to the same effect—that if the property is of a speculative character and the trustee acts on the valuer's report which has been made in the manner prescribed he will be entitled to protection. However, this approach, even though perhaps commendable as a matter of policy in enabling a trustee to rely on an expert's advice, seems contrary to principle.

(4) Purchase of land
If the trustees are only entitled to invest in trustee securities they are not entitled to *purchase* land. Moreover, even if the purchase of property is expressly authorised it will not necessarily authorise purchase for *residence* only. Thus in *Re Power*[11] the clause was to the effect that "all moneys required to be invested under this my will may be *invested* by the trustee in any manner in which he may in his absolute discretion think fit . . . including the purchase of freehold property in England and Wales." Jenkins J. held that the trustees were not entitled to

---

[5] *Ibid.*
[6] s.8(1)(c).
[7] Emphasis added.
[8] *Re Walker* (1890) 62 L.T. 449, *per* Kekewich J.; *Blyth* v. *Fladgate* [1891] 1 Ch. 337, *per* Stirling J.
[9] [1912] 1 Ch. 261.
[10] [1909] 1 Ch. 389.
[11] [1947] Ch. 572 distinguishing *Re Wragg* [1919] 2 Ch. 58 (where the property would yield income). The Law Reform Committee (23rd Report, 1982) has recommended that the rule should be reversed by statute.

purchase a dwelling-house with vacant possession for the occupation of a beneficiary: "investment" entails an income yield and the purchase of a home for occupation does not yield income.

Trustees can only purchase land in two cases:

(i) if they have an express power for this purpose under the trust instrument. A precedent investment clause commonly used in practice enables this to be done. There is also a model clause in use today which is designed to circumvent the decision in *Re Power*.[12] It gives an absolute discretion to the trustees to invest as they think fit and also empowers them to purchase property for the residence of a beneficiary. But of course the same solution can be achieved by any provision which expressly confers the power to purchase for residence; or

(ii) if they can rely on a special statutory power appropriate to the circumstances of the case. Such a statutory power will arise, first, under section 73(1)(xi) of the Settled Land Act 1925, under which capital money can be used to purchase land. Secondly, under section 28(1) of the Law of Property Act 1925 trustees for sale of land can purchase land with the proceeds of sale provided that they have not ceased to be trustees for sale within the statutory definition contained in section 205; they will have ceased to be such if they have parted with all the land held on trust for sale.[13]

It has been seen[14] that in ordinary circumstances trustees have no statutory power to mortgage trust assets in order to purchase further assets,[15] although an express power to that effect can be validly contained in the trust instrument.

V. INVESTMENT CLAUSES

The general rule is conventionally stated to be that clauses in trust deeds enlarging the trustee's powers of investment beyond the scope authorised by law are construed strictly.[16] To what extent, however, this rule is in practice followed today is debatable. Indeed it is arguable that nowadays investment clauses should be given a liberal interpretation. But this is, of course, a generalisation which cannot dogmatically be said to be either right or wrong. A number of illustrations from the case law on each side of the line—one from the late nineteenth century and the others from the present day—will be considered. A well-known case is *Bethell* v. *Abraham*,[17] where trustees were empowered to "continue or change securities from time to time as to the majority shall seem meet." This clause was strictly construed by Jessel M.R., who held that the words related merely to determining the time at which a change of

---

[12] *Ibid.*

[13] See *Re Wakeman* [1945] Ch. 177; *Re Wellsted's Will Trust* [1949] Ch. 296.

[14] *Ante*, p. 396.

[15] *Re Suenson-Taylor's Settlement, Moores* v. *Moores* [1974] 3 All E.R. 397.

[16] *Re Peczenic's Settlement Trusts* [1964] 1 W.L.R. 720 at p. 722, *per* Buckley J.

[17] (1873) L.R. 17 Eq. 24.

securities was to be made: it did not authorise a substantive change of investment outside the authorised range. This case may be compared with the more recent decision in *Re Harari's Settlement Trusts*[18] where the clause empowered the trustees to invest in such investments outside the authorised range. A similarly liberal result was arrived at in *Re Peczenic's Settlement*[19] by Buckley J.—with the exception only of investments on personal security which were clearly excluded by the trust instrument. These illustrations may be thought to manifest a difference in attitude to investment clauses in the modern law. But the true position would seem to be that it is entirely a question of construction of the particular investment clause before the court and although previous cases may be helpful they will not necessarily be decisive.[20]

Use of one of the well-known model clauses which clearly give to the trustees unrestricted investment powers (including a power to purchase property for residence purposes,[21] and also invest on personal credit[22]) will, of course, avoid any difficulties of construction. The use of such a power is often advised today. At the same time it will be appreciated that even if the trustees have this power they must still act with reasonable care and impartiality in deciding on their investments.[23]

VI. ANCILLARY STATUTORY POWERS

(1) Redeemable stock

The trustees are entitled to invest in authorised securities[24] notwithstanding the fact that they are redeemable and even if the price paid exceeds the redemption value[25]; and the trustees are entitled to retain them until redemption.[26]

(2) Bearer securities

A trustee is entitled, unless expressly prohibited by the instrument creating the trust, to retain or invest in securities payable to bearer which, if they had not been made thus payable, would have been authorised investments.[27] But it is required that until sold the bearer securities should be deposited by the trustee with a bank for safe

---

[18] [1949] 1 All E.R. 430.

[19] [1964] 1 W.L.R. 720.

[20] See also, in addition to the cases cited in text, *Re Maryon-Wilson's Estate* [1912] 1 Ch. 55; *Re McEacharn's Settlement Trusts* [1939] Ch. 858; *Re Hart's Will Trusts* [1943] 2 All E.R. 557; *Re Douglas' Will Trusts* [1959] 1 W.L.R. 744 (affirmed on another point [1959] 1 W.L.R. 1212); *Re Kob's Will Trusts* [1962] Ch. 531 (interpretation of various investment clauses).

[21] See *Re Power* [1947] Ch. 572 and *ante*, p. 454.

[22] Only an express power to lend on personal security will enable such a loan to be made: see *Khoo Tek Kong* v. *Ching Joo Tuan Neoh* [1934] A.C. 529 (P.C.); *Re Peczenic* [1964] 1 W.L.R. 720; *cf. Re Laing's Settlement* [1899] 1 Ch. 593. See also *Tucker* v. *Tucker* [1894] 1 Ch. 724.

[23] See *ante*, p. 430.

[24] *i.e.* under the T.I.A. 1961.

[25] T.A. 1925, s.2(1).

[26] *Ibid.* s.2(2).

[27] *Ibid.* s.7(1).

custody and collection of income.[28] If this deposit is made accordingly the trustee will not be liable for any loss incurred,[29] and, moreover, it is provided that any sum paid in respect of the deposit itself or collection of income is to be paid out of the income of the trust property.[30]

(3) Lending on mortgage

A supplementary power is conferred on trustees properly lending money on the security of trust property[31] to contract that the money will not be called in for a fixed period not exceeding seven years provided that interest is paid within a specified time not exceeding 30 days after it becomes due and provided also that the mortgagor is not in breach of any covenant contained in the mortgage for the maintenance and protection of the trust property.[32]

(4) Sale of land

If land is sold by trustees in fee simple or for a term having at least 500 years to run they may contract that the payment of any part of the purchase-money not exceeding two-thirds be left on mortgage.[33] But it is essential that the mortgage contains a covenant by the mortgagor to keep any buildings insured to their full value.[34] So far as this situation is concerned, it is not necessary for the trustees to obtain a report as to value, and they are not liable for loss by reason of the security being insufficient.[35]

(5) Capital reorganisations and bonus issues

(i) Where any securities[36] of a company are subject to a trust, the trustees may concur in any scheme or arrangement (a) for the reconstruction of the company; (b) for the sale of all or any part of its property or undertaking to another company; (c) for the acquisition of the securities of the company, or of control thereof, by another company[37]; (d) for its amalgamation with another company; (e) for the release, modification or variation of any rights, privileges or liabilities attached to the securities. They are also entitled to take up any new securities in lieu of the old securities, and furthermore are not responsible for any loss if they act in good faith. They can also retain any new securities for any period for which they could properly have retained the original ones.[38]

(ii) If any conditional or preferential right to subscribe for any securities in a company is offered to trustees in respect of their holdings in the company, they may (a) exercise the right and apply capital money

---

[28] *Ibid.* s.7(1), proviso.
[29] *Ibid.* s.7(2).
[30] *Ibid.*
[31] *Ante,* p. 451.
[32] T.A. 1925, s.10(1).
[33] *Ibid.* s.10(2).
[34] *Ibid.*
[35] *Ibid.*
[36] This term includes shares and stock: *ibid.* s.68(13).
[37] Para. (*c*) was added by T.I.A. 1961, s.9(1).
[38] s.10(3); T.I.A. 1961, s.9(1).

subject to the trust in payment of the consideration or (b) renounce such
right or (c) sell it for the best consideration that can be reasonably
obtained to any person including a beneficiary. They are not liable for
any loss, provided they act in good faith. If the right is sold the consideration will be capital money.[39] The power to subscribe for securities
includes a power to retain them as if they were the original holding, but
subject to any conditions which attach to that holding.[40]

(6) Consents.　The supplementary powers of investment considered
under heads (3), (4) and (5) above are exercisable subject to the consent
of any person whose consent to a change of investment is required by
law or by the trust instrument.[41]

(7) Deposits and payment of calls
Pending the negotiation and preparation of any mortgage or during any
time when an investment is being sought, the trustees may deposit the
trust money in a bank. Any interest payable is applicable as income.[42]
They may also apply capital money subject to a trust in payment of the
calls on any shares subject to the same trust.[43]

VII. Continuing Supervision

In addition to making investments, trustees are under a duty to keep
them under review to the same extent as would a prudent businessman
when dealing with his own affairs. In the case of holdings in large
quoted public companies, a periodic review will usually be sufficient.
However, where the trustees have a majority holding or some other
special position of influence, they will be expected to take advantage of
it. If a reasonably prudent businessman would require information
about the company's affairs which is not generally available, trustees
will need to obtain it. If a reasonably prudent businessman would insist
on board representation, or board control, trustees will themselves need
to insist on it.

In *Bartlett* v. *Barclays Bank Trust Co. Ltd. (No. 1)*,[44] a person incorporated a company to manage his properties. He then settled almost the
whole of the shares in the company upon trust for his wife and issue.
Initially the board included members of the settlor's family, but that
gradually changed. The trustees, however, while sending a representative to statutory meetings of the company, did not seek representation
on the board. The company purchased a property opposite the Old
Bailey, at a price well in excess of its investment value, in the hope that
it would obtain permission for development. It did not succeed in
doing so and later disposed of the property at a loss. Brightman J. held

---

[39] T.A. 1925, s.10(4).
[40] T.I.A. 1961, s.9(2).
[41] T.A. 1925, s.10(5).
[42] s.11(1).
[43] s.11(2).
[44] [1980] Ch. 515.

that the trustees were in breach of their duty to obtain the information which, as majority shareholders, was open to them.

Information is not, however, an end in itself,[45] and must be used to protect the interest of the beneficiaries. If necessary, a trustee must intervene to remove directors[46] and procure the appointment of his own nominees.[47]

Some professional trustees and trust corporations are reluctant to assume this responsibility, and look for a provision in a trust instrument which negatives what would otherwise be their duty to interfere in the management of companies in which they are shareholders.

VIII. INSIDER DEALING

A particular problem arises with regard to "insider dealing". Part V of the Criminal Justice Act 1993, which came into force on March 1, 1994, repealing the previous legislation—the Insider Dealing Act 1985, imposes wide-ranging prohibitions on insider dealing. Section 52 provides that a person will be guilty of insider dealing in three situations: first, if he deals in securities about which he has unpublished price-sensitive information (a person is defined as dealing in securities if he acquires or disposes of them or procures, directly or indirectly, an acquisition or disposal of the securities by an agent, nominee or other person acting at his direction); secondly, if he encourages another person to deal with the securities, knowing or having reasonable cause to believe that the acquisition or disposal would take place on a regulated market; and, thirdly, if he discloses the information, other than in the course of his employment or profession, to another person. If a person who is a director or other officer of a company and thereby obtains unpublished price-sensitive information about the company, is also a trustee of a trust which holds shares in the company he is immediately placed in a position of conflict of duty. On the one hand, he must not contravene the Criminal Justice Act 1993, which creates criminal offences. On the other hand, he must do the best he can for the trust.

The previous legislation contained an express provision dealing with the position of such a trustee. Section 7 of the Insider Dealing Act 1985 provided that a trustee who, in that capacity, dealt in securities was presumed to have done so otherwise than with a view to financial advantage (and so not to have committed an offence) if he acted on the advice of a person who appeared to him to be an appropriate person from whom to seek such advice and did not appear to him to be prohibited by the legislation from dealing in the securities. However, there was no corresponding presumption in relation to the disclosure of the information. The legislation thus appeared to suggest that, where a trustee had obtained inside information, he should obtain advice from

---

[45] See, *e.g. Re Lucking's Will Trust* [1968] 1 W.L.R. 866; *ante*, p. 270 where trustees had information but did not use it.
[46] [1980] Ch. 515 at p. 530.
[47] Criminal Justice Act 1993, Part V.

the trust's investment advisers about that security, without arousing their suspicions and without disclosing his own information, and that subsequently to act, or to join with his co-trustess in acting, on that advice would not amount to an offence. There is no provision in the Criminal Justice Act 1993 expressly dealing with the position of trustees. However, Section 53 provides that a person will not be guilty of either dealing or encouraging dealing if he shows that he would have done what he did even if he had not had the information (as in the previous legislation, the defence does not apply to disclosure). The Economic Secretary to the Treasury[48] explained in Standing Committee that this defence "allows a trustee who possesses insider information to deal in price-affected securities on the basis of independent investment advice"[49]. This suggests that the protection expressly given to trustees by the Insider Dealing Act 1985 has survived, although not explicitly, in the Criminal Justice Act 1993. While the advice to a trustee in this difficult position must therefore remain the same, the fact is that in many cases where a trustee is known to be in a position in which he is likely to be able to obtain inside information, it will be impossible for him to seek advice from the trust's investment advisers without arousing suspicion by so doing. In such circumstances, the only prudent course may well be for him to resign his trusteeship.

---

[48] Mr. Anthony Nelson.
[49] *Hansard*, June 10, 1993, Standing Committee B, col. 175.

CHAPTER 16

APPORTIONMENTS

It has already been seen[1] that a fundamental rule is that a trustee must not allow a conflict of interest to arise between his own personal position and his duties to the beneficiaries. The sister rule is that, where there is a conflict between the interests of different beneficiaries, a trustee must hold a balance between them. This is not so much because this is what the settlor actually did intend, for he may well never have given the matter any thought, but rather because equity presumes that this is what the settlor would have intended had he directed his mind to the point. It is therefore not necessary to find any actual evidence of intention on the part of the settlor for this principle to apply, yet on the other hand he is able to provide expressly or by implication that the principle shall not operate. Avoidance of a conflict of interest is of particular importance in relation to investments: it is also this principle which underlies the rules governing apportionments.[2] These formal rules apply as between tenants for life and remaindermen. However, other conflicts of interest can arise. In *Lloyds Bank* v. *Duker*,[3] the conflict of interest was between majority and minority beneficiaries. The testator who owned 999 of the 1,000 shares of a private company, left 46/80ths of the 999 shares to his wife. It was held that the 574 shares which represented this proportion could not be transferred to her because such a majority holding would give her the control of the company and, in relation to the remaining minority shares, would be worth more than her due proportion. Consequently, the trustees were directed to sell all 999 shares and distribute the proceeds of sale in the appropriate proportions.

I. APPORTIONMENTS BETWEEN CAPITAL AND INCOME

(1) The principle
Let us suppose that Basil settles property upon trust for Clare for life, with remainder to Priscilla absolutely. Let us also suppose that the trust property consists of

---

[1] *Ante*, p. 221.
[2] The Law Reform Committee (23rd Report, 1982) has recommended that the rules of conversion and apportionment referred to in the first part of this chapter should be replaced by a new statutory duty to hold a fair balance between beneficiaries with different interests.
[3] [1987] 1 W.L.R. 1324.

(a) £5,000 3½ per cent. War Stock;
(b) the cow Buttercup;
(c) the right under his grandfather's will to receive £15,000 on the death of his father, Bert. (This right is called a reversionary interest.)

If these assets are retained in their present form the holding of War Stock will produce a steady income, and a capital sum will be available to Priscilla on the death of Clare. Buttercup, a fine milk-yielding cow, may produce at first a high income, but as she grows old and her milk production decreases, she will become less and less valuable. She may well die before Clare, and if this is the case, Clare will have derived the whole of the benefit from her, and Priscilla will have had none. The opposite is the case with the reversionary interest. Until Bert dies, income is paid to neither Clare nor Priscilla, and if Clare dies before Bert, she will have received no benefit at all from this asset. Equity presumes that it was not Basil's intention that the beneficiaries should be treated so haphazardly and their fortunes left so much to chance. The basic solution is, therefore, that Buttercup and the reversionary interest should be sold and the proceeds invested in authorised securities, so that the income may be paid to Clare, and a capital sum preserved intact for Priscilla. The rules which follow prescribe how this is to be done. However, once any necessary apportionment between capital and income according to these rules has been made, the trustees are apparently entitled to make investments which produce either high or low income depending on the relative wealth of the tenant for life and the remainderman.[4]

This basic solution is not, however, always easy to apply and in working it out there are three questions to consider:

1. Is there a duty to convert a particular asset into an authorised investment?
2. If so, does the income have to be apportioned between the date when the duty arises, and the date when the conversion actually takes place?
3. If so, how is such apportionment calculated?

These questions are progressive so that if the answer to any one is "no," there is no need to consider the questions which follow it.

(2) Is there a duty to convert?

The duty to convert the trust property into authorised investments may arise

(a) if the trust instrument so directs; or
(b) by operation of the rule in *Howe* v. *Lord Dartmouth*.[5]

The most frequent case of an express direction to convert occurs when

---

[4] *Nestlé* v. *National Westminster Bank* [1993] 1 W.L.R. 1260.
[5] (1802) 7 Ves. 137.

there is a trust for sale, but any direction to convert is for this purpose equally adequate. The rule in *Howe* v. *Lord Dartmouth*[6] directs conversion of an asset to take place where there is no express direction in the trust instrument, but only where all the following conditions are satisfied:

(a) the trust was created by will;
(b) there are at least two beneficiaries, and they are entitled in succession;
(c) the property consists of residuary personalty;
(d) the asset is wasting, reversionary or of an unauthorised character; and
(e) there is no contrary intention in the will.

The rule does not apply to a settlement *inter vivos* for here it is said that the terms of such settlements must be observed strictly, as the settlor knew exactly the state of the assets when the settlement was created.[7]

The only one of the foregoing conditions which is likely to cause difficulty is to decide whether there is a contrary intention. In *Re Sewell's Estate*[8] the trustees were give a *discretion* as to what part of the testator's estate should be converted. This was held to have excluded the rule in *Howe* v. *Lord Dartmouth* because a discretion to convert was inconsistent with a *duty* to convert which *Howe* v *Lord Dartmouth* would impose. However, in order to exclude the rule, the power must be consciously exercised.[9] In *Alcock* v. *Sloper*[10] property was left upon trust for a life tenant and after his death upon trust for it to be sold and the proceeds divided between various named beneficiaries. Here too it was held that the rule in *Howe* v. *Lord Dartmouth* was excluded, because the express duty to convert on the death of the life tenant was inconsistent with an implied duty to convert on the death of the testator, which would be implied under *Howe* v. *Lord Dartmouth*.

The decision in *Alcock* v. *Sloper*[11] must be contrasted with that in *Re Evans*,[12] where property was given to trustees upon trust for a life tenant and after her death upon trust to be divided into three equal shares and distributed to three other members of the family. It was held here that *Howe* v. *Lord Dartmouth* did apply, because the division on the death of the life tenant could be of property in either its converted or unconverted form so that the directions in the will were not inconsistent with a duty to convert implied by *Howe* v. *Lord Dartmouth*. Where the settlor shows an intention that the property should be enjoyed *in specie* this clearly negatives the rule.[13] Bennett J. took this a stage further

---

[6] For an up-to-date account of the rule, see L.A. Sheridan, "*Howe* v. *Lord Dartmouth* Re-examined" (1952) 16 Conv. (N.S.) 349.
[7] *Per* Cozens-Hardy J. in *Re Van Straubenzee* [1901] 2 Ch. 779; and see *Milford* v. *Peile* (1854) 2 W.N. 181; *Hope* v. *Hope* (1855) 1 Jur. (N.S.) 770.
[8] (1870) L.R. 11 Eq. 80; see also *Simpson* v. *Earles* (1847) 11 Jur. 921.
[9] *Re Guinness* [1966] 1 W.L.R. 1355.
[10] (1833) 2 My. & K. 699; *Daniel* v. *Warren* (1843) 2 Y. & Coll. C.C. 290.
[11] (1833) 2 My. & K. 699.
[12] [1920] 2 Ch. 309.
[13] *Macdonald* v. *Irvine* (1878) 8 Ch.D. 101.

in *Re Fisher*[14] by saying that, where there is a trust for conversion with a power to postpone, the settlor thereby shows that he intends that the property may be enjoyed *in specie*, and that this also is inconsistent with a duty to convert which would be imposed by *Howe* v. *Lord Dartmouth*. However, in the later case of *Re Berry*,[15] Pennycuick J. refused to follow *Re Fisher*. Although the logical basis of *Re Fisher* is clear, Pennycuick J. commented that that decision was "contrary to the whole current of authority". It was an attempt to extend the scope of the exceptions from *Howe* v. *Lord Dartmouth* too far.

The cases turn on fine differences in wording and, while it may be very difficult to say on any particular set of facts whether *Howe* v. *Lord Dartmouth* is excluded, the rule itself is clear: has the testator made any provision which is expressly or impliedly inconsistent with a duty to convert at the date of death? If he has not done so and the other conditions listed above are fulfilled, *Howe* v. *Lord Dartmouth* will apply.

(3) Whether there is a need to apportion income

If there is a duty to convert, it is explained below that conversion should take place either at the date of death, or as at one year from the date of death.[16] It will be obvious that in the former case it is impossible to effect actual conversion at that date and in the latter case actual conversion will often be delayed. The question therefore arises whether, in the event of conversion being delayed, the tenant for life is entitled to the actual income produced by the asset until it is converted or whether he is entitled only to an apportioned part of it. The primary rule is that if the testator has provided, expressly or by implication, that the tenant for life is to enjoy the actual income which the property produces, then that intention prevails. Where it cannot be shown that the testator expressed any such intention, then the following rules apply.

First, where the trustees improperly postpone conversion, an apportionment will be ordered. Thus in *Wentworth* v. *Wentworth*[17] the trustees had a power to postpone conversion until a certain date. The trustees improperly postponed conversion beyond that date and the Privy Council held that apportionment should be made as from that date.

Secondly, where the property is realty, the tenant for life is entitled to the actual income which the property produces. It will be remembered that *Howe* v. *Lord Dartmouth* never operates to impose a duty to convert realty so that, if such a duty exists in respect of realty, it must be as a result of an express trust for conversion.

Thirdly, in the case of personalty, the tenant for life is entitled only to an apportioned part of the income, unless there is an intention that he shall enjoy the asset *in specie*.[18] Thus the presumption is in favour of the

---

[14] [1943] Ch. 377.
[15] [1962] Ch. 97.
[16] *Post*.
[17] [1900] A.C. 163.
[18] *Re Chaytor* [1965] 1 Ch. 233. Where there is a trust for conversion with a power to postpone, the beneficiary will only receive an apportioned part of the income; *Re Berry* [1962] Ch. 97.

enjoyment of actual income in the case of realty and of only an apportioned part of the income in the case of personalty.

(4) How is the apportionment calculated?

If there is a duty to convert and if, because the property has not been converted by the due date, the income has to be apportioned until conversion takes place, how is such apportionment calculated? Where the asset concerned is a reversionary interest, the rule in *Re Earl of Chesterfield's Trusts*[19] applies. This is dealt with below. As regards other property which has to be converted, it is necessary first to ascertain the valuation date. At common law there was a presumption that the executor's functions in administering the estate ought to be completed within one year from the death of the testator. From this the rule evolved that where there is no power to postpone sale, conversion ought to be effected within one year from the date of death and in this case, in order to calculate apportionments of income, the asset is valued as at one year from the date of death.[20] If, however, there is a power to postpone, this negatives the intention that the property should be valued as at one year from the date of death, and, because a better date could not be thought of, in this case the property is valued at the date of death.[21]

Thus

(a) if there is no power to postpone, the valuation date is one year from the date of death, but

(b) if there is a power to postpone, the valuation date is the date of death.

Whichever is the valuation date, the tenant for life is entitled to interest on the value of the asset as at the valuation date from the date of death until the date of actual conversion. Traditionally, the rate of interest applied has been 4 per cent.[22] but, as this is unrealistically low, it may be that the court would now adopt the rate which is equivalent to the court's short-term investment account.[23] If the actual income is larger, the balance is added to capital. If the actual income is smaller than the appropriate rate, the tenant for life receives that actual income, and is entitled to have it made up from future surpluses of income, or, if there are none, from capital when the asset is sold. The deficiency cannot be made good from previous surpluses of income, because these have already been notionally added to capital.

An example may assist. Suppose that copyrights of a book are left upon trust for Angela for life, with remainder to Mary. Suppose also

---

[19] (1883) 24 Ch.D. 643.

[20] *Re Eaton, Daines* v. *Eaton* (1894) 70 L.T. 761.

[21] *Re Owen, Slater* v. *Owen* [1912] 1 Ch. 519; *Re Parry, Brown* v. *Parry* [1947] Ch. 23.

[22] The actual rate of interest is in the discretion of the court, but 4 per cent. is usually taken as the appropriate figure: see *Re Lucas* [1947] Ch. 558: *Re Parry* [1947] Ch. 23; *Re Berry* [1962] Ch. 97.

[23] See *Bartlett* v. *Barclays Bank Trust Co. Ltd.* (*No. 2*) [1980] Ch. 515 and *Jaffray* v. *Marshall* [1993] 1 W.L.R. 1285; *post*, p. 586. See also *Re Fawcett* [1940] Ch. 402; *Re Parry* [1947] Ch. 23.

that the copyrights are worth £1,200 at the date of death and £1,000 one year from the date of death. Suppose further that the copyrights are not sold until three years after the date of death, and that for these three years the royalties actually received are

Year 1 £70
Year 2 £32
Year 3 £48

It is necessary first to ascertain the valuation date. Where there is a power to postpone, this will be the date of death. At this date the copyrights are worth £1,200, so that, if the appropriate rate of interest is 4 per cent., Angela is entitled to 4 per cent. × £1,200 = £48 a year. In year 1 she will receive £48, the balance of £22 being added to capital. In year 2 she will receive £32, with the right to make good the deficiency of £16 in the future. In year 3 she will receive £48, and will be entitled to a further £16 from the sale of the copyrights to make good the deficiency in year 2. If, however, there is no power to postpone, the valuation date is one year from the date of death. Angela is therefore entitled to receive 4 per cent. × £1,000 = £40 p.a. In year 1 she will receive £40, with £30 being added to capital. In year 2 she will receive £32. In year 3 she will receive £40, plus £8 to make good the shortfall in year 2.

At this point it is again stressed that the questions posed at the beginning of this discussion—is there a duty to convert; if so, does the income have to be apportioned; if so, how is such apportionment calculated—are progressive. Therefore it is only if there is a duty to convert that it is necessary to consider whether the income has to be apportioned, and it is only if there is a duty to convert and if the income does have to be apportioned that it is necessary to make the type of calculation just considered.

(5) Re Earl of Chesterfield's Trusts[24]

A special method is necessary for calculating apportionment of reversionary interests, because these do not actually produce any income until they fall into possession. At the outset it may be noted that reversionary interests are saleable. Thus, going back to the example on pages 461–462 one of the assets which Basil left upon Clare for life, with remainder to Priscilla, was the right to receive £15,000 on the death of his father, Bert. At Basil's death the trustees could have sold that reversionary interest. The price which they would obtain would be largely governed by Bert's age at the date of Basil's death, but whatever they would have received could have been invested in authorised securities, the income paid to Clare for life, and the capital held for Priscilla. But it is usually economically better not to sell, but to retain the reversionary interest until it falls into possession. If this is done, before the money that is eventually received is invested, it is clearly equitable to pay part of the amount received to Clare as compensation for the fact that she has had no income from the asset since the trust came into operation. The rule in *Re Earl of Chesterfield's Trusts* provides that,

---

[24] (1883) 24 Ch.D. 643.

where a reversionary interest which ought to be converted is retained until it falls into possession, part of it is to be treated as arrears of income and paid to the tenant for life and only the balance is to be regarded as capital.

The rule itself says that the proportion of the amount actually received which is to be regarded as capital is that which if invested at 4 per cent. compound interest with yearly rests would, after allowing for the deduction of income tax at the basic rate for the time being in force, have produced the sum actually received. It remains to be decided whether 4 per cent. is still the appropriate rate of interest to be applied.[25] "Yearly rests" are the intervals at which the interest is compounded.[26]

In this example, suppose that Bert lived for three-and-a-quarter years after the trust came into operation and, assuming that the basic rate of tax throughout that period was 25 per cent. the trustees would find that £13,625.22 invested when the trust came into operation at 4 per cent. compound interest with yearly rests would, after allowing for the deduction of tax at 25 per cent. have produced £15,000 at the date when this sum was actually received.[27] The £13,625.22 would therefore be

---

[25] See *supra*.

[26] The calculation can be complicated, but, for those who do not have super mathematical skills, the most straightforward method of making the calculation will be to follow these steps:

1. Determine the gross rate of interest to be applied. Traditionally this has been 4 per cent. but, as has been noted, a higher rate may be appropriate.

2. Deduct the basic rate of income tax, to give a net rate of interest.

3. Calculate the amount which £100 would produce if invested for the period between the date of death and the date when the reversionary interest falls in at the net rate of interest compounded annually.

4. Multiply the amount received when the reversionary interest falls in by the following fraction.

$$\frac{£100}{\text{the sum calculated by 3}}$$

5. The product is the capital element.

6. The balance is the income element.

[27] Following the steps outlined in note 23, the calculation is:

1. Gross rate: taken as 4 per cent.

2. Basic rate of income tax: 25 per cent. The net rate is, therefore,

$$4 \text{ per cent.} \times \frac{75}{100} = 3 \text{ per cent.}$$

3. The compounded amount £110.09 is calculated as follows:

Period	Amount on which calculated	Rate	Interest for period	Total at end of period
Year 1	£100.00	3%	£3.00	£103.00
Year 2	£103.00	3%	£3.09	£106.09
Year 3	£106.09	3%	£3.18	£109.27
Last 3 months	£109.27	3%	£0.82	£110.09

4. The capital element of the amount received, £15,000 is:

$$£15,000 \times \frac{100}{110.09} = £13,625.22 = 5$$

6. The income element is (£15,000 − £13,625.22) = £1,374.78

invested by the trustees as capital, and the remaining £1,374.78 would
be paid to Clare as income for the preceding three-and-a-quarter years.

The same rule applies to other property which does not produce any
income. Thus it applied in *Re Duke of Cleveland's Equity*[28] to a debt
which bore no interest and was not receivable immediately. And in *Re
Chance*[29] compensation for the refusal of planning permission under
Part I of the Town and Country Planning Act 1954[30] was held to be
apportionable.

(6) Leaseholds

In view of the decision in *Re Brooker*[31] it is necessary to give special consideration to apportionments involving leaseholds. Before 1926, a
residuary gift of leaseholds was treated in the same way as any other
gift of residuary personalty. However, in *Re Trollope*[32] Tomlin J. said
that the effect of *Re Brooker* was that "so far as leaseholders are
concerned, the rule of *Howe* v. *Lord Dartmouth* is gone".[33]

Section 28(2) of the Law of Property Act 1925 provides that, where
"land" is held upon trust for sale, then, subject to any contrary direction
in the trust instrument, the net rents and profits of the land until sale are
to be paid in the same manner as if they were income from authorised
investments made with the proceeds of sale of the land. Pending conversion of land, therefore, a tenant for life is entitled to the actual rents
and profits so received. In *Re Brooker* there was an express trust for conversion of leaseholds and it was held that as the definition in the Law of
Property Act of land included land of any tenure, the tenant for life was
entitled by virtue of section 28(2) to the actual income from leasehold
property as if it were the actual income from an authorised investment.

In the light of this decision, in general terms it seems desirable that
the position should be the same where the duty to convert arises by
virtue of the rule in *Howe* v. *Lord Dartmouth* and not, as in *Re Brooker*,
where there was an express direction to convert. As has been shown,

---

[28] [1895] 2 Ch. 542.
[29] [1962] Ch. 593.
[30] The Town and Country Planning Act 1947 provided, in general terms, that an owner of
land could not carry out any building or other works on his land without obtaining the
permission of the local authority, and without paying a "development charge". The
value of land was often less after the passing of this Act than before it, and in an effort to
give to the landowner compensation, it was proposed that a £300 million fund would be
established, on which landowners could make a claim for the depreciation in the value
of their land. The fund was, in fact, never set up and the system was changed under the
Town and Country Planning Act 1954, whereby the amount of the landowner's claim,
plus one-seventh of it for interest (less payments for certain events made before the
1954 Act came into force), formed what is known as an "unexpended balance of
established development value." Where such a balance exists, in certain cases
compensation is payable up to the amount of that balance where an application for
planning permission is refused. This was the situation in *Re Chance*. Part of the interest
of the decision lies in the fact that an unexpended balance of established development
value, and so of money paid under the system, represents interest and the amount of
that interest could be determined. Wilberforce J. however, took the whole amount of the
compensation received, and apportioned that.
[31] [1926] W.N. 93.
[32] [1927] 1 Ch. 596.
[33] [1927] 1 Ch. 596 at 601.

the rules previously discussed in this chapter equate the position when the duty to convert arises expressly with that where it is implied by *Howe* v. *Lord Dartmouth* and *Re Brooker* has been followed in the case of a trust for sale imposed by statute.[34]

Nevertheless, it has been suggested[35] that where the duty to convert leaseholds arises only by virtue of *Howe* v. *Lord Dartmouth* the pre-1926 position still applies. The basis of this suggestion is that section 28 of the Law of Property Act refers to a "disposition on trust for sale" and that this does not apply where the duty to convert is only implied by *Howe* v. *Lord Dartmouth*, for then there is not a gift of property on trust for sale, but a gift of property upon which a trust for sale is imposed by operation of law. Further, it is said, *Howe* v. *Lord Dartmouth* only applies where there is no express duty to convert and as there was an express duty in *Re Brooker*, *Howe* v. *Lord Dartmouth* was, strictly, irrelevant to *Re Brooker*.

Despite these objections, however, *Re Brooker* has been generally accepted as establishing that in the case of leaseholds, the tenant for life is entitled to the actual income however the duty to convert arises, and it is now very doubtful whether this will be altered. It would surely be regrettable if it were.

Leaseholds with over 60 years to run are authorised investments,[36] and so cannot be subject to *Howe* v. *Lord Dartmouth*.[37]

II. OTHER APPORTIONMENTS

(1) The rule in Allhusen v. Whittell[38]

There will always be an interval of time between the date of death and the date when an asset is realised. Where a person creates a trust by will in favour of persons in succession, and there are debts and liabilities to be paid, it would appear that the tenant for life will gain increasingly as that delay increases. Suppose, for example, that the gross assets of an estate amount to £20,000 and that debts amount to £5,000 and suppose that the estate is held upon trust for persons in succession. If the debts are paid forthwith, the tenant for life will have the income from the remaining £15,000. If, however, the debts are not paid for a year, the tenant for life will receive the income for that year of £20,000. The essence of the rule of apportionment laid down in *Allhusen* v. *Whittell* is to charge the tenant for life with interest on the amount subsequently used for the payment of debts so that, broadly, the tenant for life is placed in the same position as if the debts had been paid on death.

In its modern form[39] the rule requires a calculation of the average

---

[34] *Re Berton* [1939] Ch. 200.
[35] Bailey (1930–32) 4 C.L.J. 357.
[36] Settled Land Act 1925, s.73; Law of Property Act 1925, s.28. By contrast, sometimes houses held on a shorter lease may be a burden rather than an asset, for example, where the cost of repairs is high, and the rent obtainable is controlled. In these cases, the court may sanction a payment of capital to the lessor to induce him to accept a surrender of the lease: *Re Shee* [1934] Ch. 345. See also Trustee Investments Act 1961.
[37] *Re Gough* [1957] Ch. 323.
[38] (1867) L.R. 4 Eq. 295.
[39] *Re McEwen* [1913] 2 Ch. 704; Re Wills [1915] 1 Ch. 769; *Corbett* v. *C.I.R.* [1938] 1 K.B. 567.

income of the estate from the date of death to the date of payment, taken net after deduction of income tax at the basic rate.[40] The tenant for life is charged with interest at that rate, so that the debt once paid is regarded as being paid partly from income and partly from capital.

A simple example will show the operation of the rule. Suppose that a debt of £500 is paid one year from the date of death; that the average income of the estate taken throughout that period is £4 per cent.; and that the basic rate of income tax during that year is 25 per cent. The calculation is therefore:

Take a basic unit of		£100.00
Add		
Average income for one year at £4 per cent	£4.00	
Less tax	£1.00	
		£3.00
		£103.00

Each debt paid one year from death is therefore regarded as being paid in the proportion:

$$\frac{100.00}{103.00} \text{ from capital; and}$$

$$\frac{3.00}{103.00} \text{ from income.}$$

Thus, the debt of £500 will be paid:

$$\frac{100.00}{103.00} \times £500 = £485.44 \text{ from capital; and}$$

$$\frac{3.00}{103.00} \times £500 = £14.56 \text{ from income.}$$

This £14.56 will be charged to the tenant for life.

It is easy to appreciate the theoretical justification for this rule and it is also easy to see its practical defects. In particular, a separate calculation is necessary for each debt paid at a different time. Further, where payments are to be made a considerable time after death, as where the testator in his lifetime entered into a covenant to pay an annuity and the annuity was charged on the residue of his estate, the proportion borne by income steadily increases.[41] Except where very

---

[40] *Re Oldham* (1927) 71 S.J. 491.
[41] *Re Dawson* [1906] 2 Ch. 211; *Re Perkins* [1907] 2 Ch. 596; *Re Poyser* [1910] 2 Ch. 444.

large debts are involved or where a very long delay occurs in payment, the trouble of making the calculation does not justify the small adjustment between tenant for life and remainderman so that it is now very common to exclude the operation of the rule.

(2) The rule in Re Atkinson[42]

Where an authorised mortgage forms part of the estate and, upon realisation of the security by sale, the proceeds of sale are insufficient to pay the outstanding principal and interest in full, the proceeds of sale are apportioned between the tenant for life and remainderman in the proportion which the amount due for arrears bears to the amount due in respect of principal. This is the rule in *Re Atkinson*[43] and it applies to any mortgage which was received from the testator or settlor, and any *authorised* mortgage taken by the trustee himself.

Suppose that during his lifetime the testator made a mortgage advance of £25,000 upon the security of a house at £12 per cent. interest. Suppose also that the mortgagor pays a total of £1,200 interest and that the property is sold for £23,000 three years after death, no part of the capital secured by the mortgage having been repaid. The apportionment of the £23,000 is as follows:

Capital outstanding		£25,000
Interest outstanding:		
3 Years at £12 per cent. on £25,000	£9,000	
less: actually paid	£1,200	
	£ 7,800	
Total capital and interest due		£32,800

$$\text{Capital element of proceeds of sale} = \frac{£25,000}{£32,800} \times £23,000 = £17,530$$

$$\text{Income element of proceeds of sale} = \frac{£7,800}{£32,800} \times £23,000 = £5,470$$

Total proceeds of sale £23,000

The scope of the rule is in doubt. In principle it ought to apply whenever an asset carrying both capital and interest at a fixed rate is realised at a loss and it has been held to apply to an amount received in a liquidation on account of principal and arrears of interest due under a holding of debenture stock.[44] However, the rule is not applied where preference dividends are in arrears.[45]

---

[42] [1904] 2 Ch. 160.
[43] *Ibid.*
[44] *Re Walker* [1936] Ch. 280; *cf. Re Taylor* [1905] 1 Ch. 734.
[45] *Re Sale* [1913] 2 Ch. 697; *Re Wakley* [1920] 2 Ch. 205.

The rule in *Re Atkinson* is applied only to a capital sum realised on the sale of a security and not to income received from the asset. Thus, if under a power contained in a mortgage the trustees take possession of the property and let it, the net rents are applied entirely in the discharge of arrears of interest and only when they have been paid in full is the surplus applied as capital.[46] If there are arrears of interest outstanding at the date of death, those are paid in full before interest due to the estate from the period from the date of death to the date of extinction of the mortgage.[47]

Where the trustees foreclose under a mortgage, the mortgagor then loses all title to the property and the property itself becomes an asset of the estate. Accordingly, from the date of foreclosure the tenant for life is entitled to the whole of the net rents and profits until sale[48] but, if there are arrears of interest before foreclosure, it seems that a *Re Atkinson* apportionment will be made when the property is ultimately sold.[49]

There is no authority whether income tax should be deducted in making a calculation for the purposes of the rule in *Re Atkinson*. It is suggested that the appropriate method of applying the rule is first to ascertain the arrears of interest, and the proportion due to income without taking into account income tax. When that proportion has been calculated, the tenant for life's entitlement should be reduced by an amount equal to income tax at the basic rate on that sum.

III. APPORTIONMENTS RELATING TO STOCKS AND SHARES

In contrast to the apportionments already considered, which apply to unauthorised investments, apportionments of a different type are sometimes necessary in the case of authorised investments.

1. *Dividends*

The first case is of apportionment of dividends received for shares. Thus, if shares are left on trust for Peter for life, with remainder to Paul for life, it may be necessary, on the death of Peter, to apportion dividends between Peter's estate and Paul. The Apportionment Act 1870 applies to most types of periodical payment which are deemed to accrue from day to day. If, therefore, Peter dies on the fifty-ninth day of a year, and the company declares a dividend amounting to £150 for that calendar year, 59/365ths of £150 will belong to Peter's estate, and the balance will be payable to Paul. The period stated by the company in respect of that dividend will govern all beneficiaries. Suppose a company pays no dividend in 1994 and 1995, but pays a dividend in 1996, three times as large as normal, which is stated by the company to be for 1996. Suppose also that Peter dies on the fifty-ninth day of 1996. As the company has stated that the dividend is for 1996, Peter will only be entitled to 59/ 365ths. It may have been thought more equitable in

---

[46] *Re Coaks* [1911] 1 Ch. 171.
[47] *Ibid.*
[48] L.P.A. 1925, s.31; *Re Horn* [1924] 2 Ch. 222.
[49] *Re Horn* [1924] 2 Ch. 222 at p. 226.

some circumstances for Peter to have received 789/1096ths (being the fraction of days for the period 1994, 1995 and 1996 for which Peter has lived) but this is not the rule.[50]

It is necessary to make a time apportionment when there is an alteration in the class of income beneficiaries. In *Re Joel*,[51] for example, a fund was held upon trust for the testator's grandchildren contingently on their attaining the age of 21. The gift carried the intermediate income, which could accordingly be used for the grandchildren.[52] Goff J. held that each time a member of the class died under 21, or a new grandchild was born, the income of the trust ought to be apportioned so that each member of the class enjoyed only that part of the income attributable to the period for which he was alive.

The taxation rules, however, differ from those laid down by the Apportionment Act. For taxation purposes, the whole of the dividend is treated as the income of the person who, under the trust, is entitled to income on the day on which the income is payable.[53] Suppose, therefore, a fund is held upon trust for Roger for life, with remainder to Susan for life; that Roger dies on February 15, 1995; that one of the assets of the trust fund is a holding of shares in a company which pays dividends in respect of a year ending on March 31; and that in June 1995 the company declares a dividend for the year ended March 31, 1995. Roger's estate will be entitled to most of the dividend, although the whole of the dividend will form part of Susan's taxable income for the year of assessment 1995/96.

2. *Scrip Dividends*

Companies sometimes give shareholders a choice between receiving their dividends in cash and receiving additional shares. Dividends paid in the form of shares are known as scrip dividends. This choice does not pose any particular problems for the trustees if the value of the scrip offered is more or less the same as the cash dividend. In both cases the dividend will belong to the tenant for life and in such circumstances trustees have traditionally opted to take the dividend in cash. However, there have recently been a large number of enhanced scrip dividends, where the value of the scrip on offer can be as much as 50 per cent. more than the cash dividend with, sometimes, the possibility of converting the scrip into cash by selling it on at a pre-arranged price, not as high as the value of the scrip but still substantially more than the cash dividend. Trustees are clearly under an obligation to consider whether to take up such an offer. If they do, the question arises as to whether the tenant for life is entitled to the whole of the scrip or the pre-arranged

---

[50] *Re Wakley* [1920] 1 Ch. 205. The Law Reform Committee (23rd Report, 1982) has recommended that the statutory rule should not apply on the death of a testator by whose will a trust is created.

[51] [1967] Ch. 14. The Law Reform Committee (23rd Report, 1982) has recommended that the rule in this case should be abrogated.

[52] See *post*, p. 485.

[53] *I.R.C.* v. *Henderson's Executors* (1931) 16 T.C. 282; *Bryan* v. *Cassin* [1942] 2 All E.R. 262; *Wood* v. *Owen* [1941] 1 K.B. 92; *Potel* v. *I.R.C.* [1971] 2 All E.R. 504.

purchase price for which it is sold. There is authority that in these circumstances an apportionment is necessary as between income and capital.[54] If this is indeed the case, the tenant for life will be entitled to no more than the amount of the cash dividend: the additional value of the scrip or the pre-arranged price for which it is sold will therefore have to be added to the capital of the trust. If enhanced scrip dividends continue to be popular, it is likely that a test case will at some stage be necessary to establish definitively whether or not such an apportionment is indeed necessary.

3. *Purchases and Sales Cum and Ex Dividend*

Apportionment may be thought to be appropriate where stocks and shares are bought and sold. There are several factors which affect the price of stock exchange investments, such as the yield which is obtained,[55] the stability of the company concerned, the general economic condition of the country as a whole, and the future prospects of the company but one of the short-term factors is the date when the dividend is to be paid. This will clearly be an artificial example but, assuming all other factors remain constant, if a dividend of £500 is payable on January 1 and July 1 on a holding of stock worth £20,000, on January 2 the stock is worth £20,000 but its value on June 30, the day before the payment of the next dividend, will be £20,000, plus £500, *i.e.* £20,500.[56] Suppose therefore that trustees purchase stock on January 2 for £20,000 and sell it for £20,500 on June 30, does the whole of that £20,500 belong to capital, or is the sum apportioned, £20,000 being attributed to capital and £500 to income? After all, had the holding been kept for one day longer, the £500 would have been received as a dividend, and treated as income. Somewhat surprisingly, there is no apportionment, and the whole amount received is deemed to be capital. The explanation for this apparently inequitable rule is that there are in practice so many factors which affect the value of shares that it is thought too difficult to lay down any set rules to govern how the apportionment is to be calculated. It has, however, been said that if the rule of non-apportionment leads to a "glaring injustice" apportionment will be ordered.[57]

4. *Bonus Shares*

Considerable difficulty has been caused where a company issues bonus shares. Suppose the capital of a company consists of 10,000 £1 ordinary shares, and suppose also that the company has prospered, and has made an accumulated profit, which has been retained, of £5,000. If the company distributes the £5,000 to its shareholders, this sum is clearly income. On the other hand the company may decide to retain that sum

---

[54] *Re Malam* [1894] 3 Ch. 578.
[55] *Ante*, p. 433.
[56] In fact the holder of the stock will pay income tax on the dividend, so that the additional worth is £500 less tax.
[57] *Per* Harman J. in *Re MacLaren's Settlement Trusts* [1951] 2 All E.R. 414 at p. 420.

of £5,000 permanently by using it for the issue of 5,000 additional shares, and then the new shares are distributed free to the existing shareholders in the company on the basis of one new share for each two shares already held. Are these new shares to be treated as income? The general rule is that they are capital, and must be held by the trustees as such, although of course the tenant for life will obtain benefit from them by virtue of the fact that he will be entitled to the dividends which they produce.[58] Where, however, the company has no power under its articles of association to create new shares in this way, so that it ought to have distributed the profit in cash, it was decided in *Bouch* v. *Sproule*[59] that the shares distributed are regarded as income.

Bouch v. *Sproule* was considered in the Privy Council decision of *Hill* v. *Permanent Trustee Co. of New South Wales*,[60] where Lord Russell of Killowen laid down certain principles.[61]

1. Where a company makes a distribution of money among its shareholders, it is not concerned at all with the way in which the shareholders deal with that money. Thus, where the shareholder is a trustee, the company is not itself concerned with whether the money is treated as capital or income.
2. Unless a company is in liquidation, it can only make a payment by way of a return of capital under a scheme for the reduction of capital approved by the court.[62] (Restrictions are placed on a reduction of capital by a company so that creditors of the company shall not be prejudiced.) In any other case, apart from liquidation, it follows that if the company is able to distribute money it must be profit, so far as the company is concerned.
3. Generally, therefore, where the shareholder is a trustee, he will receive the money as income, and it will be payable to the tenant for life. This will not be the case, however, if there is some provision in the trust instrument to the contrary, or if the following principle applies.
4. Where the company has power under its articles of association to utilise its profits by adding them to capital, and issuing bonus shares representing the amount of that additional capital to its shareholders, those shares are capital.
5. Where the company's capital is increased in this way, its assets are undiminished (for the cash never leaves its hands), whereas if a distribution of profits is made, the company's assets consequently are diminished.[63]

An additional principle was, in effect, added by Plowman J. in *Re Outen*,[64] to the effect that where under a power in its articles of associ-

---

[58] *I.R.C.* v. *Blott* [1921] 2 A.C. 171.
[59] (1887) 12 App.Cas. 385.
[60] [1930] A.C. 720.
[61] [1930] A.C. 720 at pp. 730–732.
[62] See now, Companies Act 1985, s.135.
[63] Though why this should be relevant to a trustee is difficult to understand.
[64] [1963] Ch. 291.

ation a company capitalises profits, not by using the profits to issue new shares, but by issuing some other investment in the company, that other investment is capital in the hands of the trustee-shareholder.

Re Outen is not without interest. In 1962 Imperial Chemical Industries made a take-over bid for Courtaulds by offering to acquire from members of Courtaulds their stock in that company. The bid was resisted by the directors of Courtaulds, who in order to persuade the stockholders not to sell stock procured the capitalisation of £40 million reserves, representing capital profits, and used this to make a free issue of a new loan stock to the stockholders. Before the take-over battle, a testatrix had left her holding of stock to trustees upon trust and in due course they, along with other stockholders in Courtaulds, were issued with a holding of the loan stock. The question arose whether this loan stock was to be treated as capital or as income. The capitalisation of the reserves was in accordance with the company's articles of association.

Plowman J. held that, although Courtauld's decision did not involve the creation of new shares in Courtaulds, it effected a capitalisation under which any further character of divisible profits was taken away from the assets that were the subject of the capitalisation. The company's decision was binding on the shareholders and the loan stock was therefore capital.

A further complication on the theme occurs where the company gives the shareholder the option either to have bonus shares, or cash. The test is whether the company intends to make a capital distribution or whether it really intends to distribute income.[65] If the intention is to make a capital distribution then, whether the trustees take the bonus shares or the cash, what is received by them will be capital (the cash offer is usually inferior in value to the offer of bonus shares and so the trustees ought normally to take the bonus shares). If the intention is to distribute income, then what is received by the trustees will be income; if the trustees take the cash, this will obviously be payable to the tenant for life but, if they take the bonus shares (which they ought normally to do), there is authority that the tenants for life will still receive only the value of the cash offer, the remainder being regarded as capital.[66]

In summary, in the ordinary case where a company issues bonus shares, the reserves or profits which are used within the company to back the bonus shares are retained by the company as long-term capital. Consequently, bonus shares are in general received by the trustees as capital. Where, on the other hand, the company has no power under its articles of association to create new shares in this way, the shares distributed are received by the trustees as income. This is also the case where the intention of the company was to distribute income. All other forms of distribution by way of money or money's worth consists of the company passing on to its shareholders a profit which it has received, and the company does not itself retain any long-term benefit from the distribution. In the ordinary case, such dividends are received by the

---

[65] *I.R.C.* v. *Fisher's Executors* [1926] A.C. 395.
[66] *Re Malam* [1894] 3 Ch. 578.

trustees as income. The best illustration of this is provided by capital profits dividends.

5. *Capital Profits Dividends*

Where a company makes a capital profit and distributes that profit either in cash or in some other valuable form, it will have made a capital profit dividend, which will normally be received by the trustees as income. A series of cases were decided in about 1951 in relation to a capital profit dividend declared by Thomas Tilling & Co. A substantial part of the business of this company consisted of operating buses and coaches. When this part of the company's business was nationalised, the company was compensated by an amount of British Transport stock, which in turn the company distributed among its shareholders as a capital profits dividend. The question arose whether the stock so distributed should be regarded as capital or as income for the purposes of a trust. In *Re Sechiari*[67] and *Re Kleinwort*[68] it was held that trustees received the stock as income, so that it belonged to the tenant for life. The position was not the same as in the case of the issue of bonus shares in the company making the distribution, in which case the increase in the number of shares entitles the holders to participate in future dividends, but an isolated payment, complete in itself, and from which no future benefit will accrue directly from the company. In *Re Kleinwort*, however, Vaisey J. considered that, where special circumstances existed, the sum received was properly apportionable between capital and income. There would, in his opinion be special circumstances where the trustees had committed a breach of trust, particularly in not maintaining a balance between the conflicting interests of different beneficiaries. Thus if in such a case the trustees acting solely with the intention of benefiting the tenant for life at the expense of the remainderman invested in shares in a company in the expectation of a capital profits distribution, they would commit a breach of trust and doubtless the court would apportion the dividend between income and capital. In *Re Rudd*,[69] however, it was held that merely because the trustees, who foresaw the capital dividend and so could have sold the stock with a large profit for capital, did not do so they did not thereby commit a breach of trust. The court thus refused to apportion the capital profit dividend received. The case seems to depend on the motive of the trustees: they did not intend to prejudice the remainderman.

Special circumstances existed, however, in *Re MacLaren*.[70] After it became known that Thomas Tilling & Co. intended to distribute the British Transport stock among its shareholders, the tenant for life consented to the purchase of the stock as a capital investment. Here it was held that the tenant for life, knowing what would happen, must be regarded as having consented to the British Transport stock being regarded as capital and that it was to be treated as capital.

---

[67] [1950] 1 All E.R. 417.
[68] [1951] Ch. 860.
[69] [1952] 1 All E.R. 254.
[70] [1951] 2 All E.R. 414.

Although it has been appropriate to illustrate the principle by reference to the Tilling cases, the principle applies to any case where the company makes a capital profit and distributes that profit either in cash or in some other valuable form. That profit will, in normal circumstances, be received by the trustees as income and will therefore be payable to the tenant for life. Where the distribution is as substantial as that made by Thomas Tilling & Co., the capital value of the fund will thereby be substantially reduced—in that case, the price of the shares fell by as much as 77 per cent. an enormous windfall for the tenant for life and a substantial loss for the remaindermen.

6. *Demergers*

Similar potential difficulties are caused by the recently fashionable practice of demerging companies, that is to say hiving off some composite part of the businesses of a company into a new company and issuing all the shareholders of the original company with fully paid up shares in the new demerged company. This is done by the original company transferring the part of its assets which relate to the businesses which are to be demerged to a new subsidiary company and then declaring a dividend out of distributable profits. There are two ways of proceeding thereafter: the "direct" method is for the original company to satisfy the dividend directly by allocating to its shareholders shares in the subsidiary company, which then becomes the demerged company; the "indirect" method is for the shares in the subsidiary company to be transferred to a quite separate company, which then satisfies the dividend indirectly by allocating its own shares to the shareholders of the original company. Both of these methods appear to amount to a capital distribution which, in accordance with the principles just discussed, appears to be received as income for the purposes of a trust and will therefore be payable to the tenant for life. In one recent demerger, that of the bioscience activities of Imperial Chemical Industries into a new company, Zeneca Group, this potentially had the effect of halving the value of the capital of any trust which held shares in I.C.I. and providing the tenant for life with a windfall of half the capital value of the shares.

A test case, *Sinclair* v. *Lee*[71] was therefore brought to establish whether the shares allocated in the new company would be treated as capital or as income for the purposes of a trust. This demerger was to be carried out by the "indirect" method. Sir Donald Nicholls V.C. stated that "no one, unversed in the arcane mysteries I shall be mentioning shortly, would have any doubt over the answer. . . . Nobody would think that the Zeneca Group shares could sensibly be regarded as income."[72] His Lordship relied on the fact that, since this demerger was to be carried out by the "indirect" method, the shares of the demerged company, Zeneca Group, would never be held or received by I.C.I.; this enabled him to distinguish the authorities discussed in the previous

---

[71] [1993] 3 W.L.R. 498.
[72] *Ibid.* at p. 501.

\

two sections and he therefore held that the distribution of Zeneca Group shares would indeed be capital for the purposes of a trust. This decision establishes that shares in a company which is demerged by the "indirect" method will be capital for the purposes of a trust. However, the decision leaves completely open the position of shares in a company which is demerged by the "direct" method. Since the ground on which Sir Donald Nicholls V.C. was able to distinguish the earlier authorities applies only to "indirect" demergers, it may well be that the opposite conclusion will be reached in respect of "direct" demergers. No doubt another test case will have to be brought to resolve this question.

7. Taxation considerations

The treatment of the various types of dividends, distributions, and shares which have just been considered for the general purposes of trust administration has to be distinguished from their treatment for the purposes of taxation. Company distributions are normally paid with a tax credit of 20 per cent. so that the sum actually received has in effect suffered tax of 20 per cent. Trustees need take no further action in respect of distributions paid over to a beneficiary who has a fixed interest: the distributions are taxed as his income so, if he is a higher rate taxpayer, he has to pay a further 20 per cent. tax. However, accumulation and discretionary settlements pay tax at a flat rate of 35 per cent. and so a further 15 per cent. tax will be payable by the trustees of these settlements. However, where the trustees elect to take scrip dividends rather than cash and where shares are held which carry with them the right to receive bonus shares,[73] then, if the company is resident in the United Kingdom,[74] the shares received are treated as income. The usual 20 per cent. tax credit will not be forthcoming from the company and so tax is payable as if a dividend had been paid of an amount which, after deducting income tax at the basic rate in force, equals the value of the scrip dividend or other shares at the date of issue.[75] If the scrip dividend or shares are passed to an income beneficiary, the notional amount of the dividend is treated as part of his income for income tax purposes. If the scrip dividend or shares are retained by the trustees as an accretion to capital for a remainderman there will be no liability on them,[76] whereas if it is retained by the trustees of a discretionary or accumulation settlement, they will have to pay a further 10 per cent. tax to bring the tax paid up to the flat rate of 35 per cent.[77] Bonus shares and capital profits dividends are treated in the same way. Where, on the

---

[73] That is, the terms upon which the shares are issued gives the shareholders the right to call for bonus shares.

[74] Income and Corporation Taxes Act 1988, s.349.

[75] If, therefore, the basic rate of income tax is 25 per cent. and an issue of scrip is made which is worth £100, the company will be treated as if it paid a dividend of £133.33 from which income tax had been deducted (£133.33 less £33.33 tax = £100).

[76] Because, in general, income received by trustees subject to deduction of tax at source is not further taxable in their hands: see *ante*, p. 411.

[77] Trustees of this type of settlement are liable for income tax at a flat rate of 35 per cent. See *ante*, p. 413. In the example given in note 75, therefore the trustees would be liable to pay in addition 10 per cent. of £133.33 = £13.33.

other hand, the company which pays the scrip dividend or in which the shares are held which carry with them the right to receive bonus shares is resident outside the United Kingdom, the shares which are received are treated as capital for taxation purposes if they would be so treated for the purposes of trust administration.[78] The transfer of shares in demerged companies is not a distribution and so does not give rise to any payment of income tax. However, there are potential difficulties as to precisely what the base cost of the shares is for the purposes of capital gains tax where the shares are treated as the property of a fixed interest beneficiary; this particular question awaits resolution.

IV. APPORTIONMENTS IN RESPECT OF NATIONAL SAVINGS CERTIFICATES

It has been seen[79] that, by virtue of the Apportionment Act 1870, it may be necessary to apportion by time dividends or other income between the person entitled to the income before an event, such as death, and the person entitled after that event. It is, however, first necessary to establish that the amount in question is of an income nature. The problem arises in particular with the increment over the purchase price which is payable on the encashment of National Savings Certificates. In *Re Holder*[80] the testator in his lifetime purchased National Savings Certificates for £375, which were encashed after his death for £534. Roxburgh J. held that, by virtue of the terms on which the certificates were issued by the Government, the increment up to the date of death was capital. It was conceded that the increment which arose between the date of death and the date of encashment was to be treated as income, but the point was not argued. Although the basis for the concession does not appear from the report of the case, it would appear to be a correct concession, following the rule in *Re Earl of Chesterfield's Trusts*.[81]

V. APPORTIONMENT OF OUTGOINGS

Subject to contrary directions in the trust instrument, expenses which relate solely to the income of a trust, such as the cost of making an income tax return, are primarily payable out of income, and other expenses, such as the cost of apportioning new trustees or of bringing legal proceedings, are payable out of capital.

Where an audit takes place, however, the trustees may apportion the cost of this between capital and income in such proportions as they think fit.[82]

---

[78] *I.R.C.* v. *Wright* (1926) 11 T.C. 181.
[79] *Ante*, p. 472.
[80] [1953] Ch. 468.
[81] (1883) 24 Ch.D. 643; see *ante*, p. 466.
[82] T.A. 1925, s.22(4).

VI. EXCLUDING APPORTIONMENTS

The apportionment rules are designed to achieve fairness and in most cases it is easy to see the logic behind them. Nevertheless, it is becoming increasingly common for them to be expressly excluded. Partly this is due to taxation considerations, but in the main it is because the calculations which have to be made under some of the rules are so complicated that it is far simpler from an administrative point of view for apportionments to be excluded. Ironically, then, the long-term effect of the rules has probably been the reverse of what equity intended.

CHAPTER 17

INCOME FROM THE TRUST FUND

THERE are five questions to be asked about the income from the trust fund, namely:

1. What is the relationship between income received by the trustees from the assets which comprise the trust fund and the income to which the beneficiaries are entitled?
2. Which beneficial interests under the trust carry the right to income?
3. Are the trustees entitled to retain income?
4. How are the trustees to apply income where the beneficiary is an infant?
5. What are the taxation consequences of entitlement to income?

I. INCOME OF THE TRUST FUND

(1) The accounting period

One of the fundamental elements in the concept of income is that of time: it is only possible to speak of the income of trustees, or, indeed, of any person, if one knows the period of time which is to be considered. For taxation purposes, the period to be considered is, generally,[1] the year of assessment which ends on April 5. Where a trust is created otherwise than on April 6, the first accounting period for taxation purposes will be from the date of the creation of the trust until the following April 5; and the final accounting period is from April 6 to the date of termination of the trust.

There are, however, no corresponding statutory rules for the purposes of general trust administration. The legislature may have assumed that the basic period of account would be 12 months,[2] but the trustees can select any period which they wish.[3] In practice, most trustees adopt for the purposes of trust administration the same accounting period as is adopted for taxation.

(2) Gross and net income

The trustees may derive income from a number of sources during an accounting period. For example, they may receive dividends, bank

---

[1] The general rule applies for income tax and capital gains tax.
[2] See, *e.g.* T.A. 1925, s.22(4) authorising trustees to have the trust accounts audited once in every three "years."
[3] Unless the trust instrument itself prescribes the accounting period.

deposit interest, and rent. From this gross income there will be deducted:

(a) the expenses of the management of the trust so far as applicable to income; and

(b) any other payments which the trustees make in the exercise of administrative powers.

However, the net income will usually only be determined at some point of time after the end of an accounting period. This is because trustees have a reasonable time[4] within which to exercise powers and discretions, and they often wish to wait until the end of an accounting period so that they can see the amount of gross income received in that period.

(3) Trust management expenses

Expenses of a recurrent nature are generally payable out of income, unless the trust instrument otherwise provides. Thus, there is payable from income council tax and rates in respect of land owned by the trust[5]; rent payable in respect of leasehold property owned by the trust[6]; income tax[7]; and the cost of preparation of annual accounts and income tax returns.[8]

The expenses which are payable from capital are discussed later.[9]

Although, in general, expenses are payable either from income or from capital according to their nature,

(a) the trust instrument can direct how the expenses are to be borne[10]; and

(b) in certain instances, the trustees are given a discretion.

Thus, where the trustees require the trust accounts to be audited under the statutory power,[11] they have an absolute discretion to pay the fees of the auditor from income or from capital, or partly from income and partly from capital.

(4) Administrative powers

In *Pearson* v. *I.R.C.*[12] the House of Lords drew a distinction between administrative powers and dispositive powers. Where payments are made by the trustees out of income in the exercise of administrative powers, these payments are treated in the same way as trust management expenses, that is, they are deducted from the gross receipts in

---

[4] See, *e.g. Re Gulbenkian's Settlement Trusts (No. 2), Stephens* v. *Maun* [1970] Ch. 408.

[5] *Fountaine* v. *Pellet* (1791) 1 Ves. Jun. 337, 342.

[6] *Re Gjers* [1899] 2 Ch. 54; *Re Betty* [1899] 1 Ch. 821.

[7] *Re Cain's Settlement* [1919] 2 Ch. 364.

[8] See *Shore* v. *Shore* (1859) 4 Drew. 501.

[9] *Post*, p. 502.

[10] However, the court may override the direction in the trust instrument: *Re Tubbs* [1915] Ch. 137; *Re Hicklin* [1917] 2 Ch. 278.

[11] T.A. 1925, s.22(4).

[12] [1981] A.C. 753.

determining the amount of the net trust income. Payments which are made in the exercise of a dispositive power are applications of net trust income.

In many respects, there is no clear authority as to what powers are to be regarded as administrative and what dispositive. However, in the absence of authority, the following classification is suggested:

Administrative powers

    (i) power to charge for services;

   (ii) power to retain commission, brokerage, directors' fees;

  (iii) power to engage and pay agents and professional advisers;

  (iv) power to hold investments in nominee name, or by a custodian, and to pay the nominee or custodian;

   (v) power to insure trust assets, and to pay the premiums;

  (vi) power to insure the life of the settlor, and to pay the premiums;

 (vii) power to pay taxes and duties (as to which see *Pearson* v. *I.R.C.* itself); and

(viii) power to use income to improve land.

Dispositive powers

    (i) power to accumulate income;

   (ii) power to pay or apply income to or for the maintenance, education, or benefit of another beneficiary;

  (iii) power to allow another beneficiary to use trust assets (even if on the exercise of that power an interest in possession in the assets is not created);

  (iv) power to pay the premiums on a policy of assurance which is effected for the benefit of another beneficiary; and

   (v) power to pay or apply income in securing the discharge of an obligation owing by another beneficiary, or in guaranteeing the performance of an obligation by another beneficiary.

Powers of advancement, although affecting beneficial entitlement, are treated as "similar to" administrative.[12a]

(5) Net trust income
The net trust income in respect of an accounting period may, therefore, be said to be:

   (a) the aggregate of the gross income received[13] in that period from all the trust assets; less

   (b) trust management expenses paid from income either by virtue of their nature or pursuant to a provision in the trust instrument; and less

   (c) other payments made from income in the exercise of an administrative power.

[12a] *Inglewood (Lord)* v. *I.R.C.* [1983] 1 W.L.R. 866.

[13] In many respects it is uncertain whether, to be taken into account, an amount must be received, or whether it can merely be receivable.

In the remainder of this chapter, the net trust income in this sense is referred to as the trust income.

II. GIFTS CARRYING INCOME

When the amount of the trust income has been ascertained, it is then necessary to determine whether any beneficiary is entitled to it. If a beneficiary is entitled, his interest is said to carry the intermediate income. The possibilities are:

(a) a beneficiary is entitled to the income without any further decision of the trustees being necessary. This will usually be the case where trustees hold a fund upon trust to pay the income to Adam for life, with remainder to Eve;

(b) no person is entitled, as where the trustees accumulate it;

(c) a beneficiary is entitled to the income, but only in the exercise of the trustees' discretion; and

(d) the income has not been effectively dealt with, and so is held on a resulting trust for the settlor, or, in the case of a will trust, for the testator's residuary beneficiaries or those entitled on intestacy.

With regard to vested gifts, a gift will carry the intermediate income unless:

(a) the trust instrument provides that it is to be paid to someone else; or

(b) the trust instrument provides that the income is to be accumulated, and added to capital.[14]

The position relating to contingent gifts is dealt with by section 175 of the Law of Property Act 1925.

This section, which applies only to wills coming into operation on or after January 1, 1926, provides that except in so far as the testator has otherwise expressly disposed of his income, the following types of gift carry the intermediate income from the testator's death:

(a) contingent or future specific devises or bequests[15] of property, whether real or personal;

(b) contingent residuary devises of freehold land;

(c) specific or residuary devises of freehold land to trustees upon trust for persons whose interests are contingent or executory.

The effect so far as vested and contingent interests under trusts coming into force after 1925 is as follows:

(a) the directions of the settlor or testator always prevail. Accordingly, if the trust instrument directs that the income is to

---

[14] *Re Stapleton, Stapleton* v. *Stapleton* [1946] 1 All E.R. 323.
[15] A "devise" is a gift of realty by will; a "bequest" is a gift of personalty by will.

be accumulated, that direction will prevent the gift from carrying the income.[16] Likewise, even if the gift is vested, and there is a direction for the payment of the income to another, that direction will prevail. An example would be if property was held in trust for a minor absolutely, but with a provision that until he attained the age of majority, the income should be paid to his cousin. Again if payment is expressly deferred until a future date, the gift will not carry the intermediate income.[17] If there is no such direction:

(b) in the following cases it is assumed that there is no provision in the trust instrument to bring the gift within the scope of para. (a);

(c) a vested interest will carry the intermediate income with one exception, the case of a gift by will of residuary personalty which is expressly deferred to a future date[17A];

(d) a contingent interest arising from a settlement carries the intermediate income provided the contingency is attaining the age of majority or the happening of some event before that age;

(e) a contingent gift by will carries the intermediate income if it is of
   (i) residuary personalty[18] unless it is expressly deferred to a future date[18A];
   (ii) residuary realty[19] unless it is expressly deferred to a future date[19A];
   (iii) a specific gift of personalty, other than a pecuniary legacy, or realty[20] even if it is expressly deferred to a future date[20A];

(f) in general a pecuniary legacy does not carry the intermediate income. To this general principle there are two exceptions, when the gift does carry the intermediate income, namely,
   (i) if the gift was by the father of the infant, or by some other person who stood *in loco parentis* to him, and
   (1) if the gift is contingent, the contingency is not the attaining of an age greater than 18[21] and
   (2) there is no other fund set aside for the maintenance of the legatee.[22]
   This is the effect of the words in section 31(3) of the Trustee Act that the section "applies to a future or contingent legacy by the parent of . . . the legatee if and for such period as, under the general law, the legacy carries interest for the maintenance of the legatee";

---

[16] *Re Turner's Will Trusts* [1967] Ch. 15; *Re Ransome* [1957] Ch. 348; *Re Reade-Revell* [1930] 1 Ch. 52.

[17] *Re Geering, Gulliver v. Geering* [1964] Ch. 136.

[17A] *Re Oliver* [1947] 2 All E.R. 162. *Re Gillett's Will Trusts* [1950] Ch. 102.

[18] *Re Adams, Adams v. Adams* [1893] 1 Ch. 329; unaffected by the 1925 legislation.

[18A] *Re Geering* [1964] Ch. 136.

[19] L.P.A. 1925, s.175.

[19A] This situation is not covered by L.P.A. 1925, s.175.

[20] L.P.A. 1925, s.175.

[20A] *Re McGeorge* [1963] Ch. 544.

[21] *Re Jones, Meacock v. Jones* [1932] 1 Ch. 642; F.L.R.A. 1969, s.1.

[22] *Re West* [1913] 2 Ch. 245.

(ii) the testator directs the legacy to be set apart from the rest of his estate for the benefit of the legatee.[23]

Of course, if the testator shows an intention that the gift shall carry the intermediate income, this will prevail under the first rule considered.

It should be emphasised that, as has already been mentioned, where the intermediate income is not carried, it is undisposed of and is held on resulting trust for the settlor or, in the case of a will trust, for the testator's residuary beneficiaries or those entitled on intestory.

There is little logic in the distinction between contingent pecuniary legacies and other contingent gifts of personalty.

III. RETENTION OF INCOME

Where trustees do not pay out or apply the income they will have either

(a) accumulated it; or
(b) retained it in its character as income.

(1) Accumulation

Accumulation is the conversion of what was income into capital. It occurs at the moment at which the trustees decide to accumulate the income and while no formality is required, the desirable practice is for the decision to accumulate to be recorded carefully in the trust's minutes.

Income will only be accumulated if:

(a) there is a trust or power to do so;
(b) the trust or power is not for an excessive period; and
(c) the trustees decide to give effect to the trust, or exercise the power.

(2) Trust or power to accumulate

Trustees have no general power to accumulate income. In *Re Gourju's Will Trusts*[24] trustees held a fund upon protective trusts,[25] after the fixed interest of the principal beneficiary had come to an end.[26] They sought to accumulate the income, but Simonds J. said[27]:

"I come to the conclusion that the obligation of the trustees is to apply the trust income as and when they receive it for the purposes indicated in the subsection. . . .

Putting it in a negative way, they are not entitled, regardless of the needs of the beneficiaries, to retain in their hands the income of the trust estate."

The trust or power to accumulate may arise:

---

[23] *Re Medlock* (1886) 55 L.J. Ch. 738.
[24] [1943] Ch. 24.
[25] Under T.A. 1925, s.33.
[26] See *ante*, p. 183.
[27] [1943] Ch. 24 at p. 34.

(a) by statute[28] in the case of income which is held for the benefit of an infant beneficiary, to the extent that the income is not used for his maintenance[29]; or

(b) by provisions in the trust instrument.

(3) Excessive powers

Where the trust is subject to English law, a trust to accumulate can only be prescribed for a maximum of one of the following periods[30];

(a) the life of the settlor;

(b) a period of 21 years from the death of the settlor;

(c) the duration of the minority or respective minorities of any person or persons living or *en ventre sa mère* at the death of the settlor;

(d) the duration of the minority or respective minorities of infant beneficiaries who, if of full age, would be entitled to the income;

(e) a term of 21 years from the creation of the settlement; and

(f) the duration of the minority or respective minorities of any person or persons in being when the settlement is created, whether or not they are beneficiaries or have any other connection with the settlement.

Usually the period of 21 years in (e) above is taken.

If, at the end of the prescribed period, the income is payable to a beneficiary who is an infant, the income can still be accumulated under the statutory trust to accumulate.[31]

If a trust power prescribes accumulation for a period which is longer than that prescribed by statute, the provision is void only as to the excess.[32]

Where it is desired to accumulate for a period longer than the maximum permitted by statute, it is possible to establish the trust under a jurisdiction which recognises a longer period. Northern Ireland is popular for this purpose.[33]

(4) Exercise of power

Trustees must exercise any discretion within a reasonable time. What is reasonable depends on the facts of each case. In *Re Gulbenkian's Settlement Trusts (No. 2)*[34] trustees learned in April 1957 of a decision[35] which cast doubt on the validity of a provision in the trust instrument, and they then retained the income without accumulating it. The doubt

---

[28] T.A. 1925, s.31.

[29] See, *post*, p. 490.

[30] L.P.A. 1925, s.164; Perpetuities and Accumulations Act, 1964, s.13. These periods do not apply where the settlor is a body corporate; *Re Dodwell & Co. Ltd.'s Trust Deed* [1978] 3 All E.R. 738.

[31] T.A. 1925, s.31(2).

[32] *Re Joel's Will Trusts* [1967] Ch. 14.

[33] For an example of the use of trusts governed by the law of Northern Ireland for this purpose, see *Vestey* v. *I.R.C.* [1980] A.C. 1148.

[34] [1970] Ch. 408.

[35] *Re Gresham's Settlement* [1956] 1 W.L.R. 573, subsequently overruled.

was not resolved until the decision of the House of Lords in *Re Gulbenkian's Settlement Trusts (No. 1)*[36] in October 1968. Plowman J., held that their retention of the income was not unreasonable in the circumstances, and they could still exercise their discretion in respect of the income which had arisen since 1957. It follows that if they act reasonably, trustees can retain income as income for a considerable time and then accumulate it.

If the trustees are under a duty to accumulate, that duty is not extinguished by lapse of time. In this case, the trustees can give effect to that duty long after the income has arisen, and, if they do not do so, the court will direct them to do so.[37] If, however, the trustees merely have a power to accumulate, that is, a duty to consider whether to accumulate, but not a duty to exercise the power, the power is lost if they do not act within a reasonable time.[38]

(5) Taxation effects of accumulation

It is frequently found that instruments which impose trusts or confer powers to accumulate also provide that payments from capital can be made to beneficiaries. It may well be, then, that in a particular case the trustees have a power to distribute income as it arises to members of a discretionary class and a power to accumulate the income. There may also be a trust or power at some later date to distribute the accumulations as capital to the same persons. What is the difference to the beneficiary? The position is often largely governed by tax considerations. Suppose that the trustees of a fund receive a gross income of £1,000 p.a., and that they have a discretion either to distribute it as income, or to accumulate it. Suppose that two of the discretionary objects are George, whose top tax rate[39] is 25 per cent.[40] and Harry, whose top tax rate is 40 per cent. The trustees are themselves liable for tax at a total of 35 per cent. on income which may be accumulated.[41] Of the £1,000 received by them, they will, therefore, be required to pay £350 in tax.[42] If they then distribute it as income, before it is accumulated, the beneficiary is treated as having received a gross payment of £1,000, from which tax at 35 per cent. has been deducted. In the case of George, his top rate is 25 per cent., and he could recover by way of a repayment claim the difference between the tax which he ought to have suffered on the £1,000, namely £250, and the tax which he has actually suffered, namely £350. In the final result, therefore, he receives £650 from the trustees, and £100 by way of tax reclaim. On the

---

[36] [1970] A.C. 508.

[37] *Re Locker's Settlement Trusts* [1977] 1 W.L.R. 1323 see, *ante*, p. 274.

[38] *Re Gourju's Will Trusts* [1943] Ch. 24; *Re Wise* [1896] 1 Ch. 281; *Re Allen-Meyrick's Will Trusts* [1968] 1 W.L.R. 499.

[39] See *ante*, p. 411.

[40] These examples assume that the top tax rate will not be altered if the beneficiaries receive another £1,000 gross income.

[41] The provision also applies to income subject to a discretion. Income and Corporation Taxes Act 1988, s.686 (as amended by Finance Act 1993).

[42] In this example, the expenses of the trust are ignored. That part of the income which is applicable to the expenses of the trust payable out of income is not subject to the additional charge.

other hand Harry, who is liable to tax at 40 per cent., will be required to pay to the Revenue the difference between the tax which he has suffered on the £1,000 and the tax which is appropriate to his top rate. He will have received £650 from the trustees, but will have to pay £50 of this to the Revenue. Suppose, however, that the trustees accumulate the net income of £650, and then at some later stage distribute it as a capital payment. In this case it is treated as capital for all income tax purposes, so that no repayment claim can be made, and no further liability can arise. Thus, George will be worse off, because he will not be able to recover the £100 from the Revenue, but Harry is better off, for he will not have to pay the additional tax of £50.

A distribution from capital which has been derived from accumulated income will, however, be treated in the same way as any other distribution of capital. It may, therefore, give rise to a liability to inheritance tax.[43]

(6) Retained income
As income can be converted into capital only by the decision of the trustees to accumulate it, in strict theory the income will never be accumulated without that decision. However, if the trustees are under a duty to accumulate, the longer a period elapses the greater will be the willingness of the courts to hold that there has been an accumulation. Likewise, the courts will infer that the decision to accumulate has been taken if the trustees act in a manner which indicates that income has been accumulated. This will be so, for example, where trustees complete an income tax return for the trust showing the income as having been accumulated.

(7) Beneficial entitlement
Special rules apply where income has been accumulated during the minority of an infant beneficiary.[44] Apart from these, and subject to any provision in the trust instrument, income which has been accumulated will be added to capital, and the beneficiary entitled to capital will become entitled also to the accumulations. Income which is retained by the trustees without being accumulated will belong to the beneficiary, if any, who is entitled to income.

IV. MAINTENANCE OF INFANT BENEFICIARIES

(1) Trust instrument prevails
Section 31 of the Trustee Act 1925 confers upon trustees a power to apply income in the maintenance of infant beneficiaries.[45] However, it was decided in *Re Turner*[46] that all the provisions of section 31, whether they are expressed as powers or as duties, are in fact only "powers conferred by this Act" for the purposes of section 69(2) of the Act. Section 69(2) provides that "the powers conferred by this Act on

---

[43] Inheritance Tax Act 1984, s.65. See, *ante*, p. 420.
[44] See *post*, p. 494.
[45] There is no statutory power to maintain adult beneficiaries.
[46] [1937] Ch. 15.

trustees" apply only in so far as there is no intention expressed in the trust instrument that they should not apply. Although, therefore, the general principle is that the statutory powers, including the power of maintenance, may be expressly excluded under section 69(2).

The statutory power of maintenance will be excluded:

   (a) if there is an express power of maintenance, to the extent that the express power is inconsistent with the statutory power;

   (b) if there is any other inconsistent provision in the trust instrument, such as a direction to accumulate the whole of the income; or

   (c) there is a provision expressly excluding the statutory power.

Re Erskine's Settlement Trusts[47] is an example of the second and third of these circumstances.

In that case the settlor created a settlement for the benefit of his grandson Richard, who became entitled to the capital of the fund upon attaining the age of 22. The question concerned the entitlement to income until Richard attained that age. The trust instrument provided that the income should be accumulated during the lifetime of the settlor and thereafter until Richard reached the age of 22. It also provided that the statutory powers of maintenance and advancement should not apply. The provision for accumulation was void,[48] and Stamp J., following *Re Turner*, held that the statutory power of maintenance was effectively excluded. In the result the income was undisposed of, and belonged to the settlor's estate.

While, however, it is possible to exclude the statutory power, it will only be excluded if there is a clear expression of intention to that effect. If the trust instrument is silent on the point, the statutory power will apply.

(2) The statutory power

The statutory power to maintain is contained in section 31 of the Trustee Act 1925. This provides[49] that where property is held upon trust for any infant, then during the infancy of that person the trustees may, if in their discretion they think fit, pay the whole or part of the income to the parent or guardian of the infant beneficiary or otherwise apply it for or towards his maintenance, education, or benefit. The trustees are under a duty to accumulate the whole of the income which is not paid or applied in this way.[50]

It follows from what has been said earlier in this chapter that the trustees will have a power to maintain unless:

   (a) the gift to the infant beneficiary does not carry the intermediate income[51]; or

---

[47] [1971] 1 W.L.R. 162.
[48] Because it was contrary to L.P.A. 1925, s.164.
[49] T.A. 1925, s.31(1).
[50] s.31(2).
[51] *Ante*, p. 485.

(b) the power has been excluded.[52]

The statutory power has the following noteworthy features:

(a) it applies where the interest of the beneficiary is vested and to this extent overrides the apparent provisions of the trust instrument. Suppose, for example, that trustees hold a fund upon trust for Cedric for life, with remainder to Edmund; that the statutory power applies; and that Cedric is under the age of 18. The terms of the trust instrument would suggest that Cedric is entitled to the whole of the income, yet section 31 has the effect that, while Cedric is under the age of 18, he will be entitled only to that part, if any, of the income which the trustees decide to pay or apply for his maintenance;

(b) it also applies where the interest of the beneficiary is contingent. An example is where the trust fund is held upon trust for Fergus if he attains the age of 30[53];

(c) although section 31 refers to vested interests, it applies also to vested interests which are defeasible, as where a fund is held upon trust for Solly but, if he dies under the age of 30, then for Holly;

(d) the power only applies while the beneficiary is under the age of 18[54];

(e) where section 31 is not excluded, the trustees are under a duty to consider whether to exercise their power, but they need not exercise it. In deciding whether, and, if so, to what extent, to exercise the power, the trustees are directed by section 31 *to have regard to*

the age of the infant;
what other income, if any, is available for his maintenance;
his requirements; and
"generally to the circumstances of the case."

If the trustees know that other income is available for the maintenance of the infant, and the total amount available exceeds the needs of the infant, then so far as is practicable a proportionate part only of each fund should be paid or applied for his maintenance.

The trustees may pay the money which they decide to use either to the infant's parent or guardian,[55] or they may directly apply it for his maintenance, education or benefit;

(f) the statutory power applies whatever the nature of the property[56]; and

---

[52] *Supra.*

[53] Where the interest is contingent, it must also be shown that the gift carries the intermediate income: see p. 485, *ante.* If it does not do so, there will be no income available for the trustees to pay or apply.

[54] Family Law Reform Act 1969, Sched. 3, para. 5. See *post* p. 494, as to the position when the beneficiary reaches the age of 18.

[55] *Sowarsby* v. *Lacy* (1819) 4 Madd. 142.

[56] *Stanley* v. *I.R.C.* [1944] K.B. 255; *Re Baron Vestey* [1951] Ch. 209.

(g) where the power is to be exercised, the trustees must exercise it positively and not merely pay out the money for the infant's maintenance without considering whether it is desirable to do so. In one case[57] where the trustees made automatic payments to the infant's father without exercising any discretion, the court ordered that money to be repaid to the trust fund. But as long as the trustees exercise their discretion in good faith the court will not interfere with their decision.[58]

(3) Accumulation of surplus income

All income which is not paid to the parent or guardian of the infant beneficiary, or applied by the trustees for his maintenance, education, or benefit is to be accumulated.[59]

Although, by being accumulated, the surplus income becomes capital, the trustees may use the income accumulated in previous years as if it were income of a later year, provided that the interest of the beneficiary continues in that later year.[60]

(4) Income arising after age 18

There is no statutory power to maintain an adult beneficiary. The general principle is that the beneficiary is thereafter entitled either to the whole of the income[61] or none. It is, however, possible for the trust instrument to confer an express power to maintain.[62]

In *Re McGeorge*,[63] a testator devised land to his daughter, but declared that the devise should not take effect until the death of his wife. It was held that this was a future specific devise within section 175 of the Law of Property Act, and so prima facie carried the intermediate income. The daughter was over 18 and claimed the intermediate income, but her claim was defeated. Cross J. held that by deferring the enjoyment of the property until after the widow's death the testator expressed the intention that the daughter should not have the intermediate income. The income was, therefore, to be accumulated.

Where, on attaining the age of 18, the beneficiary has only a contingent interest in the trust property, he would, in the absence of any other provision, have no entitlement until he satisfied the contingency. However, section 31(1)(ii) has the effect of accelerating the beneficiary's interest. It provides that after attaining the age of 18, the trustees shall[64] thenceforth pay to the beneficiary the income from the

---

[57] *Wilson* v. *Turner* (1883) 22 Ch.D. 521; and see p. 145.

[58] *Re Bryant* [1894] 1 Ch. 324; *Re Lofthouse* (1885) 29 Ch.D. 921.

[59] T.A. 1925, s.31(2). The manner in which the accumulations are dealt with is discussed at *infra*.

[60] *Ibid.*

[61] *Re Jones' Will Trusts* [1947] Ch. 48.

[62] *Re Turner* [1937] Ch. 15.

[63] [1963] Ch. 544.

[64] Despite this apparently mandatory provision, the section can be excluded: *Re Turner* [1937] Ch. 15.

trust fund, and the income from accumulations[65] until either the contingency is satisfied, or until the contingency fails.

(5) Accumulations at age 18

When the infant beneficiary attains the age of 18, the trustees will hold the accumulations, including income from the accumulated fund which has itself been accumulated:

(a) in accordance with any provision of the trust instrument; and, if there is no such provision
(b) either
  (i) for the beneficiary absolutely; or
  (ii) as an accretion to the capital of the trust property.[66]

A beneficiary will become entitled to the accumulations.

(a) in any circumstances in which the trust instrument so provides; or
(b) if:
  (i) during infancy, his interest was according to the settlement vested; *and*
  (ii) he attains the age of 18[67]; or
(c) if:
  (i) he attains the age of 18; *and*
  (ii) is then entitled to capital.[68]

For this purpose, he is entitled to capital if

(a) the property is realty, and the beneficiary is entitled to:
  (i) a fee simple absolute; or
  (ii) a fee simple determinable; or
  (iii) an entailed interest[69]; or
(b) the property is personalty, and the beneficiary is entitled to the property:
  (i) absolutely; or
  (ii) for an entailed interest.[70]

In any other case, the accumulations are added to the capital of the property from which they arose.[71] Where they arose from a share of a fund, and that share continued to exist as a separate share, the accumu-

---

[65] T.A. 1925, s.31(1)(ii).

[66] T.A. 1925, s.31(2).

[67] s.31(2)(i)(*a*). This also applies if he marries under the age of 18, and had a vested interest until marriage.

[68] s.31(2)(i)(*b*). This also applies if he marries under the age of 18.

[69] See *Re Sharp's Settlement Trusts* [1972] 3 W.L.R. 765, *per* Pennycuick V.-C. at 768.

[70] *Re Sharp's Settlement Trusts, ante.*

[71] s.32(2)(ii).

lations are an accretion to that share, and not to the fund as a whole.[72] This is in contrast to the position where the beneficiary dies before attaining the age of 18 (or marrying under that age), in which case, subject to any provision in the trust instrument, the accumulations are an accretion to the fund as a whole.[73]

This point arose for consideration in *Re Sharp's Settlement Trusts*.[74] A settlement was created by which a power of appointment was conferred over a fund, and the children of the settlor were entitled equally in default of appointment. The settlor had three children, Penelope, who attained her majority in 1964; Russell, who attained his majority in 1967; and Joanne who was still an infant. Income had arisen under the settlement since 1966, and the trustees allocated it to the three children equally. Between 1966 and when Russell attained his majority in 1967 his share of accumulated income amounted to about £5,000. Since 1967, his share of the income had been paid to him. Between 1966 and the date of the hearing, in May 1972, Joanne's share of accumulated income amounted to about £41,000 and the accumulation was continuing. The question was as to the entitlement to the accumulation which had arisen of Russell's share and of the accumulation which was arising of Joanne's share. The fund was of personalty, and Pennycuick V.C. held that the entitlement of Russell and Joanne was not absolute, because their shares were subject to the power of appointment which could still be exercised. There is an anomaly here[75] because, if the property had been realty and the interest of the beneficiaries had been a determinable fee,[76] they would have been entitled to the accumulations. However, in this case, Russell and Joanne were not entitled outright to the accumulation. Penelope said that the accumulations were accretions to their shares only, as those accumulations were derived from income which the trustees had allocated to their shares. Pennycuick V.C. held in their favour, so that the accumulations from Russell's share were held, with that share itself, for Russell subject to any future exercise of the power of appointment, and Joanne's share was likewise to be held, contingently on her attaining her majority. So far as Russell was concerned, therefore, he would be entitled to the income from his share, as increased by the accumulations.

The manner in which trustees deal with accumulations when a beneficiary reaches the age of 18 is illustrated by the following table. For the purposes of the table:

(a) "Conditions A" means that the beneficiary had a vested interest during infancy and attains the age of 18; and
(b) "Conditions B" means that the beneficiary attains the age of 18 and becomes entitled to the capital.

---

[72] *Re Sharp's Settlement Trusts, ante.*
[73] See *Re Joel* [1967] Ch. 14; *ante,* p. 339.
[74] *Re Sharp's Settlement Trusts, Ibbotson* v. *Bliss* [1972] 3 W.L.R. 765.
[75] See Pennycuick V.C. at p. 156.
[76] Although not a fee simple on condition. As to the distinction, see Megarry and Wade, *The Law of Real Property* (5th ed.), pp. 67 *et seq.*

Trust instrument provides for fund to be held for	Circumstances	Entitlement	Remarks
Andrew absolutely[77]	Andrew attains 18	Andrew	Conditions B
	Andrew dies under 18	Andrew's estate	The entitlement is by virtue of the original gift, not s. 31
Brian for life	Brian attains 18	Brian	Conditions A
	Brian dies under 18	Added to capital	Neither Conditions satisfied
Charles for life if he attains 18	Charles attains 18	Added to capital	Charles' interest during infancy was contingent only; and he does not become entitled to the capital
	Charles dies under 18	Added to capital	Neither Conditions satisfied
Douglas if he attains 18	Douglas attains 18	Douglas	Conditions B
	Douglas dies under 18	Added to capital	Neither Conditions satisfied
Edward if he attains 30	Edward attains 18	Added to capital	Neither Conditions satisfied
	Edward dies under 18	Added to capital	Neither Conditions satisfied
Frank, but if he dies under 30, for George	Frank attains 18	Frank	Although Frank's interest was defeasible, it was vested, and Conditions A is satisfied
	Frank dies under 18	Added to capital	Neither Conditions satisfied
Henry, but if he dies under 18, for Ian	Henry attains 18	Henry	Conditions A
	Henry dies under 18	Added to capital	Neither Conditions satisfied

It will be seen from this table that:

(a) where the beneficiary dies under the age of 18, the accumulations will always be added to capital, except where the property was held for an infant beneficiary absolutely (the example of Andrew);

(b) where the beneficiary has a life interest which is contingent on his attaining the age of 18, or some later age, then, notwithstanding that he satisfies the contingency, the accumulations are added to capital (the examples of Charles and Edward); and

(c) the distinction between a contingent interest (the examples of Charles and Edward) and a vested interest which is defeasible (the example of Frank) is crucial.

---

[77] Andrew's infancy being the only reason why he could not call for the capital to be transferred to him.

V. TAXATION CONSEQUENCES

Section 31 and the action taken by trustees under it can have a material effect on the tax position of the beneficiary. In considering these taxation consequences it is necessary to keep in mind that:

(a) section 31 can be excluded; and
(b) where, according to the terms of the settlement, an infant bene-ficiary has a vested life interest, by section 31 that interest is converted into a life interest contingent on his attaining 18 in respect of any income which is accumulated. This is because, notwithstanding the terms of the settlement,
    (i) during the minority of the beneficiary the trustees will have a power to maintain and a trust to accumulate the remaining income; and
    (ii) the beneficiary (or his estate) will only become entitled to the accumulations if he attains the age of 18.

The latter point can lead to confusion. In order to determine the destination of accumulations, whether or not a beneficiary had during his infancy a vested interest, regard is paid to the terms of the trust instrument. For other purposes, however, the nature of the benefici-ary's interest is determined by the terms of the trust instrument as modified by the section itself.

(1) Income tax

It has been seen[78] that the trustees are liable to income tax at the basic rate[79] on all income which they receive, regardless of whether it is used for the payment of trust management expenses, paid to a beneficiary, or accumulated; and if they have a discretion with regard to income, or are directed to accumulate it, they are liable to income tax at a flat rate of 35 per cent.[80]

If section 31 applies, then whether or not under the terms of the trust instrument the beneficiary's interest was vested or contingent, the trustees have a discretion, in that they have a power to maintain, so that there is a liability to the flat rate of 35 per cent.[81] However, there is no further liability on the beneficiary unless the income was actually paid out to him, or applied for his benefit.

There is, however, a further rule, under which a beneficiary will be taxable on the whole of the net trust income if he has a vested interest in it. He is taxable according to the income tax rates which govern his own income, but he is entitled to credit for the income tax paid by the trustees in respect of the trust income paid to him. Suppose, therefore,

---

[78] *Ante*, p. 411.
[79] At present (1994–1995) this is 25 per cent. except for company distributions, taxed at 20 per cent.
[80] The additional rate is not payable in respect of that part of the gross income which was paid out in trust management expenses.
[81] Assuming that none of the income is from company distributions. The example becomes more complex if some part is from this source.

that Harry has income apart from the trust of £36,000, of which £10,000 is unearned; that the income of the trust fund is £2,000, on which the trustees pay tax, at 25 per cent. of £500, that £250 is used for trust management expenses; and that £1,250 is paid to Harry. Harry's liability is as follows:

The trustees have received	£2,000
on which they have paid tax at 25% of	£ 500
leaving	£1,500
from which they have paid trust management expenses of	£ 250
leaving net income paid to Harry of	£1,250
This is treated as a gross sum of	£1,666.67
from which income tax [81a] has been deducted of	£ 416.67
	£1,250.00

So that Harry's trust income is:

the amount paid to him	£1,250.00	
and the tax deducted	£ 416.67	
		£ 1,666.67
which is added to his other income of		£36,000.00
		£37,666.67

On the "slice" of income between £36,000 and £37,666.67 the present rate of income tax[82] is 40% to give a liability of (40% × £1,666.67) £ 666.67
Harry suffered by deductions £ 416.67

and has a further liability of £ 250.00

Using the figures of this example:
(a)   if the whole of the income is accumulated, the total liability will be that of the trustees, as follows:

[81A] In effect, the £500 paid by the trustees is attributed: as to

$\frac{250}{1500} \times 500 = 83.\,33$ to trust management expenses

$\frac{1250}{1500} \times 500 = 416.67$ to income paid to Harry.

[82] For 1994–95.

Gross income		£2,000
less: tax at the basic rate, as before	£500	
less: tax at the flat rate of 35%, discounting the 25% already paid, on that part of the gross income of the trust £2,000 as is not used in the payment of trust management expenses		
	£ 250	£ 250
	£1,750	£1,750
that is: 10% × £1,750	£ 175	
so that the total tax paid is	£ 675	£ 675
and net amount accumulated is		£1,075

(b) if the whole of the income is treated as
Harry's the total tax payable, as before is   £ 666.67

leaving the benefit[83]   £1,000

The income will be treated as that of Harry, during Harry's minority, if:

(a) he is absolutely entitled to both capital and income, so that his infancy is the sole reason why he cannot call for the capital to be transferred to him, and either he, if he lives, or his estate, if he does not, will be entitled to the accumulations[84]; or

(b) according to the terms of the trust instrument, Harry is entitled to the whole of the income, and section 31 is excluded, so that the trustees do not have power to accumulate any part of it.

In all other circumstances, only that income which is actually paid to Harry, or applied for his benefit, is treated as his for income tax purposes.[85] The remainder of the income, which is accumulated, is taxable in the hands of the trustees at the effective rate of 35 per cent.

(2) Inheritance tax

It was explained earlier[86] that the tax legislation[87] divides settled property into two main categories, according to whether or not there is, at the time being considered, an interest in possession in it. A beneficiary has an interest in possession if he is entitled to the trust income

---

[83] The net income paid to Harry, £1,250, less the further tax payable by him in respect of it, £250.
[84] *Roberts* v. *Hanks* (1926) 10 T.C. 351; *Edwardes Jones* v. *Down* (1936) 20 T.C. 279.
[85] *Stanley* v. *I.R.C.* [1944] K.B. 255.
[86] *Ante*, p. 420.
[87] Finance (No. 2) Act 1987.

without any further decision of the trustees being requisite.[88] Subject to certain exceptions, a charge to tax arises whenever an interest in possession terminates.[89]

In general, if there is no interest in possession in settled property, and one arises, there is a charge to inheritance tax at that time.[90]

However, special inheritance tax privileges are given to "accumulation and maintenance settlements." These are governed by section 71 of the Inheritance Tax Act 1984, which was drafted with section 31 of the Trustee Act in mind. Section 71 of the 1984 Act provides that a settlement is an accumulation and maintenance settlement at a given time if,[91] at that time:

(a) there is no interest in possession in it;
(b) the income is applied for the maintenance, education or benefit of a beneficiary, and to the extent that it is not so applied, it is to be accumulated; and
(c) it can be said that one or more beneficiaries will, on attaining a specified age not exceeding 25, become beneficially entitled either
    (i) to the settled property itself; or
    (ii) to an interest in possession in the settled property.

Where the conditions for an accumulation and maintenance settlement are satisfied:

(a) the trust is not subject to what would otherwise be a charge to tax on every tenth anniversary of the date of its creation[92]; and
(b) there is no charge to tax when a beneficiary becomes entitled either to an interest in possession in the settled property or to the settled property itself.[93]

The following table[94] illustrates the interaction of section 31 of the Trustee Act and the inheritance tax provisions. In the table, "I.H.T." means Inheritance Tax, "Acc. & Mtce" means accumulation and maintenance settlement, "I.I.P." means interest in possession and "D.T." means discretionary trust.

---

[88] *Pearson* v. *I.R.C.* [1981] A.C. 753; *ante*, p. 483.
[89] Inheritance Tax Act 1984, ss.51, 52.
[90] Inheritance Tax Act 1984, s.65.
[91] Only the basic conditions are given in the text: certain further ancilliary conditions must also be satisfied: Inheritance Tax Act 1984, s.65.
[92] By virtue of Inheritance Tax Act 1984, ss.64, 66.
[93] Inheritance Tax Act 1984, s.65.
[94] Do not try to learn this table. It is intended to show how it is necessary to consider (a) the terms of the trust instrument; (b) whether the gift carries the intermediate income and (c) whether s.31 is or is not excluded.

Inter-action of Trustee Act 1925, s.31 and Inheritance tax provisions

Trust instrument provides for	Section 31 Applies			Section 31 Excluded		
	I.H.T. category during minority	Whether charge to tax on death under age 18	I.H.T. effect on attaining 18	I.H.T. category during minority	Whether charge to tax on death under age 18	I.H.T. effect on attaining 18
Andrew absolutely	Personal	Yes	Continues to be personal	Personal	Yes	Continues to be personal
Brian for life	Acc. & Mtce.[1]	No	Brian becomes entitled to I.I.P.	I.I.P.	Yes	I.I.P. continues
Charles for life if he attains 18	Acc. & Mtce.[2]	No	Charles becomes entitled to I.I.P.	(i) I.I.P. if gift carries intermediate income (ii) D.T. otherwise	Yes / No	I.I.P. continues / I.I.P. arises, if gift then carries intermediate income; and charge to tax
Douglas absolutely if he attains 18	Acc. & Mtce.[3]	No	Personal	(i) I.I.P. if gift carries intermediate income (ii) D.T. otherwise	Yes / No	Personal No charge to tax / Personal Charge to tax
Edward if he attains 30	(i) Acc. & Mtce.[4] if gift carries intermediate income (ii) D.T. otherwise	No	(i) I.I.P. if gift carries intermediate income (ii) D.T. otherwise	(i) I.I.P. if gift carries intermediate income (ii) D.T. otherwise	Yes / No	I.I.P. if gift continues to carry the intermediate income (i) I.I.P. arises if gift begins to carry intermediate income. Charge to tax (ii) Otherwise D.T. continues
Frank, but if he dies under 30, for George	Acc. & Mtce. if gift carries intermediate income	No	I.I.P. if gift carries intermediate income. No charge to tax	I.I.P. if gift carries intermediate income	Yes	If gift carries intermediate income, I.I.P. continues
Henry, but if he dies under 18, for Ian	Acc. & Mtce. if gift carries intermediate income	No	Personal. No charge to tax	I.I.P. if gift carries intermediate income / D.T. if gift does not carry intermediate income	Yes / No	Personal. No charge to tax if gift has carried intermediate income Personal. Charge to tax

(1) The apparent interest in possession of Brian is removed by s.31.
(2) The conditions for an accumulation and maintenance settlement are prima facie satisfied because Charles will become entitled at an age not exceeding 25.
(3) Provided that the gift carries the intermediate income.
(4) The vested defeasible interest of Edward is converted by s.31.

CHAPTER 18

APPLICATIONS OF TRUST CAPITAL

In general, entitlement to capital will depend on the terms of the trust instrument in the case of a fixed interest trust, or on the decision of the trustees in the case of a discretionary trust. However:

(a) as in the case of entitlement to income, the quantum of capital which is available for beneficiaries will be determined after the payment of those costs and expenses which are attributable to capital[1]; and

(b) even in the case of a fixed interest trust, the trustees may take decisions which will (i) alter the time at which a beneficiary will take capital; or (ii) which will affect the quantum of his entitlement.

The main powers which will affect the quantum of entitlement are the three "A"s, namely Advancement, Appointment, and Appropriation. Appointments have been dealt with previously. Accordingly, after dealing with expenses payable from capital, this chapter is concerned primarily with the powers of advancement and appropriation.

I. EXPENSES FROM CAPITAL

It has been seen[2] that, in general, recurrent expenses are generally payable out of the income of the trust fund. This is partly because of the recurrent nature of these expenses, and partly because such expenses are generally for the benefit primarily of the beneficiary who is entitled to income. The corollary is that, in principle, there is payable out of the capital of the trust fund expenses which

(a) constitute capital expenditure on one or more assets of the trust; or

(b) apply to the trust as a whole, and can, therefore, be said to be for the benefit of all beneficiaries.

Examples of expenses which are treated as capital expenditure on an asset are calls on shares which are partly paid[3]; sums applied in

---

[1] As to net income, see *ante*, p. 483.

[2] *Ante*, p. 483.

[3] *Todd* v. *Moorhouse* (1874) L.R. 19 Eq. 69; Trustee Act 1925, s.11(2).

discharging mortgage debts[4]; and sums applied in improving land and buildings.[5] Where a building is purchased by the trustees in a derelict state, the cost of putting it into good condition at the outset will be treated as if it were part of the purchase price, and so be chargeable to capital.[6] Ordinary repairs are, in principle, payable out of income, but where the repairs can be said to be for the benefit of all beneficiaries, the court may direct that the whole or part of the cost is to be borne by capital.[7]

The second category of expense which is borne by capital covers those items relating to the trust as a whole, and which can be said to be for the benefit of all beneficiaries. Examples are the costs of the appointment of new trustees[8]; of making changes in investment; of obtaining legal advice as to the extent of the trustees' powers[9]; and taking or defending court proceedings for the protection of trust assets.[10]

It has been mentioned[11] that in certain circumstances, either by statute or the trust instrument, trustees are given a discretion whether outgoings are to be paid from income or capital. This power must be exercised so that the particular outgoings will be borne equitably between the beneficiaries with different interests.[12]

II. ADVANCEMENT

(1) The concept

In essence, advancement consists of the payment or application of a capital sum in order to establish a person in life, or to make permanent provision for him.[13] An advancement is often of an amount which, in the light of the circumstances of the recipient, is large, and where a payment is large in this sense, there is a presumption that it is made by way of advancement.[14]

It is not now generally necessary to consider in the administration of trusts[15] whether a payment is, strictly, by way of advancement, because either under the statutory power, which is considered below, or under an express power in the trust instrument, the trustees will usually have

---

[4] *Whitbread* v. *Smith* (1854) 3 De G.M. & G. 727; *Marshall* v. *Crowther* (1874) 2 Ch.D. 199.

[5] *Earl of Cowley* v. *Wellesley* (1866) L.R. 1 Eq. 656; *Re Walker's Settled Estate* [1894] 1 Ch. 189.

[6] *Re Courtier* (1886) Ch.D. 136.

[7] Under the Settled Land and Trustee Acts (Courts' General Powers) Act 1943 and Emergency Powers (Miscellaneous Provisions) Act 1953.

[8] *Re Fulham* (1850) 15 Jur. 69; *Re Fellows' Settlement* (1856) 2 Jur. (N.S.) 62.

[9] *Poole* v. *Pass* (1839) 1 Beav. 600.

[10] *Re Earl of Berkeley's Will Trusts* (1874) 10 Ch. App. 56; *Re Earl De La Warr's Estates* (1881) 16 Ch.D. 587; *Stott* v. *Milne* (1884) 25 Ch.D. 710.

[11] *Ante*, p. 397.

[12] *Re Lord De Tabley* (1896) 75 L.T. 328; *Re Earl of Stamford and Warrington* [1916] 1 Ch. 404.

[13] *Boyd* v. *Boyd* (1867) L.R. 4 Eq. 305; *Taylor* v. *Taylor* (1875) L.R. 20 Eq. 155; *Re Hayward, Kerrod* v. *Hayward* [1957] Ch. 528; *Hardy* v. *Shaw* [1975] 2 All E.R. 1052.

[14] Per Jessel M.R., *Taylor* v. *Taylor* (1875) L.R. 20 Eq. 155 at p. 157; per Goff J., *Hardy* v. *Shaw* [1975] 2 All E.R. 1052 at p. 1056.

[15] It is otherwise in the administration of estates; see Administration of Estates Act 1925, s.46(1).

a power to apply capital for the advancement or other benefit of a beneficiary.

(2) The statutory power

The statutory power is contained in section 32 of the Trustee Act 1925. This section gives trustees a power to pay or apply capital for the benefit of any beneficiary who is interested in the capital of the trust fund, whether his interest is vested or contingent, and whether or not it is liable to be defeated by the exercise of a power. If the power is exercised, there is always one and there may be two important effects:

1. The beneficiary who is advanced receives benefit from the capital earlier than he otherwise would. If, for example, trustees hold a fund upon trust for Gerald for life, with remainder to Harry, and if, during the lifetime of Gerald,[16] the trustees pay part of the fund to Harry, Harry takes the benefit of that part at that time, rather than having to wait until the death of Gerald; and
2. The beneficiary who is advanced receives benefit from the capital whereas otherwise he might not have received any benefit. Suppose that trustees hold a fund upon trust for Ian if he attains the age of 30, but, if he dies under that age, for John. Suppose also that the trustees pay part of the trust fund to Ian when he is aged 22, and that he dies when he is aged 25. Had that payment not been made, because Ian did not satisfy the condition he would have received no capital benefit.

There are four limitations on the statutory power, which are now to be considered.

(a) **Extent of power.** The trustees can make payments by way of advancement or benefit on more than one occasion, provided that the total which is paid or applied does not exceed one half of the presumptive or vested share of the beneficiary.[17] It was decided in *The Marquess of Abergavenny* v. *Ram*[18] that where, at the time of the advancement, the trustees pay out one half of the share, then the power is exhausted, and no further advancement can be made even if the value of the remaining trust assets appreciates.[19] Suppose that there have been no previous advancements; that the trustees made an advancement of £25,000 in 1990; that the value of the whole of the trust fund at that time was £50,000; and that in 1995 the value of the remainder of the trust fund is £80,000. The trustees fully exhausted their power in 1990, and can make no further advancement in 1995. If, however, they only advanced

---

[16] As to the need for Gerald to give his consent, see *infra*.

[17] T.A. 1925, s.32(1), proviso (*a*).

[18] [1981] 1 W.L.R. 843.

[19] The decision was on a provision of the Marquess of Abergavenny's Estate Act 1946, but it is of equal application to s.32 of the Trustee Act 1925.

£24,000 in 1990, so that their power was not fully exhausted, in 1995 they could advance the further sum of £28,000.[20]

(b) Bringing into account.   The second limitation is that if, after a beneficiary has been advanced, he is, or becomes, absolutely and indefeasibly entitled to the trust property, or a share in it, he must bring into account the amount of his advancement.[21] Suppose, therefore, that trustees hold a fund upon trust for James and John in equal shares if and when they attain the age of 30; that the trustees paid £20,000 by way of advancement to James when he was aged 26; and that when they attain the age of 30 the fund is worth £100,000. On the distribution of the trust fund, the amounts which James and John receive are:

Value of fund	£100,000
Amount advanced	£ 20,000
Total	£120,000

Entitlement

	James	John
$\frac{1}{2} \times$ £120,000	£60,000	£60,000
Less: advancement	£20,000	—
Net entitlement	£40,000	£60,000

When an advancement was not made in cash but in *specie*, the amount to be brought into account is the value of the asset at the time when the beneficiary becomes absolutely and indefeasibly entitled to his share.[22]

If the beneficiary had only a contingent or defeasible interest, and never becomes absolutely and indefeasibly entitled, there is no clawback of the amount advanced to him. By making an advance to a contingent beneficiary, therefore, the trustees can partially defeat the interests of other beneficiaries.

(c) Consent where prior interests.   If a beneficiary has a prior interest, he must be of full age and consent in writing to the advancement. This is because any advancement will prejudice his interest. Thus

---

[20] The calculation is:

Value of fund in 1995	£ 80,000
Add: amount previously advanced	£ 24,000
	£104,000
One half thereof	£ 52,000
less: previously advanced	£ 24,000
Maximum further advance	£28,000

[21] T.A. 1925, s.32(1), proviso (*b*). The Law Reform Committee (23rd Report, 1982) has recommended that the amount to be brought into account should be increased by reference to movements in the Index of Retail Prices.
[22] See, *e.g. Hardy* v. *Shaw* [1975] 2 All E.R. 1052.

if £10,000 is settled upon trust for Mary for life, with remainder to Derek, the trustees have a power to advance £5,000 to Derek, but only if Mary consents. If Mary consents and the advancement is made, thereafter her income will be that produced by the remaining £5,000 and not, as previously, by £10,000. A person on whom property is settled on protective trusts will not normally forfeit his life interest by consenting to an advancement.[23]

(d) **Nature of trust property.** The fourth limitation on the statutory power is that it applies only to money or securities, or to land which is held on trust for sale, and is treated as being converted into money.[24]

(3) Extensions and exclusions of statutory power
The statutory power will apply even where there is no mention of it in the trust instrument, but the power is one which falls within the scope of section 69(2)[25] and so may be excluded by the settlor or testator in the trust instrument. Thus, in *Re Evans's Settlement*[26] Stamp J. held that where the trust instrument provided that the trustees could advance up to £5,000, this by implication excluded the statutory power of advancing up to one-half of the prospective interest. Further, in *I.R.C.* v. *Bernstein*,[27] where there was a direction to accumulate income during the settlor's lifetime, the Court of Appeal held that this was a sufficient indication that the settlor did not intend the statutory power of advancement to apply.

It is more likely, however, that the statutory power will be extended. The most usual extensions give the trustees a power to advance up to the whole and not merely half of the beneficiary's share; extend the power to realty; and in some cases, do away with the need to obtain the consent of beneficiaries having prior interests.

(4) Purpose of advancement
It has been seen[28] that, originally, a power of advancement was held to relate to some substantial preferment in life. Examples were the purchasing of a commission in the Army[29]—the modern equivalent would be purchasing a partnership in a practice—purchasing or furnishing a house,[30] or even establishing a husband in business.[31] It has also been seen that this need for substantial setting up in life is now modified by the inclusion in the statutory power of "benefit", which is a word of wide import. But the trustees must still consider whether a particular gift is for the benefit of the beneficiary. In *Lowther* v. *Bentinck*[32] it was held that the payment of his debts was not for the

---

[23] See *ante*, p. 187.
[24] T.A. 1925, s.32(2).
[25] *Ante*, p. 490.
[26] [1967] 1 W.L.R. 1294.
[27] [1960] Ch. 444.
[28] *Ante*, p. 503.
[29] *Lawrie* v. *Bankes* (1857) 4 Kay & J. 142.
[30] *Perry* v. *Perry* (1870) 18 W.R. 482.
[31] *Re Kershaw's Trust* (1868) L.R. 6 Eq. 322.
[32] (1875) L.R. 19 Eq. 166.

benefit of a beneficiary, though in special circumstances a payment to a beneficiary to enable him to discharge his debts might be a benefit for this purpose. It is, however, quite clear that the trustees must not make an advancement to benefit themselves. In *Molyneux* v. *Fletcher*,[33] where the trustees made an advance to a daughter-beneficiary to enable her to pay her father's debts to one of the trustees, this was held to be an improper exercise of the power.

In most cases the "benefit" for which an advancement is made is material benefit. In some circumstances, however, the court will authorise an advancement to be made for the moral, and not necessarily material, benefit of the beneficiary. In *Re Clore*[34] the beneficiary was entitled to an interest in a trust fund of considerable value and he felt a moral obligation to make payments to charity. Pennycuick J. authorised this on the basis, it seems, that as the beneficiary felt this obligation payment by the trustees was only relieving him of a financial obligation which he would otherwise have sought to meet from his personal funds. The judge made it clear, however, that the beneficiary must feel the moral obligation and that the trustees were not at liberty to make payments in satisfaction of what *they* considered to be the beneficiary's moral obligation if the beneficiary did not share their view. Except where, perhaps, small amounts are involved, it is prudent for trustees to seek the prior sanction of the court before making advancements of this nature.

Just as trustees cannot properly make an advancement to benefit themselves,[35] they cannot make an advancement with a view to benefiting some other person. In *Re Pauling's Settlement Trusts*[36] the bankers Messrs. Coutts & Co. were trustees of a fund which was held upon trust for a wife for her life, with remainder on her death to her children. The trust instrument contained an express power for the trustees to advance to the children up to one-half of their share with the consent of the wife. The husband of the life-tenant, who was the father of the children, lived beyond his means and sought to obtain part of the trust moneys. A series of advancements were made, nominally to the children, but the money was used for the benefit of their father, or generally for the family. Thus the proceeds of one advancement were used to purchase a house for the father in the Isle of Man and the proceeds of another advancement to discharge a loan incurred by the mother. The trustees had been advised by counsel that so far as the trustees were concerned they were paying the money to the children for their own absolute use and that, in effect, what the children did with the money was not the trustees' concern. This view was unanimously rejected by the Court of Appeal (Willmer, Harman and Upjohn L.JJ.), who considered that "the power [of advancement] can be exercised only if it is for the benefit of the child or remoter issue to be advanced or, as was said during argument, it is thought to be 'a good thing' for the

---

[33] [1898] 1 Q.B. 648.
[34] [1966] 1 W.L.R. 955.
[35] *Molyneux* v. *Fletcher, supra.*
[36] [1964] Ch. 303.

advanced person to have a share of capital before his or her due time. . . . [A] power of advancement [can] be exercised only if there is some good reason for it. That good reason must be beneficial to the person to be advanced; [the power] cannot be exercised capriciously or with some other benefit in view."[37]

In their consideration of the circumstances in which an advancement could properly be made, the Court of Appeal drew a distinction between the situation where the *beneficiary* applies for an advancement for a particular purpose and the situation where the trustees themselves stipulate the purpose to which the advancement is to be put. As Willmer L.J. said: "if the trustees make the advance for a particular purpose which they state, they can quite properly pay it over to the advancee if they reasonably think they can trust him or her to carry out the prescribed purpose. What they cannot do is to prescribe a particular purpose and then raise and pay the money over to the advancee, leaving him or her entirely free, legally and morally, to apply it for that purpose or to spend it in any way he or she chooses . . . this much is plain, that if such misapplication [of the money advanced] came to [the trustees'] notice, they could not safely make further advances for particular purposes without making sure that the money was in fact applied to that purpose, since the advancee would have shown him or herself quite irresponsible."[38]

The court expressly left open the question whether, in the event of money which was advanced for a particular purpose being used for something different, that money could be recovered by the trustees. This possibility apart, once the trustees have paid over the money, they have no further legal control over it, and they must, therefore, ensure that the beneficiary is under a moral obligation to apply the money to the purpose intended.

(5) Adult beneficiaries
While, as has been seen,[39] the statutory power of maintenance applies only to infant beneficiaries, the statutory power of advancement can be exercised in favour of beneficiaries of any age.[40]

(6) Taxation
Where there is an advancement, there may be a liability both to capital gains tax and inheritance tax. If the advancement is made in cash, there can be no liability to capital gains tax in respect of the advancement itself although, if the trustees disposed of chargeable assets in order to produce funds with which to make the advancement, a liability to capital gains tax may have arisen according to general principles.[41] If, however, the advancement is made *in specie*, at the time when the trustees decide to make the advancement, they will be deemed to have

---

[37] *Ibid.* at 333; [1963] 3 All E.R. 1 at p. 8.
[38] [1964] Ch. 303 at pp. 334, 335.
[39] *Ante*, p. 490.
[40] In *Hardy* v. *Shaw* [1975] 2 All E.R. 1052 there was an advancement, in the strict sense, in favour of persons who were middle-aged.
[41] *Ante*, p. 416.

disposed of the asset at its market value at that time, and then to have re-acquired it at that value as nominees for the beneficiary.[42] If the asset had risen in value since it was acquired, the same capital gains tax results will ensue as if the asset were actually sold for that value. However, provided that the beneficiary is resident in the United Kingdom, the trustees and the beneficiary can elect that "hold-over" relief shall apply if the assets settled comprise business property[43] or if the creation of the trust involves a chargeable transfer for the purposes of inheritance tax.[44]

With regard to inheritance tax, if the advancement is to a beneficiary who immediately before the advancement had an interest in possession, there will be no liability to inheritance tax by virtue of the advancement.[45] In any other case there will be a liability,[46] although in the case of small advancements, this liability may be reduced by the use of the annual exemption[47] of the beneficiary who has the interest in possession.

III. Settled Advances

(1) Generally

Originally, an advancement consisted of an outright payment of money or transfer of an asset to a beneficiary, but during this century[48] it has become established that a power of advancement can, in principle, be exercised so that the money or property is not transferred outright, but becomes held on new trusts for the benefit of the beneficiary to be advanced.[49] This is usually done in one of three ways:

    (a) if the beneficiary is *sui juris*, the trustees might make an outright payment to him, thereby putting him in the position of creating a new settlement[50]; or

    (b) the trustees might exercise a power given to them in the trust instrument by declaring that thenceforth they will hold a part of trust fund on separate trusts for the benefit of the beneficiary to be advanced[51]; or

    (c) a new settlement might be created, either by the trustees or by some other person, usually with a nominal sum of money, so that

---

[42] Taxation of Chargeable Gains Act 1992, s.71(1).

[43] *Ibid*. s.165.

[44] See *ante*, p. 417.

[45] Finance Act 1975, Sched. 5, para. 4(3).

[46] Para. 4(2).

[47] For 1994–95 this is £3,000. There will be no tax payable if the taxpayer has not used his 7 year nil rate band.

[48] Following certain decisions at the end of the last century.

[49] The principle has long been established. See *Re Halstead's Will Trusts* [1937] 2 All E.R. 570; *Re Moxon's Will Trusts* [1958] 1 W.L.R. 165; *Re Ropner's Settlement Trusts* [1956] 1 W.L.R. 902; *Re Wills' Will Trusts* [1959] Ch. 1; *Re Abraham's Will Trusts* [1969] 1 Ch. 463; *Re Hastings-Bass* [1975] Ch. 25; *Pilkington* v. *I.R.C.* [1964] A.C. 612.

[50] In *Roper-Curzon* v. *Roper-Curzon* (1871) L.R. 11 Eq. 452, where it was necessary for the court to give its sanction to an advancement, it refused to give that sanction unless the beneficiary did resettle the amount to be advanced.

[51] See, for example, *Hoare Trustees* v. *Gardner* [1978] 1 All E.R. 791.

a convenient "vehicle" is established. The trustees of the existing settlement then transfer the amount to be advanced to the trustees of the new settlement to be held on the trusts declared by it, as an addition to the funds of that settlement.[52]

It follows that the trustees of the original settlement may, but will not necessarily, be the trustees of the advanced fund.

Whichever method is used, whether by way of resettlement, appointment, or transfer to a new settlement, it will be convenient in this chapter to refer to funds passing from an existing settlement into a new settlement.

Where there is to be an advance into settlement in one of these ways, the questions which arise are:

(i) is the proposed advance for the benefit of the beneficiary to be advanced?

(ii) can the proposed advance be also for the benefit of other beneficiaries?

(iii) to what extent can the new settlement confer an effective dispositive discretion on the trustees? and

(iv) what perpetuity period applies to the new settlement?

(2) Benefit of the advanced beneficiary

Any advancement, whether outright or into settlement, must be for the benefit of the beneficiary to be advanced. The cases establish the following principles:

(a) In general, "benefit" means direct financial benefit, so that it is likely that there will not be a valid exercise of the power of advancement if the quantum of the beneficiary's interest is reduced. The point is likely to arise where the trustees wish to advance into a protective trust for the benefit of the beneficiary to be advanced. In *Re Morris*[53] Jenkins L.J. laid down the principle that a "power of advancement is a purely ancillary power, enabling the trustee to anticipate by means of an advance under it the date of actual enjoyment by a beneficiary . . . and it can only affect the destination of the fund indirectly in the event of the person advanced failing to attain a vested interest." So he held that an advance into settlement upon protective trusts was not valid because it altered the beneficial interests.

As will be seen,[54] however, some advances into settlement upon protective trusts are valid. This requirement that the advancement is to be for the direct financial benefit of the beneficiary is, however, subject to the following points.

(b) An advance into settlement will be for the benefit of the beneficiary if the tax liability which would otherwise arise in respect of the

---

[52] See, for example, *Hart* v. *Briscoe* [1978] 1 All E.R. 791; *Pilkington* v. *I.R.C.* [1964] A.C. 612.

[53] [1951] 2 All E.R. 528.

[54] *Infra.*

funds held for the beneficiary is mitigated.[55] The position was summarised by Viscount Radcliffe in *Pilkington* v. *I.R.C.*[56] when he said[57] that " . . . if the advantage of preserving the funds of a beneficiary from the incidence of [tax][58] is not an advantage personal to that beneficiary, I do not see what is."

(c) If, in order to effect the tax mitigation, it is necessary for the beneficiary not to take any, or any direct, financial interest in the advanced fund, the advancement may still be proper. The decision in *Re Clore's Settlement Trusts*[59] has been mentioned.[60] That case was concerned with the transfer of funds into a charitable settlement under which the beneficiary took no beneficial interest.[61]

(d) In determining whether an advancement into settlement is for the benefit of a beneficiary, there must be considered all the terms of the instrument which constitutes the new settlement and not merely those under which the trustees are in practice likely to act. In *Re Hunter*[62] where a testator settled property upon trust for his sister for life, with remainder to her children with "such provision for their respective advancement maintenance and education" as the sister should appoint, one of the sister's sons was financially unstable and became bankrupt shortly after she made her will. In an attempt to enable her son to enjoy the benefit of part of the trust property, she purported to appoint that property upon protective trusts for her son. Cross J. held the trust invalid, following the dictum of Jenkins L.J. in *Re Morris*[63] that protective trusts should not be regarded "merely as a device to enable a forfeiting life-tenant to enjoy the income notwithstanding purported alienation and so forth or the event of his or her bankruptcy, and that the discretionary trust should be regarded merely as machinery to that end and not as really designed to confer any beneficial interest on the issue nominally included in it. The validity or otherwise of the discretionary trust declared in the event of forfeiture must, in my view, be determined by reference to what the trustees are empowered to do under such a trust, and not be reference to what they would in fact be likely to do, or be expected to do, under it."

(e) A beneficiary may derive a benefit from knowing that financial provision is being made for his wife and children. So, in *Re Halsted's Will Trusts*,[64] Farwell J. held that trustees in exercising a power of advancement for a beneficiary could properly settle funds upon trust for the beneficiary, his wife and his children.

(f) There is no necessary connection between "benefit" and "need."

---

[55] *Re Ropner's Settlement Trusts* [1956] 3 All E.R. 332; Re Meux [1958] Ch. 154; *Re Wills' Will Trusts* [1959] Ch. 1.
[56] [1964] A.C. 612.
[57] At p. 640.
[58] In this case, the tax was estate duty.
[59] [1966] 1 W.L.R. 955.
[60] *Ante*, p. 507.
[61] The decision may depend on its particular facts.
[62] [1963] Ch. 372.
[63] [1951] 2 All E.R. 528; *supra*.
[64] [1937] 2 All E.R. 570.

Thus, the advancement of funds may be valid if the trustees consider that it is for the benefit of the beneficiary, irrespective of his need.[65]

(3) Other beneficiaries

Property will only be settled if at least one person other than the beneficiary to be advanced has some interest in it, whether vested or contingent. The fact that one or more other persons will or might benefit does not in itself make defective an advance into settlement. This is one of the several points which the House of Lords decided in *Pilkington* v. *I.R.C.*[66] In that case a testator set up a will trust under which the trustees were directed to hold the trust fund upon trust, broadly, for the benefit of the testator's nephew Richard, for life, with remainder to such of his children as he should appoint, or, in default of appointment, for all of his children in equal shares. Richard had three children, all born after the death of the testator, of whom one was Richard's daughter Penelope. When Penelope was still very young, the trustees wished to advance funds into a new settlement for her benefit. Accordingly, her grandfather proposed to create a settlement under which the income would be accumulated, or used for Penelope's maintenance until she reached the age of 21. Penelope was to be entitled to income on attaining that age, and to the capital on attaining the age of 30. Other members of the family were to benefit if Penelope died under the age of 30. The trustees of the original settlement proposed to transfer one half of Penelope's share under that settlement to the trustees of the proposed new settlement. The House of Lords held that, in principle,[67] this would be within the trustees' power of advancement, notwithstanding the fact that other members of the family might benefit.

(4) Dispositive discretions under new settlement

In *Re Wills Will Trusts*[68] Upjohn J. said[69] that "a settlement created in exercise of the power of advancement cannot in general delegate any powers or discretions, at any rate in relation to beneficial interests, to any trustees or other persons, and in so far as the settlement purports to do so, it is *pro tanto* invalid." This has led to the view that an advance into a discretionary settlement would be unauthorised. It has also led to the view that if there is an effective advancement into a settlement upon protective trusts, the discretionary trusts which would otherwise arise on the termination of the principal beneficiary's life interest would be ineffective. Both the dictum of Upjohn J. and the views developed from it follow the maxim *delegatus non potest delegare*.

It is submitted that the better view is that discretions can be conferred on the trustees of the new settlement. In the first place, in

---

[65] In *Re Pilkington's Will Trusts* [1961] Ch. 466 the Court of Appeal had held that there could only be a valid advancement into settlement where the benefit to be conferred was related to the real or personal needs of the beneficiary. This was rejected by the House of Lords in *Pilkington* v. *I.R.C.* [1964] A.C. 612.

[66] [1964] A.C. 612.

[67] The actual appointment was void as a contravention of the perpetuity rules.

[68] [1959] Ch. 1.

[69] At p. 13.

Pilkington v. *I.R.C.*[70] Viscount Radcliffe said[71]: "I am unconvinced by the argument that the trustees would be improperly delegating their trust by allowing the money raised to pass over to new trustees under a settlement conferring new powers on the latter. In fact I think the whole issue of delegation is here beside the mark. The law is not that trustees cannot delegate: it is that trustees cannot delegate unless they have authority to do so. If the power of advancement which they possess is so read as to allow them to raise money for the purpose of having it settled[72] then they do have the necessary authority to let the money pass out of the old settlement into the new trusts. No question of delegation of their powers or trust arises." It is submitted that this means that, provided that the power in the original settlement is sufficiently wide, the advancement can properly be made into a new settlement which does confer dispositive powers on the trustees; and that the statutory power, or an express power to the like effect, will be construed as being sufficiently wide.

Furthermore, where there is an advancement into settlement, the principle of *delegatus non potest delegare* will rarely be observed in its entirety. It is clear that the new settlement may itself include powers of advancement.[73] While in concept a power of advancement may be a power merely to bring forward the date at which a beneficiary would otherwise enjoy the trust property,[74] it has been seen[75] that the exercise of such a power may well alter the beneficial entitlement to the funds advanced.

Thirdly, if in appropriate circumstances,[76] there can be a valid advancement into a settlement under which the beneficiary to be advanced takes no beneficial interest, it is absurd if there cannot be a valid advance into a settlement under which he is a discretionary beneficiary.[77]

While it is thought, therefore, that there is no fundamental objection to the new settlement conferring upon the trustees dispositive powers, in any particular case it is still necessary to show that that is for the benefit of the beneficiary who is being advanced.

(5) The perpetuity period

Where the trustees of an existing settlement make an advance into a new settlement, for the purposes of the perpetuity rules they are treated as if they had exercised a special power of appointment. Accordingly, the interests limited by the new settlement, as read back into the original settlement, must comply with the perpetuity rule. It was on this

---

[70] [1964] A.C. 612.

[71] At p. 639.

[72] Which was how the power was read by the House of Lords.

[73] *Re Mewburn* [1934] Ch. 112; *Re Morris* [1951] 2 All E.R. 528; *Re Hunter's Will Trusts* [1963] Ch. 372.

[74] *Re Morris* [1951] 2 All E.R. 528; *ante,* p. 510.

[75] *Ante,* p. 510.

[76] As in *Re Clore's Settlement Trust* [1966] 1 W.L.R. 955; *ante,* p. 507.

[77] Although the issues of benefit and delegation are separate, much greater tax mitigation may be achieved by using discretionary, rather than fixed interest, trusts.

ground that the House of Lords held that the proposed appointment in
Pilkington v. *I.R.C.*[78] would have been void.

The Perpetuities and Accumulations Act 1964 will only apply to the
advancement if the original settlement itself was made after July 15,
1964,[79] so that the old perpetuity rule must still govern many advancements. Where, however, the 1964 Act does apply, the interests under
the new settlement will be treated as valid until, if at all, it becomes
established that they will vest outside the perpetuity period.[80]

If all of the interests purportedly conferred by the new settlement will
not vest within the perpetuity period, the result will depend on
whether the effective provisions of the new settlement when taken by
themselves, will be for the benefit of the beneficiary to be advanced,
and will not be totally different in effect from what the trustees
intended. This is shown by the decision in *Re Hastings-Bass (deceased)*.[81]
In that case trustees transferred from an existing settlement the sum of
£50,000 to be held upon the trusts of a new settlement, intending that
transfer to be an advancement for the primary benefit of a beneficiary.
William. The trustees misunderstood the effect of the new settlement,
under which William took a life interest, but all the remaining
provisions of which were void because of contravention of the rule
against perpetuities. The first question was whether the statutory
power of advancement could be exercised where the effect was to give
the advanced beneficiary, in this case William, only an interest in
income, and no interest in capital. The court held that this was a
sufficient "application" of the funds and that the appointment was not
necessarily defective on that ground.

The second question was one of more general application: was the
purported exercise of the power effective when the trustees did not fully
appreciate the effects of the new settlement and so could not take into
account all the relevant circumstances? The court held that where
trustees purport to exercise a power in good faith then, even if the effect
of that purported exercise is different from that intended by the
trustees, the court would only interfere with the purported exercise in
two circumstances. First, the court would interfere if the result actually
achieved was not authorised by the trustees' power. Secondly, the court
would interfere if it was clear that the trustees would not have acted as
they did had they not taken into account considerations which they
ought not to have taken into account or if they had not failed to take into
account considerations which they ought to have taken into account. In
this case, the effect of conferring upon William an effective life interest
was to achieve a substantial saving of estate duty.[82] It was likely,
therefore, that the trustees would have acted, broadly, as they did if

---

[78] [1964] A.C. 612; *ante*, p. 511.
[79] Section 15(4) will apply to exclude the Act in the case of original settlements made
before that date.
[80] Section 3; *ante*, p. 168.
[81] [1975] Ch. 25.
[82] The inheritance tax rules are different, and no tax would be saved if the facts were
repeated at the present time.

they had appreciated the true effect of the advancement, and the court held that the exercise of their power was valid.

If, however, had they appreciated the true effect of their action, the trustees would not have acted as they did, their purported exercise of the power would have been void.[83]

(6) Taxation

Just as a liability to capital gains tax may arise in the case of an ordinary advancement,[84] so it may arise in the case of a settled advance. The capital gains tax legislation treats most settlements as if they were a separate legal person, so that if an asset is transferred from one settlement to another settlement, the asset is deemed to be disposed of by the trustees of the transferring settlement and acquired by the trustees of the acquiring settlement. However, the capital gains tax legislation does not prescribe rules for determining what constitutes a separate settlement. For example, if the trustees of a settlement declare that they will thenceforth hold part of the trust fund on separate trusts for the benefit of a beneficiary to be advanced, does that part become subject to a new settlement, or does it remain within the original settlement. In *Roome* v. *Edwards*[85] Lord Wilberforce said[86] "Since 'settlement' and 'trusts' are legal terms, which are also used by businessmen or laymen in a business or practical sense, I think that the question whether a particular set of facts amounts to a settlement should be approached by asking what a person, with a knowledge of the legal context of the word under established doctrine and applying this knowledge in a practical and commonsense manner to the facts under examination, would conclude."

If the resettlement occurs only as the result of the exercise by the trustees of their powers under the original settlement, it seems that the exercise of a special power of appointment will not amount to a resettlement and a consequential deemed disposal of the property in question[87]; on the other hand, while the exercise of a wider power, such as a power of advancement, will not necessarily amount to a resettlement, it will have this effect if the new settlement is complete in itself and is sufficiently separate to require no further reference back for any purpose to the original settlement.[88] If there is such a resettlement, the trustees of the original settlement are deemed to dispose of all the assets which become subject to the new settlement at their market value at the time and the assets are then reacquired at that value. However, if the acquiring settlement is resident in the United Kingdom hold over relief is available if the assets comprise business property[89] or if the creation

---

[83] *e.g. Re Abraham's Will Trust* [1969] 1 Ch. 463.
[84] *Ante*, p. 508.
[85] [1981] 1 All E.R. 736, H.L.
[86] At p. 739.
[87] *Roome* v. *Edwards* [1981] S.T.C. 96, *Bond* v. *Pickford* [1983] S.T.C. 517.
[88] *Swires* v. *Renton* [1991] S.T.C. 490.
[89] Taxation of Chargeable Gains Act 1992, s.165.

of the new settlement involves a chargeable transfer for the purposes of inheritance tax.[90]

There may also be a liability to inheritance tax if there was an interest in possession under the original settlement and the same beneficiary does not have an immediate interest in possession under the new settlement.[91] There will not usually be a liability if there was no interest in possession either under the original or the new settlement,[92] but in other cases there usually will be.

IV. OTHER APPLICATIONS OF CAPITAL

In some cases, the power of maintenance and advancement contained in the trust instrument, or the statutory powers, will not be sufficient for a beneficiary's needs. Where this is so there are four other possibilities:

(a) maintenance from capital;
(b) application to the court under section 53 of the Trustee Act 1925;
(c) application to the court under its inherent jurisdiction;
(d) application to the court to vary the trust. This is considered at page 541.

(1) Maintenance out of capital

Although, in principle, income is to be used for the maintenance of a beneficiary,[93] it is just possible that trustees can use capital for this purpose.

Section 31 of the Trustee Act 1925 clearly envisages that only income will be used for maintenance and in a note to the old case of *Barlow* v. *Grant*[94] it was said that "the court will not permit executors and trustees to break in upon the capital of infants' legacies without the sanction of the court, and the court itself, though it will break in upon the capital for the purpose of advancement, will rarely do so for maintenance." But however rarely a court might exercise its power to use capital for an infant's maintenance, it does have such a power. Lord Alvanley said in *Lee* v. *Brown*[95] that: "The principle is now established that if an executor does without application what the court would have approved, he shall not be called to account, and forced to undo that merely because it was done without application." The extent of this dictum—the case was on advancement—is not clear and it is just possible that a trustee who maintained out of capital would not be called upon to make good the capital if the court would itself have ordered maintenance out of capital.

Quite apart from its doubtful legality, however, there would be taxation disadvantages in doing so, for in respect of every £1 taken out of the capital for this purpose the trustees would have to deduct income

---

[90] See *ante*, p. 417.
[91] Inheritance Tax Act 1984, ss.51, 52.
[92] *Ibid.* s.81; however, for tax purposes the property remains comprised in the first settlement.
[93] See *ante*, p. 490.
[94] (1684) 1 Vern. 255.
[95] (1798) 4 Ves. 362.

tax at the basic rate and pay it over to the Revenue.[96] Where, however, an advancement of capital is made, no income tax is payable and by making an advancement, the same result can now usually be achieved as a purported maintenance out of capital.

(2) Section 53

Section 53 of the Trustee Act 1925 provides that where an infant is beneficially entitled to any property, the court may "with a view to the application of the capital or income thereof for the maintenance, education, or benefit of the infant" make an order appointing a person to convey the infant's interest on his behalf. This section is chiefly used where the infant's interest is small, and produces very little income, but where, if the interest were sold, the proceeds could be used for the infant's maintenance or benefit.[97] It was, however, pointed out in *Re Meux*[98] that this section does not give a power to dispose of the infant's interest whenever it is merely for the infant's benefit: there must be "a view to the application" of the capital or income for the maintenance, education or benefit of the infant. It seems that it must be intended to *apply* the capital or income in some way for the benefit of the infant. In *Re Heyworth's Contingent Reversionary Interest*[99] the court refused to give its consent under section 53 to a proposal merely to sell the infant's interest and hand over a cash sum, without there being any clear idea as to what was to happen to that money thereafter. On the other hand, where it is proposed to resettle the money and the transaction as a whole is for the infant's benefit, the court has held that the fact of resettling was a sufficient "application" to come within section 53.[1]

An example of the use of this power is contained in *Re Bristol's Settled Estates*.[2] In that case there were two tenants in tail of settled land, the Marquess of Bath and his infant son Lord Jermyn. The estate was a large one and to save estate duty it was, in essence, intended that the existing settlement should be terminated, part of the property paid absolutely to the Marquess, and the remaining part resettled. Provided the Marquess lived for a period of five years (and an insurance policy was to be taken out to cover this) both he and the ultimate beneficiaries would gain by the arrangement, the only loser being the Revenue. Before the scheme could be put into operation, it was necessary for the entailed interest to be barred. The Marquess could bar his entail, and were he not a minor, Lord Jermyn could have barred his entail with the consent of the Marquess as the protector of the settlement. The court made an order under section 53 appointing a named person to execute with the consent of the protector of the settlement an assurance on behalf of Lord Jermyn barring his entailed interest in the property, so that the capital

---

[96] See *ante*, p. 411.
[97] *Ex p. Green* (1820) 1 Jac. & W. 253; *Ex p. Chambers* (1829) 1 Russ. & M. 577; *Ex p Swift* (1828) 1 Russ. & M. 575.
[98] [1958] Ch. 154.
[99] [1956] Ch. 364.
[1] *Re Meux, ante.*
[2] [1965] 1 W.L.R. 469; [1964] 3 All E.R. 939.

and income could, under the proposed scheme, be appointed for his benefit.[3]

Clearly within the terms of the provisions of section 53 are schemes for raising money for the education of an infant, or to provide a house or purchase a share in a partnership for him.[4]

(3) Inherent jurisdiction

In limited circumstances the court has an inherent jurisdiction (quite apart from the Variation of Trusts Act 1958) to modify the terms of the trust.[5] One of the occasions in which it will do so is where a settlor or testator has made some provision for a family, but has postponed the enjoyment, for example, by directing accumulation of the income for a set period. Where this is done, the trustees cannot themselves use the income to maintain an infant, but the court will assume from the fact that the settlor has made provision for the family that he did not intend to leave the children inadequately provided for. The court has, therefore, in some cases directed that the income or part of it is not to be accumulated but is to be used for the maintenance of the infant.[6]

V. APPROPRIATION

Appropriation occurs when trustees effectively set aside part of the trust property and earmark it for a specific purpose. For the purposes of trust law generally, the effect of appropriation is that beneficiaries who have an interest in the appropriated fund have no rights in respect of the non-appropriated property, and the beneficiaries of the non-appropriated property have no rights in respect of the appropriated fund.

The position is as follows:

(i) trustees do not have any general power to appropriate[7];

(ii) the trust instrument may direct appropriation, or confer on the trustees a power to appropriate;

(iii) if the trust instrument directs different property to be held on different trusts, that will be treated as an implied direction to appropriate.[8] If, therefore, the trust instrument directs one-quarter of the property to be held on trust for Pinky for life, with remainder to her issue, and the other three quarters to be held on trust for Perky for life with remainder to her issue, then separate funds should be appropriated;

---

[3] See also *Re Lansdowne's Will Trusts* [1967] Ch. 603.

[4] *Re Baron Vestey's Settlement* [1951] Ch. 541.

[5] See further, as to the circumstances in which the court may vary beneficial interests in this and other cases, *post.* p. 541.

[6] *Havelock* v. *Havelock* (1881) 17 Ch. D. 807; *Re Collins* (1886) 32 Ch.D. 229; *Revel* v. *Watkinson* (1748) 1 Ves. Sen. 93; *Re Walker* [1901] 1 Ch. 879; *Greenwell* v. *Greenwell* (1800) 5 Ves. 194; *Cavendish* v. *Mercer* (1776) 5 Ves. 195; *Errat* v. *Barlow* (1807) 14 Ves. 202.

[7] The Law Reform Committee (23rd Report, 1982) has recommended that trustees should be given a statutory power of appropriation.

[8] *Fraser* v. *Murdoch* (1881) 6 App. Cas. 855; *Re Walker* (1890) 62 L.T. 449; *Re Nicholson* [1939] 3 All E.R. 832.

(iv) it seems that if property is held on trust for sale, the trustees have an implied power to appropriate, unless there is a direction to the contrary in the trust instrument[9];

(v) a mere power to appropriate, whether express or implied, will require the consent of adult beneficiaries affected, although not of infant or unborn beneficiaries. However, the power may go beyond one merely to appropriate, so that it is a power to appropriate without any consent being requisite. Consents are not requisite where the trust instrument directs appropriation;

(vi) personal representatives are given a statutory power of appropriation,[10] but this does not apply to trustees.

---

[9] *Re Nickels* [1898] 1 Ch. 630; *Re Brooks* (1897) 76 L.T. 771.
[10] By s.41 of the Administration of Estates Act 1925.

Chapter 19

THE POSITION OF A BENEFICIARY UNDER A TRUST

In general terms, as long as a trust is being properly administered and is continuing, a beneficiary has no right to interfere in its administration, but has passively to wait to receive the benefit appropriate to him under the trust. If, however, the trust is not being properly administered, the beneficiary can take steps to compel its proper administration, and in any case may take certain action to preserve his position. Ultimately, however, the destiny of the trust may lie in his hands, for if various conditions are fulfilled, he can bring the trust to an end even if this appears contrary to the wording of the trust instrument.

I. Control of Trustees' Discretion

Two fundamental principles govern the control of trustees by beneficiaries:

(a) so long as the trust continues, decisions which have to be made in the administration of the trust are to be made by the trustees alone; and

(b) all the beneficiaries under the trust, if *sui juris* and between them absolutely entitled, may bring the trust to an end.[1]

The court is jealous to preserve the trustee's powers, largely because the main function of trustees is to control the trust as a whole, and the right to exercise all the decisions necessary goes to the root of trusteeship. Thus, even where it has power to do so under the Variation of Trusts Act 1958, the court will not approve an arrangement which could override the discretionary powers which the trustees intend to exercise.[2] The leading case on the subject is *Re Brockbank*.[3] It was mentioned in an earlier chapter[4] that where no person is named in a trust instrument as having a power to appoint new trustees, then the existing trustee or trustees are given that power by section 36 of the Trustee Act 1925. In *Re Brockbank* the beneficiaries, all *sui juris* and between them absolutely entitled to the whole of the beneficial interest under the trust, wished to appoint a person as a new trustee, against the

---

[1] See *post*, p. 524.
[2] *Re Steed's Will Trusts* [1960] Ch. 407, also discussed *post*, p. 552.
[3] [1948] Ch. 206.
[4] *Ante*, p. 369.

wishes of the existing trustee. It was held that the appointment of new trustees was a power given to the existing trustees, and this power could not be exercised by the beneficiaries.

It has been suggested,[5] probably correctly, that while the beneficiaries cannot cut down the trustees' powers, they can add to them. This right, if it exists, is to add only to the trustees' powers, and not to their duties, so that their discretion is preserved intact, but is enlarged.

The main areas in which beneficiaries seek to control the trustees' discretion is with regard to investments, and in respect of the exercise of the discretion under discretionary trusts. In both respects the trustees' position is essentially the same. They must take note of any representation made to them, for these representations may properly affect the exercise of their discretion. Thus, if one of the beneficiaries passes to the trustees confidential information that shares in a particular company are likely to improve rapidly, the trustees will give that full consideration in deciding whether to buy. But the decision must be theirs, for they are the persons who can best judge the interests of all beneficiaries, and they are the persons who are answerable.

To the general rule that the trustees should listen, but must alone make the decisions, there are certain exceptions:

(a) the trustees' discretion may be limited by contract. Thus, where a person acts as nominee for another, the terms of the arrangement between them may require the trustee-nominee to act in accordance with the directions of the beneficiary;

(b) the trustees' discretion may be limited by the terms of the trust instrument itself. The usual form of this limitation is to require the consent of a beneficiary or other person to the sale of a particular asset, but there is no reason in principle why it should not be restricted in some other way;

(c) there is a third exception of uncertain extent, which arises from the decision of the Court of Appeal in *Butt* v. *Kelson*.[6]

In *Butt* v. *Kelson* the trustees of a trust held a large proportion of the shares in a private limited company, of which they were also directors by virtue of their trust shareholding. The question arose how far the beneficiaries could control the votes of the trustees both as directors and as shareholders. It was held that the trustees' votes as directors could not be controlled by the beneficiaries, while their votes as shareholders could be controlled. The apparent inconsistency of this curious result may be explained on the basis that under company law directors have duties to all the shareholders, and not only to those shareholders, if any, whom they represent, with the result that it would have been inconsistent with this obligation if the trustees were compelled to vote as directors solely in accordance with the wishes of the beneficiaries. But their votes as shareholders were not subject to this conflict of duty. Nevertheless, it would seem at first sight that the manner in which the

---

[5] *Underhill & Hayton: Law of Trusts and Trustees* (14th ed., 1987) p. 633.
[6] [1952] Ch. 197.

voting power was to be exercised should be a matter for the trustees' discretion, free from interference by the beneficiaries. On this ground *Butt* v. *Kelson* was criticised by Upjohn J. in *Re Whichelow*[7] as being inconsistent with *Re Brockbank*. It is, however, possible to regard a right to vote in a company as a property right and for special considerations to apply to such votes, but *Butt* v. *Kelson* is probably incorrect in so far as it allows beneficiaries to control the votes of trustee-shareholders and should not be extended.

II. RIGHT TO COMPEL DUE ADMINISTRATION

Whether or not a beneficiary suspects any improper conduct on the part of the trustees, he may insist that the accounts of the trust are audited by any solicitor or accountant who is acceptable to the trustees. If agreement cannot be reached on the auditor, the audit is carried out by the Public Trustee. Unless special circumstances exist, the audit cannot be carried out more than once in every three years and if a beneficiary does require more frequent audits he will be ordered personally to pay the costs.[8] Although it is convenient to consider this provision here, the position is the same where the trustee requires an audit to be carried out.

Where the beneficiary thinks that the trust is not being properly administered, where there is some point of doubt relating to the administration of the trust, and in certain other circumstances, he may make an application to the court.[9] There are two types of application:

(a) an application on summons for the determination of a specific question or questions; and
(b) an action for general administration of the trust.

It is desirable for the former method to be used where possible, because it is cheaper, quicker and simpler than the latter.

The following are examples of the circumstances in which it may be appropriate to apply to the court on summons.

(a) for the approval of a specific transaction for which permission is not given by the general law, or by the trust instrument, but which is thought to be in the interests of the beneficiaries as a whole.[10] In most cases, of course, this type of application will be made by the trustee[11];
(b) to direct the trustees to do a particular act which they ought to do or to refrain from doing a particular act which they ought not to

---

[7] [1954] 1 W.L.R. 5.
[8] Trustee Act 1925, s.22(4); Public Trustee Act 1906, s.13(5). The Law Reform Committee (23rd Report, 1982) has recommended that s.13 of the 1906 Act should be repealed.
[9] For the comparable circumstances in which the trustee might wish to make an application to the court, see *ante*, p. 393.
[10] See *Boardman* v. *Phipps* [1967] 2 A.C. 46 (which was, at least in the opinion of the court, an example of the circumstances where an application should have been made); and *ante*, p. 393.
[11] See *ante*, p. 393.

do. The act referred to must be one which the trustees are under a definite obligation to do or not to do: it is not appropriate for a beneficiary to question by this means an act which a trustee has a discretion to do[12];

(c) to direct the payment of money in the hands of the trustees into court[13];

(d) as to the construction of the provisions of the trust instrument, or to ascertain the class of beneficiaries;

(e) to determine any other specific question which arises in the administration of a trust.

Generally it is not appropriate to use this method where the subject-matter of the proposed application will involve third parties, or in an action against trustees for breach of trust where the facts are in dispute.

It will be seen that almost all specific questions which arise in the administration of a trust can be dealt with by summons in this way. An action for the general administration of a trust, that is, where the court itself is to become responsible for the whole administration of the trust, will accordingly usually only be necessary where there is constant dispute between the trustees; where the circumstances of the trust give rise to recurring difficulties which would require frequent single applications to the court; and where prima facie doubt exists as to the bona fides of the trustees.

III. Right to Enforce Claims

As part of his right to compel the due administration of the trust, a beneficiary can apply to the court if the trustees fail to take action to preserve the trust property.[14] A cause of action against a third party might itself be an item of trust property. The court might direct the trustees to enforce that claim, or it might allow the beneficiary to sue direct for the benefit of the trust, where necessary using the name of the trustee.[15] Alternatively, a beneficiary is able to sue the trustees, and make those who are alleged to be under obligations to the trust co-defendants.

In *Wills* v. *Cooke*[16] the trust property included a farm which was subject to a tenancy. The trustees retained solicitors to advise them with regard to the administration of the trust but, it was alleged, the solicitors failed to advise the trustees to take action to increase the rent in accordance with the Agricultural Holdings Act 1948. One of the beneficiaries sued the solicitors direct, claiming that the trustees had a right of action against them and that that right was an item of trust property. On an interlocutory application, Slade J. held that that right might be an item of trust property and that the statement of claim should not be

---

[12] *Syffolk* v. *Lawrence* (1884) 32 W.R. 899.
[13] As to the circumstances in which money is payable into court, see Trustee Act. 1925, s.63.
[14] *Fletcher* v. *Fletcher* (1844) 4 Hare 67.
[15] As in *Foley* v. *Burnell* (1783) 1 Bro. C.C. 274, a case of trespass to trust land.
[16] (1979) L.S.G., July 11.

struck out. He also said, however, that the right would not have been an item of trust property if the trustees had entered into the contract with the solicitors solely for their own protection and benefit.

IV. RIGHT TO TERMINATE A TRUST

If there is only one beneficiary under a trust who is *sui juris*, or if there are two or more beneficiaries and they are all *sui juris* and they are all in agreement, he or they can bring the trust to an end irrespective of the wishes of the trustees or of the creator of the trust. This is the rule in *Saunders* v. *Vautier*.[17] There are two reasons for this rule. First, equity regards the trustees as primarily holding the balance between various beneficiaries with conflicting interests. Where all the beneficiaries are of the same mind, the basic reason for the trustees' existence has gone. But as has been seen, if the beneficiaries still want the trust to continue, they cannot generally control the trustees' discretion: either the trust must be terminated, or the trustees must be allowed to get on with their job. Secondly, a voluntary trust is in equity the equivalent of a gift at common law,[18] so that as a general principle once a trust is created the settlor has no longer any control over it, just as, if he had made an outright gift of property, he would have had no control over what was done with that property. Thus, if all the beneficiaries are *sui juris* and between them entitled to the whole of the beneficial interest in the trust property, the settlor's provisions expressed in the trust instrument will not prevent them from bringing the trust to an end.

In *Saunders* v. *Vautier* itself, a trustee held a sum of money upon trust to accumulate the income until a specified date, and then to pay it to a beneficiary. The beneficiary reached the age of 21, and so became *sui juris*, before the date specified for distribution. He successfully claimed that the capital and accumulated income to date should be paid over to him.

If, however, the trust instrument had provided that the beneficiary did not obtain a vested interest until he survived to the specified date, then he would not have been able to invoke the rule without the concurrence of the person entitled in default of his attaining that age.[19]

If the beneficial interest is sold, the purchaser stands in the same position as the vendor, and if the vendor could have brought the trust to an end the purchaser will be able to do so if he is *sui juris*. If the beneficial interest is mortgaged, the mortgagee cannot bring the trust to an end as long as the beneficiary still has a right under the mortgage to have his beneficial interest redeemed upon payment of the amount secured.[20]

The rule also applies where beneficiaries are entitled in succession.

---

[17] (1841) Cr. & Ph. 240. See also *Josselyn* v. *Josselyn* (1837) 9 Sim. 63; *Gosling* v. *Gosling* (1859) Johns, 265; *Wharton* v. *Masterman* [1895] A.C. 186; *Re Johnston* [1894] 3 Ch. 204; *Re Smith* [1928] Ch. 915; *Re Lord Nunburnholme* [1911] 2 Ch. 510; *Berry* v. *Green* [1938] A.C. 575.

[18] *Re Bowden* [1936] Ch. 71.

[19] *Gosling* v. *Gosling* (1859) Johns. 265; *Re Lord Nunburnholme* [1912] 1 Ch. 489.

[20] This is the conclusion from *Re Bell, Jeffrey* v. *Sales* [1896] 1 Ch. 1.

So if property is held upon trust for Andrew for life, with remainder to Brian for life, with remainder to Charles, if Andrew, Brian and Charles are all alive and *sui juris* and they all join in, they can bring the trust to an end. Where a trust is brought to an end in this way, the beneficiaries can compel the trustees to convey the property to whomsoever they direct[21] and, if the trustees refuse, they will personally have to pay the cost of the beneficiaries' application to the court.

Use may be made of the rule in *Saunders* v. *Vautier* to overcome the specific difficulty in *Re Brockbank*[22] Thus, if beneficiaries dislike the existing trustees, or the existing trustees' choice of a new trustee, they may combine together, bring the existing trust to an end, set up a new trust on exactly the same terms, but with their nominees as trustees, and direct the old trustees to convey the trust property to the new trustees. This method is effective, but it may be expensive. *Ad valorem* stamp duty was formerly payable on the formation of a trust *inter vivos* but this is now only the case in the relatively unlikely case that consideration in money or money's worth is furnished.[23] In certain circumstances, there can also be certain taxation disadvantages in the breaking of a trust.

On the termination of a trust there will often be a liability both to capital gains tax and to inheritance tax. If a trust is terminated, and the trustees sell the investments comprising the trust fund, they will be liable to capital gains tax on any increase in value which has accrued while the investments have been subject to the trust. If, however, the trustees distribute the assets *in specie*, the beneficiaries will become absolutely entitled to the assets as against the trustees,[24] and, in principle, a liability to capital gains tax will arise as if the trustees had disposed of the assets on the open market for their full value at the time when the beneficiaries became entitled.[25] However, if the beneficiaries are resident in the United Kingdom, they may claim holdover relief if the assets in question comprise business property[26] or if the vesting of the property in the beneficiaries involves a chargeable transfer for the purposes of inheritance tax. Under this relief the beneficiaries are treated for capital gains[27] tax purposes as acquiring the assets at their base cost to the trustees. By claiming this relief, the liability for the tax is deferred until the beneficiaries actually dispose of the assets.

The position with regard to inheritance tax is more complicated. Suppose that a fund of £100,000 is held upon trust for Elizabeth for life with remainder to Angela, and that it is agreed to bring the trust to an end by paying £40,000 to Elizabeth and £60,000 to Angela. It has been seen[28] that where a beneficiary has an interest in possession in settled property he is treated for inheritance tax purposes as if he was bene-

---

[21] *Re Marshall* [1914] 1 Ch. 192; *Re Sandeman's Will Trusts* [1937] 1 All E.R. 368.
[22] [1948] Ch. 206; *ante,* p. 520.
[23] See *ante,* p. 408.
[24] This concept was considered at p. 418, *ante.*
[25] Taxation of Chargeable Gains Act 1992, s.71(1).
[26] Taxation of Chargeable Gains Act 1992, s.165.
[27] See *ante,* p. 416.
[28] *Ante,* p. 425.

526 The Position of a Beneficiary Under a Trust

ficially entitled to the settled property itself.[29] Accordingly, immediately before the termination Elizabeth would be treated for inheritance tax purposes as being beneficially entitled to £100,000, whereas after the termination she would only be entitled to the actual sum of £40,000. There would, therefore, be a potentially exempt transfer by Elizabeth of £60,000.[30]

So far as concerns Angela, she has given up a reversionary interest in a fund of £100,000 in order to obtain an immediate outright payment of £60,000. There is no liability to inheritance tax upon her, because usually[31] no tax is payable where a person disposes of a reversionary interest.[32]

---

[29] Inheritance Tax Act 1984, s.49.
[30] No inheritance tax would be payable if Elizabeth survived for a further seven years. If she failed to do so, the tax payable would be calculated by reference to her lifetime transfers.
[31] This rule does not apply where the person disposing of the reversionary interest acquired it for value, or was himself the settlor (Inheritance Tax Act 1984, s.48(1)).
[32] Ibid. ss.47, 48(1).

Chapter 20

TRUSTEES' REMUNERATION AND BENEFITS

THE fundamental rule is that the office of trustee is gratuitous, that is, that the duties must be performed by the trustee without remuneration or profit. The development of this rule was due in part to the fact that trustees were often members of the family and persons of substance, who were prepared to act as trustees as part of the general obligations of kinship. In more recent years, however, it has come to be recognised that the management of money and assets is an activity which requires skill, aptitude, and often considerable technical support. Accordingly, it is now very common for trustees to be either professional advisers, such as solicitors and accountants, who act as part of their ordinary professional practice, or banks and similar trust companies. Such trustees are generally prepared to act only if given adequate recompense.

I. Modern Commercial Remuneration Terms

Throughout this chapter, it will be helpful to keep in mind what a professional trustee or a commercial trust company may wish to obtain. The main items are:

1. Fees for acting as a trustee, including the administration of the trust.
2. Where the trust property includes shares in a company and the trustees act as directors of that company, fees for acting as a director of the company.
3. Commissions customarily paid by third parties in respect of business transacted on behalf of the trust. For example, where a person is appointed as an agent of an insurance company, he will usually receive commission in respect of business placed by him with that company. Likewise, stockbrokers pay commission to certain agents in respect of stock exchange business placed with them. Where a trustee carries on a professional practice or commercial business, he will wish to retain these commissions.
4. Profits made by the trustee from services performed for the trust as its customer. For example, if a bank acts as a trustee but also acts as a banker to the trust, it will wish to retain for itself its ordinary commercial profit derived from acting as banker.

The remainder of this chapter considers the extent to which the trustee will achieve these objectives.

II. FEES: THE GENERAL RULE

The general rule has already been stated, namely that a trustee is not entitled to claim any salary or remuneration for carrying out the trusteeship.[1] This extends to the case where the trusteeship involves running a business belonging to the trust. In *Barrett* v. *Hartley*,[2] for example, a trustee had managed a business for six years, and had done so with such success that a large profit accrued to the beneficiaries. But when the trustee claimed remuneration he was unsuccessful, it being held that his efforts were merely part of the duties imposed upon him by accepting the trusteeship. It has even been held, in *Re Gates*,[3] that when a solicitor-trustee employs his firm to act as solicitors to the trust, if there is no charging clause in the trust instrument, the firm is not entitled to charge for its services, despite the fact that the solicitor-trustee had agreed with his partner that he himself would receive no part of the fee. Where, however, there is a charging clause, the remuneration is not regarded for income tax purposes as mere bounty, with the result that the solicitor is entitled to treat it as earned income.[4]

In some cases the rule can operate inequitably, and sometimes even harshly. But it can also operate illogically. In Chapter 13 it was explained that, even in the absence of any provision in the trust instrument, a trustee has wide powers under section 23 of the Trustee Act 1925 to appoint agents to do most of the work (although not to take the decisions) relating to the trust and the trustee is entitled to pay the agent for so doing. The result is, therefore, that if there is no provision in the trust instrument for the payment of the trustee, the trustee can out of the trust funds pay an agent to do most of the work, but, if he does the work himself, as was presumably intended by the settlor, then he cannot be paid. The general rule that a trustee may not be paid for his services was firmly established in the eighteenth century, at which time an agent could only be employed in very limited circumstances. Having regard to the wide power that now exists of appointing agents, the rule may now require revision. Although a trustee cannot obtain remuneration, he is, of course, entitled to be reimbursed actual payments which he has properly made in connection with his trusteeship. This extends to the costs of taking or defending proceedings where he has acted reasonably in so doing.[5] His right to reimbursement is contractual.[6]

---

[1] *Robinson* v. *Pett* (1734) 3 P. Wms. 249; *Re Thorpe* [1891] 2 Ch. 360; *Re Barker* (1886) 34 Ch.D. 77.

[2] [1866] L.R. 2 Eq. 789.

[3] [1933] Ch. 913; followed in *Re Hill* [1934] Ch. 623 and *Re French Protestant Hospital* [1951] Ch. 567.

[4] *Dale* v. *I.R.C.* [1954] A.C. 11.

[5] Where the trustee acts in a manner hostile to the beneficiaries, no costs will be recoverable; see *Holding and Management* v. *Property Holding and Investment Trust* [1989] 1 W.L.R. 1313.

[6] *Re Spurling's Will Trusts* [1966] 1 W.L.R. 920.

III. Fees: Exceptions to the General Rule

There are the following exceptions[7] to the general rule:

(1) Power in trust instrument

The creator of the trust can authorise the trustees to be paid for their services, and it is common for this to be done where a professional person is appointed a trustee. Provisions to this effect are, however, construed strictly, and against the trustee, so that a very wide clause is necessary if, for example, a solicitor-trustee is to be entitled to charge for work done by him in the administration of a trust which could have been done by someone not a solicitor.[8]

Accordingly, the usual form of charging clause is to the following effect:

"Any trustee for the time being hereof being a solicitor accountant or other person engaged in any profession shall be entitled to charge and be paid all usual professional or other charges for business transacted time expended and acts done by him or any partner of his in connection with the trustees hereof including business and acts which a trustee not being engaged in a profession or business could have done personally."

Provided that the charging clause is wide enough, a trustee is entitled to engage a company which he controls to carry out on behalf of the trust, and to pay that company for so doing. In *Re Orwell's Will Trusts*[9] George Orwell created a trust by his will, the will containing a clause authorising the trustee[10] to charge for services performed by him or his company.[11] Vinelott J. held that the company could be paid and, further, that the trustee need not account for the remuneration which he himself received from the company.[12] The remuneration payable may be expressed to be the income from a part of the estate[13] or even part of the capital by virtue of a power of appointment.[14]

If there is a charging clause, the trustee cannot charge what he likes, but only what is reasonable. Where the trustee is a solicitor, the beneficiaries can insist on having his charges taxed, that is assessed by an officer of the court. Whether or not the trustee is a solicitor, if the trustee takes from the trust fund an amount in excess of what the beneficiaries

---

[7] In *Tito v. Waddell (No. 2)* [1977] Ch. 106 (*ante*, p. 9) it may be thought that there was a clear conflict of interest, but the type of "trust" considered in that case is not dealt with in this book.

[8] *Harbin v. Darby* (1860) 28 Beav. 325; *Re Chapple, Newton v. Chapple* (1884) 27 Ch.D. 584.

[9] [1982] 3 All E.R. 177.

[10] The case concerned the literary executor of the will, who, for the purposes of remuneration, was held to be in the same position as a trustee.

[11] The clause authorised the trustee to charge for work done by him "or his firm." Although, generally, the expression "firm" denotes an unincorporated partnership, the court held that in this clause it extended to a private company.

[12] *cf. Re Gee* [1948] 1 All E.R. 498; see *post* p. 537.

[13] *Public Trustee v. I.R.C.* [1960] A.C. 398.

[14] *Re Beatty's Will Trusts* [1990] 1 W.L.R. 1503.

consider is reasonable, they may bring an action against the trustee for breach of trust.[15]

It is customary for commercial trust companies, as well as the Public Trustee, to make a charge on an *ad valorem* basis. As an illustration, the fees charged by the Public Trustee[16] for acting as the trustee of an ordinary trust are:

(a) *Acceptance fee*

On the first £50,000	1.25 per cent.
On the excess over £50,000	0.5 per cent.
Minimum fee £175	

(b) *Administration fee.* Due annually on April 1 on the net capital value of funds under administration: the valuation date is whichever of the following dates most recently precedes the date on which the fee is payable: July 1, 1987, in the case of any estate or trust in which the Public Trustee was acting on that day; September 30, 1991, in the case of any estate or trust in which the Public Trustee was acting on that day; and, in any other case, the date of the acceptance of the trust by the Public Trustee or such convenient date as he may select.

On the first £30,000	1.5 per cent.
On the excess over £30,000 up to £150,000	1.25 per cent.
On the excess over £150,000 up to £375,000	0.75 per cent.
On any excess over £375,000 up to £2,500,000	0.5 per cent.
On any excess over £2,500,000	0.2 per cent.
Minimum fee £25	

(c) *Activity fees*
(i) *Insurance and stockbroker's commission fee.*
A fee equal to the amount of any commission allowed.

(ii) *Income collection fee*
On the gross income actually received by the Public Trustee $3\frac{1}{2}$ per cent. (There is no fee on income paid direct from source to a beneficiary.)

(iii) *Additional work*
A reasonable additional fee may be charged according to work involved for various matters including:
(i) dealing with a business
(ii) dealing with assets outside the United Kingdom
(iii) dealing with freehold or leasehold property or a mortgage and for duties of an unusual, complex or exacting nature.

---

[15] *Re Wells, Wells* v. *Wells* [1962] 1 W.L.R. 784.
[16] From 1992: Public Trustee (Fees) Order 1985 as amended by Public Trustee (Fees) (Amendment) Orders 1987, 1988 & 1992.

(d) *Withdrawal fee*
6.5 times the administration fee for the year previous to the withdrawal.

The position where the trustee has agreed a fixed level of remuneration and wishes to increase it is considered below.[17]

(2) With authority of the court
The second exception to the general rule is that under its inherent jurisdiction the court may:

(a) authorise a trustee to be remunerated where there is no charging clause[18];

(b) authorise a trustee to retain remuneration which he has already received[19]; and

(c) authorise a trustee to charge in excess of what the trustee agreed to receive when accepting appointment.[20]

In some of the older cases, the court was not averse to allowing the trustee reasonable remuneration. In the case of *Brown v. Litton,*[21] for example, the captain of a merchant ship took with him on a voyage a sum of money to use in trade. During the voyage he died and his mate, on assuming command of the vessel, took possession of the money and with it made considerable profits in trade. The mate was ordered to account for his profits but Harcourt L.K. nevertheless held him entitled to a fair remuneration, which was to be fixed by the court, for his trouble.

More recently, the policy adopted by the court was that it would only authorise a trust to receive remuneration where his services were of exceptional benefit to the trust.[22] Such a case was *Boardman v. Phipps.*[23] Boardman was the solicitor to the trustees of a will, who held among other assets 8,000 out of an issued 30,000 shares in a private company. Boardman, thinking there was considerable scope for making a profit, considered with the trustees whether they should acquire the remaining shares in the company, but the trustees refused, partly because under the terms of the trust instrument they had no power to acquire additional shares in the company.[24] Boardman then, by using knowledge which he had gained as a solicitor to the trust, fought a takeover battle for control of the company. As Wilberforce J. observed at first instance, "it is interesting, and at times fascinating to watch, through the long correspondence that has been put in [evidence], the manner in which [Mr. Boardman] drives [the chairman of the company]

---

[17] *Post*, p. 533.
[18] *Bainbridge* v. *Blair* (1845) 8 Beav. 558; *Re Freeman's Settlement Trusts* (1887) 37 Ch.D. 148; *Re Masters* [1953] 1 All E.R. 19; *Re Worthington (deceased)* [1954] 1 All E.R. 677.
[19] *Forster* v. *Ridley* (1864) 4 De G.J. & Sm. 452.
[20] *Re Duke of Norfolk's Settlement Trusts* [1981] 3 W.L.R. 455, C.A.
[21] (1711) 1 P.Wms. 140.
[22] See, *e.g. Protheroe* v. *Protheroe* [1968] 1 W.L.R. 519, where the trustee was only entitled to reimbursement of his actual expenses. See *ante*, p. 243.
[23] [1967] 2 A.C. 46; see also *ante*, p. 248.
[24] The court said that application should have been made to the court for permission to purchase these shares.

from one prepared position to another until the fruit is ready to drop into his hand."[25] Eventually the fruit did indeed drop. Boardman acquired virtually all the shares in the company other than those held by the trust, some at a price of £3, and others at a price of £4.50. Having gained control of the company, he was able to dispose of some of the assets, and to reorganise the business, as a result of which the shares became worth over £8 each. He had therefore made a profit of over £75,000 on the shares which he had acquired, as well as substantially increasing the value of the shares held by the trust. The beneficiaries then claimed that profit. On the facts, it was held that Boardman would have been unable to have conducted negotiations without the knowledge gained as solicitor to the trust and as such he became a constructive trustee and so was liable to account for his profit. The Court of Appeal and the House of Lords[26] considered, however, that Boardman was "a man of conspicuous ability, of great energy, clarity of mind and persistence . . . with a flair for negotiation," and although he was made to disgorge his profit, he was allowed by the court "generous remuneration." He was allowed remuneration because he had exceptional abilities in this respect, and had exercised them for the benefit of the trust. In other words, the average trustee, and even the average professional trustee, would not have been able to have achieved the results which Boardman achieved. In this case, remuneration was awarded even though Boardman had committed a breach of fiduciary duty. In *O'Sullivan* v. *Management Agency and Music*,[27] remuneration was ordered even in favour of a fiduciary who had been guilty of undue influence. A fiduciary agent, whose contract with a performer was set aside for undue influence, was held to be entitled to remuneration, together with a reasonable sum by way of profit, on the basis that he had contributed significantly to the performer's success. On the other hand, in *Guinness* v. *Saunders*,[28] a claim for remuneration by a director who had acted in good faith but in a situation where there was a clear conflict between his interest and his duty was denied by the House of Lords—in fact the House of Lords doubted whether such remuneration would ever be ordered in favour of a director. Lord Goff[29] felt that the jurisdiction could not be exercised where it would encourage trustees to put themselves into a conflict situation—however, in this respect, the authorities are not consistent.

In *Re Duke of Norfolk's Settlement Trusts*[30] a trust company accepted the trusteeship of a discretionary trust on the basis that it would receive a low, fixed, annual fee. It became involved in an extensive re-development programme in the Strand and applied (a) for special remuneration in respect of the re-development, which was granted,[31] and (b) an

---

[25] [1965] Ch. 922 at p. 1014.
[26] Upholding Wilberforce J.
[27] [1985] Q.B. 428.
[28] [1990] 2 A.C. 663.
[29] On the grounds that this would constitute interference by the court in the administration of the company's affairs.
[30] [1981] 3 W.L.R. 455, C.A.
[31] At first instance ([1978] 3 W.L.R. 655), and not reversed by the Court of Appeal.

increase in the ordinary standard of remuneration. The Court of Appeal held that it could authorise an increase in the agreed level of remuneration, but it would only do so if the experience and skill of the trustee made it in the interest of the beneficiaries to do so. The Court of Appeal also held that it was relevant to take into account remuneration charged by other trust companies, but it is not clear how much reliance is to be placed on that.

(3) Agreement with all beneficiaries
The third exception to the general rule is that if the beneficiaries are all *sui juris* and between them absolutely entitled to the whole of the beneficial interest under the trust, they can validly agree with the trustees that they shall be paid. Such agreements are construed strictly, in the same way as provisions for payment in the trust instrument.[32]

Where all the beneficiaries do not agree, or some are not *sui juris*, individual beneficiaries can agree with a trustee for his remuneration, but that agreement binds only the individual beneficiary, and not the trust property as such.

(4) Judicial trustees
A judicial trustee may always charge for his services.[33]

(5) Custodian trustees
A custodian trustee is entitled to charge fees equivalent to those which the Public Trustee could charge for acting as a custodian trustee.[34] However, this only enables the custodian trustee to charge for the services which he performs in that capacity. In *Forster* v. *Williams Deacon's Bank*[35] an attempt was made to use the device of custodian trusteeship to overcome the absence of a charging clause in the trust instrument. In that case Williams Deacon's Bank had been appointed both managing trustee and custodian trustee. It was appreciated that the bank could not charge *qua* managing trustee, but it was anticipated that it could derive its remuneration from its capacity as a custodian trustee. The Court of Appeal rejected the device, however, holding that the deed merely constituted the bank the sole trustee so that the inability to charge remained. A similar attempt in a later case was held to be totally ineffective.[36]

Although when he has been validly appointed a custodian trustee may always charge for his services, he may only charge for his services in his capacity as custodian trustee. Thus in *Re Brooke Bond*[37] an insurance company was a custodian trustee under the trust deed securing the pension scheme of Brooke Bond & Co.Ltd. Under the terms of the trust deed the managing trustees were entitled to effect with any

---

[32] It seems that the agreement has to be concluded with the beneficiaries before the trustee takes up his office: *Douglas* v. *Archbutt* (1858) 2 De G. & J. 148; *Re Sherwood* (1840) 3 Beav. 338. This appears to be contrary to principle.
[33] Judicial Trustees Act 1896, ss.1(5), 4(1).
[34] Public Trustee Act 1906, s.4.
[35] [1935] Ch. 359.
[36] *Arning* v. *James* [1936] Ch. 158.
[37] [1963] Ch. 357.

insurance company a policy assuring the payment of the pensions under the scheme. The managing trustees proposed to effect the policy with the custodian trustee. Cross J. held that the custodian trustee could not without the authority of the court contract with the managing trustee for its own benefit but, application having been made to the court, the learned judge authorised the managing trustees to effect the policy with the custodian trustee on the basis that the latter need not account for its profit, on condition that the terms of the policy were approved by an independent actuary.

(6) The Public Trustee

The Public Trustee is always entitled to charge for his services.[38] Details of some of the fees which he currently charges have been given previously.[39]

(7) Trust corporations

As has been seen,[40] the court has a power to appoint a trustee, and will do so principally where one cannot be appointed without the assistance of the court. When the court does so, it has power to authorise the trustee to be paid and where it appoints a trust corporation to be a trustee, it will almost invariably authorise that corporation to be paid. But in principle, as regards remuneration, a trust corporation is in exactly the same position as an individual trustee. While, in principle, it is not entitled to charge merely because it is a trust corporation,[41] it may well be that the court will approve the payment of fees according to the trust corporation's ordinary scale of fees, particularly where the beneficiaries do not object.[42]

Once a trustee has been appointed by the court, he generally has no further connection with the court but the court may also, on the application of any person interested in the trust, appoint someone to be a judicial trustee. A judicial trustee, who is usually the Public Trustee, the Official Solicitor, or a trust corporation, becomes for the purpose an officer of the court and as such he is able at any time to obtain the directions of the court without formality. Unless there has been mismanagement, the court will only in exceptional circumstances appoint a judicial trustee where suitable private persons are willing to act as trustees.[43] A judicial trustee may always charge for his services.[44]

(8) The role in Cradock v. Piper

The rule known as the rule in *Cradock* v. *Piper*[45] is a curious exception to the principle that a solicitor trustee, like any other trustee, may not pay

---

[38] Public Trustee Act 1906, s.9. Administration of Justice Act 1965, s.2; Public Trustees (Fees) Act 1957.

[39] *Ante*, p. 530.

[40] *Ante*, p. 375.

[41] See also *Re Barbour's Settlement, ante.*

[42] *Re Codd's Will Trust* [1975] 1 W.L.R. 1139.

[43] *Re Chisholm* (1898) 43 S.J. 43.

[44] Judicial Trustees Act 1896, s.1.

[45] (1850) 1 Mac. & G. 664.

either himself or another member of his firm for work done for the trust[46] (in the absence of authorisation by the trust instrument or by the court) save where he can properly employ an outside solicitor in which case he may employ and pay another member of his firm provided that it has been expressly agreed that the solicitor-trustee will not take any share in the profits.[47] The effect of this rule is that, where a solicitor-trustee acts as a solicitor for himself and his co-trustees in litigation relating to the trust and the costs of acting for both of them do not exceed the expense which would have been incurred if he had been acting for the co-trustees alone, then he may be paid his usual costs.

The rule is firmly established[48] but it is quite illogical. If it is proper for a solicitor to be paid his usual fees for litigation, why is it not proper for him to be paid his usual fees for non-litigious work? In *Re Corsellis*[49] Cotton L.J. made a feeble attempt to justify the difference. "There may be this reason for it," he said, "that in an action, although costs are not always hostilely taxed, yet there may be a taxation where parties other than the trustee-solicitor may appear and test the propriety of the costs, and the court can disallow altogether the costs of any proceedings which may appear to be vexatious or improperly taken." There is, however, little merit in this explanation. In the first place, even where there is the usual charging clause, or remuneration for non-contentious business is authorised by the court, this will not authorise payment for acts which are not properly done. Further, where there is an express power for a solicitor-trustee to charge, a beneficiary can always insist that a solicitor-trustee's bill of costs be taxed,[50] and it has even been decided that where the beneficiaries are dissatisfied with a bill, it is the solicitor-trustee's duty to inform the beneficiaries of their right to have it taxed.[51] There remains, therefore, no logic in the distinction between court proceedings and other business for this purpose. But the rule is firm.

(9) Trust property abroad

Where the trust property is situated abroad, and the law of the country where the property is situated allows payment the trustees appear to be entitled to retain their emoluments. In *Re Northcote*[52] English executors had to get in assets of the deceased in America. To do so they had to obtain a grant of probate in the State of New York, under the law of which they were entitled to a commission on the value of the assets. They deducted this for themselves and the English court held they need not account for it to the trust.

---

[46] *Christophers* v. *White* (1847) 10 Beav. 523.
[47] *Clack* v. *Carton* (1866) 30 L.J. Ch. 639.
[48] *Broughton* v. *Broughton* (1855) 5 De G.M. & G. 160; *Lincoln* v. *Windsor* (1851) 9 Hare 158; *Re Baker* (1886) 24 Ch.D. 77.
[49] (1887) 34 Ch.D. 675 at p. 682.
[50] *Re Fish* [1893] 2 Ch. 413.
[51] *Re Webb* [1894] 1 Ch. 73.
[52] [1949] 1 All E.R. 442.

IV. Directors' Fees

The second type of remuneration which a trustee might seek to retain is fees paid to him as a director of a company in which the trust fund is invested. There are three questions:

1. Is the trustee-director in principle liable to account for his director's fees?
2. If so, are there any exceptions to the principle?
3. If he does account, how are the fees treated in the administration of the trust?

(1) Liability to account

There are two preliminary points. First, in the case of private companies, the articles of association often endeavour to prevent the directors from acting contrary to the interests of shareholders by providing that any person who becomes a director must himself hold, or must within a short, specified time acquire, a number of shares in that company. In this way it is hoped that as the director will wish to advance the value of his own shares, he will also be acting in the interests of the other shareholders. Secondly, by section 360 of the Companies Act 1985[53] a company is not allowed to take notice of the fact that shares might be held upon trust, and as far as the company is concerned, it deals with trustees who are registered holders of shares in exactly the same way as shareholders who are beneficially entitled. It will therefore be apparent that directors can use shares which they hold as trustees as their share qualification: if they do so, will they be allowed to keep their directors' fees?

The first case was *Re Francis*.[54] Under the articles of association of a company, the holders of a certain number of shares were entitled to vote themselves directorships. Such shares were held by the trustees on behalf of the trust, and they procured their appointment as directors. Kekewich J., following the general principle that a trustee cannot profit from his trusteeship, held that they had to account to the trust for their fees. This case, however, was not even cited in *Re Dover Coalfield Extension*,[55] which introduced new considerations. The Dover company held shares in the Consolidated Kent Collieries Corporation, with whom they did business. In order to protect the interests of the Dover company, a director of the Dover company was appointed a director of the Kent company. As a director, he had a contract with the Kent company which governed the services which he was to perform for the company, and it regulated his remuneration. The articles of association of the Kent company required directors to acquire 1,000 shares within one month from being appointed a director. So that he should be registered with the appropriate number of shares, the Dover company therefore transferred to the director this number of shares, which he held upon trust for the Dover company. It was not disputed that he had

---

[53] Replacing provisions of previous Acts.
[54] (1905) 74 L.J.Ch. 198.
[55] [1908] 1 Ch. 65.

to account to the Dover company for the dividends on those shares, and he did in fact do so, but he claimed that he did not have to account for his directors' fees. The Court of Appeal held he could retain his directors' fees; although he could not have continued in office without the shares, he was appointed a director by an independent board of directors before he had acquired the shares and his directorship did not therefore automatically flow from his trusteeship.

In *Re Macadam*,[56] following *Re Francis*,[57] trustees who by virtue of the trust shareholding were able to elect themselves directorships and in fact did so were held liable to account for their fees but this was distinguished in *Re Gee*,[58] where Harman J. said that in some circumstances, even where a trustee is able through his voting rights to compel his appointment as director, he is nevertheless entitled to retain his fees, if his appointment was in fact independent of his trust shareholding.

In his judgment in *Re Gee* Harman J. reviewed the previous cases. He concluded that the test was: has the trustee used powers vested in him *qua* trustee to procure his appointment as a director? To be liable to account the trustee therefore

(a) must have powers *qua* trustee
(b) which he himself uses
(c) to procure his appointment as director.

If any of these elements is missing, he may retain his fees—as in *Re Dover Coalfield*, where he has his directorship first and, although he has powers *qua* trustee, he does not use those powers to procure his appointment as a director. Similarly, if he has a majority shareholding in a company beneficially, as well as a minority holding *qua* trustee, and votes himself a directorship, his directorship will be the result of his beneficial voting power, and not that *qua* trustee. Likewise, where others hold the majority shareholding, the trustee has a minority shareholding, and he is appointed a director by the votes of the others, although he has powers *qua* trustee he does not use those powers to procure his appointment. The court will consider all the circumstances to see whether or not the appointment was truly independent of the voting powers held *qua* trustee.

In *Re Orwell's Will Trusts*,[59] the facts of which have already been given,[60] Vinelott J. distinguished *Re Gee*. He held that while the general rule is that a trustee must account for any benefit, such as remuneration, which a person obtains from a company as a result of his position as a trustee, this rule does not apply if the company was properly entitled to be paid from the trust fund, and there is no other nexus between the company with which the trustee is connected and the trust fund.

---

[56] [1946] Ch. 73.
[57] (1905) 74 L.J.Ch. 198.
[58] [1948] Ch. 284.
[59] [1982] 1 W.L.R. 1337.
[60] *Ante,* p. 529.

(2) Exceptions

Where a trustee-director is, in principle, not entitled to retain his director's fees, there are two circumstances in which, nevertheless, he may do so.

(a) *Power in trust instrument.* The settlor can include an effective power in the trust instrument authorising the retention of director's fees. This power may be express or implied. So, in *Re Llewellin*[61] where the testator had expressly provided that the trustees could use the trust shares to acquire directorships, it was held that he had also impliedly authorised them to retain their directors' fees.

(b) *With authority of the court.* The court can authorise a trustee-director to retain his director's fees. In deciding whether to exercise this power, it will consider the extent of the skill and effort which has been applied. The general rule is that a trustee is expected to exercise in the discharge of his trusteeship the effort and skill which a prudent man of business would in general undertake in the management of his own investments. A trustee-director is expected to exercise the same standard when acting as a director. So, in *Re Keeler's Settlement Trusts*[62] the court directed that an inquiry should be held as to the extent to which trustee-directors had exerted effort and skill above that standard, and held that they could retain their directors' fees, but to that extent only.

(3) Application of fees

Where a trustee-director is obliged to account for his director's fees, and does so, it seems that, notwithstanding the revenue character of those sums so far as the company is concerned, in the administration of the trust they are to be treated as an addition to the settled property, and added to capital.[63]

V. Commissions

The third category of payment which a trustee might seek to retain is commissions paid by third parties.

(1) The general rule

The general rule is that the trustee is accountable for commissions which he receives in respect of trust business.[64]

The test is not whether the trust has suffered a loss, but whether the trustee has made a profit. Thus, in *Williams* v. *Barton*[65] the trustee was a stockbrokers' clerk who was paid commission earned on business introduced by him to his firm. He arranged for his firm to value the trust assets, and was duly paid his commission. It was held that he had to

---

[61] [1949] Ch. 225.
[62] [1981] 2 W.L.R. 499.
[63] *Re Francis* (1905) 74 L.J. Ch. 198.
[64] This question is discussed more fully *ante*, p. 227.
[65] [1927] 2 Ch. 9.

account for that commission. There was no suggestion that the valuation of the trust assets was improper or unnecessary, but nevertheless the trustee was not entitled to make a profit from it. The trustee might have been tempted to have the assets valued more frequently than was in fact necessary.

(2) Exceptions

The trust instrument can, and often does, empower trustees to retain commissions. The court, no doubt, also has power to authorise this, but there appears to be no reported case in which it has exercised this power.

Furthermore, the rule does not apply where the recipient of the commission is discharging a duty imposed by statute, and in so doing does not act harshly or oppressively. So in *Swain* v. *The Law Society*[66] the House of Lords held that the Law Society was entitled to retain the equivalent of commission paid in respect of the compulsory insurance against negligence which solicitors are obliged to maintain.[67] The Law Society was required to apply that commission for the benefit of the profession as a whole.

VI. Commercial Profits

The last category of benefit which, in ordinary circumstances, a trustee might seek to keep is profits derived by him in carrying on a business, where the trust is a customer of that business.

(1) The general rule

As in the case of commissions, it seems that the trustee is liable to account for the profit.[68]

(2) Exceptions

The trust instrument can empower trustees to retain their profit. So, in *Re Sykes*[69] two brothers who were wine merchants were appointed the trustees of a will under which one of the assets of the trust was a public house. Under the terms of the will, they were authorised to supply wine to the public house, and they were held entitled to their usual profit for doing so. Similarly, in *Space Investments* v. *Canadian Imperial Bank of Commerce*,[70] a bank trustee was entitled under a settlement to deposit trust funds with itself on a normal commercial basis; no breach of trust was committed by the bank in so doing and the position of the trust was no better than any other depositor or general creditor, even when the bank went into liquidation.

The court also has power to authorise trustees to retain a commercial profit.

---

[66] [1983] A.C. 598, H.L. see *ante*, p. 15.
[67] The Solicitors Act 1974, s.37.
[68] *Re Sykes* [1909] 2 Ch. 241.
[69] [1909] 2 Ch. 241.
[70] [1986] 1 W.L.R. 1072.

VII. Other Financial Benefits

Finally, it should be noted that there is a general rule that a trustee is not to be entitled to profit in any way from his trusteeship unless he is authorised to do so by the trust instrument or by the court. An extreme, if unusual, example is *Sugden* v. *Crossland*[71] where a person was anxious to become a trustee of a will. He therefore paid the existing trustee £75 to retire and appoint him in his place. It was held that the retirement and appointment was ineffective, and also that the £75 belonged to the trust.

A further example is *Webb* v. *Earl of Shaftesbury*,[72] where Lord Eldon held that trustees were not entitled to exercise sporting rights over land held by them as trustees. He held that either the rights should be let for the benefit of the beneficiaries or, if they could not be let, should be held for the heirs of the settlor on a resulting trust. The trustees could not themselves derive any benefit.

In view of the foregoing, it need hardly be said that, quite apart from the rules relating to investments,[73] a trustee must not use trust moneys in his own trade or business. If he does so, he will be liable to account for the profit he makes or, at the beneficiaries' option, compound interest.[74]

The rule applies not only to profits which are made at the expense of the trust, but also to profits which are made without any loss to the trust at all, but which are derived by virtue of the trusteeship. This principle has already been considered in Chapter 8.[75]

---

[71] (1856) 3 Sm. & G. 192.
[72] (1802) 7 Ves. 480.
[73] *Ante*, pp. 430 *et seq.*
[74] *Post*, pp. 586 *et seq.*
[75] See *ante*, p. 239.

CHAPTER 21

VARIATION OF TRUSTS

IF the beneficiaries are *sui juris* and absolutely entitled they can, if they think fit, terminate the trust and if they so choose, set up new trusts in respect of the trust property.[1] But if the beneficiaries are not thus qualified it is necessary that an application be made to the court for a variation of the trusts. It is important to make a distinction for this purpose between two classes of variation by the court: (i) variation concerned with the *management or administration* of the trusts, and (ii) variation of the *beneficial interests* arising under the trusts.

I. MANAGEMENT AND ADMINISTRATION

(1) The inherent jurisdiction of the court

The court has always had an inherent jurisdiction to sanction a departure from the terms of a trust, but it is now clearly established that this applies only to the management or administration of the trust. It does not apply to any rearrangement of the rights of the beneficiaries to the beneficial interests themselves,[2] with the exception only of cases of "maintenance"[3] and "compromise,"[4] assuming that the latter amounts to a variation in the true sense of the word.[5] The jurisdiction, although still somewhat nebulous, was defined by Romer L.J. in *Re New*[6] to cover an "emergency" which has arisen in the administration of the trust, that is to say, something for which no provision is made in the trust and which could not have been foreseen or anticipated by the author of the trust. The inherent jurisdiction is, therefore, of distinctly limited scope. In *Re New* itself the trustees of shares in a company were authorised by the court as a matter of emergency to concur in a scheme under which shares were exchanged for more realisable shares in a new company. The sanction of the court was required because the trustees had no power of investment in the new shares under the terms of the trust

---

[1] See *ante*, p. 524.
[2] *Chapman* v. *Chapman* [1954] A.C. 428 at pp. 454, 455.
[3] See *post*, p. 544.
[4] See *post*, p. 544.
[5] This is perhaps doubtful because it seems that the court's sanction to a compromise of disputed rights (which is what "compromise" in this context means) does not result in a variation of the beneficial trusts but only brings to an end any dispute about them. See *post*, p. 544, for further discussion of "compromise" in this sense.
[6] [1910] 2 Ch. 524.

instrument. This was in the circumstances a transaction in the nature of "salvage" of the trust property.[7]

(2) Trustee Act 1925, s.57

The inherent jurisdiction has been largely superseded by section 57 of the Trustee Act 1925. This is based on a concept wider than that of emergency. The basis of the section is *expediency*. It provides in effect that the court may empower trustees (but not Settled Land Act trustees[8]) in the management or administration of the trust property to perform any act which is not authorised by the trust instrument if in the opinion of the court it is expedient. The ambit of the section was considered by the Court of Appeal in *Re Downshire's Settled Estates, Re Chapman's Settlement Trusts* and *Re Blackwell's Settlement Trusts.*[9] According to Lord Evershed and Romer L.J. in their joint judgment, "The object of section 57 was to secure that trust property should be managed as advantageously as possible in the interests of the beneficiaries, and, with that object in view, to authorise specific dealings with the property which the court might have felt itself unable to sanction under the inherent jurisdiction, either because there was no actual 'emergency' or because of inability to show that the position which called for intervention was one which the creator of the trust could not reasonably have foreseen; but it was no part of the legislative aim to disturb the rule that the court will not rewrite a trust."[10] Moreover, the court must be satisfied that the proposed transaction is for the benefit of the whole trust and not simply for a beneficiary.[11]

The section does not, therefore, confer on the court any general jurisdiction to vary beneficial interests. It is limited to the managerial supervision and control of trust property by the trustees and cannot be stretched further than that.

However, subject to this decisive limitation, it is an overriding provision to be read into every trust.[12] And it has been used for various purposes, for example, to authorise the partitioning of land where the necessary consent could not be obtained,[13] the sale of a reversionary interest which the trustees had no power to sell until it fell into possession,[14] or to blend two charitable funds into one.[15] Indeed the section has also been used to extend trustees' investment powers[16] most

---

[7] The principle was applied in *Re Tollemache* [1903] 1 Ch. 955.

[8] Trustee Act 1925, s.57(4).

[9] [1953] Ch. 218; Denning L.J. dissented. On appeal to the House of Lords in *Re Chapman's Settlement Trusts*: affirmed *sub nom. Chapman* v. *Chapman* [1954] A.C. 429, it was conceded s.57 did not apply. In the House of Lords, the statement of law in the Court of Appeal regarding s.57 was neither approved or disapproved and, therefore, is still good law.

[10] *Ibid.*

[11] *Re Craven's Estate (No.2)* [1937] Ch. 431.

[12] *Re Mair* [1935] Ch. 562.

[13] *Re Thomas* [1930] 1 Ch. 194.

[14] *Re Cockerell's Settlement Trusts* [1956] Ch. 372; *cf. Re Heyworth's Contingent Reversionary Interest* [1956] Ch. 364.

[15] *Re Shipwrecked Fishermen and Mariners' Benevolent Fund* [1959] Ch. 220.

[16] *Re Brassey's Settlement* [1955] 1 W.L.R. 192; *Re Shipwrecked Fishermen and Mariners' Benevolent Fund supra* not following *Re Royal Society's Charitable Trusts* [1956] Ch. 87.

recently in *Mason* v. *Farbrother*[17] and *Anker-Petersen* v. *Anker-Petersen*.[18] It used to be thought that an application for this purpose should now preferably be made under the Variation of Trusts Act 1958.[19] However, *Anker-Petersen* v. *Anker-Petersen* has now established that, provided the beneficial interests are not affected by the proposed extension of investment powers, section 57 should be used in preference to the Variation of Trusts Act 1958.

II. VARIATION OF BENEFICIAL INTERESTS

It has been seen that the foregoing relates only to variations in pursuance of the management and administration of the trust. We are now concerned with the more drastic rewriting of a trust which is involved in the variation of the beneficial interests themselves. The cases in which the class of variation is permissible will now be considered.

(1) Settled Land Act 1925, s.64

This provides that the court may sanction any transaction *affecting or concerning the settled land or any part thereof or any other land* (not being a transaction otherwise authorised by the Act or by the settlement) which in the opinion of the court would be *for the benefit* of the settled land, or any part thereof, or the persons interested under the settlement.[20] Furthermore, the word "transaction" is widely defined to include (*inter alia*) a "compromise or other dealing or other arrangement."[21] And it is now clear that the section—as was held by the majority of the Court of Appeal in *Re Downshire*[22]—confers an ampler jurisdiction than that conferred by section 57 of the Trustee Act 1925.[23] Indeed it enables the beneficial interests under the settlement to be remoulded,[24] and is not restricted to steps of an administrative character.

The section is applied not only to settled land but also to land held on trust for sale. In *Re Simmons*[25] Danckwerts J. reached this conclusion on the ground that section 28 of the Law of Property Act 1925 gave to trustees for sale the powers conferred by the Settled Land Act 1925, and these included the power conferred by section 64.

(2) Matrimonial Causes Act 1973, s.24

Under this Act, replacing earlier legislation of longstanding, the Family Division of the High Court has a wide jurisdiction, after pronouncing a

---

[17] [1983] 2 All E.R. 1078.
[18] [1991] 88/16 L.S. Gaz. 32.
[19] See *post*, p. 546, and see *Re Coates' Will Trusts* [1959] 1 W.L.R. 375, *Re Byng's Will Trusts* [1959] 2 All E.R. 54 at p. 57. It was held that this was not possible in *Mason* v. *Farbrother* [1983] 2 All E.R. 1078 because the parties were not fully representative.
[20] s.64(1) (emphasis added). The powers have been extended by the Settled Land and Trustee Acts (Court's General Powers) Act 1943, s.1., as amended by the Emergency Laws (Miscellaneous Provisions) Act 1953, s.9.
[21] s.64(2). *Raikes* v. *Lygon* [1988] 1 W.L.R. 281.
[22] [1953] Ch. 218.
[23] *Ante*, p. 542.
[24] *Raikes* v. *Lygon* [1988] 1 W.L.R. 281.
[25] [1956] Ch. 125.

decree of divorce or nullity of marriage, to vary the trusts contained in any ante-nuptial or post-nuptial settlement which has been made for the benefit of the parties to the marriage or the children of that marriage.[26] It is clearly established that the jurisdiction extends to a rearrangement of beneficial interests: and the fact that a saving of inheritance tax or other taxes will result will have no bearing on the exercise of this jurisdiction.[27]

(3) Mental Health Act 1983, s.96(3)

This gives the Court of Protection power to make a settlement of the property of the patient and subsequently to vary it if any material fact was not initially disclosed, or there has been a substantial change in circumstances.

(4) Maintenance

The position here is and has long been that where a testator or settlor has made his disposition in such a way—and this will especially occur in trusts for accumulation—that the immediate beneficiaries have no fund for their present maintenance the court will assume that the intention to provide sensibly for the family is so paramount that it will order maintenance in disregard of the trusts.[28] An order for maintenance will obviously result in a variation of the beneficial interests. Morever, the jurisdiction is not restricted to cases of "emergency",[29] nor is it dependent on the beneficiaries being infants.[30]

(5) Compromise

It was the decision of the House of Lords in *Chapman* v. *Chapman*[31] on the question of compromise which led directly to the passing of the Variation of Trusts Act 1958.[32] It has long been clearly established that the court may sanction a "compromise" on behalf of an infant or unborn person where proposed by persons beneficially interested in the trusts who are *sui juris* and may protect the trustees accordingly. This is, like the power to award maintenance,[33] part of the inherent jurisdiction of the court, and also enables, where it applies, beneficial interests to be varied. But the important question is, what is meant by a "compromise"?

The Court of Appeal in *Re Downshire Settled Estates, Re Chapman's Settlement Trusts* and *Re Blackwell's Settlement Trusts*,[34] in the majority opinion of Evershed M.R. and Romer L.J., held that the word "compro-

---

[26] Matrimonial Causes Act 1973, s.24.

[27] See *Thomson* v. *Thomson and Whitmee* [1956] P. 384.

[28] *Re Downshire Settled Estates* [1953] Ch. 218 at p. 238, *per* Evershed M.R. and Romer L.J., considered in *Chapman* v. *Chapman* [1954] A.C. 529 at pp. 445, 455–457, 469, 471; see *ante*, p. 543. See also *Re Collins* (1886) 32 Ch.D. 229 at p. 232; *Havelock* v. *Havelock* (1881) 17 Ch.D. 807.

[29] See *supra*, p. 409, and see *Hayley* v. *Bannister* (1820) 4 Madd. 275.

[30] *Revel* v. *Watkinson* (1748) 1 Ves.Sen. 93.

[31] [1954] A.C. 429.

[32] *Post*, p. 546.

[33] *Supra*.

[34] *Supra*.

mise" should not be construed narrowly so as to be confined to a compromise of *disputed* rights, but covered any arrangement between tenant for life and remainderman. In *Re Downshire* and *Re Blackwell* the court held that the arrangement proposed was in the nature of a compromise in the wider sense of the word, and sanctioned it accordingly. But in *Re Chapman* they refused to do so because there was no compromise even in this extended sense: the court was merely being asked to destroy trusts which had been expressly declared. In *Re Chapman* Denning L.J. dissented on the broad principle that the court had the power to deal with the property and interests of infants or other persons under disability in a manner not authorised by the trust whenever the court was satisfied that what was proposed was most advantageous for them, provided that everyone of full age agreed to it. He was prepared to give a very wide meaning indeed to the inherent jurisdiction of the Court.

The majority of the Court of Appeal in *Re Chapman* had shown the jurisdiction to be limited in some degree by holding that the word "compromise," however widely construed, would not cover every kind of arrangement. But it was the House of Lords in *Chapman* v. *Chapman*,[35] in affirming the decision of the Court of Appeal, which re-examined the meaning of the term for this purpose. Lords Simonds, Morton and Asquith were in no doubt that the power of the court to sanction a compromise in a suit to which a person was not a party, such as an infant or unborn person, did not extend to cases where there was no real dispute between the parties. Lord Cohen alone was prepared to hold that the jurisdiction of the court extended to compromise in the wide sense between tenant for life on the one hand and remainderman on the other. This decision establishes clearly that a compromise means a compromise of a disputed right and this is as far as the inherent jurisdiction of the court goes.[36]

Consequences of Chapman v. Chapman. It appeared from this decision that in *Re Downshire* and *Re Blackwell* the Court of Appeal had gone too far in giving the word "compromise" an unnatural meaning. But quite apart from this there had been a number of schemes approved in the Chancery Division shortly before the decision of the House of Lords, on the basis of what may perhaps be called the "quasi-compromise" principle which then held the field, and the orders there made had accordingly been made without jurisdiction.[37] Moreover, it now became fashionable to scrutinise settlements with a view to finding a provision of sufficient ambiguity or uncertainty in its effect on the

---

[35] *Supra.*

[36] Not a compromise of a simulated dispute (*Re Powell-Cotton's Resettlement* [1956] 1 W.L.R. 23) nor a variation of the existing investment powers (*Mason* v. *Farbrother* [1983] 2 All. E.R. 1078).

[37] See, *e.g. Re Leeds (Duke) and Re the Coal Acts 1938 to 1943* [1947] Ch. 525. *Re Downshire Settled Estates, supra,* and *Re Blackwell's Settlements Trusts, supra,* may also be taken to be overruled on this point, but the decisions may still stand on the application of Settled Land Act 1925, s.64; see *ante,* p. 543.

beneficial interests to form a peg on which to hand a compromise of a "genuine" dispute.

This bizarre situation could not long continue, and the Law Reform Committee was invited in 1957 to consider the position. They reached the conclusion that the result produced by *Chapman* v. *Chapman* was most unsatisfactory. It was pointed out that on a decree of divorce or nullity the Divorce Court had the power to sanction variations in the marriage settlement even if these were designed to produce a saving in estate duty or tax. And the Committee asked: why should an infant whose parents are happily married be in a worse position than an infant whose parents are divorced? The recommendations of the Committee were given legislative effect in the Variation of Trusts Act 1958.

(6) Variation of Trusts Act 1958[38]

The reason behind the anxiety to invoke the jurisdiction of the court to vary beneficial interests on the basis of a "compromise" was to minimise tax or estate duty liabilities which would be attracted with full force if the trust remained unaltered. For example, the old-fashioned settlement with its succession of limited interests had, in particular, fallen out of favour, because on the death of each limited owner estate duty was leviable on the value of the whole settled funds. And a great deal of ingenuity was and is devoted to the formulation of schemes dividing up the trust funds between those interested in capital and income respectively, in such a way that tax is saved.

Tax.[39]   These schemes were formerly presented to the court for its sanction under the head of "compromise" and are now presented under the Variation of Trusts Act 1958. Although Lord Morton said in *Chapman* v. *Chapman*[40] that if the court had power to approve and did approve schemes for the purpose of avoiding taxation "the way would be open for a most undignified game of chess between the Chancery Division and the legislature", the plain fact remains that very many applications under the Act have been made successfully for this very purpose alone.[41]

Yet despite these realities, echoes of judicial repugnance towards tax avoidance can still occasionally be heard and it is arguable, if only faintly, as a result of the controversial decision in *Re Weston's Settlements*,[42] that certain forms of tax avoidance may be regarded as illegitimate. In this case the applicants applied for an order for approval of an arrangement by which property settled on English trusts should be freed from those trusts and settled on a Jersey settlement. The

---

[38] For a detailed discussion of the relevant case law, see Harris (1969) 33 Conv. (N.S.) 113, 183.

[39] See also *post*, p. 562.

[40] *Ante*, at p. 545.

[41] See, *e.g. Re Norfolk's Will Trusts, The Times* March 23, 1966 (purpose to reduce duty on estates worth £3m.).

[42] [1968] 2 W.L.R. 1154 (Stamp J.); [1969] 1 Ch. 223, C.A.; and see *post*, p. 573 for further discussions of this decision.

purpose of the exercise was to avoid a heavy liability to capital gains tax and estate duty.[43] Stamp J. at first instance said: "I am not persuaded that this application represents more than a cheap exercise in tax avoidance which I ought not to sanction, as distinct from a legitimate avoidance of liability to taxation."[44] The Court of Appeal, however, tended to place emphasis on other factors, nor indeed did Stamp J. ignore them. As is shown in the next chapter,[45] the primary basis of the Court of Appeal decision appears to be that no administrative benefits would accrue in transferring the settlement to Jersey because the family had been living in Jersey for only a few months and probably they would not stay there. There was also doubt as to the competency of Jersey courts to administer trusts.[46] And finally the element of moral or social benefit was stressed. On this Lord Denning M.R. said:

> "There are many things in life more worthwhile than money. One of these things is to be brought up in this our England which is still 'the envy of less happier lands.' I do not believe that it is for the benefit of children to be uprooted from England and transported to another country simply to avoid tax. . . . Children are like trees: they grow stronger with firm roots."[47]

The case can be legally justified on the grounds just mentioned. But to introduce notions of "legitimate" and "illegitimate" tax avoidance would seem to be uncontrollably vague and unworkable.[48]

The taxation results of the termination of a trust described at page 388 apply equally on the termination of a trust by order of the court.

The Act. The Variation of Trusts Act, which came into force on July 23, 1958, applies to trusts of real and personal property, whether the trusts arise before or after the passing of the Act, under any will, settlement or other disposition.[49] The court may, if it thinks fit, by order approve an arrangement varying or revoking all or any of the trusts, or enlarging the powers of the trustees of managing or administering any of the trust property, on behalf of four classes of beneficiaries or potential beneficiaries. These are as follows:

(A) persons having, directly or indirectly, a vested or contingent interest who by reason of infancy or other incapacity are incapable of assenting;

---

[43] Approximately £160,000.

[44] [1968] 2 W.L.R. 1154 at p. 1162.

[45] At p. 573.

[46] [1968] 2 W.L.R. 1154 at p. 1162 *per* Stamp J.; [1969] 1 Ch. 223 at p. 247, *per* Harman L.J.: a doubt which appears to be unfounded: see *post*, p. 574.

[47] [1969] 1 Ch. 223 at p. 245, and see *post*, p. 573.

[48] The issue here is of "tax avoidance," not "tax evasion". The latter amounts to a criminal offence and clearly a scheme which "evaded" tax could not be sanctioned. But to take advantage of the existing tax laws for a person's own benefit and thereby "avoid" tax is generally regarded as being a legitimate exercise: see also Bretten [1968] 32 Conv. (N.S.) 194; Harris [1969] 33 Conv. (N.S.) 183 at 191 *et seq.*

[49] s.1(1).

(B) persons, whether ascertained or not, who may become, directly
     or indirectly, entitled to an interest at a future date or on the
     happening of a future event, if they then answer a specified des-
     cription or qualify as members of a specified class, but not
     including such persons if the future event had happened at the
     date of application to the court[50];
(C) persons unborn;
(D) persons who will be interested as discretionary beneficiaries
     under protective trusts[51] if the interest of the principal benefici-
     ary should fail or determine.[52]

In classes (A), (B) and (C) above the court will only approve the
arrangement if it is for the benefit of the persons mentioned in those
classes. But in class (D) the benefit of the persons there mentioned need
not be considered.[53] And if a beneficiary falls within class (D) and also
within one of the other classes so that different heads of jurisdiction
may apply, it is only necessary to apply for approval under (D). The four
paragraphs are alternative, so that if the case can be brought within (D)
it is not necessary to establish a benefit.[54]

(i) *General effect of the Act.* The Act largely gives to the court the
jurisdiction for which Denning L.J. contended in *Re Chapman's
Settlement Trust.*[55] It has commendably done away with the hair-
splitting technicalities involved in a "compromise" and it has attracted
a great many applications to the court since it was passed. But it must
be emphasised that, although the jurisdiction is wide in many respects,
it is in particular limited in the sense that it only empowers the court to
authorise arrangements on behalf of the persons designated in the Act,
as if they were all ascertained and *sui juris.* It does not enable the court
to override any objection—even if it is unreasonable—or dispense with

---

[50] For decisions on the meaning of this paragraph, see *Re Suffert's Settlement* [1961] Ch. 1; *Re Moncrieff's Settlement Trusts* [1962] 1 W.L.R. 1344. Briefly, however, if the class in question is, for example, the statutory next-of-kin of a living propositus, then the latter is treated as having died at the date of application to the court, and thereupon the next-of-kin become ascertainable. Since the "future event" (the death of the propositus) has notionally happened, a member of the class of next-of-kin who is in existence cannot be bound by an order for variation without his consent (see *Re Suffert's Settlement, supra.*). Further, persons who have contingent interests, however remote, are already entitled; they are not persons who "may become entitled." Consequently, in *Knocker v. Youille* [1986] 1 W.L.R. 934, it was held that consent could not be given on behalf of a very numerous class of contingently entitled beneficiaries, whose approval it was not practical to obtain.
[51] See *ante*, p. 182.
[52] s.1(1) and see also s.1(2), which defines "protective trusts" as the trusts specified in Trustee Act 1925, s.33(1)(i) and (ii) or "any like trusts." For the meaning of this last expression, see *Re Wallace's Settlement* [1968] 1 W.L.R. 711 at 716, *per* Megarry J.: "The word 'like' requires not identity but similarity; and similarity in substance suffices without the need for similarity in form or detail or wording." See also *Gibbon v. Mitchell* [1990] 1 W.L.R. 1304.
[53] s.1(1), proviso, and see also *post*, p. 552.
[54] *Re Turner's Will Trusts* [1960] Ch. 122.
[55] *Supra.* In *Re Chapman's Settlement Trusts (No. 2)* [1959] 1 W.L.R. 372 an application to create substantially the same scheme was granted under the Variation of Trusts Act 1958.

the consent—even it is is unreasonably withheld—of any beneficiary who is in fact ascertained and *sui juris*: in such circumstances, the Act cannot be invoked.

(ii) *Trusts to which Act applies.* Section 1(1) of the Act provides that the Act applies where "property, whether real or personal, is held on trusts arising . . . under any will, settlement or other disposition." It seems, however, that the Act does not apply to every type of trust. Proceedings had been commenced on behalf of children who were alleged to have been born with physical deformities as a result of their mothers having taken the drug thalidomide during pregnancy. These proceedings had been settled upon the basis that the manufacturers of the drug paid into court nearly £6m. on terms that there should be paid out or applied various sums "in such manner as the judge may direct to or for the benefit of each (deformed) child". In *Allen* v. *Distillers Co. (Biochemicals) Ltd.*[56] an application was made for the payment of money out of court to be held by trustees on the terms of a draft which was submitted to the court for approval. Under the terms of settlement of the original proceedings, each child was entitled to payment on attaining the age of majority, whereas under the proposed draft settlement deed, the trustees were to be empowered to defer the date upon which the child would be entitled. The court held that it had no jurisdiction under the Act to approve the "variation" of the terms upon which the money had been paid into court. Eveleigh J.[57] said[58] that the terms upon which the money had been paid into court was not "a trust of the kind referred to in the 1958 Act. The Act contemplates a situation where a beneficial interest is created which did not previously exist and probably one which is related to at least one other beneficial interest." Similarly in *Mason* v. *Farbrother*[58A] an application under the 1958 Act for the variation of the existing investment powers of a pension fund was not pursued because of doubts about whether the parties were truly representative of the classes of beneficiaries whom they purported to represent.

(iii) *Specific considerations*

(a) **Benefit.** The only essential guidance specifically provided in the Act as to the principles on which the exercise of the jurisdiction is based is that, with the exception of Class (D) above (discretionary beneficiaries under protective trusts), the arrangements should be for the *benefit* of the persons designated in the Act[59] on whose behalf approval of the arrangement is sought. There must be a definite benefit, even if it is not purely financial, conferred on such persons. Thus in *Re Van Gruisen's*

---

[56] [1974] 2 All E.R. 365.
[57] As he says in the judgment, "a common lawyer with this problem" of what constitutes a trust.
[58] At p. 374.
[58A] [1983] 2 All E.R. 1078.
[59] s.1(1), proviso.

Will Trusts[60] it was shown that actuarially the provisions for infants and unborn persons were more beneficial to them under the proposed arrangement than under the trusts of the will, and the arrangement was approved. But Ungoed-Thomas J. sounded a warning note when he said: "The court is not merely concerned with the actuarial calculation . . . the court is also concerned whether the arrangement as a whole in all the circumstances, is such that it is proper to approve it. The court's concern involves, *inter alia*, a practical and businesslike consideration of the arrangement, including the total amount of the advantages which the various parties obtain and their bargaining strength." The same reasoning was applied in the earlier decision of *Re Clitheroe's Settlement Trusts*,[61] where the arrangement was designed to exclude any future wife from the class of objects of an immediate discretionary trust[62] but in compensation gave her the benefit of a covenant by the settlor to pay the trustees an annual sum for her benefit. Danckwerts J. sanctioned the arrangements in principle but required evidence to show that it was in fact for the benefit of a future wife.

The rule that a "benefit" is all-important has caused some, though very few, applications to fail. For example, the Court of Appeal in *Re Steed's Will Trusts*[63] refused to sanction a variation sought by the beneficiary enabling her to take the whole beneficial interest, because it did not take sufficient account of a "spectral spouse" for whom the trusts were also designed and whom the beneficiary might conceivably marry. Again, in *Re Tinker's Settlement*,[64] Russell J. declined to accept the argument that it was for the benefit of unborn persons as members of a family viewed as a whole that something reasonable and fair, but to their financial detriment, should be done.

The test was applied once more in *Re T.'s Settlement Trusts*[65] though this was only one ground of the decision. In this case Wilberforce J. refused to approve a proposed arrangement to transfer an infant female's share of settled funds to trustees to hold on protective trusts for her life, with remainders over. The infant would otherwise have become absolutely entitled in possession to the funds on attaining 21, and the arrangement had been devised because she had shown herself to be irresponsible in matters of money. The judge based his refusal (*inter alia*) on the ground that the proposals were not confined simply to dealing in a beneficial way with the special requirements of the infant. Another proposal for variation was later approved: this was to the effect

---

[60] [1964] 1 W.L.R. 449.
[61] [1959] 1 W.L.R. 1159.
[62] It was not a protective trust, so the proviso to s.1(1) did not apply.
[63] [1960]Ch. 407. See also *Re Cohen's Settlement Trusts* [1965] 1 W.L.R. 1229. (Here it was proposed to substitute June 14, 1973 in lieu of the applicant's death as the date when the persons to take were to receive the capital of the settled funds. Stamp J. refused the application on behalf of unborn beneficiaries because it could happen (even if it was a remote eventuality) that the applicant might survive the proposed date, and under the arrangement such persons would have no interest in the fund, whereas they would under the original settlement.)
[64] [1960] 1 W.L.R. 1011.
[65] [1964] Ch. 158.

that the infant's right to capital should be deferred for a time, she being given a protected life interest in the meantime.

The principle adumbrated by Danckwerts J. in *Re Cohen's Will Trusts*[66] may arguably be something of an aberration to the trend of authority. It was submitted that in the unlikely event of one of the testator's children predeceasing his widow, then aged nearly 80, the proposed arrangement would not be advantageous to his grandchildren, some of whom were infants. But it was held that risk of some kind was inherent in every application under the Act and this risk being one which would be reasonable for an adult, the court would take it on behalf of the infant.

In practice it seems that with a variation which is, when viewed broadly, for the financial benefit of the beneficiaries, but involves risks (particularly if a beneficiary were to die within a short time after the variation is made), the court is inclined to require such risks to be covered by insurance, even if the premiums are paid for out of income, and so at the expense of an infant beneficiary.[67]

But in some cases it is unnecessary to apply to the court because the risks are non-existent. Thus it has been held[68] that trustees can properly and with complete safety deal with their funds on the basis that a woman of 70 will not have a further child and an application under the Act is inappropriate: "the Act is concerned to vary trusts applicable in events which will or may happen and not to cover impossible contingencies."[69]

Moral or social benefit. Practically all the cases have been concerned with *financial* benefit which is a mundane consideration admitting of reasonable proof. But it is now established that this is not necessarily the only consideration to be taken into account by the court. Thus in *Re T.'s Settlement Trusts*[70] the judge approved the alternative scheme of variation because on the special facts of the case the evidence showed that the infant beneficiary was irresponsible and immature: "there appears to me to be a definite benefit for this infant for a period during which it is to be hoped that independence may bring her into maturity and responsibility to be protected against creditors."[71] This decision was followed by Megarry J. in *Re Holt's Settlement*[72] where he said (on a scheme postponing vesting of interests in children from 21 years to 30 years): "The word 'benefit' in the proviso to section 1 of the Act of 1958 is . . . plainly not confined to financial benefit, but may extend to moral or social benefit. . . ."[73] This rule was confirmed by the decision of the

---

[66] [1959] 1 W.L.R. 865, *cf. Re Cohen's Settlement Trusts* [1965] 1 W.L.R. 1229 (*ante*, fn. 63).

[67] For an example, see *Re Robinson's Settlement Trusts* [1976] 3 All E.R. 61.

[68] *Re Pettifor's Will Trusts* [1966] Ch. 257.

[69] *Ibid.* at pp. 260, 261, *per* Pennycuick J. See also *Re Westminster Bank Ltd.'s Declaration of Trust* [1963] 1 W.L.R. 820 where an order was made under V.T.A. 1958, in respect of a woman aged 50.

[70] [1964] Ch. 158.

[71] *Ibid.* at 162.

[72] [1969] 1 Ch. 100.

[73] *Ibid.* at p. 121.

Court of Appeal in *Re Weston's Settlement*.[74] For this purpose it was decided that it was for the benefit of children to be educated in England rather than in Jersey.

Perhaps an even broader view of "benefit" in this context was taken in *Re Remnant's Settlement Trusts*,[75] where Pennycuick J. approved an arrangement deleting forfeiture clauses whereby the interests of certain children were subject to forfeiture if they practised Roman Catholicism or married a Roman Catholic. The basis of the case appears to be that such provisions might operate as a deterrent to them in the selection of a husband and also as a source of possible family dissension.

Benefit in administration. An arrangement which results in improvement in the general administration of the trust may also be a "benefit" within the meaning of the Act. As will be shown,[76] it is on this ground that the courts have approved applications for the export of trusts to countries abroad where the beneficiaries are resident.

(b) Discretionary beneficiaries under protective trusts. It has already been stated that it is unnecessary, by way of exception to the general rule, to show a benefit to the persons falling within class (D).[77] Nevertheless, it is clearly established that their interests cannot be simply ignored. As Wilberforce J. held in *Re Burney's Settlement Trusts*,[78] in approving an arrangement varying discretionary trusts, the discretionary power conferred on the court has still to be judicially exercised and it is incumbent on the applicant to make out a case for interfering with protective trusts. Indeed, the basic principle had been stated earlier, more generally, by Lord Evershed M.R. in *Re Steed's Will Trusts*,[79] where he said that "the court is bound to look at the scheme as a whole and when it does so, to consider, as surely it must, what really was the intention of the benefactor." The requirements were spelt out in *Re Baker's Settlement Trusts*,[80] where Ungoed-Thomas J. said that where property was held on protective trusts for the benefit of the applicant and an application was made to vary those trusts, evidence (including in this case that of the financial position of the applicant and her husband) should be laid before the court to show to what extent the protective trusts continued to serve any useful purpose.

(c) Meaning of "arrangement". There is no doubt that the term has been widely construed to cover many classes of variation. "It is," as Lord Evershed M.R. has said in *Re Steed's Will Trusts*,[81] "deliberately

---

[74] [1969] 1 Ch. 223; for further discussion of this case, see *post*, p. 573 and *infra*. See also *Re C.L.* [1969] 1 Ch. 587 (mental patient surrendered his protected life interest and contingent interest in remainder. Held (Cross J.), that it was for the patient's benefit because in all probability it was what the patient would have done if of sound mind).

[75] [1970] Ch. 560, *cf. Re Tinker's Settlement* [1960] 1 W.L.R. 1011.

[76] *Post*, p. 570.

[77] s.1(1), proviso.

[78] [1961] 1 W.L.R. 545.

[79] [1960] Ch. 407 at p. 421.

[80] [1964] 1 W.L.R. 336.

[81] [1960] Ch. 407 at p. 419.

used in the widest possible sense to cover any proposal which any person may put forward for varying or revoking trusts." It need not, therefore, necessarily be *inter partes*. Views of the trustees are relevant but not conclusive and, if necessary, will be overridden.[82]

The wide meaning attached to an arrangement was, however, modified in *Re T.'s Settlement Trusts*.[83] Here Wilberforce J. refused, as the alternative and primary ground for his decision, to sanction the arrangement initially proposed because it amounted to a completely new settlement and that was beyond the jurisdiction conferred by the Act. If this represents the true position there are limits to the conception of an "arrangement", but it might be thought to be an unjustified abridgment of the court's jurisdiction.

Nevertheless subsequent case law seems to have accepted the distinction between "variation" and "resettlement". For example, in *Re Ball's Settlement*[84] Megarry J. laid down the following test to be applied: "If an arrangement changes the whole substratum of the trust, it may well be that it cannot be regarded as merely varying that trust. But if an arrangement, while leaving the substratum effectuates the purpose . . . by other means, it may still be possible to regard that arrangement as merely varying the original trusts, even though the means employed are wholly different and even though the form is completely changed." In this case the judge held that although the arrangement sought rescinded all beneficial and administrative trusts of the settlement and substituted new provisions, he could approve it because it preserved the "general drift" of the old trusts.

The fact remains that a pedantic distinction has grown up between "variation" and "resettlement" for which there appears to be no sanction in the words of the Act, nor any practical justification.

Court orders. It now seems to be established that it is the arrangement itself and not the order of the court which effects the variation.[85] But it is necessary (so it seems) to regard the order of the court and the arrangement as having been made at the same time.[86] The arrangement will, however, be embodied in, or referred to in, the order, and where this causes a disposition of beneficial interests, stamp duty was formerly payable—such voluntary dispositions are no longer subject thereto. In *Thorn* v. *I.R.C.*,[87] Walton J. had to consider the nature of the disposition affected. A trust fund was held upon protective trusts for the settlor's wife for life, with remainder to the settlor's daughter for life, and ultimately for the children and remoter issue of the daughter.

---

[82] *Ibid.* at p. 420.

[83] [1964] Ch. 158; and *ante*, p. 550.

[84] [1968] 1 W.L.R. 899. See also *Re Holt's Settlement* [1969] 1 Ch. 100 at p. 117 (Megarry J.).

[85] *Re Holt's Settlement* [1969] 1 Ch. 100. See also *Re Holmden's Settlement* [1968] A.C. 685 at pp. 701, 705, 713; *Spens* v. *I.R.C.* [1970] 1 W.L.R. 1173 at pp. 1183, 1184. Megarry J. in *Re Holt* followed *Re Joseph's Will Trusts* [1959] 1 W.L.R. 1019, not *Re Hambledon's Will Trusts* [1960] 1 W.L.R. 82, which held that the court order effected the variation.

[86] *Re Holt, supra* at p. 115. The main reason for this requirement seems to be that decisions made on the basis of *Re Hambleden (supra)* would have been made without jurisdiction.

[87] [1976] 2 All E.R. 622.

An order had been made under the Act approving a variation on behalf of the unborn and unascertained issue of the daughter. The trustees contended that in giving its approval the court, in effect, dealt with the interest of each unborn or unascertained person. Each interest, looked at separately, would have had almost no value. However, Walton J. held that the order effected the disposition of the totality of the separate interests which therefore fell to be valued as a composite whole. This decision will once again become important if *ad valorem* duty is ever reimposed on voluntary dispositions.

(d) Fraud and public policy. It is a statement of the obvious that if a variation is fraudulent or contrary to public policy it will not be sanctioned. A case of some interest on this point is *Re Robertson's Will Trusts*,[88] where the applicant had exercised a special power of appointment in favour of his children as a preliminary to the proposed arrangement. His purpose and intention in making the appointment was to benefit his children and not himself. Later he was advised that his financial position would in fact be improved if the appointment were made and the scheme approved. But Russell J. held that to suppose his original purpose and intention had been changed or added to was unjustified. It followed that there was no fraud on the power, though, if there had been, the court would not have been able to approve the scheme.

However, subsequent case law appears to indicate a certain conflict as to the precise principles to be applied. In *Re Wallace's Settlement*[89] Megarry J. said that the fact that protected life tenants had executed appointments in favour of their children in itself raised a case for inquiry because the life tenants benefited by the arrangement; but on the evidence he was satisfied that there was no fraud on the power because the benefit to the life tenants was not substantial and they had intended to make the appointment before the arrangement was approved. However, in *Re Brook's Settlement*[90] Stamp J. adopted a rather different approach. He held that the exercise of a special power of appointment amounted to a fraud on the power and he was unable to approve the variation. Here one of the purposes of the appointment (by a protected life tenant in favour of his children from which he would also benefit from a division of the capital) was to enable the life tenant to obtain what he could not otherwise get, namely capital rather than income. This was enough to invalidate the appointment.

The important feature of *Re Brook* is that the judge emphasised that the question is whether the *purpose* of the appointment amounted to a fraud, not, as was apparently suggested in *Re Wallace*, the *effect* of the appointment on the financial position of the appointor. It is thought that *Re Brook* applies the correct principle.

---

[88] [1960] 1 W.L.R. 1050.
[89] [1968] 1 W.L.R. 711.
[90] [1968] 1 W.L.R. 1661.

Release. The difficulties that may thus arise as a result of a fraud on the power, however inadvertent, may in some circumstances be avoided by releasing the power. For no question of a fraud on a power can arise on a mere release. And it has been held that, provided that the power in question can be released,[91] the court will approve an arrangement varying a settlement even though the objects of the power are ignored.[92] There appears to be some doubt whether the release should be effected by deed, or whether it can be inferred from the facts. The latter would seem sufficient.[93]

Even if the power cannot be released (*e.g.* if it was given to the donee *qua* trustee)[94] it still seems possible to apply to the court for an arrangement extinguishing the power because this amounts to varying or revoking a trust within section 1 of the 1958 Act. But because the power is not of itself releasable the court is likely to impose conditions on the release. Thus Stamp J. in *Re Drewe's Settlement*[95] in approving an arrangement insisted that it could only be effected by deed and with the consent of the trustees.

Public policy. Considerations of public policy were neatly side-stepped by Buckley J. in *Re Michelham's Will Trusts*.[96] Approval was sought to an arrangement whereby trust property was transferred to the applicants absolutely. The efficacy of the scheme depended on their continuing to remain unmarried. Insurance policies were therefore to be effected which would ensure that, if either did in fact marry, certain sums would become available to replace the funds thus transferred. The policies included a stipulation that the insurers should be indemnified by a Swiss bank if the policy moneys became payable. The bank proposed to give the indemnity on terms that it, in turn, should be indemnified by one or other of the applicants if the moneys became payable. The judge, in approving the arrangement, held that, although the counter-indemnities given by the applicants to the bank ought to be regarded as tending to discourage the applicants from marrying, that would not affect its validity. This was so because if the counter-indemnities were unenforceable by the bank on grounds of public policy—and that was a question of Swiss law—that fact alone would not relieve the bank from its obligation to indemnify the insurers.

(e) Form of application. An application should normally be made by a life-tenant or other person entitled to the income of the trust funds. It should only be made by the trustees, as Russell J. said in *Re Druce's Settlement Trusts*,[97] where "they are satisfied that the proposals are

---

[91] See *Re Will's Trust Deeds* [1964] Ch. 219, and *ante*, p. 151 and see Hawkins (1968) 84 L.Q.R. 64.

[92] *Re Christie-Miller's Settlement* [1961] 1 W.L.R. 462; *Re Courtland's Settlement* [1965] 1 W.L.R. 1385; *Re Ball's Settlement* [1968] 1 W.L.R. 899.

[93] In *Re Ball* Megarry J. insisted on a formal release, but in *Re Christie-Miller* and *Re Courtland* an inferred release was regarded as sufficient.

[94] See *ante*, p. 153.

[95] [1966] 1 W.L.R. 1518.

[96] [1964] Ch. 550.

[97] [1962] 1 W.L.R. 363.

beneficial to the persons interested and have a good prospect of being approved by the court, and further, that if they do not make the application no one else will." As these principles were satisfied in this case it was held to be a proper case for an application by the trustees. In the ordinary way the trustees will be respondents, as will be all the existing beneficiaries, adult and infant and the Attorney-General[98] if the existing settlement contains a charitable trust. It is, moreover, the duty of persons appointed guardians *ad litem* for an infant to take proper legal advice and apprise themselves fully of the nature of the application and the manner in which the beneficial interest of the infant is proposed to be affected.[99] At the same time it is recognised that there is a limit to the necessity for joinder of parties. So it seems unnecessary, for reasons of practicality and expense, to join persons who are merely potential members of a class. Thus, it has been held that it is unnecessary to join persons who are only interested as the objects of a power which may never be exercised.[1] And the same has been applied to persons interested under protective trusts which it is proposed to vary: as Wilberforce J. said in *Munro's Settlement Trusts*,[2] the court looks prima facie to the trustees as watchdogs to see that interested parties' interests are protected.

(f) **Extent of jurisdiction.** The Act does not extend to Scotland[3] or Northern Ireland.[4] Jurisdiction is accordingly withheld from the courts of these countries. But this does not oust the jurisdiction of the *English* courts to vary a Northern Ireland or Scottish or indeed any foreign settlement. And it has been held in *Re Ker's Settlement Trusts*[5] that the court has jurisdiction to vary a settlement of which the proper law was that of Northern Ireland and in *Re Paget's Settlement*[6] where the proper law was believed to be that of New York.

(g) **Trustee Investments Act 1961.** The Trustee Investments Act 1961[7] expressly preserves the discretion of the court under the Variation of Trusts Act 1958 to extend the trustees' powers of investment. And many applications have been made under the Variation of Trusts Act 1958 to extend the trustees' investment powers as well as to vary the beneficial trusts. The question, however, is: are the trustees entitled under the Act of 1958 to obtain investment powers greater than those conferred by the Act of 1961? The answer in most of the reported cases was originally negative. Thus, in *Re Cooper's Settlement*,[8] Buckley J. held that the court must be satisfied that there are "special circumstances" in which the trustees should be given wider powers than the "normally

---

[98] See *Re Longman's Settlement Trusts* [1962] 1 W.L.R. 455.
[99] *Re Whittall* [1973] 1 W.L.R. 1027.
[1] *Re Christie-Miller's Marriage Settlement* [1961] 1 W.L.R. 462.
[2] [1963] 1 W.L.R. 145. *cf. Re Courtland's Settlement* [1965] 1 W.L.R. 1385.
[3] s.2(1).
[4] s.2(2).
[5] [1963] Ch. 553.
[6] [1965] 1 W.L.R. 1046.
[7] s.15; and see *ante*, p. 450.
[8] [1962] Ch. 826.

appropriate" powers indicated by the Act of 1961. The fact that the extension of investment powers proposed was part of an arrangement to vary beneficial interests was specifically rejected as amounting to a special circumstance justifying a departure from the scope of the statutory scheme. Likewise in *Re Kolb's Will Trusts*,[9] where the settlor clearly wished to invest the whole fund in equities and it was only because of the wording of the instrument that the trustees did not have the power to do so, Cross J. doubted whether this fact alone constituted such special circumstances as to justify an extension of the powers of investment conferred by the Act of 1961. Further, in *Re Clarke's Will Trusts*[10] Russell J. was only prepared to go so far as to substitute the requirements of the dividend history demanded of wider-range securities, in place of those provided for in the trust instrument.

Only in one reported case from this period were "special circumstances" justifying an extension been found. This is *Re University of London Charitable Trusts*,[11] a case relating to charitable trusts. Wilberforce J. held (*inter alia*[12]) that he was entitled to extend the range of investment beyond that permitted by the Act of 1961 because, if he did not, the benefits of a proposed combined investment pool which would arise from the saving of administrative expenses, convenience of administration and the practicability of dividing the combined pool into parts would be frustrated. However, the courts have now accepted that the Trustee Investments Act 1961 has become outdated and are now once again prepared to authorise extensions of investment powers. Thus in *Trustees of the British Museum* v. *Attorney-General*[13] Sir Robert Megarry V.C. took the view that the principle laid down in *Re Kolb* should no longer be followed. However, as has already been seen, it has now been held[14] that, provided the beneficial interests are not affected by the proposed extension of investment powers, section 57 of the Trustee Act 1925 should be used in preference to the Variation of Trusts Act 1958.

(h) Law of Property Act 1925, s.53(1)(c). In *Re Holt's Settlement*[15] Megarry J. held that trusts are varied effectively by the arrangement (taking effect when the court order is made) even though it does not comply with section 53(1)(*c*) of the Law of Property Act 1925. This requires that the disposition of an equitable interest should be in writing.[16] In coming to this conclusion the judge relied on *Oughtred* v. *I.R.C.*,[17] on the basis that the arrangement gave rise to a constructive trust and therefore the requirements of section 53(1)(*c*) could be ignored because of section 52(2) which exempts constructive trusts from these

---

[9] [1962] Ch. 531.
[10] [1961] 1 W.L.R. 1471.
[11] [1964] Ch. 282.
[12] See also *ante*, p. 355.
[13] [1984] 1 W.L.R. 418.
[14] In *Anker-Petersen* v. *Anker-Petersen* (1991) 88/16 L.S. Gaz. 32.
[15] [1969] 1 Ch. 100.
[16] For further discussion of this section and the cases, see *ante*, p. 35.
[17] [1960] A.C. 206. See *ante*, p. 42.

requirements. In the House of Lords in *Oughtred* v. *I.R.C.* this view was in fact adopted only by Lord Radcliffe, who was dissenting on the main issue, to which this point was, in the view of the majority, irrelevant.[18] However, this view is consistent with subsequent authority,[19] although it is clearly limited to pure personalty because all contracts for the sale of land are now required to be in writing.[20]

(i) **Trustee Act 1925, s.53.**[21] Under this section the court has the power to make vesting orders in relation to an infant's beneficial interest. In some cases it may prove necessary to combine an application under this section with one under the Variation of Trusts Act 1958. This happened in *Re Bristol's Settled Estates*,[22] where Buckley J. authorised the execution of a disentailing assurance on behalf of an infant tenant in tail in remainder so that the property could be dealt with for his benefit under a proposed "arrangement" which the judge also approved.

(j) **Perpetuity.** The Perpetuities and Accumulations Act 1964[23] applies only to instruments taking effect after the commencement of the Act.[24] The question is how far this provision affects variations made under the Act of 1958. In *Re Holt's Settlement*[25] Megarry J. held that an arrangement (taken with the court order[26]) was an "instrument" for this purpose, with the result that provisions deriving their validity from the 1964 Act might be included in the arrangement; and this would apply not only to trusts created since the commencement of the 1964 Act but also to those created before this date.[27]

But one difficulty does remain. The problem is whether the instrument must take effect as a "disposition". The 1964 Act tends to suggest that this is necessary.[28] The point did not arise in *Holt's* case because the applicant there surrendered a life interest and this amounted to a "disposition". It seems, however, that if the arrangement does not involve a disposition, then the benefits of the 1964 Act cannot be utilised in respect of subsequent variations of the original trusts.[29]

---

[18] See *ante*, p. 28.
[19] *D.H.N. Food Distributors* v. *Tower Hamlets L.B.C.* [1976] 1 W.L.R. 852, *Chinn* v. *Collins* [1981] A.C. 533.
[20] Under the Law of Property (Miscellaneous Provisions) Act 1989, s.2.
[21] *Supra.*
[22] [1965] 1 W.L.R. 469; see also *Re Lansdowne's Will Trusts* [1967] Ch. 603.
[23] See *ante*, p. 164.
[24] s.15(5).
[25] [1969] 1 Ch. 100.
[26] See *ante*, p. 553.
[27] The same principle was applied but no reasons given in *Re Lloyd's Settlement* [1967] 2 W.L.R. 1078 in relation to s.13 and the accumulation periods.
[28] See ss.1, 3(5).
[29] See *Re Holmden's Settlement* [1968] A.C. 685 where it was suggested that a mere alteration of the period for which discretionary trusts should continue was not a "disposition."

CHAPTER 22

EXPORTING TRUSTS

I. MOTIVES

A PERSON may wish to create a new trust abroad, or to export an existing trust for a variety of reasons. Generally, these are one or more of the following:

1. The beneficiaries or a majority of them are resident abroad, or are intending to reside abroad, and it will be most convenient for the trust to be administered in the country in which they are resident.[1]
2. There is a widespread fear that future United Kingdom legislation might aim to achieve a more even distribution of wealth among members of the community and that this can only be achieved by, in effect, confiscating part of the assets of those who are thought to be wealthy. A wealth tax is only one form which such legislation might take. It is not for us to comment here on the ethics or political wisdom of any such measures, but man is an essentially greedy animal and, having acquired assets, will usually go to great lengths to retain them. Some have thought that if assets are transferred abroad, and held by trustees, then they will be safe from the tax gatherer's preying hands, particularly if the present owner does not retain any legal entitlement to them.
3. From time to time, there is an associated fear that as a currency, sterling may not be stable, and that the value and security of wealth may be enhanced if it is held abroad.
4. Occasionally, it is desired to take advantage of foreign rules of law. Although it is not "foreign" in this sense, a particular example is Northern Ireland where it is possible to direct accumulation for a period of 60 years.
5. But in most cases there are two predominant motives. The first is to ensure so far as possible that funds are protected from any re-introduction of United Kingdom exchange control.

---

[1] This was the reason for the approval of the court given in *Re Seale's Marriage Settlement* [1961] Ch. 574; and in *Re Windeatt's Will Trusts* [1969] 1 W.L.R. 692; [1969] 2 All E.R. 324. See *post*, p. 438. See also *Re Whitehead's Will Trusts* [1971] 1 W.L.R. 833; *post*, p. 571.

6. The second predominant motive is to save tax.

This chapter is concerned with the extent to which these two last objectives can effectively be achieved. It examines the main aspects of the law which apply when a person resident in the United Kingdom wishes to create a new trust abroad or when an existing United Kingdom trust is transferred abroad. Trusts which are administered abroad are commonly referred to as "off-shore"[2] trusts.

II. EXCHANGE CONTROL

United Kingdom exchange control legislation is currently[3] in suspense. It was intended, when enacted, to conserve the United Kingdom's gold and foreign currency resources, and to assist the balance of payments by restricting the outflow of funds from the United Kingdom. While the legislation was in operation, very broadly a person resident in the United Kingdom[4] who wished to purchase an investment or other asset abroad[5] had to do so in one of three ways, namely:

(a) with currency purchased through the official foreign exchange market. This was controlled strictly by the Bank of England, acting as the exchange control authority. In principle, the Bank of England gave permission for the use of foreign currency purchased at the official rate of exchange only where the investment was likely directly to promote United Kingdom exports, or where it promised an early benefit to the balance of payments. Permission was not generally given for personal investment.

(b) With "investment currency". After the introduction of exchange control, persons who were resident in the United Kingdom and who had foreign currency securities[6] were obliged, when they sold them, to sell them through controlled channels for sterling. The proceeds of sale, known as investment currency, were available for sale to other United Kingdom residents but, because of the shortage of investment currency, this was at a premium often in excess of 40 per cent. This applied even where the resident investor wished to sell one foreign currency security and to re-invest the proceeds in another such security.

(c) With the proceeds of foreign currency borrowings. These were sums borrowed abroad in a currency other than sterling. A

---

[2] The expression includes anywhere outside the U.K., and so includes the Channel Islands and the Isle of Man.

[3] Since October 24, 1979.

[4] Or in the other Scheduled Territories, namely the Channel Islands, the Isle of Man, the Republic of Ireland and Gibraltar.

[5] That is, outside the Scheduled Territories. A special relaxation applied in the case of investment in other EEC countries.

[6] *i.e.* securities denominated or payable in any currency other than sterling.

foreign currency borrowing required the permission of the Bank of England. This was not generally available to private investors.

When foreign currency securities were purchased, irrespective of the source of the funds, the certificates of the securities had to be held by depositories designated by the Bank of England.[7]

While the control was in force, an individual who wished to invest abroad was therefore subject to numerous restrictions and almost invariably substantial extra cost. Furthermore, there was always the risk, that in acute national financial circumstances the Government would take action to compel those securities to be realised. Furthermore, there was a general prohibition on maintaining foreign currency bank accounts.

In 1979 the legislation was suspended but not repealed.[8] It can be brought into operation again by Order made by H.M. Treasury.[9] Since 1979, many individuals resident in the United Kingdom have created trusts with a view to enabling their funds to be free of any reintroduction of the control. The strategy is based on the premise that where the trustees are resident abroad, and the investments are situated abroad, the trustees will not themselves be subject to United Kingdom exchange control legislation; and the beneficiary, not having the power to control the trustees, will himself not be able to procure that the funds are brought within the scope of the control. In current jargon, such non-resident trustees are said to be "non-compellable".

The fear that exchange control might be re-introduced has, therefore, been a powerful stimulus to the formation of new off-shore trusts.

In the case of existing trusts, when the legislation was in force all trusts were classified as resident or non-resident. This depended on the residential status of the settlor, in the case of an *inter vivos* trust, or of the deceased at the date of his death in the case of a will trust. Where the trust was resident, there was no restriction on the appointment of non-resident trustees as such; but the assets could only be transferred to them with the consent of the Bank of England which was only sparingly given. In general, permission was always refused unless it could be shown that all possible beneficiaries were themselves non-resident. On the other hand, there were very few onerous restrictions on trusts which had throughout their existence been non-resident, or which had been made non-resident before the original introduction of exchange control.[10]

Accordingly, there is also a movement towards making existing trusts non-resident and taking the assets abroad, while there is no restriction on so doing.

---

[7] Most banks and practising solicitors were so designated.

[8] By the Exchange Control (General Exemption) Order 1979 (S.I. 1979 No. 1660) and the Exchange Control (Revocation) (No. 2) Direction 1979 (S.I. 1979 No. 1162).

[9] Under the Exchange Control Act 1947.

[10] By the Defence (Finance) Regulations 1939, issued under the Emergency Powers (Defence) Acts.

III. TAXATION

1. *Taxation generally*

In order to determine the taxation advantages of a trust which is for the time being non-resident[11] it is necessary to consider the taxation liability of:

    (a) the trustees; and
    (b) the beneficiaries.

2. *Income Tax*

(1) The trustees

An underlying principle of United Kingdom income tax law is that a person is liable to income tax

    (a) if he is resident here, on his total world-wide income; but
    (b) if he is not resident here, only on income which is derived from a source in the United Kingdom.

It follows that, in the case of non-resident trustees:

    (a) they will not be liable in respect of income derived from sources outside the United Kingdom; but
    (b) they will be liable in respect of income derived from sources within the United Kingdom to the same extent as trustees who are resident here. It has been seen[12] that, in principle, this liability will be
        (i) at 25 per cent. (20 per cent. in the case of company distributions) in the case of fixed interest trusts; and
        (ii) at 35 per cent. in the case of accumulation and discretionary settlements.[13]

Accordingly, the trustees will be free of United Kingdom income tax if all the investments are made abroad.

(2) The beneficiaries: actual income

Where a beneficiary is entitled to income from a foreign trust, he is liable to income tax on that income[14] whether or not he actually receives it.[15] This is so irrespective of the territory in which the trust assets are situated. No income tax saving is effected, therefore, where the beneficiary is actually entitled to the income.

---

[11] For the sake of simplicity, in this chapter the expression "non-resident" is used to mean both non-resident in the strict sense, and non-ordinarily resident.

[12] *Ante*, p. 412.

[13] *Ante*, p. 413.

[14] Under Case V of Schedule D.

[15] Liability is deferred if it is impossible to remit the income to the United Kingdom: s.418. If the person entitled to the income is resident but not domiciled in the United Kingdom, foreign income is only liable to United Kingdom income tax if remitted to the United Kingdom.

(3) The beneficiaries: other benefits from income

Were there no other provision, the beneficiaries would escape liability if income was accumulated abroad, and either retained abroad, or paid to them as capital. To counter this, there are two far-reaching anti-avoidance provisions.

(a) *Section 739 Income and Corporation Taxes Act 1988.* Section 739 of the Income and Corporation Taxes Act 1988 applies where:

  (i) an asset[16] is transferred to a person abroad.[17] This requirement is satisfied even if the asset has not been transferred from the United Kingdom. So, if Andrew, a resident of, say, South Africa, offers to make a gift of R2,000 to Bertram, who is a United Kingdom resident, but Bertram directs Andrew to pay that sum to trustees on his behalf in Guernsey,[18] the payment of that sum will constitute a transfer of an asset for this purpose. In *I.R.C. v. Brackett*, the taxpayer entered into a contract of employment with a Jersey company and was held to be caught by the section because rights created by the contract were assets transferred to a person abroad;

  (ii) the transfer was by the tax payer or his spouse[19];

  (iii) by virtue of, or as a consequence of, that transfer, either directly or indirectly[20] the income is payable to a person or company resident abroad[21]; and

  (iv) a United Kingdom resident enjoys, or has power to enjoy, that income. The definition of "power to enjoy" is very wide indeed.[22]

---

[16] The expression includes money, and property or rights of any kind.

[17] *I.e.* out of the United Kingdom.

[18] Which is "abroad" for this purpose.

[19] *Vestey* v. *I.R.C.* [1980] A.C. 1148.

[20] This follows from the application of the general principle to a transfer by "an associated operation". S.739 defines "associated operation" in relation to any transfer as "an operation of any kind effected by any person in relation to any of the assets transferred or any assets representing, whether directly or indirectly, any of the assets transferred, or to the income arising from any such assets, or to any assets representing, whether directly or indirectly, the accumulations of income arising from any such assets."

[21] For this purpose, "income" does not include director's remuneration.

[22] S.742(2) provides that for the purposes of the section an individual is deemed to have power to enjoy the income of a person resident or domiciled out of the United Kingdom if

"(a) the income is in fact so dealt with by any person as to be calculated, at some point of time, and whether in the form of income or not, to enure for the benefit of the individual, or

(b) the receipt or accrual of the income operates to increase the value to the individual of any assets held by him for his benefit, or

(c) the individual receives or is entitled to receive, at any time, any benefit provided or to be provided out of that income or out of moneys which are or will be available for the purpose by reason of the effect or successive effects of the associated operations on that income and on any assets which directly or indirectly represent that income, or

(d) the individual has power, by means of the exercise of any power of appointment or power of revocation or otherwise, to obtain for himself, whether with or without the consent of any other person, the beneficial enjoyment of the income, or may, in the

Where the section applies the income arising abroad is treated as the income of the United Kingdom resident for income tax purposes[23] to the extent to which it is not actually distributed to others. There are two exceptions to this provision:

(a) where the Board of Inland Revenue is satisfied that tax avoidance was not the purpose or one of the purposes for which the transfer was effected. Even if the avoidance of tax was not the primary purpose of the transfer, it will almost invariably be one of the purposes, so that this exception is more apparent than real;

(b) where the transfer was part of a *bona fide* commercial transaction, and not designed for the purpose of avoiding tax.

In most cases, therefore, where a United Kingdom resident forms a trust abroad, and places money or other assets in that trust, under which he or his spouse is a beneficiary, section 739 will apply, and there will be no saving of income tax. Indeed, the liability can be greater than if the income arose within the United Kingdom. In *Lord Chetwode* v. *I.R.C.*,[24] Lord Chetwode created a settlement in the Bahamas, which owned the entire share capital of a Bahamian investment company. It was held that Lord Chetwode was assessable on the whole[25] of the income of the investment company, and that he could not even deduct the expenses of the management of that company in computing the amount of income to be brought into account for tax.

Income and Corporation Taxes Act 1988, s.740. Section 739 applies only where, *inter alia*, the transfer of assets was made by the taxpayer or his spouse. Section 740 applies where an individual who is resident in the United Kingdom can benefit under a foreign trust but who was not a settlor in relation to it. If, therefore, Edward creates a non-resident discretionary settlement under which he and his son Frank are discretionary beneficiaries, during Edward's lifetime section 739 will apply. However, after Edward's death, provided Frank took no part in setting up the arrangements, he will only be liable, if at all, under section 740 in respect of income which he does not receive as income.

Under section 740, it is necessary to calculate the income of a foreign trust which arose after March 9, 1981 directly or indirectly from a transfer of assets, and which can be used for providing a benefit for an individual who is ordinarily resident in the United Kingdom. Thus, in the example, income which is accumulated after the death of Edward is relevant income for this purpose, because it is capable of providing a benefit for Frank at some time in the future. A running notional record

event of the exercise of any power vested in any other person, become entitled to the beneficial enjoyment of the income, or
(e) the individual is able in any manner whatsoever, and whether directly or indirectly, to control the application of the income."
Even this is extended by 742(3).
[23] This does not apply to income which the foreign resident actually distributes to others.
[24] [1977] 1 All E.R. 638.
[25] In practice, the Revenue do allow a very limited deduction from the gross income in respect of the costs of collecting that income.

is then kept of this income, but no liability arises at that stage. When, however, the individual receives a benefit from the trust which is not taxable as ordinary income, the value of that benefit is treated as forming part of his income for the year in which he actually receives it. Thus, if the trustees made a discretionary capital payment to Frank, he will be subject to income tax on it to the extent that it is covered by income which has arisen to the trustees.

In summary, therefore, the general position is that:

(a) a beneficiary resident in the United Kingdom will be liable to income tax on the actual income which he receives or to which he is entitled;

(b) the settlor will be liable to income tax on income retained within the trust unless it cannot be applied for his benefit, this liability being to tax when the income arises; but

(c) other beneficiaries[26] will only be liable to income tax retained within the trust when they actually receive benefit from it.

Non-resident trusts are, therefore, a useful means by which the liability to income tax can be deferred.

3. *Capital Gains Tax*

(1) Types of non-resident trust

For capital gains tax purposes, a trust will, in principle, only be regarded as non-resident if

(a) the general administration of the trust is ordinarily carried on outside the United Kingdom. There is no definition of this, but it probably means where the trustees meet, or, if it is large enough to have its own secretariat, where that secretariat is situated; and

(b) the majority of the trustees are not resident or ordinarily resident in the United Kingdom.[27]

This is so even if the settlor was resident in the United Kingdom at the time when the trust was created.

However, a trust will also be regarded as non-resident if:

(a) all the trust property is derived from a person who is not domiciled or resident in the United Kingdom;

(b) some or all of the trustees are individuals or companies whose business consists of or includes the management of trusts or of acting as trustees; and

(c) a majority of the trustees are either such persons, or persons who are actually non-resident.[28]

These trusts are regarded as being non-resident even if their general administration is actually carried on in the United Kingdom.

---

[26] Apart from the settlor's widow.
[27] Taxation of Chargeable Gains Act 1992, s.69(1).
[28] *Ibid.* s.69(2).

Trusts which are treated as non-resident trusts for capital gains tax purposes are divided into two categories, which are known[29] as

(a) section 87 trusts; and
(b) fully foreign trusts.

A "section 87" trust, that is, a trust which is within section 87 of the Taxation of Chargeable Gains Act 1992, is one in which, during the year of assessment[30] being considered:

(i) the trustees are non-resident;
(ii) if the trust was created *inter vivos*, and the settlor is still alive, the settlor
    (a) was domiciled and resident in the United Kingdom at the time when the settlement was created; or
    (b) is domiciled and resident in the United Kingdom in the year of assessment being considered; or
(iii) if the settlement was created *inter vivos* and the settlor is dead, he was domiciled and resident in the United Kingdom when the settlement was created; or
(iv) if the settlement was created by will, the testator was domiciled and resident in the United Kingdom at the date of his death.

A "fully foreign trust" is one which is non-resident, and which is outside the scope of section 87.

(2) The trustees
In common with non-resident individuals, non-resident trustees are not chargeable to captial gains tax in respect of gains arising on the disposal of assets, even if the assets are situated in the United Kingdom.[31] This is so whether the trust is a section 87 trust, or a fully foreign trust.

(3) The beneficiaries: section 87 trusts
The provisions of section 87 of the Taxation of Chargeable Gains Act 1992 are similar to those of section 740 of the Income and Corporation Taxes Act 1988.[32] A notional record is maintained of all gains which accrue to the trustees after March 9, 1981. These are known as "trust gains". When the trustees make a capital payment to a beneficiary[33] that payment is treated as representing a capital gain to the extent of the available trust gains. Suppose, therefore, that the trustees realise the following gains, and make the following capital payments:

---

[29] Colloquially, not by statute.
[30] From April 6 to the following April 5.
[31] Taxation of Chargeable Gains Act 1992, s.2(1). There is, however, a liability if the non-resident carries on a trade in the United Kingdom and disposes of trading assets (*ibid.*, s.10(1)).
[32] *Ante*, p. 564.
[33] Whether resident or non-resident.

Year of assessment	Gains	Capital Payment
1991/92	nil	£8,000 to Andrew
1992/93	£20,000	nil
1993/94	£20,000	£15,000 to Brian
1994/95	£20,000	£50,000 to Charles
1995/96	£20,000	nil

The trust gains for 1991/92 are nil. Of the gains realised in 1992/93, £8,000 are attributed to Andrew for 1992/93, and the balance of £12,000 is carried forward to 1993/94. The trust gains for 1993/94 are (a) the balance brought forward from 1992/93, £12,000, and (b) the gains arising in the year, £20,000, less (c) £15,000 which is attributed to Brian. The balance of £17,000 is carried forward. In 1994/95 the trust gains total £37,000[34] so that £37,000 is attributed to Charles for 1994/95. The remaining £13,000 which he has received in that year will have the gains for 1995/96 attributed to it. If any of Andrew, Brian or Charles is domiciled and resident in the United Kingdom in the year in which any of these gains is attributed to a capital payment made to him, he will have to pay the appropriate capital gains tax thereon in accordance with the normal rules; thus, he can deduct from the attributed gain any losses and his annual exemption and will be taxed on the balance at the same rate as that at which he pays income tax. However, no capital gains tax will be payable by any beneficiary who is not domiciled and resident in the United Kingdom in the year in question.

However, in addition to the basic capital gains tax payable in the manner illustrated in this example, beneficiaries who receive capital payments after April 5, 1992 and are liable to pay capital gains tax because they are domiciled and resident in the United Kingdom also have to pay a supplementary interest charge of 10 per cent. per annum of the tax actually payable in respect of any period up to six years during which payment of capital gains tax has been deferred.[35] In the example above, the capital payment to Andrew is not liable to this interest charge because it was made before April 6, 1992 and, in any event, no capital gains tax was actually deferred. However, the capital payments made to Brian and Charles will be liable to this payment. Of the £15,000 attributed to Brian in 1993/94, £12,000 was brought forward from 1992/93; if he is domiciled and resident in the United Kingdom in 1993/94, he will therefore have to pay an extra 10 per cent. of the tax due in respect of that £12,000 (no interest will be payable in respect of the other £3,000 since that gain arose in the year in which he received the capital payment). In the same way, Charles will, if domiciled and resident in the United Kingdom in 1994/95, have to pay an extra 10 per cent. of the tax due in respect of £17,000 of the £37,000 attributed to him in 1994/95.

The provisions seem complicated but they have the effect that no liability can attach to a resident beneficiary until he actually receives a capital payment. Accordingly, even where the trust is within section 87,

---

[34] I.e. £17,000 brought forward from 1993/94, and the £20,000 which arises in 1994/95.
[35] Taxation of Chargeable Gains Act 1992, ss.91–97.

deferment of capital gains tax can be achieved merely by retaining all capital within the trust, although such deferment will of course now be liable to an interest payment of 10 per cent. per annum of the tax due in respect of any gains during the six years prior to the receipt of a capital payment by a resident beneficiary.

(4) The beneficiaries: fully foreign trusts
No liability attaches to beneficiaries, even if resident in the United Kingdom, in respect of gains realised by the trustees of a fully non-resident trust. This is so whether or not the trustees make capital payments to the beneficiaries.

However, where a beneficiary becomes absolutely entitled to assets as against the trustees of a fully foreign trust, he will in general be treated as acquiring those assets at a nil base cost, so that he will be taxable on the whole of the proceeds of sale when he disposes of the asset.

(5) Exporting trusts
Since March 19, 1991, the export of a trust has constituted a deemed disposal by the trustees[36] similar to that which occurs when a beneficiary becomes absolutely entitled to the whole or any part of the trust property.[37] The deemed disposal is said to take place immediately before the trustees cease to become resident and ordinarily resident in the United Kingdom. Consequently, it is the retiring United Kingdom trustees who make the disposal and become primarily liable for the tax. This obviously means that exporting a trust involves the payment of capital gains tax on all gains made prior to export; only subsequent gains will escape tax and then only to the extent that the trust when exported does not become a section 87 trust (which it will usually do,[38] in which case tax will be payable if any capital payments are made to beneficiaries who are domiciled and resident in the United Kingdom). The introduction of this exit charge has made exporting trusts considerably less attractive than hitherto. Nevertheless there is still some merit in hiving off and exporting those assets in a trust which are likely to make substantial capital gains in the future and there is everything to be said for hiving off and exporting those assets in a trust which are actually showing a capital loss.

4. *Inheritance Tax*

Where settled property is situated in the United Kingdom, inheritance tax will be payable in any event according to the ordinary rules discussed earlier, which depend on whether or not there is an interest in possession in that property.[39]

Where settled property is situated outside the United Kingdom, that property is "excluded property" for inheritance tax purposes if, but

---

[36] Taxation of Chargeable Gains Act 1992, s.80(2).
[37] See *ante*, p. 416.
[38] Because of the domiciliary and residential status of the settlor: see p. 566, *ante*.
[39] See *ante*, pp. 420 and 424.

only if, the settlor was domiciled outside the United Kingdom at the time when the settlement was made.[40] If property is excluded property, there will be no liability upon the coming to an end of an interest in possession, or upon any of the occasions on which inheritance tax is normally payable in the case of a discretionary trust, such as the making of a capital distribution out of the settled property, or the decennial anniversaries of the creation of the settlement.

The settlor will be treated as being domiciled in some part of the United Kingdom at the time when the settlement was created if:

(a) he would be treated as so domiciled according to the general law; or

(b) he would be treated as being so domiciled according to the general law within three years prior to the creation of the settlement[41]; or

(c) he was resident in the United Kingdom for at least 17 out of the 20 years ending with that in which the settlement was made.[42]

The last two categories only have full application where the property became settled after December 9, 1974.

Where, at the time when a settlement was made, the settlor was domiciled in some part of the United Kingdom, that settlement will, in principle, be permanently within the purview of inheritance tax. Strictly, inheritance tax will be payable even if the settlor, trustees, and all possible beneficiaries are resident outside the United Kingdom, and all the settled property is situated outside the United Kingdom.

In some circumstances, where a settlement is being exported, the parties are content to rely on the rule that one state will not enforce the tax laws of another. In other words, although inheritance tax may be payable, the parties will so conduct themselves that the tax cannot be recovered.

In other circumstances it may be possible to rely on a specific exemption which applies to Government securities. Most United Kingdom Government securities issued before 18 March, 1977[43] are exempt from all United Kingdom taxation, including inheritance tax,[44] while they are in the beneficial ownership of persons who are neither domiciled,[45] nor ordinarily resident in the United Kingdom. This exemption applies to settled property where a person who is neither domiciled nor ordinarily resident in the United Kingdom has an interest in possession in the securities.[46] If there is no interest in possession in the securities, the exemption only applies if it can be shown that all known persons for whose benefit the settled property or

---

[40] Inheritance Tax Act 1984, s.6(1).

[41] Inheritance Tax Act 1984, s.267(1)(a).

[42] Inheritance Tax Act 1984, s.6(2). Ibid. s.267(1)(b).

[43] Inheritance Tax Act 1984, s.6(2).

[44] But the requirements for the exemption in the inheritance tax legislation must be satisfied: Van Ernst & Cie S.A. v. I.R.C. [1980] 1 All E.R. 677, C.A.

[45] "Domiciled" here has its ordinary, and not extended, meaning.

[46] Inheritance Tax Act 1984, s.48(4).

income from it has been or might be applied are neither domiciled nor ordinarily resident in the United Kingdom.[47] Anti-avoidance provisions prevent exempt securities from being channelled from a trust with resident discretionary beneficiaries to one without any.[48]

It follows that where, for example, a fund is held upon trust for Andrew for life, with remainder to Hamish, inheritance tax will be avoided if, at the death of Andrew, he is neither domiciled nor ordinarily resident in the United Kingdom and the fund is invested in exempt Government securities.

However, generally the liability to inheritance tax does not depend on the residential status of the trust. If the settlement was created by a non-domiciled settlor, and the property is situated abroad, the excluded property rules apply whether the trust is resident or non-resident. If the trust property consists of exempt British Government securities, and the beneficiaries are non-domiciled and non-ordinarily resident, the exemption will also apply whether the trust is resident or non-resident. Exporting a trust will, therefore, neither mitigate nor exacerbate the liability to inheritance tax.

5. *Taxation Summary*

The preceding parts of this chapter have attempted to describe the effect of highly complex legislation. It will have been seen that if a new non-resident trust is created, or if an existing resident trust is exported:

(a) there will be no income tax saving in respect of income received, or receivable by a resident beneficiary;

(b) liability to income tax on accumulated or withheld income may be deferred until the benefit of it is received;

(c) liability to capital gains tax will be eliminated, in the case of a fully foreign trust, or deferred until a capital payment is received in the case of a section 87 trust subject to the payment of interest in respect of the period of deferment, but only after the exit charge has been paid, thus restricting benefit to subsequent capital gains; and

(d) liability to inheritance tax will be the same as if the trust had remained resident.

IV. When Exporting is Proper

Trusts are a peculiar creation of English law, and for several centuries it would not have occurred to trustees or beneficiaries to seek to export that trust. However, since the middle of the last century, when the question first arose and more particularly during the last 40 years, certain principles have been developed by the courts on an ad hoc basis. The present position is as follows:

---

[47] *Ibid.*
[48] *Ibid* s.48(5).

(1) The English court does have power to appoint non-resident trustees of an English settlement[49] and it also has power to approve an arrangement under the Variation of Trusts Act by which non-resident trustees are appointed and the trust fund is exported.[50] The appointment of foreign trustees is not, therefore, *ipso facto* bad.

(2) Where the court would itself be prepared to appoint non-resident trustees and there are adequate powers under the Trustee Act 1925 or the trust instrument, an effective appointment can be made without the intervention of the court. In *Re Whitehead's Will Trusts*,[51] the main beneficiary had emigrated to Jersey in 1959, and was found to be permanently resident there.[52] In 1969 the trustees, who were resident in the United Kingdom, executed a deed under section 36 of the Trustee Act 1925[53] appointing persons resident in Jersey as new trustees and retiring from the trusts. The resident trustees wished to be fully protected, however, and the deed of retirement and appointment was made conditional upon the main beneficiary obtaining from the court a declaration that the resident trustees were effectively discharged. The court made the declaration. The decision shows that in a proper case[54] the appointment of a non-resident trustee without the intervention of the court is fully effective and valid.

(3) If the court does not itself make the appointment but there is a purported retirement of resident trustees and the appointment of non-resident trustees without the intervention of the court, the appointment is not void but is voidable. In *Re Whitehead's Will Trusts*[55] Pennycuick V.C. said[56] " . . . the law has been quite well established for upwards of a century that there is no absolute bar to the appointment of persons resident abroad as trustees of an English trust. I say 'no absolute bar,' in the sense that such an appointment would be prohibited by law and would consequently be invalid. On the other hand, apart from exceptional circumstances, it is not proper to make such an appointment, that is to say, the court would not, apart from exceptional circumstances, make such an appointment, nor would it be right for the donees of the power to make such an appointment out of court. If they did, presumably the court would be likely to interfere at the instance of the beneficiaries. There do, however, exist exceptional circumstances in which such an appointment can properly be made. The most obvious exceptional circumstances are those in which the beneficiaries have settled permanently in some country outside the United Kingdom and what is proposed to be done is to appoint new trustees in that country."

---

[49] *Meinertzhagen* v *Davis* (1844) 1 Coll.N.C. 355; *Re Long's Settlement* (1869) 17 W.R. 218; *Re Seale's Marriage Settlement* [1961] Ch. 574; *Re Whitehead's Will Trusts* [1971] 1 W.L.R. 833.
[50] *Re Seale's Marriage Settlement, supra; Re Windeatt's Will Trusts* [1969] 1 W.L.R. 692; *Re Whitehead's Will Trusts, supra.*
[51] [1971] 1 W.L.R. 833.
[52] [1971] 1 W.L.R. 833 at p. 838.
[53] See *ante*, p. 371.
[54] *i.e.* where the court itself makes the appointment.
[55] [1971] 1 W.L.R. 833.
[56] At p. 837.

(4) It is therefore necessary to know in what circumstances the court will itself appoint non-resident trustees. The fundamental principle is that the court will do so if is in the interest of the beneficiaries.

(5) Subject to the following points, it will usually be in the interest of the beneficiaries for the trust to be administered and for the trustees to be resident in the same territory as that in which the beneficiaries, or a majority of them, reside. Thus, *Re Seale's Marriage Settlement*[57] was concerned with a marriage settlement made in 1931 at a time when the husband and wife were domiciled in England. The husband and wife subsequently emigrated to Canada with their children, and at the date of the hearing in 1961 they had been living in Canada for some years, and were domiciled in Canada. Buckley J. found as a fact that they intended to continue to reside there. It was desired to export the trust to Quebec by two stages: the appointment of a Canadian trust corporation to be a trustee of the marriage settlement and for the discharge of the English trustees; and then for the property subject to the marriage settlement to be transferred to the Canadian corporation as trustee of a new Quebec settlement. The new settlement followed as closely as possible the terms of the English settlement, but without certain protective life interests which were not recognised by the law of Quebec. Buckley J. was satisfied that it was to the advantage of all beneficiaries for the settlement to be exported, and he approved the arrangements. This was followed by *Re Windeatt's Will Trusts*.[58] The testator who was domiciled in England, created a will trust for the benefit of, *inter alios*, his daughter and her children. The daughter and her children had lived in Jersey for 19 years prior to the application, and were held to be permanently resident there. Pennycuick J. approved an arrangement for two Jersey residents to be appointed, and for the trust assets to be transferred to them.

(6) In certain circumstances it will be in the interests of the beneficiaries for non-resident trustees to be appointed even if they are resident in a territory different from that where the trustees are resident. For example, it may be in the interests of the beneficiaries for the trust to be exported from the United Kingdom, so that it may cease to be liable to United Kingdom taxation. However, if the beneficiaries are resident in a territory which does not recognise, or is not fully acquainted with, trusts, it may be appropriate for the trust to be exported to a territory which does. In *Re Chamberlain*[59] where some of the beneficiaries were resident in France and the others in Indonesia the court approved an arrangement to export an English trust by the appointment of trustees resident in Guernsey.

(7) There have been no reported decisions in which the court has approved the export of an English trust where the beneficiaries are resident in England, and the purpose is to mitigate the liability to tax. However, in view of the attitude which the court has taken in the case

---

[57] [1961] Ch. 574.
[58] [1969] 1 W.L.R. 692; [1969] 2 All E.R. 324.
[59] [1976] N.L.J. 1934.

of applications to mitigate tax in other circumstances[60] there seems to be no insuperable objection to the export of a trust in these circumstances.

(8) All the circumstances must, however, be taken into account. If the proposed exploration is not clearly in the interest of the beneficiaries, a predominant tax avoidance motive may lead the court to refuse to make the appointment. In *Re Weston's Settlements*[61] two settlements were made in 1964 for the benefit of the two sons of the settlor. A total of 500,000 shares in The Stanley Weston Group were transferred to the trustees of those settlements. However, the settlor obviously could not have anticipated that by the Finance Act of the very next year a capital gains tax would be introduced. The shares rose in value and, by the time of the hearing at first instance in 1968, there was a prospective liability to capital gains tax of £163,000. The settlor lived in England until 1967, and in the first half of that year he made three visits of a few days each to Jersey. He then purchased a house, in which he lived from August 1967. The application to the court was commenced in November 1967. This sought the appointment of two professional men in Jersey of impeccable standing as trustees of the two English settlements and the approval of an arrangement under which the property subject to the English settlements could be transferred to Jersey settlements in identical terms. It was hoped that in doing this the property subject to the settlements would be free of capital gains tax and would also be free of estate duty under section 28 of the Finance Act 1949.[62] Both Stamp J., at first instance, and the Court of Appeal refused to sanction the arrangement. The courts were influenced by two main facts:

(a) there was clearly some doubt whether the settlor and his children, the main beneficiaries, would live in Jersey permanently; particularly as they had only been there for a few months prior to the date of the hearing. That was insufficient to show a settled intention and the court was worried at the possibility that shortly after the arrangement was approved, and the shares sold free of tax, the beneficiaries would return to England[63]; and

(b) as was mentioned in the previous chapter[64] this was, according to Stamp J. "a cheap exercise in tax avoidance" which ought not to be sanctioned.[65] In the Court of Appeal Harman L.J. also described it as "an essay in tax avoidance naked and unashamed."[66] This seems to have disturbed the court despite the fact that numerous applications under the Variation of Trusts

---

[60] See *e.g. Pilkington* v. *I.R.C.* [1964] A.C. 612, *ante*, p. 512; and decisions on the variation of trusts at p. 546 *et seq., ante*.

[61] [1969] 1 Ch. 223, C.A.; [1968] 3 All E.R. 338; and see also *ante*, p. 546.

[62] Now replaced by inheritance tax.

[63] [1969] 1 Ch. at pp. 245, 246 (Lord Denning M.R.).

[64] *Ante*, p. 546.

[65] [1968] 2 W.L.R. 1154 at p. 1162.

[66] *Supra* at p. 246.

Act have had tax minimisation as one of their main factors.[67] It is impossible to avoid wondering whether the court was influenced by the feeling that the settlor, who was the son of a Russian immigré, and who had built up his fortune in England during the 1939–45 war, should not be permitted to escape his normal tax liability.

With the advantage of hindsight, it seems that the trustees were unfortunately advised, and that the arrangement would have been approved if it had been made a few years later, when it could have been shown that the beneficiaries were genuinely settled there. Although in *Re Windeatt's Will Trusts*[68] Pennycuick J. expressed himself[69] to be "in the most complete agreement" with the decision in *Re Weston's Settlement*,[70] it is highly likely that that decision will be confined to its own facts.

(9) The court will not approve the appointment of non-resident trustees if they are resident in a territory which may be reluctant to enforce the trust. If both the trustees are resident abroad and the assets are situated abroad, the English court will be incapable of protecting the beneficiaries and it will, therefore, wish to be satisfied that, in the case of any maladministration, the beneficiaries will be given protection by the local law. A third factor which influenced the Court of Appeal in *Re Weston's Settlement*[71] was that there was no equivalent of the Trustee Act 1925 in Jersey,[72] and that the Jersey court had not had to enforce any *inter vivos* settlement. While the general principle is clear, the particular objection in *Re Weston's Settlement* to Jersey appears to have been misconceived. In both *Re Windeatt's Will Trusts*[73] and *Re Whitehead's Will Trusts*[74] the court approved the export of trusts to Jersey.

V. METHODS OF EXPORTING

A trust can be exported simply by the resident trustees[75] appointing non-resident new trustees, and then retiring. At the time, the assets will be transferred to the new trustees, or will automatically vest in them.[76] This method is only likely to be satisfactory, however, if the new trustees are resident in a territory which either has a trust law based closely on English law, or which will give effect to English trust law.

In other circumstances, it may be necessary to alter the form of the settlement to take account of differences between English trust law and the law of the country to which the settlement is to be exported. This alteration can sometimes be effected by using a power in the trust

---

[67] See *ante*, p. 546.
[68] [1969] 1 W.L.R. 692; [1969] 2 All E.R. 324.
[69] [1969] 1 W.L.R. at p. 696; [1969] 2 All E.R. at p. 327.
[70] *Supra.*
[71] [1969] 1 Ch. 223, C.A., *supra.*
[72] Comprehensive trust legislation has now been enacted in Jersey.
[73] [1969] 1 W.L.R. 692, *ante*, p. 572.
[74] [1971] 1 W.L.R. 833, *ante*, p. 571.
[75] Or such other person who has the power of appointing new trustees (see *ante*, p. 367).
[76] Under T.A. 1925, s.40; *ante*, p. 381.

instrument to revoke existing trusts, and to declare new ones. However, the usual form of this power could only be used to declare new "trusts" in the sense in which that term is understood by English law. Wider powers which may become more common include a provision to declare new beneficial interests as nearly as possible equating to trusts under English law. If there is no power in the trust instrument, an application to the court will be necessary under the Variation of Trusts Act 1958.[77]

VI. Exporting Part of the Trust

There may be circumstances in which it is designed to appoint non-resident trustees of part but not the whole of the trust fund. Assuming that the circumstances are those in which the court would appoint non-resident trustees, there is no fundamental objection to this. In particular, section 37(1)(b) of the Trustee Act 1925 provides that a separate set of trustees may be appointed for any part of the trust property held on trusts distinct from those relating to any other part of the trust property. Under this provision, separate trustees can be appointed even although there is no alteration to the trustees of the remainder of the trust fund.

But as the trustees in *Roome* v. *Edwards*[78] found out, there are major risks in so doing. In that case, the House of Lords was concerned with a marriage settlement created in 1944. In 1955, a power of appointment was exercised in respect of a comparatively small part of the trust fund, whereby the part was thenceforth to be held upon trusts, to accumulate the income until a daughter of the marriage reached the age of 25, and then to transfer the capital of that part to her. From 1955, the appointed fund was administered as if it were a trust separate from the main fund. One of the assets of the main trust appreciated very substantially in value, and steps were taken with a view to the saving of capital gains tax. The main fund, but not the 1955 fund, was exported, by the retirement of the United Kingdom trustees, and the appointment of trustees resident in the Cayman Islands. Shortly thereafter, the gain was realised, and the Crown claimed the tax from the trustees of the 1955 appointed fund, who were still resident. The House of Lords held that the 1955 fund and the main fund together comprised one settlement for capital gains tax purposes; and that the claim of the Crown succeeded by virtue of the fact that, where part of the property comprised in a settlement is vested in one set of trustees, and part in another, they shall be treated as together constituting and acting on behalf of a single body of trustees. The resident trustees (of the 1955 fund) were therefore liable to pay the tax on the gain realised by the non-resident trustees (of the main fund). Lord Roskill gave a clear warning[79]: "Persons, whether professional men or not, who accept appointment as trustees of settlements such as these are clearly at risk under the [1979] Act and have only themselves to blame if they accept the obligations of trustees in these

---

[77] See *ante*, p. 546.
[78] [1981] 1 All E.R. 736, H.L.
[79] [1981] 1 All E.R. 736 at p. 744.

circumstances without ensuring that they are sufficiently and effectively protected whether by their beneficiaries or otherwise for fiscal or
other liabilities which may fall on them personally as a result of the
obligations which they had felt able to assume." Not only are there particular risks in the export of part but not the whole of a trust, but the
decision in *Roome* v. *Edwards* is taken to reinforce the view that, where
resident trustees retire in favour of non-resident trustees without the
intervention of the court, they should always seek adequate
indemnities.

CHAPTER 23

BREACH OF TRUST

A BREACH of trust occurs if a trustee does any act which he ought not to do, or fails to do any act which he ought to do with regard to the administration of the trust, or with regard to the beneficial interests arising under the trust. It would be undesirable to attempt an exhaustive list of circumstances in which a breach of trust can be committed, but the following are examples:

(a) investment of trust moneys in unauthorised investments;
(b) taking a profit from the trust not authorised by the trust instrument or by the court;
(c) manipulating the investments to benefit one beneficiary at the expense of another;
(d) negligently allowing trust property to remain under the control of one trustee only;
(e) paying trust property to the wrong person;
(f) purchasing trust property without authority;
(g) failing to exercise a proper discretion with regard to trust decisions.

Where there is an allegation of breach of trust, it is desirable to pose the following questions:

1. Has a breach of trust been committed?
2. If so, is the proposed defendant liable?
3. If so, what is the prima facie measure of liability?
4. Is there any right to contribution or indemnity?
5. Is the proposed plaintiff in time to sue?
6. May the proposed defendant be relieved from liability by the court or otherwise?

If these questions are applied to the problem involving breach of trust, they should be adequate to ensure that no relevant point is overlooked when looking at the position from the point of view of the trustee. If the matter is being looked at from the point of view of the beneficiary, it is also necessary to ask whether the beneficiary can take any other action if sufficient redress cannot be obtained from the trustees. This aspect of the problem is the subject of the last part of this chapter.

I. Own Acts of the Trustee

There will usually be little difficulty in ascertaining whether a breach of trust has been committed by a trustee during his trusteeship. Complications sometimes arise, however, in respect of acts done at the beginning and end of a trusteeship.

On appointment, a trustee should take certain steps. He should inspect the trust instrument to ascertain the terms of the trust, and to see whether any notices are indorsed. He should ensure that all the trust property is transferred into his name jointly with the other trustees, for he may be liable if he allows the property to remain in the hands of another.[1] He may wish to go through the trust papers to familiarise himself with the circumstances of the trust. If in doing so, or in any other way, he learns that a breach of trust has been committed, he must obtain satisfaction from the person responsible. Should the new trustee not do so, he will himself be liable for breach of trust for his own omission. The only exception to this principle is if he is reasonably satisfied that it would be useless to institute proceedings because, for example, the former trustee cannot be found, or is destitute.[2]

On the other hand, unless he has knowledge that a breach of trust has been committed, or there are suspicious circumstances, a new trustee may assume that there has been no breach of trust.[3]

When a trustee retires from a trust, in principle he remains liable for breaches of trust committed during his trusteeship, and his estate will be liable if he is dead. He is only relieved from liability if and to such extent as he may have been released by the continuing trustees, or by the beneficiaries being in possession of the relevant facts at the time.

It may sometimes happen that a breach of trust may occur shortly after one trustee retires. The retiring trustee will be liable if he contemplated that a breach of trust would occur, and he retired with the intention of facilitating it, or believing that it would occur, he retired to avoid being involved in it. He is liable because his motive in retiring was to enable the breach of trust to occur. If he merely realised that his retirement would facilitate the breach of trust, he will not *ipso facto* be liable,[4] but he will be liable if in addition to realising that his retirement would facilitate the breach, he foresaw, or ought reasonably to have foreseen, that such breach would in fact take place. In this case he would be failing in his duty to prevent a breach of trust occurring. It follows that, if the retiring trustee did not foresee what would happen, but the remaining trustees took advantage of his absence to perpetrate the breach, the retiring trustee has not himself failed in any of his duties and he will not be liable.[5]

Apart from this, a trustee is not liable for breaches of trust which occur after his retirement.

---

[1] He will only be liable if loss is caused as a result of the property being left in the hands of others: *Re Miller's Deed Trusts*, L.S.G. May 3, 1978.

[2] *Re Forest of Dean Coal Co.* [1878] 10 Ch.D. 450.

[3] *Re Stratham, ex p. Geaves* [1856] 8 De G.M. & G. 291.

[4] *Head* v. *Gould* [1898] 2 Ch. 250.

[5] *Head* v. *Gould, supra.*

II. ACTS OF CO-TRUSTEES

A trustee can never be liable for the acts of his co-trustee as such, but in certain circumstances he will be liable where a breach of trust is committed by his co-trustee if he himself has been in some way at fault. The position is governed by section 30 of the Trustee Act 1925, which was discussed earlier,[6] as interpreted by *Re Vickery*[7] which applied *Re City Equitable Fire Insurance Company*.[8]

The general intention of section 30 is clear. It is that a person is responsible for his own acts, neglects and defaults, and not for loss caused through the acts, neglects or defaults of any other person, including co-trustees and agents, unless the loss occurs "through his own wilful default."

It will be recalled that the difficulty arises from the meaning of the words "wilful default."

It was explained previously[9] that the interpretation of "wilful default" given in *Re Vickery* and *Re City Equitable Fire Insurance Co.* has been criticised by several writers because it does not represent the pre-1926 position. Section 30 of the Trustee Act 1925 replaced the now repealed section 31 of the Law of Property Amendment Act 1859, which itself merely incorporated the indemnity clause which it was usual practice to insert in trust instruments.[10] Cases decided on that indemnity clause and on the 1859 Act show clearly that the form of words purporting to exclude liability for loss unless it occurred through the wilful default of the trustee did not exclude liability even for purely passive and innocent breaches of trust.[11] It was thus formerly the law that a trustee would be liable for a breach of trust arising through the act or default of his co-trustee if he merely left a matter in the hands of his co-trustee without inquiry. The majority of pre-1926 cases fall into the following categories:

(a) where the trustee leaves a matter in the hands of his co-trustee without inquiry[12];

(b) where he stands by while a breach of trust of which he is aware is being committed[13];

---

[6] *Ante*, p. 403.

[7] [1931] 1 Ch. 572.

[8] [1925] Ch. 407.

[9] *Ante*, p. 403.

[10] See *Re Brier* (1884) 26 Ch.D. 238 at p. 243 (Lord Selborne).

[11] *Chambers* v. *Minchin* (1802) 7 Ves. 186; *Shipbrook* v. *Hinchinbrook* (1810) 16 Ves. 477; *Hanbury* v. *Kirkland* (1829) 3 Sim. 265; *Broadhurst* v. *Balguy* (1841) 1 Y. & C.C.C. 16; *Thompson* v. *Finch* (1865) 8 De G.M. & G. 560; *Mendes* v. *Guedalla* (1862) 8 Jur. 878; *Hale* v. *Adams* (1873) 21 W.R. 400; *Wynee* v. *Tempest* (1897) 13 T.L.R. 360; *Re Second East Dulwich Building Society* (1899) 68 L.J.Ch. 196.

[12] See the authorities quoted in note 11.

[13] In *Styles* v. *Guy* (1849) 1 Mac. & G. 422 at 433, Lord Cottenham stated that it is the duty of executors and trustees "to watch over, and if necessary, to correct, the conduct of each other." See also *Booth* v. *Booth* (1838) 1 Beav. 125; *Gough* v. *Smith* [1872] W.N. 18.

   (c) where he allows trust funds to remain in the sole control of his co-trustee[14];

   (d) where, on becoming aware of a breach of trust committed or contemplated by his co-trustee, he takes no steps to obtain redress.[15]

These rules sometimes operated inequitably in the case of passive breaches of trust. Thus, in *Underwood* v. *Stevens*[16] a trustee in good faith allowed trust funds to remain in the hands of his co-trustee, and when he made inquiries of his co-trustee as to certain transactions with those funds, the co-trustee gave false information. The trustee was held liable, however, notwithstanding that the trust instrument provided that trustees should not be liable for loss unless it occurred through their wilful default. The effect of the indemnity clause was, therefore, markedly different from the prima facie meaning of the words used. The effect of the decision in *Re Vickery*[17] has, in effect, been to modify the third of the rules stated above, in interpreting "wilful default" as a consciousness of negligence or a recklessness in the performance of a duty.

Section 30(1) of the Trustee Act 1925 specifically exempts trustees from liability for signing receipts for the sake of conformity, unless they have actually received the trust money or securities. As all trustees have, as a general principle, to sign receipts, it will be appreciated that these documents frequently circulate among trustees prior to a transaction so that all necessary signatures are obtained by the time that the transaction is to be completed. A trustee is not liable if any breach of trust occurs merely as a result of his having signed such a receipt, though of course if, for example, having signed it he allows his co-trustee to obtain money with the document, and to retain that money for an unreasonable time, he will thereby have acted recklessly and will accordingly make himself liable.

The circumstances in which a trustee is liable for the acts of his agents have been considered in Chapter 13.

III. MEASURE OF LIABILITY

If the trustee has committed a breach of trust, what is the extent of his liability? The basic principles are:

   (a) a remedy for breach of trust is most commonly awarded in order to compensate the trust fund for a loss sustained; "the obligation of a defaulting trustee [to compensate the trust fund for such a

---

[14] *English* v. *Willats* (1831) 1 L.J.Ch. 84; *Ex p. Booth* (1831) Mont. 248; *Child* v. *Giblett* (1834) 3 L.J.Ch. 124; *Hewitt* v. *Foster* (1843) 6 Beav. 259; *Wiglesworth* v. *Wiglesworth* (1852) 16 Beav. 269; *Byass* v. *Gates* (1854) 2 W.R. 487; *Trutch* v. *Lamprell* (1855) 20 Beav. 116; *Cowell* v. *Gatcombe* (1859) 27 Beav. 568; *William* v. *Higgins* (1868) 17 L.T. 525; *Rodbard* v. *Cooke* (1877) 25 W.R. 555; *Lewis* v. *Nobbs* (1878) 8 Ch.D. 591.

[15] *Boadman* v. *Mosman* (1779) 1 Bro.C.C. 68; *Wilkins* v. *Hogg* (1861) 8 Jur. (N.S.) 25 at 26 (Lord Westbury).

[16] (1816) 1 Mer. 712.

[17] [1931] 1 Ch. 572. *cf.*, however, *Re Lucking's Will Trusts* [1968] 1 W.L.R. 866.

loss] is essentially one of effecting restitution to the estate. The obligation is of a personal character and its extent is not to be limited by common law principles governing the remoteness of damage"[17A]; nor is it relevant that the loss would have been suffered even if the breach of trust had not occurred.[17B]

(b) a remedy for breach of trust is also awarded in order to obtain for the trust fund any profit made by the trustee without authority; the nature of the obligation of a trustee to account for advantages of this kind was considered in Chapter 8.

(c) such remedies are not awarded in order to punish the trustee but, if he has been fraudulent or has otherwise behaved particularly badly, the court will reflect its displeasure by increasing the amount of interest payable by the trustee above that which he would otherwise have been ordered to pay.

The following examples will illustrate these principles. All are concerned with the prima facie liability of the trustee and do not take into account the possibility of some protection or relief being given to the trustee as discussed below.

(1) Payment to wrong person

Where the trustees pay trust money to the wrong person, their liability is to make good to the trust fund that amount, so that the correct beneficiary can be paid out the capital sum wrongly paid, together with interest.[18] An unusual recent illustration of the operation of this principle is provided by *Target Holdings* v. *Redferns*.[18A] The plaintiff had agreed to lend £1,525,000 on the security of two properties which were apparently being purchased for £2,000,000 but which were in fact being acquired for £775,000. The defendant solicitors, who were acting in the normal way both for the purchasers and for the plaintiff mortgagee, were holding the mortgage advance on trust for the plaintiff with authority to release it to the purchasers only upon receipt of the duly executed conveyances and mortgages of the properties. However, they released the funds several days before the execution of these documents. The subsequent loss made by the plaintiff as a result of the insufficiency of the mortgage securities would have been incurred even if the defendants had complied with their instructions. Nevertheless, the Court of Appeal held that the obligation of a trustee who had committed a breach of trust was to put the trust fund in the same position as it would have been if no breach had taken place and that, where the breach consisted in the wrongful payment of trust moneys to a stranger so that there was an immediate loss, it was not necessary for there to be any inquiry as to whether the loss would have occurred if there had been no breach. This decision is wholly consistent with all the other authorities. While it is hard to have any sympathy for a firm of solicitors who acted with such blatant disregard for their instructions, it

---

[17A] *Re Dawson* [1966] 2 N.S.W.R. 211 at p. 214.
[17B] *Target Holdings* v. *Redferns* [1994] 2 All E.R. 337.
[18] See, *post*, p. 586, as to the rate of interest.
[18A] [1994] 2 All E.R. 337.

will nevertheless be interesting to see whether the House of Lords carries out any general review of the authorities in the event that the appeal for which leave has been given actually proceeds.

(2) Improper sale of authorised investments

If trustees improperly sell an authorised investment, and reinvest the proceeds in unauthorised investments, which are then sold at a loss, the beneficiaries have a choice.They can compel the trustees either to make good the difference between the sale price of the authorised investment and the proceeds of sale of the unauthorised investment, or to repurchase for the trust the authorised security, taking credit for the proceeds of sale of the unauthorised security. Suppose, therefore, that the trustees hold 400 I.C.I. shares (authorised by the Trustee Investments Act 1961) which they sell for £1,000. That £1,000 is reinvested in the purchase of shares in the Uranium Exploration Co., which are not authorised. A year later these shares are sold for £200. The beneficiaries can compel the trustees to pay to the trust fund £1,000, the proceeds of the I.C.I shares, less the £200 which they have paid in from the sale of the uranium shares. Alternatively, they can compel the trustees to purchase for the trust 400 I.C.I. shares, however much they might cost. If I.C.I. shares have doubled in price, the trustees will have to pay £2,000 for them, less the £200 received from the sale of the authorised investments.

This principle was taken a stage further in *Re Massingberd*.[19] In that case the trustees sold Consols and reinvested in an unauthorised security. The unauthorised security was in due course sold without loss, but by this time the price of Consols had risen. The court held that the trustees should place the beneficiaries in the same position as they would have been had no sale taken place, with the result that they had themselves to pay the increase in the price of the Consols.

In assertaining their liability, trustees are not entitled to take into account any loss which would have been sustained if they had strictly performed the trust.[20] Suppose, therefore, trustees are directed to invest in one particular investment. They improperly sell that investment for £1,000 and invest that sum in another investment. The latter declines in value and is sold for £800, but the investment which the trustees were directed to make has also declined and its market price is £700. The trustees are liable to make good, at the option of the beneficiaries, the difference between £800 and £1,000, and they are not excused from liability by virtue of the fact that if the investment which they had been directed to make had been retained, the holding would have been worth only £700.

(3) Unauthorised investments

It is clear that trustees who invest in unauthorised investments may be called upon to sell those investments, and make good the loss.[21] On the

---

[19] (1890) 63 L.T. 296.
[20] *Shepherd* v. *Mouls* (1845) 4 Hare 500 at p. 504; *Watts* v. *Girdlestone* (1843) 6 Beav. 188; *Byrchall* v. *Bradford* (1822) 6 Madd. 235.
[21] *Re Salmon* (1889) 42 Ch.D. 351.

other hand, if a profit is made, the profit accrues to the trust; similarly, with interest. If the trustees make an improper investment in a security which yields a very high income, the income beneficiary is entitled to interest at the ordinary rate, and the balance is then added to capital.[22] Once added to capital, it cannot then be set off against future deficiencies, either of capital on realisation of the investment, or of income.

If all the beneficiaries are ascertained and *sui juris* they may decide to accept an improper investment. In *Thornton* v. *Stokill*[23] it was held that if the beneficiaries did so, they could not in addition claim the difference between the value of the improper investment and the value which authorised investments would have if retained. But in the case of *Re Lake*[24] it was held that they could do so.

(4) Failure to invest properly

Section 11(1) of the Trustee Act 1925 gives trustees the power to pay trust money into a bank while an investment is being sought. It seems, however, that this does not affect cases decided before the Act to the effect that moneys must not be left uninvested for an unreasonable time.[25] On the basis that the old rules still apply:

(a) if the trustees ought to have invested in a *range* of investments, as will usually be the case, their liability is limited to making good the difference between any interest actually received and the rate of interest fixed by the court.[26] The trustees are not liable for any capital loss, because it is impossible to ascertain it.[27]

(b) if the trustees ought to have invested in one specified security only, but did not do so, in the event of the price rising they can be compelled to purchase such an amount of that specified security as they could have purchased with the trust fund at the proper time.

Trustees may erroneously regard their investment powers as more limited than they actually are and, as a result invest in a more restricted range of investments than they were actually obliged to. This occurred in *Nestlé* v. *National Westminster Bank*.[28] The Court of Appeal held that a beneficiary who could prove that loss had been suffered thereby could obtain compensation. However, save in extreme cases (the court used as an example the investment of the entire trust fund in fixed interest securities when the trustees had power to invest in equities), such a loss will be extremely difficult to prove and could not be established in that case.

---

[22] *Re Emmet's Estate* (1881) 17 Ch.D. 142. As to the "ordinary" rate of interest, see *post*, p. 587.

[23] (1855) 1 Jur. 151.

[24] [1903] 1 K.B. 439.

[25] *Cann* v. *Cann* (1884) 33 W.R. 40.

[26] As to which, see *post*, p. 587.

[27] *Per* Wigram V.C., *Shepherd* v. *Mouls* (1845) 4 Hare 500 at p. 504.

[28] [1993] 1 W.L.R. 1260.

(5) Use for personal purposes

If the trustees use the trust money for their personal purposes, they are liable to pay back the amount used, or the value[29] of property improperly sold to provide the funds which the trustees use.

Special rules apply as to interest.[30] However, instead of receiving interest, the beneficiaries can require the trustees to pay over the actual profit received.[31] If the trustee has mixed the trust money with his own money, the beneficiaries may in some circumstances be able to claim a proportionate share of the profits,[32] but this appears only to be the case if the profits were actually enhanced by the use of the trust money.[33]

(6) Profit to trust fund

It follows from the principle that the measure of liability is to compensate the trust fund for loss that, if there is a loss neither of income nor of capital, although the trustees may have committed a breach of trust, they will not be held liable. In *Vyse* v. *Foster*,[34] for example, trustees held land and money upon a common trust. Without authority they erected a bungalow on the land for £1,600 and this benefited the trust fund to a greater degree than £1,600. An attempt was made to say that the trustees were liable to pay £1,600 because this expenditure was unauthorised, but at the same time to say that the beneficiaries were entitled to the benefit of the bungalow which was trust property. The Court of Appeal and House of Lords rejected this argument, and it is only surprising that it was accepted at first instance.

(7) Date at which loss to be assessed

Where a trustee improperly deals with an asset which thereby ceases to be under his control, it is necessary to determine the date at which the loss to the trust fund is to be measured. Previously, when the values of many assets were more stable than at the present time, the loss was ascertained at the date when proceedings were commenced. Thus in *Re Massingberd*,[35] where trustees improperly sold Consols, the Court of Appeal ordered them to pay the cost of replacing the Consols as at the date of the writ. Much more recently, in *Re Bell's Indenture*,[36] Vinelott J. said[37] that this was incorrect, and that the general principle was that the loss should be ascertained at the date of judgment. However, in *Jaffray* v. *Marshall*,[38] it was held that this question had not actually had to be

---

[29] Ascertained as at the date of judgment: *infra*.
[30] *Post*, p. 586.
[31] *Newman* v. *Bennett* (1784) 1 Bro.C.C. 359; *Ex p. Watson* (1814) 2 V. & B. 414; *Walker* v. *Woodward* (1826) 1 Russ. 107 at p. 111; *Att-Gen.* v. *Solly* (1829) 2 Sim 518; *Wedderburn* v. *Wedderburn* (1838) 4 My. & Cr. 41 at p. 46; *Jones* v. *Foxall* (1852) 15 Beav. 388; *Williams* v. *Powell* (1852) 15 Beav. 388; *Macdonald* v. *Richardson* (1858) 1 Giff. 81; *Townend* v. *Townend* (1859) 1 Giff. 201; *Re Davis, Davis* v. *Davis* (1902) 2 Ch. 314.
[32] *Docker* v. *Somes* (1834) 2 My. & K. 655; *Edinburgh Town Council* v. *Lord Advocate* (1879) 4 App.Cas. 823.
[33] *Re Tilley's Will Trusts* [1967] Ch. 1179 (see *post*, p. 623).
[34] (1872) L.R. 8 Ch. 309; affirmed (1874) L.R. 7 H.L. 318.
[35] (1890) 63 L.T. 296, C.A.
[36] (1980) 1 W.L.R. 1217.
[37] At p. 1233.
[38] [1993] 1 W.L.R. 1285.

decided in either of these cases which were therefore of no assistance. This was a case where trust property had, in breach of trust, been mortgaged to secure the debts of the tenant for life and was subsequently lost as the result of a sale by the mortgagee. It was held that, since there had been a continuing breach of trust, the trustees were liable to compensate the trust at the highest intermediate value of the property between the date of breach and the date of judgment. This view seems consistent with the general nature of the liability of trustees for breach of trust; it remains to be seen whether it is generally adopted.

However, whatever the general rule is, if the trustees improperly dispose of an asset but, had that disposal not taken place, they would at a later date properly have disposed of it, the loss is to be ascertained at that later date, and not at any subsequent date. In *Re Bell's Indenture*[39] the court was concerned with a marriage settlement made in 1907 and a voluntary settlement made in 1930. One person, Alexander, was a trustee of both settlements, and was a beneficiary under both settlements. In 1947, the trustees of the marriage settlement improperly sold a farm for £8,200, the purchasers being the trustees of the voluntary settlement. In 1949 the trustees of the voluntary settlement properly sold the farm to a third party for £12,400. If the trustees of the marriage settlement had not sold the farm in 1947, they would have done so when the trustees of the voluntary settlement did so in 1949. Vinelott J. held that the liability of the trustees of the marriage settlement was to be limited to the value of the farm in 1949. He also held that no account should be taken of the fact that, if the trustees of the marriage settlement had sold in 1949, they would probably have reinvested the proceeds of sale in another farm, because it was impossible to determine how any such other farm would have appreciated or depreciated. Similarly, in *Jaffray* v. *Marshall*,[40] the probability that the trust property would have fallen in value in line with a general reduction in land values was not taken into account so as to reduce the compensation payable; the trustees had had the right to sell the property at any time and it was the breach of trust which had deprived them of the opportunity of so doing.

Where in other circumstances a defaulting trustee is liable to make a payment by way of restitution, that liability continues until restitution is actually made and this is so even if the settlement has in the meantime come to an end. In *Bartlett* v. *Barclays Bank Trust Co Ltd. (No. 1)*[41] trustees were held liable for permitting a company in which they had a controlling interest to engage in hazardous property speculation and for the loss which ensued from the reduction in the value of the shares in the company. Three of the beneficiaries became absolutely entitled to their shares in 1974, but the trust company continued to hold the shares as nominees of the beneficiaries until September 1978 when the company disposed of all its speculative investments and all the shares were sold. In *Bartlett* v. *Barclays Bank Trust Co Ltd. (No. 2)*[42] it was

---

[39] [1980] 1 W.L.R. 1217.
[40] [1993] 1 W.L.R. 1285.
[41] [1980] 2 W.L.R. 430.
[42] [1980] 2 W.L.R. 448.

held that the loss suffered by the beneficiaries was to be assessed as at September 1978.

(8) No allowance for tax

Where a trustee takes trust moneys and applies them for his own purposes, he is liable to restore the moneys which he has taken, and he is not allowed to benefit from any reduction in the liability to tax which ensues from the misapplication.[43] A further point which arose in *Re Bell's Indenture*[44] was that, if the trustees of the marriage settlement had not improperly sold the farm in 1947 but had retained it until 1949, sold it then, and reinvested the proceeds of sale, the value of the trust fund would have been much larger than it in fact was. This would have given rise to greater liabilities to estate duty[45] on the deaths of successive beneficiaries. It was held, however, that the defaulting trustee was not entitled to reduce the amount which he had to pay to make good the breach of trust by the amount of that saving in duty. This was followed in *Bartlett* v. *Barclays Bank Trust Co Ltd. (No. 2)*.[46] If the trustee in that case had not permitted the company to engage in loss-making speculative property investments, the company would have made larger dividend payments. This would have increased the income, and so the income tax liability of the beneficiaries. Likewise, if the company had not sustained losses, the shares could have been sold for a higher price, which would probably have increased the liability to capital gains tax. Brightman, L.J held, however, that the trustees were liable to make good the gross loss, and could not take into account the tax savings which has occurred, even though this produced "a somewhat unjust bias"[47] against the trustees.

(9) Interest

Where a trustee has misapplied trust funds, he is liable not only to replace those funds, but also to pay interest. Likewise, a trustee is liable to pay interest where, by neglecting to make an investment, income is lost.[48]

There are two questions:

(a) at what rate is the interest to be calculated? and
(b) is the interest to be simple or compounded, and, if compounded, at what frequency?[49]

The approach of the courts, particularly with regard to the rate of

---

[43] Thus, the rule in *British Transport Commission* v. *Gourley* [1956] A.C. 185, H.L. does not apply.
[44] [1980] 1 W.L.R. 1217; *ante*, p. 584.
[45] The forerunner of inheritance tax.
[46] [1980] 2 W.L.R. 448.
[47] At p. 451.
[48] *Stafford* v. *Fiddon* (1857) 23 Beav. 386.
[49] The differences are striking. On £10,000, 10 per cent. simple interest for 10 years will amount to £10,000; 10 per cent. interest compounded yearly will amount to £15,937; and 10 per cent. interest compounded half-yearly will amount to £16,533.

interest, has changed in recent years, but the present position appears to be as follows:

(i) Although in the nineteenth century the ordinary rate was 4 per cent.[50] this is totally out of line with modern rates, and the general rule is now to be, broadly, a current commercial rate.

(ii) A current commercial rate has been taken as 1 per cent. above the minimum lending rate,[51] but another recent trend[52] has been to take the rate allowed from time to time on the court's short term investment account.[53] This rate, which is generally in line with that offered by the National Savings Bank, is varied from time to time by statutory instrument. The changes are usually made towards the beginning of a calendar year, and because the changes are made much less frequently than those of the lending rate, the calculation is more straightforward.

(iii) If a trustee uses trust money for his own purposes, he will be ordered to pay a higher rate if it is a reasonable conclusion that he would have realised a higher rate.[54] This is so without proof that the trustee did in fact derive a higher rate.

(iv) In the absence of special circumstances, the general obligation of the trustee is to pay simple interest,[55] but the court has a discretion to order interest to be compounded.

(v) The trustee will be ordered to pay interest compounded annually if there is an obligation to accumulate.[56] If, however, the trustee should have invested the fund in a specified investment, and there was an obligation to accumulate, the interest must be compounded at the intervals at which interest or dividends would have been received on that investment. So if the trustees would have received interest on the investment half-yearly, the compounding is half-yearly.[57]

(vi) The trustee will also be ordered to pay interest compounded annually if he has used trust money in his own business[58] or for commercial purposes, but probably not if he has used it in his professional practice.[59]

(vii) Although the purpose of ordering a trustee to pay compound

---

[50] *A.G.* v. *Alford* (1855) 4 De G.M. & G. 843; *Fletcher* v. *Green* (1864) 33 Beav. 426.

[51] *Wallersteiner* v. *Moir (No. 2)* [1975] Q.B. 373; *Belmont Finance Corporation* v. *Williams Furniture Ltd (No. 2)* [1980] 1 All E.R. 393. *Guardian Ocean Cargoes* v. *Banco do Brasil (No. 3)* [1992] 2 Lloyd's Rep. 193.

[52] *Bartlett* v. *Barclays Bank Trust Co Ltd (No. 2)* [1980] 2 W.L.R. 448, *Jaffray* v. *Marshall* [1993] 1 W.L.R. 1285.

[53] Established under s.6(1) of the Administration of Justice Act 1965.

[54] *A.G.* v. *Alford* (1855) De G.M. & G. 852.

[55] *Stafford* v. *Fiddon* (1857) 23 Beav. 386; *Burdick* v. *Garrick* (1870) 5 Ch. App. 233; *Vyse* v. *Foster* (1874) L.R. 7 H.L. 318; *Belmont Finance Corporation* v. *Williams Furniture Ltd. (No. 2)* [1970] 1 All E.R. 393.

[56] *Raphael* v. *Boehm* (1805) 11 Ves. 92; *Re Barclay* [1899] 1 Ch. 674.

[57] *Re Emmet's Estate* (1881) 17 Ch.D. 142; *Gilroy* v. *Stephens* (1882) 30 W.R. 745.

[58] *Wallersteiner* v. *Moir (No. 2)* [1975] Q.B. 373, *Guardian Ocean Cargoes* v. *Banco do Brasil (No. 3)* [1992] 2 Lloyd's Rep. 193.

[59] *Burdick* v. *Garrick* (1870) 5 Ch. App. 233; *Hale* v. *Sheldrake* (1889) 60 L.T. 292.

rather than simple interest has been stated[60] to be not to punish the trustees, compounding does appear to be used for this purpose in certain cases of active and deliberate fraud or misconduct.[61]

Where a trustee pays interest, it seems that it is for the court to decide whether the income beneficiaries are entitled to the whole of that interest. In *Bartlett* v. *Barclays Bank Trust Co Ltd. (No. 2)*[62] Brightman, L.J. said[63]: "To some extent the high interest rates payable on money lent reflect and compensate for the continual erosion in the value of money by reason of galloping inflation. It seems to me arguable, therefore, that if a high rate of interest is payable in such circumstances, a proportion of that interest should be added to capital in order to help maintain the value of the corpus of the trust estate. It may be, therefore, that there will have to be some adjustment as between life tenant and remainderman."

This approach, which reflects that adopted where there is an unauthorised investment in a high income producing security, was applied in *Jaffray* v. *Marshall*,[64] in which judicial notice was taken of the fact that high rates of interest contain a large element which merely preserves capital values (which should belong to the remaindermen) while, in times when inflation was at a less high level, the rate of return needed to preserve capital was not as high. Since the period in question was of the latter kind, the interest (at the short term investment account rate) was apportioned equally between the tenant for life and the remainderman.

(10) Losses on mortgage

Where an unauthorised investment is made which results in loss, the trustees are generally liable for the whole of that loss. But in the case of mortgages section 9 of the Trustee Act 1925 provides that where trust moneys are invested on "mortgage security which would at the time of the investment be a proper investment in all respects for a smaller sum" the trustee will only be liable for the excess over that smaller sum, although that may not represent the loss to the estate. A trustee is not, however, protected by this section where he ought not to have invested on the security of such property at all.[65]

(11) Set-off

If a trustee commits more than one breach of trust, he cannot set off a gain made in one transaction against a loss in another. But each transaction is considered as a whole. In *Fletcher* v. *Green*[66] trustees made an

---

[60] By Lord Hatherley in *Burdick* v. *Garrick* (1870) 5 Ch. App. 233.
[61] *e.g. Jones* v. *Foxall* (1852) 15 Beav. 388; *Gordon* v. *Gonda* [1955] 1 W.L.R. 885.
[62] [1980] 2 W.L.R. 448.
[63] At p. 452.
[64] [1993] 1 W.L.R. 1285.
[65] *Re Walker* (1809) 59 L.J. Ch. 386, and *see ante*, p. 451.
[66] (1864) 33 Beav. 426.

authorised investment on mortgage. The property was in due course sold at a loss, and the proceeds were paid into court. The court authorities invested the money in Consols, which rose in price. It was held that the trustees could offset the gain in the Consols against the loss on the mortgage, as these were two incidents in the same transaction. On the other hand, in *Dimes* v. *Scott*[67] trustees committed a breach of trust by failing to realise an unauthorised investment, which they ought to have sold and invested in Consols. Much later, some of the property was sold and invested in Consols. By that time, however, the market price had fallen considerably below the price at which Consols were standing when the investment should have been made. The trustees sought to offset the gain made in the Consols against the loss on the sale of the unauthorised investment. It was held that they could not do so, for there were here two transactions, not one. The breach of trust was in not realising the unauthorised investment. The gain arose from the authorised investment being at an unusually low figure. The decision is a hard one, and were similar facts to be put before the court today, the court might well strive to reach a different result. *Dimes* v. *Scott* was followed in *Wiles* v. *Gresham*,[68] where trustees of a marriage settlement committed a breach of trust by negligently failing to recover from the husband the sum of £2,000 which he had covenanted to pay to them. They committed a further breach of trust by investing some of the other trust funds in the purchase of land without authority. The husband, however, with his own money improved the land considerably, so that it became worth considerably more than when the trustees purchased it. When a claim was made against them for failure to recover the £2,000, the trustees sought to set off the profit made on the investment in the land but were unable to do so because the transactions were distinct.

The cases show that while the rule is clear—that a gain can only be set of against a loss in the *same* transaction—it may well be difficult to decide whether two or more events are stages in the same transaction, or are separate transactions. The test seems to be whether all the individual steps taken in pursuance of a common policy can be treated as one "transaction" for this purpose. Thus, in *Bartlett* v. *Barclays Bank Trust Co Ltd. (No. 1)*,[69] where the trustee allowed the company to embark on two speculative property developments as part of the company's policy of seeking to increase the cash funds available to it, the trustee was allowed to offset the profit from one development against the loss arising from the other.

IV. Position of Trustees Inter Se

Trustees are under a duty to act jointly, and unless the trust instrument provides to the contrary, they do not have authority to act individually. Decisions of trustees usually must be unanimous[70] and there is no question of a vote of the majority binding them all. Also, they may and

---

[67] (1828) 4 Russ. 195.
[68] (1854) 2 Drew. 258; 24 L.J.Ch. 264.
[69] [1980] 2 W.L.R. 430. See also *ante*, p. 458.
[70] See *ante*, p. 388.

should ensure that all the trust property and investments are placed in the names of them all. In principle, then, each trustee takes an equal part in the administration of the trust, and has an equal say in what happens to the trust property. Thus, if a breach of trust has been committed, each trustee should be equally liable. But the wronged beneficiary need not sue each trustee: he may sue them all, or on the other hand he may sue only one or two of them. For this reason the liability of trustees is joint and several.

If an action is successfully brought against only one trustee, the general rule is that he has a right of contribution against his co-trustees, so that in the result each trustee contributes equally to the plaintiff's damages. Despite the principle of contribution, a trustee who is sued may sometimes be in a very difficult position. If there are three trustees, Timothy, Titus and Tom, who commit a breach of trust involving the loss of £30,000, the beneficiary, Bruce, may choose to sue Timothy alone: Bruce has a right to recover £30,000 from Timothy, and he is not concerned with Timothy's right of contribution. Timothy can of course claim £10,000 each from Titus and Tom, but if Titus has now disappeared and Tom has gone bankrupt, Timothy's claim will be unsatisfied. In the result, Timothy will have paid out £30,000 and will not have received anything. In order to achieve a greater degree of flexibility and a more equitable result, the operation of the rules of contribution between trustees for breach of trust was somewhat relaxed by the Civil Liability (Contribution) Act 1978. Under this Act, where the loss occasioned by the breach of trust occurs after 1978[71] the court has power to award, in favour of one trustee against another, contribution of such amount as is found to be just and equitable, having regard to the extent of the responsibility of the other trustee for the loss.[72]

The right of contribution does not exist where the trustees have been guilty of fraud.[73]

Under the old rules of equity which are now affected by the Civil Liability (Contribution) Act 1978,[74] there were three cases in which the defendant trustee might claim a complete indemnity from one of his co-trustees. These were:

(1) Breach of trust committed on advice of solicitor-trustee

Where one of the trustees is a solicitor, and the breach of trust was committed solely in reliance on his advice, then the solicitor-trustee must indemnify his co-trustees.[75] It is not sufficient to show merely that one of the trustees at the time of the breach was a solicitor: it must be shown that the other trustees were relying entirely on his advice. Thus in *Head* v. *Gould*[76] Miss Head and a solicitor, Mr. Gould, were the trustees of a settlement. They sold a house forming part of the trust property and instead of reinvesting the proceeds, in breach of trust paid

---

[71] ss.7(1), 10(1).
[72] ss.1(1), 2(1).
[73] *Bahin* v. *Hughes* (1886) 31 Ch.D. 390.
[74] s.2(2): see *infra*.
[75] *Lockhart* v. *Reilly* (1856) 25 L.J.Ch. 697.
[76] *Head* v. *Gould* [1898] 2 Ch. 250.

the proceeds to the life-tenant, Miss Head's mother. Following an action by the remainderman against the two trustees, Miss Head sought to be indemnified by the solicitor, but she was unsuccessful. Kekewich J. found that she did not rely on Mr. Gould, but actively urged Mr. Gould to commit the breach. Where the breach of trust was committed principally on the advice of the solicitor-trustee, in order to resist successfully a claim by his co-trustee for indemnity it is for the solicitor-trustee to show that his co-trustee was in full possession of all relevant facts, and made an independent judgment. *Re Partington*[77] was a case involving improper investments. There, Stirling J. said: "I have got to consider the question, has [the solicitor] communicated what he did to Mrs. Partington [the co-trustee] in such a way as to enable her to exercise her judgment upon the investments, and to make them, really and in truth, her act as well as his own?" The judge found in favour of Mrs. Partington, who was entitled to the indemnity.

(2) One trustee alone benefiting from breach

In *Bahin* v. *Hughes*[78] Cotton L.J. refused to limit the circumstances in which an indemnity would be ordered. "I think it wrong," he said, "to lay down any limitation of the circumstances under which one trustee would be held liable to the others for indemnity, both having been held liable to the *cestui que trust*; but so far as cases have gone at present, relief has only been granted against a trustee who has himself got the benefit of the breach of trust, or between whom and his co-trustees there has existed a relation which will justify the court in treating him as solely liable for the breach of trust. . . . " In *Bahin* v. *Hughes* there were two trustees, one of whom was content to leave the administration of the trust to the other trustee. The other trustee acted honestly, but made an improper investment which caused loss. The passive trustee claimed an indemnity, but was unsuccessful. It is by no means clear how far Cotton L.J.'s dictum goes.

(3) Where trustee also a beneficiary

It was held in *Chillingworth* v. *Chambers*[79] that a trustee who was also a beneficiary and who had participated in a breach of trust must indemnify his co-trustee to the extent of his beneficial interest. This only applied if the trustee-beneficiary had, as between himself and his co-trustees, exclusively benefited from the breach of trust. Suppose therefore that Abraham and Ambrose were trustees of a trust, in which Ambrose had a beneficial interest worth £2,000, but in which Abraham had no interest. Suppose also a breach of trust was committed from which Ambrose derived some benefit, but Abraham did not—*e.g.* investment in authorised securities to bring in a higher income—causing a loss of £4,000. Ambrose would be liable to indemnify Abraham to the extent of £2,000, leaving the remaining liability of £2,000 to be shared by them equally. It is not clear whether for the rule

---

[77] (1887) 57 L.T. 654.
[78] (1886) 31 Ch.D. 390.
[79] [1896] 1 Ch. 685.

in *Chillingworth* v. *Chambers* to apply it is necessary for the trustee-beneficiary actually to receive a benefit from the breach, or whether it is sufficient if the breach was committed with the intention to give him a benefit, but the latter view seems preferable.

Civil Liability (Contribution) Act 1978.   Such questions of indemnity are now regulated by the Civil Liability (Contribution) Act 1978. It is provided[80] that in proceedings where contribution is claimed, the court has power to exempt any person from liability to contribute, or to direct that the contribution to be recovered shall amount to a complete indemnity. It appears to be unlikely that this provision will add materially to the cases in which indemnity was available under the old law.

V. Limitation of Actions

Assuming a breach of trust has been committed, and that some loss has occurred, the question then arises whether the beneficiaries are in time to sue. The history of limitation of actions in respect of breaches of trust has been highly complicated, but the position is now governed by the Limitation Act 1980, coupled with the application in certain respects of the equitable doctrine of laches. "Laches" is delay in bringing action for so long that by his conduct the person wronged is deemed to have waived his claim.

There are two distinct situations, which will now be considered.

(1) No statutory period of limitation

Section 21(1) of the Limitation Act 1980, provides that there shall be no statutory period of limitation in respect of an action by a beneficiary under a trust if the action is one:

> "(a) in respect of any fraud or fraudulent breach of trust to which the trustee was a party or privy, or
> (b) to recover from the trustee trust property or the proceeds thereof in the possession of the trustee, or previously received by the trustee and converted to his use."

It follows that whenever trustees have committed fraud or retained any of the capital of the trust, there is no question of any defence under the statute. Thus, in *Re Howlett*[81] where a trustee occupied property belonging to the trust, he was held to be outside the scope of the Act. Likewise, in *Wassell* v. *Leggatt*,[82] where a husband forcibly took property belonging to his wife, thereby becoming a trustee of it for her, and kept it until his death, his executors were unable to plead the statute.

Where the statute does not apply, the defence of laches may be raised.

---

[80] s.2(1).
[81] [1949] Ch. 767.
[82] [1896] 1 Ch. 554; see also *Re Tufnell* (1902) 18 T.L.R. 705; *Re Eyre-Williams* [1923] 2 Ch. 533.

To establish this defence, it is necessary to show that the beneficiary has known of the breach of trust for a substantial period of time and has acquiesced in it. There are no fixed rules as to the period of time which must elapse: it must in the particular case be sufficiently long to enable the court to impute acquiescence. Likewise, if the beneficiaries clearly acquiesce after only a fairly short time, that will be a sufficient defence. It will be seen, therefore, that the essence of the defence is acquiescence of the part of the beneficiary when in full knowledge of the facts. Accordingly, it is generally considered that delay in taking action is merely evidence of acquiescence[83] although it has been suggested that mere delay may in itself constitute a separate defence apart from acquiescence.[84]

(2) Defence under the statute

(a) **Generally.** In other cases, the Limitation Act 1980 applies. Section 21(3) of that Act, which applies both to express trustees[85] and to implied or constructive[86] trustees, provides that actions to recover trust property or in respect of breach of trust are to be brought within six years from the date on which the right of action accrued. In the case of breach of trust, this is the date on which the breach occurred, and not when the loss was sustained.[87] Suppose, therefore, that a beneficiary knows that the trustees invest in unauthorised investments. At first the investments do well, but later lead to loss. Even though the loss may not be sustained for several years, the limitation period runs from when the unauthorised investment was made. Accordingly, in *Re Swain*[88] trustees were under an obligation to convert the deceased's assets into authorised investments. In breach of trust, they continued to carry on the deceased's business until the youngest beneficiary attained the age of 21. Eight years later, one of the other beneficiaries sought to make the trustees liable for the loss caused through carrying on the business, but they were held entitled to plead the statute.

Although in general no statutory period runs where the trustee has received trust property, a special rule applies where the trustee is also a beneficiary. If the trustee distributed the trust fund honestly and

---

[83] *Morse* v. *Royal* (1806) 12 Ves. 355; *Life Association of Scotland* v. *Siddal* (1861) 3 De G.F. & J. 58.

[84] *Per* Lindley L.J. in *Re Sharpe* [1892] 1 Ch. 154 at p. 168. See also *Smith* v. *Clay* (1767) 3 Bro.C.C. 639n.

[85] The section does not apply to an action by the Attorney-General against the trustee of charitable trusts which in this sense have no beneficiaries; *Attorney-General* v. *Cocke* [1988] Ch. 414.

[86] s.19(2) only applies where the action is against a "trustee," and not where the action is against someone who, although in a fiduciary capacity, is not a trustee. In *Tito* v. *Waddell (No. 2)* [1977] Ch. 106 (*ante*, p. 9) the Crown was held not to be in a fiduciary position. However, Megarry V.C. said (at p. 249) that, even if the Crown had been in a fiduciary position, it would not have been a trustee, so that the claim would not have been barred by s.19(2) of the Limitation Act 1939, which is now re-enacted as s.21(3) of the 1980 Act. Further, the doctrine of laches applied, but was no bar in this case because it had not been pleaded.

[87] *Re Somerset* [1894] 1 Ch. 231.

[88] [1891] 3 Ch. 233.

reasonably, but made an over-distribution to himself, the statutory period applies to the extent of his own share, and the excess is subject only to the doctrine of laches.[89]

Section 21(3) also provides that where a beneficiary has a future interest, for the purposes of the Limitation Act the right of action is deemed not to have accrued until his interest falls into possession. The effect of this is that a remainderman can take action in respect of breach of trust at any time during the subsistence of a prior life interest, or within six years from becoming entitled. The operation of section 21(3) is shown by *Re Pauling's Settlement Trusts*.[90] In that case improper advancements were made to beneficiaries, and the trustees pleaded, among other defences, that the period of limitation ran in their favour from the time when the advancements were made. In rejecting this, the Court of Appeal said that the interests of the children to whom the advancements were made were future interests, within the terms of the proviso to section 21(3), and that if an improper advancement was made, that did not start the limitation period running. As the advancement was improper, it did not bind the children at all. They could, therefore, sue at the time when they ought to have received the whole of their share.

Section 21(3), however, must be read in conjunction with section 21(4), which provides that where the statute can be pleaded against a beneficiary, he cannot benefit from an action brought by a beneficiary against whom the statute cannot be pleaded.[91] Suppose, therefore, that trustees hold investments upon trust for Daphne for life, with remainder to Chloe. Suppose also that they sell one of those investments and improperly hand over the proceeds to Daphne's daughter. In the absence of fraudulent concealment Daphne will be debarred from suing after six years. Chloe may wait until Daphne's death before suing, but she may sue before then. If she sues before then, she can compel the trustees to make good the capital loss, but during the lifetime of Daphne the trustees can themselves retain the income from that property.[91A]

(b) Fraud. As has been stated, there is no statutory period of limitation for action in respect of a fraudulent breach of trust, but it will be appreciated that a non-fraudulent breach of trust may have been committed, and subsequently concealed by fraud. Special provision is made, therefore, for actions based on fraud, or actions concealed by fraud. Section 32 which is of general application and is not confined to actions for breach of trust, provides that where an action is based upon the fraud of the defendant or his agent, or where a right of action is concealed by fraud, "the period of limitation shall not begin to run until the plaintiff has discovered the fraud . . . or could with reasonable diligence have discovered it." For the purposes of this section, "fraud"

---

[89] Limitation Act, 1980, s.21(2).

[90] [1964] Ch. 303.

[91] *Re Somerset* (1894) 1 Ch. 231.

[91A] On the basis that Daphne, by not suing, has in effect consented to the breach of trust and so the trustees, having repaired the breach, are entitled to the income which she would otherwise have received; *Fletcher* v. *Collis* [1905] 2 Ch. 24.

is wider than the type of conduct which would give rise to an independent action, and in *Beaman* v. *A.R.T.S Ltd.*[92] Lord Greene M.R. pointed out that the fraudulent conduct "may acquire its character as such from the very manner in which that act is performed."

The scope of section 32[93] was illustrated by *Eddis* v. *Chichester Constable.*[94] One of the assets of the trust in that case was a painting of St. John the Baptist by Caravaggio. The painting used to hang in a stately home where the life tenant lived, and in 1950 he lent it for an exhibition at Burlington House. During that exhibition he sold it to a consortium of art dealers, who subsequently sold it to an art gallery in Kansas City. The life tenant had no title to the painting, and when the trustees discovered the loss of painting in 1963 they brought an action against, *inter alios*, the estate of the life tenant, who was by then dead, for damages for breach of trust. In the course of his judgment, Lord Denning M.R. said[95] "one thing is quite clear: the right of action was 'concealed by the fraud' of the [life tenant]. I do not know that he did anything actively to deceive the trustees, but that does not matter. His wrongful sale of the heirloom was enough. It was a fraud; and by saying nothing about it, he concealed the fraud."

(3) Applicability to actions for an account

Section 23 of the Limitation Act 1980 provides that "an action for an account shall not be brought after the expiration of any time limit under this Act which is applicable to the claim which is the basis of the duty to account." The section may be intended to prevent any action for an account being brought in respect of a breach of trust which is already statute-barred, although a separate provision hardly seems necessary for this purpose. It is certainly difficult to see what further purpose the section serves. In *Attorney-General* v. *Cocke*[96] the Attorney-General brought an action against the executors and trustees of an estate held on charitable trusts, seeking *inter alia* accounts and enquiries as to the estate. Section 21(3) of the Limitation Act 1980 was clearly inapplicable; first, because the action was being brought by the Attorney-General and not by a beneficiary and, secondly, because the claim was neither to recover trust property nor in respect of any breach of trust. Harman J. held that all fiduciaries were under a permanent duty to account arising out of their fiduciary relationships; such claims were not subject to any period of limitation under the Act and so there was no time limit to which section 23 could apply in respect of such a claim. Consequently, it appears that a claim for an account against a fiduciary, based simply on the existence of a fiduciary relationship, can be brought at any time. It is therefore difficult to see in what circumstances section 23 will ever operate to bar an action for an account which is not related to a cause of action which is itself already statute-barred.

---

[92] [1949] 1 K.B. 550.
[93] The decision was on s.26 of the 1939 Act, which corresponded with s.32 of the 1980 Act.
[94] [1969] 2 Ch. 345.
[95] At p. 356.
[96] [1988] Ch. 414.

VI. If Trustee Prima Facie Liable, Obtaining Relief or Exemption from Liability

Even if an action can prima facie be brought against a trustee, it may nevertheless be possible for him to claim total or partial relief. The possibilities are:

    (a) by virtue of a provision in the trust instrument;
    (b) by means of an application to the court;
    (c) by virtue of an act of the beneficiaries, whether concurrence in or waiver of the breach;

and in addition the trustees may benefit

    (d) by virtue of indemnity from the beneficiaries.

1. *Provision in the Trust Instrument*

It has already been stated that the trust instrument can authorise a large number of acts which would not otherwise be open to the trustee. If the trustee takes advantage of such a provision, he is, of course, not guilty of a breach of trust. But even if he is guilty of a breach, he can still be relieved from liability. Thus one clause in use is:

> "In the professional execution of the trusts hereof no trustee shall be liable for any loss to the trust property arising by reason of any improper investment made in good faith or by reason of any mistake or omission made in good faith by any trustee hereof or by reason of any other matter of thing except wilful and individual fraud or wrongdoing on the part of the trustee who is sought to be made liable."

The golden rule is, therefore, always have a look at the trust instrument.

2. *Application to Court*

The court has power over a wide field before an act is actually carried out to sanction acts even if they would otherwise be a breach of trust.[97] Where no such application has been made prior to the act being carried out, however, by virtue of section 61 of the Trustee Act 1925 the court has a discretion to grant relief. The section provides that if it appears to the court that a trustee is or may be personally liable for any breach of trust but has acted honestly and reasonably, and ought fairly to be excused for the breach of trust or for omitting to obtain the directions of the court in the matter in which he committed such breach, then the court may relieve him either wholly or partially for personal liability.

    Thus the trustee must

    (a) have acted honestly;

---

[97] For example, see *Boardman* v. *Phipps* [1967] 2 A.C. 46, discussed *ante*, p. 248.

(b) have acted reasonably; and

(c) ought fairly to be excused.

"Honestly" here means in good faith. "Reasonably" is a question of fact which depends on the circumstances of each case. The courts have consistently refused to lay down any rules[98] but there have been numerous applications under the section, and under the provisions which it replaced. In *Re Kay*[99] the applicant was an executor and trustee of a will of a testator who left over £22,000 with apparent liabilities of only about £100. Before advertising for claims, the executor paid to the widow a legacy of £300, and only afterwards learned of liabilities which exceeded the value of the estate. It was held that it was reasonable for the executor to assume that with an estate of this size liabilities would not approach the value of the estate, so that he could safely pay the legacy. The court therefore granted him relief.

Difficulties sometimes arise when a trustee has taken legal advice but such advice was wrong. Although it is hard on the trustee, the fact that he has taken and has followed legal advice does not automatically excuse him from liability. In *National Trustee Co. of Australia* v. *General Finance Co. of Australia*,[1] for example, trustees followed the advice of their solicitors but this advice was wrong. It was held in the special circumstances that they should not be granted relief. One of the factors to be taken into account is the size of the trust property. If the property is of low value, trustees would probably be reasonable in taking merely the advice of a solicitor, whereas if the trust fund were very large, the advice of a Queen's Counsel might well be warranted.

Two aspects of the section were considered by Plowman J. in *Re Rosenthal*.[2] The testator devised his house to his sister and left the remainder of his estate to his widow. The estate duty payable in respect of the house, amounting to £1,700, should have been paid by the sister, but the executors, who for this purpose were treated as trustees,[3] transferred the house to the sister without making any arrangements with her to secure the payment of the duty.[4] They paid £270 on account of the duty liability and were left to pay £1,500. One of the trustees, who was a solicitor and who was acting in connection with the administration of the estate, claimed to be entitled to rely on section 61. Plowman J. rejected this contention on two grounds. First, in respect of the £270 which had been paid, improperly, from residue, although the trustee had acted honestly, he had not acted reasonably and had not shown that he ought fairly to be excused. In this respect, Plowman J. took account of

---

[98] *Per* Byrne J. in *Re Turner* [1897] 1 Ch. 536; *per* Romer J. in *Re Kay* [1897] 2 Ch., at p. 524.

[99] [1897] 2 Ch. 518.

[1] [1905] A.C. 373.

[2] *Re Rosenthal, Schwarz* v. *Bernstein* [1972] 1 W.L.R. 1273.

[3] One of the persons appointed as an executor had purported to resign from his office by means of the appointment of new trustees. This was probably invalid but the so-called new trustees were treated by the judge as trustees for the purposes of the case.

[4] The liability of the sister arose under the Finance Act 1894, s.9(1). See *Re the Countess of Orford* [1896] 1 Ch. 257.

the fact that he was a professional trustee[5] and appears to have adopted a more stringent approach. Secondly, in respect of the question of whether section 61 could apply to an *anticipated* breach of trust (the remaining £1,500 which was still to be paid had not been paid from residue and so no breach of trust had actually occurred in respect of it), the solicitor was in effect seeking a declaration that he was entitled to take this sum from residue. Plowman J. held that the section was incapable of giving relief in respect of a breach of trust which had not yet occurred.

It does not follow that, when it is shown that a trustee has acted honestly and reasonably, he will automatically be excused: it is only when these conditions are fulfilled that the court has a *discretion* to grant relief. It has been suggested that, where a trustee takes the wrong advice of his solicitor, he ought to sue his solicitor. Where he does not seek to recover the loss from the solicitor (assuming the solicitor to be liable for negligence) the court will probably not excuse the trustee.

It is clear that it is far more difficult for a paid trustee to obtain relief than it is for an unpaid trustee to do so. In the *National Trustee Co. of Australia* case the court had in mind the fact that the trustees were paid. But in *Re Pauling*[6] the Court of Appeal said that relief under section 61 can be granted to a paid trustee if the circumstances are appropriate, and a degree of relief was granted in that case to paid trustees who were bankers. But in its judgment the Court of Appeal held that "Where a banker undertakes to act as a paid trustee of a settlement created by a customer, and so deliberately places itself in a position where its duty as trustee conflicts with its interest as a banker, we think that the court should be very slow to relieve such a trustee under the provisions of the section."[7]

If the court does decide to grant relief, it has a discretion to grant partial or total relief.

3. *Act of the Beneficiaries*

A beneficiary who has once agreed to, or concurred in, a breach of trust cannot afterwards sue the trustees in respect of it. This applies only if three conditions are satisfied:

   (a) that the beneficiary was of full and sound mind at the time when he agreed or concurred;
   (b) that he had full knowledge of all relevant facts, and of the legal effect of his agreement or concurrence; and

---

[5] [1972] 1 W.L.R. 1273, at p. 1278.

[6] [1964] Ch. 303.

[7] See also *Re Windsor Steam Coal Company [1901] Ltd.* [1929] 1 Ch. 151, and *Re Waterman's Will Trusts* [1952] 2 All E.R. 1054. In *Re Cooper* (No. 2) (1978) 21 O.R. (2d) 579 (Ontario) the two trustees were the senior partner in a trustee law firm, and one of his junior partners. The whole of the conduct of the administration was left in the hands of the senior partner, who stole Can. $180,000 and was sentenced to seven and a half years imprisonment. The court found that the junior partner had no reason to suspect the fraud of his senior partner, and that he had acted honestly and reasonably. It therefore granted him relief under the Ontario equivalent of s.61.

(c) that he was an entirely free agent and was not under any undue influence.

A good example of the working of this rule is *Nail* v. *Punter*.[8] In that case trustees held stock upon trust for a married woman for life, with remainder to such person as she should by will appoint. During her lifetime, the woman's husband persuaded the trustees to sell the stock and pay him the proceeds. The wife then brought an action against the trustees but, before it was concluded, died, having by her will appointed the stock to her husband. The husband endeavoured to claim the same remedy as his wife had sought. But the husband, having become a beneficiary by virtue of the exercise of the power of appointment, could not succeed because he had been a party to the breach.

A trustee is also protected from action if the beneficiaries subsequently learn of the breach, and acquiesce in it, or give the trustee a release. Again, the beneficiaries must be *sui juris*, have full knowledge of the relevant facts, and act as free agents. Often releases are granted formally by deed, but an informal release, if supported by consideration, will be effective. In *Ghost* v. *Waller*,[9] for example, part of the trust property was lost through a breach of trust. The beneficiary agreed through her solicitors by letter that in consideration of the trustees undertaking to assist in recovering part of the loss she would "give up all claims if she has any against her trustees for negligence." It was held that this was an effective release.

Neither a formal nor an informal release will be effective if the beneficiary was not in full possession of the facts. In *Thompson* v. *Eastwood*[10] the beneficiary was entitled to a legacy under a will. The trustee denied the beneficiary's right to that legacy by virtue of alleged illegality, and the dispute was settled on the payment by the trustee of a smaller sum than that to which the beneficiary was entitled. A formal deed of release was executed, but when the beneficiary discovered the true position, he was held entitled to claim the full legacy, despite the deed of release, and despite an interval of over 25 years from the breach.

In *Re Pauling*,[11] one of the defences put forward by the trustees was that the beneficiaries, when over 21, had consented to the improper advances being made. It is clear that, had those consents been effective, the beneficiaries could not afterwards have succeeded in an action against the trustees. It has, however, long been clearly established that, where an infant makes a gift in favour of his parent, there will be a presumption of undue influence on the part of the parent[12] and that this presumption will continue for a short time—the exact period is undefined and depends on the circumstances of each case—after the infant attains his majority.[13] As far as the trustees are concerned, what

---

[8] (1832) 5 Sim. 555.
[9] (1846) 9 Beav. 497.
[10] (1877) 2 App.Cas. 215; and see *Re Freeston's Charity* [1978] 1 W.L.R. 741, C.A. (no acquiescence in a breach of a charitable trust).
[11] [1964] Ch. 303, and see *ante*, p. 507.
[12] *Huguenin* v. *Baseley* (1807) 14 Ves. 273.
[13] See *Lancashire Looms Ltd.* v. *Black* [1943] 1 K.B. 380.

is the effect on an advancement to favour a parent and not a child of a consent given by that child which may be the result of undue influence? The Court of Appeal in *Re Pauling* said: "Without expressing a final opinion, we think that the true view may be that a trustee carrying out a transaction in breach of trust may be liable if he knew, or ought to have known, that the beneficiary was acting under the undue influence of another, or may be presumed to have done so, but will not be liable if it cannot be established that he so knew or ought to have known." A trustee who is asked to commit a breach of trust for the benefit of a parent on the basis of consent by a beneficiary just turned 18 ought, therefore, to be reasonably sure that the child is emancipated from the parent.

4. *Indemnification by Beneficiary of Trustee*

It has already been shown that, subject to the conditions just mentioned, a beneficiary who with full knowledge concurs in a breach of trust cannot afterwards sue his trustees. This would not, however, affect the right of other beneficiaries to take action, and if such action is taken the trustee may be able to claim an indemnity out of the beneficial interest of the beneficiary who is concerned in the breach. In particular, if the beneficiary who has concurred in the breach of trust is the tenant for life and the trustee repairs the breach at the behest of the remainder-man, he is entitled to the income which the tenant for life would otherwise have received during the remainder of his lifetime.[13A] Outside this special situation, there are two rules which overlap:

(i) under the inherent jurisdiction, the court has power to order a beneficiary to give the trustee an indemnity
  (a) if he instigated[14] or requested[15] a breach of trust with the intention of obtaining a personal benefit (whether or not such personal benefit was in fact received) or
  (b) if he concurred in a breach of trust and actually derived a personal benefit from it[16]
(ii) under section 62 of the Trustee Act 1925 the court may impound the interest of a beneficiary in the trust fund if he instigates or requests or consents in writing to a breach of trust by the trustee. Where the section applies, the court has a discretion whether to impound, and, if so, whether to impound the whole or only part of the beneficiary's interest.

It will be seen that section 62 applies irrespectively of personal benefit, or of a motive for personal benefit. On the other hand, section 62 only applies in the case of mere consent to a breach of trust if such consent was in writing, whereas the general jurisdiction of the court operates whether or not the consent is in writing. The court will not

---

[13A] *Fletcher* v. *Collis* [1905] 2 Ch. 24.
[14] *Trafford* v. *Boehm* (1746) 3 Atk. 440.
[15] *Fuller* v. *Knight* (1843) 6 Beav. 205.
[16] *Montford* v. *Cadogan* (1816) 19 Ves. 635.

exercise its power to impound the beneficiary's interest unless the trustee can show that the beneficiary fully appreciated that the proposed action would constitute a breach of trust.

By a fairly robust construction, it was held in *Re Pauling (No. 2)*[17] that the power under section 62 can be exercised in favour of a person who is not a trustee at the time when the breach of trust occurred. In coming to this decision, Wilberforce J. was clearly influenced by the consideration that, if the section only applied to persons who were trustees at the time of the application, the court might be loath to remove trustees before such application has been made, even if from the other circumstances of the case their removal was desirable.

Where a beneficiary unsuccessfully brings proceedings against a trustee alleging breach of trust, the trustee will be entitled to take his costs out of the trust fund and only if that is insufficient will an order be made against the beneficiary personally.[18]

VII. PERSONAL AND PROPRIETARY BASIS OF REMEDIES FOR BREACH OF TRUST

So far this chapter has been concerned with the actions against trustees *personally* for breach of trust. So far as a beneficiary is concerned, this may be inadequate, and clearly will be if the trustees are insolvent. In these circumstances the beneficiaries may seek either a *personal* remedy against persons who have wrongly received the trust property or a *proprietary* remedy operating against the trust property itself. Such circumstances involve considering the legal basis of remedies for breach of trust. In the leading case of *Re Diplock*,[19] Caleb Diplock by his will directed his executors to apply his residuary estate "for such charitable institution or institutions or other charitable or benevolent object or objects" as they should in their absolute discretion think fit. His executors distributed the residue amounting to over £200,000 among 139 charities. This was in fact done before the testator's next-of-kin challenged the validity of the bequest. The House of Lords, in the litigation that followed, held in *Chichester Diocesan Fund and Board of Finance (Inc.)* v. *Simpson*[20] that the bequest was invalid. *Re Diplock* was concerned with the next-of-kin's claims to recover the money from the executors and the charities which had received it.

The claims of the next-of-kin against the executors were eventually compromised, with the approval of the court. But actions continued for the considerable balance against the institutions which had participated in the distribution. The money had been devoted by the institutions to diverse purposes. In the majority of cases, the cheques sent to them had been paid into their general accounts at the bank.

---

[17] [1963] Ch. 576.
[18] *Re Spurling's Will Trusts* [1966] 1 W.L.R. 920.
[19] [1948] Ch. 465; affirmed by H.L. *sub nom. Ministry of Health* v. *Simpson* [1951] A.C. 251.
[20] [1944] A.C. 341; and see *ante*, p. 333.

Some of such accounts were in credit: some were overdrawn, and some of the latter secured and some unsecured. In a few cases payment had been made into a special account. In others it had been earmarked for some designated purpose. In yet others the money had been spent on altering or enlarging existing buildings owned by the charity. The next-of-kin were concerned with recovering the money from the recipients. They based their claim under two heads. These were: *(i) in personam* and *(ii) in rem*. The claim *in personam* amounted to a claim against the charities personally by reason of the "equity" which the next-of-kin had to recover the money. They contended that any unpaid creditor, legatee or next-of-kin possessed such an "equity" as against an overpaid beneficiary or stranger to the estate. The claim *in rem* amounted to a claim to trace identifiable assets—whether unmixed or part of a mixed fund—into the hands of volunteers, which the charities who had wrongly received the assets undoubtedly were. Both claims succeeded.

It should be noted that, although *Re Diplock* was concerned with claims against innocent volunteers who had received property from the personal representatives, similar general principles apply where (as more usually happens) the claim is directly against trustees or persons in a fiduciary position. Furthermore, the proprietary remedy *in rem* is of more significance in the law of trusts than the claim *in personam* because, if it lies, it enables the beneficiaries to trace the trust money into the property acquired with it, in priority to the general creditors of the trustee or fiduciary if he is insolvent—this is because a trust or fiduciary obligation attaches to that property. However, it is nevertheless necessary to discuss the basis of the claim *in personam* as well.

1. *Personal Claims*

Re Diplock remains the principal authority governing personal claims. Consequently, any discussion of such claims must focus almost entirely on that decision. This is not the case for proprietary claims, in respect of which *Re Diplock* is only one of a number of leading authorities.

(1) The moral claim of the charities
It was argued for the charities that, notwithstanding the formal invalidity of the bequest, it should at any rate be taken that Caleb Diplock intended the institutions to enjoy the residuary estate in preference to his blood-relations and, therefore, it did not lie in the months of the next-of-kin to allege any "unconscientiousness" on the part of those whose claim was in accordance with the wishes of the testator, however ineffectually those wishes had been expressed. But this argument, based as it was on the postulate that the conscience of the recipients should be in some degree affected by their retention of the moneys, was rejected by the court as wholly untenable: "it is impossible to contend that a disposition which according to the general law of the land is held to be entirely invalid can yet confer upon those who, *ex hypothesi*, have improperly participated under the disposition

some moral or equitable right to retain what they have received against those whom the law declares to be properly entitled."[21]

(2) Recipient's notice of the invalidity of the gift

It was argued for the next-of-kin that by the terms of the letter which accompanied all the executors' payments, and which, though not entirely accurately, set out the terms of the gift, the charities had been given notice of the invalidity of the trusts, or at least were put on enquiry as regards their validity. Therefore (the argument ran) the charities were subjected to a constructive trust of the moneys received in favour of the next-of-kin. But this argument, although admittedly it had some attraction, was rejected. "Persons in the position of the respondents, themselves unversed in the law, are entitled in such circumstances as these to assume that the executors are properly administering the estate."[22]

(3) The next-of-kin's equitable right of recovery

This argument, which the Court of Appeal subjected to an exhaustive analysis, was to the effect, as the court put it: "Apart from any notice which the respondents may have had of the true effect of the testator's will, they had in truth no right to receive any of the moneys paid to them and that . . . the unpaid next-of-kin had a direct claim, recognised and established by the courts of equity, to recovery from the respondents of the sums improperly paid to the respondents and properly belonging to the next-of-kin."

(a) **Mistake of law.** It was on this question that the judge in the court below[23] (Wynn-Parry J.) came to the conclusion that an unpaid beneficiary could only sue the wrongly paid recipient in equity when the payment had been made under a mistake of fact; and here there was a mistake of law.

It was acknowledged by the Court of Appeal that the mistake was one of law and, moreover, as Wynn-Parry J. had held, that as regards *common law* claims for money had and received the action would not lie where money had been paid under a mistake of law.[24] But the fundamental point on which the court differed from the judge was that the common law claim was in no sense derived from equity but had a lineage altogether independent of it.[25] The court, taking the view that there was no "necessity in logic for the claim as being clothed, as it were, with all the attributes or limitations appropriate to the common law action for money had and received,"[26] went on to consider the relevant cases dating back as far as the days of Lord Keeper Bridgman and Lord Keeper Finch (afterwards Lord Nottingham L.C.) to see what

---

[21] [1948] Ch. 465, at p. 476.
[22] *Ibid.* at pp. 478–479.
[23] [1947] Ch. 716.
[24] This was certainly the law then but it may not be so for much longer following the decision of the House of Lords in *Woolwich Equitable Building Society* v. *I.R.C.* [1993] A.C. 70.
[25] [1948] Ch. 465, at p. 480.
[26] *Ibid.* at p. 481.

principles had been established by them.[27] And having done so, the court rejected the contention that in equity the mistake under which the payment is made must be one of fact. As Lord Simonds said[28] in the House of Lords, where the decision was affirmed:

"It would be a strange thing if the Court of Chancery having taken upon itself to see that the assets of a deceased person were duly administered was deterred from doing justice to the creditor, legatee or next-of-kin because the executor had done him wrong under a mistake of law. If in truth this were so, I think that the father of Equity would not recognise his own child."

It will also be appreciated that the unpaid creditor, legatee or next-of-kin would not himself be a party to the wrongful payment: the executor would be responsible for that. It is, therefore, difficult to see, as Lord Simonds said, what relevance the distinction between mistake of fact and law can have to such a situation.[29]

(b) Administration of the estate by the court. Wynn-Parry J. had also held that it was necessary that there must be or have been administration by the court before the equitable remedy *in personam* would lie. But the Court of Appeal, after analysing the cases,[30] came to the conclusion that they wholly negatived any such requirement[31]: if the court had administered the estate there would be every reason why equity should come to the rescue of an underpaid legatee if a wrong payment were made, but there seemed no reason why such administration should be essential.

(c) Stranger to the estate. The cases mentioned above[32] also established that it is irrelevant to the applicability of the remedy that the original recipient had no title at all and was a stranger to the estate.[33] No doubt many of the cases are concerned with providing equality between the original recipient and other persons having a like title to that of the recipient—for example, next-of-kin—but there is no reason why the remedy should not be applied as against a stranger even

---

[27] *Supra*, at p. 482. The cases cited and discussed at length included *Nelthrop* v. *Hill* (1669) 1 Ch.Cas. 135; *Grove* v. *Banson, ibid.* at p. 148; *Chamberlain* v. *Chamberlain* (1675) 1 Ch.Cas. 256; *Noel* v. *Robinson* (1682) 1 Vern. 90; *Anonymous* (1682) 1 Vern. 162; *Newman* v. *Barton* (1690) 2 Vern. 205; *Anonymous* (1718) 1 P.Wms. 495; *Orr* v. *Kaines* (1750) 2 Ves.Sen. 194; *Walcot* v. *Hall* (1788) 2 Bro.C.C. 304; *Gillespie* v. *Alexander* (1827) 3 Russ. 130; *Greig* v. *Somerville* (1830) 1 Russ. & My. 338; *David* v. *Frowd* (1833) 1 My. & K. 200; *Sawyer* v. *Birchmore* (1836) 1 Keen 391; *Thomas* v. *Griffith* (1860) 2 Giff. 504; *Fenwick* v. *Clarke* (1862) 4 De G.F. & J. 240; *Peterson* v. *Peterson* (1866) L.R. 3 Eq. 111; *Rogers* v. *Ingham* (1876) 3 Ch.D. 351; *Re Robinson* [1911] 1 Ch. 502; *Re Hatch* [1919] 1 Ch. 351; *Re Rivers* [1920] 1 Ch. 320; *Re Mason* [1928] Ch. 385; [1929] 1 Ch. 1, C.A.; *Re Blake* [1932] 1 Ch. 54.

[28] *Ministry of Health* v. *Simpson* [1951] A.C. 251, at p. 270.

[29] *Ibid.*

[30] See cases cited in note 27, *supra*.

[31] [1948] Ch. 465, at p. 489.

[32] See cases cited in note 27, *supra*.

[33] [1948] Ch. 465, at p 502.

though the effect of the refund will be actually to dispossess him rather than to produce equality.

(d) The "conscience" of the recipient. It had been argued that the conscience of the recipient, on which equity must fasten, was not affected in circumstances such as these. But the Court of Appeal decided that it is prima facie at least a sufficient circumstance that the charities had received some share of the estate to which they were not entitled.[34] As Sir John Leach said long before in *David* v. *Frowd*,[35] "a party claiming under such circumstances has no great reason to complain that he is called upon to replace what he has received against his right."

(e) Conditions for the application of the equitable remedy. The foregoing has shown that *Re Diplock* established (a) that an equitable remedy is available equally to an unpaid or underpaid creditor, legatee or next-of-kin, and (b) that a claim by the next-of-kin will not be liable to be defeated merely (i) in the absence of administration by the court; or (ii) because the mistake under which the original payment was made was one of law rather than fact; or (iii) because the original recipient had no title at all and was a stranger to the estate.[36]

But there is one important qualification that must be fulfilled before a claim by an unpaid beneficiary can succeed. This was stated by the Court of Appeal in *Re Diplock* as follows.[37]

"Since the original wrong payment was attributable to the blunder of the personal representatives, the right of the unpaid beneficiary is in the first instance against the wrongdoing executor or adminis-trator: and the beneficiary's direct claim in equity against those overpaid or wrongly paid should be limited to the amount which he cannot recover from the party responsible. In some cases the amount will be the whole amount of the payment wrongly made, *e.g.* where the executor or administrator is shown to be wholly without assets or is protected from attack by having acted under an order of the court."[38]

In the actual case the claims of the next-of-kin against the executors or their estates had already been compromised. Accordingly it was held that the amount recovered from the executors should be apportioned among the charities in proportion to the money the latter had wrongly received. This meant that the maximum recoverable from an individual charity by the next-of-kin should be rateably reduced.[39]

---

[34] *Ibid.* at p. 503.
[35] (1883) 1 My. & K 200, at p. 211.
[36] [1948] Ch. 465, at p. 502.
[37] *Ibid.* at p. 503.
[38] For early authority for this proposition, see *Orr* v. *Kaines* (1750) 2 Ves.Sen. 195; *Hodges* v. *Waddington* (1684) 2 Vent. 360.
[39] [1948] Ch. 465 at p. 506.

(f) No liability for interest. The Court of Appeal established that the recipients were only liable for the principal sum claimed and not for any interest.[40]

(4) Possible limitations of the remedy in personam

Re Diplock was concerned with any claim in respect of the administration of an estate and was dealt with by the Court of Appeal and by the House of Lords[41] strictly on that basis. It is not, therefore, so clearly established that the principles laid down will apply with equal force between beneficiaries under a trust pure and simple, although there seems no cogent reason why they should not. In *Butler* v. *Broadhead*,[42] the plaintiffs purchased land from a company in the course of being wound up. Some years later, it transpired that the company had had no title to the land and so the plaintiffs attempted to utilise the *in personam* claim in *Re Diplock* in order to claim against the contributories of the company, to whom its surplus assets had been distributed. It was argued that such an *in personam* claim was limited to the administration of estates but Templeman J. did not dismiss the claim on this ground but rather on the ground that it was barred by the Companies Act 1948[43] (it was assumed that the plaintiffs had failed to respond to the liquidator's advertisement seeking claims by the creditors of the company). This decision suggested that there was no reason in principle why the *in personam* claim should not apply to *inter vivos* trusts. Subsequently, in *Re J. Leslie Engineers Company*,[44] Oliver J. accepted the theoretical availability of such a claim to the liquidator of a company who was attempting to recover payments made to a creditor by a director after the liquidation had commenced; however, he denied the claim because the creditor had given value and the liquidator had not exhausted his remedies against the director. These decisions suggest that in an appropriate claim, the *in personam claim* could be applied at least to *inter vivos* trusts and possibly also to companies in liquidation. A further limitation of the remedy *in personam* has presumably been created by the recognition by the House of Lords in *Lipkin Gorman* v. *Karpnale*[45] of a general defence of change of position. In *Re Diplock* itself, the House of Lords had actually refused to recognise any such defence, a decision which produced very considerable hardship for those charities who had used the funds to improve their buildings and, consequently, provoked very considerable criticism. This defence will be considered in detail in the next section of this Chapter. However, now that it has been established, the *in personam* remedy will be able to operate in a much more reasonable manner. Consequently, there seems no reason whatever why it should not now be extended to *inter vivos* trusts and perhaps also to companies in liquidation.

---

[40] The authority is *Gittins* v. *Steele* (1818) 1 Swanst. 200.
[41] *Sub nom. Ministry of Health* v. *Simpson* [1951] A.C. 251.
[42] [1975] Ch. 97.
[43] Now Companies Act 1985, s.557.
[44] [1976] 1 W.L.R. 292.
[45] [1991] 2 A.C. 548.

2. *Proprietary Claims*[46]

In *Re Diplock* the Court of Appeal also subjected to an exhaustive analysis the question of the next-of-kin's proprietary rights to trace identifiable assets—whether unmixed or part of a mixed fund—into the hands of the charities. They did so primarily in case their decision as to the personal remedy of the next-of-kin was reversed by the House of Lords. However, in *Ministry of Health* v. *Simpson*, the House of Lords, in affirming the decision of the Court of Appeal as to the *in personam* claim, did not find it necessary to consider the question of proprietary rights. The Court of Appeal actually upheld the proprietary claim of the next-of-kin, subject to certain defences which will be considered later on. However, their analysis of proprietary rights of this kind constitutes merely one of a number of important judicial discussions of claims of this type. The totality of these authorities, rather than the decision in *Re Diplock* alone, will be considered in the discussion which follows. Proprietary claims have an important advantage over any claim *in personam*. If the claimant can identify his property in the hands of the defendant, he will be entitled to recover that property in full in priority to the claims of the general creditors of the defendant.[47] He will also normally be able to take advantage of any increase in the value of the property[48] and will also be able to claim its income or fruits from the date when it reached the hands of the defendant (the earliest date from which the payment of interest will be awarded in a personal claim is from the date when the writ was issued[49] and, in many cases, the payment of interest will only be ordered as from the date of judgment).[50]

The attitudes of the common law and of equity to claims *in rem* are quite distinct. It is in fact questionable how far proprietary claims recognised by the common law are rights *in rem* at all, although a successful proprietary claim in equity clearly gives the claimant a right *in rem* over the subject matter. It is therefore necessary to consider legal and equitable proprietary claims separately.

(1) Proprietary claims at common law

A person who seeks to assert a proprietary claim at law will use the action appropriate to the type of property which he is claiming. If he is claiming land, he will use the action for the recovery of land; he merely needs to show a better title than the defendant and, if he can do so, he will not be defeated by the defence of bona fide purchase for value without notice although his action may become statute-barred as a result of the adverse possession of the defendant. A successful claim will produce an order for the specific recovery of the land so that a legal

---

[46] The best discussion of proprietary claims is found in Goff & Jones: *The Law of Restitution* (4th ed. (1993)) pp. 73–102. See also Birks: *An Introduction to the Law of Restitution*: Chap. XI.

[47] Insolvency Act 1986, s.283.

[48] *Re Tilley's Will Trusts* [1967] Ch. 1179; see *post*, p. 623.

[49] *Jaffray* v. *Marshall* [1993] 1 W.L.R. 1285.

[50] *Re Diplock* [1948] Ch. 465.

proprietary right to land is indeed a right *in rem*. If the claim is instead for specific chattels, the claimant will use a tortious action for wrongful interference with goods under the Torts (Interference with Goods) Act 1977.[51] Bona fide purchase for value without notice will only be a defence to such a claim if the property has been purchased in market overt or is protected by the provisions of the Sale of Goods Act 1979.[52] However, a successful plaintiff is not entitled to specific recovery of the chattel, although the court has a discretion to so order.[53] Thus a legal proprietary right to chattels will only rarely amount to a right *in rem*. Finally, if the claim is for choses in action or money, the claimant will only be able to use the action for money had and received, which imposes only a personal liability on the defendant. Thus, a legal proprietary right to property of this type will never amount to a right *in rem*. However, all the legal proprietary rights mentioned will now be presumably subject to the defence of change of position, which will be discussed in detail later in this section.

(a) **Who can bring a legal proprietary claim?** Only the legal owner of property is entitled to bring a proprietary claim at common law. Since the legal owner of property subject to a trust will be the trustees, this requirement will in many cases prevent the beneficiaries of a trust from bringing such a claim for in a case such as *Re Diplock* the trustees will themselves have been responsible for the property reaching the hands of the defendant and so are prevented from reclaiming it by the principle of non-derogation from grant. Only where the trustees have themselves been defrauded by the defendant is a legal proprietary claim likely to be available to a trust.

(b) **What property can be traced at law?**

(i) **Property in its original form.** Where the property which it is sought to trace remains in its original form, the legal owner will, subject to the defences mentioned above, be able to trace it into the hands of anyone in the world and obtain the appropriate remedy. Difficulties may arise, however, when chattels are intermingled with other chattels of the same nature so that it cannot precisely be ascertained which belong to the claimant.[54] In these circumstances, it seems that a tortious action will still be available despite the mixing. This follows from *Jackson* v. *Anderson*,[55] where it was held that an action of conversion could be maintained against someone who had mixed the plaintiff's gold coins in a barrelful of the same description. So far as ownership of the intermingled chattels is concerned, this has traditionally depended on whether the mixing was accidental or deliberate. If chattels are mixed accidentally so that they cannot be separated or identified, then the original owners are treated as tenants in common of the whole in

---

[51] s.1.
[52] ss.22(1), 23. See also Consumer Credit Act 1974, Sched. IV, Pt. I, para. 22.
[53] Torts (Interference with Goods) Act 1977, s.3.
[54] See R.A. Pearce: 40 Conveyancer (N.S.) (1976) 277.
[55] (1811) 4 Taunt. 24.

proportion to their contributions. This was held in *Spence* v. *Union Marine Insurance Company*,[56] where bales of wool belonging to different owners became indistinguishable as the result of a shipwreck. On the other hand, in the same case[57] it was suggested that, where a person deliberately mixed the property of another with his own, then the whole must be taken to be the property of the other unless and until the mixer unmixed the chattels. However, this rule has now been described as no longer appropriate given the availability of modern and sophisticated methods of measurement. This was in *Indian Oil Corporation* v. *Greenstone Shipping Company*,[58] where the owners of a vessel had mixed with their own crude oil a cargo of crude oil which they were shipping. The owners of the cargo claimed the whole of the crude oil. However, since it was possible to determine exactly the amounts of oil belonging to each party, it was held that the mixture was held in common and that the owners of the cargo were entitled to receive a quantity of the mixed oil equal to that which had gone into the mixture, any doubts being resolved in their favour, together with damages for any loss which they had suffered. While this view seems more appropriate in modern conditions, it remains to be seen which way the conflict of authority thus produced is finally resolved. Legal proprietary claims to money, on the other hand, suffer from the difficulty that money has no earmark (it is rare for a note to be taken of the numbers of banknotes and there is no way of doing so in the case of coins). Further, since money is the universal medium of exchange, the transferor of money normally makes that money the property of the transferee. However, if a claimant can identify money in the hands of another as belonging to him (as would be the case where bank notes of known serial numbers were stolen and found in the possession of the thief), then that money could be recovered by an action for money had and received.

(ii) **Property following a change of form.** Can property be followed at law through a change of form? Can money which has been deposited with an agent or stolen by a thief be followed at law into any property which the money is used to purchase? The conventional answer to this question is that at law property can be followed into its product and anything into which it is turned can be recovered, provided only that the property or its product has at all times remained identifiable. However, if the property or its product has at any time become unidentifiable by, for example, being mixed with other money in a bank account, then the right to trace at law will be lost. In *Taylor* v. *Plumer*,[59] the defendant had given his stockbroker a draft for £22,000 to be disbursed on Exchequer Bills. The stockbroker, having cashed the draft and used £6,500 for this purpose, paid for certain American securities which he had already agreed to purchase and also obtained some bullion with a draft which he had exchanged for cash. He then

---

[56] (1868) L.R. 3 C.P. 427.
[57] *Ibid.*, at pp. 437–438. This is the rule in equity—see *Lupton* v. *White* (1808) 15 Ves. 432.
[58] [1987] 2 Lloyd's Rep. 286.
[59] (1815) 3 M. & S.562.

attempted to flee the country but was intercepted at Falmouth, where he surrendered the securities and the bullion. His trustee in bankruptcy tried to recover these assets or their value from the defendant on the basis that the latter's title could not survive these transactions; had he succeeded, the defendant would have had to take his turn with the general creditors. However, Lord Ellenborough C.J. held that the defendant could at all times have traced the product of his draft into the hands of the stockbroker since his property was at all times completely identifiable; consequently, he could claim the assets in priority to the general creditors. His lordship stated that only when property was turned into money *and* mixed with other money did the right to trace disappear.

Although it has been contended[60] that this decision is no authority for the right to trace at law surviving a change of form of the property unless the nature of the transaction by which the change of form occurs is such as to vest title in the new form of the property in the claimant, *Taylor* v. *Plumer* has been repeatedly followed. In *Re J. Leslie Engineers Company*,[61] the liquidator of a company was held entitled to follow at law a cheque drawn on the company account to cash into the postal orders which had been purchased with the cash and sent to the defendant. Similarly, in *Lipkin Gorman* v. *Karpnale*,[62] the House of Lords held that the plaintiff firm of solicitors could follow at law its right of action against its bankers in respect of the credit balance of its client account into the funds drawn in cash from the account by one of its partners and exchanged for gaming chips at the defendant's casino. *Taylor* v. *Plumer* was, if anything, extended in *Banque Belge pour l'Etranger* v. *Hambrouck*,[63] where the Court of Appeal emphasised that it is not the mere payment of money into a bank account which matters but the identifiability of the property. The defendant had fraudulently obtained £6,000 from the plaintiff by drawing cheques on his employers in favour of himself. He paid these cheques into his own account with another bank, an account into which no other substantial sums were ever paid. From this account, he drew out cash which he paid over to his mistress in consideration for the continuance of their relationship; she paid these sums into a deposit account, whose outstanding balance was successfully claimed by the plaintiff. The majority of the Court of Appeal[64] held that the plaintiff was entitled at law to trace the money through the defendant's bank account because it was possible to distinguish the money at every stage; the fact that, to all intents and

---

[60] By S. Khurshid & P. Matthews: (1979) 95 L.Q.R. 78, who argue that the references in *Taylor* v. *Plumer* to the right of the defendant to trace were to tracing in equity, rather than to tracing at law. This argument is convincing historically and there is much to be said for it as a matter of principle; however, it is inconsistent with the authorities in which *Taylor* v. *Plumer* has been applied.

[61] [1976] 1 W.L.R. 292.

[62] [1991] 2 A.C. 548 (in fact, only a personal claim was being pursued in the House of Lords).

[63] [1921] 1 K.B. 321.

[64] Bankes and Atkin L.JJ. Scrutton L.J. held that the plaintiff was entitled only to trace in equity.

purposes, no other sums had been paid into that account meant that the funds abstracted from the plaintiff had never lost their identity.[65]

However, where property or its product has been turned into money and mixed with other money, the right to trace will be lost. This will be the case not only where the funds have actually been mixed in a bank account but also where the funds have passed through an inter-bank clearing system. In *Agip (Africa)* v. *Jackson*,[66] the name of the payee on a payment order issued by the plaintiff was fraudulently altered and the sum in question was transferred by the plaintiff's bank in Tunis through its correspondent bank in New York, and presumably then through the New York clearing system, to an account at Lloyds Bank in London in the name of a shell English company controlled by the defendants, a firm of accountants from the Isle of Man. The plaintiff subsequently claimed to be entitled to follow this payment through the account of the shell company into an account of the defendants in the Isle of Man, to which it had subsequently been transferred. The shell company's account had contained no other funds at the relevant time so there would have been no difficulty about following the funds from that account to the account of the defendants. However, Millett J. (whose decision was affirmed on appeal[67]) held that the funds could not be traced at law into the account of the shell company. Given that the money had been transmitted by telegraphic transfer and had almost certainly passed through the New York clearing system, "nothing passed between Tunisia and London but a stream of electrons. It is not possible to treat the money received by Lloyds Bank in London or its correspondent bank in New York as representing the proceeds of the payment order or of any other physical asset previously in its hands and delivered by it in exchange for the money."[68] This decision emphasises the restrictions of proprietary claims at law. It does not necessarily mean that payments made by cheque can never be followed at law; where both payer and payee have their accounts at the same branch, it will clearly be possible to follow the payment at law from one account to another and this will almost certainly also be possible where the accounts are at different branches of the same bank. However, it may well be that the intervention of any inter-bank clearing system will cause the funds to lose their identity and be prevented from being traced at law despite the existence of the original cheque, simply because no funds may actually have been transferred from the payer's bank to the payee's bank on the day in question (this will depend on the overall balance of cleared transactions between the two banks on that day). Whether or not this is actually the case, the restrictions on legal proprietary claims are clearly highly inconvenient; however, these difficulties have been substantially alleviated by the intervention of equity.

---

[65] Atkin L.J. went so far as to say that it was possible to trace at law even into a mixed fund. However, this view is generally regarded more as an expression of hope than as a statement of reality.

[66] [1989] 3 W.L.R. 1367.

[67] [1991] 3 W.L.R. 116.

[68] [1989] 3 W.L.R. 1367 at p. 1383.

(2) Proprietary claims in equity

A person who seeks to assert a proprietary claim in equity will be relying on the existence of an equitable proprietary interest in the property in question which he will be endeavouring to enforce against the defendant. However, no such claim will be able to be made against a defendant who is a bona fide purchaser for value of a legal estate in the property without notice of the interest of the claimant (such a person inevitably takes the property free of such an equitable proprietary interest) or against any defendant who is able to invoke the recently recognised defence of change of position. A successful equitable proprietary claim will, in effect, involve the imposition of a constructive trust upon the defendant, who will hold the property on trust for the claimant to give effect to his equitable proprietary interest therein. If the claimant is able to show that any particular item of property in the hands of the defendant is, in equity, either entirely his own property or entirely the product of his own property, then he will obviously be able to call for that property to be transferred to him. If, on the other hand, he is able to show that any particular item of property in the hands of the defendant is only partially the product of his own property, then he will normally have a lien or charge over it for the amount of his contribution thereto and will enjoy the rights appropriate to the holder of such an interest in the type of property in question.[69] In all cases, his equitable proprietary right will amount to a right *in rem*, provided of course that it is actually enforceable against the defendant in the first place.

(a) Who can bring an equitable proprietary claim?

It is generally said that a claimant is able to trace an equitable proprietary interest into its product only if he can point to the existence of a fiduciary relationship. In *Agip (Africa)* v. *Jackson*,[70] Millett J. held that:

> "the only restriction on the ability of equity to follow assets is the requirement that there must be some fiduciary relationship which permits the assistance of equity to be invoked. The requirement has been widely condemned and depends on authority rather than principle."

Historically there was no such requirement. In *Re Hallett's Estate*,[71] the defendant solicitor sold bonds belonging partly to his own marriage settlement and partly to a client and mixed the proceeds with his own funds in a bank account. The beneficiaries of the marriage settlement could clearly point to the existence of a fiduciary relationship but the client was also permitted to trace in equity on the basis that she was the legal and beneficial owner of the property which she had deposited with the defendant. Similarly, in *Banque Belge pour l'Etranger* v. *Hambrouck*,[72] Scrutton L.J. who had doubted the availability of a tracing claim at law, held that the plaintiff was entitled to trace in equity and

---

[69] *Re Hallett's Estate* (1880) 13 Ch.D. 696.
[70] [1989] 3 W.L.R. 1367 at p. 1386.
[71] (1880) 13 Ch.D. 696. See [1975] C.L.P. 64.
[72] [1921] 1 K.B. 321.

both the other members of the court stated that, had they not held the plaintiff able to trace at law, they also would have permitted an equitable tracing claim. None of the members of the court stated any requirement for the existence of a fiduciary relationship as a prerequisite to an equitable proprietary claim. There is, of course, no doubt whatever that the necessary fiduciary relationship could have been found in both these cases had it been necessary. As Millett J. went on to say in *Agip (Africa)* v. *Jackson*,[73] "the requirement may be circumvented since it is not necessary that the fund to be traced should have been the subject of fiduciary obligations before it got into the wrong hands; it is sufficient that the payment to the defendant itself gives rise to a fiduciary relationship." Both the defaulting solicitor in *Re Hallett's Estate* and the fraudulent employee in *Banque Belge pour l'Etranger* v. *Hambrouck* could undoubtedly have been held to be constructive trustees of, respectively, the proceeds of the bonds and the proceeds of the cheques. The significant fact is that none of the judges felt it necessary to look for and find such a fiduciary relationship.

However, it is generally thought that in *Re Diplock*[74] the Court of Appeal interpreted the decision of the House of Lords in *Sinclair* v. *Brougham*[75] as establishing, in the words of Goulding J. in *Chase Manhattan Bank* v. *Israel-British Bank (London)*[76] "that an initial fiduciary relationship is a necessary foundation of the equitable right of tracing." It is questionable both whether this was really the opinion of the Court of Appeal in *Re Diplock* and whether *Sinclair* v. *Brougham* imposed any such requirement. The latter case arose out of the liquidation of the Birkbeck Permanent Benefit Building Society, in the course of which it became apparent that a banking business which the Society had been running was in fact *ultra vires*. A question of priorities therefore arose between the shareholders of the society and the depositors in the banking business (both had agreed that the outside creditors should be paid off first). The possibility of an equitable proprietary claim being available to the depositors was raised for the first time in the House of Lords as a result of a suggestion to counsel by Viscount Haldane L.C. A majority of the House of Lords subsequently held that the depositors did indeed have an equitable proprietary interest arising under a trust.[77] It is, frankly, hard to justify the existence of such a trust[78]; what is more its existence would also have given the depositors priority over

---

[73] [1989] 3 W.L.R. 1367 at p. 1386.

[74] [1948] Ch. 465.

[75] [1914] A.C. 398.

[76] [1980] 2 W.L.R. 202 at p. 209.

[77] Viscount Haldane L.C. and Lord Atkinson held that the trust in question was "a resulting trust, not of an active character," while Lord Parker of Waddington held that it was a constructive trust. Lord Sumner did not indicate with which of these two views he agreed.

[78] A person who deposits money with a bank must necessarily make the bank absolute legal and beneficial owner thereof since otherwise the bank would be unable to utilise the funds other than in accordance with the rules governing trust investments and certainly would not be able to use the funds to make unsecured loans. Such a depositor clearly has no more than a chose in action against the bank—see *Space Investments* v. *Canadian Imperial Bank of Commerce Trust Co. (Bahamas)* [1986] 1 W.L.R. 1072.

the outside creditors and it must be at least questionable whether such a trust could possibly have been found to exist had it not already been agreed that these creditors should be paid off first. The House of Lords had to look for and find a fiduciary relationship in this case because that was the only way of establishing that the depositors had an equitable proprietary interest. This does not, however, of itself necessarily mean that a fiduciary relationship is required where the claimant already has a pre-existing equitable proprietary right. Indeed, in *Re Diplock*[79] the Court of Appeal did no more than state that "equity may operate on the conscience not merely of those who acquire a legal title in breach of some trust, express or constructive, or of some other fiduciary obligation, but of volunteers provided that as a result of what has gone before some equitable proprietary interest has been created and attaches to the property in the hands of the volunteer." It is not obvious that this passage has the effect of requiring a fiduciary relationship where the claimant already has a pre-existing equitable proprietary interest. However, that is the way in which it has always been sub-sequently interpreted, both at first instance and in the Court of Appeal.[80]

The issue is not purely technical. As will be seen shortly the now well-established requirement for a fiduciary relationship is satisfied in the vast majority of cases where the claimant is able to rely on the existence of a proprietary interest in the property in question—indeed, it is arguable that the courts have on occasions strained the concept of fiduciary relationship to its limits, if not well beyond them, in order to satisfy this requirement. Even so, however, an absolute legal and beneficial owner of property cannot possibly point to any such relation-ship and so, according to the present understanding of the law, is therefore apparently not entitled to trace in equity. Consequently, if the property of such a person is stolen and its product is mixed with other money in a bank account, the victim of the theft will be entitled to trace neither at law (because of the mixing) nor in equity (because of the absence of a fiduciary relationship). This ridiculous anomaly can only be rectified either by challenging the requirement for a fiduciary rela-tionship (something which is much advocated but which is realistically only possible in the House of Lords) or by holding that a theif holds stolen money on trust for his victim, who is therefore entitled to trace it in equity into a mixed fund. Such a conclusion was reached by the High Court of Australia in *Black* v. *S. Freeman & Co.*,[81] a decision which was cited with approval by Lord Templeman in *Lipkin Gorman* v. *Karpnale*,[82] which did not of course concern an equitable tracing claim. If this Australian decision is one day incorporated into English law, then the requirement for a fiduciary relationship, although still unjustifiable historically, will cease to have any negative effects.

---

[79] [1948] Ch. 465 at p. 530.
[80] In *Aluminium Industrie Vaassen* v. *Romalpa Aluminium* [1976] 1 W.L.R. 676 and in *Agip (Africa)* v. *Jackson* [1991] 3 W.L.R. 116.
[81] [1910] 12 C.L.R. 105.
[82] [1992] 2 A.C. 548.

Given that, at least for the moment, the existence of a fiduciary relationship is a necessary prerequisite of an equitable proprietary claim, it is necessary to consider in what circumstances such a fiduciary relationship will be held to exist. It is obvious that the requirement for a fiduciary relationship will be satisfied where the person against whom the equitable proprietary claim is being brought is an express trustee of the property in question and it was held in *Re Diplock*[82A] that the requirement will also be satisfied where the property in question was originally subject to an express trust, even though the equitable proprietary claim is in fact being brought against a subsequent holder thereof. The requirement will equally be satisfied where, as in *Attorney-General for Hong Kong* v. *Reid*,[82B] the person against whom the equitable proprietary claim is being brought has been held to be a constructive trustee of the property in question and where, as in *Agip (Africa)* v. *Jackson*,[82C] the property in question became subject to a constructive trust as a result of an improper disposition thereof. It has also been held, more controversially, that the recipient of property under a transaction which is void, voidable, or mistaken holds that property on trust for the transferor, thus providing him with both the existing prerequisites of an equitable proprietary claim, namely an equitable proprietary interest and a fiduciary relationship.

In *Sinclair* v. *Brougham*[82D] four of the members of the House of Lords regarded such a trust as the basis of the right of the depositors in the *ultra vires* banking business to bring an equitable proprietary claim.[82E] As has already been mentioned,[82F] it is hard to justify the existence of such a trust; the depositors had made their deposits with the intention of becoming general creditors of the building society and there is no obvious reason why they should have been held to have had an equitable proprietary interest and the consequential priority over its other general creditors. *Sinclair* v. *Brougham* was expressly applied recently in *Westdeutsche Landesbank Girozentrale* v. *Islington London Borough Council*,[82G] where the Court of Appeal held that £2,500,000 paid by the bank to the local authority pursuant to an interest rate swap agreement subsequently held by the House of Lords to be *ultra vires* and void[82H] had, from the time of its receipt by the local authority, been held on resulting trust for the bank. Here too the bank entered into the transaction with the intention of becoming a general creditor of the local authority and there is no obvious reason for the priority accorded to it. Both these decisions concerned transactions which were void *ab*

[82A] [1948] Ch. 465.

[82B] [1993] A.C. 713

[82C] [1989] 3 W.L.R. 1367, [1991] 3 W.L.R. 116.

[82D] [1914] A.C. 398.

[82E] Viscount Haldane L.C. and Lord Atkinson held that the trust in question was "a resulting trust, not of an active character", while Lord Parker of Waddington held that it was a constructive trust. Lord Sumner did not indicate with which of these two views he agreed.

[82F] *Supra.*

[82G] December 17, 1993 (as yet unreported).

[82H] In *Hazell* v. *Hammersmith and Fulham London Borough Council* [1992] A.C. 1.

initio but a similar conclusion was reached by Millett J. in relation to a voidable transaction in *El Ajou* v. *Dollar Land Holdings*.[821] He held that persons who had been induced to purchase shares by fraudulent misrepresentations were "entitled to rescind the transaction and revest the equitable title to the purchase money in themselves, at least to the extent necessary to support an equitable tracing claim", stating that "the trust which is operating in these cases is not some new model remedial constructive trust, but an old fashioned institutional resulting trust".[83] Unless the existence of fraud is in itself a ground for obtaining an equitable proprietary interest, there is no obvious justification for the priority given here either.

More controversial still was the much earlier decision in *Chase Manhattan Bank* v. *Israel-British Bank (London)*[84] to attribute the same consequences to a payment made as a result of a mistake. In this case, the plaintiff New York bank as the result of a clerical error made twice rather than once a payment of $2,000,000 to another New York bank for the credit of the defendant London bank, which subsequently became insolvent. The plaintiff duly proved in the liquidation in respect of the second payment made under a mistake of fact but this gave no priority over the other creditors of the defendant. The plaintiff therefore also claimed to be entitled to trace the second payment in equity against the defendant. The legal effects of the mistaken payment had to be determined in accordance with the law of the State of New York, where a payment under a mistake of fact of money which the payee cannot conscientiously withhold gives rise to the imposition of a constructive trust. Goulding J. held that this was "also in accord with the general principles of equity as applied in England".[85] He justified this conclusion on the grounds that "a person who pays money to another under a factual mistake retains an equitable property in it and the conscience of that other is subjected to a fiduciary duty to respect his proprietary right."[86] This decision is even more questionable. It is not obvious how either an equitable proprietary interest or a fiduciary duty could conceivably have arisen as the result of a payment made through a third party bank intended to be in settlement of a commercial debt.

The decision in *Chase Manhattan Bank* v. *Israel-British Bank (London)* was expressly applied in the New Zealand Court of Appeal in *Liggett* v. *Kensington*.[87] A gold-dealer had offered its purchasers' the option of leaving their bullion in its custody on the purchasers' behalf as "non-allocated bullion". Purchasers who did so were issued with a certificate of ownership and were entitled to take physical possession of their bullion on seven days' notice. The gold-dealer subsequently became insolvent and the question arose as to whether these purchasers were entitled to an equitable proprietary claim in priority to a debenture

---

[821] [1993] B.C.L.C. 735, affirmed by the Court of Appeal without discussion of this particular point [1994] 1 B.C.L.C. 464.

[83] [1993] B.C.L.C. 735 at p. 753.

[84] [1980] 2 W.L.R. 202.

[85] *Ibid.* at p. 208

[86] *Ibid.* at p. 209.

[87] [1993] 1 N.Z.L.R. 257

holder. As has already been mentioned,[88] the majority of the New Zealand Court of Appeal (Cooke P. and Gault J.) held that the gold-dealer was in a fiduciary relationship with the purchasers, breach of which led to the imposition of a constructive trust and thus in turn to the purchasers having an equitable proprietary interest in the purchase moneys and their product, the remaining bullion. Cooke P., however, also held, applying *Chase Manhattan Bank* v. *Israel-British Bank (London)*, that the mistaken belief of the purchasers that they were acquiring gold, not merely contractual rights, meant that they had throughout retained an equitable proprietary interest in the purchase moneys. However, when this case reached the Privy Council under the name of *In re Goldcorp Exchange*,[89] the decison of the New Zealand Court of Appeal was reversed. Lord Mustill held that there was no fiduciary relationship between the gold-dealer and the purchasers so that no equitable proprietary interest could arise in that way. Further, in relation to the claim based on the retention by the purchasers of an equitable proprietary interest in the purchase money, Lord Mustill held that, whether this claim was based on mistake, misrepresentation or a total failure of consideration, the purchasers had at no time sought to rescind their contracts with the gold-dealer on any of these grounds but had, on the contrary, "throughout the proceedings asserted various forms of proprietary interest in the bullion, all of them derived in one way or another from the contracts of sale". This stance was "wholly inconsistent with the notion that the contracts were and are so ineffectual that the customers are entitled to get their money back". This of course meant that the Board did not have to consider the validity of the principle enunciated by Goulding J. in *Chase Manhattan Bank* v. *Israel-British Bank*. However, Lord Mustill declined to express an opinion as to whether or not that case was correctly decided. It cannot therefore now be assumed that the conclusion of Goulding J. that the law of the State of New York was "in accord with the general principles of equity as applied in England" would necessarily be adopted by an appellate court. However, there is no doubt that his conclusion and the recent statements in *Westdeutsche Landesbank Girozentrale* v. *Islington London Borough Council* and *El Ajou* v. *Dollar Holdings* constitute English law at present. Whether they should do so is questionable. It has of course often been contended[89A] that, as in the United States of Amercia, equitable proprietary claims should be made available in order to remedy unjust enrichment. If English law wishes to introduce such a principle, a question on which widely differing opinions have been expressed,[89B] it should do so openly and not by adopting strained interpretations of both law and fact in order to find the equitable proprietary interest and the fiduciary relationship required by existing English law.

In conclusion, although the requirement for a fiduciary relationship is undoubtedly satisfied in the vast majority of cases where the claimant is

---

[88] *Ante*, pp. 224–225.

[89] [1994] 3 W.L.R. 199.

[89A] See Goff & Jones: *op. cit.*

[89B] Compare the views expressed in Goff & Jones: *op cit.* with the views expressed *ante*, pp. 224–225.

able to rely on the existence of a proprietary interest in the property in question, some uncertainty remains as to whether such a relationship arises as the result of a transfer of property under a transaction which is void, voidable, or mistaken. It is to be hoped that the House of Lords soon has an opportunity to consider not only whether or not a fiduciary relationship is indeed a prerequisite for an equitable proprietary claim but also whether such a claim should arise as a result of a transfer of property under a transaction which is void, voidable or mistaken.

(b) What property can be traced in equity? From its earliest days, equity has always been prepared to permit a beneficiary of a trust to enforce that trust against every transferee of the trust property save where the latter can show that he is a bona fide purchaser of a legal estate therein for value without notice or, today, can make out a defence of change of position. There seems no reason why such a claim should ever have been confined to the trust property in its original form for, otherwise, any alteration in the form of the trust property would have defeated the interests of the beneficiaries. Thus, equity was prepared to allow a beneficiary to follow the trust property into its product.[90] However, at this stage equity, like the common law, only permitted a tracing claim so long as the property or its product remained identifiable; consequently, the payment of the property or its product into a mixed fund was at this stage as fatal to a tracing claim in equity as it was (and still is) to a tracing claim at law. However, in 1852 in *Pennell* v. *Deffell*,[91] the Court of Appeal in Chancery held that the fact that property had become unidentifiable in a mixed fund was no bar to a tracing claim in equity. The fact that it is thus possible to trace in equity property which has been mixed with the property of another has made equitable proprietary claims attractive to the suppliers of goods to manufacturers. They have sought, by means of what are known as retention of title clauses, to ensure that title to the goods which they have supplied does not pass to the manufacturers until the goods have been paid for. This has meant that the rules of equitable tracing have had to be applied in a commercial context very different from the trust context in which they were originally developed.

(i) Property which has not been mixed. Where the claimant has an equitable proprietary interest in property which has not been mixed, whether that property is still in its original form or has suffered a change of form, he will often be able to compel the holder of the legal proprietary interest in that property to trace it at law. Thus, if property is stolen from a trust, the trustee will have the right to trace that property at law and the beneficiary will have the right to trace that property in equity. In such circumstances, because of the absence of a defence of bona fide purchase for value without notice at law, the beneficiary will be better advised to compel the trustee to trace the property or its product at law. However, this will not be possible where, as in *Re*

---

[90] See *Ryall* v. *Ryall* (1739) 1 Atk. 59 and the other authorities citied in [1975] C.L.P. 64.
[91] (1853) De M. & G. 372.

Diplock,[92] the trustee has himself in breach of trust disposed of the property in question since he will be estopped from tracing at law by the principle of non-derogation from grant. In such circumstances, the beneficiaries will have to trace the property or its product in equity. The only defence to such a claim will be bona fide purchase for value of a legal estate without notice or, now, change of position. A successful claimant will be entitled, according to Sir George Jessel M.R. in *Re Hallett's Estate*,[93] to elect between calling for the property or its product to be transferred to him or taking a charge thereon for the amount of his property which was laid out in its acquisition.

Claims of this kind are not confined to cases in which the beneficiaries of a trust recover the original trust property or its unmixed product from a third party into whose hands it has been transferred in breach of trust. They have also been made in many of the cases involving retention of title clauses. In *Aluminium Industrie Vaassen* v. *Romalpa Aluminium*,[94] a company selling aluminium foil was, under the terms of the contract of sale, expressed to remain the owner of the foil until such time as the purchaser had paid the purchase price in full (it was also provided that the vendor would become owner of any new objects made as a result of mixing the foil with other materials). This did not prevent the purchaser from giving a good title to third parties but, as between vendor and purchaser, the goods remained the property of the vendor. The purchaser went into liquidation owing substantial sums in respect of unpaid foil. The vendor claimed to be entitled to such foil as remained in the possession of the purchaser and to the proceeds of sale of unmixed foil sold to third parties which had been paid by them to the receiver and had been placed by him in a separate bank account. Once it had been held that the terms of the contract were indeed as has been stated (this was in fact disputed by the purchaser), the vendor was clearly entitled to the foil which was still in the possession of the purchaser (the nature of this claim was not discussed at all but the vendor, as legal owner thereof, was clearly entitled to recover this property at law). However the vendor's claim to the proceeds of sale of the unmixed foil sold to third parties was based on *Re Hallett's Estate*.[95] The Court of Appeal held that the purchaser held the foil as a fiduciary agent of the vendor. Consequently, the vendor was entitled to trace the foil in equity into its product, the proceeds of sale. Given that neither the foil nor its proceeds of sale had ever become unidentifiable by being mixed with other property, there seems no reason why the vendor should not equally have been able to trace the proceeds of sale at law. However, the decision clearly establishes that, provided the necessary fiduciary relationship can be established,[96] a vendor will be able to

---

[92] [1948] Ch. 465.

[93] (1880) 13 Ch.D. 676 at p. 709.

[94] [1976] 1 W.L.R. 676.

[95] (1880) 13 Ch.D. 696.

[96] This has not been possible in a number of subsequent cases concerning retention of title clauses. Consequently, the vendors have necessarily had to trace at law. See *Clough Mill* v. *Martin* [1985] 1 W.L.R. 111 and *Hendy Lennox (Industrial Engines)* v. *Grahame Puttick* [1984] 1 W.L.R. 485.

recover property subject to a retention of title clause by means of an equitable proprietary claim.

(ii) Property which has been mixed. Where the claimant has an equitable proprietary interest in property which has been mixed, the mixing will usually have occurred as a result of the property or its product having been mixed with other money in a bank account. In such circumstances, if the mixed fund has subsequently remained intact, the claimant will clearly be entitled to a lien or charge on the mixed fund for the amount of his property and, presumably, in the event that any interest has been earned, to the part thereof paid in respect of his property.[97] (In practice, however, sums will inevitably have been withdrawn from the mixed fund, in which case it is necessary to have recourse to a series of presumptions in order to establish whether such withdrawals have been made from the mixed funds rateably or from one or more of its component parts.) In the same way, at least in principle, a claimant who can show that his property has been mixed with other property to form a new object should be entitled to trace his property in equity into its product, provided that he can show the necessary fiduciary relationship. This has indeed been attempted in a number of cases concerning retention of title clauses. If, as in *Aluminium Industrie Vaassen* v. *Romalpa Aluminium*,[98] such a claimant can show both the necessary fiduciary relationship and a clear intention that any such new objects should become the property of the vendor in whole or in part, such a claim should in principle be able to succeed (no such claim was in fact brought in that case but in *Bordon (U.K.)* v. *Scottish Timber Products*[99] the formulation used was described as "presumably effective" for this purpose). However, for a variety of reasons, such claims as have been brought have been unsuccessful. It has sometimes[1] been held that the terms of the contract have not had the effect of giving the vendor any proprietary interest in the new object; it has sometimes[2] been held that there has been no sufficient fiduciary relationship; and it has sometimes[3] been held that any interest created in the new object amounts to a charge which should have been registered under what is now the Companies Act 1985[4] and in default is consequently void for non-registration.

Where sums have been withdrawn from a mixed fund and it is necessary to have recourse to a series of presumptions in order to establish whether such withdrawals have been made from the mixed funds rateably or from one or more of its component parts, the pre-

---

[97] There is some uncertainty about the right of the claimant to increases in value in the mixed fund; see *post*, p. 623.
[98] [1976] 1 W.L.R. 676.
[99] [1979] 3 W.L.R. 672, *per* Bridge L.J. at p. 684.
[1] In *Bordon (U.K.)* v. *Scottish Timber Products* [1979] 3 W.L.R. 672 and *Re Peachdart* [1983] 3 W.L.R. 878.
[2] In *Re Bond Worth* [1979] 3 W.L.R. 629, *Re Andrabell* [1984] 3 All E.R. 407 and *Hendy Lennox (Industrial Engines)* v. *Grahame Puttick* [1984] 1 W.L.R. 485.
[3] In *Re Bond Worth* [1979] 3 W.L.R. 629, *Re Peachdart* [1984] 3 W.L.R. 878, *Re Weldtech Equipment* [1991] B.C.C. 16 and *Compaq Computer* v. *Abercorn Group* [1991] B.C.C. 484.
[4] ss.395–404.

sumptions differ depending on whether the mixed fund consists of funds of the claimant and funds of a fiduciary, of funds of two claimants both entitled to trace in equity into the mixed fund, or of funds of the claimant and funds of an innocent volunteer (it is obviously also possible for a mixed fund to consist of the funds of two claimants and the funds of a fiduciary or of the funds of two claimants and the funds of an innocent volunteer; in these circumstances, the situation is resolved by treating the two claimants as one and ascertaining first what they together can recover out of the mixed fund and then what part of this sum can be recovered by each individual claimant).

(a) Mixed funds consisting of funds of the claimant and funds of a fiduciary. In *Space Investments* v. *Canadian Imperial Bank of Commerce Trust Company*[5] a bank trustee, which was expressly authorised to deposit trust funds with itself, did so and subsequently went into liquidation. A person who deposits money with a bank normally[6] necessarily makes the bank absolute legal and beneficial owner thereof—were this not the case, the bank would have considerable difficulty in earning the interest payable to the depositor since it would be unable to utilise the funds other than in accordance with the rules governing trust investments and certainly would not be able to use the funds to make unsecured loans. The Privy Council therefore held that, since the mixing of the trust funds with the trustee's own funds had been entirely lawful, the beneficiaries had retained no proprietary interest in the funds deposited and so could not trace them in equity; they were therefore no more than general creditors of the bank. However, Lord Templeman emphasised that, if the mixing had been carried out without such an express authorisation, it would have been unlawful. In such circumstances, the beneficiaries would have been allowed "to trace the trust money to all the assets of the bank and to recover the trust money by an equitable charge over all the assets of the bank."[7] If this is indeed the case, the rights of persons entitled to trace in equity into a mixed fund consisting of funds of the claimant and funds of a fiduciary are considerably wider than has previously been thought (hitherto, such a claimant has only been permitted to trace into property which can be demonstrated to be the product of the mixed fund). Giving the claimant an equitable charge over all the assets of the bank converts him to all intents and purposes into a debenture holder since he obtains priority over the general creditors even in respect of assets which were not the product of the mixed fund. This seems wholly unfair to the general creditors and it is to be hoped that this dictum is not in fact ever

---

[5] [1986] 1 W.L.R. 1072.

[6] The depositors in an *ultra vires* banking business were of course held to have an equitable proprietary interest in *Sinclair* v. *Brougham* [1914] A.C. 398, *ante* p. 613, a decision which, surprisingly, was not cited. The imposition of the trust necessary to give rise to this equitable proprietary interest has already been criticised, principally because of its potential effects on the general creditors had they not already been paid off.

[7] [1986] 1 W.L.R. 1072 at p. 1074.

applied.[8] These criticisms were considered by the Privy Council recently in *In re Goldcorp Exchange*[8A] where Lord Mustill expressed the view that "the law relating to the creation and tracing of equitable proprietary interests is still in a state of development" but concluded that it was not necessary or appropriate to consider the scope and ambit of the observations in *Space Investments* or their application to trustees other than bank trustees". The scope and effect of Lord Templeman's dictum therefore still awaits clarification.

The traditional rules governing tracing into a mixed fund consisting of funds of the claimant and funds of a fiduciary are based on the decision of the Court of Appeal in *Re Hallett's Estate*.[9] The defendant solicitor sold bonds belonging partly to his own marriage settlement and partly to a client and mixed the proceeds with his own funds in a bank account. Subsequently, he made various withdrawals from the mixed fund, which on his death was insufficient to satisfy all the claims thereon. The Court of Appeal, having held unanimously that both the beneficiaries and the client were entitled to trace in equity,[10] held by a majority[11] that the funds drawn out must be debited to Hallett's share of the mixed fund on the basis that, where a man does an act which may be rightfully performed, he cannot be heard to say that that act was intentionally and in fact done wrongfully. The balance left in the mixed fund was sufficient to satisfy both tracing claims so that it was not necessary to decide any question of priorities as between them.[12] The presumption, therefore, is that a fiduciary draws his own funds out first and so any balance left in the mixed fund represents the property of the claimant. His claim thereto is of course limited to the amount of his funds which were originally mixed (together with, presumably, any interest which has been earned in respect of the part thereof which is his property). Nor does his claim extend to sums paid into the account after the original mixing. In *Roscoe* v. *Winder*,[13] the balance of the mixed fund fell to £25 as a result of repeated dissipation by the fiduciary. However, at his death the fund contained a balance of £358. Sarjant J. held the beneficiaries entitled to trace only £25; the sums which had been paid in went to the general creditors, with whom the beneficiaries

---

[8] See R.M. Goode, (1987) 103 L.Q.R. 433. An equally unorthodox, but this time excessively narrow, view of equitable tracing claims of this type was taken in *Re Attorney-General's Reference (No. 1) of 1985* [1986] Q.B. 491. However, this view was based on *Lister & Co.* v. *Stubbs* (1890) 45 Ch.D. 1 and therefore presumably cannot survive the overruling of that decision by the Privy Council in *Attorney-General for Hong Kong* v. *Reid* [1993] 3 W.L.R. 1143, *ante* p. 229.

[8A] [1994] 3 W.L.R. 199. Lord Templeman was a member of the Board.

[9] (1880) 13 Ch.D. 696.

[10] See *ante*, p. 612.

[11] Thesiger L.J. dissented, holding that payments out of the mixed fund should, in accordance with the decision of the Court of Appeal in Chancery in *Pennell* v. *Deffell* (1853) De M. & G. 372, be governed by the Rule in *Devaynes* v. *Noble, Clayton's Case* (1816) 1 Mer. 572 (see *post*, p. 625).

[12] Had this not been the case, priorities as between the two claimants would have been determined by the Rule in *Devaynes* v. *Noble, Clayton's Case* (1816) 1 Mer. 572 (see *post*, p. 625), as had indeed been held by Fry J. at first instance.

[13] [1915] 1 Ch. 62.

could of course prove for the residue of their claim. This conclusion was approved and applied by the Privy Council in *In re Goldcorp Exchange*.[13A]

If the balance of the mixed fund is insufficient fully to discharge the liability of the fiduciary to the claimant, the latter can nevertheless follow the withdrawals into any identifiable product thereof and claim an equitable charge therein. In *Re Oatway*,[14] a trustee, having mixed the trust money with his own, first withdrew sums which he invested and later withdrew and dissipated the remainder. His trustee in bankruptcy suggested that, according to *Re Hallett's Estate*, what he had first withdrawn was his own money; consequently, the investments belonged to him and it was the trust money which had been dissipated. This unmeritorious claim was predictably rejected; Joyce J. held that the beneficiaries were entitled to the investments on the basis that their claim must be satisfied from any identifiable part of the mixed fund or its product before the trustee could assert any claim thereto.

The precise scope of this right to follow the withdrawals from the mixed fund into their product is uncertain. In *Re Hallett's Estate*[15] Sir George Jessel M.R. stated that, where a claimant was seeking to trace into property which was the product of a mixed fund containing funds of the claimant and funds of a fiduciary, the only remedy available to him was to take a charge thereon for the amount of his property which was laid out in its acquisition. If this is indeed the case, the claimant's right to trace will be limited to his original contribution to the purchase price of the property and will not extend to any increase in its value. This view was followed in *Re Oatway*, where Joyce J. held that the trust had a charge on the investments which had been purchased by the trustee and went on to say that, because this charge was for an amount superior to their value, the investments and their proceeds of sale belonged to the trust.[16] On the other hand, a different view was expressed in *Re Tilley's Will Trusts*.[17] An executrix, who was also tenant for life, paid the estate's funds into her own bank account and used the mixed fund as part payment for two houses, the remainder of the purchase money being provided by extensive overdraft facilities. She continued to engage in property transactions of this kind until her death. The remaindermen claimed to be entitled to a rateable share of the proceeds of the two houses. It was conceded, contrary to the view expressed by Sir George Jessel M.R. in *Re Hallett's Estate*, that where property is the product of a mixed fund the claimant has the right to "require the asset to be treated as trust property with regard to that proportion of it which the trust moneys contributed to its purchase."[18] Ungoed-Thomas J. clearly accepted this proposition as good law. However, on the facts, he held that the trust funds had not in fact been invested in the two properties since the use by the tenant for life of the

---

[13A] [1994] 3 W.L.R. 199.

[14] [1903] 2 Ch. 356.

[15] (1880) 13 Ch.D. 696 at p. 709.

[16] This remark is a potential cause of confusion; however, there is no doubt that Joyce J. followed *Re Hallett's Estate*.

[17] [1967] 2 W.L.R. 1533.

[18] *Ibid.* at p. 1542.

estate's funds had merely prevented her from having to use more extensive overdraft facilities, which were clearly available to her. Hence the remaindermen were entitled only to the funds of the estate which had been mixed together with interest thereon. It is questionable whether it should in fact be open to a fiduciary who has committed a clear breach of trust by mixing trust funds with his own successfully to contend that any profits so made were not actually due to the use of the trust funds. While *Re Tilley's Will Trusts* clearly establishes that such a contention is possible, the opposite view has been taken in other jurisdictions.[19] In relation to the more general question as to whether the claimant's right to trace is limited to his original contribution to the purchase price of the property, the view that it should be so limited has been supported[20] on the grounds that the priority of the claimant over the general creditors of the fiduciary should be limited to whatever is necessary to enable him to recuperate his lost funds and should not extend to any profit made thereby. Adoption of this view would protect the general creditors of the fiduciary without enabling the fiduciary to profit personally since, in the event that he was solvent, he would be liable to account to his principal for any profit which he had made as a result of his breach of trust under the principles discussed in Chapter 8.[21]

A further question, on which there is no direct authority, is whether a claimant can elect to recover an asset which is the product of the mixed fund rather than taking any balance of the mixed fund to which he is entitled. It will be of interest for him so to do if, contrary to the view suggested above, he is entitled to any increase in the value of such an asset or if any part of the mixed fund to which he is prima facie entitled has subsequently been invested in some other asset which has fallen in value. This situation has never arisen in any of the authorities since in no case have there been both a credit balance in the mixed fund and assets purchased with funds withdrawn from it. However, the observations of all the judges, particularly those of Sir George Jessel M.R. in *Re Hallett's Estate*, indicate the mixed fund as the recourse primarily available to the claimant. The interests of the claimant and of the general creditors of the fiduciary are very evenly balanced where any part of the mixed fund to which the claimant is prima facie entitled has subsequently been invested in some other asset which has fallen in value. However, on the grounds of simplicity and consistency, it is suggested that the claimant must take any balance of the mixed fund to which he is entitled before proceeding to follow the withdrawals from the mixed fund into their product.

Finally, it must be emphasised that all the rules which have been discussed are no more than presumptions. Consequently, these presumptions can be rebutted in any given case if either the claimant or the fiduciary is able to establish to the satisfaction of the court that any par-

---

[19] In Australia in *Scott* v. *Scott* (1963) 36 A.L.J.R. 345 and in the United States of America in *Primeau* v. *Granfield* (1911) 184 Fed. 480.

[20] See G.H. Jones, (1988) 37 King's Counsel 15 at p. 16.

[21] See *ante*, pp. 239–251.

ticular withdrawal was intended to be made from some specific part of the mixed fund or that any subsequent payment back into the mixed fund was intended to replace a previous withdrawal.

(b) Mixed funds consisting of funds of two claimants. Where a mixed fund consists of the funds of two claimants, both of whom are entitled to trace in equity into the mixed fund, withdrawals from the mixed fund are presumed to be made rateably from the funds held by each claimant. Since each claimant necessarily has an equitable proprietary interest in his part of the funds which have been mixed, the attribution of profits and losses rateably between them is entirely in accordance with principle. However, in the event that the mixed fund in question is an active unbroken bank account (the only relevant example is a current (but not a deposit) account), then the presumption that withdrawals from the mixed fund are presumed to be made rateably is displaced by a principle enunciated by Grant M.R. in *Devaynes* v. *Noble, Clayton's Case*,[22] which is generally known as the Rule in *Clayton's Case*. In such an account, "there is no room for any other appropriation than that which arises from the order in which the receipts and payments take place, and are carried into the account. Presumably, it is the sum first paid in, that is first drawn out. It is the first item on the debit side of the account, that is discharged, or reduced, by the first item on the credit side. The appropriation is made by the very act of setting the two items against each other. Upon that principle, all accounts current are settled, and particularly cash accounts."[23] *Devaynes* v. *Noble* did not concern a tracing claim but rather a question as to the appropriation of payments. The Rule was, however, applied to equitable tracing claims in the first case in which tracing was permitted in equity into a mixed fund, *Pennell* v. *Deffell*[24] in 1852. As has already been seen, the Court of Appeal decided by a majority in *Re Hallett's Estate*[25] that the Rule should no longer apply to mixed funds containing funds of a claimant and funds of a fiduciary. However, had any question of priorities between the two claimants in *Re Hallett's Estate* had to be determined, there is no doubt that the Rule in *Clayton's Case* would have been applied for this purpose, as it had indeed been applied by Fry J. at first instance; this was expressly recognised by all three members of the court.[26] The same conclusion was reached in *Hancock* v. *Smith*.[27] Recently, in *Barlow Clowes International* v. *Vaughan*,[28] the Court of Appeal confirmed that the rule provided a convenient method of determining competing claims where the funds

[22] (1817) 1 Mer. 572.
[23] *Ibid.* at pp. 608–609.
[24] (1853) De M. & G. 372.
[25] (1880) 13 Ch.D. 696.
[26] Sir George Jessel M.R. and Baggallay L.J., who had held that the Rule in *Clayton's Case* did not apply to a mixed fund consisting of funds of a claimant and funds of a fiduciary, agreed with Thesiger L.J., who had taken the opposite view, that the *Rule in Clayton's Case* clearly applied to mixed funds consisting of funds of two claimants.
[27] (1889) 41 Ch.D. 456, *per* Lord Halsbury L.C. and Cotton L.J. (Fry L.J. did not deal with the point).
[28] [1992] 4 All E.R. 22.

of several beneficiaries had been blended in one account and there was a deficiency or where there had been a wrongful mixing of different sums of trust money in a single account. However, where its application would be impracticable or would result in injustice between the investors, because a relatively small number of investors would obtain most of the funds, or would be contrary to the express or implied intention of the investors, the rule would not be applied if a preferable alternative method of distribution was available. The Court of Appeal held that there had been such a presumed intention as between the various subscribers to a collective investment scheme by which their money would be mixed together and invested through a common fund; consequently, the assets which remained available for distribution would be distributed rateably between them.

However, the Rule in *Clayton's Case* is just as capable of enabling a relatively small number of investors to obtain most of the funds when applied to mixed funds consisting of the funds of two claimants as when it is applied to common funds in collective investment schemes. Suppose that a trustee mixes the funds of two trusts in a current banking account, paying in £2,000 of the funds of Trust A on one day and £1,000 of the funds of Trust B on the following day. If on the third day he withdraws £2,000 from the mixed fund and invests it in securities, those securities will have been purchased entirely with the funds of Trust A. If on the fourth day he withdraws £700 from the mixed fund and loses this sum gambling at a casino, the entire loss will fall on Trust B, whose only right will be to the £300 left in the mixed fund. (Were, on the other hand, the mixed fund a deposit account, both profits and losses would be shared rateably; Trust A and Trust B would respectively be entitled to two-thirds and one-third of the securities and £200 and £100 of the balance of the mixed fund.) Why is this result any more absurd than it would have been to have permitted the later investors in a collective investment scheme to have recovered almost all their investment and the earlier investors to have recovered almost none of theirs (the consequence of the application of the Rule in *Clayton's Case* which induced the Court of Appeal to find the implied intention necessary to displace it in *Barlow Clowes International* v. *Vaughan*)?

The Rule in *Clayton's Case* was trenchantly condemned by Learned Hand J. in *Re Walter J. Schmidt*,[29] although he was nevertheless compelled by precedent to apply it. However, unless and until a court is prepared to recognise the absurdity of the illustration set out above, the Rule will continue to apply to mixed funds consisting of funds of two claimants who are both entitled to trace in equity and also, as will be seen in the next section, to mixed funds consisting of funds of the claimant and funds of an innocent volunteer.

(c) Mixed funds consisting of funds of the claimant and funds of an innocent volunteer. Where a mixed fund consists of the funds of a claimant and the funds of an innocent volunteer, withdrawals from the

---

[29] (1923) 298 Fed. 314 (United States of America).

mixed fund are presumed to be made in exactly the same way as withdrawals from a mixed fund consisting of the funds of two claimants, that is to say rateably unless the mixed fund in question is an active unbroken bank account, in which case the Rule in *Clayton's Case* applies.[30]

However, while the attribution of profits and losses rateably is entirely in accordance with principle in the case of a mixed fund consisting of the funds of two claimants, both of whom have equitable proprietary interests therein, it is highly questionable in the case of a mixed fund consisting of the funds of a claimant and the funds of an innocent volunteer. The claimant necessarily has an equitable proprietary interest in the mixed fund; if he did not, he would not be entitled to trace in equity. How can an innocent volunteer resist a claim by the holder of an equitable proprietary interest to recover his property? What defence, other than the defence of change of position, can an innocent volunteer have to an equitable proprietary claim? In principle, the claimant should be able to recover his funds in full out of the mixed fund quite irrelevant of what withdrawals have been made therefrom by the innocent volunteer.

However, this is clearly not the law. In *Re Diplock*[31] Lord Greene M.R. held that the positions of the claimant and the innocent volunteer were equivalent. "This burden on the conscience of the volunteer is not such as to compel him to treat the claim of the equitable owner as paramount. That would be to treat the volunteer as strictly as if he himself stood in a fiduciary relationship to the equitable owner which *ex hypothesi* he does not. The volunteer is under no greater duty of conscience to recognise the interest of the equitable owner than that which lies upon a person having an equitable interest in one of two trust funds of 'money' which have become mixed towards the equitable owner of the other. Such a person is not in conscience bound to give precedence to the equitable owner of the other of the two funds." He therefore relied on *Sinclair* v. *Brougham*[32] as authority for the attribution of profits and losses rateably in mixed funds consisting of funds of a claimant and funds of an innocent volunteer. However, the analogy with *Sinclair* v. *Brougham* is not in fact sound. The House of Lords indeed held that the shareholders and the depositors in the *ultra vires* banking business should share the remaining assets rateably but the depositors were held to be entitled to trace in equity by virtue of the existence of a trust in their favour. Therefore both they and the shareholders in fact had proprietary interests. This was not the case in *Re Diplock*, where only the claimants had an equitable proprietary interest.

It is of course highly unlikely, given the decision in *Re Diplock*, that an innocent volunteer will ever be held liable for the whole of the losses suffered by a mixed fund. It seems generally to be accepted that as at present losses should be attributed rateably between the claimant and

---

[30] *Re Diplock* [1948] Ch. 465 (in respect of the claim against the National Institute for the Deaf).
[31] *Ibid.* at p. 524.
[32] [1914] A.C. 398.

the innocent volunteer. At present, subject to the defence of change of position, profits are also attributed rateably. However, it has been suggested that, provided the claimant is in a position to recover his original contribution to the mixed fund in full by means of a charge on the mixed fund or on the property which constitutes its product, the innocent volunteer should be entitled to retain the benefit of any improvements which he has made or profits which he has obtained.[33] Depriving the holder of an equitable proprietary interest of profits while retaining his rateable liability for losses does not seem very consistent with the nature of an equitable proprietary claim. However, suggestions of this type clearly demonstrate that the leniency shown at present towards innocent volunteers is more likely to be amplified than taken away.

(c) Defences to equitable proprietary claims. No equitable proprietary claim can succeed if the property in question has simply disappeared as a result of dissipation. If, for example, funds which are susceptible of being traced are expended on a case of wine which is then consumed, no proprietary claim will be able to be brought against the person who has expended the funds (nor will any proprietary claim be able to be brought against the vendor of the wine, who will be a bona fide purchaser for value without notice). The disappearance of the property is not, formally, a defence to an equitable proprietary claim but its effect is the same as if it were a defence. Quite apart from this situation, there are of course a number of formal defences which can be made out to an equitable proprietary claim.

(i) Bona fide purchase for value of a legal estate without notice. It is, of course, axiomatic that no equitable proprietary interest of any type can survive the bona fide purchase for value of a legal estate or interest in the property in question to a person who has no notice of any kind of the equitable proprietary interest in question. Thus, if trust property is sold by the trustees to a bona fide purchaser for value who has no notice of the interests of the beneficiaries, the latter cannot pursue any equitable proprietary claim against the purchaser; their only possible proprietary claim will be to attempt to trace into the proceeds of sale.

(ii) Change of position. English law has traditionally denied any general defence of change of position[34] although in *Re Diplock*[35] the Court of Appeal held that innocent volunteers could rely on two limited (and controversial) manifestations of this defence as against equitable proprietary claims. However, in *Lipkin Gorman* v. *Karpnale*[36] the House of Lords upheld for the first time the existence of such a defence. This case was, in the House of Lords, concerned principally with an action for money had and received; no proprietary claim was being pursued. However, it is clear that the defence so enunciated is generally

---

[33] See D.J. Hayton, (1990) 106 L.Q.R. 87 at p. 100.
[34] See particularly *Ministry of Health* v. *Simpson* [1951] A.C. 251.
[35] [1948] Ch. 465 at pp. 546–548.
[36] [1991] A.C. 548, [1991] 3 W.L.R. 10.

applicable and will therefore apply to both legal and equitable proprietary claims.

All the members of the House of Lords agreed that, on the facts, the defendant casino could invoke the defence of change of position against the claim by the plaintiff solicitors to recover funds which had been stolen from its client account and subsequently lost at the casino but only to the extent that the casino had paid out winnings to the gambler. However, the House took considerable care not to preempt the subsequent development of the defence. Lord Bridge stated[37] that "in expressly acknowledging the availability of this defence for the first time it would be unwise to attempt to define its scope in abstract terms." Lord Goff said this[38]:

"I am most anxious that, in recognising this defence to actions of restitution, nothing should be said at this stage to inhibit the development of the defence on a case by case basis, in the usual way. It is, of course, plain that the defence is not open to one who has changed his position in bad faith, as where the defendant has paid away the money with knowledge of the facts entitling the plaintiff to restitution; and it is commonly accepted that the defence should not be open to a wrongdoer. These are matters which can, in due course, be considered in depth in cases where they arise for consideration. . . . It is not appropriate in the present case to identify all those actions in restitution to which change of position may be a defence. . . . At present I do not wish to state the principle any less broadly than this: that the defence is available to a person whose position has so changed that it would be inequitable in all the circumstances to require him to make restitution, or alternatively to make restitution in full. I wish to stress, however, that the mere fact that the defendant has spent the money, in whole or in part, does not of itself render it inequitable that he should be called upon to repay, because the expenditure might in any event have been incurred by him in the ordinary course of things. . . .

"I wish to add two further footnotes. The defence of change of position is akin to the defence of bona fide purchase; but we cannot simply say that bona fide purchase is a species of change of position. This is because change of position will only avail a defendant to the extent that his position has been changed; whereas, where bona fide purchase is invoked, no inquiry is made (in most cases) into the adequacy of the consideration. Even so, the recognition of change of position as a defence should be doubly beneficial. It will enable a more generous approach to be taken of the recognition of the right of restitution, in the knowledge that the defence is, in appropriate cases, available; and, while recognising the different functions of property at law and in equity, there may also in due course develop a more consistent approach to tracing

---

[37] [1991] 3 W.L.R. 10 at p. 15.
[38] *Ibid.* at pp. 34–35.

claims, in which common defences are recognised as available to such claims, whether advanced at law or in equity."

It is clear from the final passage of this quotation that Lord Goff envisaged the application of the defence of change of position to both legal and equitable proprietary claims and that he did not regard this defence as supplanting the defence of bona fide purchase for value without notice. Only Lord Templeman gave any further illustrations of circumstances in which the defence of change of position would be available. He envisaged a situation in which a donee of stolen money has expended it "in reliance on the validity of the gift before he receives notice of the victim's claim for restitution. Thus if the donee spent £20,000 in the purchase of a motor car which he would not have purchased but for the gift, it seems to me that the donee has altered his position on the faith of the gift and has only been unjustly enriched to the extent of the secondhand value of the motor car at the date when the victim of the theft seeks restitution. If the donee spends the £20,000 in a trip round the world, which he would not have undertaken without the gift, it seems to me that the donee has altered his position on the faith of the gift and that he is not unjustly enriched when the victim of the faith seeks restitution."[39]

Applying the various observations of the members of the House of Lords to legal and equitable proprietary claims, it is clear that a defaulting fiduciary will never be able to utilise the defence of change of position since he cannot have acted in good faith. On the other hand, a person who has received property in good faith and subsequently engaged in some expenditure which he would not otherwise have made will be entitled to invoke the defence of change of position to the extent that he is worse off as a result of the transaction. At law, if a person purchases stolen property in good faith and subsequently sells it on at a loss, he will be entitled to invoke the defence of change of position to the extent of his loss on the sale and repurchase. In equity, if an innocent volunteer receives in good faith property transferred to him in breach of trust, he will be able to invoke the defence of change of position to the extent that he has spent the property or its product in ways which have provided no lasting benefit to him, provided that he would not have engaged in the expenditure in question in any event. Thus a charity which, as in *Re Diplock*, receives in good faith a payment which has been made in breach of trust, will be able to invoke the defence of change of position to the extent that it discharges unsecured debts or spends the funds on improvements to its properties which increases their value by less than the amount expended. A private individual will additionally be able to invoke the defence to the extent that he has spent the sum received on some item of one-off expenditure, such as a holiday, which he would not otherwise have made.

It obviously remains to be seen how the defence of change of position is developed by the courts. However, its effect on proprietary claims

---

[39] *Ibid.* at p. 16.

seems likely to be confined to cases of resales at a loss and of one-off non-productive expenditure.

(iii) Where tracing would be inequitable.   In *Re Diplock*[40] the Court of Appeal held that it would be inequitable for a claimant to trace in equity where an innocent volunteer had used the claimant's property either to alter or improve his land or to pay off his debts. These defences must now have been subsumed within the general defence of change of position enunciated in *Lipkin Gorman* v. *Karpnale* to the extent that the expenditure has produced no lasting benefit for the innocent volunteer and would not have been engaged in but for the receipt of the claimant's property. However, the defences enunciated by the Court of Appeal are not limited to this situation. The court clearly envisaged that improvements made to land would constitute a complete defence whether or not the value of the land had thereby increased in value. If it has indeed increased in value, there seems no reason why the claimant should not be entitled to obtain a charge over the land for the amount by which its value has increased. Further, although it is of course axiomatic that the payment of unsecured debts prevents any subsequent equitable proprietary claim (because the discharged creditor will be a bona fide purchaser for value without notice), there seems no reason why secured debts should be treated in the same way. If secured debts of an innocent volunteer are discharged by the use of the funds of the claimant, why should the claimant not be subrogated to the security discharged with his money and be entitled to enforce that security against the innocent volunteer?[41]

(iv) Where compensation has been recovered from the fiduciary who perpetrated the breach of trust in question.   It has already been seen[42] that any *in personam* claim available against an innocent volunteer will be reduced to the extent that compensation can be obtained from any fiduciary responsible for having made any relevant disposition of trust property in breach of trust. In *Re Diplock*,[43] the Court of Appeal took the view that "prima facie and subject to discussion" any equitable proprietary claim should similarly be reduced by any amounts which the claimant had recovered from any fiduciary responsible for having made such a disposition. The court did not actually suggest that it was necessary for the claimant to sue any such fiduciary prior to embarking on an equitable proprietary claim, merely that if any compensation had been recovered it should constitute a rateable bar to any such equitable proprietary claim. It is, frankly, difficult to see why the existence of a personal liability should constitute a bar to a proprietary claim. However, if it is ever held that it is in fact necessary for such a claimant to sue any fiduciary first, it is to be hoped that the fiduciary will be subrogated to that part of the claim "which represents the difference between the total of the sum recovered from the [fiduciary] and the

---

[40] [1948] Ch. 465 at pp. 546–548.
[41] See Goff & Jones: *The Law of Restitution* (4th ed., 1993) 600.
[42] See *ante*, p. 605.
[43] [1948] Ch. 465 at p. 556.

volunteer and the loss suffered by [the claimant]."[44] It would in fact be preferable to require the claimant to proceed against the innocent volunteer before suing the fiduciary, who would then be liable only for any amount which cannot be recovered from the innocent volunteer; however, such a solution could only be imposed by statute.[45]

---

[44] Goff & Jones: *op. cit.*, p. 92.
[45] As in New Zealand (Administration Act 1952, s.30B(5)) and in Western Australia (Western Australia Trustee Act 1962, s.65(7)).

INDEX

[All references are to page number]